NOTES FROM UNDERGROUND
and Other Stories

NOTES FROM UNDERGROUND
and Other Stories

◆

Fyodor Dostoevsky

Translation by
CONSTANCE GARNETT

Introduction and Notes by
DAVID RAMPTON

WORDSWORTH CLASSICS

For my husband
ANTHONY JOHN RANSON
with love from your wife, the publisher.
Eternally grateful for your unconditional love.

Readers who are interested in other titles from
Wordsworth Editions are invited to visit our website at
www.wordsworth-editions.com

For our latest list and a full mail-order service, contact
Bibliophile Books, 5 Datapoint, South Crescent, London E16 4TL
TEL: +44 (0)20 7474 2474 FAX: +44 (0)20 7474 8589
ORDERS: orders@bibliophilebooks.com
WEBSITE: www.bibliophilebooks.com

This edition published 2015 by Wordsworth Editions Limited
8B East Street, Ware, Hertfordshire SG12 9HJ

ISBN 978 1 84022 577 8

Wordsworth Editions
is the company founded in 1987 by
MICHAEL TRAYLER

Typeset in Great Britain by Antony Gray
Printed and bound by Clays Ltd, St Ives plc

CONTENTS

GENERAL INTRODUCTION

Wordsworth Classics are inexpensive editions designed to appeal to the general reader and students. We commissioned teachers and specialists to write wide ranging, jargon-free introductions and to provide notes that would assist the understanding of our readers rather than interpret the stories for them. In the same spirit, because the pleasures of reading are inseparable from the surprises, secrets and revelations that all narratives contain, we strongly advise you to enjoy this book before turning to the Introduction.

General Adviser
KEITH CARABINE

INTRODUCTION

The more spirit and inner substance there is in us, the more beautiful our place and life is. Of course it is a terrible dissonance, a terrible disequilibrium which society presents to us. The *external* must be balanced by the *inner* life. Otherwise, with the absence of external occurrences, the inner world will take the upper hand too dangerously. The nerves and imagination would take a very great place in one's being. Every external occurrence, because one hasn't got used to it, appears colossal and in some way terrifying. You begin to be afraid of life.

Dostoevsky in an 1847 letter to his brother Mikhail

Fyodor Dostoevsky (1821–1881) was a genius and a supremely gifted writer. No one has written more interestingly about psychology, society and politics. 'Notes from Underground', *Crime and Punishment*, *The Demons* and *The Brothers Karamazov* figure on every list of the most important books ever written. Literature in Russia has always been much more than belles-lettres, and Dostoevsky made an extraordinary contribution to the debates it facilitated. After a period of decidedly mixed success, he ended up engaging an enormous readership, as well as a cult following, that grows more numerous by the day.

All this is clear, yet Dostoevsky and his work also offer us an impressive series of intriguing contradictions. He is one of the most Russian of Russian writers – a Slavophile, a patriot, a fervent supporter of the Orthodox Church – yet he immersed himself in the literature and ideas of Western Europe. Even as he attacked Western values and beliefs because of the threats he thought they posed for Russia, Dostoevsky admired its great literary figures, Balzac and E. T. A. Hoffmann, Shakespeare and Dickens, and praised their contributions to world literature. In his twenties he frequented radical circles (Beketov, Petrashevsky) and swooned to the romantic strains of utopian thinking, only to become ferociously conservative in middle age. Sentenced to mock execution and penal servitude for talking about how Russia might be improved as a nation, he immersed himself in a life of solitude, agony and despair, and managed to transmute his encounters with sadists and murderers into sublime works of literature. Despite suffering from nervous strain, fears of madness, insomnia, nightmares, fainting fits and epilepsy, he produced an astonishingly large and diverse body of work, edited important literary/political journals, and played an active role in the events of his era. The author of a significant number of stunning masterpieces, he is sometimes dismissed as a slapdash writer producing stale and formulaic melodramas. His name is inextricably bound up with the realist novel as a form, yet his work is an extraordinary mix of tragic seriousness, a 'higher realism' as he called it, and a sort of low comedy that challenges all kinds of generic conventions. During his lifetime he was not recognised as one of Russia's important thinkers; now he is among its most revered. His fiction is carefully set in a particular time and place, Russia (and Western Europe) in the middle of the nineteenth century, yet the issues he discusses – the rival claims of free will and determinism, reason and emotion, faith and doubt, sin and forgiveness, love and egoism – are of universal interest. He is deeply invested in history, yet often singled out as one of those very special writers who keep their finger on the pulse of modernity. A man of God who consistently preached Christian compassion, Dostoevsky nonetheless loathed and feared the Jesuits, insisted that the Pope was conspiring to take over the world with the support of European socialists, and maintained that the Jews were a bunch of money-grubbing bankers bent on world domination, profiting to the maximum from the industrialisation of Russia. For a writer who infinitely preferred the blue of the sky or the green of a leaf to the greyness of theory, he has attracted an impressive number of theoretically minded critics, Bakhtin, Shklovsky, Todorov, Tynyanov *et al*.[1] Seen from a certain perspective his life is a lurching from one disaster to another, particularly if one thinks of all the suffering he and his family underwent, yet even in death he was hailed as a prophet, thirty thousand admirers followed his coffin to the cemetery, and he became a national icon.

Dostoevsky's stories are important because they show his extra-ordinary range, serve as helpful introductions to the large subjects that preoccupy him in the great novels, and give his career a distinctive shape. For example, more than half of the stories in this volume were published in the space of three years, between 1846 and 1849, and constitute an important aesthetic achievement in their own right; and there are many others in this collection – 'Uncle's Dream', 'An Unpleasant Predicament' and 'A Gentle Spirit' – that deserve to be better known. Even extraordinarily inventive works such as 'The Crocodile' and 'Bobok' are often ignored when Dostoevsky's fiction is discussed. A brief introduction to the salient features of the stories included here should help the reader get oriented in this impressive body of work.

Marginalised Characters

Dostoevsky wrote a lot about lonely people, and with a minimum of forcing we could probably bundle all of his stories into one capacious group with that title. That said, some distinctions in this regard might be useful. His characters are cut off from different things in different ways. In this section I want to look at some of Dostoevsky's more straightforward treatments of such figures, before going on to examine other ways in which his stories might be characterised.

In an 1846 story called 'Mr Prohartchin', the narrator first lists the food ('onion, curd, salted cucumber') that the parsimonious hero can afford, and then pauses and makes this remark: 'Here the biographer confesses that nothing would have induced him to allude to such realistic and low details, positively shocking and offensive to some lovers of the heroic style' (p. 3). In such passages Dostoevsky lays claim to his right to represent the marginal, the lowly, the dispossessed, the meek of the earth, and the need to find a new lexical register for such humdrum details. Gogol had played a crucial role in making these people legitimate subjects for fiction; Dostoevsky was keen to carry on that tradition. In this story, nothing much happens. Mr Prohartchin, 'a man utterly insignificant, with nothing but a trunk and

---

1 For details see the Select Bibliography at the end of the Introduction.

a German lock' (p. 21), eventually dies of inanition and old age. Yet the story does come to a surprise end: the other lodgers in the house find some 2,500 roubles hidden in Prohartchin's mattress. They lay out the money, offer their various impressions and treat the dead man rather unceremoniously. A blackish humour obtains.

At one point things are described as 'utterly incomprehensible muddle, from which everyone withdrew baffled' (p. 13). That is indeed a frequent state of affairs in Dostoevsky's fiction, but it is not the last word on the meaning of Prohartchin's life or this story. In the end, the character himself uncannily manages to have that. Reading the expression on his dead face, the assembled seem to hear him saying: 'Here I am dead now, but look here, what if – that is, perhaps it can't be so – but I say what if I'm not dead, what if I get up, do you hear? What would happen then?' (p. 27). A number of stories are destined to end with this sort of ambiguity, this uncomprehending questioning, the hesitant uncertainties of the dead and the dying, and the pregnant silences such imagined ramblings elicit. Dostoevsky was fascinated by conceptions of heaven and the afterlife, but this story is not about that. Wisely resisting the temptation to say the last word about life in this world, Dostoevsky makes such moments that much more impressive for being so difficult to articulate.

One of his last stories, 'The Heavenly Christmas Tree', begins and ends in similar fashion, but Dostoevsky takes a very different route to arrive at his conclusion. It was first published in *A Writer's Diary*[2] and Dostoevsky begins by commenting on the anomaly of including a fiction in his musings on life and writing. In the first few lines he both confesses to the story's invention and insists on its truth. It is about a young boy left utterly alone, whose mother has just died of starvation. With nothing to eat and no means to buy more, he walks about the brightly lit city, shunned by all who might have helped him. He eventually lies down, goes to sleep and freezes to death. Once again, the last word on this death both can and cannot be said. Yes, the boy is a reproach to us all and a truly pathetic sight, lying dead on a woodstack, not far from his mother's corpse. But, no, the idea that he rejoined her in heaven, where with the other dead children he frolics around Christ's Christmas tree, this cannot be asserted with such certainty. 'I cannot tell you whether that could have happened or not,' writes Dostoevsky. Instead of a saccharine parable, he gives us a *cri de coeur*.

2 Collections of essays, sketches, impressions, and anecdotes that Dostoevsky published in the 1870s.

'Polzunkov' introduces another version of Dostoevsky's archetypal marginalised figure, the 'ridiculous man' who is featured so prominently in nineteenth-century Russian fiction, in Pushkin's *Eugene Onegin*, Lermontov's *Hero of Our Time*, Turgenev's *Rudin*, and so on. Dostoevsky's narrator hits upon the perfect phrase for describing him: 'This external equality and internal inequality, his uneasiness about himself and at the same time his continual self-depreciation – all this was strikingly incongruous and provocative of laughter and pity' (p. 184). Polzunkov himself tells the story of how he is cheated by an unscrupulous boss and played for a fool on 1 April. Such a story turns on the kind of tragicomedy that makes Pushkin and Gogol such important precursors, and prepares readers for the powerful incongruities in Dostoevsky's late fiction.

In 'A Faint Heart' the subject is again the vulnerability of the outsider. Vasya Shumkov is the victim of ordinary life here. Despite a loving fiancée, a bosom friend, an understanding (if somewhat exploitative) boss, an excellent hand for calligraphy and a bright future, he loses his mind when he is unable to meet a deadline for some copying task assigned to him at work. His madness detaches him from everyone, and the tale concludes with Arkady trying to make sense of his friend Vasya's catastrophe as he walks along the Neva River in St Petersburg:

> he stood still for a minute and turned a keen glance up the river into the smoky frozen thickness of the distance, which was suddenly flushed crimson with the last purple and blood-red glow of sunset, still smouldering on the misty horizon . . . Night lay over the city, and the wide plain of the Neva, swollen with frozen snow, was shining in the last gleams of the sun with myriads of sparks of gleaming hoar frost. There was a frost of twenty degrees. A cloud of frozen steam hung about the over-driven horses and the hurrying people. The condensed atmosphere quivered at the slightest sound, and from all the roofs on both sides of the river columns of smoke rose up like giants and floated across the cold sky, intertwining and untwining as they went, so that it seemed new buildings were rising up above the old, a new town was taking shape in the air . . . It seemed as if all that world, with all its inhabitants, strong and weak, with all their habitations, the refuges of the poor or the gilded palaces for the comfort of the powerful, was at that twilight hour like a fantastic vision of fairyland, like a dream which in its turn would vanish and pass away like vapour into the dark-blue sky. A strange thought came to poor Vasya's forlorn friend. He started, and his heart seemed at

that instant flooded with a hot rush of blood kindled by a powerful, overwhelming sensation he had never known before. He seemed only now to understand all the trouble, and to know why his poor Vasya had gone out of his mind, unable to bear his happiness. His lips twitched, his eyes lighted up, he turned pale, and, as it were, had a clear vision into something new.   [pp. 181–2]

Reading such passages, we remember that St Petersburg for Dostoevsky is an artificial city, inspired by European models, in marked contrast to Moscow; a special kind of city, imagined into being by Peter the Great, erected in the Finnish swamps on the bones of all the serfs who died building it. In this eschatological vision, suffering seems part of some larger, vaguely providential plan, even if there is no rational explanation for or much evidence of such a plan. Vasya's tragedy is part of something bigger, something no more fantastical than the extraordinary capital that Russia constructed for itself. This is hinted at in the description of the landscape, part romantic sublime, part menacingly apocalyptic. The meek may be destined to fail in nineteenth-century St Petersburg, but they can be crushed by happiness as well as misfortune. Ultimately they may be the ones to inherit the earth, as the Bible tells us, but that looks unlikely to happen any time soon. Meanwhile, the life of the poor and the rich, the hovels and the palaces, the threatening nightmare of the sunset and the town that takes shape in the air, will all continue to be interrogated by those intent on understanding the meaning of our imaginings.

'An Honest Thief' and 'The Peasant Marey' are also stories about marginalised characters, but they have a social component that distinguishes them from the ones examined thus far. In the first, a drunkard on his deathbed confesses to having committed a petty crime. He is one of those human beings whom Dostoevsky had in mind when he ostensibly said – the story is probably apocryphal – that Russian literature all came out from under Gogol's overcoat. The Christian ending proves that even the lowly serfs have a conscience and that it is as active and powerful and says the same thing to them as ours does to us. So too 'The Peasant Marey', an anecdote about a man who does something particularly kind to soothe a frightened child, an altruistic act that compels the narrator to speculate about the meaning of this 'deep and humane civilised feeling' (p. 641), shown by an ignorant peasant no less. Dostoevsky juxtaposes this incident with the inhumanity and squalor of a group of convicts, the most abject and brutal image of the human species that one could possibly conceive.

Again, the story was first published in *A Writer's Diary*, inviting us to read it, at least in part, as a record of the author's own childhood experiences. The distinguishing features of this character's dignity and humanity suggest he too is representative of Russia's underclass and help make the story an affirmation of faith and enriched understanding. His isolation enables him to see with special clarity why it is incumbent on society to protect and comfort the vulnerable.

The Cruelty of Sensuality

The unconsummated desires felt by those who find themselves so isolated constitute another of Dostoevsky's great subjects in the stories. It hovers in the background of 'A Faint Heart', and someone wonders if there is a 'Mrs Polzunkov' in that tale of loss, but the workings of sensuality in Dostoevsky's fiction are explored in more detail in stories such as 'The Landlady', 'White Nights', 'Uncle's Dream', 'A Little Hero' and 'A Christmas Tree and a Wedding'.

'The Landlady' is all about the smoky allure of a young woman named Katerina for one Ordynov, a recluse whose only passion thus far has been science. We first meet him roaming St Petersburg, unconsciously seeking to assuage some vague desire. He finds its object in the woman who lets him his room in his new lodgings . She in turn is in thrall to his landlord, an old man named Murin, described as 'pale as death', and constantly staring at Katerina (his wife? his daughter? his slave?) 'with a leaden, fixed, searching gaze' (p. 38). One of his momentary glances is described as a 'strange mingling of contempt, mocking, impatient, angry uneasiness and at the same time sly, spiteful curiosity' (p. 78). No writer ever made jealousy more harrowing. Meanwhile, Ordynov's giddy heart beats violently, his existence resembles a state of chaos, he is attacked by fever and chills, he swoons with ecstasy, he loses consciousness completely, and these are just the highlights of the first five pages of his emotional ups and downs, fated to last for another sixty.

Emotions continue to be writ large in this story, and oxymorons pullulate in the writer's attempt to describe them. Ordynov has 'moments of insufferable, devastating happiness' (p. 45), he wants to 'scream with ecstasy', a kiss makes him languish 'in unquenchable torture' (p. 45), he suffers from a 'chill, icy sweat' (p. 47). Murin is fairly busy on the emotional front as well: he has an epileptic seizure, tries to murder Ordynov with a gun, cultivates a reputation as a mystic 'always reading religious books' (p. 55), is hinted at being responsible for corrupting Katerina by taking her from her family before the age of consent, is accused of being a wizard who can tell fortunes (pp. 78-9), and successfully resists a knife attack from his unhappy lodger. One thinks of Matthew Arnold's reviewing Tolstoy's *Anna Karenina* and assuring his readers that, if the emotions seem larger than life in the novel, that is because Russians have larger emotions than the rest of us. At any rate, sexual attraction in 'The Landlady' appears to be one of those euphemism-strewn no-go areas, in which every desire has its transgressive effect and repressed counterpart, neither of which can be named directly.

White Nights features more of the same. Here a self-confessed recluse wanders St Petersburg in search of real life, an antidote to his own existence. The emphasis is on the changing seasons. Spring is to the city what a flash of fire is to the sad pensive eyes of a consumptive girl, the means by which a totally unexpected transformation takes place. So the weather report, given the imminent arrival of Petersburg's ultra-long evenings, is all 'bosom heaving', 'mortal anguish' and 'fleeting distraction' (p. 224) as the city, like a woman, reveals its hidden, promising, passionate side. As if conjured up by this incantation, an actual woman named Nastenka appears – with 'black eyelashes' on which 'glistened a tear' (she has just been accosted by a potential villain), 'the gleam of a smile' (p. 226), faint blushes – and the lonely man claims her for his own.

They meet again on the following night. He tells her he is a 'type', a 'dreamer' (p. 231), cut off from everyone, living and partly living. He talks at her for a very long time, finally eliciting her comment: 'You talk as though you were reading it out of a book' (p. 233). And he is, in the sense that he rhapsodises about the sky *à la* Schiller, quotes the Russian poet Zhukovsky on 'the Goddess of Fancy' (p. 234), conjures up a 'whole kingdom of fancies' (p. 235), watches that kingdom disintegrate, uses it as a preface for reconstituting another, introduces a bevy of characters from literature in general and Scott's romances in particular, creates another fairyland, pronounces himself an artist, and ends with a 'morbidly overwrought spirit' and 'a weary sweet ache in his heart' (p. 237). The coda to this extraordinary outburst is that the torments of pure love, however delusional, are too great to suffer, and he consoles himself with celebrating 'the anniversary of [his] own sensations' (p. 239).

Then it is Nastenka's turn, and here the sound of a human voice, unmediated by literature, actually threatens to come through. Her autobiographical account reveals that, a year or so ago, a man was smitten by her. He overcame her grandmother's disapproval of his suit by taking them to Rossini's *Barber of Seville*, proposed, was accepted, had to leave town, pledged his undying love, returned, but hasn't exactly hastened to seek her out. Here readers interested in a story's predictive sequences can choose one of three options: the man in question could come looking for her and declare his true love; she could reconcile herself to living without love; or she could enlist the aid of her new admirer to win back the old. No prizes for guessing: Nastenka chooses option three and, revealingly, her new lover could not be more eager to help her. In *The Barber of Seville*, Figaro suggests that the young and innocent Rosina write her beloved a letter, and she promptly pulls such a letter from her bosom: i.e., she is not quite as innocent as she appears. The scene from the opera is reduplicated in the story, one of Dostoevsky's many artfully allusive ploys in this carefully constructed tale. But Nastenka's lover is a no-show, prompting more impossibly literary speeches, more incomprehension on Nastenka's part, more failed communication. In this hot-house atmosphere, she finally proposes to our hero and, 'breathless with sobs' (p. 259), he accepts. Just as he has taken her in his arms, a young man walks by. He turns out to be her former lover, recognises Nastenka, and calls out to her. At which point she gives her would-be protector a tender kiss and rushes off with her first beau. A letter of apology is in the post the next day, in which the abandoned lover is invited to come and live with them as a 'friend' and 'brother' (p. 262). His room is instantly transformed into something dingy and dark, and he has a horrific vision of himself, fifteen years hence, in the same room, only more decrepit, greyer, darker. Even the spiders' webs are 'thicker than ever' (pp. 262-3). Unconvincingly, but poignantly, he tells himself that he has had a moment of happiness and must settle for that.

'Uncle's Dream' features Dostoevsky's particular sort of comedy with a bittersweet aftertaste. Sexual desire is the cause of much of the conflict that takes place. The wealthy and aged widower Prince Gravila is lured into proposing to the ravishing Zinaida, by a mother fanatically dedicated to her daughter's getting the highest possible yield on her assets, as it were. The prince keeps mentioning certain curves of Zinaida's body that he particularly admires, even while he assures anyone who will listen that he is soon off to spend some serious time in a monastery. Finally, in a drunken stupor, he proposes and is accepted. Meanwhile, his nephew, Mozglyakov, who is only a pretend nephew, a fraud with his eye on the main chance, convinces his 'uncle' that his proposal was just a dream. Which makes the title an intriguing misnomer: the uncle in question is not an uncle – until he dies suddenly at the end and his real nephew arrives on the scene – and the dream is not a dream, until the prince's death makes supererogatory whatever proposals he has made, real and imagined. Through it all Dostoevsky emphasises the transience of sexual attraction, even as he conjures with its destructive power. Zinaida's real love dies of self-induced consumption, a shell of his former, handsome self. The prince's death follows ignominiously soon after. Everyone is scandalised, until life reassumes its particular rhythms the next day.

The ending of the story is another one of those non-endings that Dostoevsky uses so adroitly, one that ignores and simultaneously drives home the point about the ephemeral nature of the desire that has propelled the events of the story. Mozglyakov encounters Zinaida by chance in a new city where he has travelled for work and is spurned one last time. He watches her at a ball, with 'a biting Mephistophelean smile' on his face, leaning 'in a picturesque attitude against a column'. We know this pose, the superfluous man in his new guise, self-consciously playing a role. She refuses to play along and he leaves town the next day. Gloom, isolation, deep and nameless regret? Not a bit of it. The story ends:

> He felt positively lighter-hearted as he drove out of the town. Snow was lying like a dazzling shroud over the boundless, deserted plain. In the distance on the very horizon stretched dark forests.
>
> The mettlesome horses dashed along, flinging the powdery snow with their hoofs. The sledge bell tinkled, Pavel Alexandrovitch sank into thought, and then into dreams, and then into a sweet sleep. He woke at the third posting station, feeling fresh and well, with quite different thoughts in his mind.   [p. 408]

For someone like Mozglyakov, all that posing, yearning, desiring, despairing seems vaguely silly the next day, the mere stuff of romantic novels. Life simply goes on, and not being able to feel anything very profoundly can actually turn out to be an advantage.

Children do not figure prominently in Russian fiction, but Dostoevsky is fascinated by them. He is also the first writer to discuss children and sex in any kind of systematic way. In 'A Little Hero' a boy of ten comes of age, smitten as he is by a married woman, who may well be cheating on her husband. He is meanwhile constantly being teased by her friend. He describes his feelings this way:

> But there was for all that another secret, strange and foolish reason, which I concealed, at which I shuddered as at a skeleton. At the very thought of it, brooding, utterly alone and overwhelmed, in some dark

mysterious corner to which the inquisitorial mocking eye of the blue-eyed rogue could not penetrate, I almost gasped with confusion, shame and fear – in short, I was in love.   [p. 271]

This is not the sort of language Rousseau would use to describe his first love in *The Confessions* or Tolstoy for similar revelations in *Boyhood* or *Youth*. Shame figures much more prominently than pleasure here, and passive suffering supersedes any hint of sensuality. This is primal guilt without the primal lust.

Compare such an avowal to the language used at the end of the story, when, having given the 'little hero' a kiss, the lady vanishes for ever:

Hardly able to breathe, leaning on my elbow on the grass, I stared unconsciously before me at the surrounding slopes, streaked with cornfields, at the river that flowed twisting and winding far away, as far as the eye could see, between fresh hills and villages that gleamed like dots all over the sunlit distance – at the dark-blue, hardly visible forests, which seemed as though smoking at the edge of the burning sky, and a sweet stillness inspired by the triumphant peacefulness of the picture gradually brought calm to my troubled heart. I felt more at ease and breathed more freely, but my whole soul was full of a dumb, sweet yearning, as though a veil had been drawn from my eyes as though at a foretaste of something. My frightened heart, faintly quivering with expectation, was groping timidly and joyfully towards some conjecture . . . and all at once my bosom heaved, began aching as though something had pierced it, and tears, sweet tears, gushed from my eyes. I hid my face in my hands, and quivering like a blade of grass, gave myself up to the first consciousness and revelation of my heart, the first vague glimpse of my nature. My childhood was over from that moment.   [p. 294]

The ending of 'A Little Hero' recalls that of 'A Faint Heart' because the sheer gorgeousness of the setting evoked serves as a kind of relief for the hero, while the juxtaposition of splendid setting and infinite yearning conveys the power of the epiphanic moment. Keep in mind too that this is a man talking about his feelings as a ten-year-old: i.e., this is pre-pubescent love seen retrospectively. It is content to go on existing and gently torturing its victim in the absence of its object, who has escaped, gone back to the fallen world, for which he is heading.

Juxtaposed with these innocent but powerful emotions in children is the lust of the adult male for young children. Both Svidrigailov

(*Crime and Punishment*) and Stavrogin (*The Demons*) are guilty of having raped young girls. This makes Dostoevsky's 'A Christmas Tree and a Wedding' a particularly important story, for it anatomises in a few devastating pages a socially sanctioned version of such behaviour.

Anyone interested in testing the proposition that Dostoevsky is a slapdash writer is advised to read carefully the opening of this unassuming little story:

> The other day I saw a wedding . . . but no, I had better tell you about the Christmas tree. The wedding was nice, I liked it very much; but the other incident was better. I don't know how it was that, looking at that wedding, I thought of that Christmas tree. This was what happened. Just five years ago, on New Year's Eve, I was invited to a children's party.   [p. 213]

So far, so innocuous. Yet of all the different ways in which Dostoevsky could have begun this story, why choose this one we might ask. How are these two seemingly disparate events linked if the narrator doesn't know? And how is a Christmas tree an event anyway? Why was he invited to the party? Why is that five-year slippage introduced so quietly? These questions are important, because their answers show us that for whatever reason the narrator has deliberately misled us. The wedding wasn't 'nice'; he didn't like it 'very much'. The wedding and the tree are indeed linked, and the narrator knows why. In fact their linkage is the whole point of the story. And the Christmas tree is an event, because while attending the party and seeing the children receive their presents, the narrator has watched Julian Mastakovitch, a rich, successful, ambitious middle-aged man drooling over an eleven-year-old girl. By the time the party is over, to judge by the sycophantic response he elicits from her parents and assembled guests, he is destined to be betrothed to the girl.

Fast forward five years, and the story concludes with a very brief but devastating account of the victim being led to the altar as a sacrificial lamb. 'The classic severity of every feature of her face gave a certain dignity and seriousness to her beauty. But through that sternness and dignity, through that melancholy, could be seen the look of childish innocence; something indescribably naïve, fluid, youthful, which seemed mutely begging for mercy.' Julian Mastakovitch is overheard at one point figuring out the income that the girl's large dowry will create, and the last word emphasises the financial angle as opposed to the lascivious one. That said, the image that stays in the mind is the tear-stained face of innocence contemplating an incomprehensible future.

Experiments

Many of Dostoevsky's stories are examples of experiments with genres that intrigued him. 'Novel in Nine Letters' is his imitation or parody of the epistolary novels so popular at one point in the history of the European novel. Richardson (*Pamela*, *Clarissa*), Montesquieu (*Lettres persanes*), Rousseau (*Julie*), Laclos (*Les Liaisons dangereuses*), Goethe (*Die Leiden des jungen Werthers*). In *Clarissa*, Richardson needed 538 letters to get his story told. Yet, in a way, nothing is omitted in this much briefer account of love and loss: the two correspondents have fallen out after some murky business affair, have been cuckolded by the same young man, and have sat idly by while their relationship becomes mere debt and threatening. The reader is left to infer all this, even while the letters fill in the details of lives gone vaguely astray and represent the masks we adopt to disguise such things from ourselves.

The missives in 'A Novel in Nine Letters' must abide by the accepted conventions, all the while bristling with the irritation and indignation that have occasioned the exchange. In 'Another Man's Wife, or The Husband under the Bed', Dostoevsky tries his hand at bedroom farce that has its own conventions and acquits himself admirably. This is a comic tale about infidelity using the intonations of Paul de Kock, the nineteenth-century French novelist who wrote a hundred novels with titles such as *The Wife, the Husband, and the Lover*, slightly *louche* accounts of the mores of low- and middle-class Parisians. (Molly Bloom, unsurprisingly, is a great fan of de Kock.) In Dostoevsky's hands it consists of hysterical excess piled on hysterical excess. During a good part of the story there are two men under the bed, not just one. And when the family lapdog sniffs them out, one of the hapless cuckolds strangles it. The story concludes with his attempt to explain to his now indignant wife how he ended up with a dead dog in his pocket.

In 'The Crocodile' and 'Bobok', Dostoevsky conducts even more interesting experiments, this time using his own idiosyncratic version of magic realism. The former is his version of Gogol's 'The Nose', a black comedy in which a couple of quasi-impossible or outright impossible things happen: first, a barber discovers his client's nose in his morning loaf of bread; then the nose becomes a person, walking about St Petersburg, taking a carriage, visiting a church, and so on. Its owner, feeling seriously deprived, hunts it down and reclaims it. The elevation of the nose to the status of independent entity makes every reaction, every commentary, every speculation about the future, every attempt to be rational, in short, every perfectly commonsensical suggestion to deal with what has happened, a self-evident absurdity.

So too with 'The Crocodile'. On page one we learn that Ivan Matveitch is on the point of going to Europe for a visit. Hence the trip to see the crocodile: a look at one of Europe's 'indigenous inhabitants' (p. 547), he surmises, might well be helpful. A minute's reflection on that remark will have readers puzzling over their atlases. (This observation is book-ended by the repeated claims at the end of the story identifying the crocodile as a 'mammal'.) Things get so goofy by page two, when the crocodile swallows our erstwhile traveller whole, that 'making sense' no longer means what it did. In his new surroundings the somewhat pompous, self-absorbed, garrulous Ivan Matveitch holds forth as if his new position will serve as the ideal platform for communicating his progressive views. Anyone who sees himself as 'the cynosure of all eyes' (p. 563), developing 'a new economic theory' (p. 563), incarnating 'a pattern of resignation to fate and the will of Providence' (p. 564) is certainly willing to dream big. Once the suggestion is made that a man can exist indefinitely inside a crocodile – a thousand-year lifespan is mentioned at one point – then every straight-faced observation made about how that time is to be spent simply adds to the fun.

The parable-like features of Gogol's story are brilliantly reproduced in Dostoevsky's, and attempts at reading both as allegories are ubiquitous, ingenious and ultimately unsatisfying. In effect, the reader's desire to find a meaning is redoubled precisely because of the challenge to verisimilitude that the story poses. Because Europe figures so prominently in the story, various critics have suggested that it is a lampoon directed against Europeanisation. As Samuel Cioran remarks: 'By some sleight of hand Dostoevsky managed to create a single unappetising salad of all the disparate and unwelcome Europeanisms (liberalism, progressivism, utilitarianism, scientific determinism, materialism, etc.) under the catchall title of "nihilism" and flavour it with a generous dressing of xenophobia whose recipe was concocted during his visits to Western Europe.'[3] A committed proponent of Russia's mystical nationalism, Dostoevsky believed in Russian exceptionalism *avant la lettre*. Russia was superior to the West, its people more potentially homogenous, its literature more impressive and comprehensive, its capacity for self-criticism greater, and so on. Dostoevsky was impatient with the liberal and conservative press, and

3 'Introduction', *The Crocodile*, Ann Arbor, 1985, p. 12.

said so in a series of brilliant polemical exchanges, but he saved his special venom for radical writers and thinkers.

For example, at one point Ivan Matveitch announces that, working out of his new location in the crocodile, he will be 'the New Fourier'. The reference is to Charles Fourier (1772–1837), a French philosopher and economist. He became famous when his proposals for the founding of communes were adopted by literally hundreds of groups of people keen to live together on different terms. The communes he proposes are little solar systems organised around sexual passion writ large, each planned on the basis of the 810 types of characters, which makes for 1620 people in each commune or *phalenstère*. Fourier believed that the universe is a gigantic, ongoing exercise in creation. People, planets, stars – all feel passion and yearn for sexual intercourse. In fact, each of us is a microscopic star, and we must liberate our passion to restore the harmony of the universe. This will in turn facilitate the activity that will make life, industry, agriculture, etc. an infinity of passionate experiences and the subject of vast transformations. Nothing would then be impossible. By a simple act of will we will step from one planet to the next; the sea will become lemonade; human life as we know it will be utterly transformed. When Fourier was not dreaming on this scale, he was busy talking about planet Earth. He coined the word 'feminism' and argued that there was nothing wrong with homosexuality.

Dostoevsky mocks such utopian notions but his characters are haunted by them. One can see the decadent West looming in Fourierist formulas like 'free love' and references to the intense pleasures of social, sexual, economic relations etc. encouraged by membership in the commune. There is an abstract, schematic, rational approach to the complexities of human behaviour here that Dostoevsky finds laughable. And all the talk of transcendence, the soaring into the ether in unimaginably exciting new guises, is for him mere intellectual indulgence, a fairytale that militates against the pursuit of a genuine understanding of what society is and how it might be changed. For all these reasons Fourier is mentioned prominently in Dostoevsky's amusing take on political and social changes in Russia, disguised as a light-hearted farce. We hear at the end of the revisionist accounts of the incident in the local press, the critique of Russia's inferior status vis-à-vis Europe, and the suggestion that the story of the man in the crocodile is going to run and run. This conclusion bodes well for the triumph of comedy, and the victory of the imagination in a world as absurd as the one sketched in here.

'Bobok' represents another generic departure for Dostoevsky. As a story it has a curious genesis. An article from a Petersburg journal compared Dostoevsky's *Writer's Diary* to Gogol's 'Diary of a Madman', claiming that, as a portrait of its author, it resembles exactly the painting of Dostoevsky hanging in the Academy of Arts, a portrait described as being of a man gravely ill. Dostoevsky's riposte is 'Bobok'. We learn from the subtitle that this is not Dostoevsky's diary but 'somebody's'. He speaks of the madness that often afflicts literary figures, and he hears voices. Unlike the ones telling his counterpart in the Gogol story that he is the King of Spain, they say simply 'bobok'. This means 'a small bean' in Russian, but what on earth does that mean? The problem is not semantic but contextual. More clues are needed, and more are forthcoming.

Mr Somebody visits a Petersburg cemetery (probably Volkovo, to the south of the city, where for years water was the bane of those who dug graves). There he learns that life beyond the tomb is a staging area of a few months, before decomposition starts in earnest. During that time the dead converse, play cards, invoke the past, insult each other, and yearn to have another chance at something more real. There's a lot of talk about 'getting naked', of opportunity lost, of a desire to satiate passions now etiolated. The effect on the 'somebody' relating these events is striking. He emphasises the repugnance occasioned by rotting flesh, the banality of the last gasps in these meaningless lives, in this meaningless life in death. And he hears about the word bobok again. This time it is associated with a phenomenon that anticipates Samuel Beckett. Every six weeks a corpse shows 'an imperceptible speck of life' by mumbling the word. As the last sound made by a decaying body about to drift into permanent silence, bobok starts to look like a random two-syllable noise, a nonsense word, a mantra that will disappear along with the people who pronounce it.

The sprightly dialogue among the deceased is truncated when the narrator sneezes and everything becomes as quiet as the grave. The rest of the story is a meditation on this silence. At least half a dozen explanations for it are suggested. First, it could be that the dead are ashamed, but if that is the case why all the talk about casting off shame? Then it is suggested that they share 'some secret' unknown to the living: that is, something too occult for syntax, something to remind us that graveyards may have a lot to tell us but they are firmly in this world. The 'undiscovered country' Hamlet refers to will always be undiscovered by definition. But it is also possible that the narrator is mad to suppose the existence of such a secret. What if he is refusing to acknowledge what is in effect an open secret, namely that the end of life is a watery grave and the stink of mortality? At one point the narrator seems to be saying that 'bobok' explains everything: 'The bobok case does not trouble me (so that is what that bobok signified!)'. But, again, does this mean that the value of human life equals a pair of nonsense syllables? Or does it mean that the suggestion that that's what life is needn't bother us because it's as nonsensical as the word that expresses it, that it is a non-explanation? This flurry of questions confirms the reader's sense that an allegorical reading is just too tidy for all the competing, jostling suggestions in this strange story.

Which brings us to its conclusion. In a sense, Dostoevsky's end is his beginning. We learn that the editor of the *Citizen* has also had his portrait exhibited in the St Petersburg Academy of Arts. Perhaps he will agree to print this answer to the accusation included in the original article. The in-joke or the open secret hovering over this solution is that Dostoevsky himself is the editor of the *Citizen*. Like any search for the meaning of life, this interrogation of the dead – the narrator is intent on hearing more 'biographies and anecdotes', keen to go to other cemeteries – seems fated to take us round in circles.

Four Masterpieces

Any comprehensive collection of Dostoevsky's short fiction reveals not only how many good stories Dostoevsky wrote but also how varied the best of them are. The ones in this final section, 'An Unpleasant Predicament', 'A Gentle Spirit', 'The Dream of a Ridiculous Man' and 'Notes from Underground', are bound together in a number of ways: they are about four ridiculous men, whose ignominious trajectories are carefully described; they all suffer from the cognitive dissonance created by the contradictory narratives that inform their lives; and their stories conclude equivocally. Yet how different these four characters are. The first story features a pompous government official who makes a disastrous attempt to ingratiate himself with his employees, the second, an abusive husband who slowly learns the truth about himself as he retells the story of his wife's suicide, the third, a man who almost kills himself but is saved by a revelation about the nature of heaven and earth, and, lastly, a petty civil servant whose sardonic, outrageous, devastating exercise in self-analysis explains why he is fated to shrink away from life and love for ever.

'An Unpleasant Predicament' tells the story of Ivan Pralinsky, a middle-aged man in government service, recently promoted to General. When we first meet him it is 1862, a year after the emancipation of the serfs. He has had a few drinks and is imparting to two acquaintances from work his somewhat hazy vision of what additional reforms should be tried and what a new Russia might look like. He likes what he calls syllogistic argument: a common humanity equals love, which induces confidence, which bespeaks trust, 'and so there is love' (p. 413) – no wonder his friends start laughing at him. In a long interior monologue he tries out other logical constructions to show how humanity can lead to love and happiness, with predictable results. It is not so much that Dostoevsky mocks would-be reformers as that he wants us to be wary of the clichés in which such sentiments are often expressed. Pralinsky's language resembles nothing so much as a bunch of cotton wadding, something that wraps up a problem and makes it invisible. The reforms that Russia needs will involve much more than a lot of words. Meanwhile he badmouths his coachman while professing eternal blood brotherhood with the peasants.

On his way home, Pralinsky learns in an evil hour about the wedding of one of his subordinates, a lowly clerk. What about dropping in on the celebration? Why is that so unthinkable? Shouldn't a new era imply new relations between the powerful and their underlings? Going to the party becomes 'an action normal, patriarchal, lofty and moral' (p. 418), the General concludes, revolutionary in its implications, an event tantamount to the last days of Pompeii. He comforts himself with the thought: 'I am morally elevating the humiliated, I restore him to himself' (p. 420). Dropping in and acting like a humble guest is a sure way to improve social relations and make himself a reputation as an egalitarian. Of course it all turns out the way it would in a Chekhov story. Copious amounts of vodka and champagne do him in. His impromptu speech on 'the contemporary significance of Russia among the European States' (p. 439) falls flat. One of the braver guests denounces him for what he is, a popularity-seeking, hypocritical reactionary who confuses his sentimental maunderings with a new social policy. He sleeps half the night away in a drunken stupor and then makes his escape. The catastrophe steels him at work against any sort of conviviality or exchange and permanently disabuses him of the notion that there can be any genuine equality between the different classes.

'A Gentle Spirit' opens with the narrator musing on his wife's recent suicide. Her body is lying on the table in the drawing room; he is trying to make sense of what has happened. Dostoevsky likes to explore the difference between 'why' questions. One answer is because of the callous way in which everyone treated her, him included, a second is more teleologically oriented: what purpose was served by such a death? Two suicides by young women about which Dostoevsky read before writing this story provide another context. One was Herzen's teenage daughter, who left a breezy, mocking suicide note, suggesting they could toast her new life with champagne should her attempt fail. The other involved a woman jumping out of a window, holding an icon of the Virgin Mary to her chest, like the young wife in 'A Gentle Spirit'.

The narrator and the girl in question (neither is named in the story) first meet when she comes to his shop to pawn inexpensive family treasures. She is just sixteen, he is forty-one. In one of their first conversations, the pawnbroker impresses her with an allusion to *Faust*, a legend in which the hero, suicidal, bored, jaded, makes a pact with Mephistopheles for magical powers that will enable him to live again. In the different versions of the myth, there is always the idea of a trade-off between moral integrity on the one hand, power and success on the other. In some versions the beautiful female whom Faust meets succeeds in interceding for him with the devil; in this story she doesn't.

As he retells the story, looking for the answer to his question, he discovers a cold, tyrannical, withdrawn, manipulative person in the mirror who must shoulder a good deal of the blame. Like so many of Dostoevsky's lovers, there is an element of voyeurism in his attitude to the beloved. He arranges to overhear a seducer's attempt to get her into bed, but 'the holy contempt of virtue for vice' (p. 616) wins out. Even after her death, the narrator muses about how his love is now unencumbered by jealousy, that he is willing to watch her 'from the other side of the street' (p. 635), while she walks laughing with her lover. All of this is noble but too late. Now he must spend long years alone, paying with bitter remorse for his stupidity and brutality. His last question is ' "Men, love one another" – who said that? Whose commandment is that?' Dostoevsky is to strike this note again and again in these stories.

'The Dream of a Ridiculous Man' invites readers to think again about suicide. In it, the eponymous hero decides to commit suicide but is saved by a child, or rather by his own concern for a terrified and defenceless child, a concern that makes no sense if one has decided to end one's life that very day. It turns out that a pernicious and insidious solipsism must be resisted at such a juncture.

Here is Dostoevsky's 'ridiculous man' on the subject:

'I may almost say that the world now seemed created for me alone: if I shot myself the world would cease to be at least for me. I say nothing of its being likely that nothing will exist for anyone when I am gone, and that as soon as my consciousness is extinguished the whole world will vanish too and become void like a phantom, a mere appurtenance of my consciousness, for possibly all this world and all these people are only me myself.'   [p. 647]

Obviously ridding oneself of such a conviction is essential if abstract ideas about ethics are to exist. In Dostoevsky's view, the writer's task is to facilitate that escape, which is one of the reasons why suicide comes up so often in his work. It has important religious implications as well. As G. K. Chesterton puts it in a famous passage: 'The man who kills a man, kills a man. The man who kills himself, kills all men; as far as he is concerned he wipes out the world. His act is worse (symbolically considered) than any rape or dynamite outrage. For it destroys all buildings: it insults all women.'[4] Such a conviction helps explain why Dostoevsky sees the nihilists as so dangerous.

At the end of 'Dream of a Ridiculous Man', the narrator, having decided not to kill himself, has an extraordinary dream about a perfect day in paradise. The 'Children of the Sun' are there in all their Edenic splendour, serene, luminous, enchanting, like the ones that play around Christ's Christmas tree in the story discussed above. Of course this respite in paradise cannot last. Some combination of a debilitating self-consciousness, an exposure to cruel sensuality, a decision to divide themselves into groups, an interest in devising legal codes, and an obliviousness of the past has apparently made these children lose track of the object of their faith. Or, rather, such changes lead them to a new object, a new conviction. As one of them says,

We have science, and by the means of it we shall find the truth and we shall arrive at it consciously. Knowledge is higher than feeling, the consciousness of life is higher than life. Science will give us wisdom, wisdom will reveal the laws, and the knowledge of the laws of happiness is higher than happiness.   [p. 657]

Here Dostoevsky has all his ducks in a row: for him, the rationalist account of how life should be understood gets the accent exactly wrong every time. If you're convinced that knowing the laws of happiness is preferable to being happy, you are destined to make a lot of potentially happy people miserable. However, the story concludes on an uplifting if somewhat vague note: if we pledge to love one another Eden can be

4 'The Flag of the World', *Orthodoxy* http://www.leaderu.com/cyber/books/ orthodoxy/ch5.html

retrofitted in an hour: 'If only everyone wants it, it can be arranged at once' (p. 659). The new commandment seems not to have lost all of its force after all.

'Notes from Underground' is the best of Dostoevsky's short stories and the most discussed. The treatment of the social, psychological and philosophical ideas that so intrigued him finds its apotheosis here. A. D. Nuttall, one of Dostoevsky's most insightful critics, offers this summary of the *Notes*: It is 'a long rambling diatribe purportedly set down by a shabby government official, against the body of doctrine we know as utilitarianism; that is, the view that man must always act to maximise happiness and to minimise pain, that from this simple proposition we can deduce the only accurate psychology, the only legitimate morality.'[5] In the story, Dostoevsky shows how reducing human beings to this sort of calculus is a kind of 'philosophy of swine' (Carlyle's phrase).[6] Another problem is that in such an equation, the private and the public are at odds. The Underground Man absolutely refuses to admit that maximising his pleasure could do the same for the pleasure of the greatest number. A third difficulty stems from the fact that he gets as much pleasure from self-abasement as another might get from prosperity. After all, people are quirky and whimsical, for all our talk about an undifferentiated majority whose desires can be easily predicted. Besides, no matter what scientists, psychologists and philosophers propose as they seek to redefine nineteenth-century ideas about human nature, mankind is always capable of acting contrary to their definitions, simply by choosing to do so.

In *Notes from Underground* Dostoevsky is also mocking *What is to be Done?*, a utopian socialist novel by Nikolay Chernyshevsky inspired by the utilitarians' ideas. Chernyshevsky argues that the 'rational egoism' championed in that book will facilitate the establishment of communally held property and collective labour, and create a utilitarian paradise. His book was widely read, and Lenin called him the Great Precursor. For Dostoevsky, the radical critic's thoughts on psychology, property and human nature more generally look nasty. Besides, in Dostoevsky's view, Chernyshevsky completely ignores the spiritual dimension of man's life. How can his characters strive to imitate Christ's ideal and live by his new commandment if they take a materialist view of our nature?

5 *Crime and Punishment: Murder as Philosophic Experiment*, Edinburgh, 1978, p. 15.

6 Roger Crisp, 'Well-Being', *Stanford Encyclopaedia of Philosophy* http://plato. stanford.edu/entries/well-being/

In Part Two of the story, Dostoevsky puts some flesh on the bones of these propositions. There is a hilarious account of the Underground Man's successful attempt to imitate Chernyshevsky's new man by refusing to yield to him on the pavement. The time he passes as a self-invited guest at a friend's party is almost as amusingly awful as poor Pralinsky's wedding celebration. And of course the Underground Man meets up with a woman and the craziness begins in earnest. This one is called Liza and she works in a brothel. Once he has had sex with her, he describes a prostitute's funeral to frighten her, condemns her for immorality but exonerates himself for engaging her, and conjures up the mother of all sentimental domestic scenes to show her what she has missed. At the end of it, Liza says to her tormentor what Nastenka in 'White Nights' tells her strange suitor: 'Why, you . . . speak somehow like a book' (p. 523). A bad book, too, to judge by all the clichés. When Liza becomes distraught, the only comfort he can offer is a detailed account of the long sojourn rotting in the cemetery that awaits her.

When she subsequently comes to his place he continues in the same vein, but Liza is undeterred. The more ashamed and spiteful he becomes, the more compassion she shows him. That sounds hopeful, but of course with the Underground Man the consequences of such a response could not be more dire. Through it all he is lucidity itself in anatomising his own incapacities: e.g., 'I was angry with myself, but, of course, it was she who would have to pay for it' (p. 165); 'I shall never forgive [her] for having found me in this wretched dressing-gown' (p. 540); 'with me loving meant tyrannising and showing my moral superiority' (p. 543). The inevitable male downward spiral into the contradictory selfishness and self-hatred that characterises so many of Dostoevsky's would-be lovers begins again. When she offers compassion, he pulls out a five-rouble note to pay her off. This is the most bookish, that is, the most hatefully impersonal thing that he could do but, again, his analysis of his motivations and choices is impeccable: the insult he has given her might end up being a 'purification': 'Tomorrow I should have defiled her soul and exhausted her heart, while now the feeling of insult will never die in her heart . . . ' Instead of 'cheap happiness', she will have 'exalted suffering' (p. 545). Lest we start feeling too 'holier than thou', he has some dismissive words for us as well: 'I have only in my life carried to an extreme what you have not dared to carry halfway, and what's more, you have taken your cowardice for good sense, and have found comfort in deceiving yourselves' (p. 546).

In the end he is left alone with his enjoyable pain. The questions raised by his narrative are manifold: If history offers no finite goal, what are we to make of Dostoevsky's conviction about the importance of striving for a transcendent ideal? If suffering has a value, how are we to judge the value of making other people suffer? Is the Underground Man a prophet or a warning? Does his definition of freedom anticipate the existentialists or help to discredit them? Whatever we decide about these or a hundred other such questions, we will still have the Underground Man's voice in our head as we close the book, still feel the tension of his paradoxes, still register the intensity of his sense of loss. Nuttall puts it well: 'As we turn the last page the words die into our mixed awareness of the whole book: a book full of chattering arguments, of self-defeating propositions; and at the same time (for the imagination will hold all these together, as it is implied by the nature of literature that they are in a way the same thing) a book about darkness, about narrow, dirty rooms with no fresh air, no windows, about failure to touch.'[7] That Dostoevsky manages to make those voices speak so cogently to us a hundred and fifty years later is a tribute to his genius and to the inspirational quality of great literature.

7 *Crime and Punishment*, p. 36.

SELECT BIBLIOGRAPHY

Bakhtin, M., *Problems of Dostoevsky's Poetics*, edited and translated by Caryl Emerson, Minneapolis, 1984

Berdyaev, Nicholas, *Dostoevsky*, translated by Donald Attwater, Cleveland and New York, 1973

Berlin, Isaiah, *Russian Thinkers*, edited by Henry Hardy and Aileen Kelly, Harmondsworth, 1978

Catteau, Jacques, *Dostoevsky and the Process of Literary Creation*, translated by Audrey Littlewood, Cambridge, 1989

Cioran, Samuel David (trans.), *The Crocodile*, Ann Arbor, 1985

Frank, Joseph, *Dostoevsky: The Seeds of Revolt, 1821–1849*, Princeton, 1976

———, *Dostoevsky: The Years of Ordeal, 1850–1859*, Princeton, 1983

———, *Dostoevsky: The Stir of Liberation, 1860–1865*, Princeton, 1986

———, *Dostoevsky: The Miraculous Years, 1865–1871*, Princeton, 1995

———, *Dostoevsky: The Mantle of the Prophet, 1871–1881*, Princeton, 2002

Jackson, Robert Louis, *Dostoevsky's Underground Man in Russian Literature*, The Hague, 1958

———, *Dostoevsky's Quest for Form: A Study of his Philosophy of Art*, New Haven, 1966

———, *The Art of Dostoevsky: Deliriums and Nocturnes*, Princeton, 1981

Jackson, Robert Louis, *Dialogues with Dostoevsky: The Overwhelming Questions*, Stanford, 1993

Jones, John, *Dostoevsky*, Oxford, 1985

———, *Dostoevsky after Bakhtin: Readings in Dostoyevsky's Fantastic Realism*, Cambridge, 1990

Katz, Michael R. (ed. and trans.), *Notes from Underground*, New York, 2001

Knapp, Liza, *The Annihilation of Inertia: Dostoevsky and Metaphysics*, Evanston, 1996

Leatherbarrow, W. J. (ed.), *The Cambridge Companion to Dostoevskii*. Cambridge, 2002

Lodge, Kirsten (ed. and trans.), *Notes from the Underground*, Peterborough, 2014

Meyer, Priscilla and Rudy, Stephen (eds), *Dostoevsky & Gogol: Texts and Criticism*, Ann Arbor, 1979

Meyer, Ronald (ed. and trans.), *The Gambler and Other Stories*, Harmondsworth, 2010

Morson, Gary Saul, *The Boundaries of Genre: Dostoevsky's 'Diary of a Writer' and the Traditions of Literary Utopia*, Austin, 1981

———, *Narrative and Freedom: The Shadows of Time*, New Haven, 1994

Nuttall, A. D., *'Crime and Punishment': Murder as Philosophic Experiment*, Edinburgh, 1978

Offord, Derek, 'Dostoevsky and Chernyshevsky', *Slavonic and East European Review*, 57 (1979), pp. 509–30

Steiner, George, *Tolstoy or Dostoevsky: An Essay in the Old Criticism*, New York, 1959

Straus, Nina Pelikan, *Dostoevsky and the Woman Question: Rereadings at the End of a Century*, New York, 1994

Terras, Victor, *The Young Dostoevsky, 1846–49: A Critical Study*, The Hague, 1969

———, *Reading Dostoevsky*, Madison, 1998

Todorov, Tzvetan, *Genres in Discourse*, translated by Catherine Porter, Cambridge, UK, 1990

Tynyanov, Yu, *Dostoevskii i Gogol: K teorii parodii* (Dostoevsky and Gogol: Towards a Theory of Parody), Moscow, 1921

Wilks, Ronald (trans.), *Notes from Underground and The Double*, Harmondsworth, 2009

NOTES FROM UNDERGROUND
and Other Stories

Mr Prohartchin

I N THE DARKEST and humblest corner of Ustinya Fyodorovna's flat lived Semyon Ivanovitch Prohartchin, a well-meaning elderly man, who did not drink. Since Mr Prohartchin was of a very humble grade in the service, and received a salary strictly proportionate to his official capacity, Ustinya Fyodorovna could not get more than five roubles a month from him for his lodging. Some people said that she had her own reasons for accepting him as a lodger; but, be that as it may, as though in despite of all his detractors, Mr Prohartchin actually became her favourite, in an honourable and virtuous sense, of course. It must be observed that Ustinya Fyodorovna, a very respectable woman, who had a special partiality for meat and coffee, and found it difficult to keep the fasts, let rooms to several other boarders who paid twice as much as Semyon Ivanovitch, yet not being quiet lodgers, but on the contrary all of them 'spiteful scoffers' at her feminine ways and her forlorn helplessness, stood very low in her good opinion, so that if it had not been for the rent they paid, she would not have cared to let them stay, nor indeed to see them in her flat at all. Semyon Ivanovitch had become her favourite from the day when a retired, or, perhaps more correctly speaking, discharged clerk, with a weakness for strong drink, was carried to his last resting-place in Volkovo.[1] Though this gentleman had only one eye, having had the other knocked out owing, in his own words, to his valiant behaviour; and only one leg, the other having been broken in the same way owing to his valour; yet he had succeeded in winning all the kindly feeling of which Ustinya Fyodorovna was capable, and took the fullest advantage of it, and would probably have gone on for years living as her devoted satellite and toady if he had not finally drunk himself to death in the most pitiable way. All this had happened at Peski,[2] where Ustinya Fyodorovna only had three lodgers, of whom, when she moved into a new flat and set up on a larger scale, letting to about a dozen new boarders, Mr Prohartchin was the only one who remained.

Whether Mr Prohartchin had certain incorrigible defects, or whether his companions were, every one of them, to blame, there seemed to be misunderstandings on both sides from the first. We must observe here that all Ustinya Fyodorovna's new lodgers without exception got on together like brothers; some of them were in the same office; each one of them by turns lost all his money to the others at faro,[3] preference[4] and *bixe*;[5] they all liked in a merry hour to enjoy what they called the fizzing moments of life in a crowd together; they were fond, too, at times of discussing lofty subjects, and though in the end things rarely passed off without a dispute, yet as all prejudices were banished from the whole party the general harmony was not in the least disturbed thereby. The most remarkable among the lodgers were Mark Ivanovitch, an intelligent and well-read man; then Oplevaniev; then Prepolovenko, also a nice and modest person; then there was a certain Zinovy Prokofy-evitch, whose object in life was to get into aristocratic society; then there was Okeanov, the copying clerk, who had in his time almost wrested the distinction of prime favourite from Semyon Ivanovitch; then another copying clerk called Sudbin; the plebeian Kantarev; there were others too. But to all these people Semyon Ivanovitch was, as it were, not one of themselves. No one wished him harm, of course, for all had from the very first done Prohartchin justice, and had decided in Mark Ivanovitch's words that he, Prohartchin, was a good and harmless fellow, though by no means a man of the world, trustworthy, and not a flatterer, who had, of course, his failings; but that if he were sometimes unhappy it was due to nothing else but lack of imagination. What is more, Mr Prohartchin, though deprived in this way of imagination, could never have made a particularly favourable impression from his figure or manners (upon which scoffers are fond of fastening), yet his figure did not put people against him. Mark Ivanovitch, who was an intelligent person, formally undertook Semyon Ivanovitch's defence, and declared in rather happy and flowery language that Prohartchin was an elderly and respectable man, who had long, long ago passed the age of romance. And so, if Semyon Ivanovitch did not know how to get on with people, it must have been entirely his own fault.

The first thing they noticed was the unmistakable parsimony and niggardliness of Semyon Ivanovitch. That was at once observed and noted, for Semyon Ivanovitch would never lend anyone his teapot, even for a moment; and that was the more unjust as he himself hardly ever drank tea, but when he wanted anything, drank, as a rule, rather a pleasant decoction of wild flowers and certain medicinal herbs, of which he always had a considerable store. His meals, too, were quite different from the other lodgers'. He never, for instance, permitted himself to partake of the whole dinner provided daily by Ustinya Fyodorovna for the other boarders. The dinner cost half a rouble; Semyon Ivanovitch paid only twenty-five kopecks in copper, and never exceeded it, and so took either a plate of soup with pie, or a plate of beef; most frequently he ate neither soup nor beef, but he partook in moderation of white bread with onion, curd, salted cucumber, or something similar, which was a great deal cheaper, and he would only go back to his half-rouble dinner when he could stand it no longer . . . Here the biographer confesses that nothing would have induced him to allude to such realistic and low details, positively shocking and offensive to some lovers of the heroic style, if it were not that these details exhibit one peculiarity, one characteristic, in the hero of this story; for Mr Prohartchin was by no means so poor as to be unable to have regular and sufficient meals, though he sometimes made out that he was. But he acted as he did regardless of obloquy and people's prejudices, simply to satisfy his strange whims, and from frugality and excessive carefulness: all this, however, will be much clearer later on. But we will beware of boring the reader with the description of all Semyon Ivanovitch's whims, and will omit, for instance, the curious and very amusing description of his attire; and, in fact, if it were not for Ustinya Fyodorovna's own reference to it we should hardly have alluded even to the fact that Semyon Ivanovitch never could make up his mind to send his linen to the wash, or if he ever did so it was so rarely that in the intervals one might have completely forgotten the existence of linen on Semyon Ivanovitch. From the landlady's evidence it appeared that 'Semyon Ivanovitch, bless his soul, poor lamb, for twenty years had been tucked away in his corner, without caring what folks thought, for all the days of his life on earth he was a stranger to socks, handkerchiefs, and all such things,' and what is more, Ustinya Fyodorovna had seen with her own eyes, thanks to the decrepitude of the screen, that the poor dear man sometimes had had nothing to cover his bare skin.

Such were the rumours in circulation after Semyon Ivanovitch's death. But in his lifetime (and this was one of the most frequent occasions of dissension) he could not endure it if anyone, even some-body on friendly terms with him, poked his inquisitive nose uninvited into his corner, even through an aperture in the decrepit screen. He was a taciturn man, difficult to deal with and prone to ill health. He did not like people to give him advice, he did not care for people who put themselves forward either, and if anyone jeered at him or gave him advice unasked, he would fall foul of him at once, put him to shame, and settle his business. 'You are a puppy, you are a featherhead, you are not one to give advice, so there – you mind your own business, sir. You'd better count the stitches in your own socks, sir, so there!'

Semyon Ivanovitch was a plain man, and never used the formal mode of address to anyone. He could not bear it either when someone who knew his little ways would begin from pure sport pestering him with questions, such as what he had in his little trunk . . . Semyon Ivanovitch had one little trunk. It stood under his bed, and was guarded like the apple of his eye; and though everyone knew that there was nothing in it except old rags, two or three pairs of damaged boots and all sorts of rubbish, yet Mr Prohartchin prized his property very highly, and they used even to hear him at one time express dissatisfaction with his old, but still sound, lock, and talk of getting a new one of a special German pattern with a secret spring and various complications. When on one occasion Zinovy Prokofyevitch, carried away by the thoughtlessness of youth, gave expression to the very coarse and unseemly idea that Semyon Ivanovitch was probably hiding and treasuring something in his box to leave to his descendants, everyone who happened to be by was stupefied at the extraordinary effects of Zinovy Prokofyevitch's sally. At first Mr Prohartchin could not find suitable terms for such a crude and coarse idea. For a long time words dropped from his lips quite incoherently, and it was only after a while they made out that Semyon Ivanovitch was reproaching Zinovy Prokofyevitch for some shabby action in the remote past; then they realised that Semyon Ivanovitch was predicting that Zinovy Prokofyevitch would never get into aristocratic society, and that the tailor to whom he owed a bill for his suits would beat him – would certainly beat him – because the puppy had not paid him for so long; and finally, 'You puppy, you,' Semyon Ivanovitch added, 'here you want to get into the hussars,[6] but you won't, I tell you, you'll make a fool of yourself. And I tell you what, you puppy, when your superiors know all about it they will take and make you a copying clerk; so that will be the end of it! Do you hear, puppy?' Then Semyon Ivanovitch subsided, but after lying down for five hours to the intense astonishment of everyone he seemed to have reached a decision, and began suddenly reproaching and abusing the young man again, at first to himself and afterwards addressing Zinovy Prokofyevitch. But the matter did not end there, and in the evening, when Mark Ivanovitch and Prepolovenko made tea and asked Okeanov to drink it with them, Semyon Ivanovitch got up from his bed, purposely joined them, subscribing his fifteen or twenty kopecks, and on the pretext of a sudden desire for a cup of tea began at great length going into the subject, and explaining that he was a poor man, nothing but a poor man, and that a poor man like him had nothing to save. Mr Prohartchin confessed that he was a poor man on this occasion, he said, simply because the subject had come up; that the day before yesterday he had meant to borrow a rouble from that impudent fellow, but now he should not borrow it for fear the puppy should brag that that was the fact of the matter, and that his salary was such that one could not buy enough to eat, and that finally, a poor man, as you see, he sent his sister-in-law in Tver[7] five roubles every month, that if he did not send his sister-in-law in Tver five roubles every month his sister-in-law would die, and if his sister-in-law, who was dependent on him, were dead, he, Semyon Ivanovitch, would long ago have bought himself a new suit . . . And Semyon Ivanovitch went on talking in this way at great length about being a poor man, about his sister-in-law and about roubles, and kept repeating the same thing over and over again to impress it on his audience till he got into a regular muddle and relapsed into silence. Only three days later, when they had all forgotten about him, and no one was thinking of attacking him, he added something in conclusion to the effect that when Zinovy Prokofyevitch went into the hussars the impudent fellow would have his leg cut off in the war, and then he would come with a wooden leg and say: 'Semyon Ivanovitch, kind friend, give me something to eat!' and then Semyon Ivanovitch would not give him something to eat, and would not look at the insolent fellow; and that's how it would be, and he could just make the best of it.

All this naturally seemed very curious and at the same time fearfully amusing. Without much reflection, all the lodgers joined together for further investigation, and simply from curiosity determined to make a final onslaught on Semyon Ivanovitch *en masse*. And as Mr Prohartchin, too, had of late – that is, ever since he had begun living in the same flat with them – been very fond of finding out everything about them and asking inquisitive questions, probably for private reasons of his own, relations sprang up between the opposed parties without any preparation or effort on either side, as it were by chance and of itself. To get into relations Semyon Ivanovitch always had in reserve his peculiar, rather sly, and very ingenuous manoeuvre, of which the reader has learned something already. He would get off his bed about teatime, and if he saw the others gathered together in a group to make tea he would go up to them like a quiet, sensible, and friendly person, hand over his twenty kopecks, as he was entitled to do, and announce that he wished to join them. Then the young men would wink at one another, and so indicating that they were in league together against Semyon Ivanovitch, would begin a conversation, at first strictly proper and decorous. Then one of the wittier of the party would, apropos of nothing, fall to telling them news consisting most usually of entirely false and quite incredible details. He would say, for instance, that someone had heard His

Excellency that day telling Demid Vassilyevitch that in his opinion married clerks were more trustworthy than unmarried, and more suitable for promotion; for they were steady, and that their capacities were considerably improved by marriage, and that therefore he – that is, the speaker – in order to improve and be better fitted for promotion, was doing his utmost to enter the bonds of matrimony as soon as possible with a certain Fevronya Prokofyevna. Or he would say that it had more than once been remarked about certain of his colleagues that they were entirely devoid of social graces and of well-bred, agreeable manners, and consequently unable to please ladies in good society, and that, therefore, to eradicate this defect it would be suitable to deduct something from their salary, and with the sum so obtained, to hire a hall, where they could learn to dance, acquire the outward signs of gentlemanliness and good-breeding, courtesy, respect for their seniors, strength of will, a good and grateful heart and various agreeable qualities. Or he would say that it was being arranged that some of the clerks, beginning with the most elderly, were to be put through an examination in all sorts of subjects to raise their standard of culture, and in that way, the speaker would add, all sorts of things would come to light, and certain gentlemen would have to lay their cards on the table – in short, thousands of similar very absurd rumours were discussed. To keep it up, everyone believed the story at once, showed interest in it, asked questions, applied it to themselves; and some of them, assuming a despondent air, began shaking their heads and asking everyone's advice, saying what were they to do if they were to come under it? It need hardly be said that a man far less credulous and simple-hearted than Mr Prohartchin would have been puzzled and carried away by a rumour so unanimously believed. Moreover, from all appearances, it might be safely concluded that Semyon Ivanovitch was exceedingly stupid and slow to grasp any new unusual idea, and that when he heard anything new, he had always first, as it were, to chew it over and digest it, to find out the meaning, and struggling with it in bewilderment, at last perhaps to overcome it, though even then in a quite special manner peculiar to himself alone . . . In this way curious and hitherto unexpected qualities began to show themselves in Semyon Ivanovitch . . . Talk and tittle-tattle followed, and by devious ways it all reached the office at last, with additions. What increased the sensation was the fact that Mr Prohart-chin, who had looked almost exactly the same from time immemorial, suddenly, apropos of nothing, wore quite a different countenance. His face was uneasy, his eyes were timid and had a scared and rather suspicious expression. He took to walking softly, starting and listening, and to put the finishing touch to his new characteristics developed a passion for investigating the truth. He carried his love of truth at last to such a pitch as to venture, on two occasions, to enquire of Demid Vassilyevitch himself concerning the credibility of the strange rumours that reached him daily by dozens, and if we say nothing here of the consequence of the action of Semyon Ivanovitch, it is for no other reason but a sensitive regard for his reputation. It was in this way people came to consider him as misanthropic and regardless of the proprieties. Then they began to discover that there was a great deal that was fantastical about him, and in this they were not altogether mistaken, for it was observed on more than one occasion that Semyon Ivanovitch completely forgot himself, and sitting in his seat with his mouth open and his pen in the air, as though frozen or petrified, looked more like the shadow of a rational being than that rational being itself. It sometimes happened that some innocently gaping gentleman, on suddenly catching his straying, lustreless, questioning eyes, was scared and all of a tremor, and at once inserted into some important document either a smudge or some quite inappropriate word. The impropriety of Semyon Ivanovitch's behaviour embarrassed and annoyed all really well-bred people . . . At last no one could feel any doubt of the eccentricity of Semyon Ivanovitch's mind, when one fine morning the rumour was all over the office that Mr Prohartchin had actually frightened Demid Vassilyevitch himself, for, meeting him in the corridor, Semyon Ivanovitch had been so strange and peculiar that he had forced his superior to beat a retreat . . . The news of Semyon Ivanovitch's behaviour reached him himself at last. Hearing of it he got up at once, made his way carefully between the chairs and tables, reached the entry, took down his overcoat with his own hand, put it on, went out, and disappeared for an indefinite period. Whether he was led into this by alarm or some other impulse we cannot say, but no trace was seen of him for a time either at home or at the office . . . We will not attribute Semyon Ivanovitch's fate simply to his eccentricity, yet we must observe to the reader that our hero was a very retiring man, unaccustomed to society, and had, until he made the acquaintance of the new lodgers, lived in complete unbroken solitude, and had been marked by his quietness and even a certain mysteriousness; for he had spent all the time that he lodged at Peski lying on his bed behind the screen, without talking or having any sort of relations with anyone. Both his old fellow-lodgers lived exactly as he did: they, too were, somehow mysterious people and spent fifteen years lying behind their screens. The happy, drowsy hours and days trailed by, one after the other, in patriarchal stagnation, and as everything around them went its way in the same happy fashion, neither Semyon Ivanovitch nor Ustinya Fyodorovna could remember exactly when fate had brought them together.

'It may be ten years, it may be twenty, it may be even twenty-five altogether,' she would say at times to her new lodgers, 'since he settled with me, poor dear man, bless his heart!' And so it was very natural that the hero of our story, being so unaccustomed to society was disagreeably surprised when, a year before, he, a respectable and modest man, had found himself, suddenly in the midst of a noisy and boisterous crew, consisting of a dozen young fellows, his colleagues at the office, and his new house-mates.

The disappearance of Semyon Ivanovitch made no little stir in the lodgings. One thing was that he was the favourite; another, that his passport, which had been in the landlady's keeping, appeared to have been accidentally mislaid. Ustinya Fyodorovna raised a howl, as was her invariable habit on all critical occasions. She spent two days in abusing and upbraiding the lodgers. She wailed that they had chased away her lodger like a chicken, and all those spiteful scoffers had been the ruin of him; and on the third day she sent them all out to hunt for the fugitive and at all costs to bring him back, dead or alive. Towards evening Sudbin first came back with the news that traces had been discovered, that he had himself seen the runaway in Tolkutchy Market[8] and other places, had followed and stood close to him, but had not dared to speak to him; he had been near him in a crowd watching a house on fire in Crooked Lane.[9] Half an hour later Okeanov and Kantarev came in and confirmed Sudbin's story, word for word; they, too, had stood near, had followed him quite close, had stood not more than ten paces from him, but they also had not ventured to speak to him, but both observed that Semyon Ivanovitch was walking with a drunken cadger. The other lodgers were all back and together at last, and after listening attentively they made up their minds that Prohartchin could not be far off and would not be long in returning; but they said that they had all known beforehand that he was about with a drunken cadger. This drunken cadger was a thoroughly bad lot, insolent and cringing, and it seemed evident that he had got round Semyon Ivanovitch in some way. He had turned up just a week before Semyon Ivanovitch's disappearance in company with Remnev, had spent a little time in the flat telling them that he had suffered in the cause of justice, that he had formerly been in the service in the provinces, that an inspector had come down on them, that he and his associates had somehow suffered in a good cause, that he had come to Petersburg and fallen at the feet of Porfiry Grigoryevitch, that he had been got, by interest, into a department; but through the cruel persecution of fate he had been discharged from there too, and that afterwards through reorganisation the office itself had ceased to exist, and that he had not been included in the new revised staff of clerks owing as much to direct incapacity for official work as to capacity for something else quite irrelevant – all this mixed up with his passion for justice and of course the trickery of his enemies. After finishing his story, in the course of which Mr Zimoveykin more than once kissed his sullen and unshaven friend Remnev, he bowed down to all in the room in turn, not forgetting Avdotya the servant, called them all his benefactors, and explained that he was an undeserving, troublesome, mean, insolent and stupid man, and that good people must not be hard on his pitiful plight and simplicity. After begging for their kind protection Mr Zimoveykin showed his livelier side, grew very cheerful, kissed Ustinya Fyodorovna's hands, in spite of her modest protests that her hand was coarse and not like a lady's; and towards evening promised to show the company his talent in a remarkable character dance. But next day his visit ended in a lamentable *dénouement*. Either because there had been too much character in the character-dance, or because he had, in Ustinya Fyodorovna's own words, somehow 'insulted her and treated her as no lady, though she was on friendly terms with Yaroslav Ilyitch himself, and if she liked might long ago have been an officer's wife', Zimoveykin had to steer for home next day. He went away, came back again, was again turned out with ignominy, then wormed his way into Semyon Ivanovitch's good graces, robbed him incidentally of his new breeches, and now it appeared he had led Semyon Ivanovitch astray.

As soon as the landlady knew that Semyon Ivanovitch was alive and well, and that there was no need to hunt for his passport, she promptly left off grieving and was pacified. Meanwhile some of the lodgers determined to give the runaway a triumphal reception; they broke the bolt and moved away the screen from Mr Prohartchin's bed, rumpled up the bed a little, took the famous box, put it at the foot of the bed; and on the bed laid the sister-in-law, that is, a dummy made up of an old kerchief, a cap and a mantle of the landlady's, such an exact counterfeit of a sister-in-law that it might have been mistaken for one. Having finished their work they waited for Semyon Ivanovitch to return, meaning to tell him that his sister-in-law had arrived from the country and was there behind his screen, poor thing! But they waited and waited.

Already, while they waited, Mark Ivanovitch had staked and lost half a month's salary to Prepolovenko and Kantarev; already Okeanov's nose had grown red and swollen playing 'flips on the nose'[10] and 'three cards';[11] already Avdotya the servant had almost had her sleep out and had twice been on the point of getting up to fetch the wood and light the stove, and Zinovy Prokofyevitch, who kept running out every minute to see whether Semyon Ivanovitch were coming, was wet to the skin; but there was no sign of anyone yet – neither Semyon Ivanovitch nor the drunken cadger. At last everyone went to bed, leaving the sister-in-law behind the screen in readiness for any emergency; and it was not till four o'clock that a knock was heard at the gate, but when it did come it was so loud that it quite made up to the expectant lodgers for all the wearisome trouble they had been through. It was he – he himself – Semyon Ivanovitch, Mr Prohartchin, but in such a condition that they all cried out in dismay, and no one thought about the sister-in-law. The lost man was unconscious. He was brought in, or more correctly carried in, by a sopping and tattered night-cabman. To the landlady's question where the poor dear man had got so groggy, the cabman answered: 'Why, he is not drunk and has not had a drop, that I can tell you, for sure; but seemingly a faintness has come over him, or some sort of a fit, or maybe he's been knocked down by a blow.'

They began examining him, propping the culprit against the stove to do so more conveniently, and saw that it really was not a case of drunkenness, nor had he had a blow, but that something else was wrong, for Semyon Ivanovitch could not utter a word, but seemed twitching in a sort of convulsion, and only blinked, fixing his eyes in bewilderment first on one and then on another of the spectators, who were all attired in night array. Then they began questioning the cabman, asking where he had got him from. 'Why, from folks out Kolomna[12] way,' he answered. 'Deuce knows what they are, not exactly gentry, but merry, rollicking gentlemen; so he was like this when they gave him to me; whether they had been fighting, or whether he was in some sort of a fit, goodness knows what it was; but they were nice, jolly gentlemen!'

Semyon Ivanovitch was taken, lifted high on the shoulders of two or three sturdy fellows, and carried to his bed. When Semyon Ivanovitch on being put in bed felt the sister-in-law, and put his feet on his sacred box, he cried out at the top of his voice, squatted up almost on his heels, and trembling and shaking all over, with his hands and his body he cleared a space as far as he could in his bed, while gazing with a tremulous but strangely resolute look at those present, he seemed as it were to protest that he would sooner die than give up the hundredth part of his poor belongings to anyone . . . Semyon Ivanovitch lay for two or three days closely barricaded by the screen, and so cut off from all the world and all its vain anxieties. Next morning, of course, every one had forgotten about him; time, meanwhile, flew by as usual, hour followed hour and day followed day. The sick man's heavy, feverish brain was plunged in something between sleep and delirium; but he lay quietly and did not moan or complain; on the contrary he kept still and silent and controlled himself, lying low in his bed, just as the hare lies close to the earth when it hears the hunter. At times a long depressing stillness prevailed in the flat, a sign that the lodgers had all gone to the office, and Semyon Ivanovitch, waking up, could relieve his depression by listening to the bustle in the kitchen, where the landlady was busy close by; or to the regular flop of Avdotya's downtrodden slippers as, sighing and moaning, she cleared away, rubbed and polished, tidying all the rooms in the flat. Whole hours passed by in that way, drowsy, languid, sleepy, wearisome, like the water that dripped with a regular sound from the locker into the basin in the kitchen. At last the lodgers would arrive, one by one or in groups, and Semyon Ivanovitch could very conveniently hear them abusing the weather, saying they were hungry, making a noise, smoking, quarrelling and making friends, playing cards and clattering the cups as they got ready for tea. Semyon Ivanovitch mechanically made an effort to get up and join them, as he had a right to do at tea; but he at once sank back into drowsiness, and dreamed that he had been sitting a long time at the tea-table, having tea with them and talking, and that Zinovy Prokofyevitch had already seized the opportunity to introduce into the conversation some scheme concerning sisters-in-law and the moral relation of various worthy people to them. At this point Semyon Ivanovitch was in haste to defend himself and reply. But the mighty formula that flew from every tongue – 'It has more than once been observed' – cut short all his objections, and Semyon Ivanovitch could do nothing better than begin dreaming again that today was the first of the month and that he was receiving money in his office.

Undoing the paper round it on the stairs, he looked about him quickly, and made haste as fast as he could to subtract half of the lawful wages he had received and conceal it in his boot. Then on the spot, on the stairs, quite regardless of the fact that he was in bed and asleep, he made up his mind when he reached home to give his landlady what was due for board and lodging; then to buy certain necessities, and to show anyone it might concern, as it were casually and unintentionally, that some of his salary had been deducted, that now he had nothing left to send his sister-in-law; then to speak with commiseration of his sister-in-law, to say a great deal about her the next day and the day after, and ten days later to say something casually again about her poverty, that his companions might not forget. Making this determination he observed that Andrey Efimovitch, that everlastingly silent, bald little man who sat in the office three rooms from where Semyon Ivanovitch sat, and hadn't said a word to him for twenty years, was standing on the stairs, that he, too, was counting his silver roubles, and shaking his head, he said to him: 'Money!' – 'If there's no money there will be no porridge,' he added grimly as he went down the stairs, and just at the door he ended: 'And I have seven children, sir.' Then the little bald man, probably equally unconscious that he was acting as a phantom and not as a substantial reality, held up his hand about thirty inches from the floor, and waving it vertically, muttered that the eldest was going to school, then glancing with indignation at Semyon Ivanovitch, as though it were Mr Prohartchin's fault that he was the father of seven, pulled his old hat down over his eyes, and with a whisk of his overcoat he turned to the left and disappeared. Semyon Ivanovitch was quite frightened, and though he was fully convinced of his own innocence in regard to the unpleasant accumulation of seven under one roof, yet it seemed to appear that in fact no one else was to blame but Semyon Ivanovitch. Panic-stricken he set off running, for it seemed to him that the bald gentleman had turned back, was running after him, and meant to search him and take away all his salary, insisting upon the indisputable number seven, and resolutely denying any possible claim of any sort of sisters-in-law upon Semyon Ivanovitch. Prohartchin ran and ran, gasping for breath . . . Beside him was running, too, an immense number of people, and all of them were jingling their money in the tail pockets of their skimpy little dress-coats; at last everyone ran up, there was the noise of fire engines, and whole masses of people carried him almost on their shoulders up to that same house on fire which he had watched last time in company with the drunken cadger. The drunken cadger – alias Mr Zimoveykin – was there now, too, he met Semyon Ivanovitch, made a fearful fuss, took him by the arm, and led him into the thickest part of the crowd. Just as then in reality, all about them was the noise and uproar of an immense crowd of people, flooding the whole of Fontanka Embankment[13] between the two bridges, as well as all the surrounding streets and alleys; just as then, Semyon Ivanovitch, in company with the drunken cadger, was carried along behind a fence, where they were squeezed as though in pincers in a huge timber yard full of spectators who had gathered from the street, from Tolkutchy Market and from all the surrounding houses, taverns and restaurants. Semyon Ivanovitch saw all this and felt as he had done at the time; in the whirl of fever and delirium all sorts of strange figures began flitting before him. He remembered some of them. One of them was a gentleman who had impressed everyone extremely, a man seven feet high, with whiskers half a yard long, who had been standing behind Semyon Ivanovitch's back during the fire, and had given him encouragement from behind when our hero had felt something like ecstasy and had stamped as though intending thereby to applaud the gallant work of the firemen, of which he had an excellent view from his elevated position. Another was the sturdy lad from whom our hero had received a shove by way of a lift on to another fence, when he had been disposed to climb over it, possibly to save someone. He had a glimpse, too, of the figure of the old man with a sickly face, in an old wadded dressing-gown, tied round the waist, who had made his appearance before the fire in a little shop buying sugar and tobacco for his lodger, and who now, with a milk-can and a quart pot in his hands, made his way through the crowd to the house in which his wife and daughter were burning together with thirteen and a half roubles in the corner under the bed. But most distinct of all was the poor, sinful woman of whom he had dreamed more than once during his illness – she stood before him now as she had done then, in wretched bark shoes and rags, with a crutch and a wicker-basket on her back. She was shouting more loudly than the firemen or the crowd, waving her crutch and her arms, saying that her own children had turned her out and that she had lost two coppers in consequence. The children and the coppers, the coppers and the children, were mingled together in an utterly incomprehensible muddle, from which everyone withdrew baffled, after vain efforts to understand. But the woman would not desist, she kept wailing, shouting and waving her arms, seeming to pay no attention either to the fire to which she had been carried by the crowd from the street or to the people about her, or to the misfortune of strangers, or even to the sparks and red-hot embers which were beginning to fall in showers on the crowd standing near. At last Mr Prohartchin felt that a feeling of terror was coming upon him; for he saw clearly that all this was not, so to say, an accident, and that he would not get off scot-free. And, indeed, upon the wood stack, close to him, was a peasant, in a torn smock that hung loose about him, with his hair and beard singed, and he began stirring up all the people against Semyon Ivanovitch. The crowd pressed closer and closer, the peasant shouted, and foaming at the mouth with horror, Mr Prohartchin suddenly realised that this peasant was a cabman whom he had cheated five years before in the most inhuman way, slipping away from him without paying through a side gate and jerking up his heels as he ran as though he were barefoot on hot bricks. In despair Mr Prohartchin tried to speak, to scream, but his voice failed him. He felt that the infuriated crowd was twining round him like a many-coloured snake, strangling him, crushing him. He made an incredible effort and awoke. Then he saw that he was on fire, that all his corner was on fire, that his screen was on fire, that the whole flat was on fire, together with Ustinya Fyodorovna and all her lodgers, that his bed was burning, his pillow, his quilt, his box, and last of all, his precious mattress. Semyon Ivanovitch jumped up, clutched at the mattress and ran dragging it after him. But in the landlady's room into which, regardless of decorum, our hero ran just as he was, barefoot and in his shirt, he was seized, held tight, and triumphantly carried back behind the screen, which meanwhile was not on fire – it seemed that it was rather Semyon Ivanovitch's head that was on fire – and was put back to bed. It was just as some tattered, unshaven, ill-humoured organ-grinder puts away in his travelling box the Punch who has been making an upset, drubbing all the other puppets, selling his soul to the devil, and who at last ends his existence, till the next performance, in the same box with the devil, the negroes, the Pierrot, and Mademoiselle Katerina with her fortunate lover, the captain.

Immediately everyone, old and young, surrounded Semyon Ivanovitch, standing in a row round his bed and fastening eyes full of expectation on the invalid. Meantime he had come to himself, but from shame or some other feeling began pulling up the quilt over him, apparently wishing to hide himself under it from the attention of his sympathetic friends. At last Mark Ivanovitch was the first to break silence, and as a sensible man he began saying in a very friendly way that Semyon Ivanovitch must keep calm, that it was too bad and a shame to be ill, that only little children behaved like that, that he must get well and go to the office. Mark Ivanovitch ended by a little joke, saying that no regular salary had yet been fixed for invalids, and as he knew for a fact that their grade would be very low in the service, to his thinking anyway, their calling or condition did not promise great and substantial advantages. In fact, it was evident that they were all taking genuine interest in Semyon Ivanovitch's fate and were very sympathetic. But with incomprehensible rudeness, Semyon Ivanovitch persisted in lying in bed in silence, and obstinately pulling the quilt higher and higher over his head. Mark Ivanovitch, however, would not be gainsaid, and restraining his feelings, said something very honeyed to Semyon Ivanovitch again, knowing that that was how he ought to treat a sick man. But Semyon Ivanovitch would not feel this: on the contrary he muttered something between his teeth with the most distrustful air, and suddenly began glancing askance from right to left in a hostile way, as though he would have reduced his sympathetic friends to ashes with his eyes. It was no use letting it stop there. Mark Ivanovitch lost patience, and seeing that the man was offended and completely exasperated, and had simply made up his mind to be obstinate, told him straight out, without any softening suavity, that it was time to get up, that it was no use lying there, that shouting day and night about houses on fire, sisters-in-law, drunken cadgers, locks, boxes and goodness knows what, was all stupid, improper and degrading, for if Semyon Ivanovitch did not want to sleep himself he should not hinder other people, and please would he bear it in mind.

This speech produced its effects, for Semyon Ivanovitch, turning promptly to the orator, articulated firmly, though in a hoarse voice, 'You hold your tongue, puppy! You idle speaker, you foul-mouthed man! Do you hear, young dandy? Are you a prince, eh? Do you understand what I say?'

Hearing such insults, Mark Ivanovitch fired up, but realising that he had to deal with a sick man, magnanimously overcame his resentment and tried to shame him out of his humour, but was cut short in that too; for Semyon Ivanovitch observed at once that he would not allow people to play with him for all that Mark Ivanovitch wrote poetry. Then followed a silence of two minutes; at last, recovering from his amazement, Mark Ivanovitch, plainly, clearly, in well-chosen language, but with firmness, declared that Semyon Ivanovitch ought to understand that he was among gentlemen, and 'you ought to understand, sir, how to behave with gentlemen.'

Mark Ivanovitch could on occasion speak effectively and liked to impress his hearers, but, probably from the habit of years of silence, Semyon Ivanovitch talked and acted somewhat abruptly; and, moreover, when he did on occasion begin a long sentence, as he got further into it every word seemed to lead to another word, that other word to a third word, that third to a fourth and so on, so that his mouth seemed brimming over; he began stuttering, and the crowding words took to flying out in picturesque disorder. That was why Semyon Ivanovitch, who was a sensible man, sometimes talked terrible nonsense. 'You are lying,' he said now. 'You booby, you loose fellow! You'll come to want – you'll go begging, you seditious fellow, you – you loafer. Take that, you poet!'

'Why, you are still raving, aren't you, Semyon Ivanovitch?'

'I tell you what,' answered Semyon Ivanovitch, 'fools rave, drunkards rave, dogs rave, but a wise man acts sensibly. I tell you, you don't know your own business, you loafer, you educated gentleman, you learned book! Here, you'll get on fire and not notice your head's burning off. What do you think of that?'

'Why . . . you mean . . . How do you mean, burn my head off, Semyon Ivanovitch?'

Mark Ivanovitch said no more, for everyone saw clearly that Semyon Ivanovitch was not yet in his sober senses, but delirious.

But the landlady could not resist remarking at this point that the house in Crooked Lane had been burnt owing to a bald wench; that there was a bald-headed wench living there, that she had lighted a candle and set fire to the lumber room; but nothing would happen in her place, and everything would be all right in the flats.

'But look here, Semyon Ivanovitch,' cried Zinovy Prokofyevitch, losing patience and interrupting the landlady, 'you old fogey, you old crock, you silly fellow – are they making jokes with you now about your sister-in-law or examinations in dancing? Is that it? Is that what you think?'

'Now, I tell you what,' answered our hero, sitting up in bed and making a last effort in a paroxysm of fury with his sympathetic friends. 'Who's the fool? You are the fool, a dog is a fool, you joking gentleman. But I am not going to make jokes to please you, sir; do you hear, puppy? I am not your servant, sir.'

Semyon Ivanovitch would have said something more, but he fell back in bed helpless. His sympathetic friends were left gaping in perplexity, for they understood now what was wrong with Semyon Ivanovitch and did not know how to begin. Suddenly the kitchen door creaked and opened, and the drunken cadger – alias Mr Zimoveykin – timidly thrust in his head, cautiously sniffing round the place as his habit was. It seemed as though he had been expected, everyone waved to him at once to come quickly, and Zimoveykin, highly delighted, with the utmost readiness and haste jostled his way to Semyon Ivanovitch's bedside.

It was evident that Zimoveykin had spent the whole night in vigil and in great exertions of some sort. The right side of his face was plastered up; his swollen eyelids were wet from his running eyes, his coat and all his clothes were torn, while the whole left side of his attire was bespattered with something extremely nasty, possibly mud from a puddle. Under his arm was somebody's violin, which he had been taking somewhere to sell. Apparently they had not made a mistake in summoning him to their assistance, for seeing the position of affairs, he addressed the delinquent at once, and with the air of a man who knows what he is about and feels that he has the upper hand, said: 'What are you thinking about? Get up, Senka. What are you doing, a clever chap like you? Be sensible, or I shall pull you out of bed if you are obstreperous. Don't be obstreperous!'

This brief but forcible speech surprised them all; still more were they surprised when they noticed that Semyon Ivanovitch, hearing all this and seeing this person before him, was so flustered and reduced to such confusion and dismay that he could scarcely mutter through his teeth in a whisper the inevitable protest.

'Go away, you wretch,' he said. 'You are a wretched creature – you are a thief! Do you hear? Do you understand? You are a great swell, my fine gentleman, you regular swell.'

'No, my boy,' Zimoveykin answered emphatically, retaining all his presence of mind. 'You're wrong there, you wise fellow, you regular Prohartchin,' Zimoveykin went on, parodying Semyon Ivanovitch and looking round gleefully. 'Don't be obstreperous! Behave yourself, Senka, behave yourself, or I'll give you away, I'll tell them all about it, my lad, do you understand?'

Apparently Semyon Ivanovitch did understand, for he started when he heard the conclusion of the speech, and began looking rapidly about him with an utterly desperate air.

Satisfied with the effect, Mr Zimoveykin would have continued, but Mark Ivanovitch checked his zeal, and waiting till Semyon Ivanovitch was still and almost calm again began judiciously impressing on the uneasy invalid at great length that 'to harbour ideas such as he now had in his head was, first, useless, and secondly, not only useless, but harmful; and, in fact, not so much harmful as positively immoral; and the cause of it all was that Semyon Ivanovitch was not only a bad example, but led them all into temptation.'

Everyone expected satisfactory results from this speech. Moreover by now Semyon Ivanovitch was quite quiet and replied in measured terms. A quiet discussion followed. They appealed to him in a friendly way, enquiring what he was so frightened of. Semyon Ivanovitch answered, but his answers were irrelevant. They answered him, he answered them. There were one or two more observations on both sides and then everyone rushed into discussion, for suddenly such a strange and amazing subject cropped up that they did not know how to express themselves. The argument at last led to impatience, impatience led to shouting, and shouting even to tears; and Mark Ivanovitch went away at last foaming at the mouth and declaring that he had never known such a blockhead. Oplevaniev spat in disgust, Okeanov was frightened, Zinovy Prokofyevitch became tearful, while Ustinya Fyodorovna positively howled, wailing that her lodger was leaving them and had gone off his head, that he would die, poor dear man, without a passport and without telling anyone, while she was a lone, lorn woman and that she would be dragged from pillar to post. In fact, they all saw clearly at last that the seed they had sown had yielded a hundred-fold, that the soil had been too productive, and that in their company, Semyon Ivanovitch had succeeded in over-straining his wits completely and in the most irrevocable manner. Everyone subsided into silence, for though they saw that Semyon Ivanovitch was frightened, the sympathetic friends were frightened too.

'What?' cried Mark Ivanovitch; 'but what are you afraid of? What have you gone off your head about? Who's thinking about you, my good sir? Have you the right to be afraid? Who are you? What are you? Nothing, sir. A round nought, sir, that is what you are. What are you making a fuss about? A woman has been run over in the street, so are you going to be run over? Some drunkard did not take care of his pocket, but is that any reason why your coat-tails should be cut off? A house is burnt down, so your head is to be burnt off, is it? Is that it, sir, is that it?'

'You . . . you . . . you stupid!' muttered Semyon Ivanovitch, 'if your nose were cut off you would eat it up with a bit of bread and not notice it.'[14]

'I may be a dandy,' shouted Mark Ivanovitch, not listening; 'I may be a regular dandy, but I have not to pass an examination to get married – to learn dancing; the ground is firm under me, sir. Why, my good man, haven't you room enough? Is the floor giving way under your feet, or what?'

'Well, they won't ask you, will they? They'll shut one up and that will be the end of it?'

'The end of it? That's what's up? What's your idea now, eh?'

'Why, they kicked out the drunken cadger.'

'Yes; but you see that was a drunkard, and you are a man, and so am I.'

'Yes, I am a man. It's there all right one day and then it's gone.'

'Gone! But what do you mean by it?'

'Why, the office! The off-off-ice!'

'Yes, you blessed man, but of course the office is wanted and necessary.'

'It is wanted, I tell you; it's wanted today and it's wanted tomorrow, but the day after tomorrow it will not be wanted. You have heard what happened?'

'Why, but they'll pay you your salary for the year, you doubting Thomas,[15] you man of little faith. They'll put you into another job on account of your age.'

'Salary? But what if I have spent my salary, if thieves come and take my money? And I have a sister-in-law, do you hear? A sister-in-law! You battering-ram . . . '

'A sister-in-law! You are a man . . . '

'Yes, I am; I am a man. But you are a well-read gentleman and a fool, do you hear? – you battering-ram – you regular battering-ram! That's what you are! I am not talking about your jokes; but there are jobs such that all of a sudden they are done away with. And Demid – do you hear? – Demid Vassilyevitch says that the post will be done away with . . . '

'Ah, bless you, with your Demid! You sinner, why, you know . . . '

'In a twinkling of an eye you'll be left without a post, then you'll just have to make the best of it.'

'Why, you are simply raving, or clean off your head! Tell us plainly, what have you done? Own up if you have done something wrong! It's no use being ashamed! Are you off your head, my good man, eh?'

'He's off his head! He's gone off his head!' they all cried, and wrung their hands in despair, while the landlady threw both her arms round Mark Ivanovitch for fear he should tear Semyon Ivanovitch to pieces.

'You heathen, you heathenish soul, you wise man!' Zimoveykin besought him. 'Senka, you are not a man to take offence, you are a polite, prepossessing man. You are simple, you are good . . . do you hear? It all comes from your goodness. Here I am a ruffian and a fool, I am a beggar; but good people haven't abandoned me, no fear; you see they treat me with respect, I thank them and the landlady. Here, you see, I bow down to the ground to them; here, see, see, I am paying what is due to you, landlady!' At this point Zimoveykin swung off with pedantic dignity a low bow right down to the ground.

After that Semyon Ivanovitch would have gone on talking; but this time they would not let him, they all intervened, began entreating him, assuring him, comforting him, and succeeded in making Semyon Ivanovitch thoroughly ashamed of himself, and at last, in a faint voice, he asked leave to explain himself.

'Very well, then,' he said, 'I am prepossessing, I am quiet, I am good, faithful and devoted; to the last drop of my blood, you know . . . do you hear, you puppy, you swell? . . . granted the job is going on, but you see I am poor. And what if they take it? do you hear, you swell? Hold your tongue and try to understand! They'll take it and that's all about it . . .

it's going on, brother, and then not going on . . . do you understand? And I shall go begging my bread, do you hear?'

'Senka,' Zimoveykin bawled frantically, drowning the general hubbub with his voice. 'You are seditious! I'll inform against you! What are you saying? Who are you? Are you a rebel, you sheep's head? A rowdy, stupid man they would turn off without a character. But what are you?'

'Well, that's just it.'

'What?'

'Well, there it is.'

'How do you mean?'

'Why, I am free, he's free, and here one lies and thinks . . . '

'What?'

'What if they say I'm seditious?'

'Se-di-tious? Senka, you seditious!'

'Stay,' cried Mr Prohartchin, waving his hand and interrupting the rising uproar, 'that's not what I mean. Try to understand, only try to understand, you sheep. I am law-abiding. I am law-abiding today, I am law-abiding tomorrow, and then all of a sudden they kick me out and call me seditious.'

'What are you saying?' Mark Ivanovitch thundered at last, jumping up from the chair on which he had sat down to rest, running up to the bed and in a frenzy shaking with vexation and fury. 'What do you mean? You sheep! You've nothing to call your own. Why, are you the only person in the world? Was the world made for you, do you suppose? Are you a Napoleon?[16] What are you? Who are you? Are you a Napoleon, eh? Tell me, are you a Napoleon?'

But Mr Prohartchin did not answer this question. Not because he was overcome with shame at being a Napoleon, and was afraid of taking upon himself such a responsibility – no, he was incapable of disputing further, or saying anything . . . His illness had reached a crisis. Tiny teardrops gushed suddenly from his glittering, feverish, grey eyes. He hid his burning head in his bony hands that were wasted by illness, sat up in bed, and sobbing, began to say that he was quite poor, that he was a simple, unlucky man, that he was foolish and unlearned, he begged kind folks to forgive him, to take care of him, to protect him, to give him food and drink, not to leave him in want, and goodness knows what else Semyon Ivanovitch said. As he uttered this appeal he looked about him in wild terror, as though he were expecting the ceiling to fall or the floor to give way. Everyone felt his heart soften and move to pity as he looked at the poor fellow. The landlady, sobbing and wailing like a peasant woman at her forlorn condition, laid the invalid back in bed with her own hands. Mark Ivanovitch, seeing the uselessness of touching upon the memory of Napoleon, instantly relapsed into kindliness and came to her assistance. The others, in order to do something, suggested raspberry tea, saying that it always did good at once and that the invalid would like it very much; but Zimoveykin contradicted them all, saying there was nothing better than a good dose of camomile or something of the sort. As for Zinovy Prokofyevitch, having a good heart, he sobbed and shed tears in his remorse for having frightened Semyon Ivanovitch with all sorts of absurdities, and gathering from the invalid's last words that he was quite poor and needing assistance, he proceeded to get up a subscription for him, confining it for a time to the tenants of the flat. Everyone was sighing and moaning, everyone felt sorry and grieved, and yet all wondered how it was a man could be so completely panic-stricken. And what was he frightened about? It would have been all very well if he had had a good post, had had a wife, a lot of children; it would have been excusable if he were being hauled up before the court on some charge or other; but he was a man utterly insignificant, with nothing but a trunk and a German lock; he had been lying more than twenty years behind his screen, saying nothing, knowing nothing of the world nor of trouble, saving his halfpence, and now at a frivolous, idle word the man had actually gone off his head, was utterly panic-stricken at the thought he might have a hard time of it . . . And it never occurred to him that everyone has a hard time of it! 'If he would only take that into consideration,' Okeanov said afterwards, 'that we all have a hard time, then the man would have kept his head, would have given up his antics and would have put up with things, one way or another.'

All day long nothing was talked of but Semyon Ivanovitch. They went up to him, enquired after him, tried to comfort him; but by the evening he was beyond that. The poor fellow began to be delirious, feverish. He sank into unconsciousness, so that they almost thought of sending for a doctor; the lodgers all agreed together and undertook to watch over Semyon Ivanovitch and soothe him by turns through the night, and if anything happened to wake all the rest immediately. With the object of keeping awake, they sat down to cards, setting beside the invalid his friend, the drunken cadger, who had spent the whole day in the flat and had asked leave to stay the night. As the game was played on credit and was not at all interesting they soon got bored. They gave up the game, then got into an argument about something, then began to be loud and noisy, finally dispersed to their various corners, went on for a long time angrily shouting and wrangling, and as all of them felt suddenly ill-humoured they no longer cared to sit up, so went to sleep.

Soon it was as still in the flat as in an empty cellar, and it was the more like one because it was horribly cold. The last to fall asleep was Okeanov. 'And it was between sleeping and waking,' as he said afterwards, 'I fancied just before morning two men kept talking close by me.' Okeanov said that he recognised Zimoveykin, and that Zimoveykin began waking his old friend Remnev just beside him, that they talked for a long time in a whisper; then Zimoveykin went away and could be heard trying to unlock the door into the kitchen. The key, the landlady declared afterwards, was lying under her pillow and was lost that night. Finally – Okeanov testified – he had fancied he had heard them go behind the screen to the invalid and light a candle there, 'and I know nothing more,' he said, 'I fell asleep, and woke up,' as everybody else did, when everyone in the flat jumped out of bed at the sound behind the screen of a shriek that would have roused the dead, and it seemed to many of them that a candle went out at that moment. A great hubbub arose, everyone's heart stood still; they rushed pell-mell at the shriek, but at that moment there was a scuffle, with shouting, swearing and fighting. They struck a light and saw that Zimoveykin and Remnev were fighting together, that they were swearing and abusing one another, and as they turned the light on them, one of them shouted: 'It's not me, it's this ruffian,' and the other who was Zimoveykin, was shouting: 'Don't touch me, I've done nothing! I'll take my oath any minute!' Both of them looked hardly like human beings; but for the first minute they had no attention to spare for them; the invalid was not where he had been behind the screen. They immediately parted the combatants and dragged them away, and saw that Mr Prohartchin was lying under the bed; he must, while completely unconscious, have dragged the quilt and pillow after him so that there was nothing left on the bedstead but the bare mattress, old and greasy (he never had sheets). They pulled Semyon Ivanovitch out, stretched him on the mattress, but soon realised that there was no need to make trouble over him, that he was completely done for; his arms were stiff, and he seemed all to pieces. They stood over him, he still faintly shuddered and trembled all over, made an effort to do something with his arms, could not utter a word, but blinked his eyes as they say heads do when still warm and bleeding, after being just chopped off by the executioner.

At last the body grew more and more still; the last faint convulsions died away. Mr Prohartchin had set off with his good deeds and his sins. Whether Semyon Ivanovitch had been frightened by something, whether he had had a dream, as Remnev maintained afterwards, or there had been some other mischief – nobody knew; all that can be said is, that if the head clerk had made his appearance at that moment in the flat and had announced that Semyon Ivanovitch was dismissed for sedition, insubordination and drunkenness; if some old draggle-tailed beggar woman had come in at the door, calling herself Semyon Ivanovitch's sister-in-law; or if Semyon Ivanovitch had just received two hundred roubles as a reward; or if the house had caught fire and Semyon Ivanovitch's head had been really burning – he would in all probability not have deigned to stir a finger in any of these eventualities. While the first stupefaction was passing over, while all present were regaining their powers of speech, were working themselves up into a fever of excitement, shouting and flying to conjectures and suppositions; while Ustinya Fyodorovna was pulling the box from under his bed, was rummaging in a fluster under the mattress and even in Semyon Ivanovitch's boots; while they cross-questioned Remnev and Zimoveykin, Okeanov, who had hitherto been the quietest, humblest and least original of the lodgers, suddenly plucked up all his presence of mind and displayed all his latent talents, by taking up his hat and under cover of the general uproar slipping out of the flat. And just when the horrors of disorder and anarchy had reached their height in the agitated flat, till then so tranquil, the door opened and suddenly there descended upon them, like snow upon their heads, a personage of gentlemanly appearance, with a severe and displeased-looking face, behind him Yaroslav Ilyitch, behind Yaroslav Ilyitch his subordinates and the functionaries whose duty it is to be present on such occasions, and behind them all, much embarrassed, Mr Okeanov. The severe-looking personage of gentlemanly appearance went straight up to Semyon Ivanovitch, examined him, made a wry face, shrugged his shoulders and announced what everybody knew, that is, that the dead man was dead, only adding that the same thing had happened a day or two ago to a gentleman of consequence, highly respected, who had died suddenly in his sleep. Then the personage of gentlemanly, but displeased-looking, appearance walked away saying that they had troubled him for nothing, and took himself off. His place was at once filled (while Remnev and Zimoveykin were handed over to the custody of the proper functionaries) by Yaroslav Ilyitch, who questioned someone, adroitly took possession of the box, which the landlady was already trying to open, put the boots back in their proper place, observing that they were all in holes and no use, asked for the pillow to be put back, called up Okeanov, asked for the key of the box which was found in the pocket of the drunken cadger, and solemnly, in the presence of the proper officials, unlocked Semyon Ivanovitch's property. Everything was displayed: two rags, a pair of socks, half a handkerchief, an old hat, several buttons, some old soles and the uppers of a pair of boots – that is, all sorts of odds and ends, scraps, rubbish, trash, which had a stale smell. The only thing of any value was the German lock. They called up Okeanov and cross-questioned him sternly; but Okeanov was ready to take his oath. They asked for the pillow, they examined it; it was extremely dirty, but in other respects it was like all other pillows. They attacked the mattress, they were about to lift it up, but stopped for a moment's consideration, when suddenly and quite unexpectedly something heavy fell with a clink on the floor. They bent down and saw on the floor a screw of paper and in the screw some dozen roubles. 'A-hey!' said Yaroslav Ilyitch, pointing to a slit in the mattress from which hair and stuffing were sticking out. They examined the slit and found that it had only just been made with a knife and was half a yard in length; they thrust hands into the gap and pulled out a kitchen knife, probably hurriedly thrust in there after slitting the mattress. Before Yaroslav Ilyitch had time to pull the knife out of the slit and to say 'A-hey!' again, another screw of money fell out, and after it, one at a time, two half-roubles, a quarter-rouble, then some small change, and an old-fashioned, solid five-kopeck piece – all this was seized upon. At this point it was realised that it would not be amiss to cut up the whole mattress with scissors. They asked for scissors.

Meanwhile, the guttering candle lighted up a scene that would have been extremely curious to a spectator. About a dozen lodgers were grouped round the bed in the most picturesque costumes, all unbrushed, unshaven, unwashed, sleepy-looking, just as they had gone to bed. Some were quite pale, while others had drops of sweat upon their brows: some were shuddering, while others looked feverish. The landlady, utterly stupefied, was standing quietly with her hands folded waiting for Yaroslav Ilyitch's good pleasure. From the stove above, the heads of Avdotya, the servant, and the landlady's favourite cat looked down with frightened curiosity. The torn and broken screen lay cast on the floor, the open box displayed its uninviting contents, the quilt and pillow lay tossed at random, covered with fluff from the mattress, and on the three-legged wooden table gleamed the steadily growing heap of silver and other coins. Only Semyon Ivanovitch preserved his composure, lying calmly on the bed and seeming to have no foreboding of his ruin. When the scissors had been brought and Yaroslav Ilyitch's assistant, wishing to be of service, shook the mattress rather impatiently to ease it from under the back of its owner, Semyon Ivanovitch with his habitual civility made room a little, rolling on his side with his back to the searchers; then at a second shake he turned on his face, finally gave way still further, and as the last slat in the bedstead was missing, he suddenly and quite unexpectedly plunged head downward, leaving in view only two bony, thin, blue legs, which stuck upwards like two branches of a charred tree. As this was the second time that morning that Mr Prohartchin had poked his head under his bed it at once aroused suspicion, and some of the lodgers, headed by Zinovy Prokofyevitch, crept under it, with the intention of seeing whether there were something hidden there too. But they knocked their heads together for nothing, and as Yaroslav Ilyitch shouted to them, bidding them release Semyon Ivanovitch at once from his unpleasant position, two of the more sensible seized each a leg, dragged the unsuspected capitalist into the light of day and laid him across the bed. Meanwhile the hair and flock were flying about, the heap of silver grew – and, my goodness, what a lot there was! . . . Noble silver roubles, stout solid rouble-and-a-half pieces, pretty half-rouble coins, plebeian quarter-roubles, twenty kopeck pieces, even the unpromising old crone's small fry of ten- and five-kopeck silver pieces – all done up in separate bits of paper in the most methodical and systematic way; there were curiosities also, two counters of some sort, one *napoléon d'or*, one very rare coin of some unknown kind . . . Some of the roubles were of the greatest antiquity: there were rubbed and hacked coins of Elizabeth, German kreutzers,[17] coins of Peter, of Catherine; there were, for instance, old fifteen-kopeck pieces, now very rare, pierced for wearing as earrings, all much worn, yet with the requisite number of dots . . . there was even copper, but all of that was green and tarnished . . . They found one red note, but no more. At last, when the dissection was quite over and the mattress case had been shaken more than once without a clink, they piled all the money on the table and set to work to count it. At the first glance one might well have been deceived and have estimated it at a million, it was such an immense heap. But it was not a million, though it did turn out to be a very considerable sum – exactly 2,497 roubles and a half – so that if Zinovy Prokofyevitch's subscription had been raised the day before there would perhaps have been just 2,500 roubles. They took the money, they put a seal on the dead man's box, they listened to the landlady's complaints, and informed her when and where she ought to lodge information in regard to the dead man's little debt to her. A receipt was taken from the proper person. At that point hints were dropped in regard to the sister-in-law; but being persuaded that in a certain sense the sister-in-law was a myth, that is, a product of the defective imagination with which they had more than once reproached

Semyon Ivanovitch – they abandoned the idea as useless, mischievous and disadvantageous to the good name of Mr Prohartchin, and so the matter ended.

When the first shock was over, when the lodgers had recovered themselves and realised the sort of person their late companion had been, they all subsided, relapsed into silence and began looking distrustfully at one another. Some seemed to take Semyon Ivanovitch's behaviour very much to heart, and even to feel affronted by it. What a fortune! So the man had saved up like this! Not losing his composure, Mark Ivanovitch proceeded to explain why Semyon Ivanovitch had been so suddenly panic-stricken; but they did not listen to him. Zinovy Prokofyevitch was very thoughtful, Okeanov had had a little to drink, the others seemed rather crestfallen, while a little man called Kantarev, with a nose like a sparrow's beak, left the flat that evening after very carefully packing up and cording all his boxes and bags, and coldly explaining to the curious that times were hard and that the terms here were beyond his means. The landlady wailed without ceasing, lamenting for Semyon Ivanovitch, and cursing him for having taken advantage of her lone, lorn state. Mark Ivanovitch was asked why the dead man had not taken his money to the bank. 'He was too simple, my good soul, he hadn't enough imagination,' answered Mark Ivanovitch.

'Yes, and you have been too simple, too, my good woman,' Okeanov put in. 'For twenty years the man kept himself close here in your flat, and here he's been knocked down by a feather – while you went on cooking cabbage-soup and had no time to notice it . . . Ah-ah, my good woman!'

'Oh, the poor dear,' the landlady went on, 'what need of a bank! If he'd brought me his pile and said to me: "Take it, Ustinyushka, poor dear, here is all I have, keep and board me in my helplessness, so long as I am on earth," then, by the holy ikon I would have fed him, I would have given him drink, I would have looked after him. Ah, the sinner! ah, the deceiver! He deceived me, he cheated me, a poor lone woman!'

They went up to the bed again. Semyon Ivanovitch was lying properly now, dressed in his best, though, indeed, it was his only, suit, hiding his rigid chin behind a cravat which was tied rather awkwardly, washed, brushed, but not quite shaven, because there was no razor in the flat; the only one, which had belonged to Zinovy Prokofyevitch, had lost its edge a year ago and had been very profitably sold at Tolkutchy Market; the others used to go to the barber's.

They had not yet had time to clear up the disorder. The broken screen lay as before, and exposing Semyon Ivanovitch's seclusion, seemed like an emblem of the fact that death tears away the veil from all our secrets, our shifty dodges and intrigues. The stuffing from the mattress lay about in heaps. The whole room, suddenly so still, might well have been compared by a poet to the ruined nest of a swallow, broken down and torn to pieces by the storm, the nestlings and their mother killed, and their warm little bed of fluff, feather and flock scattered about them . . . Semyon Ivanovitch, however, looked more like a conceited, thievish old cock-sparrow. He kept quite quiet now, seemed to be lying low, as though he were not guilty, as though he had had nothing to do with the shameless, conscienceless and unseemly duping and deception of all these good people. He did not heed now the sobs and wailing of his bereaved and wounded landlady. On the contrary, like a wary, callous capitalist, anxious not to waste a minute in idleness even in the coffin, he seemed to be wrapped up in some speculative calculation. There was a look of deep reflection on his face, while his lips were drawn together with a significant air, of which Semyon Ivanovitch during his lifetime had not been suspected of being capable. He seemed, as it were, to have grown shrewder, his right eye was, as it were, slyly screwed up. Semyon Ivanovitch seemed wanting to say something, to make some very important communication and explanation and without loss of time, because things were complicated and there was not a minute to lose . . . And it seemed as though they could hear him.

'What is it? Give over, do you hear, you stupid woman? Don't whine! Go to bed and sleep it off, my good woman, do you hear? I am dead; there's no need of a fuss now. What's the use of it, really? It's nice to lie here . . . Though I don't mean that, do you hear? You are a fine lady, you are a regular fine lady. Understand that; here I am dead now, but look here, what if – that is, perhaps it can't be so – but I say what if I'm not dead, what if I get up, do you hear? What would happen then?'

The Landlady

ORDYNOV had made up his mind at last to change his lodgings. The landlady with whom he lodged, the poor and elderly widow of a petty functionary, was leaving Petersburg, for some reason or other, and setting off to a remote province to live with relations before the first of the month when his time at his lodging was up. Staying on till his time was up the young man thought regretfully of his old quarters and felt vexed at having to leave them; he was poor and lodgings were dear. The day after his landlady went away, he took his cap and went out to wander about the back streets of Petersburg, looking at all the bills stuck up on the gates of the houses, and choosing by preference the dingiest and most populous blocks of buildings, where there was always more chance of finding a corner in some poor tenant's flat.

He had been looking for a long time, very carefully, but soon he was visited by new, almost unknown, sensations. He looked about him at first carelessly and absent-mindedly, then with attention, and finally with intense curiosity. The crowd and bustle of the street, the noise, the movement, the novelty of objects and the novelty of his position, all the paltry, everyday triviality of town life so wearisome to a busy Petersburger spending his whole life in the fruitless effort to gain by toil, by sweat and by various other means, a snug little home, in which to rest in peace and quiet – all this vulgar prose and dreariness aroused in Ordynov, on the contrary, a sensation of gentle gladness and serenity. His pale cheeks began to be suffused with a faint flush, his eyes began to shine as though with new hope, and he drew deep and eager breaths of the cold fresh air. He felt unusually light-hearted.

He always led a quiet and absolutely solitary life. Three years before, after taking his degree and becoming to a great extent his own master, he went to see an old man whom he had known only at second-hand, and was kept waiting a long while before the liveried servants consented to take his name in a second time. Then he walked into a dark, lofty, and deserted room, one of those dreary-looking rooms still to be found in old-fashioned family mansions that have been spared by time, and saw in it a grey-headed old man, hung with orders of distinction, who had been the friend and colleague of his father, and was his guardian. The old man handed him a tiny screw of notes. It turned out to be a very small sum: it was all that was left of his ancestral estates, which had been sold by auction to pay the family debts. Ordynov accepted his inheritance unconcernedly, took leave for ever of his guardian, and went out into the street. It was a cold, gloomy, autumn evening; the young man was dreamy and his heart was torn with a sort of unconscious sadness. There was a glow of fire in his eyes; he felt feverish, and was hot and chilly by turns. He calculated on the way that on his money he could live for two or three years, or even on half rations for four years. It grew dusk and began to drizzle with rain. He had taken the first corner he came across, and within an hour had moved into it. There he shut himself up as though he were in a monastery, as though he had renounced the world. Within two years he had become a complete recluse.

He had grown shy and unsociable without being aware of the fact; meanwhile, it never occurred to him that there was another sort of life – full of noise and uproar, of continual excitement, of continual variety, which was inviting him and was sooner or later inevitable. It is true that he could not avoid hearing of it, but he had never known it or sought to know it: from childhood his life had been exceptional; and now it was more exceptional than ever. He was devoured by the deepest and most insatiable passion, which absorbs a man's whole life and does not, for beings like Ordynov, provide any niche in the domain of practical daily activity. This passion was science. Meanwhile it was consuming his youth, marring his rest at nights with its slow, intoxicating poison, robbing him of wholesome food and of fresh air which never penetrated to his stifling corner. Yet, intoxicated by his passion, Ordynov refused to notice it. He was young and, so far, asked for nothing more. His passion made him a babe as regards external existence and totally incapable of forcing other people to stand aside when needful to make some sort of place for himself among them. Some clever people's science is a capital in their hands; for Ordynov it was a weapon turned against himself.

He was prompted rather by an instinctive impulse than by a logical, clearly defined motive for studying and knowing, and it was the same in every other work he had done hitherto, even the most trivial. Even as a child he had been thought queer and unlike his schoolfellows. He had never known his parents; he had to put up with coarse and brutal treatment from his schoolfellows, provoked by his odd and unsociable disposition, and that made him really unsociable and morose, and little by little he grew more and more secluded in his habits. But there never had been and was not even now any order and system in his solitary studies; even now he had only the first ecstasy, the first fever, the first delirium of the artist. He was creating a system for himself, it was being evolved in him by the years; and the dim, vague, but marvellously soothing image of an idea, embodied in a new, clarified form, was gradually emerging in his soul. And this form craved expression, fretting his soul; he was still timidly aware of its originality, its truth, its independence: creative genius was already showing, it was gathering strength and taking shape. But the moment of embodiment and creation was still far off, perhaps very far off, perhaps altogether impossible!

Now he walked about the street like a recluse, like a hermit who has suddenly come from his dumb wilderness into the noisy, roaring city. Everything seemed to him new and strange. But he was so remote from all the world that was surging and clattering around him that he did not wonder at his own strange sensation. He seemed unconscious of his own aloofness; on the contrary, there was springing up in his heart a joyful feeling, a sort of intoxication, like the ecstasy of a hungry man, who has meat and drink set before him after a long fast; though, of course, it was strange that such a trivial novelty as a change of lodgings could excite and thrill any inhabitant of Petersburg, even Ordynov; but the truth is that it had scarcely ever happened to him to go out with a practical object.

He enjoyed wandering about the streets more and more. He stared about at everything like a *flâneur*.[18]

But, even now, inconsequent as ever, he was reading significance in the picture that lay so brightly before him, as though between the lines of a book. Everything struck him; he did not miss a single impression, and looked with thoughtful eyes into the faces of passing people, watched the characteristic aspect of everything around him and listened lovingly to the speech of the people as though verifying in everything the conclusions that had been formed in the stillness of solitary nights. Often some trifle impressed him, gave rise to an idea, and for the first time he felt vexed that he had so buried himself alive in his cell. Here everything moved more swiftly, his pulse was full and rapid, his mind, which had been oppressed by solitude and had been stirred and uplifted only by strained, exalted activity, worked now swiftly, calmly and boldly. Moreover, he had an unconscious longing to squeeze himself somehow

into this life which was so strange to him, of which he had hitherto
known – or rather correctly divined – only by the instinct of the artist.
His heart began instinctively throbbing with a yearning for love and
sympathy. He looked more attentively at the people who passed by
him; but they were strangers, preoccupied and absorbed in thought,
and by degrees Ordynov's careless light-heartedness began unconsciously to pass away; reality began to weigh upon him, and to inspire in
him a sort of unconscious dread and awe. He began to be weary from
the surfeit of new impressions, like an invalid who for the first time
joyfully gets up from his sick bed, and sinks down giddy and stupefied
by the movement and exhausted by the light, the glare, the whirl of life,
the noise and medley of colours in the crowd that flutters by him. He
began to feel dejected and miserable, he began to be full of dread for his
whole life, for his work, and even for the future. A new idea destroyed
his peace. A thought suddenly occurred to him that all his life he had
been solitary and no one had loved him – and, indeed, he had succeeded
in loving no one either. Some of the passers-by, with whom he had
chanced to enter into conversation at the beginning of his walk, had
looked at him rudely and strangely. He saw that they took him for a
madman or a very original, eccentric fellow, which was indeed, perfectly
correct. He remembered that everyone was always somewhat ill at ease
in his presence, that even in his childhood everyone had avoided him on
account of his dreamy, obstinate character, that sympathy for people
had always been difficult and oppressive to him, and had been unnoticed
by others, for though it existed in him there was no moral equality
perceptible in it, a fact which had worried him even as a child, when he
was utterly unlike other children of his own age. Now he remembered
and reflected that always, at all times, he had been left out and passed
over by everyone.

Without noticing it, he had come into an end of Petersburg remote
from the centre of the town. Dining after a fashion in a solitary
restaurant, he went out to wander about again. Again he passed through
many streets and squares. After them stretched long fences grey, and
yellow; he began to come across quite dilapidated little cottages, instead
of wealthy houses, and mingled with them colossal factories, monstrous,
soot-begrimed, red buildings with long chimneys. All around it was
deserted and desolate, everything looked grim and forbidding, so at
least it seemed to Ordynov. It was by now evening. He came out of a
long side-street into a square where there stood a parish church.

He went into it without thinking. The service was just over, the
church was almost empty, only two old women were kneeling near

the entrance. The verger, a grey-headed old man, was putting out the candles. The rays of the setting sun were streaming down from above through a narrow window in the cupola and flooding one of the chapels with a sea of brilliant light, but it grew fainter and fainter, and the blacker the darkness that gathered under the vaulted roof, the more brilliantly glittered in places the gilt ikons, reflecting the flickering glow of the lamps and the lights. In an access of profound depression and some stifled feeling Ordynov leaned against the wall in the darkest corner of the church, and for an instant sank into forgetfulness. He came to himself when the even, hollow sound of the footsteps of two persons resounded in the building. He raised his eyes and an indescribable curiosity took possession of him at the sight of the two advancing figures. They were an old man and a young woman. The old man was tall, still upright and hale looking, but thin and of a sickly pallor. From his appearance he might have been taken for a merchant from some distant province. He was wearing a long black full-skirted coat trimmed with fur, evidently a holiday dress, and he wore it unbuttoned; under it could be seen some other long-skirted Russian garment, buttoned closely from top to bottom. His bare neck was covered with a bright red handkerchief carelessly knotted; in his hands he held a fur cap. His thin, long, grizzled beard fell down to his chest, and fiery, feverishly glowing eyes flashed a haughty, prolonged stare from under his frowning, overhanging brows. The woman was about twenty and wonderfully beautiful. She wore a splendid blue, fur-trimmed jacket, and her head was covered with a white satin kerchief tied under her chin. She walked with her eyes cast down, and a sort of melancholy dignity pervaded her whole figure and was vividly and mournfully reflected in the sweet contours of the childishly soft, mild lines of her face. There was something strange in this surprising couple.

The old man stood still in the middle of the church, and bowed to all the four points of the compass, though the church was quite empty; his companion did the same. Then he took her by the hand and led her up to the big ikon of the Virgin, to whom the church was dedicated. It was shining on the altar, with the dazzling light of the candles reflected on the gold and precious stones of the setting. The church verger, the last one remaining in the church, bowed respectfully to the old man, the latter nodded to him. The woman fell on her face, before the ikon. The old man took the hem of the veil that hung at the pedestal of the ikon and covered her head. A muffled sob echoed through the church.

Ordynov was impressed by the solemnity of this scene and waited in impatience for its conclusion. Two minutes later the woman raised her head and again the bright light of the lamp fell on her charming face. Ordynov started and took a step forward. She had already given her hand to the old man and they both walked quietly out of the church. Tears were welling up from her dark blue eyes under the long eyelashes that glistened against the milky pallor of her face, and were rolling down her pale cheeks. There was a glimpse of a smile on her lips; but there were traces in her face of some childlike fear and mysterious horror. She pressed timidly close to the old man and it could be seen that she was trembling from emotion.

Overwhelmed, tormented by a sweet and persistent feeling that was novel to him, Ordynov followed them quickly and overtook them in the church porch. The old man looked at him with unfriendly churlishness; she glanced at him, too, but absent-mindedly, without curiosity, as though her mind were absorbed by some faraway thought. Ordynov followed them without understanding his own action. By now it had grown quite dark; he followed at a little distance. The old man and the young woman turned into a long, wide, dirty street full of hucksters' booths, corn chandlers' shops and taverns, leading straight to the city gates, and turned from it into a long narrow lane, with long fences on each side of it, running alongside the huge, blackened wall of a four-storeyed block of buildings, by the gates of which one could pass into another street also big and crowded. They were approaching the house; suddenly the old man turned round and looked with impatience at Ordynov. The young man stood still as though he had been shot; he felt himself how strange his impulsive conduct was. The old man looked round once more, as though he wanted to assure himself that his menacing gaze had produced its effect, and then the two of them, he and the young woman, went in at the narrow gate of the courtyard. Ordynov turned back.

He was in the most discontented humour and was vexed with himself, reflecting that he had wasted his day, that he had tired himself for nothing, and had ended foolishly by magnifying into an adventure an incident that was absolutely ordinary.

However severe he had been with himself in the morning for his reclusive habits, yet it was instinctive with him to shun anything that might distract him, impress and shock him in his external, not in his internal, artistic world. Now he thought mournfully and regretfully of his sheltered corner; then he was overcome by depression and anxiety about his unsettled position and the exertions before him. At last, exhausted and incapable of putting two ideas together, he made his way late at night to his lodging and realised with amazement that he had been about to pass the house in which he lived. Dumbfounded, he shook his head, and put down his absent-mindedness to fatigue and, going up the stairs, at last reached his garret under the roof. There he lighted a candle – and a minute later the image of the weeping woman rose vividly before his imagination. So glowing, so intense was the impression, so longingly did his heart reproduce those mild, gentle features, quivering with mysterious emotion and horror, and bathed in tears of ecstasy or childish penitence, that there was a mist before his eyes and a thrill of fire seemed to run through all his limbs. But the vision did not last long. After enthusiasm, after ecstasy, came reflection, then vexation, then impotent anger; without undressing he threw himself on his hard bed . . .

Ordynov woke up rather late in the morning, in a nervous, timid and oppressed state of mind. He hurriedly got ready, almost forcing himself to concentrate his mind on the practical problems before them, and set off in the opposite direction from that he had taken on his pilgrimage the day before. At last he found a lodging, a little room in the flat of a poor German called Schpies,[19] who lived alone with a daughter called Tinchen. On receiving a deposit Schpies instantly took down the notice that was nailed on the gate to attract lodgers, complimented Ordynov on his devotion to science, and promised to work with him zealously himself. Ordynov said that he would move in in the evening. From there he was going home, but changed his mind and turned off in the other direction; his self-confidence had returned and he smiled at his own curiosity. In his impatience the way seemed very long to him. At last he reached the church in which he had been the evening before. Evening service was in preparation. He close a place from which he could see almost all the congregation; but the figures he was looking for were not there. After waiting a long time he went away, blushing. Resolutely suppressing in himself an involuntary feeling, he tried obstinately to force himself to change the current of his thoughts. Reflecting on everyday practical matters, he remembered he had not had dinner and, feeling that he was hungry, he went into the same tavern in which he had dined the day before. Unconsciously he sauntered a long time about the streets, through crowded and deserted alleys, and at last came out into a desolate region where the town ended in a vista of fields that were turning yellow; he came to himself when the deathlike silence struck him by its strangeness and unfamiliarity. It was a dry and frosty day such as are frequent in Petersburg in October. Not far away was a cottage; and near it stood two haystacks; a little horse with prominent ribs was standing unharnessed, with drooping head and lip thrust out, beside a little two-wheeled gig, and seemed to be pondering over something. A watchdog, growling, gnawed a bone beside a broken wheel, and a child of three who, with nothing on but his shirt, was engaged in combing his shaggy white head, stared in wonder at the solitary stranger from the town. Behind the cottage there was a stretch of field and cottage garden. There was a dark patch of forest against the blue sky on the horizon, and on the opposite side were thick snow clouds, which seemed chasing before them a flock of flying birds moving noiselessly one after another across the sky. All was still and, as it were, solemnly melancholy, full of a palpitating, hidden suspense . . . Ordynov was walking on further and further, but the desolation weighed upon him. He turned back to the town from which there suddenly floated the deep clamour of bells, ringing for the evening service; he redoubled his pace and within a short time he was again entering the church that had been so familiar to him since the day before.

The unknown woman was there already. She was kneeling at the very entrance, among the crowd of worshippers. Ordynov forced his way through the dense mass of beggars, old women in rags, sick people and cripples, who were waiting for alms at the church door, and knelt down beside the stranger. His clothes touched her clothes and he heard the breath that came irregularly from her lips as she whispered a fervent prayer. As before, her features were quivering with a feeling of boundless devotion, and tears again were falling and drying on her burning cheeks, as though washing away some fearful crime. It was quite dark in the place where they were both kneeling, and only from time to time the dim flame of the lamp, flickering in the draught from the narrow open window pane, threw a quivering glimmer on her face, every feature of which printed itself on the young man's memory, making his eyes swim, and rending his heart with a vague, insufferable pain. But this torment had a peculiar, intense ecstasy of its own. At last he could not endure it; his breast began shuddering and aching all in one instant with a sweet and unfamiliar yearning, and, bursting into sobs, he bowed down with his feverish head to the cold pavement of the church. He saw nothing and felt nothing but the ache in his heart, which thrilled with sweet anguish.

This extreme impressionability, sensitiveness and lack of resisting power may have been developed by solitude, or this impulsiveness of heart may have been evolved in the exhausting, suffocating and hopeless silence of long, sleepless nights, in the midst of unconscious yearnings and impatient stirrings of spirit, till it was ready at last to explode and find an outlet, or it may have been simply that the time for that solemn moment had suddenly arrived and it was as inevitable as when on a sullen, stifling day the whole sky grows suddenly black and a storm pours rain and fire on the parched earth, hangs pearly drops on the emerald twigs, beats down the grass, the crops, crushes to the earth the tender cups of the flowers, in order that afterwards, at the first rays of the sun, everything, reviving again, may shine and rise to meet it, and triumphantly lift to the sky its sweet, luxuriant incense, glad and rejoicing in its new life ...

But Ordynov could not think now what was the matter with him. He was scarcely conscious.

He hardly noticed how the service ended, and only recovered his senses as he threaded his way after his unknown lady through the crowd that thronged the entrance. At times he met her clear and wondering eyes. Stopped every minute by the people passing out, she turned round to him more than once; he could see that her surprise grew greater and greater, and all at once she flushed a fiery red. At that minute the same old man came forward again out of the crowd and took her by the arm. Ordynov met his morose and sarcastic stare again, and a strange anger suddenly gripped his heart. At last he lost sight of them in the darkness; then, with a superhuman effort, he pushed forward and got out of the church. But the fresh evening air could not restore him; his breathing felt oppressed and stifled, and his heart began throbbing slowly and violently as though it would have burst his breast. At last he saw that he really had lost his strangers – they were neither in the main street nor in the alley. But already a thought had come to Ordynov, and in his mind was forming one of those strange, decisive projects, which almost always succeed when they are carried out, in spite of their wildness. At eight o'clock next morning he went to the house from the side of the alley and walked into a narrow, filthy and unclean backyard which was like an open cesspool in a house. The porter, who was doing something in the yard, stood still, leaned with his chin on the handle of his spade, looked Ordynov up and down and asked him what he wanted. The porter was a little fellow about five and twenty, a Tatar with an extremely old-looking face, covered with wrinkles.

'I'm looking for a lodging,' Ordynov answered, impatiently.

'Which?' asked the porter, with a grin. He looked at Ordynov as if he knew all about him.

'I want a furnished room in a flat,' answered Ordynov.

'There's none in that yard,' the porter answered enigmatically.

'And here?'

'None here, either.' The porter took up his spade again.

'Perhaps they will let me have one,' said Ordynov, giving the porter ten kopecks.

The Tatar glanced at Ordynov, took the ten kopecks, then took up his spade again, and after a brief silence announced that: 'No, there was no lodging.' But the young man did not hear him; he walked along the rotten, shaking planks that lay in the pool towards the one entrance from that yard into the lodge of the house, a black, filthy, muddy entrance that looked as though it were drowning in the pool. In the lower storey lived a poor coffin-maker. Passing by his cheering work-shop, Ordynov clambered by a half-broken, slippery, spiral staircase to the upper storey, felt in the darkness a heavy, clumsy door covered with rags of sacking, found the latch and opened it. He was not mistaken. Before him stood the same old man looking at him intently with extreme surprise.

'What do you want?' he asked abruptly and almost in a whisper.

'Is there a room to let?' asked Ordynov, almost forgetting everything he had meant to say. He saw over the old man's shoulder the young woman.

The old man began silently closing the door, shutting Ordynov out.

'We have a lodging to let,' the young woman's friendly voice said suddenly.

The old man let go of the door.

'I want a corner,' said Ordynov, hurriedly entering the room and addressing himself to the beautiful woman.

But he stopped in amazement as though petrified, looking at his future landlord and landlady; before his eyes a mute and amazing scene was taking place. The old man was as pale as death, as though on the point of losing consciousness. He looked at the woman with a leaden, fixed, searching gaze. She too, grew pale at first; then blood rushed to her face and her eyes flashed strangely. She led Ordynov into another little room.

The whole flat consisted of one rather large room, divided into three by two partitions. From the outer room they went straight into a narrow dark passage; directly opposite was the door, evidently leading to a bedroom the other side of the partition. On the right, the other side of the passage, they went into the room which was to let; it was narrow and pokey, squeezed in between the partition and two low windows; it was blocked up with the objects necessary for daily life; it was poor and cramped but passably clean. The furniture consisted of a plain white table, two plain chairs and a locker that ran both sides of the wall. A big, old-fashioned ikon in a gilt wreath stood over a shelf in a corner and a lamp was burning before it. There was a huge, clumsy Russian stove partly in this room and partly in the passage. It was clear that it was impossible for three people to live in such a flat.

They began discussing terms but incoherently and hardly understanding one another. Two paces away from her, Ordynov could hear the beating of her heart; he saw she was trembling with emotion and, it seemed, with fear. At last they came to an agreement of some sort. The young man announced that he should move in at once and glanced at his landlord. The old man was standing at the door, still pale, but a quiet, even dreamy smile had stolen on to his lips. Meeting Ordynov's eyes he frowned again.

'Have you a passport?' he asked suddenly, in a loud and abrupt voice, opening the door into the passage for him.

'Yes,' answered Ordynov, suddenly taken aback.

'Who are you?'

'Vassily Ordynov, nobleman, not in the service, engaged in private work,' he answered, falling into the old man's tone.

'So am I,' answered the old man. 'I'm Ilya Murin, artisan. Is that enough for you? You can go ... '

An hour later Ordynov was in his new lodging, to the surprise of himself and of his German who, together with his dutiful Tinchen, was beginning to suspect that his new lodger had deceived him.

Ordynov did not understand how it had all happened, and he did not want to understand ...

2

His heart was beating so violently that he was giddy, and everything was green before his eyes; mechanically he busied himself arranging his scanty belongings in his new lodgings: he undid the bag containing various necessary possessions, opened the box containing his books and began laying them out on the table; but soon all this work dropped from his hands. Every minute there rose before his eyes the image of the woman, the meeting with whom had so troubled and disturbed his whole existence, who had filled his heart with such irresistible, violent ecstasy – and such happiness seemed at once flooding his starved life that his thoughts grew dizzy and his soul swooned in anguish and perplexity.

He took his passport and carried it to the landlord in the hope of getting a glance at her. But Murin scarcely opened the door; he took the paper from him, said, 'Good; live in peace,' and closed the door again. An unpleasant feeling came over Ordynov. He did not know why, but it was irksome for him to look at the old man. There was something spiteful and contemptuous in his eyes. But the unpleasant impression quickly passed off. For the last three days Ordynov had, in comparison with his former stagnation, been living in a whirl of life; but he could not reflect, he was, indeed, afraid to. His whole existence was in a state of upheaval and chaos; he dimly felt as though his life had been broken in half; one yearning, one expectation possessed him, and no other thoughts troubled him.

In perplexity he went back to his room. There by the stove in which the cooking was done a little humpbacked old woman was busily at work, so filthy and clothed in such rags that she was a pitiful sight. She seemed very ill-humoured and grumbled to herself at times, mumbling with her lips. She was his landlord's servant. Ordynov tried to talk to her, but she would not speak, evidently from ill-humour. At last dinner-time arrived. The old woman took cabbage soup, pies and beef out of the oven, and took them to her master and mistress. She gave some of the same to Ordynov. After dinner there was a deathlike silence in the flat.

Ordynov took up a book and spent a long time turning over its pages, trying to follow the meaning of what he had read often before. Losing patience, he threw down the book and began again putting his room to rights; at last he took up his cap, put on his coat and went out into the street. Walking at hazard, without seeing the road, he still tried as far as he could to concentrate his mind, to collect his scattered thoughts and to reflect a little upon his position. But the effort only reduced him to misery, to torture. He was attacked by fever and chills alternately, and at times his heart beat so violently that he had to support himself against the wall. 'No, better death,' he thought; 'better death,' he whispered with feverish, trembling lips, hardly thinking of what he was saying. He walked for a very long time; at last, feeling that he was soaked to the skin and noticing for the first time that it was pouring with rain, he returned home. Not far from home he saw his porter. He fancied that the Tatar stared at him for some time with curiosity, and then went his way when he noticed that he had been seen.

'Good-morning,' said Ordynov, overtaking him. 'What are you called?'

'Folks call me porter,' he answered, grinning.

'Have you been porter here long?'

'Yes.'

'Is my landlord an artisan?'

'Yes, if he says so.'

'What does he do?'

'He's ill, lives, prays to God. That's all.'

'Is that his wife?'

'What wife?'

'Who lives with him.'

'Ye-es, if he says so. Goodbye, sir.'

The Tatar touched his cap and went off to his den.

Ordynov went to his room. The old woman, mumbling and grumbling to herself, opened the door to him, fastened it again with the latch, and again climbed on the stove where she spent her life. It was already getting dark. Ordynov was going to get a light, when he noticed that the door to the landlord's room was locked. He called the old woman, who, propping herself on her elbow, looked sharply at him from the stove, as though wondering what he wanted with the landlord's lock; she threw him a box of matches without a word. He went back into his room and again, for the hundredth time, tried to busy himself with his books and things. But, little by little, without understanding what he was doing, he sat down on the locker, and it seemed to him that he fell asleep. At times he came to himself and realised that his sleep was not sleep but the agonising unconsciousness of illness. He heard a knock at the door, heard it opened, and guessed that it was the landlord and landlady returning from evening service. At that point it occurred to him that he must go in to them for something. He stood up, and it seemed to him that he was already going to them, but stumbled and fell over a heap of firewood which the old woman had flung down in the middle of the floor. At that point he lost consciousness completely, and opening his eyes after a long, long time, noticed with surprise that he was lying on the same locker, just as he was, in his clothes, and that over him there bent with tender solicitude a woman's face, divinely beautiful and, it seemed, drenched with gentle, motherly tears. He felt her put a pillow under his head and lay something warm over him, and some tender hand was laid on his feverish brow. He wanted to say, 'Thank you,' he wanted to take that hand, to press it to his parched lips, to wet it with his tears, to kiss, to kiss it to all eternity. He wanted to say a great deal, but what he did not know himself; he would have been glad to die at that instant. But his arms felt like lead and would not move; he was as it were numb, and felt nothing but the blood pulsing through his veins, with throbs which seemed to lift him up as he lay in bed. Somebody gave him water . . . At last he fell into unconsciousness.

He woke up at eight o'clock in the morning. The sunshine was pouring through the green, mouldy windows in a sheaf of golden rays; a feeling of comfort relaxed the sick man's limbs. He was quiet and calm, infinitely happy. It seemed to him that someone had just been by his pillow. He woke up, looking anxiously around him for that unseen being; he so longed to embrace his friend and for the first time in his life to say, 'A happy day to you, my dear one.'

'What a long time you have been asleep!' said a woman's gentle voice.

Ordynov looked round, and the face of his beautiful landlady was bending over him with a friendly smile as clear as sunlight.

'How long you have been ill!' she said. 'It's enough; get up. Why keep yourself in bondage? Freedom is sweeter than bread, fairer than sunshine. Get up, my dove, get up.'

Ordynov seized her hand and pressed it warmly. It seemed to him that he was still dreaming.

'Wait; I've made tea for you. Do you want some tea? You had better have some; you'll be better. I've been ill myself and I know.'

'Yes, give me something to drink,' said Ordynov in a faint voice, and he got up on his feet. He was still very weak. A chill ran down his spine, all his limbs ached and felt as though they were broken. But there was a radiance in his heart, and the sunlight seemed to warm him with a sort of solemn, serene joy. He felt that a new, intense, incredible life was beginning for him. His head was in a slight whirl.

'Your name is Vassily?' she asked. 'Either I have made a mistake, or I fancy the master called you that yesterday.'

'Yes, it is. And what is your name?' said Ordynov, going nearer to her though hardly able to stand on his feet. He staggered.

She caught him by the arm, and laughed.

'My name is Katerina,' she said, looking into his face with her large, clear blue eyes. They were holding each other by the hands.

'You want to say something to me,' she said at last.

'I don't know,' answered Ordynov; everything was dark before his eyes.

'See what a state you're in. There, my dove, there; don't grieve, don't pine; sit here at the table in the sun; sit quiet, and don't follow me,' she added, seeing that the young man made a movement as though to keep her. 'I will be with you again at once; you have plenty of time to see as much as you want of me.' A minute later she brought in the tea, put it on the table, and sat down opposite him.

'Come, drink it up,' she said. 'Does your head ache?'

'No, now it doesn't ache,' he said. 'I don't know, perhaps it does . . . I don't want any . . . enough, enough! . . . I don't know what's the matter with me,' he said, breathless, and finding her hand at last. 'Stay here, don't go away from me; give me your hand again . . . It's all dark before my eyes; I look at you as though you were the sun,' he said, as it were tearing the words out of his heart, and almost swooning with ecstasy as he uttered them. His throat was choking with sobs.

'Poor fellow! It seems you have not lived with anyone kind. You are all lonely and forlorn. Haven't you any relations?'

'No, no one; I am alone . . . never mind, it's no matter! Now it's better; I am all right now,' said Ordynov, as though in delirium. The room seemed to him to be going round.

'I, too, have not seen my people for many years. You look at me as . . . ' she said, after a minute's silence.

'Well . . . what?'

'You look at me as though my eyes were warming you! You know, when you love anyone . . . I took you to my heart from the first word. If you are ill I will look after you again. Only don't you be ill; no. When you get up we will live like brother and sister. Will you? You know it's difficult to get a sister if God has not given you one.'

'Who are you? Where do you come from?' said Ordynov in a weak voice.

'I am not of these parts . . . You know folks tell how twelve brothers lived in a dark forest, and how a fair maiden lost her way in that forest. She went to them and tidied everything in the house for them, and put her love into everything. The brothers came home, and learned that the sister had spent the day there. They began calling her; she came out to them. They all called her sister, gave her freedom, and she was equal with all. Do you know the fairy tale?'

'I know it,' whispered Ordynov.

'Life is sweet; is it sweet to you to live in the world?'

'Yes, yes; to live for a long time, to live for ages,' answered Ordynov.

'I don't know,' said Katerina dreamily. 'I should like death, too. Is life sweet? To love, and to love good people, yes . . . Look, you've turned as white as flour again.'

'Yes, my head's going round . . . '

'Stay, I will bring you my bedclothes and another pillow; I will make up the bed here. Sleep, and dream of me; your weakness will pass. Our old woman is ill, too.'

While she talked she began making the bed, from time to time looking at Ordynov with a smile.

'What a lot of books you've got!' she said, moving away a box.

She went up to him, took him by the right arm, led him to the bed, tucked him up and covered him with the quilt.

'They say books spoil a man,' she said, shaking her head thoughtfully. 'Do you like reading?'

'Yes,' answered Ordynov, not knowing whether he were asleep or awake, and pressing Katerina's hand tight to assure himself that he was awake.

'My master has a lot of books; you should see! He says they are religious books. He's always reading to me out of them. I will show you afterwards; you shall tell me afterwards what he reads to me out of them.'

'Tell me,' whispered Ordynov, keeping his eyes fixed on her.

'Are you fond of praying?' she said to him after a moment's silence. 'Do you know, I'm afraid, I am always afraid ... '

She did not finish; she seemed to be meditating. At last she raised his hand to her lips.

'Why are you kissing my hand?' (and her cheeks flushed faintly crimson).

'Here, kiss mine,' she said, laughing and holding out both hands to him; then she took one away and laid it on his burning forehead; then she began to stroke and arrange his hair. She flushed more and more; at last she sat down on the floor by his bedside and laid her cheek against his cheek; her warm, damp breath tickled his face ... At last Ordynov felt a gush of hot tears fall from her eyes like molten lead on his cheeks. He felt weaker and weaker; he was too faint to move a hand. At that moment there was a knock at the door, followed by the grating of the bolt. Ordynov could hear the old man, his landlord, come in from the other side of the partition. Then he heard Katerina get up and, without haste and without listening, take her books; he felt her make the sign of the cross over him as she went out; he closed his eyes. Suddenly a long, burning kiss scorched his feverish lips; it was like a knife thrust into his heart. He uttered a faint shriek and sank into unconsciousness ...

Then a strange life began for him.

In moments when his mind was not clear, the thought flashed upon him that he was condemned to live in a long, unending dream, full of strange, fruitless agitations, struggles and sufferings. In terror he tried to resist the disastrous fatalism that weighed upon him, and at a moment of tense and desperate conflict some unknown force struck him again and he felt clearly that he was once more losing memory, that an impassable, bottomless abyss was opening before him and he was flinging himself into it with a wail of anguish and despair. At times he had moments of insufferable, devastating happiness, when the life force quickens convulsively in the whole organism, when the past shines clear, when the present glad moment resounds with triumph and one dreams, awake, of a future beyond all ken; when a hope beyond words falls with life-giving dew on the soul; when one wants to scream with ecstasy; when one feels that the flesh is too weak for such a mass of impressions that the whole thread of existence is breaking, and yet, at the same time, one greets all one's life with hope and renewal. At times he sank into lethargy, and then everything that had happened to him the last few days was repeated again, and passed across his mind in a swarm of broken, vague images; but his visions came in strange and enigmatic form. At times the sick man forgot what had happened to him, and wondered that he was not in his old lodging with his old landlady. He could not understand why the old woman did not come as she always used at the twilight hour to the stove, which from time to time flooded the whole dark corner of the room with a faint, flickering glow, to warm her trembling, bony hands at the dying embers before the fire went out, always talking and whispering to herself, and sometimes looking at him, her strange lodger, who had, she thought, grown mad by sitting so long over his books.

Another time he would remember that he had moved into another lodging; but how it had happened, what was the matter with him, and why he had to move he did not know, though his whole soul was swooning in continual, irresistible yearning . . . But to what end, what led him on and tortured him and who had kindled this terrible flame that stifled him and consumed his blood, again he did not know and could not remember. Often he greedily clutched at some shadow, often he heard the rustle of light footsteps near his bed, and a whisper, sweet as music, of tender, caressing words. Someone's moist and uneven breathing passed over his face, thrilling his whole being with love; hot tears dropped upon his feverish cheeks, and suddenly a long, tender kiss was printed on his lips; then his life lay languishing in unquenchable torture; all existence, the whole world, seemed standing still, seemed to be dying for ages around him, and everything seemed shrouded in a long night of a thousand years . . .

Then the tender, calmly flowing years of early childhood seemed coming back to him again with serene joy, with the inextinguishable happiness, the first sweet wonder of life, with the swarms of bright spirits that fluttered under every flower he picked, that sported with him on the luxuriant green meadow before the little house among the acacias, that smiled at him from the immense crystal lake beside which he would sit for hours together, listening to the splashing of the waves, and that rustled about him with their wings, lovingly scattering bright rainbow dreams upon his little cot, while his mother, bending over him, made the sign of the cross, kissed him, and sang him sweet lullabies in the long, peaceful nights. But then a being suddenly began to appear who overwhelmed him with a childlike terror, first bringing into his life the slow poison of sorrow and tears; he dimly felt that an unknown old man held all his future years in thrall, and, trembling, he could not turn his eyes away from him. The wicked old man followed him about everywhere. He peeped out and treacherously nodded to the boy from under every bush in the copse, laughed and mocked at him, took the shape of every doll, grimacing and laughing in his hands, like a spiteful evil gnome; he set every one of the child's inhuman schoolfellows against him, or, sitting with the little ones on the school bench, peeped out, grimacing, from every letter of his grammar. Then when he was asleep the evil old man sat by his pillow . . . he drove away the bright spirits whose gold and sapphire wings rustled about his cot, carried off his poor mother from him for ever, and began whispering to him every night long, wonderful fairy tales, unintelligible to his childish imagination, but thrilling and tormenting him with terror and un-childlike passion. But the wicked old man did not heed his sobs and entreaties, and would go on talking to him till he sank into numbness, into unconsciousness. Then the child suddenly woke up a man; the years passed over him unseen, unheeded. He suddenly became aware of his real position. He understood all at once that he was alone, an alien to all the world, alone in a corner not his own, among mysterious and suspicious people, among enemies who were always gathering together and whispering in the corners of his dark room, and nodding to the old woman squatting on her heels near the fire, warming her bony old hands, and pointing to him. He sank into perplexity and uneasiness; he wanted to know who these people were, why they were here, why he was himself in this room, and guessed that he had strayed into some dark den of miscreants, drawn on by some powerful but incompre-hensible force, without having first found out who and what the tenants were and who his landlord was. He began to be tortured by suspicion – and suddenly, in the stillness of the night, again there began a long, whispered story, and some old woman, mournfully nodding her white, grizzled head before the dying fire, was muttering it softly, hardly audibly to herself. But – and again he was overcome with horror – the story took shape before him in forms and faces. He saw everything, from his dim, childish visions upwards: all his thoughts and dreams, all his experiences in life, all he had read in books, things he had forgotten long ago, all were coming to life, all were being put together, taking shape and rising up before him in colossal forms and images, moving and swarming about him; he saw spread out before him magnificent, enchanted gardens, a whole town built up and demolished before his eyes, a whole churchyard giving up its dead, who began living over again; whole races and peoples came into being and passed away before his eyes; finally, every one of his thoughts, every immaterial fancy, now took bodily shape around his sick-bed; took bodily shape almost at the moment of its conception; at last he saw himself thinking not in immaterial ideas, but in whole worlds, whole creations, saw himself borne along like an atom in this infinite, strange world from which there was no escape, and all this life in its mutinous independence crushing and oppressing him and pursuing him with eternal, infinite irony; he felt that he was dying, dissolving into dust and ashes for ever, and even without hope of resurrection; he tried to flee; but there was no corner in all the universe to hide him. At last, in an access of despair, he made an intense effort, uttered a shriek and woke up.

He woke up, bathed in a chill, icy sweat. About him was a deadly silence; it was the dead of night. But still it seemed to him that somewhere the wonderful fairy tale was going on, that some hoarse voice was really telling a long story of something that seemed familiar to him. He heard talk of dark forests, of bold brigands, of some daring bravoes, maybe of Stenka Razin[20] himself, of merry drunken bargemen, of some fair maiden and of Mother Volga.[21] Was it not a fairy tale? Was he really hearing it? For a whole hour he lay, open-eyed, without stirring a muscle, in agonising numbness. At last he got up carefully, and joyfully felt that his strength had come back to him after his severe illness. The delirium was over and reality was beginning. He noticed that he was dressed exactly as he had been during his talk with Katerina, so that it could not have been long since the morning she had left him. The fire of resolution ran through his veins. Mechanically he felt with his hand for a big nail for some reason driven into the top of the partition near which stood his bed, seized it, and hanging his whole weight upon it, succeeded in pulling himself up to the crevice from which a hardly perceptible light stole into his room. He put his eye to the opening and, almost breathless with excitement, began peeping in.

There was a bed in the corner of the landlord's room; before it was a table covered with a cloth and piled up with books of old-fashioned shape, looking from their bindings like devotional books. In the corner was an ikon of the same old-fashioned pattern as in his room; a lamp was burning before it. On the bed lay the old man, Murin, sick, worn out with suffering and pale as a sheet, covered with a fur rug. On his knees was an open book. On a bench beside the bed lay Katerina, with her arm about the old man's chest and her head bent on his shoulder. She was looking at him with attentive, childishly wondering eyes, and seemed, breathless with expectation, to be listening with insatiable curiosity to what Murin was telling her. From time to time the speaker's voice rose higher, there was a shade of animation on his pale face; he frowned, his eyes began to flash, and Katerina seemed to turn pale with dread and expectation. Then something like a smile came into the old man's face and Katerina began laughing softly. Sometimes tears came into her eyes; then the old man tenderly stroked her on the head like a child, and she embraced him more tightly than ever with her bare arm that gleamed like snow, and nestled even more lovingly to his bosom.

At times Ordynov still thought this was part of his dream; in fact, he was convinced of it; but the blood rushed to his head and the veins throbbed painfully in his temples. He let go of the nail, got off the bed, and staggering, feeling his way like a lunatic, without understanding the impulse that flamed up like fire in his blood, he went to the door and pushed violently; the rusty bolt flew open at once, and with a bang and a crash he suddenly found himself in the middle of his landlord's bedroom. He saw Katerina start and tremble, saw the old man's eyes flash angrily under his lowering brows and his whole face contort with sudden fury. He saw the old man, still keeping close watch upon him, feel hurriedly with fumbling hand for a gun that hung upon the wall; then he saw the barrel of the gun flash, aimed straight at his breast with an uncertain hand that trembled with fury . . . There was the sound of a shot, then a wild, almost unhuman, scream, and when the smoke parted, a terrible sight met Ordynov's eyes. Trembling all over, he bent over the old man. Murin was lying on the floor; he was writhing in convulsions, his face was contorted in agony, and there was foam upon his working lips. Ordynov guessed that the unhappy man was in a severe epileptic fit. He flew, together with Katerina, to help him . . .

3

The whole night was spent in agitation. Next day Ordynov went out early in the morning, in spite of his weakness and the fever that still hung about him. In the yard he met the porter again. This time the Tatar lifted his cap to him from a distance and looked at him with curiosity. Then, as though pulling himself together, he set to work with his broom, glancing askance at Ordynov as the latter slowly approached him.

'Well, did you hear nothing in the night?' asked Ordynov.

'Yes, I heard.'

'What sort of man is he? Who is he?'

'Self took lodgings, self should know; me stranger.'

'Will you ever speak?' cried Ordynov, beside himself with an access of morbid irritability.

'What did me do? Your fault – you frightened the tenants. Below lives the coffin-maker, he deaf, but heard it all, and his wife deaf, but she heard, and in next yard, far away, they heard, too. I go to the overseer.'

'I am going to him myself,' answered Ordynov; and he went to the gate.

'As you will; self took the room . . . Master, master, stay.'

Ordynov looked round; the porter touched his hat from politeness.

'Well!'

'If you go, I go to the landlord.'

'What?'

'Better move.'

'You're stupid,' said Ordynov, and was going on again.

'Master, master, stay.' The porter touched his hat again and grinned. 'Listen, master: be not wrathful; why persecute a poor man? It's a sin to persecute a poor man. It is not God's law – do you hear?'

'You listen, too: here, take that. Come, what is he?'

'What is he?'

'Yes.'

'I'll tell you without money.'

At this point the porter took up his broom, brandished it once or twice, then stopped and looked intently, with an air of importance, at Ordynov.

'You're a nice gentleman. If you don't want to live with a good man, do as you like; that's what I say.'

Then the Tatar looked at him still more expressively, and fell to sweeping furiously again.

Making a show of having finished something at last, he went up to Ordynov mysteriously, and with a very expressive gesture pronounced: 'This is how it is.'

'How – what?'

'No sense.'

'What?'

'Has flown away. Yes! Has flown away!' he repeated in a still more mysterious tone. 'He is ill. He used to have a barge, a big one, and a second and a third, used to be on the Volga, and me from the Volga myself. He had a factory, too, but it was burnt down, and he is off his head.'

'He is mad?'

'Nay! . . . Nay! . . . ' the Tatar answered emphatically. 'Not mad. He is a clever man. He knows everything; he has read many books, many, many; he has read everything, and tells others the truth. Some bring two roubles, three roubles, forty roubles, as much as you please; he looks in a book, sees and tells the whole truth. And the money's on the table at once – nothing without money!'

At this point the Tatar positively laughed with glee, throwing himself into Murin's interests with extreme zest.

'Why, does he tell fortunes, prophesy?'

'H'm! . . . ' muttered the porter, wagging his head quickly. 'He tells the truth. He prays, prays a great deal. It's just that way, comes upon him.'

Then the Tatar made his expressive gesture again.

At that moment someone called the porter from the other yard, and then a little, bent, grey-headed man in a sheepskin appeared. He walked stumbling and looking at the ground, groaning and muttering to himself. He looked as though he were in his dotage.

'The master, the master!' the porter whispered in a fluster, with a hurried nod to Ordynov, and taking off his cap, he ran to meet the old man, whose face looked familiar to Ordynov; he had anyway met him somewhere just lately.

Reflecting, however, that there was nothing remarkable in that, he walked out of the yard. The porter struck him as an out-and-out rogue and an impudent fellow.

'The scoundrel was practically bargaining with me!' he thought. 'Goodness knows what it means!'

He had reached the street as he said this.

By degrees he began to be absorbed in other thoughts. The impression was unpleasant, the day was grey and cold; flakes of snow were flying. The young man felt overcome by a feverish shiver again; he felt, too, as though the earth were shaking under him. All at once an unpleasantly sweet, familiar voice wished him good-morning in a broken tenor.

'Yaroslav Ilyitch,' said Ordynov.

Before him stood a short, sturdy, red-cheeked man, apparently about thirty, with oily grey eyes and a little smile, dressed . . . as Yaroslav Ilyitch always was dressed. He was holding out his hand to him in a very amicable way. Ordynov had made the acquaintance of Yaroslav Ilyitch just a year before in quite a casual way, almost in the street. They had so easily become acquainted, partly by chance and partly through Yaroslav Ilyitch's extraordinary propensity for picking up everywhere good-natured, well-bred people, and his preference was for friends of good education whose talents and elegance of behaviour made them worthy at least of belonging to good society. Though Yaroslav Ilyitch had an extremely sweet tenor, yet even in conversation with his dearest friends there was something extraordinary clear, powerful and dominating in the tone of his voice that would put up with no evasions; it was perhaps merely due to habit.

'How on earth . . . ?' exclaimed Yaroslav Ilyitch, with an expression of the most genuine, ecstatic pleasure.

'I am living here.'

'Have you lived here long?' Yaroslav Ilyitch continued on an ascending note. 'And I did not know it! Why, we are neighbours! I am in this quarter now. I came back from the Ryazan province a month ago. I've caught you, my old and noble friend!' and Yaroslav Ilyitch laughed in a most good-natured way. 'Sergeyev!' he cried impressively, 'wait for me at Tarasov's, and don't let them touch a sack without me. And stir up the Olsufyev porter; tell him to come to the office at once. I shall be there in an hour . . . '

Hurriedly giving someone this order, the refined Yaroslav Ilyitch took Ordynov's arm and led him to the nearest restaurant.

'I shall not be satisfied till we have had a couple of words alone after such a long separation. Well, what of your doings?' he pronounced almost reverently, dropping his voice mysteriously. 'Working at science, as ever?'

'Yes, as before,' answered Ordynov, struck by a bright idea.

'Splendid, Vassily Mihalitch, splendid!' At this point Yaroslav Ilyitch pressed Ordynov's hand warmly. 'You will be a credit to the community. God give you luck in your career . . . Goodness! how glad I am I met you! How often I have thought of you, how often I have said: "Where is he, our good, noble-hearted, witty Vassily Mihalitch?" '

They engaged a private room. Yaroslav Ilyitch ordered lunch, asked for vodka, and looked feelingly at Ordynov.

'I have read a great deal since I saw you,' he began in a timid and somewhat insinuating voice. 'I have read all Pushkin . . . '

Ordynov looked at him absent-mindedly.

'A marvellous understanding of human passion. But first of all, let me express my gratitude. You have done so much for me by nobly instilling into me a right way of thinking.'

'Upon my word . . . '

'No, let me speak; I always like to pay honour where honour is due, and I am proud that this feeling at least has found expression.'

'Really, you are unfair to yourself, and I, indeed . . . '

'No, I am quite fair,' Yaroslav Ilyitch replied, with extraordinary warmth. 'What am I in comparison with you?'

'Good heavens!'

'Yes . . . '

Then followed silence.

'Following your advice, I have dropped many low acquaintances and have, to some extent, softened the coarseness of my manners,' Yaroslav Ilyitch began again in a somewhat timid and insinuating voice. 'In the time when I am free from my duties I sit for the most part at home; in the evenings I read some improving book and . . . I have only one desire, Vassily Mihalitch: to be of some little use to the fatherland . . . '

'I have always thought you a very high-minded man, Yaroslav Ilyitch.'

'You always bring balm to my spirit . . . you generous young man . . . '

Yaroslav Ilyitch pressed Ordynov's hand warmly.

'You are drinking nothing?' he said, his enthusiasm subsiding a little.

'I can't; I'm ill.'

'Ill? Yes, are you really? How long – in what way – did you come to be ill? If you like I'll speak . . . What doctor is treating you? If you like I'll speak to our parish doctor. I'll run round to him myself. He's a very skilful man!'

Yaroslav Ilyitch was already picking up his hat.

'Thank you very much. I don't go in for being doctored. I don't like doctors.'

'You don't say so? One can't go on like that. But he's a very clever man,' Yaroslav Ilyitch went on imploringly. 'The other day – do allow me to tell you this, dear Vassily Mihalitch – the other day a poor carpenter came. "Here," said he, "I hurt my hand with a tool; cure it for me . . . " Semyon Pafnutyitch, seeing that the poor fellow was in danger of gangrene, set to work to cut off the wounded hand; he did this in my presence, but it was done in such a gener . . . that is, in such a superb way, that I confess if it had not been for compassion for suffering humanity, it would have been a pleasure to look on, simply from curiosity. But where and how did you fall ill?'

'In moving from my lodging . . . I've only just got up.'

'But you are still very unwell and you ought not to be out. So you are not living where you were before? But what induced you to move?'

'My landlady was leaving Petersburg.'

'Domna Savishna? Really? . . . A thoroughly estimable, good-hearted woman! Do you know? I had almost a son's respect for her. That life, so near its end, had something of the serene dignity of our forefathers, and looking at her, one seemed to see the incarnation of our hoary-headed, stately old traditions . . . I mean of that . . . something in it so poetical!' Yaroslav Ilyitch concluded, completely overcome with shyness and blushing to his ears.

'Yes, she was a nice woman.'

'But allow me to ask you where you are settled now.'

'Not far from here, in Koshmarov's Buildings.'

'I know him. A grand old man! I am, I may say, almost a real friend of his. A fine old veteran!' Yaroslav Ilyitch's lips almost quivered with enthusiasm. He asked for another glass of vodka and a pipe. 'Have you taken a flat?'

'No, a furnished room in a flat.'

'Who is your landlord? Perhaps I know him, too.'

'Murin, an artisan; a tall old man . . . '

'Murin, Murin; yes, in the back court, over the coffin-maker's, allow me to ask?'

'Yes, yes, in the back court.'

'H'm! are you comfortable there?'

'Yes; I've only just moved in.'

'H'm! . . . I only meant to say, h'm! . . . have you noticed nothing special?'

'Really . . . '

'That is . . . I am sure you will be all right there if you are satisfied with your quarters . . . I did not mean that; I am ready to warn you . . . but, knowing your character . . . How did that old artisan strike you?'

'He seems to be quite an invalid.'

'Yes, he's a great sufferer . . . But have you noticed nothing? Have you talked to him?'

'Very little; he is so morose and unsociable.'

'H'm! . . . ' Yaroslav Ilyitch mused. 'He's an unfortunate man,' he said dreamily.

'Is he?'

'Yes, unfortunate, and at the same time an incredibly strange and interesting person. However, if he does not worry you . . . Excuse my dwelling upon such a subject, but I was curious . . . '

'And you have really roused my curiosity, too . . . I should very much like to know what sort of a man he is. Besides, I am living with him . . . '

'You know, they say the man was once very rich. He traded, as most likely you have heard. But through various unfortunate circumstances he was reduced to poverty; many of his barges were wrecked in a storm and lost, together with their cargo. His factory, which was, I believe, in the charge of a near and dear relation, was equally unlucky and was burnt down, and the relation himself perished in the flames. It must be admitted it was a terrible loss! Then, so they say, Murin sank into tearful despondency; they began to be afraid he would lose his reason, and, indeed, in a quarrel with another merchant, also an owner of barges plying on the Volga, he suddenly showed himself in such a strange and unexpected light that the whole incident could only be accounted for on the supposition that he was quite mad, which I am prepared to believe. I have heard in detail of some of his queer ways; there suddenly happened at last a very strange, so to say momentous, circumstance which can only be attributed to the malign influence of wrathful destiny.'

'What was it?' asked Ordynov.

'They say that in a fit of madness he made an attempt on the life of a young merchant, of whom he had before been very fond. He was so upset when he recovered from the attack that he was on the point of taking his own life; so at least they say. I don't know what happened after that, but it is known that he was several years doing penance . . . But what is the matter with you, Vassily Mihalitch? Am I fatiguing you with my artless tale?'

'Oh no, for goodness' sake . . . You say that he has been doing penance; but he is not alone.'

'I don't know. I am told he was alone. Anyway, no one else was mixed up in that affair. However, I have not heard what followed; I only know . . . '

'Well?'

'I only know – that is, I have nothing special in my mind to add . . . I only want to say, if you find anything strange or out of the ordinary in him, all that is merely the result of the misfortunes that have descended upon him one after the other . . . '

'Yes, he is so devout, so sanctimonious.'

'I don't think so, Vassily Mihalitch; he has suffered so much; I believe he is quite sincere.'

'But now, of course, he is not mad; he is all right?'

'Oh, yes, yes; I can answer for that, I am ready to take my oath on it; he is in full possession of all his faculties. He is only, as you have justly observed, extremely strange and devout. He is a very sensible man, in fact. He speaks smartly, boldly and very subtly. The traces of his stormy life in the past are still visible on his face. He's a curious man, and very well read.'

'He seems to be always reading religious books.'

'Yes, he is a mystic.'

'What?'

'A mystic. But I tell you that as a secret. I will tell you, as a secret, too, that a very careful watch was kept on him for a time. The man had a great influence on people who used to go to him.'

'What sort of influence?'

'But you'll never believe it; you see, in those days he did not live in this building. Alexandr Ignatyevitch, a respectable citizen, a man of standing, held in universal esteem, went to see him with a lieutenant out of curiosity. They arrive and are received, and the strange man begins by looking into their faces. He usually looks into people's faces if he consents to be of use to them; if not, he sends people away, and even very uncivilly, I'm told. He asks them, "What do you want, gentlemen?" "Well," answers Alexandr Ignatyevitch, "your gift can tell you that, without our saying." "Come with me into the next room," he says; then he signified which of them it was who needed his services. Alexandr Ignatyevitch did not say what happened to him afterwards, but he came out from him as white as a sheet. The same thing happened to a well-known lady of high rank: she, too, came out from seeing him as white as a sheet, bathed in tears and overcome with his predictions and his sayings.'

'Strange. But now does he still do the same?'

'It's strictly prohibited. There have been marvellous instances. A young cornet, the hope and joy of a distinguished family, mocked at him. "What are you laughing at?" said the old man, angered. "In three days' time you will be like this!" and he crossed his arms over his bosom to signify a corpse.'

'Well?'

'I don't venture to believe it, but they say his prediction came true. He has a gift, Vassily Mihalitch . . . You are pleased to smile at my guileless story. I know that you are greatly ahead of me in culture; but I believe in him; he's not a charlatan. Pushkin himself mentions a similar case in his works.'[22]

'H'm! I don't want to contradict you. I think you said he's not living alone?'

'I don't know . . . I believe his daughter is with him.'

'Daughter?'

'Yes, or perhaps his wife; I know there is some woman with him. I have had a passing glimpse of her, but I did not notice.'

'H'm! Strange . . . '

The young man fell to musing, Yaroslav Ilyitch to tender contemplation of him. He was touched both at seeing an old friend and at having satisfactorily told him something very interesting. He sat sucking his pipe with his eyes fixed on Vassily Mihalitch; but suddenly he jumped up in a fluster.

'A whole hour has passed and I forgot the time! Dear Vassily Mihalitch, once more I thank the lucky chance that brought us together, but it is time for me to be off. Will you allow me to visit you in your learned retreat?'

'Please do, I shall be delighted. I will come and see you, too, when I have a chance.'

'That's almost too pleasant to believe. You gratify me, you gratify me unutterably! You would not believe how you have delighted me!'

They went out of the restaurant. Sergeyev was already flying to meet them and to report in a hurried sentence that Vilyam Emelyanovitch was pleased to be driving out. A pair of spirited roans in a smart light gig did, in fact, come into sight. The trace horse was particularly fine. Yaroslav Ilyitch pressed his best friend's hand as though in a vice, touched his hat and set off to meet the flying gig. On the way he turned round once or twice to nod farewells to Ordynov.

Ordynov felt so tired, so exhausted in every limb, that he could scarcely move his legs. He managed somehow to crawl home. At the gate he was met again by the porter, who had been diligently watching his parting from Yaroslav Ilyitch, and beckoning to him from a distance. But the young man passed him by. At the door of his flat he ran full tilt against a little grey-headed figure coming out from Murin's room, looking on the ground.

'Lord forgive my transgressions!' whispered the figure, skipping on one side with the springiness of a cork.

'Did I hurt you?'

'No, I humbly thank you for your civility . . . Oh, Lord, Lord!'

The meek little man, groaning and moaning and muttering something edifying to himself, went cautiously down the stairs. This was the 'master' of the house, of whom the porter stood in such awe. Only then Ordynov remembered that he had seen him for the first time here at Murin's, when he was moving into the lodging.

He felt unhinged and shaken; he knew that his imagination and impressionability were strained to the utmost pitch, and resolved not to trust himself. By degrees he sank into a sort of apathy. A heavy oppressive feeling weighed upon his chest. His heart ached as though it were sore all over, and his whole soul was full of dumb, comfortless tears.

He fell again upon the bed which she had made him, and began listening again. He heard two breathings: one the heavy broken breathing of a sick man, the other soft but uneven, as though also stirred by emotion, as though that heart was beating with the same yearning, with the same passion. At times he heard the rustle of her dress, the faint stir of her soft light steps, and even that faint stir of her feet echoed with a vague but agonisingly sweet pang in his heart. At last he seemed to distinguish sobs, rebellious sighs and, at last, praying again. He knew that she was kneeling before the ikon, wringing her hands in a frenzy of despair! . . . Who was she? For whom was she praying? By what desperate passion was her heart torn? Why did it ache and grieve and pour itself out in such hot and hopeless tears?

He began to recall her words. All that she had said to him was still ringing in his ears like music, and his heart lovingly responded with a vague heavy throb at every recollection, every word of hers as he devoutly repeated it . . . For an instant a thought flashed through his mind that he had dreamed all this. But at the same moment his whole being ached in swooning anguish as the impression of her hot breath, her words, her kiss rose vividly again in his imagination. He closed his eyes and sank into oblivion. A clock struck somewhere; it was getting late; twilight was falling.

It suddenly seemed to him that she was bending over him again, that she was looking into his eyes with her exquisitely clear eyes, wet with sparkling tears of serene, happy joy, soft and bright as the infinite turquoise vault of heaven at hot midday. Her face beamed with such triumphant peace; her smile was warm with such solemnity of infinite bliss; she leaned with such sympathy, with such childlike impulsiveness on his shoulder that a moan of joy broke from his exhausted bosom. She tried to tell him something, caressingly she confided something to him. Again it was as though heart-rending music smote upon his hearing. Greedily he drank in the air, warm, electrified by her near breathing. In anguish he stretched out his arms, sighed, opened his eyes . . . She stood before him, bending down to his face, all pale as from fear, all in tears, all quivering with emotion. She was saying something to him, entreating him with half-bare arms, clasping and wringing her hands; he folded her in his arms, she quivered on his bosom . . .

'What is it? What is the matter with you?' said Ordynov, waking up completely, still pressing her in his strong, warm embrace. 'What is the matter with you, Katerina? What is it, my love?'

She sobbed softly with downcast eyes, hiding her flushed face on his breast. For a long while she could not speak and kept trembling as though in terror.

'I don't know, I don't know,' she said at last, in a hardly audible voice, gasping for breath, and scarcely able to articulate. 'I don't know how I came here . . . ' She clasped him even more tightly, with even more intensity, and in a violent irrepressible rush of feeling, kissed his shoulder, his hands, his chest; at last, as though in despair, she hid her face in her hands, fell on her knees, and buried her head in his knees. When Ordynov, in inexpressible anguish, lifted her up impatiently and made her sit down beside him, her whole face glowed with a full flush of shame, her weeping eyes sought forgiveness, and the smile that, in spite of herself, played on her lip could scarcely subdue the violence of her new feeling. Now she seemed again frightened; mistrustfully she pushed away his hand, and, with drooping head, answered his hurried questions in a fearful whisper.

'Perhaps you have had a terrible dream?' said Ordynov. 'Perhaps you have seen some vision . . . Yes? Perhaps *he* has frightened you . . . He is delirious and unconscious. Perhaps he has said something that was not for you to hear? Did you hear something? Yes?'

'No, I have not been asleep,' answered Katerina, stifling her emotion with an effort. 'Sleep did not come to me, he has been silent all the while and only once he called me. I went up, called his name, spoke to him; I was frightened; he did not wake and did not hear me. He is terribly sick, the Lord succour him! Then misery came upon my heart, bitter misery! I prayed and prayed and then this came upon me.'

'Hush, Katerina, hush, my life, hush! You were frightened yesterday . . . '

'No, I was not frightened yesterday! . . . '

'Has it ever been like this with you at other times?'

'Yes.' And again she trembled all over and huddled up to him like a child. 'You see,' she said, repressing her sobs, 'it was not for nothing that I have come to you, it was not for nothing that I could not bear to stay alone,' she repeated, gratefully pressing his hands. 'Enough, enough shedding tears over other people's sorrows! Save them for a dark day when you are lonely and cast down and there is no one with you! . . . Listen, have you ever had a love?'

'No . . . I never knew a love before you . . . '

'Before me? . . . You call me your love?'

She suddenly looked at him as though surprised, would have said something, but then was silent and looked down. By degrees her whole face suddenly flushed again a glowing crimson; her eyes shone more brightly through the forgotten tears still warm on her eyelashes, and it could be seen that some question was hovering on her lips. With bashful shyness she looked at him once or twice and then looked down again.

'No, it is not for me to be your first love,' she said. 'No, no,' she said, shaking her head thoughtfully, while the smile stole gently again over her face. 'No,' she said, at last, laughing; 'it's not for me, my own, to be your love.'

At that point she glanced at him, but there was suddenly such sadness reflected in her face, such hopeless sorrow suddenly overshadowed all her features, such despair all at once surged up from within, from her heart, that Ordynov was overwhelmed by an unaccountable, painful feeling of compassion for her mysterious grief and looked at her with indescribable distress.

'Listen to what I say to you,' she said in a voice that wrung his heart, pressing his hands in hers, struggling to stifle her sobs. 'Heed me well, listen, my joy! You calm your heart and do not love me as you love me now. It will be better for you, your heart will be lighter and gladder, and you will guard yourself from a fell foe and will win a sister fond. I will come and see you as you please, fondle you and take no shame upon myself for making friends with you. I was with you for two days when you lay in that cruel sickness! Get to know your sister! It is not for nothing that we have sworn to be brother and sister, it is not for nothing that I prayed and wept to the Holy Mother for you! You won't get another sister! You may go all round the world, you may get to know the whole earth and not find another love like mine, if it is love your heart wants. I will love you warmly, I will always love you as I do now, and I will love you because your soul is pure and clean and can be seen through; because when first I glanced at you, at once I knew you were the guest of my house, the longed-for guest, and it was not for nothing that you wanted to come to us; I love you because when you look at me your eyes are full of love and speak for your heart, and when they say anything, at once I know of all that is within you and long to give my life for your love, my freedom, because it is sweet to be even a slave to the man whose heart I have found . . . But my life is not mine but another's . . . and my freedom is bound! Take me for a sister and be a brother to me and take me to your heart when misery, when cruel weakness falls upon me; only do so that I have no shame to come to you and sit through the long night with you as now. Do you hear me? Is your heart opened to me? Do you understand what I have been saying to you? . . . '

She tried to say something more, glanced at him, laid her hand on his shoulder and at last sank helpless on his bosom. Her voice died away in convulsive, passionate sobbing, her bosom heaved, and her face flushed like an evening sunset.

'My life,' whispered Ordynov; everything was dark before his eyes and he could hardly breath. 'My joy,' he said, not knowing what he was saying, not understanding himself, trembling lest a breath should break the spell, should destroy everything that was happening, which he took rather for a vision than reality: so misty was everything around him! 'I don't know, I don't understand you, I don't remember what you have just said to me, my mind is darkened, my heart aches, my queen!'

At this point his voice broke with emotion. She clung more tightly, more warmly, more fervently to him. He got up, no longer able to restrain himself; shattered, exhausted by ecstasy, he fell on his knees. Convulsive sobs broke agonisingly from his breast at last, and the voice that came straight from his heart quivered like a harp-string, from the fullness of unfathomable ecstasy and bliss.

'Who are you, who are you, my own? Where do you come from, my darling?' he said, trying to stifle his sobs. 'From what heaven did you fly into my sphere? It's like a dream about me, I cannot believe in you. Don't check me, let me speak, let me tell you all, all! I have long wanted to speak . . . Who are you, who are you, my joy? How did you find my heart? Tell me; have you long been my sister? . . . Tell me everything about yourself, where you have been till now. Tell me what the place was called where you lived; what did you love there at first? what rejoiced you? what grieved you? . . . Was the air warm? was the sky clear? . . . Who were dear to you? who loved you before me? to whom did your soul yearn first? . . . Had you a mother? did she pet you as a child, or did you look round upon life as solitary as I did? Tell me, were you always like this? What were your dreams? what were your visions of the future? what was fulfilled and what was unfulfilled with you? – tell me everything . . . For whom did your maiden heart yearn first, and for what did you give it? Tell me, what must I give you for it? what must I give you for yourself? . . . Tell me, my darling, my light, my sister; tell me, how am I to win your heart? . . . '

Then his voice broke again, and he bowed his head. But when he raised his eyes, dumb horror froze his heart and the hair stood up on his head.

Katerina was sitting pale as a sheet. She was looking with a fixed stare into the air, her lips were blue as a corpse's and her eyes were dimmed by a mute, agonising woe. She stood up slowly, took two steps forward and, with a piercing wail, flung herself down before the ikon . . . Jerky, incoherent words broke from her throat. She lost consciousness. Shaken with horror, Ordynov lifted her up and carried her to his bed; he stood over her, frantic. A minute later she opened her eyes, sat up in the bed, looked about her and seized his hand. She drew him towards her, tried to whisper something with her lips that were still pale, but her voice would not obey her. At last she burst into a flood of tears; the hot drops scalded Ordynov's chilly hand.

'It's hard for me, it's hard for me now; my last hour is at hand!' she said at last in desperate anguish.

She tried to say something else, but her faltering tongue could not utter a word. She looked in despair at Ordynov, who did not understand her. He bent closer to her and listened . . . At last he heard her whisper distinctly: 'I am corrupted – they have corrupted me, they have ruined me!'

Ordynov lifted his head and looked at her in wild amazement. Some hideous thought flashed across his mind. Katerina saw the convulsive workings of his face.

'Yes! Corrupted,' she went on; 'a wicked man corrupted me. It was *he* who has ruined me! . . . I have sold my soul to him. Why, why did you speak of my mother? Why did you want to torture me? God, God be your judge! . . . '

A minute later she was softly weeping; Ordynov's heart was beating and aching in mortal anguish.

'He says,' she whispered in a restrained, mysterious voice, 'that when he dies he will come and fetch my sinful soul . . . I am his, I have sold my soul to him. He tortures me, he reads to me in his books. Here, look at his book! here is his book. He says I have committed the unpardonable sin. Look, look . . . '

And she showed him a book. Ordynov did not notice where it had come from. He took it mechanically – it was all in manuscript like the old heretical books which he had happened to see before, but now he was incapable of looking or concentrating his attention on anything else. The book fell out of his hands. He softly embraced Katerina, trying to bring her to reason. 'Hush, hush,' he said; 'they have frightened you. I am with you; rest with me, my own, my love, my light.'

'You know nothing, nothing,' she said, warmly pressing his hand. 'I am always like this! I am always afraid . . . I've tortured you enough, enough! . . . I go to him then,' she began a minute later, taking a breath; 'sometimes he simply comforts me with his words, sometimes he takes his book, the biggest, and reads it over me – he always reads such grim, threatening things! I don't know what, and don't understand every word; but fear comes upon me; and when I listen to his voice, it is as though it were not he speaking, but someone else, someone evil, someone you could not soften anyhow, could not entreat, and one's heart grows so heavy and burns . . . Heavier than when this misery comes upon me!'

'Don't go to him. Why do you go to him?' said Ordynov, hardly conscious of his own words.

'Why have I come to you? If you ask – I don't know either . . . But he keeps saying to me, "Pray, pray!" Sometimes I get up in the dark night and for a long time, for hours together, I pray; sometimes sleep overtakes me, but fear always wakes me, always wakes me and then I always fancy that a storm is gathering round me, that harm is coming to me, that evil things will tear me to pieces and torment me, that my prayers will not reach the saints and that they will not save me from cruel grief. My soul is being torn, my whole body seems breaking to pieces through crying . . . Then I begin praying again, and pray and pray until the Holy Mother looks down on me from the ikon more lovingly. Then I get up and go away to sleep, utterly shattered; sometimes I wake up on the floor, on my knees before the ikon. Then sometimes he wakes, calls me, begins to soothe me, caress me, comfort me, and then I feel better, and if any trouble comes I am not afraid with him. He is powerful! His word is mighty!'

'But what trouble, what sort of trouble have you? . . . And Ordynov wrung his hands in despair.

Katerina turned fearfully pale. She looked at him like one condemned to death, without hope of pardon.

'Me? I am under a curse, I'm a murderess; my mother cursed me! I was the ruin of my own mother! . . . '

Ordynov embraced her without a word. She nestled tremulously to him. He felt a convulsive shiver pass all over her, and it seemed as though her soul were parting from her body.

'I hid her in the damp earth,' she said, overwhelmed by the horror of her recollections, and lost in visions of her irrevocable past. 'I have long wanted to tell it; he always forbade me with supplications, upbraidings and angry words, and at times he himself will arouse all my anguish as though he were my enemy and adversary. At night, even as now – it all comes into my mind. Listen, listen! It was long ago, very long ago, I don't remember when, but it is all before me as though it had been yesterday, like a dream of yesterday, devouring my heart all night. Misery makes the time twice as long. Sit here, sit here beside me; I will tell you all my sorrow; may I be struck down, accursed as I am, by a mother's curse . . . I am putting my life into your hands . . . '

Ordynov tried to stop her, but she folded her hands, beseeching his love to attend, and then, with even greater agitation began to speak. Her story was incoherent, the turmoil of her spirit could be felt in her words, but Ordynov understood it all, because her life had become his life, her grief his grief, and because her foe stood visible before him, taking shape and growing up before him with every word she uttered and, as it were, with inexhaustible strength crushing his heart and cursing him malignantly. His blood was in a turmoil, it flooded his heart and obscured his reason. The wicked old man of his dream (Ordynov believed this) was living before him.

'Well, it was a night like this,' Katerina began, 'only stormier, and the wind in our forest howled as I had never heard it before . . . it was in that night that my ruin began! An oak was broken before our window, and an old grey-headed beggar came to our door, and he said that he remembered that oak as a little child, and that it was the same then as when the wind blew it down . . . That night – as I remember now – my father's barge was wrecked on the river by a storm, and though he was afflicted with illness, he drove to the place as soon as the fishermen ran to us at the factory. Mother and I were sitting alone. I was asleep. She was sad about something and weeping bitterly . . . and I knew what about! She had just been ill, she was still pale and kept telling me to get ready her shroud . . . Suddenly, at midnight, we heard a knock at the gate; I jumped up, the blood rushed to my heart; mother cried out . . . I did not look at her, I was afraid. I took a lantern and went myself to open the gate . . . It was *he*! I felt frightened, because I was always frightened when he came, and it was so with me from childhood ever since I remembered anything! At that time he had not white hair; his beard was black as pitch, his eyes burnt like coals; until that time he had never once looked at me kindly. He asked me, "Is your mother at home?" Shutting the little gate, I answered, "Father is not at home." He said, "I know," and suddenly looked at me, looked at me in such a way . . . it was the first time he had looked at me like that. I went on, but he still stood. "Why don't you come in?" "I am thinking." By then we were going up to the room. "Why did you say that your father was not at home when I asked you whether your mother was at home?" I said nothing . . . Mother was terror-stricken – she rushed to him . . . He scarcely glanced at her. I saw it all. He was all wet and shivering; the storm had driven him fifteen miles, but whence he came and where he lived neither mother nor I ever knew; we had not seen him for nine weeks . . . He threw down his cap, pulled off his gloves – did not pray to the ikon, nor bow to his hostess – he sat down by the fire . . . '

Katerina passed her hand over her face, as though something were weighing upon her and oppressing her, but a minute later she raised her head and began again: 'He began talking in Tatar to mother. Mother knew it, I don't understand a word. Other times when he came, they sent me away; but this time mother dared not say a word to her own child. The unclean spirit gained possession of my soul and I looked at my mother, exalting myself in my heart. I saw they were looking at me, they were talking about me; she began crying. I saw him clutch at his knife and more than once of late I had seen him clutch at the knife when he was talking with mother. I jumped up and caught at his belt, tried to tear the evil knife away from him. He clenched his teeth, cried out and tried to beat me back; he struck me in the breast but did not shake me off. I thought I should die on the spot, there was a mist before my eyes. I fell on the floor, but did not cry out. Though I could hardly see, I saw him. He took off his belt, tucked up his sleeve and with the hand with which he had struck me took out the knife and gave it to me. "Here, cut it away, amuse yourself over it, even as I insulted you, while I, proud girl, will bow down to the earth to you for it." I laid aside the knife; the blood began to stifle me, I did not look at him. I remember I laughed without opening my lips and looked threatening straight into mother's mournful eyes, and the shameless laugh never left my lips, while mother sat pale, deathlike . . . '

With strained attention Ordynov listened to her incoherent story. By degrees her agitation subsided after the first outburst; her words grew calmer. The poor creature was completely carried away by her memories and her misery was spread over their limitless expanse.

'He took his cap without bowing. I took the lantern again to see him out instead of mother who, though she was ill, would have followed him. We reached the gates. I opened the little gate to him, drove away the dogs in silence. I see him take off his cap and bow to me, I see him feel in his bosom, take out a red morocco box, open the catch. I look in – big pearls, an offering to me. "I have a beauty," says he, "in the town. I got it to offer to her, but I did not take it to her; take it, fair maiden, cherish your beauty; take them, though you crush them under foot." I took them, but I did not want to stamp on them, I did not want to do them too much honour, but I took them like a viper, not saying a word. I came in and set them on the table before mother – it was for that I took them. Mother was silent for a minute, all white as a hand-kerchief. She speaks to me as though she fears me. "What is this, Katya?" and I answer, "The merchant brought them for you, my own – I know nothing." I see the tears stream from her eyes. I see her gasp for breath. "Not for me, Katya, not for me, wicked daughter, not for me." I remember she said it so bitterly, so bitterly, as though she were weeping out her whole soul. I raised my eyes, I wanted to throw myself at her feet, but suddenly the evil one prompted me. "Well, if not to you, most likely to father; I will give them to him when he comes back; I will say the merchants have been, they have forgotten their wares . . . " Then how she wept, my own . . . "I will tell him myself what merchants have been, and for what wares they came . . . I will tell him whose daughter you are, whose bastard child! You are not my daughter now, you serpent's fry! You are my accursed child!" I say nothing, tears do not come to me . . . I went up to my room and all night I listened to the storm, while I fitted my thoughts to its raging.

'Meanwhile, five days passed by. Towards evening after five days, father came in, surly and menacing, and he had been stricken by illness on the way. I saw his arm was bound up, I guessed that his enemy had waylaid him upon the road, his enemy had worn him out and brought sickness upon him. I knew, too, who was his enemy, I knew it all. He did not say a word to mother, he did not ask about me. He called together all the workmen, made them leave the factory, and guard the house from the evil eye. I felt in my heart, in that hour, that all was not well with the house. We waited, the night came, another stormy, snowy one, and dread came over my soul. I opened the window; my face was hot, my eyes were weeping, my restless heart was burning; I was on fire. I longed to be away from that room, far away to the land of light, where the thunder and lightning are born. My maiden heart was beating and beating . . . Suddenly, in the dead of night – I was dozing, or a mist had fallen over my soul, and confounded it – all of a sudden I hear a knock at the window: "Open!" I look, there was a man at the window, he had climbed up by a rope. I knew at once who the visitor was, I opened the window and let him into my lonely room. It was *he*! Without taking off his hat, he sat down on the bench, he panted and drew his breath as though he had been pursued. I stood in the corner and knew myself that I turned white all over. "Is your father at home?" "He is." "And your mother?" "Mother is at home, too." "Be silent now; do you hear?" "I hear." "What?" "A whistle under the window!" "Well, fair maid, do you want to cut your foe's head off? Call your father, take my life? I am at your maiden mercy; here is the cord, tie it, if your heart bids you; avenge yourself for your insult." I am silent. "Well? Speak, my joy." "What do you want?" "I want my enemy to be gone, to take leave for good and all of the old love, and to lay my heart at the feet of a new one, a fair maid like you . . ." I laughed; and I don't know how his evil words went to my heart. "Let me, fair maid, walk downstairs, test my courage, pay homage to my hosts." I trembled all over, my teeth knocked together, but my heart was like a red-hot iron. I went. I opened the door to him, I let him into the house, only on the threshold with an effort I brought out, "Here, take your pearls and never give me a gift again," and I threw the box after him.'

Here Katerina stopped to take breath. At one moment she was pale and trembling like a leaf, at the next the blood rushed to her head, and now, when she stopped, her cheeks glowed with fire, her eyes flashed through her tears, and her bosom heaved with her laboured, uneven breathing. But suddenly she turned pale again and her voice sank with a mournful and tremulous quiver.

'Then I was left alone and the storm seemed to wrap me about. All at once I hear a shout, I hear workmen run across the yard to the factory, I hear them say, "The factory is on fire." I kept in hiding; all ran out of the house; I was left with mother; I knew that she was parting from life, that she had been lying for the last three days on her deathbed. I knew it, accursed daughter! . . . All at once a cry under my room, a faint cry like a child when it is frightened in its sleep, and then all was silent. I blew out the candle, I was as chill as ice, I hid my face in my hands, I was afraid to look. Suddenly I hear a shout close by, I hear the men running from the factory. I hung out of the window, I see them bearing my dead father, I hear them saying among themselves, "He stumbled, he fell down the stairs into a red-hot cauldron; so the devil must have pushed him down." I fell upon my bed; I waited, all numb with terror, and I do not know for whom or what I waited, only I was overwhelmed with woe in that hour. I don't remember how long I waited; I remember that suddenly everything began rocking, my head grew heavy, my eyes were smarting with smoke and I was glad that my end was near. Suddenly I felt someone lift me by the shoulders. I looked as best I could; he was singed all over and his kaftan, hot to the touch, was smoking.

' "I've come for you, fair maid; lead me away from trouble as before you led me into trouble; I have lost my soul for your sake, no prayers of mine can undo this accursed night! Maybe we will pray together!" He laughed, the wicked man. "Show me," said he, "how to get out without passing people!" I took his hand and led him after me. We went through the corridor – the keys were with me – I opened the door to the storeroom and pointed to the window. The window looked into the garden, he seized me in his powerful arms, embraced me and leapt with me out of the window. We ran together, hand-in-hand, we ran together for a long time. We looked, we were in a thick, dark forest. He began listening: "There's a chase after us, Katya! There's a chase after us, fair maid, but it is not for us in this hour to lay down our lives! Kiss me, fair maid, for love and everlasting happiness!" "Why are your hands covered with blood?" "My hands covered with blood, my own? I stabbed your dogs; they barked too loud at a late guest. Come along!"

'We ran on again; we saw in the path my father's horse, he had broken his bridle and run out of the stable, for he did not want to be burnt. "Get on it, Katya, with me; God has sent us help." I was silent. "Won't you? I am not a heathen, not an unclean pagan; here, I will cross myself if you like," and here he made the sign of the cross. I got on the horse, huddled up to him and forgot everything on his bosom, as though a dream had come over me, and when I woke I saw that we were standing by a broad, broad river. He got off the horse, lifted me down and went off to the reeds where his boat was hidden. We were getting in. "Well, farewell, good horse; go to a new master, the old masters all forsake you!" I ran to father's horse and embraced him warmly at parting. Then we got in, he took the oars and in an instant we lost sight of the shore. And when we could not see the shore, I saw him lay down the oars and look about him, all over the water.

' "Hail," he said, "stormy river-mother, who giveth drink to God's people and food to me! Say, hast thou guarded my goods, are my wares safe, while I've been away?" I sat mute, I cast down my eyes to my bosom; my face burned with shame as with a flame. And he: "Thou art welcome to take all, stormy and insatiable river, only let me keep my vow and cherish my priceless pearl! Drop but one word, fair maid, send a ray of sunshine into the storm, scatter the dark night with light!"

'He laughed as he spoke, his heart was burning for me, but I could not bear his jeers for shame; I longed to say a word, but was afraid and sat dumb. "Well, then, be it so!" he answered to my timid thought; he spoke as though in sorrow, as though grief had come upon him, too. "So one can take nothing by force. God be with you, you proud one, my dove, my fair maid! It seems, strong is your hatred for me, or I do not find favour in your clear eyes!" I listened and was seized by spite, seized by spite and love; I steeled my heart. I said: "Pleasing or not pleasing you came to me; it is not for me to know that, but for another senseless, shameless girl who shamed her maiden room in the dark night, who sold her soul for mortal sin and could not school her frantic heart; and for my sorrowing tears to know it, and for him who, like a thief, brags of another's woe and jeers at a maiden's heart!" I said it, and I could bear no more. I wept . . . He said nothing; looked at me so that I trembled like a leaf. "Listen to me," said he, "fair maid," and his eyes burned strangely. "It is not a vain word I say, I make you a solemn vow. As much happiness as you give me, so much will I be a gentleman, and if ever you do not love me – do not speak, do not drop a word, do not trouble, but stir only your sable eyebrow, turn your black eye, stir only your little finger and I will give you back your love with golden freedom; only, my proud, haughty beauty, then there will be an end to my life too." And then all my flesh laughed at his words . . . '

At this point Katerina's story was interrupted by deep emotion; she took breath, smiled at her new fancy and would have gone on, but suddenly her sparkling eyes met Ordynov's feverish gaze fixed on her. She started, would have said something, but the blood flooded her face . . . She hid her face in her hands and fell upon the pillow as though in a swoon. Ordynov was quivering all over! An agonising feeling, an unbearable, unaccountable agitation ran like poison through all his veins and grew with every word of Katerina's story; a hopeless yearning, a greedy and unendurable passion took possession of his imagination and troubled his feelings, but at the same time his heart was more and more oppressed by bitter, infinite sadness. At moments he longed to shriek to Katerina to be silent, longed to fling himself at her feet and beseech her by his tears to give him back his former agonies of love, his former pure, unquestioning yearning, and he regretted the tears that had long dried on his cheeks. There was an ache at his heart which was painfully oppressed by fever and could not give his tortured soul the relief of tears. He did not understand what Katerina was telling him, and his love was frightened of the feeling that excited the poor woman. He cursed his passion at that moment; it smothered him, it exhausted him, and he felt as though molten lead were running in his veins instead of blood.

'Ach! that is not my grief,' said Katerina, suddenly raising her head.

'What I have told you just now is not my sorrow,' she went on in a voice that rang like copper from a sudden new feeling, while her heart was rent with secret, unshed tears. 'That is not my grief, that is not my anguish, not my woe! What, what do I care for my mother, though I shall never have another mother in this world! What do I care that she cursed me in her last terrible hour? What do I care for my old golden life, for my warm room, for my maiden freedom? What do I care that I have sold myself to the evil one and abandoned my soul to the destroyer, that for the sake of happiness I have committed the unpardonable sin? Ach, that is not my grief, though in that great is my ruin! But what is bitter to me and rends my heart is that I am his shameless slave, that my shame and disgrace are dear to me, shameless as I am, but it is dear to my greedy heart to remember my sorrow as though it were joy and happiness; that is my grief, that there is no strength in it and no anger for my wrongs! . . .'

The poor creature gasped for breath and a convulsive, hysterical sob cut short her words, her hot, laboured breath burned her lips, her bosom heaved and sank and her eyes flashed with incomprehensible indignation. But her face was radiant with such fascination at that moment, every line, every muscle quivered with such a passionate flood of feeling, such insufferable, incredible beauty that Ordynov's black thoughts died away at once and the pure sadness in his soul was silenced. And his heart burned to be pressed to her heart and to be lost with it in frenzied emotion, to throb in harmony with the same storm, the same rush of infinite passion, and even to swoon with it. Katerina met Ordynov's troubled eyes and smiled so that his heart burned with redoubled fire. He scarcely knew what he was doing.

'Spare me, have pity on me,' he whispered, controlling his trembling voice, bending down to her, leaning with his hand on her shoulder and looking close in her eyes, so close that their breathing was mingled in one. 'You are killing me. I do not know your sorrow and my soul is troubled . . . What is it to me what your heart is weeping over! Tell me what you want – I will do it. Come with me, let us go; do not kill me, do not murder me! . . .'

Katerina looked at him immovably, the tears dried on her burning cheeks. She wanted to interrupt him, to take his hand, tried to say something, but could not find the words. A strange smile came upon her lips, as though laughter were breaking through that smile.

'I have not told you all, then,' she said at last in a broken voice; 'only will you hear me, will you hear me, hot heart? Listen to your sister. You have learned little of her bitter grief. I would have told you how I lived a year with him, but I will not . . . A year passed, he went away with his comrades down the river, and I was left with one he called his mother to wait for him in the harbour. I waited for him one month, two, and I met a young merchant, and I glanced at him and thought of my golden years gone by. "Sister, darling," said he, when he had spoken two words to me, "I am Alyosha, your destined betrothed; the old folks betrothed us as children; you have forgotten me – think, I am from your parts." "And what do they say of me in your parts?" "Folk's gossip says that you behaved dishonourably, forgot your maiden modesty, made friends with a brigand, a murderer," Alyosha said, laughing. "And what did you say of me?" "I meant to say many things when I came here" – and his heart was troubled. "I meant to say many things, but now that I have seen you my heart is dead within me, you have slain me," he said. "Buy my soul, too, take it, though you mock at my heart and my love, fair maiden. I am an orphan now, my own master, and my soul is my own, not another's. I have not sold it to anyone, like somebody who has blotted out her memory; it's not enough to buy the heart, I give it for nothing, and it is clear it is a good bargain." I laughed, and more than once, more than twice he talked to me; a whole month he lived on the place, gave up his merchandise, forsook his people and was all alone. I was sorry for his lonely tears. So I said to him one morning, 'Wait for me, Alyosha, lower down the harbour, as night comes on; I will go with you to your home, I am weary of my life, forlorn.' So night came on, I tied up a bundle and my soul ached and worked within me. Behold, my master walks in without word or warning. "Good-day, let us go, there will be a storm on the river and the time will not wait." I followed him; we came to the river and it was far to reach his mates. We look: a boat and one we knew rowing in it, as though waiting for someone. "Good-day, Alyosha; God be your help. Why, are you belated at the harbour, are you in haste to meet your vessels? Row me, good man, with the mistress, to our mates, to our place. I have let my boat go and I don't know how to swim." "Get in," said Alyosha, and my whole soul swooned when I heard his voice. "Get in with the mistress, too, the wind is for all, and in my bower there will be room for you, too." We got in; it was a dark night, the stars were in hiding, the wind howled, the waves rose high and we rowed out a mile from shore – all three were silent.

' "It's a storm," said my master, "and it is a storm that bodes no good! I have never seen such a storm on the river in my life as is raging now! It is too much for our boat, it will not bear three!" "No, it will not," answered Alyosha, "and one of us, it seems, turns out to be one too many," he says, and his voice quivers like a harp-string. "Well, Alyosha,

I knew you as a little child, your father was my mate, we ate at each other's boards – tell me, Alyosha, can you reach the shore without the boat or will you perish for nothing, will you lose your life?" "I cannot reach it. And you, too, good man, if it is your luck to have a drink of water, will you reach the shore or not?" "I cannot reach it, it is the end for my soul. I cannot hold out against the stormy river! Listen, Katerina, my precious pearl! I remember such a night, but the waves were not tossing, the stars were shining, and the moon was bright . . . I simply want to ask you, have you forgotten?" "I remember," said I. "Well, since you have not forgotten it, well, you have not forgotten the compact when a bold man told a fair maiden to take back her freedom from one unloved – eh?" "No, I have not forgotten that either," I said, more dead than alive. "Ah, you have not forgotten! Well, now we are in hard case in the boat. Has not his hour come for one of us? Tell me, my own, tell me, my dove, coo to us like a dove your tender word . . . " '

'I did not say my word then,' whispered Katerina, turning pale . . .

'Katerina!' A hoarse, hollow voice resounded above them. Ordynov started. In the doorway stood Murin. He was barely covered with a fur rug, pale as death, and he was gazing at them with almost senseless eyes. Katerina turned paler and paler and she, too, gazed fixedly at him, as though spellbound.

'Come to me, Katerina,' whispered the sick man, in a voice hardly audible, and went out of the room. Katerina still gazed fixedly into the air, as though the old man had still been standing before her. But suddenly the blood rushed glowing into her pale cheeks and she slowly got up from the bed. Ordynov remembered their first meeting.

'Till tomorrow then, my tears!' she said, laughing strangely; 'till tomorrow! Remember at what point I stopped: "Choose between the two; which is dear or not dear to you, fair maid!" Will you remember, will you wait for one night?' she repeated, laying her hand on his shoulder and looking at him tenderly.

'Katerina, do not go, do not go to your ruin! He is mad,' whispered Ordynov, trembling for her.

'Katerina!' he heard through the partition.

'What? Will he murder me? no fear!' Katerina answered, laughing. 'Good-night to you, my precious heart, my warm dove, my brother!' she said, tenderly pressing his head to her bosom, while tears bedewed her face. 'Those are my last tears. Sleep away your sorrow, my darling, wake tomorrow to joy.' And she kissed him passionately.

'Katerina, Katerina!' whispered Ordynov, falling on his knees before her and trying to stop her. 'Katerina!'

She turned round, nodded to him, smiling and went out of the room. Ordynov heard her go in to Murin; he held his breath, listening, but heard not a sound more. The old man was silent or perhaps unconscious again . . . He would have gone in to her there, but his legs staggered under him . . . He sank exhausted on the bed . . . .

2

For a long while he could not find out what the time was when he woke. Whether it was twilight of dawn or of evening, it was still dark in his room. He could not decide how long he had slept, but felt that his sleep was not healthy sleep. Coming to himself, he passed his hands over his face as though shaking off sleep and the visions of the night. But when he tried to step on the floor he felt as though his whole body were shattered, and his exhausted limbs refused to obey him. His head ached and was going round, and he was alternately shivering and feverish. Memory returned with consciousness and his heart quivered when in one instant he lived through, in memory, the whole of the past night. His heart beat as violently in response to his thoughts, his sensations were as burning, as fresh, as though not a night, not long hours, but one minute had passed since Katerina had gone away. He felt as though his eyes were still wet with tears – or were they new, fresh tears that rushed like a spring from his burning soul? And, strange to say, his agonies were even sweet to him, though he dimly felt all over that he could not endure such violence of feeling again. There was a moment when he was almost conscious of death, and was ready to meet it as a welcome guest; his sensations were so over strained, his passion surged up with such violence on waking, such ecstasy took possession of his soul that life, quickened by its intensity, seemed on the point of breaking, of being shattered, of flickering out in one minute and being quenched for ever. Almost at that instant, as though in answer to his anguish, in answer to his quivering heart, the familiar mellow, silvery voice of Katerina rang out – like that inner music known to man's soul in hours of joy, in hours of tranquil happiness. Close beside him, almost over his pillow, began a song, at first soft and melancholy . . . her voice rose and fell, dying away abruptly as though hiding in itself, and tenderly crooning over its anguish of unsatisfied, smothered desire hopelessly concealed in the grieving heart; then again it flowed into a nightingale's trills and, quivering and glowing with unrestrained passion, melted into a perfect sea of ecstasy, a sea of mighty, boundless sound, like the first moment of the bliss of love.

Ordynov distinguished the words, too. They were simple, sincere, composed long ago with direct, calm, pure, clear feeling, but he forgot them, he heard only the sounds. Through the simple, naïve verses of the song flashed other words resounding with all the yearning that filled his bosom, responding to the most secret subtleties of his passion, which he could not comprehend though they echoed to him clearly with full consciousness of it. And at one moment he heard the last moan of a heart swooning helplessly in passion, then he heard the joy of a will and a spirit breaking its chains and rushing brightly and freely into the boundless ocean of unfettered love. Then he heard the first vow of the beloved, with fragrant shame at the first blush on her face, with prayers, with tears, with mysterious timid murmuring; then the passion of the Bacchante, proud and rejoicing in its strength, unveiled, undisguised, turning her drunken eyes about her with a ringing laugh . . .

Ordynov could not endure the end of the song, and he got up from the bed. The song at once died away.

'Good-morning and good-day are over, my beloved,' Katerina's voice rang out. 'Good-evening to you; get up, come in to us, wake up to bright joy; we expect you. I and the master, both good people, your willing servants, quench hatred with love, if your heart is still resentful. Say a friendly word! . . .'

Ordynov had already gone out of his room at her first call and scarcely realised that he was going into the landlord's bedroom. The door opened before him and, bright as sunshine, the golden smile of his strange landlady flashed upon him. At that instant, he saw, he heard no one but her. In one moment his whole life, his whole joy, melted into one thing in his heart – the bright image of his Katerina.

'Two dawns have passed,' she said, giving him her hands, 'since we said farewell; the second is dying now – look out of the window. Like the two dawns in the soul of a maiden,' Katerina added, laughing. 'The one that flushes her face with its first shame, when first her lonely maiden heart speaks in her bosom, while the other, when a maiden forgets her first shame, glows like fire, stifles her maiden heart, and drives the red blood to her face . . . Come, come into our home, good young man! Why do you stand in the doorway? Honour and love to you, and a greeting from the master!'

With a laugh ringing like music, she took Ordynov's hand and led him into the room. His heart was overwhelmed with timidity. All the fever, all the fire raging in his bosom was quenched and died down in one instant, and he dropped his eyes in confusion and was afraid to look at her. He felt that she was so marvellously beautiful that his heart could not endure her burning eyes. He had never seen his Katerina like this. For the first time laughter and gaiety were sparkling on her face, and drying the mournful tears on her black eyelashes. His hand trembled in her hand. And if he had raised his eyes he would have seen that Katerina, with a triumphant smile, had fastened her clear eyes on his face, which was clouded with confusion and passion.

'Get up, old man,' she said at last, as though waking up; 'say a word of welcome to our guest, a guest who is like a brother! Get up, you proud, unbending old man; get up, now, take your guest by his white hand and make him sit down to the table.'

Ordynov raised his eyes and seemed only then to come to himself. Only then he thought of Murin. The old man's eyes, looking as though dimmed by the approach of death, were staring at him fixedly; and with a pang in his heart he remembered those eyes glittering at him last time from black overhanging brows contracted as now with pain and anger. There was a slight dizziness in his head. He looked round him and only then realised everything clearly and distinctly. Murin was still lying on the bed, but he was partly dressed and had already been up and out that morning. As before, he had a red kerchief tied round his neck, he had slippers on his feet. His attack was evidently over, only his face was still terribly pale and yellow. Katerina was standing by his bed, her hand leaning on the table, watching them both intently. But the smile of welcome did not leave her face. It seemed as though everything had been done at a sign from her.

'Yes! it's you,' said Murin, raising himself up and sitting on the bed. 'You are my lodger. I must beg your pardon, sir; I have sinned and wronged you all unknowingly, playing tricks with my gun the other day. Who could tell that you, too, were stricken by grievous sickness? It happens to me at times,' he added in a hoarse, ailing voice, frowning and unconsciously looking away from Ordynov. 'My trouble comes upon me like a thief in the night without knocking at the gate! I almost thrust a knife into her bosom the other day . . . ' he brought out, nodding towards Katerina. 'I am ill, a fit comes, seizes me – well, that's enough. Sit down – you will be our guest.'

Ordynov was still staring at him intently.

'Sit down, sit down!' the old man shouted impatiently; 'sit down, if that will please her! So you are brother and sister, born of the same mother! You are fond of one another as lovers!'

Ordynov sat down.

'You see what a fine sister you've got,' the old man went on, laughing, and he showed two rows of white, perfectly sound, teeth. 'Be fond of one another, my dears. Is your sister beautiful, sir? Tell me, answer! Come, look how her cheeks are burning; come, look round, sing the praises of her beauty to all the world, show that your heart is aching for her.'

Ordynov frowned and looked angrily at the old man, who flinched under his eyes. A blind fury surged up in Ordynov's heart. By some animal instinct he felt near him a mortal foe. He could not understand what was happening to him, his reason refused to serve him.

'Don't look,' said a voice behind him.

Ordynov looked around.

'Don't look, don't look, I tell you, if the devil is tempting you; have pity on your love,' said Katerina, laughing, and suddenly from behind she covered his eyes with her hands; then at once took away her hands and hid her own face in them. But the colour in her face seemed to show through her fingers. She removed her hands and, still glowing like fire, tried to meet their laughter and inquisitive eyes brightly and without a tremor. But both looked at her in silence – Ordynov with the stupefication of love, as though it were the first time such terrible beauty had stabbed his heart; the old man coldly and attentively. Nothing was to be seen in his pale face, except that his lips turned blue and quivered faintly.

Katerina went up to the old man, no longer laughing, and began clearing away the books, papers, inkstand, everything that was on the table and putting them all on the window-sill. Her breathing was hurried and uneven, and from time to time she drew an eager breath as though her heart were oppressed. Her full bosom heaved and fell like a wave on the seashore. She dropped her eyes and her pitch-black eyelashes gleamed on her bright cheeks like sharp needles . . .

'A maiden queen,' said the old man.

'My sovereign!' whispered Ordynov, quivering all over. He came to his senses, feeling the old man's eyes upon him – his glance flashed upon him for an instant like lightning – greedy, spiteful, coldly contemptuous. Ordynov would have got up from his seat but some unseen power seemed to fetter his legs. He sat down again. At times he pinched his hands as though not believing in reality. He felt as though he were being strangled by a nightmare, and as though his eyes were still closed in a miserable feverish sleep. But, strange to say, he did not want to wake up!

Katerina took the old cloth off the table, then opened a chest, took out of it a sumptuous cloth, embroidered in gold and bright silks, and put it on the table; then she took out of the cupboard an old-fashioned ancestral-looking casket, set it in the middle of the table and took out of it three silver goblets – one for the master, one for the visitor, and one for herself; then with a grave, almost pensive air, she looked at the old man and at the visitor.

'Is one of us dear to someone, or not dear?' she said. 'If anyone is not dear to someone he is dear to me, and shall drink my goblet with me. Each of you is dear to me as my own brother: so let us all drink to love and concord.'

'Drink and drown dark fancies in the wine,' said the old man, in a changed voice. 'Pour it out, Katerina.'

'Do you bid me pour?' asked Katerina, looking at Ordynov.

Ordynov held out his goblet in silence.

'Stay! If one has a secret and a fancy, may his wishes come true!' said the old man, raising his goblet.

All clinked their goblets and drank.

'Let me drink now with you, old man,' said Katerina, turning to the landlord. 'Let us drink if your heart is kindly to me! Let us drink to past happiness, let us send a greeting to the years we have spent, let us celebrate our happiness with heart and with love. Bid me fill your goblet if your heart is warm to me.'

'Your wine is strong, my love, but you scarcely wet your lips!' said the old man, laughing and holding out his goblet again.

'Well, I will sip it, but you drink it to the bottom . . . Why live, old man, brooding on gloomy thoughts? gloomy thoughts only make the heart ache! Thought calls for sorrow; with happiness one can live without thinking; drink, old man,' she went on; 'drown your thoughts.'

'A great deal of sorrow must have fermented within you, since you arm yourself against it like this! So you want to make an end of it all at once, my white dove. I drink with you, Katya! And have you a sorrow, sir, if you allow me to ask?'

'If I have, I keep it to myself,' muttered Ordynov, keeping his eyes fixed on Katerina.

'Do you hear, old man? For a long while I did not know myself, did you remember; but the time came, I remembered all and recalled it; all that has passed I have passed through again in my unsatisfied soul.'

'Yes, it is grievous if one begins looking into the past only,' said the old man dreamily. 'What is past is like wine that is drunk! What happiness is there in the past? The coat is worn out, and away with it.'

'One must get a new one,' Katerina chimed in with a strained laugh, while two big tears like diamonds hung on her eyelashes. 'One cannot live down a lifetime in one minute, and a girl's heart is eager for life –

there is no keeping pace with it. Do you understand, old man? Look. I have buried my tear in your goblet.'

'And did you buy much happiness with your sorrow?' said Ordynov – and his voice quivered with emotion.

'So you must have a great deal of your own for sale,' answered the old man, 'that you put your spoke in unasked,' and he laughed a spiteful, noiseless laugh, looking insolently at Ordynov.

'What I have sold it for, I have had,' answered Katerina in a voice that sounded vexed and offended. 'One thinks it much, another little. One wants to give all to take nothing, another promises nothing and yet the submissive heart follows him! Do not you reproach anyone,' she went on, looking sadly at Ordynov. 'One man is like this, and another is different, and as though one knew why the soul yearns towards anyone! Fill your goblet, old man. Drink to the happiness of your dear daughter, your meek, obedient slave, as I was when first I knew you. Raise your goblet!'

'So be it! Fill yours, too!' said the old man, taking the wine.

'Stay, old man! Put off drinking, and let us say a word first! . . . '

Katerina put her elbows on the table and looked intently, with passionate, kindling eyes, at the old man. A strange determination gleamed in her eyes. But all her movements were calm, her gestures were abrupt, unexpected, rapid. She was all as if on fire, and it was marvellous; but her beauty seemed to grow with her emotion, her animation; her hurried breath slightly inflating her nostrils, floated from her lips, half-opened in a smile which showed two rows of teeth white and even as pearls. Her bosom heaved, her coil of hair, twisted three times round her head, fell carelessly over her left ear and covered part of her glowing cheek, drops of sweat came out on her temples.

'Tell my fortune, old man; tell my fortune, my father, before you drown your mind in drink. Here is my white palm for you – not for nothing do the folks call you a wizard. You have studied by the book and know all of the black art! Look, old man, tell me all my pitiful fate; only mind you don't tell a lie! Come, tell me as you know it – will there be happiness for your daughter, or will you not forgive her, but call down upon her path an evil, sorrowful fate? Tell me whether I shall have a warm corner for my home, or, like a bird of passage, shall be seeking among good people for a home – a lonely orphan all my life. Tell me who is my enemy, who is preparing love for me, who is plotting against me; tell me, will my warm young heart open its life in solitude and languish to the end, or will it find itself a mate and beat joyfully in tune with it till new sorrow comes! Tell me for once, old man, in what blue sky, beyond far seas and forests, my bright falcon lives. And is he keenly searching for his mate, and is he waiting lovingly, and will he love me fondly; will he soon be tired of me, will he deceive me or not deceive me, and, once for all and altogether, tell me for the last time, old man, am I long to while away the time with you, to sit in a comfortless corner, to read dark books; and when am I, old man, to bow low to you, to say farewell for good and all, to thank you for your bread and salt, for giving me to drink and eat, for telling me your tales? . . . But mind, tell all the truth, do not lie. The time has come, stand up for yourself.'

Her excitement grew greater and greater up to the last word, when suddenly her voice broke with emotion as though her heart were carried away by some inner tempest. Her eyes flashed, and her upper lip faintly quivered. A spiteful jeer could be heard hiding like a snake under every word, but yet there was the ring of tears in her laughter. She bent across the table to the old man and gazed with eager intentness into his lustreless eyes. Ordynov heard her heart suddenly begin beating when she finished; he cried out with ecstasy when he glanced at her, and was getting up from the bench. But a flitting momentary glance from the old man riveted him to his seat again. A strange mingling of contempt, mocking, impatient, angry uneasiness and at the same time sly, spiteful curiosity gleamed in his passing momentary glance, which every time made Ordynov shudder and filled his heart with annoyance, vexation and helpless anger.

Thoughtfully and with a sort of mournful curiosity the old man looked at his Katerina. His heart was stung, words had been uttered. But not an eyebrow stirred upon his face! He only smiled when she finished.

'You want to know a great deal at once, my full-fledged nestling, my fluttering bird! Better fill me a deep goblet! and let us drink first to peace and goodwill; or I may spoil my forecast, through someone's black evil eye. Mighty is the devil! Sin is never far off!'

He raised his goblet and drank. The more wine he drank, the paler he grew. His eyes burned like red coals. Evidently the feverish light of them, and the sudden deathlike blueness of his face were signs that another fit was imminent. The wine was strong, so that after emptying one goblet Ordynov's sight grew more and more blurred. His feverishly inflamed blood could bear no more: it rushed to his heart, troubled and dimmed his reason. His uneasiness grew more and more intense. To relieve his growing excitement, he filled his goblet and sipped it again, without knowing what he was doing, and the blood raced even more rapidly through his veins. He was as though in delirium, and, straining his attention to the utmost, he could hardly follow what was passing between his strange landlord and landlady.

The old man knocked his goblet with a ringing sound against the table.

'Fill it, Katerina!' he cried, 'fill it again, bad daughter, fill it to the brim! Lay the old man in peace, and have done with him! That's it, pour out more, pour it out, my beauty! Let us drink together! Why have you drunk so little? Or have my eyes deceived me? . . . '

Katerina made him some answer, but Ordynov could not hear quite what she said: the old man did not let her finish; he caught hold of her hand as though he were incapable of restraining all that was weighing on his heart. His face was pale, his eyes at one moment were dim, at the next were flashing with fire; his lips quivered and turned white, and in an uneven, troubled voice, in which at moments there was a flash of strange ecstasy, he said to her: 'Give me your little hand, my beauty! Let me tell your fortune. I will tell the whole truth. I am truly a wizard; so you are not mistaken, Katerina! Your golden heart said truly that I alone am its wizard, and will not hide the truth from it, the simple, girlish heart! But one thing you don't see: it's not for me, a wizard, to teach you wisdom! Wisdom is not what a maiden wants, and she hears the whole truth, yet seems not to know, not to understand! Her head is a subtle serpent, though her heart is melting in tears. She will find out for herself, will thread her way between troubles, will keep her cunning will! Something she can win by sense, and where she cannot win by sense she will dazzle by beauty, will intoxicate men's minds with her black eye – beauty conquers strength, even the heart of iron will be rent asunder! Will you have grief and sorrow? Heavy is the sorrow of man! but trouble is not for the weak heart, trouble is close friends with the strong heart; stealthily it sheds a bloody tear, but does not go begging to good people for shameful comfort: your grief, girl, is like a print in the sand – the rain washes it away, the sun dries it, the stormy wind lifts it and blows it away. Let me tell you more, let me tell your fortune. Whoever loves you, you will be a slave to him, you will bind your freedom yourself, you will give yourself in pledge and will not take yourself back, you will know how to cease to love in due time, you will sow a grain and your destroyer will take back a whole ear! My tender child, my little golden head, you buried your pearl of a tear in my goblet, but you could not be content with that – at once you shed a hundred; you uttered no more sweet words, and boasted of your sad life! And there was no need for you to grieve over it – the tear, the dew of heaven! It will come back to you with interest, your pearly tear, in the woeful night when cruel sorrow, evil fancies will gnaw your heart – then for that same tear another's tear will drop upon your warm heart – not a warm tear but a tear of blood, like molten lead; it will turn your white bosom to blood, and until the dreary, heavy morning that comes on gloomy days, you will toss in your little bed, shedding your heart's blood and will not heal your fresh wound till another dawn. Fill my goblet, Katerina, fill it again, my dove; fill it for my sage counsel, and no need to waste more words.' His voice grew weak and trembling, sobs seemed on the point of breaking from his bosom, he poured out the wine and greedily drained another goblet. Then he brought the goblet down on the table again with a bang. His dim eyes once more gleamed with flame.

'Ah! Live as you may!' he shouted; 'what's past is gone and done with. Fill up the heavy goblet, fill it up, that it may smite the rebellious head from its shoulders, that the whole soul may be dead with it! Lay me out for the long night that has no morning and let my memory vanish altogether. What is drunk is lived and done with. So the merchant's wares have grown stale, have lain by too long, he must give them away for nothing! but the merchant would not of his free will have sold it below its price. The blood of his foe should be spilt and the innocent blood should be shed too, and that customer should have laid down his lost soul into the bargain! Fill my goblet, fill it again, Katerina.'

But the hand that held the goblet seemed to stiffen and did not move; his breathing was laboured and difficult, his head sank back. For the last time he fixed his lustreless eyes on Ordynov, but his eyes, too, grew dim at last, and his eyelids drooped as though they were made of lead, a deadly pallor overspread his face . . . For some time his lips twitched and quivered as though still trying to articulate – and suddenly a big hot tear hung on his eyelash, broke and slowly ran down his pale cheek . . .

Ordynov could bear no more. He got up and, reeling, took a step forward, went up to Katerina and clutched her hand. But she seemed not to notice him and did not even glance at him, as though she did not recognise him . . .

She, too, seemed to have lost consciousness, as though one thought, one fixed idea had entirely absorbed her. She sank on the bosom of the sleeping old man, twined her white arm round his neck, and gazed with glowing, feverish eyes as though they were riveted on him. She did not seem to feel Ordynov taking her hand. At last she turned her head towards him, and bent upon him a prolonged searching gaze. It seemed as though at last she understood, and a bitter, astonished smile came wearily, as it were painfully, to her lips . . .

'Go away, go away,' she whispered; 'you are drunk and wicked, you are not a guest for me . . . ' then she turned again to the old man and riveted her eyes upon him.

She seemed as it were gloating over every breath he took and soothing his slumber with her eyes. She seemed afraid to breathe, checking her full throbbing heart, and there was such frenzied admiration in her face that at once despair, fury and insatiable anger seized upon Ordynov's spirit . . .

'Katerina! Katerina!' he called, seizing her hand as though in a vice.

A look of pain passed over her face; she raised her head again, and looked at him with such mockery, with such contemptuous haughtiness, that he could scarcely stand upon his feet. Then she pointed to the sleeping old man and, as though all his enemy's mockery had passed into her eyes, she bent again a taunting glance on Ordynov that sent an icy shiver to his heart.

'What? He will murder me, I suppose?' said Ordynov, beside himself with fury. Some demon seemed to whisper in his ear that he understood her . . . and his whole heart laughed at Katerina's fixed idea.

'I will buy you, my beauty, from your merchant, if you want my soul; no fear, he won't kill me! . . . '

A fixed laugh, that froze Ordynov's whole being, remained upon Katerina's face. Its boundless irony rent his heart. Not knowing what he was doing, hardly conscious, he leaned against the wall and took from a nail the old man's expensive old-fashioned knife. A look of amazement seemed to come into Katerina's face, but at the same time anger and contempt were reflected with the same force in her eyes. Ordynov turned sick, looking at her . . . he felt as though someone were thrusting, urging his frenzied hand to madness. He drew out the knife . . . Katerina watched him, motionless, holding her breath . . .

He glanced at the old man.

At that moment he fancied that one of the old man's eyes opened and looked at him, laughing. Their eyes met. For some minutes Ordynov gazed at him fixedly . . . Suddenly he fancied that the old man's whole face began laughing and that a diabolical, soul-freezing chuckle resounded at last through the room. A hideous, dark thought crawled like a snake into his head. He shuddered; the knife fell from his hands and dropped with a clang upon the floor. Katerina uttered a shriek as though awaking from oblivion, from a nightmare, from a heavy, immovable, vision . . . The old man, very pale, slowly got up from the bed and angrily kicked the knife into the corner of the room; Katerina stood pale, deathlike, immovable; her eyelids were closing; her face was convulsed by a vague, insufferable pain; she hid her face in her hands and, with a shriek that rent the heart, sank almost breathless at the old man's feet . . .

'Alyosha, Alyosha!' broke from her gasping bosom.

The old man seized her in his powerful arms and almost crushed her on his breast. But when she hid her head upon his heart, every feature in the old man's face worked with such undisguised, shameless laughter that Ordynov's whole soul was overwhelmed with horror. Deception, calculation, cold, jealous tyranny and horror at the poor broken heart – that was what he read in that laugh, that shamelessly threw off all disguise.

'She is mad!' he whispered, quivering like a leaf, and, numb with terror, he ran out of the flat.

3

When, at eight o'clock next morning, Ordynov, pale and agitated and still dazed from the excitement of that day, opened Yaroslav Ilyitch's door (he went to see him though he could not have said why) he staggered back in amazement and stood petrified in the doorway on seeing Murin in the room. The old man, even paler than Ordynov seemed almost too ill to stand up; he would not sit down, however, though Yaroslav Ilyitch, highly delighted at the visit, invited him to do so. Yaroslav Ilyitch, too, cried out in surprise at seeing Ordynov, but almost at once his delight died away, and he was quite suddenly overtaken by embarrassment halfway between the table and the chair next it. It was evident that he did not know what to say or to do, and was fully conscious of the impropriety of sucking at his pipe and of leaving his visitor to his own devices at such a difficult moment. And yet (such was his confusion) he did go on pulling at his pipe with all his might and indeed with a sort of enthusiasm. Ordynov went into the room at last. He flung a cursory glance at Murin, a look flitted over the old man's face, something like the malicious smile of the day before, which even now set Ordynov shuddering with indignation. All hostility, however, vanished at once and was smoothed away, and the old man's face assumed a perfectly unapproachable and reserved air. He dropped a very low bow to his lodger . . . The scene brought Ordynov to a sense of reality at last. Eager to understand the position of affairs, he looked intently at Yaroslav Ilyitch, who began to be uneasy and flustered.

'Come in, come in,' he brought out at last. 'Come in, most precious Vassily Mihalitch; honour me with your presence, and put a stamp of . . . on all these ordinary objects . . . ' said Yaroslav Ilyitch, pointing towards a corner of the room, flushing like a crimson rose; confused and angry that even his most exalted sentences floundered and missed fire, he moved the chair with a loud noise into the very middle of the room.

'I hope I'm not hindering you, Yaroslav Ilyitch,' said Ordynov. 'I wanted . . . for two minutes . . . '

'Upon my word! As though you could hinder me, Vassily Mihalitch; but let me offer you a cup of tea. Hey, servant . . . I am sure you, too, will not refuse a cup!'

Murin nodded, signifying thereby that he would not. Yaroslav Ilyitch shouted to the servant who came in, sternly demanded another three glasses, then sat down beside Ordynov. For some time he turned his head like a plaster kitten to right and to left, from Murin to Ordynov, and from Ordynov to Murin. His position was extremely unpleasant. He evidently wanted to say something, to his notions extremely delicate, for one side at any rate. But for all his efforts he was totally unable to utter a word . . . Ordynov, too, seemed in perplexity. There was a moment when both began speaking at once . . . Murin, silent, watching them both with curiosity, slowly opened his mouth and showed all his teeth . . .

'I've come to tell you,' Ordynov said suddenly, 'that, owing to a most unpleasant circumstance, I am obliged to leave my lodging, and . . . '

'Fancy, what a strange circumstance!' Yaroslav Ilyitch interrupted suddenly. 'I confess I was utterly astounded when this worthy old man told me this morning of your intention. But . . . '

'*He* told you,' said Ordynov, looking at Murin with surprise.

Murin stroked his beard and laughed in his sleeve.

'Yes,' Yaroslav Ilyitch rejoined; 'though I may have made a mistake. But I venture to say for you – I can answer for it on my honour that there was not a shadow of anything derogatory to you in this worthy old man's words . . . '

Here Yaroslav Ilyitch blushed and controlled his emotion with an effort. Murin, after enjoying to his heart's content the discomfiture of the other two men, took a step forward.

'It is like this, your honour,' he began, bowing politely to Ordynov: 'His honour made bold to take a little trouble on your behalf. As it seems, sir – you know yourself – the mistress and I, that is, we would be glad, freely and heartily, and we would not have made bold to say a word . . . but the way I live, you know yourself, you see for yourself, sir! Of a truth, the Lord barely keeps us alive, for which we pray His holy will; else you see yourself, sir, whether it is for me to make lamentation.' Here Murin again wiped his beard with his sleeve.

Ordynov almost turned sick.

'Yes, yes, I told you about him, myself; he is ill, that is this *malheur*. I should like to express myself in French but, excuse me, I don't speak French quite easily; that is . . . '

'Quite so . . . '

'Quite so, that is . . . '

Ordynov and Yaroslav Ilyitch made each other a half bow, each a little on one side of his chair, and both covered their confusion with an apologetic laugh. The practical Yaroslav Ilyitch recovered at once.

'I have been questioning this honest man minutely,' he began. 'He has been telling me that the illness of this woman . . . ' Here the delicate Yaroslav Ilyitch, probably wishing to conceal a slight embarrassment that showed itself in his face, hurriedly looked at Murin with enquiry.

'Yes, of our mistress . . . '

The refined Yaroslav Ilyitch did not insist further.

'The mistress, that is, your former landlady; I don't know how . . . but there! She is an afflicted woman, you see . . . She says that she is hindering you . . . in your studies, and he himself . . . you concealed from me one important circumstance, Vassily Mihalitch!'

'What?'

'About the gun,' Yaroslav Ilyitch brought out, almost whispering in the most indulgent tone with the millionth fraction of reproach softly ringing in his friendly tenor.

'But,' he added hurriedly, 'he has told me all about it. And you acted nobly in overlooking his involuntary wrong to you. I swear I saw tears in his eyes.'

Yaroslav Ilyitch flushed again, his eyes shone and he shifted in his chair with emotion.

'I, that is, we, sir, that is, your honour, I, to be sure, and my mistress remember you in our prayers,' began Murin, addressing Ordynov and looking at him while Yaroslav Ilyitch overcame his habitual agitation; 'and you know yourself, sir, she is a sick, foolish woman; my legs will hardly support me . . . '

'Yes, I am ready,' Ordynov said impatiently; 'please, that's enough, I am going directly . . . '

'No, that is – sir, we are very grateful for your kindness' (Murin made a very low bow) – 'that is not what I meant to tell you, sir; I wanted to say a word – you see, sir, she came to me almost from her home, that is from far, as the saying is, beyond the seventh water – do not scorn our humble talk, sir, we are ignorant folk – and from a tiny child she has been like this! A sick brain, hasty, she grew up in the forest, grew up a peasant, all among bargemen and factory hands; and then their house must burn down; her mother, sir, was burnt, her father burnt to death – I dare say there is no knowing what she'll tell you . . . I don't meddle, but the Chir-chir-urgi-cal Council examined her at Moscow. You see, sir, she's quite incurable, that's what it is. I am all that's left her, and she lives with me. We live, we pray to God and trust in the Almighty; I never cross her in anything.'

Ordynov's face changed. Yaroslav Ilyitch looked first at one, then at the other.

'But, that is not what I wanted to say . . . no!' Murin corrected himself, shaking his head gravely. 'She is, so to say, such a featherhead, such a whirligig, such a loving, headstrong creature, she's always wanting a sweetheart – if you will pardon my saying so – and someone to love; it's on that she's mad. I amuse her with fairy tales, I do my best at it. I saw, sir, how she – forgive my foolish words, sir,' Murin went on, bowing and wiping his beard with his sleeve – 'how she made friends with you; you, so to say, your excellency, were desirous to approach her with a view to love.'

Yaroslav Ilyitch flushed crimson, and looked reproachfully at Murin. Ordynov could scarcely sit still in his seat.

'No . . . that is not it, sir . . . I speak simply, sir, I am a peasant, I am at your service . . . Of course, we are ignorant folk, we are your servants, sir,' he brought out, bowing low; 'and my wife and I will pray with all our hearts for your honour . . . What do we need? To be strong and have enough to eat – we do not repine; but what am I to do, sir; put my head in the noose? You know yourself, sir, what life is and will have pity on us; but what will it be like, sir, if she has a lover, too! . . . Forgive my rough words, sir; I am a peasant, sir, and you are a gentleman . . . You're a young man, your excellency, proud and hasty, and she, you know yourself, sir, is a little child with no sense – it's easy for her to fall into sin. She's a buxom lass, rosy and sweet, while I am an old man always ailing. Well, the devil, it seems, has tempted you, your honour. I always flatter her with fairy tales, I do indeed; I flatter her; and how we will pray, my wife and I, for your honour! How we will pray! And what is she to you, your excellency, if she is pretty? Still she is a simple woman, an unwashed peasant woman, a foolish rustic maid, a match for a peasant like me. It is not for a gentleman like you, sir, to be friends with peasants! But she and I will pray to God for your honour; how we will pray!'

Here Murin bowed very low and for a long while remained with his back bent, continually wiping his beard with his sleeve.

Yaroslav Iiyitch did not know where he was standing.

'Yes, this good man,' he observed in conclusion, 'spoke to me of some undesirable incidents; I did not venture to believe him, Vassily Mihalitch, I heard that you were still ill,' he interrupted hurriedly, looking at Ordynov in extreme embarrassment, with eyes full of tears of emotion.

'Yes, how much do I owe you?' Ordynov asked Murin hurriedly.

'What are you saying, your honour? Give over. Why, we are not Judases. Why, you are insulting us, sir, we should be ashamed, sir. Have I and my good woman offended you?'

'But this is really strange, my good man; why, his honour took the room from you; don't you feel that you are insulting him by refusing?' Yaroslav Ilyitch interposed, thinking it his duty to show Murin the strangeness and indelicacy of his conduct.

'But upon my word, sir! What do you mean, sir? What did we not do to please your honour? Why, we tried our very best, we did our utmost, upon my word! Give over, sir, give over, your honour. Christ have mercy upon you! Why, are we infidels or what? You might have lived, you might have eaten our humble fare with us and welcome; you might have lain there – we'd have said nothing against it, and we wouldn't have dropped a word; but the evil one tempted you. I am an afflicted man and my mistress is afflicted – what is one to do? There was no one to wait on you, or we would have been glad, glad from our hearts. And how the mistress and I will pray for your honour, how we will pray for you.'

Murin bowed down from the waist. Tears came into Yaroslav Ilyitch's delighted eyes. He looked with enthusiasm at Ordynov.

'What a generous trait, isn't it! What sacred hospitality is to be found in the Russian people.'

Ordynov looked wildly at Yaroslav Ilyitch.

He was almost terrified and scrutinised him from head to foot.

'Yes, indeed, sir, we do honour hospitality; we do honour it indeed, sir,' Murin asserted, covering his beard with his whole sleeve. 'Yes, indeed, the thought just came to me; we'd have welcomed you as a guest, sir, by God! we would,' he went on approaching Ordynov; 'and I had nothing against it; another day I would have said nothing, nothing at all; but sin is a sore snare and my mistress is ill. Ah, if it were not for the mistress! Here, if I had been alone, for instance; how glad I would have been of your honour, how I would have waited upon you, wouldn't I have waited upon you! Whom should we respect if not your honour? I'd have healed you of your sickness, I know the art . . . You should have been our guest, upon my word you should, that is a great word with us! . . . '

'Yes, really; is there such an art?' observed Yaroslav Ilyitch . . . and broke off.

Ordynov had done Yaroslav Ilyitch injustice when, just before, he had looked him up and down with wild amazement.

He was, of course, a very honest and honourable person, but now he understood everything and it must be owned his position was a very difficult one. He wanted to explode, as it is called, with laughter! If he had been alone with Ordynov – two such friends – Yaroslav Ilyitch would, of course, have given way to an immoderate outburst of gaiety without attempting to control himself. He would, however, have done this in a gentlemanly way. He would after laughing have pressed Ordynov's hand with feeling, would genuinely and justly have assured him that he felt double respect for him and that he could make allowances in every case . . . and, of course, would have made no reference to his youth. But as it was, with his habitual delicacy of feeling, he was in a most difficult position and scarcely knew what to do with himself . . .

'Arts, that is decoctions,' Murin added. A quiver passed over his face at Yaroslav Ilyitch's tactless exclamation. 'What I should say, sir, in my peasant foolishness,' he went on, taking another step forward, 'you've read too many books, sir; as the Russian saying is among us peasants, "Wit has overstepped wisdom" . . . '

'Enough,' said Yaroslav Ilyitch sternly.

'I am going,' said Ordynov. 'I thank you, Yaroslav Ilyitch. I will come, I will certainly come and see you,' he said in answer to the redoubled civilities of Yaroslav Ilyitch, who was unable to detain him further. 'Goodbye, goodbye.'

'Goodbye, your honour, goodbye, sir; do not forget us, visit us, poor sinners.'

Ordynov heard nothing more – he went out like one distraught. He could bear no more, he felt shattered, his mind was numb, he dimly felt that he was overcome by illness, but cold despair reigned in his soul, and he was only conscious of a vague pain crushing, wearing, gnawing at his breast; he longed to die at that minute. His legs were giving way under him and he sat down by the fence, taking no notice of the passing people, nor of the crowd that began to collect around him, nor of the questions, nor the exclamations of the curious. But, suddenly, in the multitude of voices, he heard the voice of Murin above him. Ordynov raised his head. The old man really was standing before him, his pale face was thoughtful and dignified, he was quite a different man from the one who had played the coarse farce at Yaroslav Ilyitch's. Ordynov got up. Murin took his arm and led him out of the crowd. 'You want to get your belongings,' he said, looking sideways at Ordynov. 'Don't grieve, sir,' cried Murin. 'You are young, why grieve?'

Ordynov made no reply.

'Are you offended, sir? . . . To be sure you are very angry now . . . but you have no cause; every man guards his own goods!'

'I don't know you,' said Ordynov; 'I don't want to know your secrets. But she, she! . . . ' he brought out, and the tears rushed in streams from his eyes. The wind blew them one after another from his cheeks . . . Ordynov wiped them with his hand; his gesture, his eyes, the involuntary movement of his blue lips all looked like madness.

'I've told you already,' said Murin, knitting his brows, 'that she is crazy? What crazed her? . . . Why need you know? But to me, even so, she is dear! I've loved her more than my life and I'll give her up to no one. Do you understand now?'

There was a momentary gleam of fire in Ordynov's eyes.

'But why have I . . . ? Why have I as good as lost my life? Why does my heart ache? Why did I know Katerina?'

'Why?' Murin laughed and pondered. 'Why, I don't know why,' he brought out at last. 'A woman's heart is not as deep as the sea; you can get to know it, but it is cunning, persistent, full of life! What she wants she must have at once! You may as well know, sir, she wanted to leave me and go away with you; she was sick of the old man, she had lived through everything that she could live with him. You took her fancy, it seems, from the first, though it made no matter whether you or another . . . I don't cross her in anything – if she asks for bird's milk I'll get her bird's milk. I'll make up a bird if there is no such bird; she's set on her will though she doesn't know herself what her heart is mad after. So it has turned out that it is better in the old way! Ah, sir! you are very young, your heart is still hot like a girl forsaken, drying her tears on her sleeve! Let me tell you, sir, a weak man cannot stand alone. Give him everything, he will come of himself and give it all back; give him half the kingdoms of the world to possess, try it and what do you think? He will hide himself in your slipper at once – he will make himself so small. Give a weak man his freedom – he will bind it himself and give it back to you. To a foolish heart freedom is no use! One can't get on with ways like that. I just tell you all this, you are very young! What are you to me? You've come and gone – you or another, it's all the same. I knew from the first it would be the same thing; one can't cross her, one can't say a word to cross her if one wants to keep one's happiness; only, you know, sir' – Murin went on with his reflections – 'as the saying is, anything may happen; one snatches a knife in one's anger, or an unarmed man will fall on you like a sheep, with his bare hands, and tear his enemy's throat with his teeth; but let them put the knife in your hands and your enemy bare his chest before you – no fear, you'll step back.'

They went into the yard. The Tatar saw Murin from a distance, took off his cap to him and stared slyly at Ordynov.

'Where's your mother? At home?' Murin shouted to him.

'Yes.'

'Tell her to help him move his things, and you get away, run along!'

They went up the stairs. The old servant, who appeared to be really the porter's mother, was getting together their lodger's belongings and peevishly tying them up in a big bundle.

'Wait a minute; I'll bring you something else of yours; it's left in there . . . '

Murin went into his room. A minute later he came back and gave Ordynov a sumptuous cushion, covered with embroidery in silks and braid, the one that Katerina had put under his head when he was ill.

'She sends you this,' said Murin. 'And now go for good and good luck to you; and mind, now, don't hang about,' he added in a fatherly tone, dropping his voice, 'or harm will come of it.'

It was evident that he did not want to offend his lodger, but when he cast a last look at him, a gleam of intense malice was unconsciously apparent in his face. Almost with repulsion he closed the door after Ordynov.

Within two hours Ordynov had moved into the rooms of Schpies the German. Tinchen was horrified when she saw him. She at once asked after his health and, when she learned what was wrong, at once did her best to nurse him.

The old German showed his lodger complacently how he had just been going down to paste a new placard on the gate, because the rent Ordynov had paid in advance had run out, that very day, to the last farthing. The old man did not lose the opportunity of commending, in a roundabout way, the accuracy and honesty of Germans. The same day Ordynov was taken ill, and it was three months before he could leave his bed.

Little by little he got better and began to go out. Daily life in the German's lodgings was tranquil and monotonous. The old man had no special characteristics: pretty Tinchen, within the limits of propriety, was all that could be desired. But life seemed to have lost its colour for Ordynov for ever! He became dreamy and irritable; his impressionability took a morbid form and he sank imperceptibly into dull, angry hypochondria. His books were sometimes not opened for weeks together. The future was closed for him, his money was being spent, and he gave up all effort, he did not even think of the future. Sometimes his old feverish zeal for science, his old fervour, the old visions of his own creation, rose up vividly from the past, but they only oppressed and stifled his spiritual energy. His mind would not get to work. His creative force was at a standstill. It seemed as though all those visionary images had grown up to giants in his imagination on purpose to mock at the impotence of their creator. At melancholy moments he could not help comparing himself with the magician's pupil who, learning by stealth his master's magic word, bade the broom bring him water[23] and choked himself drinking it, as he had forgotten how to say, 'Stop.' Possibly a complete, original, independent idea really did exist within him. Perhaps he had been destined to be the artist in science. So at least he himself had believed in the past. Genuine faith is the pledge of the future. But now at some moments he laughed himself at his blind conviction, and – and did not take a step forward.

Six months, before, he had worked out, created and jotted down on paper, a sketch of a work upon which (as he was so young) in non-creative moments he had built his most solid hopes. It was a work relating to the history of the church, and his warmest, most fervent convictions were to find expression in it. Now he read over that plan, made changes in it, thought it over, read it again, looked things up and at last rejected the idea without constructing anything fresh on its ruins. But something akin to mysticism, to fatalism and a belief in the mysterious began to make its way into his mind. The luckless fellow felt his sufferings and besought God to heal him. The German's servant, a devout old Russian woman, used to describe with relish how her meek lodger prayed and how he would lie for hours together as though unconscious on the church pavement . . . He never spoke to anyone of what had happened to him. But at times, especially at the hour when the church bells brought back to him the moment when first his heart ached and quivered with a feeling new to him, when he knelt beside her in the house of God, forgetting everything, and hearing nothing but the beating of her timid heart, when with tears of ecstasy and joy he watered the new, radiant hopes that had sprung up in his lonely life – then a storm broke in his soul that was wounded for ever; then his soul shuddered, and again the anguish of love glowed in his bosom with scorching fire; then his heart ached with sorrow and passion and his love seemed to grow with his grief. Often for hours together, forgetting himself and his daily life, forgetting everything in the world, he would sit in the same place, solitary, disconsolate; would shake his head hopelessly and, dropping silent tears, would whisper to himself: 'Katerina, my precious dove, my one loved sister!'

A hideous idea began to torment him more and more, it haunted him more and more vividly, and every day took more probable, more actual shape before him. He fancied – and at last he believed it fully – he fancied that Katerina's reason was sound, but that Murin was right when he called her 'a weak heart'. He fancied that some mystery, some secret, bound her to the old man, and that Katerina, though innocent of crime as a pure dove, had got into his power. Who were they? He did not know, but he had constant visions of an immense, over-powering despotism over a poor, defenceless creature, and his heart raged and trembled in impotent indignation. He fancied that before the frightened eyes of her suddenly awakened soul the idea of its degradation had been craftily presented, that the poor *weak* heart had been craftily tortured, that the truth had been twisted and contorted to her, that she had, with a purpose, been kept blind when necessary, that the inexperienced inclinations of her troubled passionate heart had been subtly flattered, and by degrees the free soul had been clipped of its wings till it was incapable at last of resistance or of a free movement towards free life . . .

By degrees Ordynov grew more and more unsociable and, to do them justice, his Germans did not hinder him in the tendency.

He was fond of walking aimlessly about the streets. He preferred the hour of twilight, and, by choice, remote, secluded and unfrequented places. On one rainy, unhealthy spring evening, in one of his favourite back-lanes he met Yaroslav Ilyitch.

Yaroslav Ilyitch was perceptibly thinner. His friendly eyes looked dim and he looked altogether disappointed. He was racing off full speed on some business of the utmost urgency, he was wet through and muddy and, all the evening, a drop of rain had in an almost fantastic way been hanging on his highly decorous but now blue nose. He had, moreover, grown whiskers.

These whiskers and the fact that Yaroslav Ilyitch glanced at him as though trying to avoid a meeting with an old friend almost startled

Ordynov. Strange to say, it even wounded his heart, which had till then felt no need for sympathy. He preferred, in fact, the man as he had been – simple, kindly, naïve; speaking candidly, a little stupid, but free from all pretensions to disillusionment and commonsense. It is unpleasant when a foolish man whom we have once liked, just on account of his foolishness, suddenly becomes sensible; it is decidedly disagreeable. However, the distrust with which he looked at Ordynov was quickly effaced.

In spite of his disillusionment he still retained his old manners, which, as we all know, accompany a man to the grave, and even now he eagerly tried to win Ordynov's confidence. First of all he observed that he was very busy, and then that they had not seen each other for a long time; but all at once the conversation took a strange turn.

Yaroslav Ilyitch began talking of the deceitfulness of mankind in general. Of the transitoriness of the blessings of this world, of the vanity of vanities; he even made a passing allusion to Pushkin with more than indifference, referred with some cynicism to his acquaintances and, in conclusion, even hinted at the deceitfulness and treachery of those who are called friends, though there is no such thing in the world as real friendship and never has been; in short, Yaroslav Ilyitch had grown wise.

Ordynov did not contradict him, but he felt unutterably sad, as though he had buried his best friend.

'Ah! fancy, I was forgetting to tell you,' Yaroslav Ilyitch began suddenly, as though recalling something very interesting. 'There's a piece of news! I'll tell you as a secret. Do you remember the house where you lodged?'

Ordynov started and turned pale.

'Well, only fancy, just lately a whole gang of thieves was discovered in that house; that is, would you believe me, a regular band of brigands; smugglers, robbers of all sorts, goodness knows what. Some have been caught but others are still being looked for; the sternest orders have been given. And, can you believe it! do you remember the master of the house, that pious, respectable, worthy-looking old man?'

'Well!'

'What is one to think of mankind? He was the chief of their gang, the leader. Isn't it absurd?'

Yaroslav Ilyitch spoke with feeling and judged of all mankind from one example, because Yaroslav Ilyitch could not do otherwise, it was his character.

'And they? Murin?' Ordynov articulated in a whisper.

'Ah! Murin, Murin! No, he was a worthy old man, quite respectable . . . but, excuse me, you throw a new light . . . '

'Why? Was he, too, in the gang?'

Ordynov's heart was ready to burst with impatience.

'However, as you say . . . ' added Yaroslav Ilyitch, fixing his pewtery eyes on Ordynov – a sign that he was reflecting – 'Murin could not have been one of them. Just three weeks ago he went home with his wife to their own parts . . . I learned it from the porter, that little Tatar, do you remember?'

A Novel in Nine Letters

1

From Pyotr Ivanitch to Ivan Petrovitch

DEAR SIR and most precious friend, Ivan Petrovitch, for the last two days I have been, I may say, in pursuit of you, my friend, having to talk over most urgent business with you, and I cannot come across you anywhere. Yesterday, while we were at Semyon Alexeyitch's, my wife made a very good joke about you, saying that Tatyana Petrovna and you were a pair of birds always on the wing. You have not been married three months and you already neglect your domestic hearth. We all laughed heartily – from our genuine kindly feeling for you, of course – but, joking apart, my precious friend, you have given me a lot of trouble. Semyon Alexeyitch said to me that you might be going to the ball at the Social Union's club! Leaving my wife with Semyon Alexeyitch's good lady, I flew off to the Social Union. It was funny and tragic! Fancy my position! Me at the ball – and alone, without my wife! Ivan Andreyitch meeting me in the porter's lodge and seeing me alone, at once concluded (the rascal!) that I had a passion for dances, and taking me by the arm, wanted to drag me off by force to a dancing class, saying that it was too crowded at the Social Union, that an ardent spirit had not room to turn, and that his head ached from the patchouli[24] and mignonette.[25] I found neither you, nor Tatyana Petrovna. Ivan Andreyitch vowed and declared that you would be at *Woe from Wit*,[26] at the Alexandrinsky Theatre.[27]

I flew off to the Alexandrinsky Theatre: you were not there either. This morning I expected to find you at Tchistoganov's – no sign of you there. Tchistoganov sent to the Perepalkins' – the same thing there. In fact, I am quite worn out; you can judge how much trouble I have taken! Now I am writing to you (there is nothing else I can do). My business is by no means a literary one (you understand me?); it would be better to meet face to face; it is extremely necessary to discuss something with you and as quickly as possible, and so I beg you to come to us today with Tatyana Petrovna to tea and for a chat in the evening. My Anna

Mihalovna will be extremely pleased to see you. You will truly, as they say, oblige me to my dying day. By the way, my precious friend – since I have taken up my pen I'll go into all I have against you – I have a slight complaint I must make; in fact, I must reproach you, my worthy friend, for an apparently very innocent little trick which you have played at my expense . . . You are a rascal, a man without conscience. About the middle of last month, you brought into my house an acquaintance of yours, Yevgeny Nikolaitch; you vouched for him by your friendly and, for me, of course, sacred recommendation; I rejoiced at the opportunity of receiving the young man with open arms, and when I did so I put my head in a noose. A noose it hardly is, but it has turned out a pretty business. I have not time now to explain, and indeed it is an awkward thing to do in writing, only a very humble request to you, my malicious friend: could you not somehow very delicately, in passing, drop a hint into the young man's ear that there are a great many houses in the metropolis besides ours? It's more than I can stand, my dear fellow! We fall at your feet, as our friend Semyonovitch says. I will tell you all about it when we meet. I don't mean to say that the young man has sinned against good manners, or is lacking in spiritual qualities, or is not up to the mark in some other way. On the contrary, he is an amiable and pleasant fellow; but wait, we shall meet; meanwhile if you see him, for goodness' sake whisper a hint to him, my good friend. I would do it myself, but you know what I am, I simply can't, and that's all about it. You introduced him. But I will explain myself more fully this evening, anyway. Now goodbye. I remain, etc.

P.S. – My little boy has been ailing for the last week, and gets worse and worse every day; he is cutting his poor little teeth. My wife is nursing him all the time, and is depressed, poor thing. Be sure to come, you will give us real pleasure, my precious friend.

2

From Ivan Petrovitch to Pyotr Ivanitch

DEAR SIR, PYOTR IVANITCH! I got your letter yesterday, I read it and was perplexed. You looked for me, goodness knows where, and I was simply at home. Till ten o'clock I was expecting Ivan Ivanitch Tolokonov. At once on getting your letter I set out with my wife, I went to the expense of taking a cab, and reached your house about half-past six. You were not at home, but we were met by your wife. I waited to see you till half-past ten, I could not stay later. I set off with my wife, went to the expense of a cab again, saw her home, and went on myself to the Perepalkins', thinking I might meet you there, but again I was out in my reckoning. When I got home I did not sleep all night, I felt uneasy; in the morning I drove round to you three times, at nine, at ten and at eleven; three times I went to the expense of a cab, and again you left me in the lurch.

I read your letter and was amazed. You write about Yevgeny Nikolaitch, beg me to whisper some hint, and do not tell me what about. I commend your caution, but all letters are not alike, and I don't give documents of importance to my wife for curl-papers. I am puzzled, in fact, to know with what motive you wrote all this to me. However, if it comes to that, why should I meddle in the matter? I don't poke my nose into other people's business. You can be not at home to him; I only see that I must have a brief and decisive explanation with you, and, moreover, time is passing. And I am in straits and don't know what to do if you are going to neglect the terms of our agreement. A journey for nothing; a journey costs something, too, and my wife's whining for me to get her a velvet mantle of the latest fashion. About Yevgeny Nikolaitch I hasten to mention that when I was at Pavel Semyonovitch Perepalkin's yesterday I made enquiries without loss of time. He has five hundred serfs in the province of Yaroslav, and he has expectations from his grandmother of an estate of three hundred serfs near Moscow. How much money he has I cannot tell; I think you ought to know that better. I beg you once for all to appoint a place where I can meet you. You met Ivan Andreyitch yesterday, and you write that he told you that I was at the Alexandrinsky Theatre with my wife. I write that he is a liar, and it shows how little he is to be trusted in such cases that only the day before yesterday he did his grandmother out of eight hundred roubles. I have the honour to remain, etc.

P.S. – My wife is going to have a baby; she is nervous about it and feels depressed at times. At the theatre they sometimes have firearms going off and sham thunderstorms. And so for fear of a shock to my wife's nerves I do not take her to the theatre. I have no great partiality for the theatre myself.

3

From Pyotr Ivanitch to Ivan Petrovitch

MY PRECIOUS FRIEND, IVAN PETROVITCH – I am to blame, to blame, a thousand times to blame, but I hasten to defend myself. Between five and six yesterday, just as we were talking of you with the warmest affection, a messenger from Uncle Stepan Alexeyitch galloped up with the news that my aunt was very bad. Being afraid of alarming my wife, I did not say a word of this to her, but on the pretext of other urgent business I drove off to my aunt's house. I found her almost dying. Just at five o'clock she had had a stroke, the third she has had in the last two years. Karl Fyodoritch, their family doctor, told us that she might not live through the night. You can judge of my position, dearest friend. We were on our legs all night in grief and anxiety. It was not till morning that, utterly exhausted and overcome by moral and physical weakness, I lay down on the sofa; I forgot to tell them to wake me, and only woke at half-past eleven. My aunt was better. I drove home to my wife. She, poor thing, was quite worn out expecting me. I snatched a bite of something, embraced my little boy, reassured my wife and set off to call on you. You were not at home. At your flat I found Yevgeny Nikolaitch. When I got home I took up a pen, and here I am writing to you. Don't grumble and be cross to me, my true friend. Beat me, chop my guilty head off my shoulders, but don't deprive me of your affection. From your wife I learned that you will be at the Slavyanovs' this evening. I will certainly be there. I look forward with the greatest impatience to seeing you.

I remain, etc.

P.S. – We are in perfect despair about our little boy. Karl Fyodoritch prescribes rhubarb. He moans. Yesterday he did not know anyone. This morning he did know us, and began lisping papa, mamma, boo . . . My wife was in tears the whole morning.

4

From Ivan Petrovitch to Pyotr Ivanitch

MY DEAR SIR, PYOTR IVANITCH! I am writing to you, in your room, at your bureau; and before taking up my pen, I have been waiting for more than two and a half hours for you. Now allow me to tell you straight out, Pyotr Ivanitch, my frank opinion about this shabby incident. From your last letter I gathered that you were expected at the Slavyanovs', that you were inviting me to go there; I turned up, I stayed for five hours and there was no sign of you. Why, am I to be made a laughing-stock to people, do you suppose? Excuse me, my dear sir . . . I came to you this morning, I hoped to find you, not imitating certain deceitful persons who look for people, God knows where, when they can be found at home at any suitably chosen time. There is no sign of you at home. I don't know what restrains me from telling you now the whole harsh truth. I will only say that I see you seem to be going back on your bargain regarding our agreement. And only now reflecting on the whole affair, I cannot but confess that I am absolutely astounded at the artful workings of your mind. I see clearly now that you have been cherishing your unfriendly design for a long time. This supposition of mine is confirmed by the fact that last week in an almost unpardonable way you took possession of that letter of yours addressed to me, in which you laid down yourself, though rather vaguely and incoherently, the terms of our agreement in regard to a circumstance of which I need not remind you. You are afraid of documents, you destroy them, and you try to make a fool of me. But I won't allow myself to be made a fool of, for no one has ever considered me one hitherto, and everyone has thought well of me in that respect. I am opening my eyes. You try and put me off, confuse me with talk of Yevgeny Nikolaitch, and when with your letter of the seventh of this month, which I am still at a loss to understand, I seek a personal explanation from you, you make hum-bugging appointments, while you keep out of the way. Surely you do not suppose, sir, that I am not equal to noticing all this? You promised to reward me for my services, of which you are very well aware, in the way of introducing various persons, and at the same time, and I don't know how you do it, you contrive to borrow money from me in con-siderable sums without giving a receipt, as happened no longer ago than last week. Now, having got the money, you keep out of the way, and what's more, you repudiate the service I have done you in regard to Yevgeny Nikolaitch. You are probably reckoning on my speedy departure to Simbirsk,[28] and hoping I may not have time to settle your business. But I assure you solemnly and testify on my word of honour that if it comes to that, I am prepared to spend two more months in Petersburg expressly to carry through my business, to attain my objects, and to get hold of you. For I, too, on occasion know how to get the better of people. In conclusion, I beg to inform you that if you do not give me a satisfactory explanation today, first in writing, and then personally face to face, and do not make a fresh statement in your letter of the chief points of the agreement existing between us, and do not explain fully your views in regard to Yevgeny Nikolaitch, I shall be compelled to have recourse to measures that will be highly unpleasant to you, and indeed repugnant to me also.

Allow me to remain, etc.

5

From Pyotr Ivanitch to Ivan Petrovitch)

November 11

MY DEAR AND HONOURED FRIEND, IVAN PETROVITCH! I was cut to the heart by your letter. I wonder you were not ashamed, my dear but unjust friend, to behave like this to one of your most devoted friends. Why be in such a hurry, and without explaining things fully, wound me with such insulting suspicions? But I hasten to reply to your charges. You did not find me yesterday, Ivan Petrovitch, because I was suddenly and quite unexpectedly called away to a deathbed. My aunt, Yefimya Nikolaevna, passed away yesterday evening at eleven o'clock in the night. By the general consent of the relatives I was selected to make the arrangements for the sad and sorrowful ceremony. I had so much to do that I had not time to see you this morning, nor even to send you a line. I am grieved to the heart at the misunderstanding which has arisen between us. My words about Yevgeny Nikolaitch uttered casually and in jest you have taken in quite a wrong sense, and have ascribed to them a meaning deeply offensive to me. You refer to money and express your anxiety about it. But without wasting words I am ready to satisfy all your claims and demands, though I must remind you that the three hundred and fifty roubles I had from you last week were in accordance with a certain agreement and not by way of a loan. In the latter case there would certainly have been a receipt. I will not condescend to discuss the other points mentioned in your letter. I see that it is a misunderstanding. I see it is your habitual hastiness, hot temper and obstinacy. I know that your goodheartedness and open character will not allow doubts to persist in your heart, and that you will be, in fact, the first to hold out your hand to me. You are mistaken, Ivan Petrovitch, you are greatly mistaken!

Although your letter has deeply wounded me, I should be prepared even today to come to you and apologise, but I have been since yesterday in such a rush and flurry that I am utterly exhausted and can scarcely stand on my feet. To complete my troubles, my wife is laid up; I am afraid she is seriously ill. Our little boy, thank God, is better; but I must lay down my pen, I have a mass of things to do and they are urgent. Allow me, my dear friend, to remain, etc.

6

From Ivan Petrovitch to Pyotr Ivanitch

November 14

DEAR SIR, PYOTR IVANITCH! I have been waiting for three days, I tried to make a profitable use of them – meanwhile I feel that politeness and good manners are the greatest of ornaments for everyone. Since my last letter of the tenth of this month, I have neither by word nor deed reminded you of my existence, partly in order to allow you undisturbed to perform the duty of a Christian in regard to your aunt, partly because I needed the time for certain considerations and investigations in regard to a business you know of. Now I hasten to explain myself to you in the most thoroughgoing and decisive manner.

I frankly confess that on reading your first two letters I seriously supposed that you did not understand what I wanted; that was how it was that I rather sought an interview with you and explanations face to face. I was afraid of writing, and blamed myself for lack of clearness in the expression of my thoughts on paper. You are aware that I have not the advantages of education and good manners, and that I shun a hollow show of gentility because I have learned from bitter experience how misleading appearances often are, and that a snake sometimes lies hidden under flowers. But you understood me; you did not answer me as you should have done because, in the treachery of your heart, you had planned beforehand to be faithless to your word of honour and to the friendly relations existing between us. You have proved this

absolutely by your abominable conduct towards me of late, which is
fatal to my interests, which I did not expect and which I refused to
believe till the present moment. From the very beginning of our
acquaintance you captivated me by your clever manners, by the subtlety
of your behaviour, your knowledge of affairs and the advantages to be
gained by association with you. I imagined that I had found a true
friend and well-wisher. Now I recognise clearly that there are many
people who under a flattering and brilliant exterior hide venom in their
hearts, who use their cleverness to weave snares for their neighbour
and for unpardonable deception, and so are afraid of pen and paper,
and at the same time use their fine language not for the benefit of their
neighbour and their country, but to drug and bewitch the reason of
those who have entered into business relations of any sort with them.
Your treachery to me, my dear sir, can be clearly seen from what
follows.

In the first place, when, in the clear and distinct terms of my letter, I
described my position, sir, and at the same time asked you in my first
letter what you meant by certain expressions and intentions of yours,
principally in regard to Yevgeny Nikolaitch, you tried for the most part
to avoid answering, and confounding me by doubts and suspicions, you
calmly put the subject aside. Then after treating me in a way which
cannot be described by any seemly word, you began writing that you
were wounded. Pray, what am I to call that, sir? Then when every
minute was precious to me and when you had set me running after you
all over the town, you wrote, pretending personal friendship, letters in
which, intentionally avoiding all mention of business, you spoke of
utterly irrelevant matters; to wit, of the illnesses of your good lady for
whom I have, in any case, every respect, and of how your baby had been
dosed with rhubarb and was cutting a tooth. All this you alluded to in
every letter with a disgusting regularity that was insulting to me. Of
course I am prepared to admit that a father's heart may be torn by the
sufferings of his babe, but why make mention of this when something
different, far more important and interesting, was needed? I endured it
in silence, but now when time has elapsed I think it my duty to explain
myself. Finally, treacherously deceiving me several times by making
humbugging appointments, you tried, it seems, to make me play the
part of a fool and a laughing-stock for you, which I never intend to be.
Then after first inviting me and thoroughly deceiving me, you informed
me that you were called away to your suffering aunt who had had a
stroke, precisely at five o'clock as you stated with shameful exactitude.
Luckily for me, sir, in the course of these three days I have succeeded in

making enquiries and have learnt from them that your aunt had a stroke on the day before the seventh not long before midnight. From this fact I see that you have made use of sacred family relations in order to deceive persons in no way concerned with them. Finally, in your last letter you mention the death of your relative as though it had taken place precisely at the time when I was to have visited you to consult about various business matters. But here the vileness of your arts and calculations exceeds all belief, for from trustworthy information which I was able by a lucky chance to obtain just in the nick of time, I have found out that your aunt died twenty-four hours later than the time you so impiously fixed for her decease in your letter. I shall never have done if I enumerate all the signs by which I have discovered your treachery in regard to me. It is sufficient, indeed, for any impartial observer that in every letter you style me your true friend, and call me all sorts of polite names, which you do, to the best of my belief, for no other object than to put my conscience to sleep.

I have come now to your principal act of deceit and treachery in regard to me, to wit, your continual silence of late in regard to everything concerning our common interests, in regard to your wicked theft of the letter in which you stated, though in language somewhat obscure and not perfectly intelligible to me, our mutual agreements, your barbarous forcible loan of three hundred and fifty roubles which you borrowed from me as your partner without giving any receipt, and finally, your abominable slanders of our common acquaintance, Yevgeny Nikolaitch. I see clearly now that you meant to show me that he was, if you will allow me to say so, like a billy-goat, good for neither milk nor wool, that he was neither one thing nor the other, neither fish nor flesh, which you put down as a vice in him in your letter of the sixth instant. I knew Yevgeny Nikolaitch as a modest and well-behaved young man, whereby he may well attract, gain and deserve respect in society. I know also that every evening for the last fortnight you've put into your pocket dozens and sometimes even hundreds of roubles, playing games of chance with Yevgeny Nikolaitch. Now you disavow all this, and not only refuse to compensate me for what I have suffered, but have even appropriated money belonging to me, tempting me by suggestions that I should be partner in the affair, and luring me with various advantages which were to accrue. After having appropriated, in a most illegal way, money of mine and of Yevgeny Nikolaitch's, you decline to compensate me, resorting for that object to calumny with which you have unjustifiably blackened in my eyes a man whom I, by my efforts and exertions, introduced into your house. While on the contrary, from what I hear from your friends, you are still almost slobbering over him, and give out to the whole world that he is your dearest friend, though there is no one in the world such a fool as not to guess at once what your designs are aiming at and what your friendly relations really mean. I should say that they mean deceit, treachery, forgetfulness of human duties and proprieties, contrary to the law of God and vicious in every way. I take myself as a proof and example. In what way have I offended you and why have you treated me in this godless fashion?

I will end my letter. I have explained myself. Now in conclusion. If, sir, you do not in the shortest possible time after receiving this letter return me in full, first, the three hundred and fifty roubles I gave you, and, secondly, all the sums that should come to me according to your promise, I will have recourse to every possible means to compel you to return it, even to open force, secondly to the protection of the laws, and finally I beg to inform you that I am in possession of facts, which, if they remain in the hands of your humble servant, may ruin and disgrace your name in the eyes of all the world. Allow me to remain, etc.

7

From Pyotr Ivanitch to Ivan Petrovitch

November 15

IVAN PETROVITCH! When I received your vulgar and at the same time queer letter, my impulse for the first minute was to tear it into shreds, but I have preserved it as a curiosity. I do, however, sincerely regret our misunderstandings and unpleasant relations. I did not mean to answer you. But I am compelled by necessity. I must in these lines inform you that it would be very unpleasant for me to see you in my house at any time; my wife feels the same: she is in delicate health and the smell of tar upsets her. My wife sends your wife the book, *Don Quixote de la Mancha*,[29] with her sincere thanks. As for the goloshes you say you left behind here on your last visit, I must regretfully inform you that they are nowhere to be found. They are still being looked for; but if they do not turn up, then I will buy you a new pair.

I have the honour to remain your sincere friend,

8

On the sixteenth of November, Pyotr Ivanitch received by post two letters addressed to him. Opening the first envelope, he took out a carefully folded note on pale pink paper. The handwriting was his wife's. It was addressed to Yevgeny Nikolaitch and dated 2 November. There was nothing else in the envelope. Pyotr Ivanitch read:

DEAR EUGENE – Yesterday was utterly impossible. My husband was at home the whole evening. Be sure to come tomorrow punctually at eleven. At half-past ten my husband is going to Tsarskoe and not coming back till evening. I was in a rage all night. Thank you for sending me the information and the correspondence. What a lot of paper. Did she really write all that? She has style though; many thanks, dear; I see that you love me. Don't be angry, but, for goodness sake, come tomorrow.

A.

Pyotr Ivanitch tore open the other letter :

PYOTR IVANITCH – I should never have set foot again in your house anyway; you need not have troubled to soil paper about it.

Next week I am going to Simbirsk. Yevgany Nikolaitch remains your precious and beloved friend. I wish you luck, and don't trouble about the goloshes.

9

On the seventeenth of November Ivan Petrovitch received by post two letters addressed to him. Opening the first letter, he took out a hasty and carelessly written note. The handwriting was his wife's; it was addressed to Yevgeny Nikolaitch, and dated August the fourth. There was nothing else in the envelope. Ivan Petrovitch read:

GOODBYE, YEVGENY NIKOLAITCH! The Lord reward you for this too. May you be happy, but my lot is bitter, terribly bitter! It is your choice. If it had not been for my aunt I should not have put such trust in you. Do not laugh at me nor at my aunt. Tomorrow is our wedding. Aunt is relieved that a good man has been found, and that he will take me without a dowry. I took a good look at him for the first time today. He seems good-natured. They are hurrying me. Farewell, . . . My darling!! Think of me sometimes; I shall never forget you. Farewell! I sign this last like my first letter, do you remember?

Tatyana

The second letter was as follows:

IVAN PETROVITCH – Tomorrow you will receive a new pair of goloshes. It is not my habit to filch from, other men's pockets, and I am not fond of picking up all sorts of rubbish in the streets.

Yevgeny Nikolaitch is going to Simbirsk in a day or two on his grandfather's business, and he has asked me to find a travelling companion for him; wouldn't you like to take him with you?

Another Man's Wife, or the Husband Under the Bed

'BE SO KIND, SIR . . . allow me to ask you . . . '

The gentleman so addressed started and looked with some alarm at the gentleman in raccoon furs who had accosted him so abruptly at eight o'clock in the evening in the street. We all know that if a Petersburg gentleman suddenly in the street speaks to another gentleman with whom he is unacquainted, the second gentleman is invariably alarmed.

And so the gentleman addressed started and was somewhat alarmed.

'Excuse me for troubling you,' said the gentleman in raccoon, 'but I . . . I really don't know . . . you will pardon me, no doubt; you see, I am a little upset . . . '

Only then the young man in the wadded overcoat observed that this gentleman in the raccoon furs certainly was upset. His wrinkled face was rather pale, his voice was trembling. He was evidently in some confusion of mind, his words did not flow easily from his tongue, and it could be seen that it cost him a terrible effort to present a very humble request to a personage possibly his inferior in rank or condition, in spite of the urgent necessity of addressing his request to somebody. And indeed the request was in any case unseemly, undignified, strange, coming from a man who had such a dignified fur coat, such a respectable jacket of a superb dark-green colour, and such distinguished decorations adorning that jacket. It was evident that the gentleman in raccoon was himself confused by all this, so that at last he could not stand it, but made up his mind to suppress his emotion and politely to put an end to the unpleasant position he had himself brought about.

'Excuse me, I am not myself: but it is true you don't know me . . . forgive me for disturbing you; I have changed my mind.'

Here, from politeness, he raised his hat and hurried off.

'But allow me . . . '

The little gentleman had, however, vanished into the darkness, leaving the gentleman in the wadded overcoat in a state of stupefaction.

'What a queer fellow!' thought the gentleman in the wadded overcoat. After wondering, as was only natural, and recovering at last from his stupefaction, he bethought him of his own affairs, and began walking to and fro, staring intently at the gates of a house with an endless number of storeys. A fog was beginning to come on, and the young man was somewhat relieved at it, for his walking up and down was less noticeable in the fog, though indeed no one could have noticed him but some cabman who had been waiting all day without a fare.

'Excuse me!'

The young man started again; again the gentleman in raccoon was standing before him.

'Excuse me again . . . ' he began, 'but you . . . you are no doubt an honourable man! Take no notice of my social position. . . but I am getting muddled . . . look at it as man to man . . . you see before you, sir, a man craving a humble favour . . . '

'If I can . . . What do you want?'

'You imagine, perhaps, that I am asking for money,' said the mysterious gentleman, with a wry smile, laughing hysterically and turning pale.

'Oh, dear, no.'

'No, I see that I am tiresome to you! Excuse me, I cannot bear myself; consider that you are seeing a man in an agitated condition, almost of insanity, and do not draw any conclusion . . . '

'But to the point, to the point,' responded the young man, nodding his head encouragingly and impatiently.

'Now think of that! A young man like you reminding me to keep to the point, as though I were some heedless boy! I must certainly be doting! . . . How do I seem to you in my degrading position? Tell me frankly.'

The young man was overcome with confusion, and said nothing.

'Allow me to ask you openly: have you not seen a lady? That is all that I have to ask you,' the gentleman in the raccoon coat said resolutely at last.

'Lady?'

'Yes, a lady.'

'Yes, I have seen . . . but I must say lots of them have passed . . . '

'Just so,' answered the mysterious gentleman, with a bitter smile. 'I am muddled, I did not mean to ask that; excuse me, I meant to say, haven't you seen a lady in a fox-fur cape, in a dark velvet hood and a black veil?'

'No, I haven't noticed one like that . . . no. I think I haven't seen one.'

'Well, in that case, excuse me!'

The young man wanted to ask a question, but the gentleman in raccoon vanished again; again he left his patient listener in a state of stupefaction.

'Well, the devil take him!' thought the young man in the wadded overcoat, evidently troubled.

With annoyance he turned up his beaver collar, and began cautiously walking to and fro again before the gates of the house of many storeys. He was raging inwardly.

'Why doesn't she come out?' he thought. 'It will soon be eight o'clock.'

The town clock struck eight.

'Oh, devil take you!'

'Excuse me! . . . '

'Excuse me for speaking like that . . . but you came upon me so suddenly that you quite frightened me,' said the young man, frowning and apologising.

'Here I am again. I must strike you as tiresome and queer.'

'Be so good as to explain at once, without more ado; I don't know what it is you want . . . '

'You are in a hurry. Do you see, I will tell you everything openly, without wasting words. It cannot be helped. Circumstances sometimes bring together people of very different characters . . . But I see you are impatient, young man . . . So here . . . though I really don't know how to tell you: I am looking for a lady (I have made up my mind to tell you all about it). You see, I must know where that lady has gone. Who she is – I imagine there is no need for you to know her name, young man.'

'Well, well, what next?'

'What next? But what a tone you take with me! Excuse me, but perhaps I have offended you by calling you young man, but I had nothing . . . in short, if you are willing to do me a very great service, here it is : a lady – that is, I mean a gentlewoman of a very good family, of my acquaintance . . . I have been commissioned . . . I have no family, you see . . . '

'Oh!'

'Put yourself in my position, young man (ah, I've done it again; excuse me, I keep calling you young man). Every minute is precious . . . Only fancy, that lady . . . but cannot you tell me who lives in this house?'

'But . . . lots of people live here.'

'Yes, that is so, you are perfectly right,' answered the gentleman in raccoon, giving a slight laugh for the sake of good manners. 'I feel I am rather muddled . . . But why do you take that tone? You see, I admit frankly that I am muddled, and however haughty you are, you have seen enough of my humiliation to satisfy you . . . I say a lady of honourable conduct, that is, of light tendencies – excuse me, I am so confused; it is as though I were speaking of literature – Paul de Kock[30] is supposed to be of light tendencies, and all the trouble comes from him, you see . . . '

The young man looked compassionately at the gentleman in raccoon, who seemed in a hopeless muddle and, pausing, stared at him with a meaningless smile and with a trembling hand for no apparent reason gripped the lappet of his wadded overcoat.

'You ask who lives here?' said the young man, stepping back a little.

'Yes; you told me lots of people live here.'

'Here . . . I know that Sofya Ostafyevna lives here, too,' the young man brought out in a low and even commiserating tone.

'There, you see, you see! You know something, young man?'

'I assure you I don't, I know nothing . . . I judged from your troubled air . . . '

'I have just learned from the cook that she does come here; but you are on the wrong tack, that is, with Sofya Ostafyevna . . . she does not know her . . . '

'No? Oh . . . I beg your pardon, then . . . '

'I see this is of no interest to you, young man,' said the queer man, with bitter irony.

'Listen,' said the young man, hesitating. 'I really don't understand why you are in such a state, but tell me frankly, I suppose you are being deceived?' The young man smiled approvingly. 'We shall understand one another, anyway,' he added, and his whole person loftily betrayed an inclination to make a half-bow.

'You crush me! But I frankly confess that is just it . . . but it happens to everyone! . . . I am deeply touched by your sympathy. To be sure, among young men . . . though I am not young; but you know, habit, a bachelor life, among bachelors, we all know . . . '

'Oh, yes, we all know, we all know! But in what way can I be of assistance to you?'

'Why, look here: admitting a visit to Sofya Ostafyevna . . . though I don't know for a fact where the lady has gone, I only know that she is in that house; but seeing you walking up and down, and I am walking up and down on the same side myself, I thought . . . you see, I am waiting for that lady . . . I know that she is there. I should like to meet her and explain to her how shocking and improper it is! . . . In fact, you understand me . . . '

'H'm! Well?'

'I am not acting for myself; don't imagine it; it is another man's wife!

Her husband is standing over there on the Voznesensky Bridge;[31] he wants to catch her, but he doesn't dare; he is still loath to believe it, as every husband is.' (Here the gentleman in raccoon made an effort to smile.) 'I am a friend of his; you can see for yourself I am a person held in some esteem; I could not be what you take me for.'

'Oh, of course. Well, well!'

'So, you see, I am on the lookout for her. The task has been entrusted to me (the unhappy husband!). But I know that the young lady is sly (Paul de Kock forever under her pillow); I am certain she scurries off somewhere on the sly . . . I must confess the cook told me she comes here; I rushed off like a madman as soon as I heard the news; I want to catch her. I have long had my suspicions, and so I wanted to ask you; you are walking here . . . you – you – I don't know . . . '

'Come, what is it you want?'

'Yes . . . I have not the honour of your acquaintance; I do not venture to enquire who and what you may be . . . Allow me to introduce myself, anyway; glad to meet you! . . . ' The gentleman, quivering with agitation, warmly shook the young man's hand. 'I ought to have done this to begin with,' he added, 'but I have lost all sense of good manners.'

The gentleman in raccoon could not stand still as he talked; he kept looking about him uneasily, fidgeted with his feet, and like a drowning man clutched at the young man's hand.

'You see,' he went on, 'I meant to address you in a friendly way . . . Excuse the freedom . . . I meant to ask you to walk along the other side and down the side street, where there is a back entrance. I, too, on my side, will walk from the front entrance, so that we cannot miss her; I'm afraid of missing her by myself; I don't want to miss her. When you see her, stop her and shout to me . . . But I'm mad! Only now I see the foolishness and impropriety of my suggestion! . . . '

'No, why, no! It's all right! . . . '

'Don't make excuses for me; I am so upset. I have never been in such a state before. As though I were being tried for my life! I must own indeed – I will be straightforward and honourable with you, young man; I actually thought you might be the lover.'

'That is, to put it simply, you want to know what I am doing here?'

'You are an honourable man, my dear sir. I am far from supposing that you are *he*, I will not insult you with such a suspicion; but . . . give me your word of honour that you are not the lover . . . '

'Oh, very well, I'll give you my word of honour that I am a lover, but not of your wife; otherwise I shouldn't be here in the street, but should be with her now!'

'Wife! Who told you she was my wife, young man? I am a bachelor, I – that is, I am a lover myself . . . '

'You told me there is a husband on Voznesensky Bridge.'

'Of course, of course, I am talking too freely; but there are other ties! And you know, young man, a certain lightness of character, that is . . . '

'Yes, yes, to be sure, to be sure . . . '

'That is, I am not her husband at all . . . '

'Oh, no doubt. But I tell you frankly that in reassuring you now, I want to set my own mind at rest, and that is why I am candid with you; you are upsetting me and in my way. I promise that I will call you. But I most humbly beg you to move farther away and let me alone. I am waiting for someone too.'

'Certainly, certainly, I will move farther off. I respect the passionate impatience of your heart. Oh, how well I understand you at this moment!'

'Oh, all right, all right . . . '

'Till we meet again! . . . But excuse me, young man, here I am again . . . I don't know how to say it . . . give me your word of honour once more, as a gentleman, that you are not her lover.'

'Oh, mercy on us!'

'One more question, the last: do you know the surname of the husband of your . . . that is, I mean the lady who is the object of your devotion?'

'Of course I do; it is not your name, and that is all about it.'

'Why, how do you know my name?"'

'But, I say, you had better go; you are losing time; she might go away a thousand times. Why, what do you want? Your lady's in a fox cape and a hood, while mine is wearing a plaid cloak and a pale-blue velvet hat . . . What more do you want? What else?'

'A pale-blue velvet hat! She has a plaid cloak and a pale-blue velvet hat!' cried the pertinacious man, instantly turning back again.

'Oh, hang it all! Why, that may well be . . . And, indeed, my lady does not come here!'

'Where is she, then – your lady?'

'You want to know that? What is it to you?'

'I must own, I am still . . . '

'Tfoo! Mercy on us! Why, you have no sense of decency, none at all. Well, my lady has friends here, on the third storey looking into the street. Why, do you want me to tell you their names?'

'My goodness, I have friends too, who live on the third storey, and their windows look on to the street. General – '

'General!'

'A general. If you like I will tell you what general: well, then – General Polovitsyn.'

'You don't say so! No, that is not the same! (Oh, damnation, damnation!)'

'Not the same?'

'No, not the same.'

Both were silent, looking at each other in perplexity.

'Why are you looking at me like that?' exclaimed the young man, shaking off his stupefaction and air of uncertainty with vexation.

The gentleman was in a fluster.

'I . . . I must own . . .'

'Come, allow me, allow me; let us talk more sensibly now. It concerns us both. Explain to me . . . whom do you know there?'

'You mean, who are my friends?'

'Yes, your friends . . .'

'Well, you see . . . you see! . . .'

'I see from your eyes that I have guessed right!'

'Hang it all! No, no, hang it all! Are you blind? Why, I am standing here before you, I am not with her. Oh, well! I don't care, whether you say so or not!'

Twice in his fury the young man turned on his heel with a contemptuous wave of his hand.

'Oh, I meant nothing, I assure you. As an honourable man I will tell you all about it. At first my wife used to come here alone. They are relatives of hers; I had no suspicions; yesterday I met his Excellency: he told me that he had moved three weeks ago from here to another flat, and my wi . . . that is, not mine, but somebody else's (the husband's on the Voznesensky Bridge) . . . that lady had told me that she was with them the day before yesterday, in this flat I mean . . . and the cook told me that his Excellency's flat had been taken by a young man called Bobynitsyn . . .'

'Oh, damn it all, damn it all! . . .'

'My dear sir, I am in terror, I am in alarm!'

'Oh, hang it! What is it to me that you are in terror and in alarm? Ah! Over there . . . someone flitted by . . . over there . . .'

'Where, where? You just shout, "Ivan Andreyitch", and I will run . . .'

'All right, all right. Oh, confound it! Ivan Andreyitch!'

'Here I am,' cried Ivan Andreyitch, returning, utterly breathless. 'What is it, what is it? Where?'

'Oh, no, I didn't mean anything . . . I wanted to know what this lady's name is.'

'Glaf . . .'

'Glafira?'

'No, not Glafira . . . Excuse me, I cannot tell you her name.'

As he said this the worthy man was as white as a sheet.

'Oh, of course it is not Glafira, I know it is not Glafira, and mine's not Glafira; but with whom can she be?'

'Where?'

'There! Oh, damn it, damn it!' (The young man was in such a fury that he could not stand still.)

'There, you see! How did you know that her name was Glafira?'

'Oh, damn it all, really! To have a bother with you, too! Why, you say that yours is not called Glafira! . . .'

'My dear sir, what a way to speak!'

'Oh, the devil! As though that mattered now! What is she? Your wife?'

'No – that is, I am not married . . . But I would not keep flinging the devil at a respectable man in trouble, a man, I will not say worthy of esteem, but at any rate a man of education. You keep saying, "The devil, the devil!"'

'To be sure, the devil take it; so there you are, do you understand?'

'You are blinded by anger, and I say nothing. Oh, dear, who is that?'

'Where?'

There was a noise and a sound of laughter; two pretty girls ran down the steps; both the men rushed up to them.

'Oh, what manners! What do you want?'

'Where are you shoving?'

'They are not the right ones!'

'Aha, so you've pitched on the wrong ones! Cab!'

'Where do you want to go, mademoiselle?'

'To Pokrov.[32] Get in, Annushka; I'll take you.'

'Oh, I'll sit on the other side. Off! Now, mind you drive quickly.'

The cab drove off.

'Where did they come from?'

'Oh, dear, oh, dear! Hadn't we better go there?'

'Where?'

'Why, to Bobynitsyn's . . .'

'No, that's out of the question.'

'Why?'

'I would go there, of course, but then she would tell me some other story; she would . . . get out of it. She would say that she had come on purpose to catch me with someone, and I should get into trouble.'

'And, you know, she may be there! But you – I don't know for what reason – why, you might go to the general's . . . '

'But, you know, he has moved!'

'That doesn't matter, you know. She has gone there; so you go, too – don't you understand? Behave as though you didn't know the general had gone away. Go as though you had come to fetch your wife, and so on.'

'And then?'

'Well, and then find the person you want at Bobynitsyn's. Tfoo, damnation take you, what a senseless . . . '

'Well, and what is it to you, my finding? You see, you see!'

'What, what, my good man? What? You are on the same old tack again. Oh, Lord have mercy on us! You ought to be ashamed, you absurd person, you senseless person!'

'Yes, but why are you so interested? Do you want to find out . . . '

'Find out what? What? Oh, well, damnation take you! I have no thoughts for you now; I'll go alone. Go away; get along; look out; be off!'

'My dear sir, you are almost forgetting yourself!' cried the gentleman in raccoon in despair.

'Well, what of it? What if I am forgetting myself?' said the young man, setting his teeth and stepping up to the gentleman in raccoon in a fury. 'What of it? Forgetting myself before whom?' he thundered, clenching his fists.

'But allow me, sir . . . '

'Well, who are you, before whom I am forgetting myself? W'hat is your name?'

'I don't know about that, young man; why do you want my name? . . . I cannot tell it you . . . I had better come with you. Let us go; I won't hang back; I am ready for anything . . . But I assure you I deserve greater politeness and respect! You ought never to lose your self-possession, and if you are upset about something – I can guess what about – at any rate there is no need to forget yourself . . . You are still a very, very young man! . . . '

'What is it to me that you are old? There's nothing wonderful in that! Go away. Why are you dancing about here?'

'How am I old? Of course, in position; but I am not dancing about . . . '

'I can see that. But get away with you.'

'No, I'll stay with you; you cannot forbid me; I am mixed up in it, too; I will come with you . . . '

'Well, then, keep quiet, keep quiet, hold your tongue.'

They both went up the steps and ascended the stairs to the third storey. It was rather dark.

'Stay; have you got matches?'

'Matches! What matches?'

'Do you smoke cigars?'

'Oh, yes, I have, I have; here they are, here they are; here, stay . . . ' The gentleman in raccoon rummaged in a fluster.

'Tfoo, what a senseless . . . damnation! I believe this is the door . . . '

'This, this, this?'

'This, this, this . . . Why are you bawling? Hush! . . . '

'My dear sir, overcoming my feelings, I . . . you are a reckless fellow, so there! . . . '

The light flared up.

'Yes, so it is; here is the brass plate. This is Bobynitsyn's; do you see Bobynitsyn?'

'I see it, I see it.'

'Hu-ush!'

'Why, has it gone out?'

'Yes, it has.'

'Should we knock?'

'Yes, we must,' responded the gentleman in raccoon.

'Knock, then.'

'No, why should I? You begin, you knock!'

'Coward!'

'You are a coward yourself!'

'G-et a-way with you!'

'I almost regret having confided my secret to you; you . . . '

'I – what about me?'

'You take advantage of my distress; you see that I am upset . . . '

'But do I care? I think it's ridiculous, that's all about it!'

'Why are you here?'

'Why are you here, too? . . . '

'Delightful morality!' observed the gentleman in raccoon, with indignation.

'What are you saying about morality? What are you saying?'

'Well, it's immoral!'

'What? . . . '

'Why, to your thinking, every deceived husband is a noodle!'

'Why, are you the husband? I thought the husband was on Voznesensky Bridge? So what is it to you? Why do you meddle?"

'I do believe that you are the lover! . . . '

'Listen: if you go on like this I shall be forced to think you are a noodle! That is, do you know who?'

'That is, you mean to say that I am the husband,' said the gentleman in raccoon, stepping back as though he were scalded with boiling water.

'Hush, hold your tongue. Do you hear? . . .'

'It is she.'

'No!'

'Tfoo, how dark it is!''

There was a hush; a sound was audible in Bobynitsyn's flat.

'Why should we quarrel, sir?' whispered the gentleman in raccoon.

'But you took offence yourself, damn it all!'

'But you drove me out of all patience.'

'Hold your tongue!'

'You must admit that you are a very young man.'

'Hold your tongue!'

'Of course I share your idea that a husband in such a position is a noodle.'

'Oh, will you hold your tongue? Oh! . . .'

'But why such savage persecution of the unfortunate husband? . . .'

'It is she!'

But at that moment the sound ceased.

'Is it she?'

'It is, it is, it is! But why are you – you worrying about it? It is not your trouble!'

'My dear sir, my dear sir,' muttered the gentleman in raccoon, turning pale and gulping, 'I am, of course, greatly agitated . . . you can see for yourself my abject position; but now it's night, of course, but tomorrow . . . though indeed we are not likely to meet tomorrow, though I am not afraid of meeting you – and besides, it is not I, it is my friend on the Voznesensky Bridge, it really is he! It is his wife, it is somebody else's wife. Poor fellow! I assure you, I know him very intimately; if you will allow me I will tell you all about it. I am a great friend of his, as you can see for yourself, or I shouldn't be in such a state about him now – as you see for yourself. Several times I said to him: "Why are you getting married, dear boy? You have position, you have means, you are highly respected. Why risk it all at the caprice of coquetry? You must see that." "No, I am going to be married," he said; "domestic bhss." . . . Here's domestic bliss for you! In the old days he deceived other husbands . . . now he is drinking the cup . . . you must excuse me, but this explanation was absolutely necessary . . . He is an unfortunate man, and is drinking the cup – now! . . .' At this point the gentleman in raccoon gave such a gulp that he seemed to be sobbing in earnest.

'Ah, damnation take them all! There are plenty of fools. But who are you?' The young man ground his teeth in anger.

'Well, you must admit after this that I have been gentlemanly and open with you . . . and you take such a tone!'

'No, excuse me . . . what is your name?'

'Why do you want to know my name? . . . '

'Ah!'

'I cannot tell you my name . . . '

'Do you know Shabrin?' the young man said quickly.

'Shabrin!!!'

'Yes, Shabrin! Ah!!!' (Saying this, the gentleman in the wadded overcoat mimicked the gentleman in raccoon.) 'Do you understand?'

'No, what Shabrin?' answered the gentleman in raccoon, in a fluster. 'He's not Shabrin; he is a very respectable man! I can excuse your discourtesy, due to the tortures of jealousy.'

'He's a scoundrel, a mercenary soul, a rogue that takes bribes, he steals government money! He'll be had up for it before long!'

'Excuse me,' said the gentleman in raccoon, turning pale, 'you don't know him; I see that you don't know him at all.'

'No, I don't know him personally, but I know him from others who are in close touch with him.'

'From what others, sir? I am agitated, as you see . . . '

'A fool! A jealous idiot! He doesn't look after his wife! That's what he is, if you like to know!'

'Excuse me, young man, you are grievously mistaken . . . '

'Oh!'

'Oh!'

A sound was heard in Bobynitsyn's flat. A door was opened, voices were heard.

'Oh, that's not she! I recognise her voice; I understand it all now, this is not she!' said the gentleman in raccoon, turning as white as a sheet.

'Hush!'

The young man leaned against the wall.

'My dear sir, I am off. It is not she, I am glad to say.'

'All right! Be off, then!'

'Why are you staying, then?'

'What's that to you?'

The door opened, and the gentleman in raccoon could not refrain from dashing headlong downstairs.

A man and a woman walked by the young man, and his heart stood still . . . He heard a familiar feminine voice and then a husky male voice, utterly unfamiliar.

'Never mind, I will order the sledge,' said the husky voice.

'Oh, yes, yes; very well, do . . . '

'It will be here directly.'

The lady was left alone.

'Glafira! Where are your vows?' cried the young man in the wadded overcoat, clutching the lady's arm.

'Oh, who is it? It's you, Tvorogov? My goodness! What are you doing here?'

'Who is it you have been with here?'

'Why, my husband. Go away, go away; he'll be coming out directly . . . from . . . in there . . . from the Polovitsyns'. Go away; for goodness' sake, go away.'

'It's three weeks since the Polovitsyns moved! I know all about it!'

'*Aïe!*' The lady dashed downstairs. The young man overtook her.

'Who told you?' asked the lady.

'Your husband, madam, Ivan Andreyitch; he is here before you, madam . . . '

Ivan Andreyitch was indeed standing at the front door.

'*Aïe*, it's you,' cried the gentleman in raccoon.

'Ah! *C'est vous*,'[33] cried Glafira Petrovna, rushing up to him with unfeigned delight. 'Oh, dear, you can't think what has been happening to me. I went to see the Polovitsyns; only fancy . . . you know they are living now by Izmailovsky Bridge;[34] I told you, do you remember? I took a sledge from there. The horses took fright and bolted, they broke the sledge, and I was thrown out about a hundred yards from here; the coachman was taken up; I was in despair. Fortunately Monsieur Tvorogov . . . '

'What!'

Monsieur Tvorogov was more like a fossil than like Monsieur Tvorogov.

'Monsieur Tvorogov saw me here and undertook to escort me; but now you are here, and I can only express my warm gratitude to you, Ivan Ilyitch . . . '

The lady gave her hand to the stupefied Ivan Ilyitch, and almost pinched instead of pressing it.

'Monsieur Tvorogov, an acquaintance of mine; it was at the Skorlupovs' ball we had the pleasure of meeting; I believe I told you; don't you remember, Koko?'

'Oh, of course, of course! Ah, I remember,' said the gentleman in raccoon addressed as Koko. 'Delighted, delighted!' And he warmly pressed the hand of Monsieur Tvorogov.

'Who is it? What does it mean? I am waiting . . .' said a husky voice.

Before the group stood a gentleman of extraordinary height; he took out a lorgnette and looked intently at the gentleman in the raccoon coat.

'Ah, Monsieur Bobynitsyn!' twittered the lady. 'Where have you come from? What a meeting! Only fancy, I have just had an upset in a sledge . . . but here is my husband! Jean! Monsieur Bobynitsyn, at the Karpovs' ball . . .'

'Ah, delighted, very much delighted! . . . But I'll take a carriage at once, my dear.'

'Yes, do, Jean, do; I still feel frightened; I am all of a tremble, I feel quite giddy . . . At the masquerade tonight,' she whispered to Tvorogov . . . 'Goodbye, goodbye, Mr Bobynitsyn! We shall meet tomorrow at the Karpovs' ball, most likely.'

'No, excuse me, I shall not be there tomorrow; I don't know about tomorrow, if it is like this now . . .' Mr Bobynitsyn muttered something between his teeth, made a scrape with his boot, got into his sledge and drove away.

A carriage drove up; the lady got into it. The gentleman in the raccoon coat stopped, seemed incapable of making a movement and gazed blankly at the gentleman in the wadded coat. The gentleman in the wadded coat smiled rather foolishly.

'I don't know . . .'

'Excuse me, delighted to make your acquaintance,' answered the young man, bowing with curiosity and a little intimidated.

'Delighted, delighted! . . .'

'I think you have lost your golosh . . .'

'I – oh, yes, thank you, thank you. I keep meaning to get rubber ones."

'The foot gets so hot in rubbers,' said the young man, apparently with immense interest.

'Are you coming?'

'It does make it hot. Coming directly, darling; we are having an interesting conversation! Precisely so, as you say, it does make the foot hot . . . But excuse me, I . . .'

'Oh, certainly.'

'Delighted, very much delighted to make your acquaintance! . . .'

The gentleman in raccoon got into the carriage, the carriage set off, the young man remained standing looking after it in astonishment.

The following evening tbere was a performance of some sort at the Italian opera. Ivan Andreyitch burst into the theatre like a bomb. Such furore, such a passion for music had never been observed in him before. It was known for a positive fact, anyway, that Ivan Andreyitch used to be exceeding fond of a nap for an hour or two at the Itahan opera; he even declared on several occasions how sweet and pleasant it was. 'Why, the prima donna,' he used to say to his friends, 'mews a lullaby to you like a little white kitten.'[35] But it was a long time ago, last season, that he used to say this; now, alas! even at home Ivan Andreyitch did not sleep at nights. Nevertheless he burst into the crowded opera-house like a bomb. Even the conductor started suspiciously at the sight of him, and glanced out of the corner of his eye at his side-pocket in the full expectation of seeing the hilt of a dagger hidden there in readiness. It must be observed that there were at that time two parties, each supporting the superior claims of its favourite prima donna. They were called the —sists and the —nists. Both parties were so devoted to music that the conductors actually began to be apprehensive of some startling manifestation of the passion for the good and the beautiful embodied in the two prima donnas. This was how it was that, looking at this youthful dash into the *parterre* of a grey-haired senior (though, indeed, he was not actually grey-haired, but a man of about fifty, rather bald, and altogether of respectable appearance), the conductor could not help recalling the lofty judgement of Hamlet, Prince of Denmark upon the evil example set by age to youth,[36] and, as we have mentioned above, looking out of the corner of his eye at the gentleman's side-pocket in the expectation of seeing a dagger. But there was a pocket-book and nothing else there.

Darting into the theatre, Ivan Andreyitch instantly scanned all the boxes of the second tier, and, oh – horror! His heart stood still, she was here! She was sitting in the box! General Polovitsyn, with his wife and sister-in-law, was there too. The general's adjutant – an extremely alert young man, was there too; there was a civilian too . . . Ivan Andreyitch strained his attention and his eyesight, but – oh, horror! The civilian treacherously concealed himself behind the adjutant and remained in the darkness of obscurity.

She was here, and yet she had said she would not be here!

It was this duplicity for some time displayed in every step Glafira

Petrovna took which crushed Ivan Andreyitch. This civilian youth reduced him at last to utter despair. He sank down in his stall utterly overwhelmed. Why? one may ask. It was a very simple matter . . .

It must be observed that Ivan Andreyitch's stall was close to the *baignoire*, and to make matters worse the treacherous box in the second tier was exactly above his stall, so that to his intense annoyance he was utterly unable to see what was going on over his head. At which he raged, and got as hot as a samovar. The whole of the iirst act passed unnoticed by him, that is, he did not hear a single note of it. It is maintained that what is good in music is that musical impressions can be made to fit any mood. The man who rejoices finds joy in its strains, while he who grieves finds sorrow in it; a regular tempest was howling in Ivan Andreyitch's ears. To add to his vexation, such terrible voices were shouting behind him, before him and on both sides of him that Ivan Andreyitch's heart was torn. At last the act was over. But at the instant when the curtatin was falling, our hero had an adventure such as no pen can describe.

It sometimes happens that a playbill flies down from the upper boxes. When the play is dull and the audience is yawning this is quite an event for them. They watch with particular interest the flight of the extremely soft paper from the upper gallery, and take pleasure in watching its zigzagging journey down to the very stalls, where it infallibly settles on some head which is quite unprepared to receive it. It is certainly very interesting to watch the embarrassment of the head (for the head is invariably embarrassed). I am indeed always in terror over the ladies' opera-glasses which usually lie on the edge of the boxes; I am constantly fancying that they will fly down on some unsuspecting head. But I perceive that this tragic observation is out of place here, and so I shall send it to the columns of those newspapers which are filled with advice, warnings against swindling tricks, against unconscientiousness, hints for getting rid of beetles if you have them in the house, recommendations of the celebrated Mr Princhipi, sworn foe of all beetles in the world,[37] not only Russian but even foreign, such as Prussian cockroaches, and so on.

But Ivan Andreyitch had an adventure which has never hitherto been described. There flew down on his – as already stated, somewhat bald – head, not a playbill; I confess I am actually ashamed to say what did fly down upon his head, because I am really loath to remark that on the respectable and bare – that is, partly hairless – head of the jealous and irritated Ivan Andreyitch there settled such an immoral object as a scented love-letter. Poor Ivan Andreyitch, utterly unprepared for this unforeseen and hideous occurrence, started as though he had caught upon his head a mouse or some other wild beast.

That the note was a love-letter of that there could be no mistake. It was written on scented paper, just as love-letters are written in novels, and folded up so as to be treacherously small so that it might be slipped into a lady's glove. It had probably fallen by accident at the moment it had been handed to her. The playbill might have been asked for, for instance, and the note, deftly folded in the playbill, was being put into her hands; but an instant, perhaps an accidental, nudge from the adjutant, extremely adroit in his apologies for his awkwardness, and the note had slipped from a little hand that trembled with confusion, and the civilian youth, stretching out his impatient hand, received back instead of the note the empty playbill, and did not know what to do with it. A strange and unpleasant incident lor him, no doubt, but you must admit that for Ivan Andreyitch it was still more unpleasant.

'*Prédestiné*,'[38] he murmured, breaking into a cold sweat and squeezing the note in his hands, '*prédestiné*! The bullet finds the guilty man,' the thought flashed through his mind. 'No, that's not right! In what way am I guilty? But there is another proverb, "Once out of luck, never out of trouble . . ." '

But it was not enough that there was a ringing in his ears and a dizziness in his head at this sudden incident. Ivan Andreyitch sat petrified in his chair, as the saying is, more dead than alive. He was persuaded that his adventure had been observed on all sides, although at that moment the whole theatre began to be filled with uproar and calls of encore. He sat overwhelmed with confusion, flushing crimson and not daring to raise his eyes, as though some unpleasant surprise, something out of keeping with the brilant assembly had happened to him. At last he ventured to lift his eyes.

'Charmingly sung,' he observed to a dandy sitting on his left side.

The dandy, who was in the last stage of enthusiasm, clapping his hands and still more actively stamping with his feet, gave Ivan Andreyitch a cursory and absent-minded glance, and immediately putting up his hands like a trumpet to his mouth, so as to be more audible, shouted the prima donna's name. Ivan Andreyitch, who had never heard such a roar, was delighted. 'He has noticed nothing!' he thought, and turned round; but the stout gentleman who was sitting behind him had turned round too, and with his back to him was scrutinising the boxes through his opera-glass. 'He is all right too!' thought Ivan Andreyitch. In front, of course, nothing had been seen. Timidly and with a joyous hope in his heart, he stole a glance at the *baignoire*, near which was his stall, and started with the most unpleasant sensation. A lovely lady was sitting there who, holding her handkerchief to her mouth and leaning back in her chair, was laughing as though in hysterics.

'Ugh, these women!' murmured Ivan Andreyitch, and treading on people's feet, he made for the exit.

Now I ask my readers to decide, I beg them to judge between me and Ivan Andreyitch. Was he right at that moment? The Grand Theatre,[39] as we all know, contains four tiers of boxes and a fifth row above the gallery. Why must he assume that the note had fallen from one particular box, from that very box and no other? Why not, for instance, from the gallery where there are often ladies too? But passion is an exception to every rule, and jealousy is the most exceptional of all passions. Ivan Andreyitch rushed into the foyer, stood by the lamp, broke the seal and read:

Today immediately after the performance, in G Street at the corner of X Lane, K buildings, on the third floor, the first on the right from the stairs. The front entrance. Be there, *sans faute*;[40] for God's sake.

Ivan Andreyitch did not know the handwriting, but he had no doubt it was an assignation. 'To track it out, to catch it and nip the mischief in the bud,' was Ivan Andreyitch's first idea. The thought occurred to him to unmask the infamy at once on the spot; but how could it be done? Ivan Andryitch even ran up to the second row of boxes, but judiciously came back again. He was utterly unable to decide where to run. Having nothing clear he could do, he ran round to the other side and looked through the open door of somebody else's box at the opposite side of the theatre. Yes, it was so, it was! Young ladies and young men were sitting in all the seats vertically one above another in all the five tiers. The note might have fallen from all tiers at once, for Ivan Andreyitch suspected all of them of being in a plot against him. But nothing made him any better, no probabilities of any sort. The whole of the second act he was running up and down all the corridors and could find no peace of mind anywhere. He would have dashed into the box office in hope of finding from the attendant there the names of the persons who had taken boxes on all the four tiers, but the box office was shut. At last there came an outburst of furious shouting and applause. The performance was over. Calls for the singers began, and two voices from the top gallery were particularly deafening – the leaders of the opposing factions. But they were not what mattered to

Ivan Andreyitch. Already thoughts of what he was to do next flitted
through his mind. He put on his overcoat and rushed off to G Street
to surprise them there, to catch them unawares, to unmask them., and
in general to behave somewhat more energetically than he had done
the day before. He soon found the house, and was just going in at the
front door, when the figure of a dandy in an overcoat darted forward
right in front of him, passed him and went up the stairs to the third
storey. It seemed to Ivan Andreyitch that this was the same dandy,
though he had not been able at the time to distinguish his features in
the theatre. His heart stood still. The dandy was two flights of stairs
ahead of him. At last he heard a door opened on the third floor,
and opened without the ringing of a bell, as though the visitor was
expected. The young man disappeared into the flat. Ivan Andreyitch
mounted to the third floor, before there was time to shut the door. He
meant to stand at the door, to reflect prudently on his next step, to be
rather cautious, and then to determine upon some decisive course of
action; but at that very minute a carriage rumbled up to the entrance,
the doors were flung open noisily, and heavy footsteps began ascending
to the third storey to the sound of coughing and clearing of the throat.
Ivan Andreyitch could not stand his ground, and walked into the flat
with all the majesty of an injured husband. A servant-maid rushed to
meet him much agitated, then a man-servant appeared. But to stop
Ivan Andreyitch was impossible. He flew in like a bomb, and crossing
two dark rooms, suddenly found himself in a bedroom facing a lovely
young lady, who was trembling all over with alarm and gazing at him
in utter horror as though she could not understand what was happening
around her. At that instant there was a sound in the adjoining room of
heavy footsteps coming straight towards the bedroom; they were the
same footsteps that had been mounting the stairs.

'Goodness! It is my husband!' cried the lady, clasping her hands and
turning whiter than her dressing-gown.

Ivan Andreyitch felt that he had come to the wrong place, that he
had made a silly, childish blunder, that he had acted without due consideration, that he had not been sufficiently cautious on the landing.
But there was no help for it. The door was already opening, already the
heavy husband, that is if he could be judged by his footsteps, was
coming into the room . . . I don't know what Ivan Andreyitch took
himself to be at that moment! I don't know what prevented him from
confronting the husband, telling him that he had made a mistake,
confessing that he had unintentionally behaved in the most unseemly
way, making his apologies and vanishing – not of course with flying

colours, not of course with glory, but at any rate departing in an open and gentlemanly manner. But no, Ivan Andreyitch again behaved like a boy, as though he considered himself a Don Juan[41] or a Lovelace![42] He first hid himself behind the curtain of the bed, and finally, feeling utterly dejected and hopeless, he dropped to the floor and senselessly crept under the bed. Terror had more influence on him than reason, and Ivan Andreyitch, himself an injured husband, or at any rate a husband who considered himself such, could not face meeting another husband, but was afraid to wound him by his presence. Be this as it may, he found himself under the bed, though he had no idea how it had come to pass. But what was most surprising, the lady made no opposition. She did not cry out on seeing an utterly unknown elderly gentleman seek a refuge under her bed. Probably she was so alarmed that she was deprived of all power of speech.

The husband walked in gasping and clearing his throat, said good-evening to his wife in a singsong, elderly voice, and flopped into an easy chair as though he had just been carrying up a load of wood. There was a sound of a hollow and prolonged cough. Ivan Andreyitch, transformed from a ferocious tiger to a lamb, timid and meek as a mouse before a cat, scarcely dared to breathe for terror, though he might have known from his own experience that not all injured husbands bite. But this idea did not enter his head, either from lack of consideration or from agitation of some sort. Cautiously, softly, feeling his way he began to get right under the bed so as to lie more comfortably there. What was his amazement when with his hand he felt an object which, to his intense amazement, stirred and in its turn seized his hand! Under the bed there was another person!

'Who's this?' whispered Ivan Andreyitch.

'Well, I am not likely to tell you who I am,' whispered the strange man. 'Lie still and keep quiet, if you have made a mess of things!'

'But, I say! . . . '

'Hold your tongue!'

And the extra gentleman (for one was quite enough under the bed), the extra gentleman squeezed Ivan Andreyitch's hand in his fist so that the latter almost shrieked with pain.

'My dear sir . . . '

'Sh!'

'Then don't pinch me so, or I shall scream.'

'All right, scream away, try it on.'

Ivan Andreyitch flushed with shame. The unknown gentleman was sulky and ill-humoured. Perhaps it was a man who had suffered more than once from the persecutions of fate, and had more than once been in a tight place; but Ivan Andreyitch was a novice and could not breathe in his constricted position. The blood rushed to his head. However, there was no help for it; he had to lie on his face. Ivan Andreyitch submitted and was silent.

'I have been to see Pavel Ivanitch, my love,' began the husband. 'We sat down to a game of preference. Khee-khee-khee!' (he had a fit of coughing). 'Yes . . . khee! So my back . . . khee! Bother it . . . khee-khee-khee!'

And the old gentleman became engrossed in his cough.

'My back.' he brought out at last with tears in his eyes, 'my spine began to ache . . . A damned haemorrhoid, I can't stand nor sit . . . or sit. Akkhee-khee-khee!' . . .

And it seemed as though the cough that followed was destined to last longer than the old gentleman in possession of it. The old gentleman grumbled something in its intervals, but it was utterly impossible to make out a word.

'Dear sir, for goodness' sake, move a little,' whispered the unhappy Ivan Andreyitch.

'How can I? There's no room.'

'But you must admit that it is impossible for me. It is the first time that I have found myself in such a nasty position.'

'And I in such unpleasant society.'

'But, young man! . . .'

'Hold your tongue!'

'Hold my tongue? You are very uncivil, young man . . . If I am not mistaken, you are very young; I am your senior.'

'Hold your tongue!'

'My dear sir! You are forgetting yourself. You don't know to whom you are talking!'

'To a gentleman lying under the bed.'

'But I was taken by surprise . . . a mistake, while in your case, if I am not mistaken, immorality . . .'

'That's where you are mistaken.'

'My dear sir! I am older than you, I tell you . . .'

'Sir, we are in the same boat, you know. I beg you not to take hold of my face!'

'Sir, I can't tell one thing from another. Excuse me, but I have no room.'

'You shouldn't be so fat!'

'Heavens! I have never been in such a degrading position.'

'Yes, one couldn't be brought more low.'

'Sir, sir! I don't know who you are, I don't understand how this came about; but I am here by mistake; I am not what you think . . .'

'I shouldn't think about you at all if you didn't shove. But hold your tongue, do!'

'Sir, if you don't move a little I shall have a stroke; you will have to answer for my death, I assure you . . . I am a respectable man, I am the father of a family. I really cannot be in such a position! . . .'

'You thrust yourself into the position. Come, move a little! I've made room for you, I can't do more!'

'Noble young man! Dear sir! I see I was mistaken about you,' said Ivan Andreyitch, in a transport of gratitude for the space allowed him, and stretching out his cramped limbs. 'I understand your constricted condition, but there's no help for it. I see you think ill of me. Allow me to redeem my reputation in your eyes, allow me to tell you who I am. I have come here against my will, I assure you; I am not here with the object you imagine . . . I am in a terrible fright.'

'Oh, do shut up! Understand that if we are overheard it will be the worse for us. Ssh! . . . He is talking.'

The old gentleman's cough did, in fact, seem to be over.

'I tell you what, my love,' he wheezed in the most lachrymose chant, 'I tell you what, my love . . . khee-khee! Oh, what an affliction! Fedosey Ivanovitch said to me: "You should try drinking yarrow tea," he said to me; do you hear, my love?'

'Yes, dear.'

'Yes, that was what he said, "You should try drinking yarrow tea," he said. I told him I had put on leeches. But he said, "No, Alexandr Demyanovitch, yarrow tea is better; it's a laxative; I tell you' . . . Khee-khee. Oh, dear! What do you think, my love? Khee! Oh, my God! Khee-khee! Had I better try yarrow tea? . . . Khee-khee-khee! Oh . . . Khee!' and so on.

'"I think it would be just as well to try that remedy,' said his wife.

'Yes, it would be! "You may be in consumption," he said. Khee-khee! And I told him it was gout and irritability of the stomach . . . Khee-khee! But he would have it that it might be consumption. What do you think . . . khee-khee . . . What do you think, my love; is it consumption?'

'My goodness, what are you talking about?'

'Why, consumption! You had better undress and go to bed now, my love . . . khee-khee! I've caught a cold in my head today.'

'Ouf!' said Ivan Andreyitch. 'For God's sake, do move a little.'

'I really don't know what is the matter with you; can't you lie still? . . . '

'You are exasperated against me, young man, you want to wound me, I see that. You are, I suppose, this lady's lover?'

'Shut up!'

'I will not shut up! I won't allow you to order me about! You are, no doubt, her lover. If we are discovered I am not to blame in any way; I know nothing about it.'

'If you don't hold your tongue,' said the young man, grinding his teeth, 'I will say that you brought me here. I'll say that you are my uncle who has dissipated his fortune. Then they won't imagine I am this lady's lover, anyway.'

'Sir, you are amusing yourself at my expense. You are exhausting my patience.'

'Hush, or I will make you hush! You are a curse to me. Come, tell me what you are here for? If you were not here I could lie here somehow till morning, and then get away.'

'But I can't lie here till morning. I am a respectable man, I have family ties, of course . . . What do you think, surely he is not going to spend the night here?'

'Who?'

'Why, this old gentleman . . . '

'Of course he will. All husbands aren't like you. Some of them spend their nights at home.'

'My dear sir, my dear sir!' cried Ivan Andreyitch, turning cold with terror, 'I assure you I spend my nights at home too, and this is the first time; but, my God, I see you know me. Who are you, young man? Tell me at once, I beseech you, from disinterested friendship, who are you?'

'Listen, I shall resort to violence . . . '

'But allow me, allow me, sir, to tell you, allow me to explain all this horrid business.'

'I won't listen to any explanation. I don't want to know anything about it. Be silent or . . . '

'But I cannot . . . '

A slight skirmish took place under the bed, and Ivan Andreyitch subsided.

'My love, it sounds as though there were cats hissing.'

'Cats! What will you imagine next?'

Evidently the lady did not know what to talk to her husband about. She was so upset that she could not pull herself together. Now she started and pricked up her ears.

'What cats?'

'Cats, my love. The other day I went into my study, and there was the tomcat in my study, and hissing shoo-shoo-shoo! I said to him: What is it, pussy?' and he went shoo-shoo-shoo again, as though he were whispering. I thought, 'Merciful heavens! isn't he hissing as a sign of my death?'

'What nonsense you are talking today! You ought to be ashamed, really!'

'Never mind, don't be cross, my love. I see you don't like to think of me dying; I didn't mean it. But you had better undress and get to bed, my love, and I'll sit here while you go to bed."

'For goodness' sake, leave off; afterwards . . . '

'Well, don't be cross, don't be cross; but really I think there must be mice here.'

'Why, first cats and then mice, I really don't know what is the matter with you.'

'Oh, I am all right . . . Khee . . . I . . . khee! Never mind . . . khee-khee-khee-khee! Oh! Lord have mercy on me . . . khee.'

'You hear, you are making such an upset that he hears you,' whispered the young man.

'But if you knew what is happening to me. My nose is bleeding.'

'Let it bleed. Shut up. Wait till he goes away.'

'But, young man, put yourself in my place. Why, I don't know with whom I am lying.'

'Would you be any better off if you did? Why, I don't want to know your name. By the way, what is your name?'

'No; what do you want with my name? . . . I only want to explain the senseless way in which . . . '

'Hush . . . he is speaking again . . . '

'Really, my love, there is whispering.'

'Oh, no, it's the cotton wool in your ears has got out of place.'

'Oh, by the way, talking of the cotton wool, do you know that upstairs . . . khee-khee . . . upstairs . . . khee-khee . . . ' and so on.

'Upstairs!' whispered the young man. 'Oh, the devil! I thought that this was the top storey; can it be the second?'

'Young man,' whispered Ivan Andreyitch, 'what did you say? For goodness' sake why does it concern you? I thought it was the top storey too. Tell me, for God's sake, is there another storey?'

'Really someone is stirring,' said the old man, leaving off coughing at last.

'Hush! Do you hear?' whispered the young man, squeezing Ivan Andreyitch's hands.

'Sir, you are holding my hands by force. Let me go!'

'Hush!'

A slight struggle followed and then there was a silence again.

'So I met a pretty woman . . . ' began the old man.

'A pretty woman!' interrupted his wife.

'Yes . . . I thought I told you before that I met a pretty woman on the stairs, or perhaps I did not mention it? My memory is weak. Yes. St John's wort . . . khee!'

'What?'

'I must drink St John's wort; they say it does good . . . khee-khee-khee! It does good!'

'It was you interrupted him,' said the young man, grinding his teeth again.

'You said, you met some pretty woman today?' his wife went on.

'Eh?'

'Met a pretty woman?'

'Who did?'

'Why, didn't you?'

'I? When? Oh, yes! . . . '

'At last! What a memory! Well!' whispered the young man, inwardly raging at the forgetful old gentleman.

'My dear sir, I am trembling with horror. My God, what do I hear? It's like yesterday, exactly like yesterday! . . . '

'Hush!'

'Yes, to be sure! I remember, a sly puss, such eyes . . . in a blue hat . . . '

'In a blue hat! *Aïe, aïe!*'

'It's she! She has a blue hat! My God!' cried Ivan Andreyitch.

'She? Who is she?'' whispered the young man, squeezing Ivan Andreyitch's hands.

'Hush!' Ivan Andreyitch exhorted in his turn. 'He is speaking.'

'Ah, my God, my God!'

'Though, after all, who hasn't a blue hat?'

'And such a sly little rogue,' the old gentleman went on. 'She comes here to see friends. She is always making eyes. And other friends come to see those friends too . . . '

'Foo! how tedious!' the lady interrupted. 'Really, how can you take interest in that?'

'Oh; very well, very well, don't be cross,' the old gentleman responded in a wheedling chant. 'I won't talk if you don't care to hear me. You seem a little out of humour this evening.'

'But how did you get here?' the young man began.

'Ah, you see, you see! Now you are interested, and before you wouldn't listen!'

'Oh, well, I don't care! Please don't tell me. Oh, damnation take it, what a mess!'

'Don't be cross, young man; I don't know what I am saying. I didn't mean anything; I only meant to say that there must be some good reason for your taking such an interest, . . . But who are you, young man? I see you are a stranger, but who are you ? Oh, dear, I don't know what I am saying!'

'Ugh, leave off, please!' the young man interrupted, as though he were considering something.

'But I will tell you all about it. You think, perhaps, that I will not tell you. That I feel resentment against you. Oh, no! Here is my hand. I am only feeling depressed, nothing more. But for God's sake, first tell me how you came here yourself? Through what chance? As for me, I feel no ill-will; no, indeed, I feel no ill-will, here is my hand. I have made it rather dirty, it is so dusty here; but that's nothing, when the feeling is true.'

'Ugh, get away with your hand! There is no room to turn, and he keeps thrusting his hand at me!'

'But, my dear sir, but you treat me, if you will allow me to say so, as though I were an old shoe,' said Ivan Andreyitch in a rush of the meekest despair, in a voice full of entreaty. 'Treat me a little more civilly, just a little more civilly, and I will tell you all about it! We might be friends; I am quite ready to ask you home to dinner. We can't lie side by side like this, I tell you plainly. You are in error, young man, you do not know . . . '

'When was it he met her?' the young man muttered, evidently in violent emotion. 'Perhaps she is expecting me now . . . I'll certainly get away from here!'

'She? Who is she? My God, of whom are you speaking, young man? You imagine that upstairs . . . My God, my God! Why am I punished like this?'

Ivan Andreyitch tried to turn on his back in his despair.

'Why do you want to know who she is? Oh, the devil whether it was she or not, I will get out.'

'My dear sir! What are you thinking about? What will become of me?' whispered Ivan Andreyitch, clutching at the tails of his neighbour's dress coat in his despair.

'Well, what's that to me? You can stop here by yourself. And if you won't, I'll tell them that you are my uncle, who has squandered all his property, so that the old gentleman won't think that I am his wife's lover.'

'But that is utterly impossible, young man; it's unnatural I should be your uncle. Nobody would believe you. Why, a baby wouldn't believe it,' Ivan Andreyitch whispered in despair.

'Well, don't babble then, but lie as flat as a pancake! Most likely you will stay the night here and get out somehow tomorrow; no one will notice you. If one creeps out, it is not likely they would think there was another one here. There might as well be a dozen. Though you are as good as a dozen by yourself. Move a little, or I'll get out.'

'You wound me, young man . . . What if I have a fit of coughing? One has to think of everything.'

'Hush!'

'What's that? I fancy I hear something going on upstairs again,' said the old gentleman, who seemed to have had a nap in the interval.

'Upstairs?'

'Do you hear, young man? I shall get out.'

'Well, I hear.'

'My goodness! Young man, I am going.'

'Oh, well, I am not, then! I don't care. If there is an upset I don't mind! But do you know what I suspect? I believe you are an injured husband – so there.'

'Good heavens, what cynicism! . . . Can you possibly suspect that? Why a husband? . . . I am not married.'

'Not married ? Fiddlesticks!'

'I may be a lover myself!'

'A nice lover.'

'My dear sir, my dear sir! Oh, very well, I will tell you the whole story. Listen to my desperate story. It is not I – I am not married. I am a bachelor like you. It is my friend, a companion of my youth . . . I am a lover . . . He told me that he was an unhappy man. "I am drinking the cup of bitterness," he said; "I suspect my wife." "Well," I said to him reasonably, "why do you suspect her?" . . . But you are not listening to me. Listen, listen! "Jealousy is ridiculous," I said to him; "jealousy is a vice!" . . . "No," he said; "I am an unhappy man! I am drinking . . . that is, I suspect my wife." "You are my friend," I said; "you are the companion of my tender youth. Together we culled the flowers of happiness, together we rolled in featherbeds of pleasure." My goodness, I don't know what I am saying. You keep laughing, young man. You'll drive me crazy.'

'But you are crazy now . . . '

'There, I knew you would say that . . . when I talked of being crazy. Laugh away, laugh away, young man. I did the same in my day; I, too, went astray! Ah, I shall have inflammation of the brain!'

'What is it, my love? I thought I heard someone sneeze,' the old man chanted. 'Was that you sneezed, my love?'

'Oh, goodness!' said his wife.

'Tch!' sounded from under the bed.

'They must be making a noise upstairs,' said his wife, alarmed, for there certainly was a noise under the bed.

'Yes, upstairs!' said the husband. 'Upstairs, I told you just now, I met a . . . khee-khee . . . that I met a young swell with moustaches – oh, dear, my spine! – a young swell with moustaches.'

'With moustaches! My goodness, that must have been you,' whispered Ivan Andreyitch.

'Merciful heavens, what a man! Why, I am here, lying here with you! How could he have met me? But don't take hold of my face.'

'My goodness, I shall faint in a minute.'

There certainly was a loud noise overhead at this moment.

'What can be happening there?' whispered the young man.

'My dear sir! I am in alarm, I am in terror, help me.'

'Hush!'

'There really is a noise, my love; there's a regular hubbub. And just over your bedroom, too. Hadn't I better send up to enquire?'

'Well, what will you think of next?'

'Oh, well, I won't; but really, how cross you are today!'

'Oh, dear, you had better go to bed.'

'Liza, you don't love me at all.'

'Oh, yes, I do! For goodness' sake, I am so tired.'

'Well, well; I am going!'

'Oh, no, no; don't go!' cried his wife; 'or, no, better go!'

'Why, what is the matter with you! One minute I am to go, and the next I'm not! Khee-khee! It really is bedtime, khee-khee! The Panafidins' little girl . . . khee-khee . . . their little girl . . . khee . . . I saw their little girl's Nuremburg doll[43] . . . khee-khee . . . '

'Well, now it's dolls!'

'Khee-khee . . . a pretty doll . . . khee-khee.'

'He is saying goodbye,' said the young man; 'he is going, and we can get away at once. Do you hear? You can rejoice!'

'Oh, God grant it!'

'It's a lesson to you . . . '

'Young man, a lesson for what! . . . I feel it . . . but you are young, you cannot teach me.'

'I will, though . . . Listen.'

'Oh, dear, I am going to sneeze! . . . '

'Hush, don't you dare.'

'But what can I do, there is such a smell of mice here; I can't help it. Take my handkerchief out of my pocket; I can't stir . . . Oh, my God, my God, why am I so punished?'

'Here's your handkerchief! I will tell you what you are punished for. You are jealous. Goodness knows on what grounds, you rush about like a madman, burst into other people's flats, create a disturbance. . . '

'Young man, I have not created a disturbance.'

'Hush!'

'Young man, you can't lecture to me about morals, I am more moral than you.'

'Hush!'

'Oh, my God – oh, my God!'

'You create a disturbance, you frighten a young lady, a timid woman who does not know what to do for terror, and perhaps will be ill; you disturb a venerable old man suffering from a complaint and who needs repose above everything – and all this what for? Because you imagine some nonsense which sets you running all over the neighbourhood! Do you understand what a horrid position you are in now?'

'I do very well, sir! I feel it, but you have not the right . . . '

'Hold your tongue! What has right got to do with it? Do you understand that this may have a tragic ending? Do you understand that the old man, who is fond of his wife, may go out of his mind when he sees you creep out from under the bed? But no, you are incapable of causing a tragedy! When you crawl out, I expect everyone who looks at you will laugh. I should like to see you in the light; you must look very funny.'

'And you. You must be funny, too, in that case. I should like to have a look at you too.'

'I dare say you would!'

'You must carry the stamp of immorality, young man.'

'Ah! you are talking about morals, how do you know why I'm here? I am here by mistake, I made a mistake in the storey. And the deuce knows why they let me in, I suppose she must have been expecting someone (not you, of course). I hid under the bed when I heard your stupid footsteps, when I saw the lady was frightened. Besides, it was dark. And why should I justify myself to you. You are a ridiculous, jealous old man, sir. Do you know why I don't crawl out? Perhaps you imagine I am afraid to come out? No, sir, I should have come out long ago, but I stay here from compassion for you. Why, what would you be taken for, if I were not here? You'd stand facing them, like a post, you know you wouldn't know what to do . . . '

'Why like that object? Couldn't you find anything else to compare me with, young man? Why shouldn't I know what to do? I should know what to do.'

'Oh, my goodness, how that wretched dog keeps barking!'

'Hush! Oh, it really is . . . That's because you keep jabbering. You've waked the dog, now there will be trouble.'

The lady's dog, who had till then been sleeping on a pillow in the corner, suddenly awoke, sniffed strangers and rushed under the bed with a loud bark.

'Oh, my God, what a stupid dog!' whispered Ivan Andreyitch; 'It will get us all into trouble. Here's another affliction!'

'Oh, well, you are such a coward that it may well be so.'

'Ami, Ami, come here,' cried the lady; 'ici, ici.'[44] But the dog, without heeding her, made straight for Ivan Andreyitch.

'Why is it Amishka keeps barking?' said the old gentleman. 'There must be mice or the cat under there. I seem to hear a sneezing . . . and pussy had a cold this morning.'

'Lie still,' whispered the young man. 'Don't twist about! Perhaps it will leave off.'

'Sir, let go of my hands, sir! Why are you holding them?'

'Hush! Be quiet!'

'But mercy on us, young man, it will bite my nose. Do you want me to lose my nose?'

A struggle followed, and Ivan Andreyitch got his hands free. The dog broke into volleys of barking. Suddenly it ceased barking and gave a yelp.

'Aïe!' cried the lady.

'Monster! what are you doing?' cried the young man. 'You will be the ruin of us both! Why are you holding it? Good heavens, he is strangling it! Let it go! Monster! You know nothing of the heart of women if you can do that! She will betray us both if you strangle the dog.'

But by now Ivan Andreyitch could hear nothing. He had succeeded in catching the dog and in a paroxysm of self-preservation had squeezed its throat. The dog yelled and gave up the ghost.

'We are lost!' whispered the young man.

'Amishka! Amishka,' cried the lady. 'My God, what are they doing with my Amishka? Amishka! Amishka! *Ici!* Oh, the monsters! Barbarians! Oh, dear, I feel giddy!'

'What is it, what is it?' cried the old gentleman, jumping up from his easy chair. 'What is the matter with you, my darling? Amishka! here, Amishka! Amishka! Amishka!' cried the old gentleman, snapping with his fingers and clicking with his tongue, and calling Amishka from under the bed. 'Amishka, *ici, ici*. The cat cannot have eaten him. The cat wants a thrashing, my love, he hasn't had a beating for a whole month, the rogue. What do you think? I'll talk to Praskovya Zaharyevna. But, my goodness, what is the matter, my love? Oh, how white you are! Oh, oh, servants, servants!' and the old gentleman ran about the room.

'Villains! Monsters!' cried the lady, sinking on the sofa.

'Who, who, who?' cried the old gentleman.

'There are people there, strangers, there under the bed! Oh, my God, Amishka, Amishka, what have they done to you?'

'Good heavens, what people? Amishka . . . Servants, servants, come here! Who is there, who is there?' cried the old gentleman, snatching up a candle and bending down under the bed. 'Who is there?'

Ivan Andreyitch was lying more dead than alive beside the lifeless corpse of Amishka, but the young man was watching every movement of the old gentleman. All at once the old gentleman went to the other side of the bed by the wall and bent down. In a flash the young man crept out from under the bed and took to his heels, while the husband was looking for his visitors on the other side.

'Good gracious!' exclaimed the lady, staring at the young man. 'Who are you? Why, I thought . . . '

'That monster's still there,' whispered the young man. 'He is guilty of Amishka's death!'

'*Aie!*' shrieked the lady, but the young man had already vanished from the room.

'*Aie!* There is someone here. Here are somebody's boots!' cried the husband, catching Ivan Andreyitch by the leg.

'Murderer, murderer!' cried the lady. 'Oh, Ami! Ami!'

'Come out, come out!' cried the old gentleman, stamping on the carpet with both feet; 'come out. Who are you? Tell me who you are! Good gracious, what a queer person!'

'Why, it's robbers! . . . '

'For God's sake, for God's sake,' cried Ivan Andreyitch creeping out, 'for God's sake, your excellency, don't call the servants! Your excellency, don't call anyone. It is quite unnecessary. You can't kick me out! . . . I am not that sort of person. I am a different case. Your excellency, it has all been due to a mistake! I'll explain directly, your excellency,' exclaimed Ivan Andreyitch, sobbing and gasping. 'It's all my wife that is not my wife, but somebody else's wife. I am not married, I am only . . . It's my comrade, a friend of youthful days.'

'What friend of youthful days?' cried the old gentleman, stamping. 'You are a thief, you have come to steal . . . and not a friend of youthful days.'

'No, I am not a thief, your excellency; I am really a friend of youthful days . . . I have only blundered by accident, I came into the wrong place.'

'Yes, sir, yes: I see from what place you've crawled out.'

'Your excellency! I am not that sort of man. You are mistaken. I tell you, you are cruelly mistaken, your excellency. Only glance at me, look at me, and by signs and tokens you will see that I can't be a thief. Your excellency! Your excellency!' cried Ivan Andreyitch, folding his hands and appealing to the young lady. 'You are a lady, you will understand me . . . It was I who killed Amishka . . . But it was not my fault . . . It was really not my fault . . . It was all my wife's fault. I am an unhappy man, I am drinking the cup of bitterness!'

'But really, what has it to do with me that you are drinking the cup of bitterness? Perhaps it's not the only cup you've drunk. It seems so, to judge from your condition. But how did you come here, sir?' cried the old gentleman, quivering with excitement, though he certainly was convinced by certain signs and tokens that Ivan Andreyitch could not be a thief. 'I ask you: how did you come here? You break in like a robber . . . '

'Not a robber, your excellency. I simply came to the wrong place; I am really not a robber! It is all because I was jealous. I will tell you all about it, your excellency, I will confess it all frankly, as I would to my own father; for at your venerable age I might take you for a father.'

'What do you mean by venerable age?'

'Your excellency! Perhaps I have offended you? Of course such a young lady . . . and your age . . . it is a pleasant sight, your excellency, it really is a pleasant sight such a union . . . in the prime of life . . . But don't call the servants, for God's sake, don't call the servants . . . servants would only laugh . . . I know them . . . that is, I don't mean that . . . I am only acquainted with footmen, I have a footman of my own, your excellency, and they are always laughing . . . the asses! Your highness . . . I believe I am not mistaken, I am addressing a prince? . . . '

'No, I am not a prince, sir, I am an independent gentleman . . . Please do not flatter me with your "highness". How did you get here, sir? How did you get here?'

'Your highness, that is, your excellency . . . Excuse me, I thought that you were your highness. I looked . . . I imagined . . . it does happen. You are so like Prince Korotkouhov whom I have had the honour of meeting at my friend Mr Pusyrev's . . . You see, I am acquainted with princes, too, I have met princes, too, at the houses of my friends; you cannot take me for what you take me for. I am not a thief. Your excellency, don't call the servants; what will be the good of it if you do call them?'

'But how did you come here?' cried the lady. 'Who are you?'

'Yes, who are you?' the husband chimed in. 'And, my love, I thought it was pussy under the bed sneezing. And it was he. Ah, you vagabond! Who are you? Tell me!'

And the old gentleman stamped on the carpet again.

'I cannot speak, your excellency, I am waiting till you are finished, I am enjoying your witty jokes. As regards me, it is an absurd story, your excellency; I will tell you all about it. It can all be explained without more ado, that is, I mean, don't call the servants, your excellency! Treat me in a gentlemanly way . . . It means nothing that I was under the bed, I have not sacrificed my dignity by that. It is a most comical story, your excellency!' cried Ivan Andreyitch, addressing the lady with a supplicating air. 'You, particularly, your excellency, will laugh! You behold upon the scene a jealous husband. You see, I abase myself, I abase myself of my own free will. I did indeed kill Amishka, but . . . my God, I don't know what I am saying!'

'But how, how did you get here?'

'Under cover of night, your excellency, under cover of night . . . I beg your pardon! Forgive me, your excellency! I humbly beg your pardon! I am only an injured husband, nothing more! Don't imagine, your excellency, that I am a lover! I am not a lover! Your wife is virtue itself, if I may venture so to express myself. She is pure and innocent!'

'What, what? What did you have the audacity to say?' cried the old gentleman, stamping his foot again. 'Are you out of your mind or not? How dare you talk about my wife?'

'He is a villain, a murderer who has killed Amishka,' wailed the lady, dissolving into tears. 'And then he dares! . . . '

'Your excellency, your excellency! I spoke foolishly,' cried Ivan Andreyitch in a fluster. 'I was talking foolishly, that was all! Think of me as out of my mind . . . For goodness' sake, think of me as out of my mind . . . I assure you that you will be doing me the greatest favour. I would offer you my hand, but I do not venture to . . . I was not alone, I was an uncle . . . I mean to say that you cannot take me for the lover . . . Goodness! I have put my foot in it again . . . Do not be offended, your excellency,' cried Ivan Andreyitch to the lady. 'You are a lady, you understand what love is, it is a delicate feeling . . . But what am I saying? I am talking nonsense again; that is, I mean to say that I am an old man – that is, a middle-aged man, not an old man; that I cannot be your lover; that a lover is a Richardson – that is, a Lovelace . . . I am talking nonsense, but you see, your excellency, that I am a well-educated man and know something of literature. You are laughing, your excellency. I am delighted, delighted that I have *provoked* your mirth, your excellency. Oh, how delighted I am that I have provoked your mirth.'

'My goodness, what a funny man!' cried the lady, exploding with laughter.

'Yes, he is funny, and in such a mess,' said the old man, delighted that his wife was laughing. 'He cannot be a thief, my love. But how did he come here?'

'It really is strange, it really is strange, it is like a novel! Why! At the dead of night, in a great city, a man under the bed. Strange, funny! Rinaldo-Rinaldini[45] after a fashion. But that is no matter, no matter, your excellency. I will tell you all about it . . . And I will buy you a new lapdog, your excellency . . . A wonderful lapdog! Such a long coat, such short little legs, it can't walk more than a step or two: it runs a little, gets entangled in its own coat, and tumbles over. One feeds it on nothing but sugar. I will bring you one, I will certainly bring you one.'

'Ha-ha-ha-ha-ha!' The lady was rolling from side to side with laughter. 'Oh, dear, I shall have hysterics! Oh, how funny he is!'

'Yes, yes! Ha-ha-ha! Khee-khee-khee! He is funny and he is in a mess – khee-khee-khee!'

'Your excellency, your excellency, I am now perfectly happy. I would offer you my hand, but I do not venture to, your excellency. I feel that I have been in error, but now I am opening my eyes. I am certain my wife is pure and innocent! I was wrong in suspecting her.'

'Wife – his wife!' cried the lady, with tears in her eyes through laughing.

'He married? Impossible! I should never have thought it,' said the old gentleman.

'Your excellency, my wife – it is all her fault; that is, it is my fault: I suspected her; I knew that an assignation had been arranged here – here upstairs; I intercepted a letter, made a mistake about the storey and got under the bed . . . '

'He-he-he-he!'

'Ha-ha-ha-ha!'

'Ha-ha-ha-ha!' Ivan Andreyitch began laughing at last. 'Oh, how happy I am! Oh, how wonderful to see that we are all so happy and harmonious! And my wife is entirely innocent. That must be so, your excellency!'

'He-he-he! Khee-khee! Do you know, my love, who it was?' said the old man at last, recovering from his mirth.

'Who? Ha-ha-ha.'

'She must be the pretty woman who makes eyes, the one with the dandy. It's she, I bet that's his wife!'

'No, your excellency, I am certain it is not she; I am perfectly certain.'

'But, my goodness! You are losing time,' cried the lady, leaving off laughing. 'Run, go upstairs. Perhaps you will find them.'

'Certainly, your excellency, I will fly. But I shall not find anyone, your excellency; it is not she, I am certain of it beforehand. She is at home now. It is all my fault! It is simply my jealousy, nothing else . . . What do you think? Do you suppose that I shall find them there, your excellency?'

'Ha-ha-ha!'

'He-he-he! Khee-khee!'

'You must go, you must go! And when you come down, come in and tell us!' cried the lady; 'or better still, tomorrow morning. And do bring her too, I should like to make her acquaintance.'

'Goodbye, your excellency, goodbye! I will certainly bring her, I shall be very glad for her to make your acquaintance. I am glad and happy that it was all ended so and has turned out for the best.'

'And the lapdog! Don't forget it: be sure to bring the lapdog!'

'I will bring it, your excellency, I will certainly bring it,' responded Ivan Andreyitch, darting back into the room, for he had already made his bows and withdrawn. 'I will certainly bring it. It is such a pretty one. It is just as though a confectioner had made it of sweetmeats. And it's such a funny little thing – gets entangled in its own coat and falls over. It really is a lapdog! I said to my wife : "How is it, my love, it keeps tumbling over?" "It is such a little thing," she said. As though it were made of sugar, of sugar, your excellency! Goodbye, your excellency, very, very glad to make your acquaintance, very glad to make your acquaintance!'

Ivan Andreyitch bowed himself out.

'Hey, sir! Stay, come back,' cried the old gentleman, after the retreating Ivan Andreyitch.

The latter turned back for the third time.

'I still can't find the cat, didn't you meet him when you were under the bed?'

'No, I didn't, your excellency. Very glad to make his acquaintance, though, and I shall look upon it as an honour . . . '

'He has a cold in his head now, and keeps sneezing and sneezing. He must have a beating.'

'Yes, your excellency, of course; corrective punishment is essential with domestic animals.'

'What?'

'I say that corrective punishment is necessary, your excellency, to enforce obedience in the domestic animals.'

'Ah! . . . Well, goodbye, goodbye, that is all I had to say.'

Coming out into the street, Ivan Andreyitch stood for a long time in an attitude that suggested that he was expecting to have a fit in another minute. He took off his hat, wiped the cold sweat from his brow, screwed up his eyes, thought a minute, and set off homewards.

What was his amazement when he learned at home that Glafira Petrovna had come back from the theatre a long, long time before, that she had toothache, that she had sent for the doctor, that she had sent for leeches, and that now she was lying in bed and expecting Ivan Andreyitch.

Ivan Andreyitch slapped himself on the forehead, told the servant to help him wash and to brush his clothes, and at last ventured to go into his wife's room.

'Where is it you spend your time? Look what a sight you are! What do you look like? Where have you been lost all this time? Upon my word, sir; your wife is dying and you have to be hunted for all over the town. Where have you been? Surely you have not been tracking me, trying to disturb a rendezvous I am supposed to have made, though I don't know with whom. For shame, sir, you are a husband! People will soon be pointing at you in the street.'

'My love . . . ' responded Ivan Andreyitch.

But at this point he was so overcome with confusion that he had to feel in his pocket for his handkerchief and to break off in the speech he was beginning, because he had neither words, thoughts or courage . . . What was his amazement, horror and alarm when with his handkerchief fell out of his pocket the corpse of Amishka. Ivan Andreyitch had not noticed that when he had been forced to creep out from under the bed, in an access of despair and unreasoning terror he had stuffed Amishka into his pocket with a faraway idea of burying the traces, concealing the evidence of his crime, and so avoiding the punishment he deserved.

'What's this?' cried his spouse; 'a nasty dead dog! Goodness! where has it come from? . . . What have you been up to? . . . Where have you been? Tell me at once where have you been?'

'My love,' answered Ivan Andreyitch, almost as dead as Amishka, 'my love . . .'

But here we will leave our hero – till another time, for a new and quite different adventure begins here. Someday we will describe all these calamities and misfortunes, gentlemen. But you will admit that jealousy is an unpardonable passion, and what is more, it is a positive misfortune.

A Faint Heart

UNDER the same roof in the same flat on the same fourth storey lived two young men, colleagues in the service, Arkady Ivanovitch Nefedevitch and Vasya Shumkov . . . The author, of course, feels the necessity of explaining to the reader why one is given his full title, while the other's name is abbreviated, if only that such a mode of expression may not be regarded as unseemly and rather familiar. But, to do so, it would first be necessary to explain and describe the rank and years and calling and duty in the service, and even, indeed, the characters of the persons concerned; and since there are so many writers who begin in that way, the author of the proposed story, solely in order to be unlike them (that is, some people will perhaps say, entirely on account of his boundless vanity), decides to begin straightaway with action. Having completed this introduction, he begins.

Towards six o'clock on New Year's Eve, Shumkov returned home. Arkady Ivanovitch, who was lying on the bed, woke up and looked at his friend with half-closed eyes. He saw that Vasya had on his very best trousers and a very clean shirt front. That, of course, struck him. 'Where had Vasya to go like that? And he had not dined at home either!' Meanwhile, Shumkov had lighted a candle, and Arkady Ivanovitch guessed immediately that his friend was intending to wake him accidentally. Vasya did, in fact, clear his throat twice, walked twice up and down the room, and at last, quite accidentally, let the pipe, which he had begun filling in the corner by the stove, slip out of his hands. Arkady Ivanovitch laughed to himself.

'Vasya, give over pretending!' he said.

'Arkasha, you are not asleep?'

'I really cannot say for certain; it seems to me I am not.'

'Oh, Arkasha! How are you, dear boy? Well, brother! Well, brother! . . . You don't know what I have to tell you!'

'I certainly don't know; come here.'

As though expecting this, Vasya went up to him at once, not at all anticipating, however, treachery from Arkady Ivanovitch. The other seized him very adroitly by the arms, turned him over, held him down, and began, as it is called, 'strangling' his victim, and apparently this proceeding afforded the light-hearted Arkady Ivanovitch great satisfaction.

'Caught!' he cried. 'Caught!'

'Arkasha, Arkasha, what are you about? Let me go. For goodness sake, let me go, I shall crumple my dress coat!'

'As though that mattered! What do you want with a dress coat? Why were you so confiding as to put yourself in my hands? Tell me, where have you been? Where have you dined?'

'Arkasha, for goodness' sake, let me go!'

'Where have you dined?'

'Why, it's about that I want to tell you.'

'Tell away, then.'

'But first let me go.'

'Not a bit of it, I won't let you go till you tell me!'

'Arkasha! Arkasha! But do you understand, I can't – it is utterly impossible!' cried Vasya, helplessly wriggling out of his friend's powerful clutches. 'You know there are subjects!'

'How – subjects? . . . '

'Why, subjects that you can't talk about in such a position without losing your dignity; it's utterly impossible; it would make it ridiculous, and this is not a ridiculous matter, it is important.'

'Here, he's going in for being important! That's a new idea! You tell me so as to make me laugh, that's how you must tell me; I don't want anything important; or else you are no true friend of mine. Do you call yourself a friend? Eh?'

'Arkasha, I really can't!'

'Well, I don't want to hear . . . '

'Well, Arkasha!' began Vasya, lying across the bed and doing his utmost to put all the dignity possible into his words. 'Arkasha! If you like, I will tell you; only . . . '

'Well, what? . . . '

'Well, I am engaged to be married!'

Without uttering another word Arkady Ivanovitch took Vasya up in his arms like a baby, though the latter was by no means short, but rather long and thin, and began dexterously carrying him up and down the room, pretending that he was hushing him to sleep.

'I'll put you in your swaddling clothes, Master Bridegroom,' he kept saying. But seeing that Vasya lay in his arms, not stirring or uttering a word, he thought better of it at once, and reflecting that the joke had gone too far, set him down in the middle of the room and kissed him on the cheek in the most genuine and friendly way.

'Vasya, you are not angry?'

'Arkasha, listen . . . '

'Come, it's New Year's Eve.'

'Oh, I'm all right; but why are you such a madman, such a scatter-brain? How many times have I told you? Arkasha, it's really not funny, not funny at all!'

'Oh, well, you are not angry?'

'Oh, I'm all right; am I ever angry with anyone! But you have wounded me, do do you understand?'

'But how have I wounded you? In what way?'

'I come to you as to a friend, with a full heart, to pour out my soul to you, to tell you of my happiness . . . '

'What happiness? Why don't you speak? . . . '

'Oh, well, I am going to get married!' Vasya answered with vexation, for he really was a little exasperated.

'You! You are going to get married! So you really mean it?' Arkasha cried at the top of his voice. 'No, no . . . but what's this? He talks like this and his tears are flowing . . . Vasya, my little Vasya, don't, my little son! Is it true, really?' And Arkady Ivanovitch flew to hug him again.

'Well, do you see how it is now?' said Vasya. 'You are kind, of course, you are a friend, I know that. I come to you with such joy, such rapture, and all of a sudden I have to disclose all the joy of my heart, all my rapture struggling across the bed, in an undignified way . . . You under-stand, Arkasha,' Vasya went on, half laughing. 'You see, it made it seem comic: and in a sense I did not belong to myself at that minute. I could not let this be slighted . . . What's more, if you had asked me her name, I swear, I would sooner you killed me than have answered you.'

'But, Vasya, why did you not speak! You should have told me all about it sooner and I would not have played the fool!' cried Arkady Ivanovitch in genuine despair.

'Come, that's enough, that's enough! Of course, that's how it is . . . You know what it all comes from – from my having a good heart. What vexes me is that I could not tell you as I wanted to, making you glad and happy, telling you nicely and initiating you into my secret properly . . . Really, Arkasha, I love you so much that I believe if it were not for you I shouldn't be getting married, and, in fact, I shouldn't be living in this world at all!'

Arkady Ivanovitch, who was excessively sentimental, cried and laughed at once as he listened to Vasya. Vasya did the same. Both flew to embrace one another again and forgot the past.

'How is it – how is it? Tell me all about it, Vasya! I am astonished, excuse me, brother, but I am utterly astonished; it's a perfect thunderbolt, by Jove! Nonsense, nonsense, brother, you have made it up, you've really made it up, you are telling fibs!' cried Arkady Ivanovitch, and he actually looked into Vasya's face with genuine uncertainty, but seeing in it the radiant confirmation of a positive intention of being married as soon as possible, threw himself on the bed and began rolling from side to side in ecstasy till the walls shook.

'Vasya, sit here,' he said at last, sitting upright on the bed.

'I really don't know, brother, where to begin!'

They looked at one another in joyful excitement.

'Who is she, Vasya?'

'The Artemyevs! . . . ' Vasya pronounced, in a voice weak with emotion.

'No?'

'Well, I did buzz into your ears about them at first, and then I shut up, and you noticed nothing. Ah, Arkasha, if you knew how hard it was to keep it from you; but I was afraid, afraid to speak! I thought it would all go wrong, and you know I was in love, Arkasha! My God! my God! You see this was the trouble,' he began, pausing continually from agitation, 'she had a suitor a year ago, but he was suddenly ordered somewhere; I knew him – he was a fellow, bless him! Well, he did not write at all, he simply vanished. They waited and waited, wondering what it meant . . . Four months ago he suddenly came back married, and has never set foot within their doors! It was coarse – shabby! And they had no one to stand up for them. She cried and cried, poor girl, and I fell in love with her . . . indeed, I had been in love with her long before, all the time! I began comforting her, and was always going there . . . Well, and I really don't know how it has all come about, only she came to love me; a week ago I could not restrain myself, I cried, I sobbed, and told her everything – well, that I love her – everything, in fact! . . . "I am ready to love you, too, Vassily Petrovitch, only I am a poor girl, don't make a mock of me; I don't dare to love anyone." Well, brother, you understand! You understand? . . . On that we got engaged on the spot. I kept thinking and thinking and thinking and thinking. I said to her,

"How are we to tell your mother?" She said, "It will be hard, wait a little; she's afraid, and now maybe she would not let you have me; she keeps crying, too." Without telling her I blurted it out to her mother today. Lizanka fell on her knees before her, I did the same . . . well, she gave us her blessing. Arkasha, Arkasha! My dear fellow! We will live together. No, I won't part from you for anything.'

'Vasya, look at you as I may, I can't believe it. I don't believe it, I swear. I keep feeling as though . . . Listen, how can you be engaged to be married? . . . How is it I didn't know, eh? Do you know, Vasya, I will confess it to you now. I was thinking of getting married myself; but now since you are going to be married, it is just as good! Be happy, be happy! . . .'

'Brother, I feel so light-hearted now, there is such sweetness in my soul . . . ' said Vasya, getting up and pacing about the room excitedly. 'Don't you feel the same? We shall be poor, of course, but we shall be happy; and you know it is not a wild fancy; our happiness is not a fairy tale; we shall be happy in reality! . . . '

'Vasya, Vasya, listen!'

'What?' said Vasya, standing before Arkady Ivanovitch.

'The idea occurs to me; I am really afraid to say it to you . . . Forgive me, and settle my doubts. What are you going to live on? You know I am delighted that you are going to be married, of course, I am delighted, and I don't know what to do with myself, but – what are you going to live on? Eh?'

'Oh, good heavens! What a fellow you are, Arkasha!' said Vasya, looking at Nefedevitch in profound astonishment. 'What do you mean? Even her old mother, even she did not think of that for two minutes when I put it all clearly before her. You had better ask what they are living on! They have five hundred roubles a year between the three of them: the pension, which is all they have, since the father died. She and her old mother and her little brother, whose schooling is paid for out of that income too – that is how they live! It's you and I are the capitalists! Some good years it works out to as much as seven hundred for me.'

'I say, Vasya, excuse me; I really . . . you know I . . . I am only thinking how to prevent things going wrong. How do you mean, seven hundred? It's only three hundred . . . '

'Three hundred! . . . And Yulian Mastakovitch? Have you forgotten him?'

'Yulian Mastakovitch? But you know that's uncertain, brother; that's not the same thing as three hundred roubles of secure salary, where every rouble is a friend you can trust. Yulian Mastakovitch, of course, he's a great man; in fact, I respect him, I understand him, though he is so far above us; and, by Jove, I love him, because he likes you and gives you something for your work, though he might not pay you, but simply order a clerk to work for him – but you will agree, Vasya . . . Let me tell you, too, I am not talking nonsense. I admit in all Petersburg you won't find a handwriting like your handwriting, I am ready to allow that to you,' Nefedevitch concluded, not without enthusiasm. 'But, God forbid! you may displease him all at once, you may not satisfy him, your work with him may stop, he may take another clerk – all sorts of things may happen, in fact! You know, Yulian Mastakovitch may be here today and gone tomorrow . . . '

'Well, Arkasha, the ceiling might fall on our heads this minute.'

'Oh, of course, of course, I mean nothing.'

'But listen, hear what I have got to say – you know, I don't see how he can part with me . . . No, hear what I have to say! hear what I have to say! You see, I perform all my duties punctually; you know how kind he is, you know, Arkasha, he gave me fifty roubles in silver today!'

'Did he really, Vasya? A bonus for you?'

'Bonus, indeed, it was out of his own pocket. He said: "Why, you have had no money for five months, brother, take some if you want it; thank you, I am satisfied with you." . . . Yes, really! "Yes, you don't work for me for nothing," said he. He did, indeed, that's what he said. It brought tears into my eyes, Arkasha. Good heavens, yes!'

'I say, Vasya, have you finished copying those papers? . . . '

'No . . . I haven't finished them yet.'

'Vas . . . ya! My angel! What have you been doing?'

'Listen, Arkasha, it doesn't matter, they are not wanted for another two days, I have time enough . . . '

'How is it you have not done them?'

'That's all right, that's all right. You look so horror-stricken that you turn me inside out and make my heart ache! You are always going on at me like this! He's forever crying out: Oh, oh, oh!!! Only consider, what does it matter? Why, I shall finish it, of course I shall finish it . . . '

'What if you don't finish it?' cried Arkady, jumping up, 'and he has made you a present today! And you going to be married . . . Tut, tut, tut! . . . '

'It's all right, it's all right,' cried Shumkov, 'I shall sit down directly, I shall sit down this minute.'

'How did you come to leave it, Vasya?'

'Oh, Arkasha! How could I sit down to work! Have I been in a fit state? Why, even at the office I could scarcely sit still, I could scarcely bear the beating of my heart . . . Oh! oh! Now I shall work all night, and I shall work all tomorrow night, and the night after, too – and I shall finish it.'

'Is there a great deal left?'

'Don't hinder me, for goodness' sake, don't hinder me; hold your tongue.'

Arkady Ivanovitch went on tiptoe to the bed and sat down, then suddenly wanted to get up, but was obliged to sit down again, remembering that he might interrupt him, though he could not sit still for excitement: it was evident that the news had thoroughly upset him, and the first thrill of delight had not yet passed off. He glanced at Shumkov; the latter glanced at him, smiled, and shook his finger at him, then, frowning severely (as though all his energy and the success of his work depended upon it), fixed his eyes on the papers.

It seemed that he, too, could not yet master his emotion; he kept changing his pen, fidgeting in his chair, rearranging things, and setting to work again, but his hand trembled and refused to move.

'Arkasha, I've talked to them about you,' he cried suddenly, as though he had just remembered it.

'Yes,' cried Arkasha, 'I was just wanting to ask you that. Well?'

'Well, I'll tell you everything afterwards. Of course, it is my own fault, but it quite went out of my head that I didn't mean to say anything till I had written four pages, but I thought of you and of them. I really can't write, brother, I keep thinking about you . . . '

Vasya smiled.

A silence followed.

'Phew! What a horrid pen,' cried Shumkov, flinging it on the table in vexation. He took another.

'Vasya! listen! one word . . . '

'Well, make haste, and for the last time.'

'Have you a great deal left to do?'

'Ah, brother!' Vasya frowned, as though there could be nothing more terrible and murderous in the whole world than such a question. 'A lot, a fearful lot.'

'Do you know, I have an idea – '

'What?'

'Oh, never mind, never mind; go on writing.'

'Why, what? what?'

'It's past six, Vasya.'

Here Nefedevitch smiled and winked slyly at Vasya, though with a certain timidity, not knowing how Vasya would take it.

'Well, what is it?' said Vasya, throwing down his pen, looking him straight in the face and actually turning pale with excitement.

'Do you know what?'

'For goodness' sake, what is it?'

'I tell you what, you are excited, you won't get much done . . . Stop, stop, stop! I have it, I have it – listen,' said Nefedevitch, jumping up from the bed in delight, preventing Vasya from speaking and doing his utmost to ward off all objections. 'First of all you must get calm, you must pull yourself together, mustn't you?'

'Arkasha, Arkasha!' cried Vasya, jumping up from his chair, 'I will work all night, I will, really.'

'Of course, of course, you won't go to bed till morning.'

'I won't go to bed, I won't go to bed at all.'

'No, that won't do, that won't do: you must sleep, go to bed at five. I will call you at eight. Tomorrow is a holiday; you can sit and scribble away all day long . . . Then the night and – but have you a great deal left to do?'

'Yes, look, look!'

Vasya, quivering with excitement and suspense, showed the manuscript: 'Look!'

'I say, brother, that's not much.'

'My dear fellow, there's some more of it,' said Vasya, looking very timidly at Nefedevitch, as though the decision whether he was to go or not depended upon the latter.

'How much?'

'Two signatures.'

'Well, what's that? Come, I tell you what. We shall have time to finish it, by Jove, we shall!'

'Arkasha!'

'Vasya, listen! Tonight, on New Year's Eve, everyone is at home with his family. You and I are the only ones without a home or relations . . . Oh, Vasya!'

Nefedevitch clutched Vasya and hugged him in his leonine arms.

'Arkasha, it's settled.'

'Vasya, boy, I only wanted to say this. You see, Vasya – listen, bandy-legs, listen! . . . '

Arkady stopped, with his mouth open, because he could not speak for delight. Vasya held him by the shoulders, gazed into his face and moved his lips, as though he wanted to speak for him.

'Well,' he brought out at last.

'Introduce me to them today.'

'Arkady, let us go to tea there. I tell you what, I tell you what. We won't even stay to see in the New Year, we'll come away earlier,' cried Vasya, with genuine inspiration.

'That is, we'll go for two hours, neither more nor less . . . '

'And then separation till I have finished . . . '

'Vasya, boy!'

'Arkady!'

Three minutes later Arkady was dressed in his best. Vasya did nothing but brush himself, because he had been in such haste to work that he had not changed his trousers.

They hurried out into the street, each more pleased than the other. Their way lay from the Petersburg Side to Kolomna. Arkady Ivanovitch stepped out boldly and vigorously, so that from his walk alone one could see how glad he was at the good fortune of his friend, who was more and more radiant with happiness. Vasya trotted along with shorter steps, though his deportment was none the less dignified. Arkady Ivanovitch, in fact, had never seen him before to such advantage. At that moment he actually felt more respect for him, and Vasya's physical defect, of which the reader is not yet aware (Vasya was slightly deformed), which always called forth a feeling of loving sympathy in Arkady Ivanovitch's kind heart, contributed to the deep tenderness the latter felt for him at this moment, a tenderness of which Vasya was in every way worthy. Arkady Ivanovitch felt ready to weep with happiness, but he restrained himself.

'Where are you going, where are you going, Vasya? It is nearer this way,' he cried, seeing that Vasya was making in the direction of Voznesenky.

'Hold your tongue, Arkasha.'

'It really is nearer, Vasya.'

'Do you know what, Arkasha?' Vasya began mysteriously, in a voice quivering with joy, 'I tell you what, I want to take Lizanka a little present.'

'What sort of present?'

'At the corner here, brother, is Madame Leroux's, a wonderful shop.'

'Well.'

'A cap, my dear, a cap; I saw such a charming little cap today. I enquired, I was told it was the *façon Manon Lescaut*[46] – a delightful thing. Cherry-coloured ribbons, and if it is not dear . . . Arkasha, even if it is dear . . . '

'I think you are superior to any of the poets, Vasya. Come along.'

They ran along, and two minutes later went into the shop. They were met by a black-eyed Frenchwoman with curls, who, from the first glance at her customers, became as joyous and happy as they, even happier, if one may say so. Vasya was ready to kiss Madame Leroux in his delight . . . 'Arkasha,' he said in an undertone, casting a casual glance at all the grand and beautiful things on little wooden stands on the huge table, 'lovely things! What's that? What's this? This one, for instance, this little sweet, do you see?' Vasya whispered, pointing to a charming cap farther away, which was not the one he meant to buy, because he had already from afar descried and fixed his eyes upon the real, famous one, standing at the other end. He looked at it in such a way that one might have supposed someone was going to steal it, or as though the cap itself might take wings and fly into the air just to prevent Vasya from obtaining it.

'Look,' said Arkady Ivanovitch, pointing to one, 'I think that's better.'

'Well, Arkasha, that does you credit; I begin to respect you for your taste,' said Vasya, resorting to cunning with Arkasha in the tenderness of his heart, 'your cap is charming, but come this way.'

'Where is there a better one, brother?'

'Look; this way.'

'That,' said Arkady, doubtfully.

But when Vasya, incapable of restraining himself any longer, took it from the stand from which it seemed to fly spontaneously, as though delighted at falling at last into the hands of so good a customer, and they heard the rustle of its ribbons, ruches and lace, an unexpected cry of delight broke from the powerful chest of Arkady Ivanovitch. Even Madame Leroux, while maintaining her incontestable dignity and pre-eminence in matters of taste, and remaining mute from condescension, rewarded Vasya with a smile of complete approbation, everything in her glance, gesture and smile saying at once: 'Yes, you have chosen rightly, and are worthy of the happiness which awaits you.'

'It has been dangling its charms in coy seclusion,' cried Vasya, transferring his tender feelings to the charming cap. 'You have been hiding on purpose, you sly little pet!' And he kissed it, that is the air surrounding it, for he was afraid to touch his treasure.

'Retiring as true worth and virtue,' Arkady added enthusiastically, quoting humorously from a comic paper he had read that morning. 'Well, Vasya?'

'Hurrah, Arkasha! You are witty today. I predict you will make a sensation, as women say. Madame Leroux, Madame Leroux!'

'What is your pleasure?'

'Dear Madame Leroux.'

Madame Leroux looked at Arkady Ivanovitch and smiled condescendingly.

'You wouldn't believe how I adore you at this moment . . . Allow me
to give you a kiss . . . ' And Vasya kissed the shopkeeper.

She certainly at that moment needed all her dignity to maintain her
position with such a madcap. But I contend that the innate, spontaneous
courtesy and grace with which Madame Leroux received Vasya's
enthusiasm, was equally befitting. She forgave him, and how tactfully,
how graciously, she knew how to behave in the circumstances. How
could she have been angry with Vasya?

'Madame Leroux, how much?'

'Five roubles in silver,' she answered, straightening herself with a new
smile.

'And this one, Madame Leroux?' said Arkady Ivanovitch, pointing to
his choice.

'That one is eight roubles.'

'There, you see – there, you see! Come, Madame Leroux, tell me
which is nicer, more graceful, more charming, which of them suits you
best?'

'The second is richer, but your choice *c'est plus coquet*.'[47]

'Then we will take it.'

Madame Leroux took a sheet of very delicate paper, pinned it up, and
the paper with the cap wrapped in it seemed even lighter than the paper
alone. Vasya took it carefully, almost holding his breath, bowed to
Madame Leroux, said something else very polite to her and left the
shop.

'I am a lady's man, I was born to be a lady's man,' said Vasya, laughing
a little noiseless, nervous laugh and dodging the passers-by, whom he
suspected of designs for crushing his precious cap.

'Listen, Arkady, brother,' he began a minute later, and there was a
note of triumph, of infinite affection in his voice. 'Arkady, I am so
happy, I am so happy!'

'Vasya! how glad I am, dear boy!'

'No, Arkasha, no. I know that there is no limit to your affection for
me; but you cannot be feeling one-hundredth part of what I am feeling
at this moment. My heart is so full, so full! Arkasha, I am not worthy of
such happiness. I feel that, I am conscious of it. Why has it come to
me?' he said, his voice full of stifled sobs. 'What have I done to deserve
it? Tell me. Look what lots of people, what lots of tears, what sorrow,
what workaday life without a holiday, while I, I am loved by a girl like
that, I . . . But you will see her yourself immediately, you will appreciate

her noble heart. I was born in a humble station, now I have a grade in the service and an independent income – my salary. I was born with a physical defect, I am a little deformed. See, she loves me as I am. Yulian Mastakovitch was so kind, so attentive, so gracious today; he does not often talk to me; he came up to me: "Well, how goes it, Vasya" (yes, really, he called me Vasya), "are you going to have a good time for the holiday, eh?" he laughed.

' "Well, the fact is, your excellency, I have work to do," but then I plucked up courage and said: "and maybe I shall have a good time, too, your excellency." I really said it. He gave me the money, on the spot, then he said a couple of words more to me. Tears came into my eyes, brother, I actually cried, and he, too, seemed touched, he patted me on the shoulder, and said: "Feel always, Vasya, as you feel this now." '

Vasya paused for an instant. Arkady Ivanovitch turned away, and he, too, wiped away a tear with his fist.

'And, and . . . ' Vasya went on, 'I have never spoken to you of this, Arkady . . . Arkady, you make me so happy with your affection, without you I could not live – no, no, don't say anything, Arkady, let me squeeze your hand, let me . . . thank . . . you . . . ' Again Vasya could not finish.

Arkady Ivanovitch longed to throw himself on Vasya's neck, but as they were crossing the road and heard almost in their ears a shrill: 'Hi! there!' they ran frightened and excited to the pavement.

Arkady Ivanovitch was positively relieved. He set down Vasya's outburst of gratitude to the exceptional circumstances of the moment. He was vexed. He felt that he had done so little for Vasya hitherto. He felt actually ashamed of himself when Vasya began thanking him for so little. But they had all their lives before them, and Arkady Ivanovitch breathed more freely.

The Artemyevs had quite given up expecting them. The proof of it was that they had already sat down to tea! And the old, it seems, are sometimes more clear-sighted than the young, even when the young are so exceptional. Lizanka had very earnestly maintained, 'He isn't coming, he isn't coming, mamma; I feel in my heart he is not coming;' while her mother on the contrary declared that she had a feeling that he would certainly come, that he would not stay away, that he would run round, that he could have no office work now, on New Year's Eve. Even as Lizanka opened the door she did not in the least expect to see them, and greeted them breathlessly, with her heart throbbing like a captured bird's, flushing and turning as red as a cherry, a fruit which she wonderfully resembled. Good heavens, what a surprise it was! What a joyful 'Oh!' broke from her lips. 'Deceiver! My darling!' she cried, throwing her arms round Vasya's neck. But imagine her amazement, her sudden confusion: just behind Vasya, as though trying to hide behind his back, stood Arkady Ivanovitch, a trifle out of countenance. It must be admitted that he was awkward in the company of women, very awkward indeed, in fact on one occasion something occurred . . . but of that later. You must put yourself in his place, however. There was nothing to laugh at; he was standing in the entry, in his goloshes and overcoat, and in a cap with flaps over the ears, which he would have hastened to pull off, but he had, all twisted round in a hideous way, a yellow knitted scarf, which, to make things worse, was knotted at the back. He had to disentangle all this, to take it off as quickly as possible, to show himself to more advantage, for there is no one who does not prefer to show himself to advantage. And then Vasya, vexatious insufferable Vasya, of course always the same dear kind Vasya, but now insufferable, ruthless Vasya. 'Here,' he shouted, 'Lizanka, I have brought you my Arkady? What do you think of him? He is my best friend, embrace him, kiss him, Lizanka, give him a kiss in advance; afterwards – you will know him better – you can take it back again.'

Well, what, I ask you, was Arkady Ivanovitch to do? And he had only untwisted half of the scarf so far. I really am sometimes ashamed of Vasya's excess of enthusiasm; it is, of course, the sign of a good heart, but . . . it's awkward, not nice!

At last both went in . . . The mother was unutterably delighted to make Arkady Ivanovitch's acquaintance, she had 'heard so much about him, she had . . . ' But she did not finish. A joyful 'Oh!' ringing musically through the room interrupted her in the middle of a sentence. Good heavens! Lizanka was standing before the cap which had suddenly been unfolded before her gaze; she clasped her hands with the utmost simplicity, smiling such a smile . . . Oh, heavens! why had not Madame Leroux an even lovelier cap?

Oh, heavens! but where could you find a lovelier cap? It was quite first-rate. Where could you get a better one? I mean it seriously. This ingratitude on the part of lovers moves me, in fact, to indignation and even wounds me a little. Why, look at it for yourself, reader, look, what could be more beautiful than this little love of a cap? Come, look at it . . . But, no, no, my strictures are uncalled for; they had by now all agreed with me; it had been a momentary aberration; the blindness, the delirium of feeling; I am ready to forgive them . . . But then you must look . . . You must excuse me, kind reader, I am still talking about the cap: made of tulle, light as a feather, a broad cherry-coloured ribbon covered with lace passing between the tulle and the ruche, and at the back two wide long ribbons – they would fall down a little below the nape of the neck . . . All that the cap needed was to be tilted a little to the back of the head; come, look at it; I ask you, after that . . . but I see you are not looking . . . you think it does not matter. You are looking in a different direction . . . You are looking at two big tears, big as pearls, that rose in two jet black eyes, quivered for one instant on the eyelashes, and then dropped on the ethereal tulle of which Madame Leroux's artistic masterpiece was composed . . . And again I feel vexed, those two tears were scarcely a tribute to the cap . . . No, to my mind, such a gift should be given in cool blood, as only then can its full worth be appreciated. I am, I confess, dear reader, entirely on the side of the cap.

They sat down – Vasya with Lizanka and the old mother with Arkady Ivanovitch; they began to talk, and Arkady Ivanovitch did himself credit, I am glad to say that for him. One would hardly, indeed, have expected it of him. After a couple of words about Vasya he most successfully turned the conversation to Yulian Mastakovitch, his patron. And he talked so cleverly, so cleverly that the subject was not exhausted for an hour. You ought to have seen with what dexterity, what tact, Arkady Ivanovitch touched upon certain peculiarities of Yulian Mastakovitch which directly or indirectly affected Vasya. The mother was fascinated, genuinely fascinated; she admitted it herself; she purposely called Vasya aside, and said to him that his friend was a most excellent and charming young man, and, what was of most account, such a serious, steady young man. Vasya almost laughed aloud with delight. He remembered how the serious Arkady had tumbled him on his bed for a quarter of an hour. Then the mother signed to Vasya to follow her quietly and cautiously into the next room. It must be admitted that she treated Lizanka rather unfairly: she behaved treacherously to her daughter, in the fullness of her heart, of course, and showed Vasya on the sly the present Lizanka was preparing to give him for the New Year. It was a paper-case, embroidered in beads and gold in a very choice design: on one side was depicted a stag, absolutely lifelike, running swiftly, and so well done! On the other side was the portrait of a celebrated general, also an excellent likeness. I cannot describe Vasya's raptures. Meanwhile, time was not being wasted in the parlour. Lizanka went straight up to Arkady Ivanovitch. She took his hand, she thanked him for something, and Arkady Ivanovitch gathered that she was referring to her precious Vasya. Lizanka was, indeed, deeply touched: she had heard that Arkady Ivanovitch was such a true friend of her betrothed, so loved him, so watched over him, guiding him at every step with helpful advice, that she, Lizanka, could hardly help thanking him, could not refrain from feeling grateful, and hoping that Arkady Ivanovitch might like her, if only half as well as Vasya. Then she began questioning him as to whether Vasya was careful of his health, expressed some apprehensions in regard to his marked impulsiveness of character, and his lack of knowledge of men and practical life; she said that she would in time watch over him religiously, that she would take care of and cherish his lot, and finally, she hoped that Arkady Ivanovitch would not leave them, but would live with them.

'We three shall live like one,' she cried, with extremely naïve enthusiasm.

But it was time to go. They tried, of course, to keep them, but Vasya answered point blank that it was impossible. Arkady Ivanovitch said the same. The reason was, of course, enquired into, and it came out at once that there was work to be done entrusted to Vasya by Yulian Mastakovitch, urgent, necessary, dreadful work, which must be handed in on the morning of the next day but one, and that it was not only unfinished, but had been completely laid aside. The mamma sighed when she heard of this, while Lizanka was positively scared, and hurried Vasya off in alarm. The last kiss lost nothing from this haste; though brief and hurried it was only the more warm and ardent. At last they parted and the two friends set off home.

Both began at once confiding to each other their impressions as soon as they found themselves in the street. And could they help it? Indeed, Arkady Ivanovitch was in love, desperately in love, with Lizanka. And to whom could he better confide his feelings than to Vasya, the happy man himself. And so he did; he was not bashful, but confessed everything at once to Vasya. Vasya laughed heartily and was immensely delighted, and even observed that this was all that was needed to make them greater friends than ever. 'You have guessed my feelings, Vasya,' said Arkady Ivanovitch. 'Yes, I love her as I love you; she will be my good angel as well as yours, for the radiance of your happiness will be shed on me, too, and I can bask in its warmth. She will keep house for me too, Vasya; my happiness will be in her hands. Let her keep house for me as she will for you. Yes, friendship for you is friendship for her; you are not separable for me now, only I shall have two beings like you instead of one . . . ' Arkady paused in the fullness of his feelings, while Vasya was shaken to the depths of his being by his friend's words. The fact is, he had never expected anything of the sort from Arkady. Arkady Ivanovitch was not very great at talking as a rule, he was not fond of dreaming, either; now he gave way to the liveliest, freshest, rainbow-tinted daydreams. 'How I will protect and cherish you both,' he began again. 'To begin with, Vasya, I will be godfather to all your children, every one of them; and secondly, Vasya, we must bestir ourselves about the future. We must buy furniture, and take a lodging so that you and she and I can each have a little room to ourselves. Do you know, Vasya, I'll run about tomorrow and look at the notices, on the gates! Three . . . no, two rooms, we should not need more. I really believe, Vasya, I talked nonsense this morning, there will be money enough; why, as soon as I glanced into her eyes I calculated at once that there would be enough to live on. It will all be for her. Oh, how we will work! Now, Vasya, we might venture up to twenty-five roubles for rent. A lodging is everything, brother. Nice rooms . . . and at once a man is cheerful, and his dreams are of the brightest hues. And, besides, Lizanka will keep the purse for both of us: not a farthing will be wasted. Do you suppose I would go to a restaurant? What do you take me for? Not on any account. And then we shall get a bonus and reward, for we shall be zealous in the service – oh! how we shall work, like oxen toiling in the fields . . . Only fancy,' and Arkady Ivanovitch's voice was faint with pleasure, 'all at once and quite unexpected, twenty-five or thirty roubles . . . Whenever there's an extra, there'll be a cap or a scarf or a pair of little stockings. She must knit me a scarf; look what a horrid one I've got, the nasty yellow thing, it did me a bad turn today! And you wore a nice one, Vasya, to introduce me while I had my head in a halter . . . Though never mind that now. And look here, I undertake all the silver. I am bound to give you some little present – that will be an honour, that will flatter my vanity . . . My bonuses won't fail me, surely; you don't suppose they would give them to Skorohodov? No fear, they won't be landed in that person's pocket. I'll buy you silver spoons, brother, good knives – not silver knives, but thoroughly good ones; and a waistcoat, that is a waistcoat for myself. I shall be best man, of course. Only now, brother, you must keep at it, you must keep at it. I shall stand over you with a stick, brother, today and tomorrow and all night; I shall worry you to work. Finish, make haste and finish, brother. And then again to spend the evening, and then again both of us happy; we will go in for lotto. We will spend the evening there – oh, it's jolly! Oh, the devil! How, vexing it is I can't help you. I should like to take it and write it all for you . . . Why is it our handwriting is not alike?'

'Yes,' answered Vasya. 'Yes, I must make haste. I think it must be eleven o'clock; we must make haste . . . To work!' And saying this, Vasya, who had been all the time alternately smiling and trying to interrupt with some enthusiastic rejoinder the flow of his friend's feelings, and had, in short, been showing the most cordial response, suddenly subsided, sank into silence, and almost ran along the street. It seemed as though some burdensome idea had suddenly chilled his feverish head; he seemed all at once dispirited.

Arkady Ivanovitch felt quite uneasy; he scarcely got an answer to his hurried questions from Vasya, who confined himself to a word or two, sometimes an irrelevant exclamation.

'Why, what is the matter with you, Vasya?' he cried at last, hardly able to keep up with him. 'Can you really be so uneasy?'

'Oh, brother, that's enough chatter!' Vasya answered, with vexation.

'Don't be depressed, Vasya – come, come,' Arkady interposed. 'Why, I have known you write much more in a shorter time! What's the matter? You've simply a talent for it! You can write quickly in an emergency; they are not going to lithograph your copy. You've plenty of time! . . . The only thing is that you are excited now, and preoccupied, and the work won't go so easily.'

Vasya made no reply, or muttered something to himself, and they both ran home in genuine anxiety.

Vasya sat down to the papers at once. Arkady Ivanovitch was quiet and silent; he noiselessly undressed and went to bed, keeping his eyes fixed on Vasya . . . A sort of panic came over him . . . 'What is the matter with him?' he thought to himself, looking at Vasya's face that grew whiter and whiter, at his feverish eyes, at the anxiety that was betrayed in every movement he made, 'why, his hand is shaking . . . what a stupid! Why did I not advise him to sleep for a couple of hours, till he had slept off his nervous excitement anyway.' Vasya had just finished a page, he raised his eyes, glanced casually at Arkady and at once, looking down, took up his pen again.

'Listen, Vasya,' Arkady Ivanovitch began suddenly, 'wouldn't it be best to sleep a little now? Look, you are in a regular fever.'

Vasya glanced at Arkady with vexation, almost with anger, and made no answer.

'Listen, Vasya, you'll make yourself ill.'

Vasya at once changed his mind. 'How would it be to have tea, Arkady?' he said.

'How so? Why?'

'It will do me good. I am not sleepy, I'm not going to bed! I am going on writing. But now I should like to rest and have a cup of tea, and the worst moment will be over.'

'First-rate, brother Vasya, delightful! Just so. I was wanting to propose it myself. And I can't think why it did not occur to me to do so. But I say, Mavra won't get up, she won't wake for anything . . . '

'True.'

'That's no matter, though,' cried Arkady Ivanovitch, leaping out of bed. 'I will set the samovar myself. It won't be the first time . . . '

Arkady Ivanovitch ran to the kitchen and set to work to get the samovar; Vasya meanwhile went on writing. Arkady Ivanovitch, moreover, dressed and ran out to the baker's, so that Vasya might have something to sustain him for the night. A quarter of an hour later the samovar was on the table. They began drinking tea, but conversation flagged. Vasya still seemed preoccupied.

'Tomorrow,' he said at last, as though he had just thought of it, 'I shall have to take my congratulations for the New Year . . . '

'You need not go at all.'

'Oh yes, brother, I must,' said Vasya.

'Why, I will sign the visitors' book for you everywhere . . . How can you? You work tomorrow. You must work tonight, till five o'clock in the morning, as I said, and then get to bed. Or else you will be good for nothing tomorrow. I'll wake you at eight o'clock, punctually.'

'But will it be all right, your signing for me?' said Vasya, half assenting.

'Why, what could be better? Everyone does it.'

'I am really afraid.'

'Why, why?'

'It's all right, you know, with other people, but Yulian Mastakovitch . . . he has been so kind to me, you know, Arkasha, and when he notices it's not my own signature – '

'Notices! why, what a fellow you are, really, Vasya! How could he notice? . . . Come, you know I can imitate your signature awfully well, and make just the same flourish to it, upon my word I can. What nonsense! Who would notice?'

Vasya, made no reply, but emptied his glass hurriedly . . . Then he shook his head doubtfully.

'Vasya, dear boy! Ah, if only we succeed! Vasya, what's the matter with you, you quite frighten me! Do you know, Vasya, I am not going to bed now, I am not going to sleep! Show me, have you a great deal left?'

Vasya gave Arkady such a look that his heart sank, and his tongue failed him.

'Vasya, what is the matter? What are you thinking? Why do you look like that?'

'Arkady, I really must go tomorrow to wish Yulian Mastakovitch a happy New Year.'

'Well, go then!' said Arkady, gazing at him open-eyed, in uneasy expectation. 'I say, Vasya, do write faster; I am advising you for your own good, I really am! How often Yulian Mastakovitch himself has said that what he likes particularly about your writing is its legibility. Why, it is all that Skoroplehin cares for, that writing should be good and distinct like a copy, so as afterwards to pocket the paper and take it home for his children to copy; he can't buy copybooks, the blockhead! Yulian Mastakovitch is always saying, always insisting: "Legible, legible, legible!" . . . What is the matter? Vasya, I really don't know how to talk to you . . . it quite frightens me . . . you crush me with your depression.'

'It's all right, it's all right,' said Vasya, and he fell back in his chair as though fainting. Arkady was alarmed.

'Will you have some water? Vasya! Vasya!'

'Don't, don't,' said Vasya, pressing his hand. 'I am all right. I only feel sad, I can't tell why. Better talk of something else; let me forget it.'

'Calm yourself, for goodness' sake, calm yourself, Vasya. You will finish it all right, on my honour you will. And even if you don't finish, what will it matter? You talk as though it were a crime!'

'Arkady,' said Vasya, looking at his friend with such meaning that Arkady was quite frightened, for Vasya had never been so agitated before . . . 'If I were alone, as I used to be . . . No! I don't mean that. I keep wanting to tell you as a friend, to confide in you . . . But why worry you, though? . . . You see, Arkady, to some much is given, others do a little thing as I do. Well, if gratitude, appreciation, is expected of you . . . and you can't give it?'

'Vasya, I don't understand you in the least.'

'I have never been ungrateful,' Vasya went on softly, as though speaking to himself, 'but if I am incapable of expressing all I feel, it seems as though . . . it seems, Arkady, as though I am really ungrateful, and that's killing me.'

'What next, what next! As though gratitude meant nothing more than your finishing that copy in time? Just think what you are saying, Vasya? Is that the whole expression of gratitude?'

Vasya sank into silence at once, and looked open-eyed at Arkady, as though his unexpected argument had settled all his doubts. He even smiled, but the same melancholy expression came back to his face at once. Arkady, taking this smile as a sign that all his uneasiness was over, and the look that succeeded it as an indication that he was determined to do better, was greatly relieved.

'Well, brother Arkasha, if you can,' said Vasya, 'keep an eye on me; if I fall asleep it will be dreadful. I'll set to work now . . . Arkasha?'

'What?'

'Oh, it's nothing, I only . . . I meant . . . '

Vasya settled himself, and said no more, Arkady got into bed. Neither of them said one word about their friends, the Artemyevs. Perhaps both of them felt that they had been a little to blame, and that they ought not to have gone for their jaunt when they did. Arkady soon fell asleep, still worried about Vasya. To his own surprise he woke up exactly at eight o'clock in the morning. Vasya was asleep in his chair with the pen in his hand, pale and exhausted; the candle had burnt out. Mavra was busy getting the samovar ready in the kitchen.

'Vasya, Vasya!' Arkady cried in alarm, 'when did you fall asleep?'

Vasya opened his eyes and jumped up from his chair.

'Oh!' he cried, 'I must have fallen asleep . . . '

He flew to the papers – everything was right; all were in order; there was not a blot of ink, nor spot of grease from the candle on them.

'I think I must have fallen asleep about six o'clock,' said Vasya. 'How cold it is in the night! Let us have tea, and I will go on again . . . '

'Do you feel better?'

'Yes, yes, I'm all right, I'm all right now.'

'A happy New Year to you, brother Vasya.'

'And to you too, brother, the same to you, dear boy.'

They embraced each other. Vasya's chin was quivering and his eyes were moist. Arkady Ivanovitch was silent, he felt sad. They drank their tea hastily.

'Arkady, I've made up my mind, I am going myself to Yulian Masta-kovitch.'

'Why, he wouldn't notice – '

'But my conscience feels ill at ease, brother.'

'But you know it's for his sake you are sitting here; it's for his sake you are wearing yourself out.'

'Enough!'

'Do you know what, brother, I'll go round and see . . . '

'Whom?' asked Vasya.

'The Artemyevs. I'll take them your good wishes for the New Year as well as mine.'

'My dear fellow! Well, I'll stay here; and I see it's a good idea of yours; I shall be working here, I shan't waste my time. Wait one minute, I'll write a note.'

'Yes, do brother, do, there's plenty of time. I've still to wash and shave and to brush my best coat. Well, Vasya, we are going to be contented and happy. Embrace me, Vasya.'

'Ah, if only we may, brother . . . '

'Does Mr Shumkov live here?' they heard a child's voice on the stairs.

'Yes, my dear, yes,' said Mavra, showing the visitor in.

'What's that? What is it?' cried Vasya, leaping up from the table and rushing to the entry. 'Petinka, you?'

'Good-morning, I have the honour to wish you a happy New Year, Vassily Petrovitch,' said a pretty boy of ten years old with curly black hair. 'Sister sends you her love, and so does mamma, and sister told me to give you a kiss for her.'

Vasya caught the messenger up in the air and printed a long, enthusiastic kiss on his lips, which were very much like Lizanka's.

'Kiss him, Arkady,' he said handing Petya to him, and without touching the ground the boy was transferred to Arkady Ivanovitch's powerful and eager arms.

'Will you have some breakfast, dear?'

'Thank you, very much. We have had it already, we got up early today; the others have gone to church. Sister was two hours curling my hair, and pomading it, washing me and mending my trousers, for I tore them yesterday, playing with Sashka in the street; we were snowballing.'

'Well, well, well!'

'So she dressed me up to come and see you, and then pomaded my head and then gave me a regular kissing. She said: "Go to Vasya, wish him a happy New Year, and ask whether they are happy, whether they had a good night, and . . . " to ask something else – oh yes! whether you had finished the work you spoke of yesterday . . . when you were there. Oh, I've got it all written down,' said the boy, reading from a slip of paper which he took out of his pocket. 'Yes, they were uneasy.'

'It will be finished! It will be! Tell her that it will be. I shall finish it, on my word of honour!'

'And something else . . . Oh yes, I forgot. Sister sent a little note and a present, and I was forgetting it! . . . '

'My goodness! Oh, you little darling! Where is it? where is it? That's it, oh! Look, brother, see what she writes. The darling, the precious! You know I saw there yesterday a paper-case for me; it's not finished, so she says, "I am sending you a lock of my hair, and the other will come later." Look, brother, look!'

And overwhelmed with rapture he showed Arkady Ivanovitch a curl of luxuriant, jet-black hair; then he kissed it fervently and put it in his breast pocket, nearest his heart.

'Vasya, I shall get you a locket for that curl,' Arkady Ivanovitch said resolutely at last.

'And we are going to have hot veal, and tomorrow brains. Mamma wants to make cakes . . . but we are not going to have millet porridge,' said the boy, after a moment's thought, to wind up his budget of interesting items.

'Oh! what a pretty boy,' cried Arkady Ivanovitch. 'Vasya, you are the happiest of mortals.'

The boy finished his tea, took from Vasya a note, a thousand kisses, and went out happy and frolicsome as before.

'Well, brother,' began Arkady Ivanovitch, highly delighted, 'you see how splendid it all is; you see. Everything is going well, don't be downcast, don't be uneasy. Go ahead! Get it done, Vasya, get it done. I'll be home at two o'clock. I'll go round to them, and then to Yulian Mastakovitch.'

'Well, goodbye, brother; goodbye . . . Oh! if only . . . Very good, you go, very good,' said Vasya, 'then I really won't go to Yulian Mastakovitch.'

'Goodbye.'

'Stay, brother, stay, tell them . . . well, whatever you think fit. Kiss her . . . and give me a full account of everything afterwards.'

'Come, come – of course, I know all about it. This happiness has upset you. The suddenness of it all; you've not been yourself since yesterday. You have not got over the excitement of yesterday. Well, it's settled. Now try and get over it, Vasya. Goodbye, goodbye!'

At last the friends parted. All the morning Arkady Ivanovitch was preoccupied, and could think of nothing but Vasya. He knew his weak, highly nervous character. 'Yes, this happiness has upset him, I was right there,' he said to himself. 'Upon my word, he has made me quite depressed, too, that man will make a tragedy of anything! What a feverish creature! Oh, I must save him! I must save him!' said Arkady, not noticing that he himself was exaggerating into something serious a slight trouble, in reality quite trivial. Only at eleven o'clock he reached the porter's lodge of Yulian Mastakovitch's house, to add his modest name to the long list of illustrious persons who had written their names on a sheet of blotted and scribbled paper in the porter's lodge. What was his surprise when he saw just above his own the signature of Vasya Shumkov! It amazed him. 'What's the matter with him?' he thought. Arkady Ivanovitch, who had just been so buoyant with hope, came out feeling upset. There was certainly going to be trouble, but how? And in what form?

He reached the Artemyevs with gloomy forebodings; he seemed absent-minded from the first, and after talking a little with Lizanka went away with tears in his eyes; he was really anxious about Vasya. He went home running, and on the Neva came full tilt upon Vasya himself. The latter, too, was uneasy.

'Where are you going?' cried Arkady Ivanovitch.

Vasya stopped as though he had been caught in a crime.

'Oh, it's nothing, brother, I wanted to go for a walk.'

'You could not stand it, and have been to the Artemyevs? Oh, Vasya, Vasya! Why did you go to Yulian Mastakovitch?'

Vasya did not answer, but then with a wave of his hand, he said: 'Arkady, I don't know what is the matter with me. I . . . '

'Come, come, Vasya. I know what it is. Calm yourself. You've been excited and overwrought ever since yesterday. Only think, it's not much to bear. Everybody's fond of you, everybody's ready to do anything for you; your work is getting on all right; you will get it done, you will certainly get it done. I know that you have been imagining something, you have had apprehensions about something . . . '

'No, it's all right, it's all right . . . '

'Do you remember, Vasya, do you remember it was the same with you once before; do you remember, when you got your promotion, in your joy and thankfulness you were so zealous that you spoilt all your work for a week? It is just the same with you now.'

'Yes, yes, Arkady; but now it is different, it is not that at all.'

'How is it different? And very likely the work is not urgent at all, while you are killing yourself . . . '

'It's nothing, it's nothing. I am all right, it's nothing. Well, come along!'

'Why, are you going home, and not to them?'

'Yes, brother, how could I have the face to turn up there? . . . I have changed my mind. It was only that I could not stay on alone without you; now you are coming back with me I'll sit down to write again. Let us go!'

They walked along and for some time were silent. Vasya was in haste.

'Why don't you ask me about them?' said Arkady Ivanovitch.

'Oh, yes! Well, Arkasha, what about them?'

'Vasya, you are not like yourself.'

'Oh, I am all right, I am all right. Tell me everything, Arkasha,' said Vasya, in an imploring voice, as though to avoid further explanations. Arkady Ivanovitch sighed. He felt utterly at a loss, looking at Vasya.

His account of their friends roused Vasya. He even grew talkative. They had dinner together. Lizanka's mother had filled Arkady Ivanovitch's pockets with little cakes, and eating them the friends grew more cheerful. After dinner Vasya promised to take a nap, so as to sit up all night. He did, in fact, lie down. In the morning, someone whom it was impossible to refuse had invited Arkady Ivanovitch to tea. The friends parted. Arkady promised to come back as soon as he could, by eight o'clock if possible. The three hours of separation seemed to him like three years. At last he got away and rushed back to Vasya. When he went into the room, he found it in darkness. Vasya was not at home. He asked Mavra. Mavra said that he had been writing all the time, and had not slept at all, then he had paced up and down the room, and after that, an hour before, he had run out, saying he would be back in half an hour; 'and when, says he, Arkady Ivanovitch comes in, tell him, old woman, says he,' Mavra told him in conclusion, 'that I have gone out for a walk,' and he repeated the order three or four times.

'He is at the Artemyevs,' thought Arkady Ivanovitch, and he shook his head.

A minute later he jumped up with renewed hope.

'He has simply finished,' he thought, 'that's all it is; he couldn't wait, but ran off there. But, no! he would have waited for me . . . Let's have a peep at what he has there.'

He lighted a candle, and ran to Vasya's writing-table: the work had made progress and it looked as though there were not much left to do. Arkady Ivanovitch was about to investigate further, when Vasya himself walked in . . . 'Oh, you are here?' he cried, with a start of dismay.

Arkady Ivanovitch was silent. He was afraid to question Vasya. The latter dropped his eyes and remained silent too, as he began sorting the papers. At last their eyes met. The look in Vasya's was so beseeching, imploring and broken, that Arkady shuddered when he saw it. His heart quivered and was full.

'Vasya, my dear boy, what is it? What's wrong?' he cried, rushing to him and squeezing him in his arms. 'Explain to me, I don't understand you, and your depression. What is the matter with you, my poor, tormented boy? What is it? Tell me all about it, without hiding anything. It can't be only this – '

Vasya held him tight and could say nothing. He could scarcely breathe.

'Don't, Vasya, don't! Well, if you don't finish it, what then? I don't understand you; tell me your trouble. You see it is for your sake I . . . Oh dear! oh dear!' he said, walking up and down the room and clutching at everything he came across, as though seeking at once some remedy for Vasya. 'I will go to Yulian Mastakovitch instead of you tomorrow. I will ask him – entreat him – to let you have another day. I will explain it all to him, anything, if it worries you so . . . '

'God forbid!' cried Vasya, and turned as white as the wall. He could scarcely stand on his feet.

'Vasya! Vasya!'

Vasya pulled himself together. His lips were quivering; he tried to say something, but could only convulsively squeeze Arkady's hand in silence. His hand was cold. Arkady stood facing him, full of anxious and miserable suspense. Vasya raised his eyes again.

'Vasya, God bless you, Vasya! You wring my heart, my dear boy, my friend.'

Tears gushed from Vasya's eyes; he flung himself on Arkady's bosom.

'I have deceived you, Arkady,' he said. 'I have deceived you. Forgive me, forgive me! I have been faithless to your friendship . . .'

'What is it, Vasya? What is the matter?' asked Arkady, in real alarm. 'Look!'

And with a gesture of despair Vasya tossed out of the drawer on to the table six thick manuscripts, similar to the one he had copied.

'What's this?'

'What I have to get through by the day after tomorrow. I haven't done a quarter! Don't ask me, don't ask me how it has happened,' Vasya went on, speaking at once of what was distressing him so terribly. 'Arkady, dear friend, I don't know myself what came over me. I feel as though I were coming out of a dream. I have wasted three weeks doing nothing. I kept . . . I . . . kept going to see her . . . My heart was aching, I was tormented by . . . the uncertainty . . . I could not write. I did not even think about it. Only now, when happiness is at hand for me, I have come to my senses.'

'Vasya,' began Arkady Ivanovitch resolutely, 'Vasya, I will save you. I understand it all. It's a serious matter; I will save you. Listen! listen to me: I will go to Yulian Mastakovitch tomorrow . . . Don't shake your head; no, listen! I will tell him exactly how it has all been; let me do that . . . I will explain to him . . . I will go into everything. I will tell him how crushed you are, how you are worrying yourself.'

'Do you know that you are killing me now?' Vasya brought out, turning cold with horror.

Arkady Ivanovitch turned pale, but at once controlling himself, laughed.

'Is that all? Is that all?' he said. 'Upon my word, Vasya, upon my word! Aren't you ashamed? Come, listen! I see that I am grieving you. You see I understand you; I know what is passing in your heart. Why, we have been living together for five years, thank God! You are such a kind, soft-hearted fellow, but weak, unpardonably weak. Why, even Lizaveta

Mikalovna has noticed it. And you are a dreamer, and that's a bad thing, too; you may go from bad to worse, brother. I tell you, I know what you want! You would like Yulian Mastakovitch, for instance, to be beside himself and, maybe, to give a ball, too, from joy, because you are going to get married . . . Stop, stop! you are frowning. You see that at one word from me you are offended on Yulian Mastakovitch's account. I'll let him alone. You know I respect him just as much as you do. But argue as you may, you can't prevent my thinking that you would like there to be no one unhappy in the whole world when you are getting married . . . Yes, brother, you must admit that you would like me, for instance, your best friend, to come in for a fortune of a hundred thousand all of a sudden, you would like all the enemies in the world to be suddenly, for no rhyme or reason, reconciled, so that in their joy they might all embrace one another in the middle of the street, and then, perhaps, come here to call on you. Vasya, my dear boy, I am not laughing; it is true; you've said as much to me long ago, in different ways. Because you are happy, you want everyone, absolutely everyone, to become happy at once. It hurts you and troubles you to be happy alone. And so you want at once to do your utmost to be worthy of that happiness, and maybe to do some great deed to satisfy your conscience. Oh! I understand how ready you are to distress yourself for having suddenly been remiss just where you ought to have shown your zeal, your capacity . . . well, maybe your gratitude, as you say. It is very bitter for you to think that Yulian Mastakovitch may frown and even be angry when he sees that you have not justified the expectations he had of you. It hurts you to think that you may hear reproaches from the man you look upon as your benefactor – and at such a moment! when your heart is full of joy and you don't know on whom to lavish your gratitude . . . Isn't that true? It is, isn't it?'

Arkady Ivanovitch, whose voice was trembling, paused, and drew a deep breath.

Vasya looked affectionately at his friend. A smile passed over his lips. His face even lighted up, as though with a gleam of hope.

'Well, listen, then,' Arkady Ivanovitch began again, growing more hopeful, 'there's no necessity that you should forfeit Yulian Mastakovitch's favour . . . Is there, dear boy? Is there any question of it? And since it is so,' said Arkady, jumping up, 'I shall sacrifice myself for you. I am going tomorrow to Yulian Mastakovitch, and don't oppose me. You magnify your failure to a crime, Vasya. Yulian Mastakovitch is magnanimous and merciful, and, what is more, he is not like you. He will listen to you and me, and get us out of our trouble, brother Vasya. Well, are you calmer?'

Vasya pressed his friend's hands with tears in his eyes.

'Hush, hush, Arkady,' he said, 'the thing is settled. I haven't finished, so very well; if I haven't finished, I haven't finished, and there's no need for you to go. I will tell him all about it, I will go myself. I am calmer now, I am perfectly calm; only you mustn't go . . . But listen . . .'

'Vasya, my dear boy,' Arkady Ivanovitch cried joyfully, 'I judged from what you said. I am glad that you have thought better of things and have recovered yourself. But whatever may befall you, whatever happens, I am with you, remember that. I see that it worries you to think of my speaking to Yulian Mastakovitch – and I won't say a word, not a word, you shall tell him yourself. You see, you shall go tomorrow . . . Oh no, you had better not go, you'll go on writing here, you see, and I'll find out about this work, whether it is very urgent or not, whether it must be done by the time or not, and if you don't finish it in time what will come of it. Then I will run back to you. Do you see, do you see! There is still hope; suppose the work is not urgent – it may be all right. Yulian Mastakovitch may not remember, then all is saved.'

Vasya shook his head doubtfully. But his grateful eyes never left his friend's face.

'Come, that's enough, I am so weak, so tired,' he said, sighing. 'I don't want to think about it. Let us talk of something else. I won't write either now; do you know I'll only finish two short pages just to get to the end of a passage. Listen . . . I have long wanted to ask you, how is it you know me so well?'

Tears dropped from Vasya's eyes on Arkady's hand.

'If you knew, Vasya, how fond I am of you, you would not ask that – yes!'

'Yes, yes, Arkady, I don't know that, because I don't know why you are so fond of me. Yes, Arkady, do you know, even your love has been killing me? Do you know, ever so many times, particularly when I am thinking of you in bed (for I always think of you when I am falling asleep), I shed tears, and my heart throbs at the thought . . . at the thought . . . Well, at the thought that you are so fond of me, while I can do nothing to relieve my heart, can do nothing to repay you.'

'You see, Vasya, you see what a fellow you are! Why, how upset you are now,' said Arkady, whose heart ached at that moment and who remembered the scene in the street the day before.

'Nonsense, you want me to be calm, but I never have been so calm and happy! Do you know . . . Listen, I want to tell you all about it, but I am afraid of wounding you . . . You keep scolding me and being vexed; and I am afraid . . . See how I am trembling now, I don't know why. You see, this is what I want to say. I feel as though I had never known myself before – yes! Yes, I only began to understand other people too, yesterday. I did not feel or appreciate things fully, brother. My heart . . . was hard . . . Listen how has it happened, that I have never done good to anyone, anyone in the world, because I couldn't – I am not even pleasant to look at . . . But everybody does me good! You, to begin with: do you suppose I don't see that? Only I said nothing; only I said nothing.'

'Hush, Vasya!'

'Oh, Arkasha! . . . it's all right,' Vasya interrupted, hardly able to articulate for tears. 'I talked to you yesterday about Yulian Masta-kovitch. And you know yourself how stern and severe he is, even you have come in for a reprimand from him; yet he deigned to jest with me yesterday, to show his affection and kind-heartedness, which he prudently conceals from everyone . . . '

'Come, Vasya, that only shows you deserve your good fortune.'

'Oh, Arkasha! How I longed to finish all this . . . No, I shall ruin my good luck! I feel that! Oh no, not through that,' Vasya added, seeing that Arkady glanced at the heap of urgent work lying on the table, 'that's nothing, that's only paper covered with writing . . . it's nonsense! That matter's settled . . . I went to see them today, Arkasha; I did not go in. I felt depressed and sad. I simply stood at the door. She was playing the piano, I listened. You see, Arkady,' he went on, dropping his voice, 'I did not dare to go in.'

'I say, Vasya – what is the matter with you? You look at one so strangely.'

'Oh, it's nothing, I feel a little sick; my legs are trembling; it's because I sat up last night. Yes! Everything looks green before my eyes. It's here, here – '

He pointed to his heart. He fainted. When he came to himself Arkady tried to take forcible measures. He tried to compel him to go to bed. Nothing would induce Vasya to consent. He shed tears, wrung his hands, wanted to write, was absolutely set on finishing his two pages. To avoid exciting him Arkady let him sit down to the work.

'Do you know,' said Vasya, as he settled himself in his place, 'an idea has occurred to me? There is hope.'

He smiled to Arkady, and his pale face lighted up with a gleam of hope.

'I will take him what is done the day after tomorrow. About the rest I will tell a lie. I will say it has been burnt, that it has been sopped in water, that I have lost it . . . That, in fact, I have not finished it; I cannot lie. I will explain, do you know, what? I'll explain to him all about it. I will tell him how it was that I could not. I'll tell him about my love; he has got married himself just lately, he'll understand me. I will do it all, of course, respectfully, quietly; he will see my tears and be touched by them . . . '

'Yes, of course, you must go, you must go and explain to him . . . But there's no need of tears! Tears for what? Really, Vasya, you quite scare me.'

'Yes, I'll go, I'll go. But now let me write, let me write, Arkasha. I am not interfering with anyone, let me write!'

Arkady flung himself on the bed. He had no confidence in Vasya, no confidence at all. 'Vasya was capable of anything, but to ask forgiveness for what? how? That was not the point. The point was that Vasya had not carried out his obligations, that Vasya felt guilty *in his own eyes*, felt that he was ungrateful to destiny, that Vasya was crushed, overwhelmed by happiness and thought himself unworthy of it; that, in fact, he was simply trying to find an excuse to go off his head on that point, and that he had not recovered from the unexpectedness of what had happened the day before; that's what it is,' thought Arkady Ivanovitch. 'I must save him. I must reconcile him to himself. He will be his own ruin.' He thought and thought, and resolved to go at once next day to Yulian Mastakovitch, and to tell him all about it.

Vasya was sitting writing. Arkady Ivanovitch, worn out, lay down to think things over again, and only woke at daybreak.

'Damnation! Again!' he cried, looking at Vasya; the latter was still sitting writing.

Arkady rushed up to him, seized him and forcibly put him to bed. Vasya was smiling: his eyes were closing with sleep. He could hardly speak.

'I wanted to go to bed,' he said. 'Do you know, Arkady, I have an idea; I shall finish. I made my pen go faster! I could not have sat at it any longer; wake me at eight o'clock.'

Without finishing his sentence, he dropped asleep and slept like the dead.

'Mavra,' said Arkady Ivanovitch to Mavra, who came in with the tea, 'he asked to be waked in an hour. Don't wake him on any account! Let him sleep ten hours, if he can. Do you understand?'

'I understand, sir.'

'Don't get the dinner, don't bring in the wood, don't make a noise or it will be the worse for you. If he asks for me, tell him I have gone to the office – do you understand?'

'I understand, bless you, sir; let him sleep and welcome! I am glad my gentlemen should sleep well, and I take good care of their things. And about that cup that was broken, and you blamed me, your honour, it wasn't me, it was poor pussy broke it, I ought to have kept an eye on her. "S-sh, you confounded thing," I said.'

'Hush, be quiet, be quiet!'

Arkady Ivanovitch followed Mavra out into the kitchen, asked for the key and locked her up there. Then he went to the office. On the way he considered how he could present himself before Yulian Mastakovitch, and whether it would be appropriate and not impertinent. He went into the office timidly, and timidly enquired whether his excellency were there; receiving the answer that he was not and would not be, Arkady Ivanovitch instantly thought of going to his flat, but reflected very prudently that if Yulian Mastakovitch had not come to the office he would certainly be busy at home. He remained. The hours seemed to him endless. Indirectly he enquired about the work entrusted to Shumkov, but no one knew anything about this. All that was known was that Yulian Mastakovitch did employ him on special jobs, but what they were – no one could say. At last it struck three o'clock, and Arkady Ivanovitch rushed out, eager to get home. In the vestibule he was met by a clerk, who told him that Vassily Petrovitch Shumkov had come about one o'clock and asked, the clerk went on, 'whether you were here, and whether Yulian Mastakovitch had been here'. Hearing this Arkady Ivanovitch took a sledge and hastened home, beside himself with alarm.

Shumkov was at home. He was walking about the room in violent excitement. Glancing at Arkady Ivanovitch, he immediately controlled himself, reflected, and hastened to conceal his emotion. He sat down to his papers without a word. He seemed to avoid his friend's questions, seemed to be bothered by them, to be pondering to himself on some plan, and deciding to conceal his decision, because he could not reckon further on his friend's affection. This struck Arkady, and his heart ached with a poignant and oppressive pain. He sat on the bed and began turning over the leaves of some book, the only one he had in his possession, keeping his eye on poor Vasya. But Vasya remained obstinately silent, writing and not raising his head. So passed several hours, and Arkady's misery reached an extreme point. At last, at eleven o'clock, Vasya lifted his head and looked with a fixed, vacant stare at Arkady. Arkady waited. Two or three minutes passed; Vasya did not speak.

'Vasya!' cried Arkady.

Vasya made no answer.

'Vasya!' he repeated, jumping up from the bed, 'Vasya, what is the matter with you? What is it?' he cried, running up to him.

Vasya raised his eyes and again looked at him with the same vacant, fixed stare.

'He's in a trance!' thought Arkady, trembling all over with fear. He seized a bottle of water, raised Vasya, poured some water on his head, moistened his temples, rubbed his hands in his own – and Vasya came to himself. 'Vasya, Vasya!' cried Arkady, unable to restrain his tears. 'Vasya, save yourself, rouse yourself, rouse yourself! . . . ' He could say no more, but held him tight in his arms. A look as of some oppressive sensation passed over Vasya's face; he rubbed his forehead and clutched at his head, as though he were afraid it would burst.

'I don't know what is the matter with me,' he said, at last. 'I feel torn to pieces. Come, it's all right, it's all right! Give over, Arkady; don't grieve,' he repeated, looking at him with sad, exhausted eyes. 'Why be so anxious? Come!'

'You, you comforting me!' cried Arkady, whose heart was torn. 'Vasya,' he said at last, 'lie down and have a little nap, won't you? Don't wear yourself out for nothing! You'll set to work better afterwards.'

'Yes, yes,' said Vasya, 'by all means, I'll lie down, very good. Yes! you see I meant to finish, but now I've changed my mind, yes . . . '

And Arkady led him to the bed.

'Listen, Vasya,' he said firmly, 'we must settle this matter finally. Tell me what were you thinking about?'

'Oh!' said Vasya, with a flourish of his weak hand turning over on the other side.

'Come, Vasya, come, make up your mind. I don't want to hurt you. I can't be silent any longer. You won't sleep till you've made up your mind, I know.'

'As you like, as you like,' Vasya repeated enigmatically.

'He will give in,' thought Arkady Ivanovitch.

'Attend to me, Vasya,' he said, 'remember what I say, and I will save you tomorrow; tomorrow I will decide your fate! What am I saying, your fate? You have so frightened me, Vasya, that I am using your own words. Fate, indeed! It's simply nonsense, rubbish! You don't want to lose Yulian Mastakovitch's favour – affection, if you like. No! And you won't lose it, you will see. I – '

Arkady Ivanovitch would have said more, but Vasya interrupted him. He sat up in bed, put both arms round Arkady Ivanovitch's neck and kissed him.

'Enough,' he said in a weak voice, 'enough! Say no more about that!'

And again he turned his face to the wall.

'My goodness!' thought Arkady, 'my goodness! What is the matter with him? He is utterly lost. What has he in his mind! He will be his own undoing.'

Arkady looked at him in despair.

'If he were to fall ill,' thought Arkady, 'perhaps it would be better. His trouble would pass off with illness, and that might be the best way of settling the whole business. But what nonsense I am talking. Oh, my God!'

Meanwhile Vasya seemed to be asleep. Arkady Ivanovitch was relieved. 'A good sign,' he thought. He made up his mind to sit beside him all night. But Vasya was restless; he kept twitching and tossing about on the bed, and opening his eyes for an instant. At last exhaustion got the upper hand, he slept like the dead. It was about two o'clock in the morning, Arkady Ivanovitch began to doze in the chair with his elbow on the table!

He had a strange and agitated dream. He kept fancying that he was not asleep, and that Vasya was still lying on the bed. But strange to say, he fancied that Vasya was pretending, that he was deceiving him, that he was getting up, stealthily watching him out of the corner of his eye, and was stealing up to the writing table. Arkady felt a scalding pain at his heart; he felt vexed and sad and oppressed to see Vasya not trusting him, hiding and concealing himself from him. He tried to catch hold of him, to call out, to carry him to the bed. Then Vasya kept shrieking in his arms, and he laid on the bed a lifeless corpse. He opened his eyes and woke up; Vasya was sitting before him at the table, writing.

Hardly able to believe his senses, Arkady glanced at the bed; Vasya was not there. Arkady jumped up in a panic, still under the influence of his dream. Vasya did not stir; he went on writing. All at once Arkady noticed with horror that Vasya was moving a dry pen over the paper, was turning over perfectly blank pages, and hurrying, hurrying to fill up the paper as though he were doing his work in a most thorough and efficient way. 'No, this is not a trance,' thought Arkady Ivanovitch, and he trembled all over.

'Vasya, Vasya, speak to me,' he cried, clutching him by the shoulder. But Vasya did not speak; he went on as before, scribbling with a dry pen over the paper.

'At last I have made the pen go faster,' he said, without looking up at Arkady.

Arkady seized his hand and snatched away the pen.

A moan broke from Vasya. He dropped his hand and raised his eyes to Arkady; then with an air of misery and exhaustion he passed his hand over his forehead as though he wanted to shake off some leaden weight that was pressing upon his whole being, and slowly, as though lost in thought, he let his head sink on his breast.

'Vasya, Vasya!' cried Arkady in despair. 'Vasya!'

A minute later Vasya looked at him, tears stood in his large blue eyes, and his pale, mild face wore a look of infinite suffering. He whispered something.

'What, what is it?' cried Arkady, bending down to him.

'What for, why are they doing it to me?' whispered Vasya. 'What for? What have I done?'

'Vasya, what is it? What are you afraid of? What is it?' cried Arkady, wringing his hands in despair.

'Why are they sending me for a soldier?' said Vasya, looking his friend straight in the face. 'Why is it? What have I done?'

Arkady's hair stood on end with horror; he refused to believe his ears. He stood over him, half dead.

A minute later he pulled himself together. 'It's nothing, it's only for the minute,' he said to himself, with pale face and blue, quivering lips, and he hastened to put on his outdoor things. He meant to run straight for a doctor. All at once Vasya called to him. Arkady rushed to him and clasped him in his arms like a mother whose child is being torn from her.

'Arkady, Arkady, don't tell anyone! Don't tell anyone, do you hear? It is my trouble, I must bear it alone.'

'What is it – what is it? Rouse yourself, Vasya, rouse yourself!'

Vasya sighed, and slow tears trickled down his cheeks.

'Why kill her? How is she to blame?' he muttered in an agonised, heart-rending voice. 'The sin is mine, the sin is mine!'

He was silent for a moment.

'Farewell, my love! Farewell, my love!' he whispered, shaking his luckless head. Arkady started, pulled himself together and would have rushed for the doctor. 'Let us go, it is time,' cried Vasya, carried away by Arkady's last movement. 'Let us go, brother, let us go; I am ready. You lead the way.' He paused and looked at Arkady with a downcast and mistrustful face.

'Vasya, for goodness' sake, don't follow me! Wait for me here. I will come back to you directly, directly,' said Arkady Ivanovitch, losing his head and snatching up his cap to run for a doctor. Vasya sat down at once, he was quiet and docile; but there was a gleam of some desperate resolution in his eye. Arkady turned back, snatched up from the table an open penknife, looked at the poor fellow for the last time, and ran out of the flat.

It was eight o'clock. It had been broad daylight for some time in the room.

He found no one. He was running about for a full hour. All the doctors whose addresses he had got from the house porter, when he enquired of the latter whether there were no doctor living in the building, had gone out, either to their work or on their private affairs. There was one who saw patients. This one questioned at length and in detail the servant who announced that Nefedevitch had called, asking him who it was, from whom he came, what was the matter, and concluded by saying that he could not go, that he had a great deal to do, and that patients of that kind ought to be taken to a hospital.

Then Arkady, exhausted, agitated and utterly taken aback by this turn of affairs, cursed all the doctors on earth, and rushed home in the utmost alarm about Vasya. He ran into the flat. Mavra, as though there were nothing the matter, went on scrubbing the floor, breaking up wood and preparing to light the stove. He went into the room; there was no trace of Vasya, he had gone out.

'Which way? Where? Where will the poor fellow be off to?' thought Arkady, frozen with terror. He began questioning Mavra. She knew nothing, had neither seen nor heard him go out, God bless him! Nefedevitch rushed off to the Artemyevs'.

It occurred to him for some reason that he must be there.

It was ten o'clock by the time he arrived. They did not expect him, knew nothing and had heard nothing. He stood before them frightened, distressed, and asked where was Vasya? The mother's legs gave way under her; she sank back on the sofa. Lizanka, trembling with alarm, began asking what had happened. What could he say? Arkady Ivanovitch got out of it as best he could, invented some tale which of course was not believed, and fled, leaving them distressed and anxious. He flew to his department that he might not be too late there, and he let them know that steps might be taken at once. On the way it occurred to him that Vasya would be at Yulian Mastakovitch's. That was more likely than anything: Arkady had thought of that first of all, even before the Artemyevs'. As he drove by his excellency's door, he thought of stopping, but at once told the driver to go straight on. He made up his mind to try and find out whether anything had happened at the office, and if he were not there to go to his excellency, ostensibly to report on Vasya. Someone must be informed of it.

As soon as he got into the waiting-room he was surrounded by fellow-clerks, for the most part young men of his own standing in the service. With one voice they began asking him what had happened to Vasya? At the same time they all told him that Vasya had gone out of his mind, and thought that he was to be sent for a soldier as a punishment for having neglected his work. Arkady Ivanovitch, answering them in all directions, or rather avoiding giving a direct answer to anyone, rushed into the inner room. On the way he learned that Vasya was in Yulian Mastakovitch's private room, that everyone had been there and that Esper Ivanovitch had gone in there too. He was stopped on the way. One of the senior clerks asked him who he was and what he wanted? Without distinguishing the person he said something about Vasya and went straight into the room. He heard Yulian Mastakovitch's voice from within. 'Where are you going?' someone asked him at the very door. Arkady Ivanovitch was almost in despair; he was on the point of turning back, but through the open door he saw his poor Vasya. He pushed the door and squeezed his way into the room. Everyone seemed to be in confusion and perplexity, because Yulian Mastakovitch was apparently much chagrined. All the more important personages were standing about him talking, and coming to no decision. At a little distance stood Vasya. Arkady's heart sank when he looked at him. Vasya was standing, pale, with his head up, stiffly erect, like a recruit before a new officer, with his feet together and his hands held rigidly at his sides. He was looking Yulian Mastakovitch straight in the face.

Arkady was noticed at once, and someone who knew that they lodged together mentioned the fact to his excellency. Arkady was led up to him. He tried to make some answer to the questions put to him, glanced at Yulian Mastakovitch and seeing on his face a look of genuine compassion, began trembling and sobbing like a child. He even did more, he snatched his excellency's hand and held it to his eyes, wetting it with his tears, so that Yulian Mastakovitch was obliged to draw it hastily away, and waving it in the air, said, 'Come, my dear fellow, come! I see you have a good heart.' Arkady sobbed and turned an imploring look on everyone. It seemed to him that they were all brothers of his dear Vasya, that they were all worried and weeping about him. 'How, how has it happened? How has it happened?' asked Yulian Mastakovitch. 'What has sent him out of his mind?'

'Gra-gra-gratitude!' was all Arkady Ivanovitch could articulate.

Everyone heard his answer with amazement, and it seemed strange and incredible to everyone that a man could go out of his mind from gratitude. Arkady explained as best he could.

'Good heavens! what a pity!' said Yulian Mastakovitch at last. 'And the work entrusted to him was not important, and not urgent in the least. It was not worth while for a man to kill himself over it! Well, take him away!' ... At this point Yulian Mastakovitch turned to Arkady Ivanovitch again, and began questioning him once more. 'He begs,' he said, pointing to Vasya, 'that some girl should not be told of this. Who is she – his betrothed, I suppose?'

Arkady began to explain. Meanwhile Vasya seemed to be thinking of something, as though he were straining his memory to the utmost to recall some important, necessary matter, which was particularly wanted at this moment. From time to time he looked round with a distressed face, as though hoping someone would remind him of what he had forgotten. He fastened his eyes on Arkady. All of a sudden there was a gleam of hope in his eyes; he moved with the left leg forward, took three steps as smartly as he could, clicking with his right boot as soldiers do when they move forward at the call from their officer. Everyone was waiting to see what would happen.

'I have a physical defect and am small and weak, and I am not fit for military service, your excellency,' he said abruptly.

At that everyone in the room felt a pang at his heart, and firm as was Yulian Mastakovitch's character, tears trickled from his eyes.

'Take him away,' he said, with a wave of his hands.

'Present!' said Vasya in an undertone; he wheeled round to the left and marched out of the room. All who were interested in his fate followed him out. Arkady pushed his way out behind the others. They made Vasya sit down in the waiting-room till the carriage came which had been ordered to take him to the hospital. He sat down in silence and seemed in great anxiety. He nodded to anyone he recognised as though saying goodbye. He looked round towards the door every minute, and prepared himself to set off when he should be told it was time. People crowded in a close circle round him; they were all shaking their heads and lamenting. Many of them were much impressed by his story, which had suddenly become known. Some discussed his illness, while others expressed their pity and high opinion of Vasya, saying that he was such a quiet, modest young man, that he had been so promising; people described what efforts he had made to learn, how eager he was for knowledge, how he had worked to educate himself. 'He had risen by his own efforts from a humble position,' someone observed. They spoke with emotion of his excellency's affection for him. Some of them fell to explaining why Vasya was possessed by the idea that he was being sent for a soldier, because he had not finished his work. They said that the poor fellow had lately belonged to the class liable for military service and had only received his first grade through the good offices of Yulian Mastakovitch, who had had the cleverness to discover his talent, his docility and the rare mildness of his disposition. In fact, there was a great number of views and theories.

A very short fellow-clerk of Vasya's was conspicuous as being particularly distressed. He was not very young, probably about thirty. He was pale as a sheet, trembling all over and smiling queerly, perhaps because any scandalous affair or terrible scene both frightens, and at the same time somewhat rejoices the outside spectator. He kept running round the circle that surrounded Vasya, and as he was so short, stood on tiptoe and caught at the button of everyone – that is, of those with whom he felt entitled to take such a liberty – and kept saying that he knew how it had all happened, that it was not so simple, but a very important matter, that it couldn't be left without further enquiry; then stood on tiptoe again, whispered in someone's ear, nodded his head again two or three times, and ran round again. At last everything was over. The porter made his appearance, and an attendant from the hospital went up to Vasya and told him it was time to start. Vasya jumped up in a flutter and went with them, looking about him. He was looking about for someone.

'Vasya, Vasya!' cried Arkady Ivanovitch, sobbing. Vasya stopped, and Arkady squeezed his way up to him. They flung themselves into each other's arms in a last bitter embrace. It was sad to see them. What monstrous calamity was wringing the tears from their eyes! What were they weeping for? What was their trouble? Why did they not understand one another?

'Here, here, take it! Take care of it,' said Shumkov, thrusting a paper of some kind into Arkady's hand. 'They will take it away from me. Bring it me later on; bring it . . . take care of it . . . ' Vasya could not finish, they called to him. He ran hurriedly downstairs, nodding to everyone, saying goodbye to everyone. There was despair in his face. At last he was put in the carriage and taken away. Arkady made haste to open the paper: it was Liza's curl of black hair, from which Vasya had never parted. Hot tears gushed from Arkady's eyes: oh, poor Liza!

When office hours were over, he went to the Artemyevs'. There is no need to describe what happened there! Even Petya, little Petya, though he could not quite understand what had happened to dear Vasya, went into a corner, hid his face in his little hands, and sobbed in the fullness of his childish heart. It was quite dusk when Arkady returned home. When he reached the Neva he stood still for a minute and turned a keen glance up the river into the smoky frozen thickness of the distance, which was suddenly flushed crimson with the last purple and blood-red glow of sunset, still smouldering on the misty horizon . . . Night lay over the city, and the wide plain of the Neva, swollen with frozen snow, was shining in the last gleams of the sun with myriads of sparks of gleaming hoar frost. There was a frost of twenty degrees.[48] A cloud of frozen steam hung about the over-driven horses and the hurrying people. The condensed atmosphere quivered at the slightest sound, and from all the roofs on both sides of the river columns of smoke rose up like giants and floated across the cold sky, intertwining and untwining as they went, so that it seemed new buildings were rising up above the old, a new town was taking shape in the air . . . It seemed as if all that world, with all its inhabitants, strong and weak, with all their habitations, the refuges of the poor or the gilded palaces for the comfort of the powerful, was at that twilight hour like a fantastic vision of fairyland, like a dream which in its turn would vanish and pass away like vapour into the dark-blue sky. A strange thought came to poor Vasya's forlorn friend. He started, and his heart seemed at that instant flooded with a hot rush of blood kindled by a powerful, overwhelming sensation he had never known before. He seemed only now to understand all the trouble, and to know why his poor Vasya had gone out of his mind, unable to bear his happiness. His lips twitched, his eyes lighted up, he turned pale, and, as it were, had a clear vision into something new.

He became gloomy and depressed, and lost all his gaiety. His old lodging grew hateful to him – he took a new room. He did not care to visit the Artemyevs, and indeed he could not. Two years later he met Lizanka in church. She was by then married; beside her walked a wet nurse with a tiny baby. They greeted each other, and for a long time avoided all mention of the past. Liza said that, thank God, she was happy, that she was not badly off, that her husband was a kind man and that she was fond of him . . . But suddenly in the middle of a sentence her eyes filled with tears, her voice failed, she turned away, and bowed down to the church pavement to hide her grief.

Polzunkov

I BEGAN TO SCRUTINISE the man closely. Even in his exterior there was something so peculiar that it compelled one, however far away one's thoughts might be, to fix one's eyes upon him and go off into the most irrepressible roar of laughter. That is what happened to me. I must observe that the little man's eyes were so mobile, or perhaps he was so sensitive to the magnetism of every eye fixed upon him, that he almost by instinct guessed that he was being observed, turned at once to the observer and anxiously analysed his expression. His continual mobility, his turning and twisting, made him look strikingly like a dancing doll. It was strange! He seemed afraid of jeers, in spite of the fact that he was almost getting his living by being a buffoon for all the world, and exposed himself to every buffet in a moral sense and even in a physical one, judging from the company he was in. Voluntary buffoons are not even to be pitied. But I noticed at once that this strange creature, this ridiculous man, was by no means a buffoon by profession. There was still something gentlemanly in him. His very uneasiness, his continual apprehensiveness about himself, were actually a testimony in his favour. It seemed to me that his desire to be obliging was due more to kindness of heart than to mercenary considerations. He readily allowed them to laugh their loudest at him and in the most unseemly way, to his face, but at the same time – and I am ready to take my oath on it – his heart ached and was sore at the thought that his listeners were so caddishly brutal as to be capable of laughing, not at anything said or done, but at him, at his whole being, at his heart, at his head, at his appearance, at his whole body, flesh and blood. I am convinced that he felt at that moment all the foolishness of his position; but the protest died away in his heart at once, though it invariably sprang up again in the most heroic way. I am convinced that all this was due to nothing else but a kind heart, and not to fear of the inconvenience of being kicked out and being unable to borrow money from someone. This gentleman was forever borrowing money, that is, he asked for alms in that form, when after playing the fool and entertaining them at his expense he felt in a certain sense entitled to borrow money from them. But, good heavens! what a business the borrowing was! And with what a countenance he asked for the loan! I could not have imagined that on such a small space as the wrinkled, angular face of that little man room could be found, at one and the same time, for so many different grimaces, for such strange, variously characteristic shades of feeling, such absolutely killing expressions. Everything was there – shame and an assumption of insolence, and vexation at the sudden flushing of his face, and anger and fear of failure, and entreaty to be forgiven for having dared to pester, and a sense of his own dignity, and a still greater sense of his own abjectness – all this passed over his face like lightning. For six whole years he had struggled along in God's world in this way, and so far had been unable to take up a fitting attitude at the interesting moment of borrowing money! I need not say that he never could grow callous and completely abject. His heart was too sensitive, too passionate! I will say more, indeed: in my opinion, he was one of the most honest and honourable men in the world, but with a little weakness: of being ready to do anything abject at anyone's bidding, good-naturedly and disinterestedly, simply to oblige a fellow-creature. In short, he was what is called 'a rag' in the fullest sense of the word. The most absurd thing was that he was dressed like anyone else, neither worse nor better, tidily, even with a certain elaborateness, and actually had pretentions to respectability and personal dignity. This external equality and internal inequality, his uneasiness about himself and at the same time his continual self-depreciation – all this was strikingly incongruous and provocative of laughter and pity. If he had been convinced in his heart (and in spite of his experience it did happen to him at moments to believe this) that his audience were the most good-natured people in the world, who were simply laughing at something amusing, and not at the sacrifice of his personal dignity, he would most readily have taken off his coat, put it on wrong side outwards, and have walked about the streets in that attire for the diversion of others and his own gratification. But equality he could never anyhow attain. Another trait: the queer fellow was proud, and even, by fits and starts, when it was not too risky, generous. It was worth seeing and hearing how he could sometimes, not sparing himself, consequently with pluck, almost with heroism, dispose of one of his patrons who had infuriated him to madness. But that was at moments . . . In short, he was a martyr in the fullest sense of the word, but the most useless and consequently the most comic martyr.

There was a general discussion going on among the guests. All at once I saw our queer friend jump upon his chair, and call out at the top of his voice, anxious for the exclusive attention of the company.

'Listen,' the master of the house whispered to me. 'He sometimes tells the most curious stories . . . Does he interest you?'

I nodded and squeezed myself into the group. The sight of a well-dressed gentleman jumping upon his chair and shouting at the top of his voice did, in fact, draw the attention of all. Many who did not know the queer fellow looked at one another in perplexity, the others roared with laughter.

'I knew Fedosey Nikolaitch. I ought to know Fedosey Nikolaitch better than anyone!' cried the queer fellow from his elevation. 'Gentlemen, allow me to tell you something. I can tell you a good story about Fedosey Nikolaitch! I know a story – exquisite!'

'Tell it, Osip Mihalitch, tell it.'

'Tell it.'

'Listen.'

'Listen, listen.'

'I begin; but, gentlemen, this is a peculiar story . . . '

'Very good, very good.'

'It's a comic story.'

'Very good, excellent, splendid. Get on!'

'It is an episode in the private life of your humble . . . '

'But why do you trouble yourself to announce that it's comic?'

'And even somewhat tragic!'

'Eh???!'

'In short, the story which it will afford you all pleasure to hear me now relate, gentlemen – the story, in consequence of which I have come into company so interesting and profitable . . . '

'No puns!'

'This story.'

'In short the story – make haste and finish the introduction. The story, which has its value,' a fair-haired young man with moustaches pronounced in a husky voice, dropping his hand into his coat pocket and, as though by chance, pulling out a purse instead of his handkerchief.

'The story, my dear sirs, after which I should like to see many of you in my place. And, finally, the story, in consequence of which I have not married.'

'Married! A wife! Polzunkov tried to get married!!'

'I confess I should like to see Madame Polzunkov.'

'Allow me to enquire the name of the would-be Madame Polzunkov,' piped a youth, making his way up to the storyteller.

'And so for the first chapter, gentlemen. It was just six years ago, in spring, the thirty-first of March – note the date, gentlemen – on the eve . . . '

'Of the first of April!' cried a young man with ringlets.

'You are extraordinarily quick at guessing. It was evening. Twilight was gathering over the district town of N—, the moon was about to float out . . . everything in proper style, in fact. And so in the very late twilight I, too, floated out of my poor lodging on the sly – after taking leave of my restricted[49] granny, now dead. Excuse me, gentlemen, for making use of such a fashionable expression, which I heard for the last time from Nikolay Nikolaitch. But my granny was indeed restricted: she was blind, dumb, deaf, stupid – everything you please . . . I confess I was in a tremor, I was prepared for great deeds; my heart was beating like a kitten's when some bony hand clutches it by the scruff of the neck.'

'Excuse me, Monsieur Polzunkov.'

'What do you want?'

'Tell it more simply; don't over-exert yourself, please!'

'All right,' said Osip Mihalitch, a little taken aback. 'I went into the house of Fedosey Nikolaitch (the house that he had bought). Fedosey Nikolaitch, as you know, is not a mere colleague, but the full-blown head of a department. I was announced, and was at once shown into the study. I can see it now; the room was dark, almost dark, but candles were not brought. Behold, Fedosey Nikolaitch walks in. There he and I were left in the darkness . . . '

'Whatever happened to you?' asked an officer.

'What do you suppose?' asked Polzunkov, turning promptly, with a convulsively working face, to the young man with ringlets. 'Well, gentlemen, a strange circumstance occurred, though indeed there was nothing strange in it: it was what is called an everyday affair – I simply took out of my pocket a roll of paper . . . and he a roll of paper.'

'Paper notes?'

'Paper notes; and we exchanged.'

'I don't mind betting that there's a flavour of bribery about it,' observed a respectably dressed, closely cropped young gentleman.

'Bribery!' Polzunkov caught him up.

> "Oh, may I be a Liberal,
> Such as many I have seen!"

If you, too, when it is your lot to serve in the provinces, do not warm your hands at your country's hearth . . . For as an author said: "Even the smoke of our native land is sweet to us."[50] She is our Mother, gentlemen, our Mother Russia; we are her babes, and so we suck her!'

There was a roar of laughter.

'Only would you believe it, gentlemen, I have never taken bribes?' said Polzunkov, looking round at the whole company distrustfully.

A prolonged burst of Homeric laughter[51] drowned Polzunkov's words in guffaws.

'It really is so, gentlemen . . . '

But here he stopped, still looking round at everyone with a strange expression of face; perhaps – who knows? – at that moment the thought came into his mind that he was more honest than many of all that honourable company . . . Anyway, the serious expression of his face did not pass away till the general merriment was quite over.

'And so,' Polzunkov began again when all was still, 'though I never did take bribes, yet that time I transgressed; I put in my pocket a bribe . . . from a bribe-taker . . . that is, there were certain papers in my hands which, if I had cared to send to a certain person, it would have gone ill with Fedosey Nikolaitch.'

'So then he bought them from you?'

'He did.'

'Did he give much?'

'He gave as much as many a man nowadays would sell his conscience for complete, with all its variations . . . if only he could get anything for it. But I felt as though I were scalded when I put the money in my pocket. I really don't understand what always comes over me, gentlemen – but I was more dead than alive, my lips twitched and my legs trembled; well, I was to blame, to blame, entirely to blame. I was utterly conscience-stricken; I was ready to beg Fedosey Nikolaitch's forgiveness.'

'Well, what did he do – did he forgive you?'

'But I didn't ask his forgiveness . . . I only mean that that is how I felt. Then I have a sensitive heart, you know. I saw he was looking me straight in the face. "Have you no fear of God, Osip Mihailitch?" said he. Well, what could I do? From a feeling of propriety I put my head on one side and I flung up my hands. "In what way," said I, "have I no fear of God, Fedosey Nikolaitch?" But I just said that from a feeling of propriety . . . I was ready to sink into the earth. "After being so long a friend of our family, after being, I may say, like a son – and who knows what heaven had in store for us, Osip Mihailitch? – and all of a sudden to inform against me – to think of that now! . . . What am I to think of mankind after that, Osip Mihailitch?" Yes, gentlemen, he did read me a lecture! "Come," he said, "you tell me what I am to think of mankind after that, Osip Mihailitch." "What is he to think?" I thought; and do you know, there was a lump in my throat, and my voice was quivering, and knowing my hateful weakness, I snatched up my hat. "Where are you off to, Osip Mihailitch? Surely on the eve of such a day you cannot bear malice against me? What wrong have I done you? . . . " "Fedosey Nikolaitch," I said, "Fedosey Nikolaitch . . . " In fact, I melted, gentlemen, I melted like a sugar-stick. And the roll of notes that was lying in my pocket, that, too, seemed screaming out: "You ungrateful brigand, you accursed thief!" It seemed to weigh a hundredweight . . . (if only it had weighed a hundredweight!) . . . "I see," says Fedosey Nikolaitch, "I see your penitence . . . you know tomorrow . . . " "St Mary of Egypt's day[52] . . . " "Well, don't weep," said Fedosey Nikolaitch, "that's enough: you've erred, and you are penitent! Come along! Maybe I may succeed in bringing you back again into the true path," says he . . . "maybe, my modest Penates"[53] (yes, "Penates", I remember he used that expression, the rascal) "will warm," says he, "your harden – I will not say hardened, but erring heart . . . " He took me by the arm, gentlemen, and led me to his family circle. A cold shiver ran down my back; I shuddered! I thought with what eyes shall I present myself – you must know, gentlemen . . . eh, what shall I say? – a delicate position had arisen here.'

'Not Madame Polzunkov?'

'Marya Fedosyevna, only she was not destined, you know, to bear the name you have given her; she did not attain that honour. Fedosey Nikolaitch was right, you see, when he said that I was almost looked upon as a son in the house; it had been so, indeed, six months before, when a certain retired junker[54] called Mihailo Maximitch Dvigailov was still living. But by God's will he died, and he put off settling his affairs till death settled his business for him.'

'Ough!'

'Well, never mind, gentlemen, forgive me, it was a slip of the tongue. It's a bad pun, but it doesn't matter it's being bad – what happened was far worse, when I was left, so to say, with nothing in prospect but a bullet through the brain, for that junker, though he would not admit me into his house (he lived in grand style, for he had always known how to feather his nest), yet perhaps correctly he believed me to be his son.'

'Aha!'

'Yes, that was how it was! So they began to cold-shoulder me at Fedosey Nikolaitch's. I noticed things, I kept quiet; but all at once, unluckily for me (or perhaps luckily!), a cavalry officer galloped into our little town like snow on our head. His business – buying horses for the army – was light and active, in cavalry style, but he settled himself solidly at Fedosey Nikolaitch's, as though he were laying siege to it!

I approached the subject in a roundabout way, as my nasty habit is; I said one thing and another, asking him what I had done to be treated so, saying that I was almost like a son to him, and when might I expect him to behave more like a father . . . Well, he began answering me. And when he begins to speak you are in for a regular epic in twelve cantos, and all you can do is to listen, lick your lips and throw up your hands in delight. And not a ha'p'orth of sense, at least there's no making out the sense. You stand puzzled like a fool – he puts you in a fog, he twists about like an eel and wriggles away from you. It's a special gift, a real gift – it's enough to frighten people even if it is no concern of theirs. I tried one thing and another, and went hither and thither. I took the lady songs and presented her with sweets and thought of witty things to say to her. I tried sighing and groaning. "My heart aches," I said, "it aches from love." And I went in for tears and secret explanations. Man is foolish, you know . . . I never reminded myself that I was thirty . . . not a bit of it! I tried all my arts. It was no go. It was a failure, and I gained nothing but jeers and gibes. I was indignant, I was choking with anger. I slunk off and would not set foot in the house. I thought and thought and made up my mind to denounce him. Well, of course, it was a shabby thing – I meant to give away a friend, I confess. I had heaps of material and splendid material – a grand case. It brought me fifteen hundred roubles when I changed it and my report on it for bank notes!'

'Ah, so that was the bribe!'

'Yes, sir, that was the bribe – and it was a bribe-taker who had to pay it – and I didn't do wrong, I can assure you! Well, now I will go on: he drew me, if you will kindly remember, more dead than alive into the room where they were having tea. They all met me, seeming as it were offended, that is, not exactly offended, but hurt – so hurt that it was simply . . . They seemed shattered, absolutely shattered, and at the same time there was a look of becoming dignity on their faces, a gravity in their expression, something fatherly, parental . . . the prodigal son[55] had come back to them – that's what it had come to! They made me sit down to tea, but there was no need to do that: I felt as though a samovar was toiling in my bosom and my feet were like ice. I was humbled, I was cowed. Marya Fominishna, his wife, addressed me familiarly from the first word.

' "How is it you have grown so thin, my boy?"

' "I've not been very well, Marya Fominishna," I said. My wretched voice shook.

'And then quite suddenly – she must have been waiting for a chance to get a dig at me, the old snake – she said: "I suppose your conscience felt ill at ease, Osip Mihalitch, my dear! Our fatherly hospitality was a reproach to you! You have been punished for the tears I have shed."

'Yes, upon my word, she really said that – she had the conscience to say it. Why, that was nothing to her, she was a terror! She did nothing but sit there and pour out tea. But if you were in the market, my darling, I thought you'd shout louder than any fishwife there . . . That's the kind of woman she was. And then, to my undoing, the daughter, Marya Fedosyevna, came in, in all her innocence, a little pale and her eyes red as though she had been weeping. I was bowled over on the spot like a fool. But it turned out afterwards that the tears were a tribute to the cavalry officer. He had made tracks for home and taken his hook for good and all; for you know it was high time for him to be off – I may as well mention the fact here; not that his leave was up precisely, but you see . . . It was only later that the loving parents grasped the position and had found out all that had happened . . . What could they do? They hushed their trouble up – an addition to the family!

'Well, I could not help it – as soon as I looked at her I was done for; I stole a glance at my hat, I wanted to get up and make off. But there was no chance of that, they took away my hat . . . I must confess, I did think of getting off without it. "Well!" I thought – but no, they latched the doors. There followed friendly jokes, winking, little airs and graces. I was overcome with embarrassment, said something stupid, talked nonsense about love. My charmer sat down to the piano and with an air of wounded feeling sang the song about the hussar who leaned upon the sword[56] – that finished me off!

' "Well," said Fedosey Nikolaitch, "all is forgotten, come to my arms!"

'I fell just as I was, with my face on his waistcoat.

' "My benefactor! You are a father to me!' said I. And I shed floods of hot tears. Lord, have mercy on us, what a to-do there was! He cried, his good lady cried, Mashenka cried . . . there was a flaxen-headed creature there, she cried too . . . That wasn't enough: the younger children crept out of all the corners (the Lord had filled their quiver full) and they howled too . . . Such tears, such emotion, such joy! They had found their prodigal, it was like a soldier's return to his home. Then followed refreshments, we played forfeits, and "I have a pain" – "Where is it?" – "In my heart" – "Who gave it you?" My charmer blushed. The old man and I had some punch – they won me over and did for me completely.

'I returned to my grandmother with my head in a whirl. I was laughing all the way home; for full two hours I paced up and down our little room. I waked up my old granny and told her of my happiness.

' "But did he give you any money, the brigand?"

' "He did, granny, he did, my dear – luck has come to us all of a heap: we've only to open our hand and take it."

'I woke up Sofron. "Sofron," I said, "take off my boots." Sofron pulled off my boots.

' "Come, Sofron, congratulate me now, give me a kiss! I am going to get married, my lad, I am going to get married. You can get jolly drunk tomorrow, you can have a spree, my dear soul – your master is getting married."

'My heart was full of jokes and laughter. I was beginning to drop off to sleep, but something made me get up again. I sat in thought: tomorrow is the first of April, a bright and playful day – what should I do? And I thought of something. Why, gentlemen, I got out of bed, lighted a candle, and sat down to the writing-table just as I was. I was in a fever of excitement, quite carried away – you know, gentlemen, what it is when a man is quite carried away? I wallowed joyfully in the mud, my dear friends. You see what I am like; they take something from you, and you give them something else as well and say, "Take that, too." They strike you on the cheek and in your joy you offer them your whole back.[57] Then they try to lure you like a dog with a bun, and you embrace them with your foolish paws and fall to kissing them with all your heart and soul. Why, see what I am doing now, gentlemen! You are laughing and whispering – I see it! After I have told you all my story you will begin to turn me into ridicule, you will begin to attack me, but yet I go on talking and talking and talking! And who tells me to? Who drives me to do it? Who is standing behind my back whispering to me, "Speak, speak and tell them"? And yet I do talk, I go on telling you, I try to please you as though you were my brothers, all my dearest friends . . . Ech!'

The laughter which had sprung up by degrees on all sides completely drowned at last the voice of the speaker, who really seemed worked up into a sort of ecstasy. He paused, for several minutes his eyes strayed about the company, then suddenly, as though carried away by a whirl-wind, he waved his hand, burst out laughing himself, as though he really found his position amusing, and fell to telling his story again.

'I scarcely slept all night, gentlemen. I was scribbling all night: you see, I thought of a trick. Ech, gentlemen, the very thought of it makes me ashamed. It wouldn't have been so bad if it all had been done at night – I might have been drunk, blundered, been silly and talked nonsense – but not a bit of it! I woke up in the morning as soon as it was light; I hadn't slept more than an hour or two, and was in the same mind. I dressed, I washed, I curled and pomaded my hair, put on my new dress coat and went straight off to spend the holiday with Fedosey Nikolaitch, and I kept the joke I had written in my hat. He met me again with open arms, and invited me again to his fatherly waistcoat. But I assumed an air of dignity. I had the joke I thought of the night before in my mind. I drew a step back.

' "No, Fedosey Nikolaitch, but will you please read this letter,' and I gave it him together with my daily report. And do you know what was in it? Why, "for such and such reasons the aforesaid Osip Mihalitch asks to be discharged", and under my petition I signed my full rank! Just think what a notion! Good Lord, it was the cleverest thing I could think of! As today was the first of April, I was pretending, for the sake of a joke, that my resentment was not over, that I had changed my mind in the night and was grumpy, and more offended than ever, as though to say, "My dear benefactor, I don't want to know you nor your daughter either. I put the money in my pocket yesterday, so I am secure – so here's my petition for a transfer to be discharged. I don't care to serve under such a chief as Fedosey Nikolaitch. I want to go into a different office and then, maybe, I'll inform." I pretended to be a regular scoundrel, I wanted to frighten them. And a nice way of frightening them, wasn't it? A pretty thing, gentlemen, wasn't it? You see, my heart had grown tender towards them since the day before, so I thought I would have a little joke at the family – I would tease the fatherly heart of Fedosey Nikolaitch.

'As soon as he took my letter and opened it, I saw his whole countenance change.

' "What's the meaning of this, Osip Mihalitch?"

'And like a little fool I said: "The first of April! Many happy returns of the day, Fedosey Nikolaitch!" just like a silly schoolboy who hides behind his grandmother's armchair and then shouts "oof" into her ear suddenly at the top of his voice, meaning to frighten her. Yes . . . yes, I feel quite ashamed to talk about it, gentlemen! No, I won't tell you.'

'Nonsense! What happened then?'

'Nonsense, nonsense! Tell us! Yes, do,' rose on all sides.

'There was an outcry and a hullabaloo, my dear friends! Such exclamations of surprise! And "you mischievous fellow, you naughty man," and what a fright I had given them – and all so sweet that I felt ashamed and wondered how such a holy place could be profaned by a sinner like me.

' "Well, my dear boy," piped the mamma, "you gave me such a fright that my legs are all of a tremble still, I can hardly stand on my feet! I ran to Masha as though I were crazy: 'Mashenka,' I said, 'what will become of us! See how *your* friend has turned out!' and I was unjust to you, my dear boy. You must forgive an old woman like me, I was taken in! Well, I thought, when he got home last night, he got home late, he began thinking and perhaps he fancied that we sent for him on purpose, yesterday, that we wanted to get hold of him. I turned cold at the thought! Give over, Mashenka, don't go on winking at me – Osip Mihalitch isn't a stranger! I am your mother, I am not likely to say any harm! Thank God, I am not twenty, but turned forty-five."

'Well, gentlemen, I almost flopped at her feet on the spot. Again there were tears, again there were kisses. Jokes began. Fedosey Nikolaitch, too, thought he would make April fools of us. He told us the fiery bird had flown up with a letter in her diamond beak! He tried to take us in, too – didn't we laugh? weren't we touched? Foo! I feel ashamed to talk about it.

'Well, my good friends, the end is not far off now. One day passed, two, three, a week; I was regularly engaged to her. I should think so! The wedding rings were ordered, the day was fixed, only they did not want to make it public for a time – they wanted to wait for the Inspector's visit to be over. I was all impatience for the Inspector's arrival – my happiness depended upon him. I was in a hurry to get his visit over. And in the excitement and rejoicing Fedosey Nikolaitch threw all the work upon me: writing up the accounts, making up the reports, checking the books, balancing the totals. I found things in terrible disorder – everything had been neglected, there were muddles and irregularities everywhere. Well, I thought, I must do my best for my father-in-law! And he was ailing all the time, he was taken ill, it appears; he seemed to get worse day by day. And, indeed, I grew as thin as a rake myself, I was afraid I would break down. However, I finished the work grandly. I got things straight for him in time.

'Suddenly they sent a messenger for me. I ran headlong – what could it be? I saw my Fedosey Nikolaitch, his head bandaged up in a vinegar compress, frowning, sighing, and moaning.

' "My dear boy, my son," he said, "if I die, to whom shall I leave you, my darlings?"

'His wife trailed in with all his children; Mashenka was in tears and I blubbered, too.

' "Oh no," he said. "God will be merciful, He will not visit my transgressions on you."

'Then he dismissed them all, told me to shut the door after them, and we were left alone, *tête-à-tête*.

' "I have a favour to ask of you."

' "What favour?"

' "Well, my dear boy, there is no rest for me even on my deathbed. I am in want."

' "How so?" I positively flushed crimson, I could hardly speak.

' "Why, I had to pay some of my own money into the Treasury. I grudge nothing for the public weal, my boy! I don't grudge my life. Don't you imagine any ill. I am sad to think that slanderers have blackened my name to you . . . You were mistaken, my hair has gone white from grief. The Inspector is coming down upon us and Matveyev is seven thousand roubles short, and I shall have to answer for it . . . Who else? It will be visited upon me, my boy: where were my eyes? And how can we get it from Matveyev? He has had trouble enough already: why should I bring the poor fellow to ruin?"

' "Holy saints!" I thought, "what a just man! What a heart!"

' "And I don't want to take my daughter's money, which has been set aside for her dowry: that sum is sacred. I have money of my own, it's true, but I have lent it all to friends – how is one to collect it all in a minute?"

'I simply fell on my knees before him. "My benefactor!" I cried, "I've wronged you, I have injured you; it was slanderers who wrote against you; don't break my heart, take back your money!"

'He looked at me and there were tears in his eyes. "That was just what I expected from you, my son. Get up! I forgave you at the time for the sake of my daughter's tears – now my heart forgives you freely! You have healed my wounds. I bless you for all time!"

'Well, when he blessed me, gentlemen, I scurried home as soon as I could. I got the money: ' "Here, father, here's the money. I've only spent fifty roubles."

' "Well, that's all right,' he said. "But now every trifle may count; the time is short, write a report dated some days ago that you were short of money and had taken fifty roubles on account. I'll tell the authorities you had it in advance."

'Well, gentlemen, what do you think? I did write that report, too!'

'Well, what then? What happened? How did it end?'

'As soon as I had written the report, gentlemen, this is how it ended. The next day, in the early morning, an envelope with a government seal arrived. I looked at it and what had I got? The sack! That is, instructions to hand over my work, to deliver the accounts – and to go about my business!'

'How so?'

'That's just what I cried at the top of my voice, "How so?" Gentlemen, there was a ringing in my ears. I thought there was no special reason for it – but no, the Inspector had arrived in the town. My heart sank. "It's not for nothing," I thought. And just as I was I rushed off to Fedosey Nikolaitch.

' "How is this?" I said.

' "What do you mean?" he said.

' "Why, I am dismissed."

' "Dismissed? how?"

' "Why, look at this!"

' "Well, what of it?"

' "Why, but I didn't ask for it!"

' "Yes, you did – you sent in your papers on the first of April." (I had never taken that letter back!)

' "Fedosey Nikolaitch! I can't believe my ears, I can't believe my eyes! Is this you?"

' "It is me, why?"

' "My God!"

' "I am sorry, sir. I am very sorry that you made up your mind to retire from the service so early. A young man ought to be in the service, and you've begun to be a little light-headed of late. And as for your character, set your mind at rest: I'll see to that! Your behaviour has always been so exemplary!"

' "But that was a little joke, Fedosey Nikolaitch! I didn't mean it, I just gave you the letter for your fatherly . . . that's all."

' "That's all? A queer joke, sir! Does one jest with documents like that? Why, you are sometimes sent to Siberia for such jokes. Now, goodbye. I am busy. We have the Inspector here – the duties of the service before everything; you can kick up your heels, but we have to sit here at work. But I'll get you a character – Oh, another thing: I've just bought a house from Matveyev. We are moving in in a day or two. So I expect I shall not have the pleasure of seeing you at our new residence. *Bon voyage!*"

'I ran home.

' "We are lost, granny!"

'She wailed, poor dear, and then I saw the page from Fedosey Nikolaitch's running up with a note and a birdcage, and in the cage there was a starling. In the fullness of my heart I had given her the starling. And in the note there were the words: "April 1st," and nothing more. What do you think of that, gentlemen?'

'What happened then? What happened then?'

'What then! I met Fedosey Nikolaitch once, I meant to tell him to his face he was a scoundrel.'

'Well?'

'But somehow I couldn't bring myself to it, gentlemen.'

An Honest Thief

ONE MORNING, just as I was about to set off to my office, Agrafena, my cook, washerwoman and housekeeper, came in to me and, to my surprise, entered into conversation. She had always been such a silent, simple creature that, except for her daily enquiry about dinner, she had not uttered a word for the last six years. I, at least, had heard nothing else from her.

'Here I have come in to have a word with you, sir,' she began abruptly; 'you really ought to let the little room.'

'Which little room?'

'Why, the one next to the kitchen, to be sure.'

'What for?'

'What for? Why because folks do take in lodgers, to be sure.'

'But who would take it?'

'Who would take it? Why, a lodger would take it, to be sure.'

'But, my good woman, one could not put a bedstead in it; there wouldn't be room to move! Who could live in it?'

'Who wants to live there! As long as he has a place to sleep in. Why, he would live in the window.'

'In what window?'

'In what window! As though you didn't know! The one in the passage, to be sure. He would sit there, sewing or doing anything else. Maybe he would sit on a chair, too. He's got a chair; and he has a table, too; he's got everything.'

'Who is "he" then?'

'Oh, a good man, a man of experience. I will cook for him. And I'll ask him three roubles a month for his board and lodging.'

After prolonged efforts I succeeded at last in learning from Agrafena that an elderly man had somehow managed to persuade her to admit him into the kitchen as a lodger and boarder. Any notion Agrafena took into her head had to be carried out; if not, I knew she would give me no peace. When anything was not to her liking, she at once began to brood, and sank into a deep dejection that would last for a fortnight or three weeks. During that period my dinners were spoiled, my linen was mislaid, my floors went unscrubbed; in short, I had a great deal to put up with. I had observed long ago that this inarticulate woman was incapable of conceiving a project, or originating an idea of her own. But if anything like a notion or a project was by some means put into her feeble brain, to prevent its being carried out meant, for a time, her moral assassination. And so, as I cared more for my peace of mind than for anything else, I consented forthwith.

'Has he a passport anyway, or something of the sort?'

'To be sure, he has. He is a good man, a man of experience; three roubles he's promised to pay.'

The very next day the new lodger made his appearance in my modest bachelor quarters; but I was not put out by this, indeed I was inwardly pleased. I lead as a rule a very lonely hermit's existence. I have scarcely any friends; I hardly ever go anywhere. As I had spent ten years never coming out of my shell, I had, of course, grown used to solitude. But another ten or fifteen years or more of the same solitary existence, with the same Agrafena, in the same bachelor quarters, was in truth a somewhat cheerless prospect. And therefore a new inmate, if well behaved, was a heaven-sent blessing.

Agrafena had spoken truly: my lodger was certainly a man of experience. From his passport it appeared that he was an old soldier, a fact which I should have known indeed from his face. An old soldier is easily recognised. Astafy Ivanovitch was a favourable specimen of his class. We got on very well together. What was best of all, Astafy Ivanovitch would sometimes tell a story, describing some incident in his own life. In the perpetual boredom of my existence such a storyteller was a veritable treasure. One day he told me one of these stories. It made an impression on me. The following event was what led to it.

I was left alone in the flat; both Astafy and Agrafena were out on business of their own. All of a sudden I heard from the inner room somebody – I fancied a stranger – come in; I went out; there actually was a stranger in the passage, a short fellow wearing no overcoat in spite of the cold autumn weather.

'What do you want?'

'Does a clerk called Alexandrov live here?'

'Nobody of that name here, brother. Goodbye.'

'Why, the *dvornik*[58] told me it was here,' said my visitor, cautiously retiring towards the door.

'Be off, be off, brother, get along.'

Next day after dinner, while Astafy Ivanovitch was fitting on a coat which he was altering for me, again someone came into the passage. I half opened the door.

Before my very eyes my yesterday's visitor, with perfect composure, took my wadded greatcoat from the peg and, stuffing it under his arm, darted out of the flat. Agrafena stood all the time staring at him, agape with astonishment and doing nothing for the protection of my property. Astafy Ivanovitch flew in pursuit of the thief and ten minutes later came back out of breath and empty-handed. He had vanished completely.

'Well, there's a piece of luck, Astafy Ivanovitch!'

'It's a good job your cloak is left! Or he would have put you in a plight, the thief!'

But the whole incident had so impressed Astafy Ivanovitch that I forgot the theft as I looked at him. He could not get over it. Every minute or two he would drop the work upon which he was engaged, and would describe over again how it had all happened, how he had been standing, how the greatcoat had been taken down before his very eyes, not a yard away, and how it had come to pass that he could not catch the thief. Then he would sit down to his work again, then leave it once more, and at last I saw him go down to the *dvornik* to tell him all about it, and to upbraid him for letting such a thing happen in his domain. Then he came back and began scolding Agrafena. Then he sat down to his work again, and long afterwards he was still muttering to himself how it had all happened, how he stood there and I was here, how before our eyes, not a yard away, the thief took the coat off the peg, and so on. In short, though Astafy Ivanovitch understood his business, he was a terrible slowcoach and busybody.

'He's made fools of us, Astafy Ivanovitch,' I said to him in the evening, as I gave him a glass of tea. I wanted to while away the time by recalling the story of the lost greatcoat, the frequent repetition of which, together with the great earnestness of the speaker, was beginning to become very amusing.

'Fools, indeed, sir! Even though it is no business of mine, I am put out. It makes me angry though it is not my coat that was lost. To my thinking there is no vermin in the world worse than a thief. Another takes what you can spare, but a thief steals the work of your hands, the sweat of your brow, your time . . . Ugh, it's nasty! One can't speak of it! it's too vexing. How is it you don't feel the loss of your property, sir?'

'Yes, you are right, Astafy Ivanovitch, better if the thing had been burnt; it's annoying to let the thief have it, it's disagreeable.'

'Disagreeable! I should think so! Yet, to be sure, there are thieves and thieves. And I have happened, sir, to come across an honest thief.'

'An honest thief? But how can a thief be honest, Astafy Ivanovitch?'

'There you are right indeed, sir. How can a thief be honest? There are none such. I only meant to say that he was an honest man, sure enough, and yet he stole. I was simply sorry for him.'

'Why, how was that, Astafy Ivanovitch?'

'It was about two years ago, sir. I had been nearly a year out of a place, and just before I lost my place I made the acquaintance of a poor lost creature. We got acquainted in a public-house. He was a drunkard, a vagrant, a beggar, he had been in a situation of some sort, but from his drinking habits he had lost his work. Such a ne'er-do-well! God only knows what he had on! Often you wouldn't be sure if he'd a shirt under his coat; everything he could lay his hands upon he would drink away. But he was not one to quarrel; he was a quiet fellow. A soft, good-natured chap. And he'd never ask, he was ashamed; but you could see for yourself the poor fellow wanted a drink, and you would stand it him. And so we got friendly, that's to say, he stuck to me . . . It was all one to me. And what a man he was, to be sure! Like a little dog he would follow me; wherever I went there he would be; and all that after our first meeting, and he as thin as a thread-paper! At first it was, "Let me stay the night;" well, I let him stay.

'I looked at his passport, too; the man was all right.

'Well, the next day it was the same story, and then the third day he came again and sat all day in the window and stayed the night. Well, thinks I, he is sticking to me; give him food and drink and shelter at night, too – here am I, a poor man, and a hanger-on to keep as well! And before he came to me, he used to go in the same way to a government clerk's; he attached himself to him; they were always drinking together; but he, through trouble of some sort, drank himself into the grave. My man was called Emelyan Ilyitch. I pondered and pondered what I was to do with him. To drive him away I was ashamed. I was sorry for him; such a pitiful, Godforsaken creature I never did set eyes on. And not a word said either; he does not ask, but just sits there and looks into your eyes like a dog. To think what drinking will bring a man down to!

'I keep asking myself how am I to say to him: "You must be moving, Emelyanoushka, there's nothing for you here, you've come to the wrong place; I shall soon not have a bite for myself, how am I to keep you too?"

'I sat and wondered what he'd do when I said that to him. And I seemed to see how he'd stare at me, if he were to hear me say that, how long he would sit and not understand a word of it. And when it did get home to him at last, how he would get up from the window, would take up his bundle – I can see it now, the red-check handkerchief full of holes, with God knows what wrapped up in it, which he had always with him, and then how he would set his shabby old coat to rights, so that it would look decent and keep him warm, so that no holes would be seen – he was a man of delicate feelings! And how he'd open the door and go out with tears in his eyes. Well, there's no letting a man go to ruin like that . . . One's sorry for him.

'And then again, I think, how am I off myself? Wait a bit, Emely-anoushka, says I to myself, you've not long to feast with me: I shall soon be going away and then you will not find me.

'Well, sir, our family made a move; and Alexandr Filimonovitch, my master (now deceased, God rest his soul), said, "I am thoroughly satisfied with you, Astafy Ivanovitch; when we come back from the country we will take you on again." I had been butler with them; a nice gentleman he was, but he died that same year. Well, after seeing him off, I took my belongings, what little money I had, and I thought I'd have a rest for a time, so I went to an old woman I knew, and I took a corner in her room. There was only one corner free in it. She had been a nurse, so now she had a pension and a room of her own. Well, now goodbye, Emelyanoushka, thinks I, you won't find me now, my boy.

'And what do you think, sir? I had gone out to see a man I knew, and when I came back in the evening, the first thing I saw was Emely-anoushka! There he was, sitting on my box and his check bundle beside him; he was sitting in his ragged old coat, waiting for me. And to while away the time he had borrowed a church book from the old lady, and was holding it wrong side up. He'd scented me out! My heart sank. Well, thinks I, there's no help for it – why didn't I turn him out at first? So I asked him straight off: Have you brought your passport, Emelyanoushka?'

'I sat down on the spot, sir, and began to ponder: will a vagabond like that be very much trouble to me? And on thinking it over it seemed he would not be much trouble. He must be fed, I thought. Well, a bit of bread in the morning, and to make it go down better I'll buy him an onion. At midday I should have to give him another bit of bread and an onion; and in the evening, onion again with kvass, with some more bread if he wanted it. And if some cabbage soup were to come our way, then we should both have had our fill. I am no great eater myself, and a drinking man, as we all know, never eats; all he wants is herb-brandy or green vodka. He'll ruin me with his drinking, I thought, but then another idea came into my head, sir, and took great hold on me. So much so that if Emelyanoushka had gone away I should have felt that I had nothing to live for, I do believe . . . I determined on the spot to be a father and guardian to him. I'll keep him from ruin, I thought, I'll wean him from the glass! You wait a bit, thought I; very well, Emelyanoushka, you may stay, only you must behave yourself; you must obey orders.

'Well, thinks I to myself, I'll begin by training him to work of some sort, but not all at once; let him enjoy himself a little first, and I'll look round and find something you are fit for, Emelyanoushka. For every sort of work a man needs a special ability, you know, sir. And I began to watch him on the quiet; I soon saw Emelyanoushka was a desperate character. I began, sir, with a word of advice: I said this and that to him. "Emelyanoushka," said I, "you ought to take a thought and mend your ways. Have done with drinking! Just look what rags you go about in: that old coat of yours, if I may make bold to say so, is fit for nothing but a sieve. A pretty state of things! It's time to draw the line, sure enough." Emelyanoushka sat and listened to me with his head hanging down. Would you believe it, sir? It had come to such a pass with him, he'd lost his tongue through drink and could not speak a word of sense. Talk to him of cucumbers and he'd answer back about beans! He would listen and listen to me and then heave such a sigh.

' "What are you sighing for, Emelyan Ilyitch?" I asked him.

' "Oh, nothing; don't you mind me, Astafy Ivanovitch. Do you know there were two women fighting in the street today, Astafy Ivanovitch? One upset the other woman's basket of cranberries by accident."

' "Well, what of that?"

' "And the second one upset the other's cranberries on purpose and trampled them underfoot, too."

' "Well, and what of it, Emelyan Ilyitch?"

' "Why, nothing, Astafy Ivanovitch, I just mentioned it."

' " 'Nothing, I just mentioned it!' Emelyanoushka, my boy, I thought, you've squandered and drunk away your brains!"

' "And do you know, a gentleman dropped a money-note on the pavement in Gorohovy Street, no, it was Sadovy Street. And a peasant saw it and said, 'That's my luck;' and at the same time another man saw it and said, 'No, it's my bit of luck. I saw it before you did.' "

' "Well, Emelyan Ilyitch?"

' "And the fellows had a fight over it, Astafy Ivanovitch. But a policeman came up, took away the note, gave it back to the gentleman and threatened to take up both the men."

' "Well, but what of that? What is there edifying about it, Emelyanoushka?"

' "Why, nothing, to be sure. Folks laughed, Astafy Ivanovitch."

' "Ach, Emelyanoushka! What do the folks matter? You've sold your soul for a brass farthing! But do you know what I have to tell you, Emelyan Ilyitch?"

' "What, Astafy Ivanovitch?"

' "Take a job of some sort, that's what you must do. For the hundredth time I say to you, set to work, have some mercy on yourself!"

' "What could I set to, Astafy Ivanovitch? I don't know what job I could set to, and there is no one who will take me on, Astafy Ivanovitch."

' "That's how you came to be turned off, Emelyanoushka, you drinking man!"

' "And do you know Vlass, the waiter, was sent for to the office today, Astafy Ivanovitch?"

' "Why did they send for him, Emelyanoushka?" I asked.

' "I could not say why, Astafy Ivanovitch. I suppose they wanted him there, and that's why they sent for him."

'A-ach, thought I, we are in a bad way, poor Emelyanoushka! The Lord is chastising us for our sins. Well, sir, what is one to do with such a man?

'But a cunning fellow he was, and no mistake. He'd listen and listen to me, but at last I suppose he got sick of it. As soon as he saw I was beginning to get angry, he'd pick up his old coat and out he'd slip and leave no trace. He'd wander about all day and come back at night drunk. Where he got the money from, the Lord only knows; I had no hand in that.

' "No," said I, "Emelyan Ilyitch, you'll come to a bad end. Give over drinking, mind what I say now, give it up! Next time you come home in liquor, you can spend the night on the stairs. I won't let you in!"

'After hearing that threat, Emelyanoushka sat at home that day and the next; but on the third he slipped off again. I waited and waited; he didn't come back. Well, at least I don't mind owning, I was in a fright, and I felt for the man too. What have I done to him? I thought. I've scared him away. Where's the poor fellow gone to now? He'll get lost maybe. Lord have mercy upon us!

'Night came on, he did not come. In the morning I went out into the porch; I looked, and bless me if he hadn't gone to sleep in the porch! There he was with his head on the step, and chilled to the marrow of his bones.

' "What next, Emelyanoushka, God have mercy on you! Where will you get to next!"

' "Why, you were – sort of – angry with me, Astafy Ivanovitch, the other day, you were vexed and promised to put me to sleep in the porch, so I didn't – sort of – venture to come in, Astafy Ivanovitch, and so I lay down here . . . "

'I did feel angry and sorry too.

' "Surely you might undertake some other duty, Emelyanoushka, instead of lying here guarding the steps," I said.

' "Why, what other duty, Astafy Ivanovitch?"

' "You lost soul" – I was in such a rage, I called him that – "if you could but learn tailoring work! Look at your old rag of a coat! It's not enough to have it in tatters, here you are sweeping the steps with it! You might take a needle and boggle up your rags, as decency demands. Ah, you drunken man!"

'What do you think, sir? He actually did take a needle. Of course I said it in jest, but he was so scared he set to work. He took off his coat and began threading the needle. I watched him; as you may well guess, his eyes were all red and bleary, and his hands were all of a shake. He kept shoving and shoving the thread and could not get it through the eye of the needle; he kept screwing his eyes up and wetting the thread and twisting it in his fingers – it was no good! He gave it up and looked at me.

' "Well," said I, "this is a nice way to treat me! If there had been folks by to see, I don't know what I should have done! Why, you simple fellow, I said it you in joke, as a reproach. Give over your nonsense, God bless you! Sit quiet and don't put me to shame, don't sleep on my stairs and make a laughing-stock of me."

' "Why, what am I to do, Astafy Ivanovitch? I know very well I am a drunkard and good for nothing! I can do nothing but vex you, my bene-bene-factor . . . "

'And at that his blue lips began all of a sudden to quiver, and a tear ran down his white cheek and trembled on his stubbly chin, and then poor Emelyanoushka burst into a regular flood of tears. Mercy on us! I felt as though a knife were thrust into my heart! The sensitive creature! I'd never have expected it. Who could have guessed it? No, Emelyanoushka, thought I, I shall give you up altogether. You can go your way like the rubbish you are.

'Well, sir, why make a long story of it? And the whole affair is so trifling; it's not worth wasting words upon. Why, you, for instance, sir, would not have given a thought to it, but I would have given a great deal – if I had a great deal to give – that it never should have happened at all.

'I had a pair of riding breeches by me, sir, deuce take them, fine, first-rate riding breeches they were too, blue with a check on it. They'd been ordered by a gentleman from the country, but he would not have them after all; said they were not full enough, so they were left on my hands. It struck me they were worth something. At the second-hand dealer's I ought to get five silver roubles for them, or if not I could turn them into two pairs of trousers for Petersburg gentlemen and have a piece over for a waistcoat for myself. Of course for poor people like us everything comes in. And it happened just then that Emelyanoushka was having a sad time of it. There he sat day after day: he did not drink, not a drop passed his lips, but he sat and moped like an owl. It was sad to see him – he just sat and brooded. Well, thought I, either you've not got a copper to spend, my lad, or else you're turning over a new leaf of yourself, you've given it up, you've listened to reason. Well, sir, that's how it was with us; and just then came a holiday. I went to vespers; when I came home I found Emelyanoushka sitting in the window, drunk and rocking to and fro.

'Ah! so that's what you've been up to, my lad! And I went to get something out of my chest. And when I looked in, the breeches were not there . . . I rummaged here and there; they'd vanished. When I'd ransacked everywhere and saw they were not there, something seemed to stab me to the heart. I ran first to the old dame and began accusing her; of Emelyanoushka I'd not the faintest suspicion, though there was cause for it in his sitting there drunk.

' "No," said the old body, "God be with you, my fine gentleman, what good are riding breeches to me? Am I going to wear such things? Why, a skirt I had I lost the other day through a fellow of your sort . . . I know nothing; I can tell you nothing about it," she said.

' "Who has been here, who has been in?" I asked.

' "Why, nobody has been, my good sir," says she; "I've been here all the while; Emelyan Ilyitch went out and came back again; there he sits, ask him."

' "Emelyanoushka," said I, "have you taken those new riding breeches for anything; you remember the pair I made for that gentleman from the country?"

' "No, Astafy Ivanovitch," said he; "I've not – sort of – touched them."

'I was in a state! I hunted high and low for them – they were nowhere to be found. And Emelyanoushka sits there rocking himself to and fro. I was squatting on my heels facing him and bending over the chest, and all at once I stole a glance at him . . . Alack, I thought; my heart suddenly grew hot within me and I felt myself flushing up too. And suddenly Emelyanoushka looked at me.

' "No, Astafy Ivanovitch," said he, "those riding breeches of yours, maybe, you are thinking, maybe, I took them, but I never touched them."

' "But what can have become of them, Emelyan Ilyitch?"

' "No, Astafy Ivanovitch," said he, "I've never seen them."

' "Why, Emelyan Ilyitch, I suppose they've run off of themselves, eh?"

' "Maybe they have, Astafy Ivanovitch."

'When I heard him say that, I got up at once, went up to him, lighted the lamp and sat down to work at my sewing. I was altering a waistcoat for a clerk who lived below us. And wasn't there a burning pain and ache in my breast! I shouldn't have minded so much if I had put all the clothes I had in the fire. Emelyanoushka seemed to have an inkling of what a rage I was in. When a man is guilty, you know, sir, he scents trouble far off, like the birds of the air before a storm.

' "Do you know what, Astafy Ivanovitch," Emelyanoushka began, and his poor old voice was shaking as he said the words, "Antip Prohoritch, the apothecary, married the coachman's wife this morning, who died the other day – "

'I did give him a look, sir, a nasty look it was; Emelyanoushka understood it too. I saw him get up, go to the bed, and begin to rummage there for something. I waited – he was busy there a long time and kept muttering all the while, "No, not there, where can the blessed things have got to!" I waited to see what he'd do; I saw him creep under the bed on all fours. I couldn't bear it any longer. "What are you crawling about under the bed for, Emelyan Ilyitch?" said I.

' "Looking for the breeches, Astafy Ivanovitch. Maybe they've dropped down there somewhere."

' "Why should you try to help a poor simple man like me," said I, "crawling on your knees for nothing, sir?" – I called him that in my vexation.

' "Oh, never mind, Astafy Ivanovitch, I'll just look. They'll turn up, maybe, somewhere."

' "H'm,' said I, "look here, Emelyan Ilyitch!"

' "What is it, Astafy Ivanovitch?" said he.

' "Haven't you simply stolen them from me like a thief and a robber, in return for the bread and salt you've eaten here?" said I.

'I felt so angry, sir, at seeing him fooling about on his knees before me.

' "No, Astafy Ivanovitch."

'And he stayed lying as he was on his face under the bed. A long time he lay there and then at last crept out. I looked at him and the man was as white as a sheet. He stood up, and sat down near me in the window and sat so for some ten minutes.

' "No, Astafy Ivanovitch," he said, and all at once he stood up and came towards me, and I can see him now; he looked dreadful. "No, Astafy Ivanovitch," said he, "I never – sort of – touched your breeches."

'He was all of a shake, poking himself in the chest with a trembling finger, and his poor old voice shook so that I was frightened, sir, and sat as though I was rooted to the window-seat.

' "Well, Emelyan Ilyitch," said I, "as you will, forgive me if I, in my foolishness, have accused you unjustly. As for the breeches, let them go hang; we can live without them. We've still our hands, thank God; we need not go thieving or begging from some other poor man; we'll earn our bread."

'Emelyanoushka heard me out and went on standing there before me. I looked up, and he had sat down. And there he sat all the evening without stirring. At last I lay down to sleep. Emelyanoushka went on sitting in the same place. When I looked out in the morning, he was lying curled up in his old coat on the bare floor; he felt too crushed even to come to bed. Well, sir, I felt no more liking for the fellow from that day; in fact for the first few days I hated him. I felt, as one may say, as though my own son had robbed me, and done me a deadly hurt. Ach, thought I, Emelyanoushka, Emelyanoushka! And Emelyanoushka, sir, went on drinking for a whole fortnight without stopping. He was drunk all the time, and regularly besotted. He went out in the morning and came back late at night, and for a whole fortnight I didn't get a word out of him. It was as though grief was gnawing at his heart, or as though he wanted to do for himself completely. At last he stopped; he must have come to the end of all he'd got, and then he sat in the window again. I remember he sat there without speaking for three days and three nights; all of a sudden I saw that he was crying. He was just sitting there, sir, and crying like anything; a perfect stream, as though he didn't know how his tears were flowing. And it's a sad thing, sir, to see a grown-up man and an old man, too, crying from woe and grief.

' "What's the matter, Emelyanoushka?" said I.

'He began to tremble so that he shook all over. I spoke to him for the first time since that evening.

' "Nothing, Astafy Ivanovitch."

' "God be with you, Emelyanoushka, what's lost is lost. Why are you moping about like this?' I felt sorry for him.

' "Oh, nothing, Astafy Ivanovitch, it's no matter. I want to find some work to do, Astafy Ivanovitch."

' "And what sort of work, pray, Emelyanoushka?"

' "Why, any sort; perhaps I could find a situation such as I used to have. I've been already to ask Fedosay Ivanitch. I don't like to be a burden on you, Astafy Ivanovitch. If I can find a situation, Astafy Ivanovitch, then I'll pay it you all back, and make you a return for all your hospitality."

' "Enough, Emelyanoushka, enough; let bygones be bygones – and no more to be said about it. Let us go on as we used to do before."

' "No, Astafy Ivanovitch, you, maybe, think – but I never touched your riding breeches."

' "Well, have it your own way; God be with you, Emelyanoushka."

' "No, Astafy Ivanovitch, I can't go on living with you, that's clear. You must excuse me, Astafy Ivanovitch."

' "Why, God bless you, Emelyan Ilyitch, who's offending you and driving you out of the place – am I doing it?"

' "No, it's not the proper thing for me to live with you like this, Astafy Ivanovitch. I'd better be going."

'He was so hurt, it seemed, he stuck to his point. I looked at him, and sure enough, up he got and pulled his old coat over his shoulders.

' "But where are you going, Emelyan Ilyitch? Listen to reason: what are you about? Where are you off to?"

' "No, goodbye, Astafy Ivanovitch, don't keep me now" – and he was blubbering again – "I'd better be going. You're not the same now."

' "Not the same as what? I am the same. But you'll be lost by yourself like a poor helpless babe, Emelyan Ilyitch."

' "No, Astafy Ivanovitch, when you go out now, you lock up your chest and it makes me cry to see it, Astafy Ivanovitch. You'd better let me go, Astafy Ivanovitch, and forgive me all the trouble I've given you while I've been living with you."

'Well, sir, the man went away. I waited for a day; I expected he'd be back in the evening – no. Next day no sign of him, nor the third day either. I began to get frightened; I was so worried, I couldn't drink, I couldn't eat, I couldn't sleep. The fellow had quite disarmed me. On the fourth day I went out to look for him; I peeped into all the taverns, to enquire for him – but no, Emelyanoushka was lost. "Have you managed to keep yourself alive, Emelyanoushka?" I wondered. "Perhaps he is lying dead under some hedge, poor drunkard, like a sodden log." I went home more dead than alive. Next day I went out to look for him again. And I kept cursing myself that I'd been such a fool as to let the man go off by himself. On the fifth day it was a holiday – in the early morning I heard the door creak. I looked up and there was my Emelyanoushka coming in. His face was blue and his hair was covered with dirt as though he'd been sleeping in the street; he was as thin as a match. He took off his old coat, sat down on the chest and looked at me. I was delighted to see him, but I felt more upset about him than ever. For you see, sir, if I'd been overtaken in some sin, as true as I am here, sir, I'd have died like a dog before I'd have come back. But Emelyanoushka did come back. And a sad thing it was, sure enough, to see a man sunk so low. I began to look after him, to talk kindly to him, to comfort him.

' "Well, Emelyanoushka," said I, "I am glad you've come back. Had you been away much longer I should have gone to look for you in the taverns again today. Are you hungry?"

' "No, Astafy Ivanovitch."

' "Come, now, aren't you really? Here, brother, is some cabbage soup left over from yesterday; there was meat in it; it is good stuff. And here is some bread and onion. Come, eat it, it'll do you no harm."

'I made him eat it, and I saw at once that the man had not tasted food for maybe three days – he was as hungry as a wolf. So it was hunger that had driven him to me. My heart was melted looking at the poor dear. "Let me run to the tavern," thought I, "I'll get something to ease his heart, and then we'll make an end of it. I've no more anger in my heart against you, Emelyanoushka!" I brought him some vodka. "Here, Emelyan Ilyitch, let us have a drink for the holiday. Like a drink? And it will do you good." He held out his hand, held it out greedily; he was just taking it, and then he stopped himself. But a minute after I saw him take it, and lift it to his mouth, spilling it on his sleeve. But though he got it to his lips he set it down on the table again.

' "What is it, Emelyanoushka?"

' "Nothing, Astafy Ivanovitch, I – sort of – "

' "Won't you drink it?"

' "Well, Astafy Ivanovitch, I'm not – sort of – going to drink any more, Astafy Ivanovitch."

' "Do you mean you've given it up altogether, Emelyanoushka, or are you only not going to drink today?"

'He did not answer. A minute later I saw him rest his head on his hand.

' "What's the matter, Emelyanoushka, are you ill?"

' "Why, yes, Astafy Ivanovitch, I don't feel well."

'I took him and laid him down on the bed. I saw that he really was ill: his head was burning hot and he was shivering with fever. I sat by him all day; towards night he was worse. I mixed him some oil and onion and kvass and bread broken up.

' "Come, eat some of this," said I, "and perhaps you'll be better." He shook his head. "No," said he, "I won't have any dinner today, Astafy Ivanovitch."

'I made some tea for him, I quite flustered our old woman – he was no better. Well, thinks I, it's a bad lookout! The third morning I went for a medical gentleman. There was one I knew living close by, Kostopravov by name. I'd made his acquaintance when I was in service with the Bosomyagins; he'd attended me. The doctor come and looked at him. "He's in a bad way," said he, "it was no use sending for me. But if you like I can give him a powder." Well, I didn't give him a powder, I thought that's just the doctor's little game; and then the fifth day came.

'He lay, sir, dying before my eyes. I sat in the window with my work in my hands. The old woman was heating the stove. We were all silent. My heart was simply breaking over him, the good-for-nothing fellow; I felt as if it were a son of my own I was losing. I knew that Emelyanoushkà was looking at me. I'd seen the man all the day long making up his mind to say something and not daring to.

'At last I looked up at him; I saw such misery in the poor fellow's eyes. He had kept them fixed on me, but when he saw that I was looking at him, he looked down at once.

' "Astafy Ivanovitch."

' "What is it, Emelyanoushka?"

' "If you were to take my old coat to a second-hand dealer's, how much do you think they'd give you for it, Astafy Ivanovitch?"

' "There's no knowing how much they'd give. Maybe they would give me a rouble for it, Emelyan Ilyitch."

'But if I had taken it they wouldn't have given a farthing for it, but would have laughed in my face for bringing such a trumpery thing. I simply said that to comfort the poor fellow, knowing the simpleton he was.

' "But I was thinking, Astafy Ivanovitch, they might give you three roubles for it; it's made of cloth, Astafy Ivanovitch. How could they only give one rouble for a cloth coat?"

' "I don't know, Emelyan Ilyitch," said I; "if you are thinking of taking it you should certainly ask three roubles to begin with."

'Emelyanoushka was silent for a time, and then he addressed me again –

' "Astafy Ivanovitch."

' "What is it, Emelyanoushka?" I asked.

' "Sell my coat when I die, and don't bury me in it. I can lie as well without it; and it's a thing of some value – it might come in useful."

'I can't tell you how it made my heart ache to hear him. I saw that the death agony was coming on him. We were silent again for a bit. So an hour passed by. I looked at him again: he was still staring at me, and when he met my eyes he looked down again.

' "Do you want some water to drink, Emelyan Ilyitch?" I asked.

' "Give me some, God bless you, Astafy Ivanovitch."

'I gave him a drink.

' "Thank you, Astafy Ivanovitch," said he.

' "Is there anything else you would like, Emelyanoushka?"

' "No, Astafy Ivanovitch, there's nothing I want, but I – sort of – "

' "What?"

' "I only – "

' "What is it, Emelyanoushka?"

' "Those riding breeches – it was – sort of – I who took them – Astafy Ivanovitch."

' "Well, God forgive you, Emelyanoushka," said I, "you poor, sorrowful creature. Depart in peace."

'And I was choking myself, sir, and the tears were in my eyes. I turned aside for a moment.

' "Astafy Ivanovitch – "

'I saw Emelyanoushka wanted to tell me something; he was trying to sit up, trying to speak, and mumbling something. He flushed red all over suddenly, looked at me . . . then I saw him turn white again, whiter and whiter, and he seemed to sink away all in a minute. His head fell back, he drew one breath and gave up his soul to God.'

A Christmas Tree and a Wedding

THE OTHER DAY I saw a wedding ... but no, I had better tell you about the Christmas tree. The wedding was nice, I liked it very much; but the other incident was better. I don't know how it was that, looking at that wedding, I thought of that Christmas tree. This was what happened. Just five years ago, on New Year's Eve, I was invited to a children's party. The giver of the party was a well-known and businesslike personage, with connections, with a large circle of acquaintances, and a good many schemes on hand, so that it may be supposed that this party was an excuse for getting the parents together and discussing various interesting matters in an innocent, casual way. I was an outsider; I had no interesting matter to contribute, and so I spent the evening rather independently. There was another gentleman present who was, I fancied, of no special rank or family, and who, like me, had simply turned up at this family festivity. He was the first to catch my eye. He was a tall, lanky man, very grave and very correctly dressed. But one could see that he was in no mood for merrymaking and family festivity; whenever he withdrew into a corner he left off smiling and knitted his bushy black brows. He had not a single acquaintance in the party except his host. One could see that he was fearfully bored, but that he was valiantly keeping up the part of a man perfectly happy and enjoying himself. I learned afterwards that this was a gentleman from the provinces, who had a critical and perplexing piece of business in Petersburg, who had brought a letter of introduction to our host, and for whom our host was, by no means, *con amore*,[59] using his interest, and whom he had invited, out of civility, to his children's party. He did not play cards, cigars were not offered him, everyone avoided entering into conversation with him, most likely recognising the bird from its feathers; and so my gentleman was forced to sit the whole evening stroking his whiskers simply to have something to do with his hands. His whiskers were certainly very fine. But he stroked them so zealously that, looking at him, one might have supposed that the whiskers were created first and the gentleman only attached to them in order to stroke them.

In addition to this individual, who assisted in this way at our host's family festivity (he had five fat, well-fed boys), I was attracted, too, by another gentleman. But he was quite of a different sort. He was a personage. He was called Yulian Mastakovitch. From the first glance one could see that he was an honoured guest, and stood in the same relation to our host as our host stood in relation to the gentleman who was stroking his whiskers. Our host and hostess said no end of polite things to him, waited on him hand and foot, pressed him to drink, flattered him, brought their visitors up to be introduced to him, but did not take him to be introduced to anyone else. I noticed that tears glistened in our host's eyes when he remarked about the party that he had rarely spent an evening so agreeably. I felt as it were frightened in the presence of such a personage, and so, after admiring the children, I went away into a little parlour, which was quite empty, and sat down in an arbour of flowers which filled up almost half the room.

The children were all incredibly sweet, and resolutely refused to model themselves on the 'grown-ups', regardless of all the admonitions of their governesses and mammas. They stripped the Christmas tree to the last sweetmeat in the twinkling of an eye, and had succeeded in breaking half the playthings before they knew which was destined for whom. Particularly charming was a black-eyed, curly-headed boy, who kept trying to shoot me with his wooden gun. But my attention was still more attracted by his sister, a girl of eleven, quiet, dreamy, pale, with big, prominent, dreamy eyes, exquisite as a little Cupid. The children hurt her feelings in some way, and so she came away from them to the same empty parlour in which I was sitting, and played with her doll in the corner. The visitors respectfully pointed out her father, a wealthy contractor, and someone whispered that three hundred thousand roubles were already set aside for her dowry. I turned round to glance at the group who were interested in such a circumstance, and my eye fell on Yulian Mastakovitch, who, with his hands behind his back and his head on one side, was listening with the greatest attention to these gentlemen's idle gossip. Afterwards I could not help admiring the discrimination of the host and hostess in the distribution of the children's presents. The little girl, who had already a portion of three hundred thousand roubles, received the costliest doll. Then followed presents diminishing in value in accordance with the rank of the parents of these happy children; finally, the child of lowest degree, a thin, freckled, red-haired little boy of ten, got nothing but a book of stories about the marvels of nature and tears of devotion, etc., without pictures or even woodcuts. He was the son of a poor widow, the governess of the children of the house, an oppressed and scared little boy. He was dressed in a short jacket of inferior nankin.[60] After receiving his book he walked round the other toys for a long time; he longed to play with the other children, but did not dare; it was evident that he already felt and understood his position. I love watching children. Their first independent approaches to life are extremely interesting. I noticed that the red-haired boy was so fascinated by the costly toys of the other children, especially by a theatre in which he certainly longed to take some part, that he made up his mind to sacrifice his dignity. He smiled and began playing with the other children, he gave away his apple to a fat-faced little boy who had a mass of goodies tied up in a pocket-handkerchief already, and even brought himself to carry another boy on his back, simply not to be turned away from the theatre, but an insolent youth gave him a heavy thump a minute later. The child did not dare to cry. Then the governess, his mother, made her appearance, and told him not to interfere with the other children's playing. The boy went away to the same room in which was the little girl. She let him join her, and the two set to work very eagerly dressing the expensive doll.

I had been sitting more than half an hour in the ivy arbour, listening to the little prattle of the red-haired boy and the beauty with the dowry of three hundred thousand, who was nursing her doll, when Yulian Mastakovitch suddenly walked into the room. He had taken advantage of the general commotion following a quarrel among the children to step out of the drawing-room. I had noticed him a moment before talking very cordially to the future heiress's papa, whose acquaintance he had just made, of the superiority of one branch of the service over another. Now he stood in hesitation and seemed to be reckoning something on his fingers.

'Three hundred . . . three hundred,' he was whispering. 'Eleven . . . twelve . . . thirteen,' and so on. 'Sixteen – five years! Supposing it is at four per cent – five times twelve is sixty; yes, to that sixty . . . well, in five years we may assume it will be four hundred. Yes! . . . But he won't stick to four per cent, the rascal. He can get eight or ten. Well, five hundred, let us say, five hundred at least . . . that's certain; well, say a little more for frills. H'm! . . . '

His hesitation was at an end, he blew his nose and was on the point of going out of the room when he suddenly glanced at the little girl and stopped short. He did not see me behind the pots of greenery. It seemed to me that he was greatly excited. Either his calculations had affected his imagination or something else, for he rubbed his hands and could hardly stand still. This excitement reached its utmost limit when he stopped and bent another resolute glance at the future heiress. He was about to move forward, but first looked round, then moving on tiptoe, as though he felt guilty, he advanced towards the children. He approached with a little smile, bent down and kissed her on the head. The child, not expecting this attack, uttered a cry of alarm.

'What are you doing here, sweet child?' he asked in a whisper, looking round and patting the girl's cheek.

'We are playing.'

'Ah! With him?' Yulian Mastakovitch looked askance at the boy. 'You had better go into the drawing-room, my dear,' he said to him.

The boy looked at him open-eyed and did not utter a word. Yulian Mastakovitch looked round him again, and again bent down to the little girl.

'And what is this you've got – a dolly, dear child?' he asked.

'Yes, a dolly,' answered the child, frowning, and a little shy.

'A dolly . . . and do you know, dear child, what your dolly is made of?'

'I don't know . . . ' the child answered in a whisper, hanging her head.

'It's made of rags, darling. You had better go into the drawing-room to your playmates, boy,' said Yulian Mastakovitch, looking sternly at the boy. The boy and girl frowned and clutched at each other. They did not want to be separated.

'And do you know why they gave you that doll?' asked Yulian Mastakovitch, dropping his voice to a softer and softer tone.

'I don't know.'

'Because you have been a sweet and well-behaved child all the week.'

At this point Yulian Mastakovitch, more excited than ever, speaking in most dulcet tones, asked at last, in a hardly audible voice choked with emotion and impatience: 'And will you love me, dear little girl, when I come and see your papa and mamma?'

Saying this, Yulian Mastakovitch tried once more to kiss 'the dear little girl', but the red-haired boy, seeing that the little girl was on the point of tears, clutched her hand and began whimpering from sympathy for her. Yulian Mastakovitch was angry in earnest.

'Go away, go away from here, go away!' he said to the boy. 'Go into the drawing-room! Go in there to your playmates!'

'No, he needn't, he needn't! You go away,' said the little girl. 'Leave him alone, leave him alone,' she said, almost crying.

Someone made a sound at the door. Yulian Mastakovitch instantly raised his majestic person and took alarm. But the red-haired boy was even more alarmed than Yulian Mastakovitch; he abandoned the little girl and, slinking along by the wall, stole out of the parlour into the dining-room. To avoid arousing suspicion, Yulian Mastakovitch, too, went into the dining-room. He was as red as a lobster, and, glancing into the looking-glass, seemed to be ashamed at himself. He was perhaps vexed with himself for his impetuosity and hastiness. Possibly, he was at first so much impressed by his calculations, so inspired and fascinated by them, that in spite of his seriousness and dignity he made up his mind to behave like a boy, and directly approach the object of his attentions, even though she could not be really the object of his attentions for another five years at least. I followed the estimable gentleman into the dining-room and there beheld a strange spectacle. Yulian Mastakovitch, flushed with vexation and anger, was frightening the red-haired boy, who, retreating from him, did not know where to run in his terror.

'Go away; what are you doing here? Go away, you scamp; are you after the fruit here, eh? Get along, you naughty boy! Get along, you sniveller, to your playmates!'

The panic-stricken boy in his desperation tried creeping under the table. Then his persecutor, in a fury, took out his large batiste hand-kerchief[51] and began flicking it under the table at the child, who kept perfectly quiet. It must be observed that Yulian Mastakovitch was a little inclined to be fat. He was a sleek, red-faced, solidly built man, paunchy, with thick legs; what is called a fine figure of a man, round as a nut. He was perspiring, breathless and fearfully flushed. At last he was almost rigid, so great was his indignation and perhaps – who knows? – his jealousy. I burst into loud laughter. Yulian Mastakovitch turned round and, in spite of all his consequence, was overcome with confusion. At that moment from the opposite door our host came in. The boy crept out from under the table and wiped his elbows and his knees. Yulian Mastakovitch hastened to put to his nose the handkerchief which he was holding in his hand by one end.

Our host looked at the three of us in some perplexity; but as a man who knew something of life, and looked at it from a serious point of view, he at once availed himself of the chance of catching his visitor by himself.

'Here, this is the boy,' he said, pointing to the red-haired boy, 'for whom I had the honour to solicit your influence.'

'Ah!' said Yulian Mastakovitch, who had hardly quite recovered himself.

'The son of my children's governess,' said our host, in a tone of a petitioner, 'a poor woman, the widow of an honest civil servant; and therefore . . . and therefore, Yulian Mastakovitch, if it were possible . . . '

'Oh, no, no!' Yulian Mastakovitch made haste to answer; 'no, excuse me, Filip Alexyevitch, it's quite impossible. I've made enquiries; there's no vacancy, and if there were, there are twenty applicants who have far more claim than he . . . I am very sorry, very sorry . . . '

'What a pity,' said our host. 'He is a quiet, well-behaved boy.'

'A great rascal, as I notice,' answered Yulian Mastakovitch, with a nervous twist of his lip. 'Get along, boy; why are you standing there? Go to your playmates,' he said, addressing the child.

At that point he could not contain himself, and glanced at me out of one eye. I, too, could not contain myself, and laughed straight in his face. Yulian Mastakovitch turned away at once, and in a voice calculated to reach my ear, asked who was that strange young man? They whispered together and walked out of the room. I saw Yulian Mastakovitch afterwards shaking his head incredulously as our host talked to him.

After laughing to my heart's content I returned to the drawing-room. There the great man, surrounded by fathers and mothers of families, including the host and hostess, was saying something very warmly to a lady to whom he had just been introduced. The lady was holding by the hand the little girl with whom Yulian Mastakovitch had had the scene in the parlour a little while before. Now he was launching into praises and raptures over the beauty, the talents, the grace and the charming manners of the charming child. He was unmistakably making up to the mamma. The mother listened to him almost with tears of delight. The father's lips were smiling. Our host was delighted at the general satisfaction. All the guests, in fact, were sympathetically gratified; even the children's games were checked that they might not hinder the conversation: the whole atmosphere was saturated with reverence. I heard afterwards the mamma of the interesting child, deeply touched, beg Yulian Mastakovitch, in carefully chosen phrases, to do her the special honour of bestowing upon them the precious gift of his acquaintance, and heard with what unaffected delight Yulian Mastakovitch accepted the invitation, and how afterwards the guests, dispersing in different directions, moving away with the greatest propriety, poured out to one another the most touchingly flattering comments upon the contractor, his wife, his little girl, and, above all, upon Yulian Mastakovitch.

'Is that gentleman married?' I asked, almost aloud, of one of my acquaintances, who was standing nearest to Yulian Mastakovitch. Yulian Mastakovitch flung a searching and vindictive glance at me.

'No!' answered my acquaintance, chagrined to the bottom of his heart by the awkwardness of which I had intentionally been guilty . . .

I passed lately by a certain church; I was struck by the crowd of people in carriages. I heard people talking of the wedding. It was a cloudy day, it was beginning to sleet. I made my way through the crowd at the door and saw the bridegroom. He was a sleek, well-fed, round, paunchy man, very gorgeously dressed up. He was running fussily about, giving orders. At last the news passed through the crowd that the bride was coming. I squeezed my way through the crowd and saw a marvellous beauty, who could scarcely have reached her first season. But the beauty was pale and melancholy. She looked preoccupied; I even fancied that her eyes were red with recent weeping. The classic severity of every feature of her face gave a certain dignity and seriousness to her beauty. But through that sternness and dignity, through that melancholy, could be seen the look of childish innocence; something indescribably naïve, fluid, youthful, which seemed mutely begging for mercy.

People were saying that she was only just sixteen. Glancing attentively at the bridegroom, I suddenly recognised him as Yulian Mastakovitch, whom I had not seen for five years. I looked at her. My God! I began to squeeze my way as quickly as I could out of the church. I heard people saying in the crowd that the bride was an heiress, that she had a dowry of five hundred thousand . . . and a trousseau worth ever so much.

'It was a good stroke of business, though!' I thought as I made my way into the street.

White Nights[62]

A Sentimental Story from the Diary of a Dreamer

> Or was his destiny from the start
> To be but just one moment
> Near your heart?
>
> Ivan Turgenev[63]

FIRST NIGHT

IT WAS a wonderful night, such a night as is only possible when we are young, dear reader. The sky was so starry, so bright that, looking at it, one could not help asking oneself whether ill-humoured and capricious people could live under such a sky. That is a youthful question, too, dear reader, very youthful, but may the Lord put it more frequently into your heart! . . . Speaking of capricious and ill-humoured people, I cannot help recalling my moral condition all that day. From early morning I had been oppressed by a strange despondency. It suddenly seemed to me that I was lonely, that everyone was forsaking me and going away from me. Of course, anyone is entitled to ask who 'everyone' was. For though I had been living almost eight years in Petersburg I had hardly an acquaintance. But what did I want with acquaintances? I was acquainted with all Petersburg as it was; that was why I felt as though they were all deserting me when all Petersburg packed up and went to its summer villa. I felt afraid of being left alone, and for three whole days I wandered about the town in profound dejection, not knowing what to do with myself. Whether I walked in the Nevsky,[64] went to the Gardens[65] or sauntered on the Embankment,[66] there was not one face of those I had been accustomed to meet at the same time and place all the year. They, of course, do not know me, but I know them. I know them intimately, I have almost made a study of their faces, and am delighted when they are gay, and downcast when they are under a cloud. I have almost struck up a friendship with one old man whom I meet every blessed day at the same hour in Fontanka. Such a grave, pensive countenance; he is always whispering to himself and brandishing his left arm, while in his right hand he holds a long gnarled stick with a gold knob. He even notices me and takes a warm interest in me. If I happen not to be at a certain time in the same spot in Fontanka, I am certain he feels disappointed. That is how it is that we almost bow to each other, especially when we are both in good humour. The other day, when we had not seen each other for two days and met on the third, we were actually touching our hats, but, realising in time, dropped our hands and passed each other with a look of interest.

I know the houses too. As I walk along they seem to run forward in the streets to look out at me from every window, and almost to say: 'Good-morning! How do you do? I am quite well, thank God, and I am to have a new storey in May,' or, 'How are you? I am being redecorated tomorrow;' or, 'I was almost burnt down and had such a fright,' and so on. I have my favourites among them, some are dear friends; one of them intends to be treated by the architect this summer. I shall go every day on purpose to see that the operation is not a failure. God forbid! But I shall never forget an incident with a very pretty little house of a light pink colour. It was such a charming little brick house, it looked so hospitably at me, and so proudly at its ungainly neighbours, that my heart rejoiced whenever I happened to pass it. Suddenly last week I walked along the street, and when I looked at my friend I heard a plaintive, 'They are painting me yellow!' The villains! The barbarians! They had spared nothing, neither columns, nor cornices, and my poor little friend was as yellow as a canary. It almost made me bilious. And to this day I have not had the courage to visit my poor disfigured friend, painted the colour of the Celestial Empire.[67]

So now you understand, reader, in what sense I am acquainted with all Petersburg.

I have mentioned already that I had felt worried for three whole days before I guessed the cause of my uneasiness. And I felt ill at ease in the street – this one had gone and that one had gone, and what had become of the other? – and at home I did not feel like myself either. For two evenings I was puzzling my brains to think what was amiss in my corner; why I felt so uncomfortable in it. And in perplexity I scanned my grimy green walls, my ceiling covered with a spider's web, the growth of which Matrona has so successfully encouraged. I looked over all my furniture, examined every chair, wondering whether the trouble lay there (for if one chair is not standing in the same position as it stood the day before, I am not myself). I looked at the window, but it was all in vain ... I was not a bit the better for it! I even bethought me to send for Matrona, and was giving her some fatherly admonitions in regard to the spider's web and sluttishness in general; but she simply stared at me in amazement and went away without saying a word, so that the spider's web is comfortably hanging in its place to this day. I only at last this morning realised what was wrong. Aie! Why, they are giving me the slip and making off to their summer villas! Forgive the triviality of the expression, but I am in no mood for fine language . . . for everything that had been in Petersburg had gone or was going away for the holidays; for every respectable gentleman of dignified appearance who took a cab was at once transformed, in my eyes, into a respectable head of a household who after his daily duties were over, was making his way to the bosom of his family, to the summer villa; for all the passers-by had now quite a peculiar air which seemed to say to everyone they met: 'We are only here for the moment, gentlemen, and in another two hours we shall be going off to the summer villa.' If a window opened after delicate fingers, white as snow, had tapped upon the pane, and the head of a pretty girl was thrust out, calling to a street-seller with pots of flowers – at once on the spot I fancied that those flowers were being bought not simply in order to enjoy the flowers and the spring in stuffy town lodgings, but because they would all be very soon moving into the country and could take the flowers with them. What is more, I made such progress in my new peculiar sort of investigation that I could distinguish correctly from the mere air of each in what summer villa he was living. The inhabitants of Kamenny[68] and Aptekarsky[69] Islands or of the Peterhof Road[70] were marked by the studied elegance of their manner, their fashionable summer suits and the fine carriages in which they drove to town. Visitors to Pargolovo[71] and places farther away impressed one at first sight by their reasonable and dignified air; the tripper to Krestovsky Island[72] could be recognised by his look of irrepressible gaiety. If I chanced to meet a long procession of waggoners walking lazily with the reins in their hands beside waggons loaded with regular mountains of furniture, tables, chairs, ottomans and sofas and domestic utensils of all sorts, frequently with a decrepit cook sitting on the top of it all, guarding her master's property as though it were the apple of her eye; or if I saw boats heavily loaded with household goods crawling along the Neva or Fontanka to the Black River[73] or the Islands[74] – the waggons and the boats were multiplied tenfold, a hundredfold, in my eyes. I fancied that everything was astir and moving, everything was going in regular caravans to the summer villas. It seemed as though Petersburg threatened to become a wilderness, so that at last I felt ashamed, mortified and sad that I had nowhere to go for the holidays and no reason to go away. I was ready to go away with every waggon, to drive off with every gentleman of respectable appearance who took a cab; but no one – absolutely no one – invited me; it seemed they had forgotten me, as though really I were a stranger to them!

I took long walks, succeeding, as I usually did, in quite forgetting where I was, when I suddenly found myself at the city gates. Instantly I felt light-hearted, and I passed the barrier and walked between cultivated fields and meadows, unconscious of fatigue, and feeling only all over as though a burden were falling off my soul. All the passers-by gave me such friendly looks that they seemed almost greeting me, they all seemed so pleased at something. They were all smoking cigars, every one of them. And I felt pleased as I never had before. It was as though I had suddenly found myself in Italy – so strong was the effect of nature upon a half-sick townsman like me, almost stifling between city walls.

There is something inexpressibly touching in nature round Petersburg, when at the approach of spring she puts forth all her might, all the powers bestowed on her by heaven, when she breaks into leaf, decks herself out and spangles herself with flowers . . . Somehow I cannot help being reminded of a frail, consumptive girl, at whom one sometimes looks with compassion, sometimes with sympathetic love, whom sometimes one simply does not notice; though suddenly in one instant she becomes, as though by chance, inexplicably lovely and exquisite, and, impressed and intoxicated, one cannot help asking oneself what power made those sad, pensive eyes flash with such fire? What summoned the blood to those pale, wan cheeks? What bathed with passion those soft features? What set that bosom heaving? What so suddenly called strength, life and beauty into the poor girl's face, making it gleam with such a smile, kindle with such bright, sparkling laughter? You look round, you seek for someone, you conjecture . . . But the moment passes, and next day you meet, maybe, the same pensive and preoccupied look as before, the same pale face, the same meek and timid movements, and even signs of remorse, traces of a mortal anguish and regret for the fleeting distraction . . . And you grieve that the momentary beauty has faded so soon never to return, that it flashed upon you so treacherously, so vainly, grieve because you had not even time to love her . . . And yet my night was better than my day! This was how it happened.

I came back to the town very late, and it had struck ten as I was going towards my lodgings. My way lay along the canal embankment,[75] where at that hour you never meet a soul. It is true that I live in a very remote part of the town. I walked along singing, for when I am happy I am always humming to myself like every happy man who has no friend or acquaintance with whom to share his joy. Suddenly I had a most unexpected adventure.

Leaning on the canal railing stood a woman with her elbows on the rail, she was apparently looking with great attention at the muddy water of the canal. She was wearing a very charming yellow hat and a jaunty little black mantle. 'She's a girl, and I am sure she is dark,' I thought. She did not seem to hear my footsteps, and did not even stir when I passed by with bated breath and loudly throbbing heart.

'Strange,' I thought; 'she must be deeply absorbed in something,' and all at once I stopped as though petrified. I heard a muffled sob. Yes! I was not mistaken, the girl was crying, and a minute later I heard sob after sob. Good heavens! My heart sank. And timid as I was with women, yet this was such a moment! . . . I turned, took a step towards her, and should certainly have pronounced the word 'Madam!' if I had not known that that exclamation has been uttered a thousand times in every Russian society novel. It was only that reflection stopped me. But while I was seeking for a word, the girl came to herself, looked round, started, cast down her eyes and slipped by me along the embankment. I at once followed her; but she, divining this, left the embankment, crossed the road and walked along the pavement. I dared not cross the street after her. My heart was fluttering like a captured bird. All at once a chance came to my aid.

Along the same side of the pavement there suddenly came into sight, not far from the girl, a gentleman in evening dress, of dignified years, though by no means of dignified carriage; he was staggering and cautiously leaning against the wall. The girl flew straight as an arrow, with the timid haste one sees in all girls who do not want anyone to volunteer to accompany them home at night, and no doubt the staggering gentleman would not have pursued her, if my good luck had not prompted him.

Suddenly, without a word to anyone, the gentleman set off and flew at full speed in pursuit of my unknown lady. She was racing like the wind, but the staggering gentleman was overtaking – overtook her. The girl uttered a shriek, and . . . I bless my luck for the excellent knotted stick, which happened on that occasion to be in my right hand. In a flash I was on the other side of the street; in a flash the obtrusive gentleman had taken in the position, had grasped the irresistible argument, fallen back without a word, and only when we were very far away protested against my action in rather vigorous language. But his words hardly reached us.

'Give me your arm,' I said to the girl. 'And he won't dare to annoy us further.'

She took my arm without a word, still trembling with excitement and terror. Oh, obtrusive gentleman! How I blessed you at that moment! I stole a glance at her, she was very charming and dark – I had guessed right.

On her black eyelashes there still glistened a tear – from her recent terror or her former grief – I don't know. But there was already a gleam of a smile on her lips. She too stole a glance at me, faintly blushed and looked down.

'There, you see; why did you drive me away? If I had been here, nothing would have happened . . . '

'But I did not know you; I thought that you too . . . '

'Why, do you know me now?'

'A little! Here, for instance, why are you trembling?'

'Oh, you are right at the first guess!' I answered, delighted that my girl had intelligence; that is never out of place in company with beauty. 'Yes, from the first glance you have guessed the sort of man you have to do with. Precisely; I am shy with women, I am agitated, I don't deny it, as much so as you were a minute ago when that gentleman alarmed you. I am in some alarm now. It's like a dream, and I never guessed even in my sleep that I should ever talk with any woman.'

'What? Really? . . . '

'Yes; if my arm trembles, it is because it has never been held by a pretty little hand like yours. I am a complete stranger to women; that is, I have never been used to them. You see, I am alone . . . I don't even know how to talk to them. Here, I don't know now whether I have not said something silly to you! Tell me frankly; I assure you beforehand that I am not quick to take offence? . . . '

'No, nothing, nothing, quite the contrary. And if you insist on my speaking frankly, I will tell you that women like such timidity; and if you want to know more, I like it too, and I won't drive you away till I get home.'

'You will make me,' I said, breathless with delight, 'lose my timidity, and then farewell to all my chances . . . '

'Chances! What chances – of what? That's not so nice.'

'I beg your pardon, I am sorry, it was a slip of the tongue; but how can you expect one at such a moment to have no desire . . . '

'To be liked, eh?'

'Well, yes; but do, for goodness' sake, be kind. Think what I am! Here I am, twenty-six and I have never seen anyone. How can I speak well, tactfully, and to the point? It will seem better to you when I have told you everything openly . . . I don't know how to be silent when my heart is speaking. Well, never mind . . . Believe me, not one woman, never, never! No acquaintance of any sort! And I do nothing but dream every day that at last I shall meet someone. Oh, if only you knew how often I have been in love in that way . . . '

'How? With whom? . . . '

'Why, with no one, with an ideal, with the one I dream of in my sleep. I make up regular romances in my dreams. Ah, you don't know me! It's true, of course, I have met two or three women, but what sort of women were they? They were all landladies, that . . . But I shall make you laugh if I tell you that I have several times thought of speaking, just simply speaking, to some aristocratic lady in the street, when she is alone, I need hardly say; speaking to her, of course, timidly, respectfully, passionately; telling her that I am perishing in solitude, begging her not to send me away; saying that I have no chance of making the acquaintance of any woman; impressing upon her that it is a positive duty for a woman not to repulse so timid a prayer from such a luckless man as me. That, in fact, all I ask is that she should say two or three sisterly words with sympathy, should not repulse me at first sight; should take me on trust and listen to what I say; should laugh at me if she likes, encourage me, say two words to me, only two words, even though we never meet again afterwards! . . . But you are laughing; however, that is why I am telling you . . . '

'Don't be vexed; I am only laughing at your being your own enemy, and if you had tried you would have succeeded, perhaps, even though it had been in the street; the simpler the better . . . No kind-hearted woman, unless she were stupid or, still more, vexed about something at the moment, could bring herself to send you away without those two words which you ask for so timidly . . . But what am I saying? Of course she would take you for a madman. I was judging by myself; I know a good deal about other people's lives.'

'Oh, thank you,' I cried; 'you don't know what you have done for me now!'

'I am glad! I am glad! But tell me how did you find out that I was the sort of woman with whom . . . well, whom you think worthy . . . of attention and friendship . . . in fact, not a landlady as you say? What made you decide to come up to me?'

'What made me? . . . But you were alone; that gentleman was too insolent; it's night. You must admit that it was a duty . . . '

'No, no; I mean before, on the other side – you know you meant to come up to me.'

'On the other side? Really I don't know how to answer; I am afraid to . . . Do you know I have been happy today? I walked along singing; I went out into the country; I have never had such happy moments.

You ... perhaps it was my fancy ... Forgive me for referring to it; I fancied you were crying, and I ... could not bear to hear it ... it made my heart ache ... Oh, my goodness! Surely I might be troubled about you? Surely there was no harm in feeling brotherly compassion for you ... I beg your pardon, I said compassion ... Well, in short, surely you would not be offended at my involuntary impulse to go up to you? ... '

'Stop, that's enough, don't talk of it,' said the girl, looking down, and pressing my hand. 'It's my fault for having spoken of it; but I am glad I was not mistaken in you ... But here I am home; I must go down this turning, it's two steps from here ... Goodbye, thank you! ... '

'Surely ... surely you don't mean ... that we shall never see each other again? ... Surely this is not to be the end?'

'You see,' said the girl, laughing, 'at first you only wanted two words, and now ... However, I won't say anything ... perhaps we shall meet ... '

'I shall come here tomorrow,' I said. 'Oh, forgive me, I am already making demands ... '

'Yes, you are not very patient ... you are almost insisting.'

'Listen, listen!' I interrupted her. 'Forgive me if I tell you something else ... I tell you what, I can't help coming here tomorrow. I am a dreamer; I have so little real life that I look upon such moments as this now as so rare that I cannot help going over such moments again in my dreams. I shall be dreaming of you all night, a whole week, a whole year. I shall certainly come here tomorrow, just here to this place, just at the same hour, and I shall be happy remembering today. This place is dear to me already. I have already two or three such places in Petersburg. I once shed tears over memories ... like you ... Who knows, perhaps you were weeping ten minutes ago over some memory ... But, forgive me, I have forgotten myself again; perhaps you have once been particularly happy here ... '

'Very good,' said the girl, 'perhaps I will come here tomorrow, too, at ten o'clock. I see that I can't forbid you ... The fact is, I have to be here; don't imagine that I am making an appointment with you; I tell you beforehand that I have to be here on my own account. But ... well, I tell you straight out, I don't mind if you do come. To begin with, something unpleasant might happen as it did today, but never mind that ... In short, I should simply like to see you ... to say two words to you. Only, mind, you must not think the worse of me now! Don't think I make appointments so lightly ... I shouldn't make it except that ... But let that be my secret! Only a compact beforehand ... '

'A compact! Speak, tell me, tell me all beforehand; I agree to anything,

I am ready for anything,' I cried delighted. 'I answer for myself, I will be obedient, respectful . . . you know me . . . '

'It's just because I do know you that I ask you to come tomorrow,' said the girl, laughing. 'I know you perfectly. But mind you will come on the condition, in the first place (only be good, do what I ask – you see, I speak frankly), you won't fall in love with me . . . That's impossible, I assure you. I am ready for friendship; here's my hand . . . But you mustn't fall in love with me, I beg you!'

'I swear,' I cried, gripping her hand . . .

'Hush, don't swear, I know you are ready to flare up like gunpowder. Don't think ill of me for saying so. If only you knew . . . I, too, have no one to whom I can say a word, whose advice I can ask. Of course, one does not look for an adviser in the street; but you are an exception. I know you as though we had been friends for twenty years . . . You won't deceive me, will you? . . . '

'You will see . . . the only thing is, I don't know how I am going to survive the next twenty-four hours.'

'Sleep soundly. Good-night, and remember that I have trusted you already. But you exclaimed so nicely just now, "Surely one can't be held responsible for every feeling, even for brotherly sympathy!" Do you know, that was so nicely said that the idea struck me at once that I might confide in you?'

'For God's sake do; but about what? What is it?'

'Wait till tomorrow. Meanwhile, let that be a secret. So much the better for you; it will give it a faint flavour of romance. Perhaps I will tell you tomorrow, and perhaps not . . . I will talk to you a little more beforehand; we will get to know each other better . . . '

'Oh yes, I will tell you all about myself tomorrow! But what has happened? It is as though a miracle had befallen me . . . My God, where am I? Come, tell me aren't you glad that you were not angry and did not drive me away at the first moment, as any other woman would have done? In two minutes you have made me happy for ever. Yes, happy; who knows, perhaps, you have reconciled me with myself, solved my doubts! . . . Perhaps such moments come upon me . . . But there I will tell you all about it tomorrow, you shall know everything, everything . . . '

'Very well, I consent; you shall begin . . . '

'Agreed.'

'Goodbye till tomorrow!'

'Till tomorrow!'

And we parted. I walked about all night; I could not make up my mind to go home. I was so happy . . . Tomorrow!

SECOND NIGHT

'Well, so you have survived!' she said, pressing both my hands.

'I've been here for the last two hours; you don't know what a state I have been in all day.'

'I know, I know. But to business. Do you know why I have come? Not to talk nonsense, as I did yesterday. I tell you what, we must behave more sensibly in future. I thought a great deal about it last night.'

'In what way – in what must we be more sensible? I am ready for my part; but, really, nothing more sensible has happened to me in my life than this, now.'

'Really? In the first place, I beg you not to squeeze my hands so; secondly, I must tell you that I spent a long time thinking about you and feeling doubtful today.'

'And how did it end?'

'How did it end? The upshot of it is that we must begin all over again, because the conclusion I reached today was that I don't know you at all; that I behaved like a baby last night, like a little girl; and, of course, the fact of it is that it's my soft heart that is to blame – that is, I sang my own praises, as one always does in the end when one analyses one's conduct. And therefore to correct my mistake, I've made up my mind to find out all about you minutely. But as I have no one from whom I can find out anything, you must tell me everything fully yourself. Well, what sort of man are you? Come, make haste – begin – tell me your whole history.'

'My history!' I cried in alarm. 'My history! But who has told you I have a history? I have no history . . . '

'Then how have you lived, if you have no history?' she interrupted, laughing.

'Absolutely without any history! I have lived, as they say, keeping myself to myself, that is, utterly alone – alone, entirely alone. Do you know what it means to be alone?'

'But how alone? Do you mean you never saw anyone?'

'Oh no, I see people, of course; but still I am alone.'

'Why, do you never talk to anyone?'

'Strictly speaking, with no one.'

'Who are you then? Explain yourself! Stay, I guess: most likely, like me you have a grandmother. She is blind and will never let me go anywhere, so that I have almost forgotten how to talk; and when I played some pranks two years ago, and she saw there was no holding me in, she called me to her side and pinned my dress to hers, and ever since we sit like that for days together; she knits a stocking, though she's blind, and I sit beside her, sew or read aloud to her – it's such a queer habit, here for two years I've been pinned to her . . . '

'Good Heavens! what misery! But no, I haven't a grandmother like that.'

'Well, if you haven't why do you sit at home? . . . '

'Listen, do you want to know the sort of man I am?'

'Yes, yes!'

'In the strict sense of the word?'

'In the very strictest sense of the word.'

'Very well, I am a type!'

'Type, type! What sort of type?' cried the girl, laughing, as though she had not had a chance of laughing for a whole year. 'Yes, it's very amusing talking to you. Look, here's a seat, let us sit down. No one is passing here, no one will hear us, and – begin your history. For it's no good protesting, I know you have a history; only you are concealing it. To begin with, what is a type?'

'A type? A type is an original, it's an absurd person!' I said, infected by her childish laughter. 'It's a character. Listen; do you know what is meant by a dreamer?'

'A dreamer! Indeed I should think I do know. I am a dreamer myself. Sometimes, as I sit by grandmother, all sorts of things come into my head. Why, when one begins dreaming one lets one's fancy run away with one – why, I marry a Chinese prince! . . . Though sometimes it is a good thing to dream! But, goodness knows! Especially when one has something to think of apart from dreams,' added the girl, this time rather seriously.

'Excellent! If you have been married to a Chinese emperor, you will quite understand me. Come, listen . . . But one minute, I don't know your name yet.'

'At last! You have been in no hurry to think of it!'

'Oh, my goodness! It never entered my head. I felt quite happy as it was . . . '

'My name is Nastenka.'

'Nastenka! And nothing else?'

'Nothing else! Why, is not that enough for you, you insatiable person?'

'Not enough? On the contrary, it's a great deal, a very great deal, Nastenka, you kind girl, if you are Nastenka for me from the first.'

'Quite so! Well?'

'Well, listen, Nastenka, now for this absurd history.'

I sat down beside her, assumed a pedantically serious attitude, and began as though reading from a manuscript. 'There are, Nastenka, though you may not know it, strange nooks in Petersburg. It seems as though the same sun as shines for all Petersburg people does not peep into those spots, but some other different new one, bespoken expressly for those nooks, and it throws a different light on everything. In these corners, dear Nastenka, quite a different life is lived, quite unlike the life that is surging round us, but such as perhaps exists in some unknown realm, not among us in our serious, over-serious, time. Well, that life is a mixture of something purely fantastic, fervently ideal, with something (alas! Nastenka) dingily prosaic and ordinary, not to say incredibly vulgar.'

'Foo! Good heavens! What a preface! What do I hear?'

'Listen, Nastenka. (It seems to me I shall never be tired of calling you Nastenka.) Let me tell you that in these corners live strange people – dreamers. The dreamer – if you want an exact definition – is not a human being, but a creature of an intermediate sort. For the most part he settles in some inaccessible corner, as though hiding from the light of day; once he slips into his corner, he grows to it like a snail, or, anyway, he is in that respect very much like that remarkable creature which is an animal and a house both at once and is called a tortoise. Why do you suppose he is so fond of his four walls, which are invariably painted green, grimy, dismal and reeking unpardonably of tobacco smoke? Why is it that when this absurd gentleman is visited by one of his few acquaintances (and he ends by getting rid of all his friends), why does this absurd person meet him with such embarrassment, changing countenance and overcome with confusion, as though he had only just committed some crime within his four walls; as though he had been forging counterfeit notes, or as though he were writing verses to be sent to a journal with an anonymous letter, in which he states that the real poet is dead, and that his friend thinks it his sacred duty to publish his things? Why, tell me, Nastenka, why is it conversation is not easy between the two friends? Why is there no laughter? Why does no lively word fly from the tongue of the perplexed newcomer, who at other times may be very fond of laughter, lively words, conversation about the fair sex, and other cheerful subjects? And why does this friend, probably a new friend and on his first visit – for there will hardly be a second since the friend will never come again – why is the friend himself so confused, so tongue-tied, in spite of his wit (if he has any), as he looks at the downcast face of his host, who in his turn becomes utterly helpless and at his wits' end after gigantic but fruitless efforts to smooth things over and enliven the conversation, to show his knowledge of polite society, to talk, too, of the fair sex, and by such humble endeavour, to please the poor man, who like a fish out of water has mistakenly come to visit him? Why does the gentleman, all at once remembering some very necessary business which never existed, suddenly seize his hat and hurriedly make off, snatching away his hand from the warm grip of his host, who is trying his utmost to show his regret and retrieve the lost position? Why does the friend chuckle as he goes out of the door, and swear never to come and see this queer creature again, though the queer creature is really a very good fellow, and at the same time he cannot refuse his imagination the little diversion of comparing the queer fellow's countenance during their conversation with the expression of an unhappy kitten treacherously captured, roughly handled, frightened and subjected to all sorts of indignities by children, till, utterly crestfallen, it hides away from them under a chair in the dark, and there must needs at its leisure bristle up, spit and wash its insulted face with both paws, and long afterwards look angrily at life and nature, and even at the bits saved from the master's dinner for it by the sympathetic housekeeper?'

'Listen,' interrupted Nastenka, who had listened to me all the time in amazement, opening her eyes and her little mouth. 'Listen; I don't know in the least why it happened and why you ask me such absurd questions; all I know is that this adventure must have happened word for word to you.'

'Doubtless,' I answered, with the gravest face.

'Well, since there is no doubt about it, go on,' said Nastenka, 'because I want very much to know how it will end.'

'You want to know, Nastenka, what our hero, that is I – for the hero of the whole business was my humble self – did in his corner? You want to know why I lost my head and was upset for the whole day by the unexpected visit of a friend? You want to know why I was so startled, why I blushed when the door of my room was opened, why I was not able to entertain my visitor, and why I was crushed under the weight of my own hospitality?'

'Why, yes, yes,' answered Nastenka, 'that's the point. Listen. You describe it all splendidly, but couldn't you perhaps describe it a little less splendidly? You talk as though you were reading it out of a book.'

'Nastenka,' I answered in a stern and dignified voice, hardly able to keep from laughing, 'dear Nastenka, I know I describe splendidly, but, excuse me, I don't know how else to do it. At this moment, dear Nastenka, at this moment I am like the spirit of King Solomon[76] when, after lying a thousand years under seven seals in his urn, those seven seals are at last taken off. At this moment, Nastenka, when we have met at last after such a long separation – for I have known you for ages, Nastenka, because I have been looking for someone for ages, and that is a sign that it was you I was looking for, and it was ordained that we should meet now – at this moment a thousand valves have opened in my head, and I must let myself flow in a river of words, or I shall choke. And so I beg you not to interrupt me, Nastenka, but listen humbly and obediently, or I will be silent.'

'No, no, no! Not at all. Go on! I won't say a word!'

'I will continue. There is, my friend Nastenka, one hour in my day which I like extremely. That is the hour when almost all business, work and duties are over, and everyone is hurrying home to dinner, to lie down, to rest, and on the way all are cogitating on other more cheerful subjects relating to their evenings, their nights, and all the rest of their free time. At that hour our hero – for allow me, Nastenka, to tell my story in the third person, for one feels awfully ashamed to tell it in the first person – and so at that hour our hero, who had his work too, was pacing along after the others. But a strange feeling of pleasure set his pale, rather crumpled-looking face working. He looked not with indifference on the evening glow which was slowly fading on the cold Petersburg sky. When I say he looked, I am lying: he did not look at it, but saw it as it were without realising, as though tired or preoccupied with some other more interesting subject, so that he could scarcely spare a glance for anything about him. He was pleased because till next day he was released from business irksome to him, and happy as a schoolboy let out from the classroom to his games and mischief. Take a look at him, Nastenka; you will see at once that joyful emotion has already had an effect on his weak nerves and morbidly excited fancy. You see he is thinking of something . . . Of dinner, do you imagine? Of the evening? What is he looking at like that? Is it at that gentleman of dignified appearance who is bowing so picturesquely to the lady who rolls by in a carriage drawn by prancing horses? No, Nastenka; what are all those trivialities to him now! He is rich now with his *own individual* life; he has suddenly become rich, and it is not for nothing that the fading sunset sheds its farewell gleams so gaily before him, and calls forth a swarm of impressions from his warmed heart. Now he hardly notices the road, on which the tiniest details at other times would strike him. Now "the Goddess of Fancy" (if you have read Zhukovsky,[77] dear Nastenka) has already with fantastic hand spun her golden warp and begun weaving upon it patterns of marvellous magic life – and who knows, maybe, her fantastic hand has borne him to the seventh crystal heaven[78] far from the excellent granite pavement on which he was walking his way? Try stopping him now, ask him suddenly where he is standing now, through what streets he is going – he will, probably remember nothing, neither where he is going nor where he is standing now, and flushing with vexation he will certainly tell some lie to save appearances. That is why he starts, almost cries out, and looks round with horror when a respectable old lady stops him politely in the middle of the pavement and asks her way. Frowning with vexation he strides on, scarcely noticing that more than one passer-by smiles and turns round to look after him, and that a little girl, moving out of his way in alarm, laughs aloud, gazing open-eyed at his broad meditative smile and gesticulations. But fancy catches up in its playful flight the old woman, the curious passers-by and the laughing child, and the peasants spending their nights in their barges on Fontanka (our hero, let us suppose, is walking along the canal-side at that moment), and capriciously weaves everyone and everything into the canvas like a fly in a spider's web. And it is only after the queer fellow has returned to his comfortable den with fresh stores for his mind to work on, has sat down and finished his dinner, that he comes to himself, when Matrona who waits upon him – always thoughtful and depressed – clears the table and gives him his pipe; he comes to himself then and recalls with surprise that he has dined, though he has absolutely no notion how it has happened. It has grown dark in the room; his soul is sad and empty; the whole kingdom of fancies drops to pieces about him, drops to pieces without a trace, without a sound, floats away like a dream, and he cannot himself remember what he was dreaming. But a vague sensation faintly stirs his heart and sets it aching, some new desire temptingly tickles and excites his fancy, and imperceptibly evokes a swarm of fresh phantoms. Stillness reigns in the little room; imagination is fostered by solitude and idleness; it is faintly smouldering, faintly simmering, like the water with which old Matrona is making her coffee as she moves quietly about in the kitchen close by. Now it breaks out spasmodically; and the book, picked up aimlessly and at random, drops from my dreamer's hand before he has reached the third page. His imagination is again stirred and at work, and again a new world, a new fascinating life opens vistas before him. A fresh dream – fresh happiness! A fresh rush of delicate, voluptuous poison! What is real life to him! To his corrupted eyes we live, you and I, Nastenka, so torpidly, slowly, insipidly; in his eyes we are all so dissatisfied with our fate, so exhausted by our life! And, truly, see how at first sight everything is cold, morose, as though ill-humoured among us . . . Poor things! thinks our dreamer.

And it is no wonder that he thinks it! Look at these magic phantasms, which so enchantingly, so whimsically, so carelessly and freely group before him in such a magic, animated picture, in which the most prominent figure in the foreground is of course himself, our dreamer, in his precious person. See what varied adventures, what an endless swarm of ecstatic dreams. You ask, perhaps, what he is dreaming of. Why ask that? – why, of everything ... of the lot of the poet, first unrecognised, then crowned with laurels; of friendship with Hoffmann,[79] St Bartholomew's Night,[80] of Diana Vernon,[81] of playing the hero at the taking of Kazan by Ivan Vassilyevitch,[82] of Clara Mowbray,[83] of Effie Deans,[84] of the council of the prelates and Huss[85] before them, of the rising of the dead in "Robert the Devil"[86] (do you remember the music, it smells of the churchyard!), of Minna and Brenda,[87] of the battle of Berezina,[88] of the reading of a poem at Countess V. D.'s,[89] of Danton,[90] of Cleopatra *e i suoi amanti*,[91] of a "Little House in Kolomna",[92] of a little home of one's own and beside one a dear creature who listens to one on a winter's evening, opening her little mouth and eyes as you are listening to me now, my angel ... No, Nastenka, what is there, what is there for him, voluptuous sluggard, in this life, for which you and I have such a longing? He thinks that this is a poor pitiful life, not foreseeing that for him too, maybe, sometime the mournful hour may strike, when for one day of that pitiful life he would give all his years of fantasy, and would give them not only for joy and for happiness, but without caring to make distinctions in that hour of sadness, remorse and unchecked grief. But so far that threatening time has not arrived – he desires nothing, because he is superior to all desire, because he has everything, because he is satiated, because he is the artist of his own life, and creates it for himself every hour to suit his latest whim. And you know this fantastic world of fairyland is so easily, so naturally created! As though it were not a delusion! Indeed, he is ready to believe at some moments that all this life is not suggested by feeling, is not mirage, not a delusion of the imagination, but that it is concrete, real, substantial! Why is it, Nastenka, why is it at such moments one holds one's breath? Why, by what sorcery, through what incomprehensible caprice, is the pulse quickened, does a tear start from the dreamer's eye, while his pale moist cheeks glow, while his whole being is suffused with an inexpressible sense of consolation? Why is it that whole sleepless nights pass like a flash in inexhaustible gladness and happiness, and when the dawn gleams rosy at the window and daybreak floods the gloomy room with uncertain, fantastic light, as in Petersburg, our dreamer, worn out and exhausted, flings himself on his bed and drops asleep with thrills of delight in his morbidly overwrought spirit, and with a weary sweet ache in his heart? Yes, Nastenka, one deceives oneself and unconsciously believes that real true passion is stirring one's soul; one unconsciously believes that there is something living, tangible in one's immaterial dreams! And is it delusion? Here love, for instance, is bound up with all its fathomless joy, all its torturing agonies in his bosom . . . Only look at him, and you will be convinced! Would you believe, looking at him, dear Nastenka, that he has never known her whom he loves in his ecstatic dreams? Can it be that he has only seen her in seductive visions, and that this passion has been nothing but a dream? Surely they must have spent years hand in hand together – alone the two of them, casting off all the world and each uniting his or her life with the other's? Surely when the hour of parting came she must have lain sobbing and grieving on his bosom, heedless of the tempest raging under the sullen sky, heedless of the wind which snatches and bears away the tears from her black eyelashes? Can all of that have been a dream – and that garden, dejected, forsaken, run wild, with its little moss-grown paths, solitary, gloomy, where they used to walk so happily together, where they hoped, grieved, loved, loved each other so long, 'so long and so fondly'?[93] And that queer ancestral house where she spent so many years lonely and sad with her morose old husband, always silent and splenetic, who frightened them, while timid as children they hid their love from each other? What torments they suffered, what agonies of terror, how innocent, how pure was their love, and how (I need hardly say, Nastenka) malicious people were! And, good heavens! surely he met her afterwards, far from their native shores, under alien skies, in the hot south in the divinely eternal city, in the dazzling splendour of the ball to the crash of music, in a *palazzo* (it must be in a *palazzo*), drowned in a sea of lights, on the balcony, wreathed in myrtle and roses, where, recognising him, she hurriedly removes her mask and whispering, "I am free," flings herself trembling into his arms, and with a cry of rapture, clinging to one another, in one instant they forget their sorrow and their parting and all their agonies, and the gloomy house and the old man and the dismal garden in that distant land, and the seat on which with a last passionate kiss she tore herself away from his arms numb with anguish and despair . . . Oh, Nastenka, you must admit that one would start, betray confusion, and blush like a schoolboy who has just stuffed in his pocket an apple stolen from a neighbour's garden, when your uninvited visitor, some stalwart, lanky fellow, a festive soul fond of a joke, opens your door and shouts out as though nothing were happening: "My dear boy, I have this minute come from Pavlovsk." My goodness! the old count is dead, unutterable happiness is close at hand – and people arrive from Pavlovsk!'

Finishing my pathetic appeal, I paused pathetically. I remembered that I had an intense desire to force myself to laugh, for I was already feeling that a malignant demon was stirring within me, that there was a lump in my throat, that my chin was beginning to twitch, and that my eyes were growing more and more moist.

I expected Nastenka, who listened to me opening her clever eyes, would break into her childish, irrepressible laugh; and I was already regretting that I had gone so far, that I had unnecessarily described what had long been simmering in my heart, about which I could speak as though from a written account of it, because I had long ago passed judgement on myself and now could not resist reading it, making my confession, without expecting to be understood; but to my surprise she was silent, waiting a little, then she faintly pressed my hand and with timid sympathy asked: 'Surely you haven't lived like that all your life?'

'All my life, Nastenka,' I answered; 'all my life, and it seems to me I shall go on so to the end.'

'No, that won't do,' she said uneasily, 'that must not be; and so, maybe, I shall spend all my life beside grandmother. Do you know, it is not at all good to live like that?'

'I know, Nastenka, I know!' I cried, unable to restrain my feelings longer. 'And I realise now, more than ever, that I have lost all my best years! And now I know it and feel it more painfully from recognising that God has sent me you, my good angel, to tell me that and show it. Now that I sit beside you and talk to you it is strange for me to think of the future, for in the future – there is loneliness again, again this musty, useless life; and what shall I have to dream of when I have been so happy in reality beside you! Oh, may you be blessed, dear girl, for not having repulsed me at first, for enabling me to say that for two evenings, at least, I have lived.'

'Oh, no, no!' cried Nastenka and tears glistened in her eyes. 'No, it mustn't be so any more; we must not part like that! what are two evenings?'

'Oh, Nastenka, Nastenka! Do you know how far you have reconciled me to myself? Do you know now that I shall not think so ill of myself, as I have at some moments? Do you know that, maybe, I shall leave off grieving over the crime and sin of my life? for such a life is a crime and a sin. And do not imagine that I have been exaggerating anything – for goodness' sake don't think that, Nastenka: for at times such misery comes over me, such misery . . . Because it begins to seem to me at such times that I am incapable of beginning a life in real life, because it has seemed to me that I have lost all touch, all instinct for the actual, the real; because at last I have cursed myself; because after my fantastic nights I have moments of returning sobriety, which are awful! Meanwhile, you hear the whirl and roar of the crowd in the vortex of life around you; you hear, you see, men living in reality; you see that life for them is not forbidden, that their life does not float away like a dream, like a vision; that their life is being eternally renewed, eternally youthful, and not one hour of it is the same as another; while fancy is so spiritless, monotonous to vulgarity and easily scared, the slave of shadows, of the idea, the slave of the first cloud that shrouds the sun, and overcasts with depression the true Petersburg heart so devoted to the sun – and what is fancy in depression! One feels that this *inexhaustible* fancy is weary at last and worn out with continual exercise, because one is growing into manhood, outgrowing one's old ideals: they are being shattered into fragments, into dust; if there is no other life one must build one up from the fragments. And meanwhile the soul longs and craves for something else! And in vain the dreamer rakes over his old dreams, as though seeking a spark among the embers, to fan them into flame, to warm his chilled heart by the rekindled fire, and to rouse up in it again all that was so sweet, that touched his heart, that set his blood boiling, drew tears from his eyes, and so luxuriously deceived him! Do you know, Nastenka, the point I have reached? Do you know that I am forced now to celebrate the anniversary of my own sensations, the anniversary of that which was once so sweet, which never existed in reality – for this anniversary is kept in memory of those same foolish, shadowy dreams – and to do this because those foolish dreams are no more, because I have nothing to earn them with; you know even dreams do not come for nothing! Do you know that I love now to recall and visit at certain dates the places where I was once happy in my own way? I love to build up my present in harmony with the irrevocable past, and I often wander like a shadow, aimless, sad and dejected, about the streets and crooked lanes of Petersburg. What memories they are! To remember, for instance, that here just a year ago, just at this time, at this hour, on this pavement, I wandered just as lonely, just as dejected as today. And one remembers that then one's dreams were sad, and though the past was no better one feels as though it had somehow been better, and that life was more peaceful, that one was free from the black thoughts that haunt one now; that one was free from the gnawing of conscience – the gloomy, sullen gnawing which now gives me no rest by day or by night.

And one asks oneself where are one's dreams. And one shakes one's head and says how rapidly the years fly by! And again one asks oneself what has one done with one's years. Where have you buried your best days? Have you lived or not? Look, one says to oneself, look how cold the world is growing. Some more years will pass, and after them will come gloomy solitude; then will come old age trembling on its crutch, and after it misery and desolation. Your fantastic world will grow pale, your dreams will fade and die and will fall like the yellow leaves from the trees . . . Oh, Nastenka! you know it will be sad to be left alone, utterly alone, and to have not even anything to regret – nothing, absolutely nothing . . . for all that you have lost, all that, all was nothing, stupid, simple nullity, there has been nothing but dreams!'

'Come, don't work on my feelings any more,' said Nastenka, wiping away a tear which was trickling down her cheek. 'Now it's over! Now we shall be two together. Now, whatever happens to me, we will never part. Listen; I am a simple girl, I have not had much education, though grandmother did get a teacher for me, but truly I understand you, for all that you have described I have been through myself, when grandmother pinned me to her dress. Of course, I should not have described it so well as you have; I am not educated,' she added timidly, for she was still feeling a sort of respect for my pathetic eloquence and lofty style; 'but I am very glad that you have been quite open with me. Now I know you thoroughly, all of you. And do you know what? I want to tell you my history too, all without concealment, and after that you must give me advice. You are a very clever man; will you promise to give me advice?'

'Ah, Nastenka,' I cried, 'though I have never given advice, still less sensible advice, yet I see now that if we always go on like this that it will be very sensible, and that each of us will give the other a great deal of sensible advice! Well, my pretty Nastenka, what sort of advice do you want? Tell me frankly; at this moment I am so gay and happy, so bold and sensible, that it won't be difficult for me to find words.'

'No, no!' Nastenka interrupted, laughing. 'I don't only want sensible advice, I want warm brotherly advice, as though you had been fond of me all your life!'

'Agreed, Nastenka, agreed!' I cried delighted; 'and if I had been fond of you for twenty years, I couldn't have been fonder of you than I am now.'

'Your hand,' said Nastenka.

'Here it is,' said I, giving her my hand.

'And so let us begin my history!'

NASTENKA'S HISTORY

'Half my story you know already – that is, you know that I have an old grandmother . . . '

'If the other half is as brief as that . . . ' I interrupted, laughing.

'Be quiet and listen. First of all you must agree not to interrupt me, or else perhaps I shall get in a muddle! Come, listen quietly.

'I have an old grandmother. I came into her hands when I was quite a little girl, for my father and mother are dead. It must be supposed that grandmother was once richer, for now she recalls better days. She taught me French, and then got a teacher for me. When I was fifteen (and now I am seventeen) we gave up having lessons. It was at that time that I got into mischief; what I did I won't tell you; it's enough to say that it wasn't very important. But grandmother called me to her one morning and said that as she was blind she could not look after me; she took a pin and pinned my dress to hers, and said that we should sit like that for the rest of our lives if, of course, I did not become a better girl. In fact, at first it was impossible to get away from her: I had to work, to read and to study all beside grandmother. I tried to deceive her once, and persuaded Fekla to sit in my place. Fekla is our charwoman, she is deaf. Fekla sat there instead of me; grandmother was asleep in her armchair at the time, and I went off to see a friend close by. Well, it ended in trouble. Grandmother woke up while I was out, and asked some questions; she thought I was still sitting quietly in my place. Fekla saw that grandmother was asking her something, but could not tell what it was; she wondered what to do, undid the pin and ran away . . . '

At this point Nastenka stopped and began laughing. I laughed with her. She left off at once.

'I tell you what, don't you laugh at grandmother. I laugh because it's funny . . . What can I do, since grandmother is like that; but yet I am fond of her in a way. Oh, well, I did catch it that time. I had to sit down in my place at once, and after that I was not allowed to stir.

'Oh, I forgot to tell you that our house belongs to us, that is to grandmother; it is a little wooden house with three windows, as old as grandmother herself, with a little upper storey; well, there moved into our upper storey a new lodger.'

'Then you had an old lodger,' I observed casually.

'Yes, of course,' answered Nastenka, 'and one who knew how to hold his tongue better than you do. In fact, he hardly ever used his tongue at all. He was a dumb, blind, lame, dried-up little old man, who at last could not go on living, so he died; then we had to find a new lodger, for we could not live without a lodger – the rent, together with grand-mother's pension, is almost all we have. But the new lodger, as luck would have it, was a young man, a stranger not of these parts. As he did not haggle over the rent, grandmother accepted him, and only afterwards did she ask me: "Tell me, Nastenka, what is our lodger like – is he young or old?" I did not want to lie, so I told grandmother that he wasn't exactly young and that he wasn't old.

' "And is he pleasant looking?" asked grandmother.

'Again I did not want to tell a lie: "Yes, he is pleasant looking, grand-mother,' I said.

'And grandmother said: "Oh, what a nuisance, what a nuisance! I tell you this, grandchild, that you may not be taking notice of him. What times these are! Why, a paltry lodger like this, and he must be pleasant looking too; it was very different in the old days!" '

'Grandmother was always regretting the old days – she was younger in the old days, and the sun was warmer in the old days, and cream did not turn so sour in the old days – it was always the old days! I would sit still and hold my tongue and think to myself: why did grandmother suggest it to me? Why did she ask whether the lodger was young and good-looking? But that was all, I just thought it, began counting my stitches again, went on knitting my stocking, and forgot all about it.

'Well, one morning the lodger came in to see us; he asked about a promise to paper his rooms. One thing led to another. Grandmother was talkative, and she said: "Go, Nastenka, into my bedroom and bring me my reckoner." I jumped up at once; I blushed all over, I don't know why, and forgot I was sitting pinned to grandmother; instead of quietly undoing the pin, so that the lodger should not see – I jumped so that grandmother's chair moved. When I saw that the lodger knew all about me now, I blushed, stood still as though I had been shot, and suddenly began to cry – I felt so ashamed and miserable at that minute, that I didn't know where to look! Grandmother called out, "What are you waiting for?" and I went on worse than ever. When the lodger saw that I was ashamed on his account, he bowed and went away at once!

'After that I felt ready to die at the least sound in the passage. "It's the lodger," I kept thinking; I stealthily undid the pin in case. But it always turned out not to be him; he never came. A fortnight passed; the lodger sent word through Fekla that he had a great number of French books, and that they were all good books that I might read, so would not grandmother like me to read them that I might not be dull?

Grandmother agreed with gratitude, but kept asking if they were moral books, for if the books were immoral it would be out of the question, one would learn evil from them.

' "And what should I learn, grandmother? What is there written in them?"

' "Ah," she said, "what's described in them, is how young men seduce virtuous girls; how, on the excuse that they want to marry them, they carry them off from their parents' houses; how afterwards they leave these unhappy girls to their fate, and they perish in the most pitiful way. I read a great many books," said grandmother, "and it is all so well described that one sits up all night and reads them on the sly. So mind you don't read them, Nastenka," said she. "What books has he sent?"

' "They are all Walter Scott's novels, grandmother."

' "Walter Scott's novels! But stay, isn't there some trick about it? Look, hasn't he stuck a love-letter among them?"

' "No, grandmother," I said, "there isn't a love-letter."

' "But look under the binding; they sometimes stuff it under the binding, the rascals!"

' "No, grandmother, there is nothing under the binding."

' "Well, that's all right."

'So we began reading Walter Scott, and in a month or so we had read almost half. Then he sent us more and more. He sent us Pushkin, too; so that at last I could not get on without a book and left off dreaming of how fine it would be to marry a Chinese prince.

'That's how things were when I chanced one day to meet our lodger on the stairs. Grandmother had sent me to fetch something. He stopped, I blushed and he blushed; he laughed, though, said good-morning to me, asked after grandmother, and said, "Well, have you read the books?" I answered that I had. "Which did you like best?" he asked. I said, "*Ivanhoe*,[94] and Pushkin best of all," and so our talk ended for that time.

'A week later I met him again on the stairs. That time grandmother had not sent me, I wanted to get something for myself. It was past two, and the lodger used to come home at that time. "Good-afternoon," said he. I said, "Good-afternoon," too.

' "Aren't you dull," he said, "sitting all day with your grandmother?"

'When he asked that, I blushed, I don't know why; I felt ashamed, and again I felt offended – I suppose because other people had begun to ask me about that. I wanted to go away without answering, but I hadn't the strength.

' "Listen," he said, "you are a good girl. Excuse my speaking to you like that, but I assure you that I wish for your welfare quite as much as your grandmother. Have you no friends that you could go and visit?"

'I told him I hadn't any, that I had had no friend but Mashenka, and she had gone away to Pskov.

' "Listen," he said, "would you like to go to the theatre with me?"

' "To the theatre. What about grandmother?"

' "But you must go without your grandmother's knowing it," he said.

' "No," I said, "I don't want to deceive grandmother. Goodbye.'

' "Well, goodbye,' he answered, and said nothing more.

'Only after dinner he came to see us; sat a long time talking to grandmother; asked her whether she ever went out anywhere, whether she had acquaintances, and suddenly said: "I have taken a box at the opera for this evening; they are giving *The Barber of Seville*. My friends meant to go, but afterwards refused, so the ticket is left on my hands.'

' "*The Barber of Seville*,"[95] cried grandmother; "why, the same they used to act in the old days?"

' "Yes, it's the same barber," he said, and glanced at me. I saw what it meant and turned crimson, and my heart began throbbing with suspense.

' "To be sure, I know it," said grandmother; "why, I took the part of Rosina myself in the old days, at a private performance!"

' "So wouldn't you like to go today?" said the lodger. "Or my ticket will be wasted."

' "By all means let us go," said grandmother; "why shouldn't we? And my Nastenka here has never been to the theatre."

'My goodness, what joy! We got ready at once, put on our best clothes, and set off. Though grandmother was blind, still she wanted to hear the music; besides, she is a kind old soul, what she cared most for was to amuse me; we should never have gone of ourselves.

'What my impressions of *The Barber of Seville* were I won't tell you; but all that evening our lodger looked at me so nicely, talked so nicely, that I saw at once that he had meant to test me in the morning when he proposed that I should go with him alone. Well, it was joy! I went to bed so proud, so gay, my heart beat so that I was a little feverish, and all night I was raving about *The Barber of Seville*.

'I expected that he would come and see us more and more often after that, but it wasn't so at all. He almost entirely gave up coming. He would just come in about once a month, and then only to invite us to the theatre. We went twice again. Only I wasn't at all pleased with that; I saw that he was simply sorry for me because I was so hardly treated by grandmother, and that was all. As time went on, I grew more and more restless. I couldn't sit still, I couldn't read, I couldn't work; sometimes I laughed and did something to annoy grandmother, at another time I would cry. At last I grew thin and was very nearly ill. The opera season was over, and our lodger had quite given up coming to see us; whenever we met – always on the same staircase, of course – he would bow so silently, so gravely, as though he did not want to speak, and go down to the front door, while I went on standing in the middle of the stairs, as red as a cherry, for all the blood rushed to my head at the sight of him.

'Now the end is near. Just a year ago, in May, the lodger came to us and said to grandmother that he had finished his business here, and that he must go back to Moscow for a year. When I heard that, I sank into a chair half dead; grandmother did not notice anything; and having informed us that he should be leaving us, he bowed and went away.

'What was I to do? I thought and thought and fretted and fretted, and at last I made up my mind. Next day he was to go away, and I made up my mind to end it all that evening when grandmother went to bed. And so it happened. I made up all my clothes in a parcel – all the linen I needed – and with the parcel in my hand, more dead than alive, went upstairs to our lodger. I believe I must have stayed an hour on the staircase. When I opened his door he cried out as he looked at me. He thought I was a ghost, and rushed to give me some water, for I could hardly stand up. My heart beat so violently that my head ached, and I did not know what I was doing. When I recovered I began by laying my parcel on his bed, sat down beside it, hid my face in my hands and went into floods of tears. I think he understood it all at once, and looked at me so sadly that my heart was torn.

' "Listen," he began, "listen, Nastenka, I can't do anything; I am a poor man, for I have nothing, not even a decent berth. How could we live, if I were to marry you?"

'We talked a long time; but at last I got quite frantic. I said I could not go on living with grandmother, that I should run away from her, that I did not want to be pinned to her, and that I would go to Moscow if he liked, because I could not live without him. Shame and pride and love were all clamouring in me at once, and I fell on the bed almost in convulsions, I was so afraid of a refusal.

'He sat for some minutes in silence, then got up, came up to me and took me by the hand.

' "Listen, my dear good Nastenka, listen; I swear to you that if I am ever in a position to marry, you shall make my happiness. I assure you that now you are the only one who could make me happy. Listen, I am going to Moscow and shall be there just a year; I hope to establish my position. When I come back, if you still love me, I swear that we will be happy. Now it is impossible, I am not able, I have not the right to promise anything. Well, I repeat, if it is not within a year it will certainly be some time; that is, of course, if you do not prefer anyone else, for I cannot and dare not bind you by any sort of promise."

'That was what he said to me, and next day he went away. We agreed together not to say a word to grandmother: that was his wish. Well, my history is nearly finished now. Just a year has past. He has arrived; he has been here three days, and, and – '

'And what?' I cried, impatient to hear the end.

'And up to now has not shown himself!' answered Nastenka, as though screwing up all her courage. 'There's no sign or sound of him.'

Here she stopped, paused for a minute, bent her head, and covering her face with her hands broke into such sobs that it sent a pang to my heart to hear them. I had not in the least expected such a dénouement.

'Nastenka,' I began timidly in an ingratiating voice, 'Nastenka! For goodness' sake don't cry! How do you know? Perhaps he is not here yet . . . '

'He is, he is,' Nastenka repeated. 'He is here, and I know it. We *made an agreement* at the time, that evening, before he went away: when we said all that I have told you, and had come to an understanding, then we came out here for a walk on this embankment. It was ten o'clock; we sat on this seat. I was not crying then; it was sweet to me to hear what he said . . . And he said that he would come to us directly he arrived, and if I did not refuse him, then we would tell grandmother about it all. Now he is here, I know it, and yet he does not come!'

And again she burst into tears.

'Good God, can I do nothing to help you in your sorrow?' I cried jumping up from the seat in utter despair. 'Tell me, Nastenka, wouldn't it be possible for me to go to him?'

'Would that be possible?' she asked suddenly, raising her head.

'No, of course not,' I said pulling myself up; 'but I tell you what, write a letter.'

'No, that's impossible, I can't do that,' she answered with decision, bending her head and not looking at me.

'How impossible – why is it impossible?' I went on, clinging to my idea. 'But, Nastenka, it depends what sort of letter; there are letters and letters and . . . Ah, Nastenka, I am right; trust to me, trust to me, I will not give you bad advice. It can all be arranged! You took the first step – why not now?'

'I can't. I can't! It would seem as though I were forcing myself on him . . . '

'Ah, my good little Nastenka,' I said, hardly able to conceal a smile; 'no, no, you have a right to, in fact, because he made you a promise. Besides, I can see from everything that he is a man of delicate feeling; that he behaved very well,' I went on, more and more carried away by the logic of my own arguments and convictions. 'How did he behave? He bound himself by a promise: he said that if he married at all he would marry no one but you; he gave you full liberty to refuse him at once . . . Under such circumstances you may take the first step; you have the right; you are in the privileged position – if, for instance, you wanted to free him from his promise . . . '

'Listen; how would you write?'

'Write what?'

'This letter.'

'I tell you how I would write: "Dear sir" . . . '

'Must I really begin like that, "Dear sir"?'

'You certainly must! Though, after all, I don't know, I imagine . . . '

'Well, well, what next?'

' "Dear sir – I must apologise for – " But, no, there's no need to apologise; the fact itself justifies everything. Write simply:

I am writing to you. Forgive me my impatience; but I have been happy for a whole year in hope; am I to blame for being unable to endure a day of doubt now? Now that you have come, perhaps you have changed your mind. If so, this letter is to tell you that I do not repine, nor blame you. I do not blame you because I have no power over your heart, such is my fate!

You are an honourable man. You will not smile or be vexed at these impatient lines. Remember they are written by a poor girl; that she is alone; that she has no one to direct her, no one to advise her, and that she herself could never control her heart. But forgive me that a doubt has stolen – if only for one instant – into my heart. You are not capable of insulting, even in thought, her who so loved and so loves you.'

'Yes, yes; that's exactly what I was thinking!' cried Nastenka, and her eyes beamed with delight. 'Oh, you have solved my difficulties: God has sent you to me! Thank you, thank you!'

'What for? What for? For God's sending me?' I answered, looking delighted at her joyful little face.

'Why, yes; for that too.'

'Ah, Nastenka! Why, one thanks some people for being alive at the same time with one; I thank you for having met me, for my being able to remember you all my life!'

'Well, enough, enough! But now I tell you what, listen: we made an agreement then that as soon as he arrived he would let me know, by leaving a letter with some good simple people of my acquaintance who know nothing about it; or, if it were impossible to write a letter to me, for a letter does not always tell everything, he would be here at ten o'clock on the day he arrived, where we had arranged to meet. I know he has arrived already; but now it's the third day, and there's no sign of him and no letter. It's impossible for me to get away from grandmother in the morning. Give my letter tomorrow to those kind people I spoke to you about: they will send it on to him, and if there is an answer you bring it tomorrow at ten o'clock.'

'But the letter, the letter! You see, you must write the letter first! So perhaps it must all be the day after tomorrow.'

'The letter . . . ' said Nastenka, a little confused, 'the letter . . . but . . . '[96]

But she did not finish. At first she turned her little face away from me, flushed like a rose, and suddenly I felt in my hand a letter which had evidently been written long before, all ready and sealed up. A familiar sweet and charming reminiscence floated through my mind.

'R, o – Ro; s, i – si; n, a – na,' I began.

'Rosina!' we both hummed together; I almost embracing her with delight, while she blushed as only she could blush, and laughed through the tears which gleamed like pearls on her black eyelashes.

'Come, enough, enough! Goodbye now,' she said speaking rapidly. 'Here is the letter, here is the address to which you are to take it. Goodbye, till we meet again! Till tomorrow!'

She pressed both my hands warmly, nodded her head, and flew like an arrow down her side street. I stood still for a long time following her with my eyes.

'Till tomorrow! till tomorrow!' was ringing in my ears as she vanished from my sight.

THIRD NIGHT

Today was a gloomy, rainy day without a glimmer of sunlight, like the old age before me. I am oppressed by such strange thoughts, such gloomy sensations; questions still so obscure to me are crowding into my brain – and I seem to have neither power nor will to settle them. It's not for me to settle all this!

Today we shall not meet. Yesterday, when we said goodbye,

the clouds began gathering over the sky and a mist rose. I said that tomorrow it would be a bad day; she made no answer, she did not want to speak against her wishes; for her that day was bright and clear, not one cloud should obscure her happiness.

'If it rains we shall not see each other,' she said. 'I shall not come.'

I thought that she would not notice today's rain, and yet she has not come.

Yesterday was our third interview, our third white night . . . But how fine joy and happiness makes anyone! How brimming over with love the heart is! One seems longing to pour out one's whole heart; one wants everything to be gay, everything to be laughing. And how infectious that joy is! There was such a softness in her words, such a kindly feeling in her heart towards me yesterday . . . How solicitous and friendly she was; how tenderly she tried to give me courage! Oh, the coquetry of happiness! While I . . . I took it all for the genuine thing. I thought that she . . . But, my God, how could I have thought it? How could I have been so blind, when everything had been taken by another already, when nothing was mine; when, in fact, her very tenderness to me, her anxiety, her love . . . yes, love for me, was nothing else but joy at the thought of seeing another man so soon, desire to include me, too, in her happiness? . . . When he did not come, when we waited in vain, she frowned, she grew timid and discouraged. Her movements, her words, were no longer so light, so playful, so gay; and, strange to say, she redoubled her attentiveness to me, as though instinctively desiring to lavish on me what she desired for herself so anxiously, if her wishes were not accomplished. My Nastenka was so downcast, so dismayed, that I think she realised at last that I loved her, and was sorry for my poor love. So when we are unhappy we feel the unhappiness of others more; feeling is not destroyed but concentrated . . . I went to meet her with a full heart, and was all impatience. I had no presentiment that I should feel as I do now, that it would not all end happily. She was beaming with pleasure; she was expecting an answer. The answer was himself. He was to come, to run at her call. She arrived a whole hour before I did. At first she giggled at everything, laughed at every word I said. I began talking, but relapsed into silence.

'Do you know why I am so glad,' she said, 'so glad to look at you? – why I like you so much today?'

'Well?' I asked, and my heart began throbbing.

'I like you because you have not fallen in love with me. You know that some men in your place would have been pestering and worrying me, would have been sighing and miserable, while you are so nice!'

Then she wrung my hand so hard that I almost cried out. She laughed.

'Goodness, what a friend you are!' she began gravely a minute later. 'God sent you to me. What would have happened to me if you had not been with me now? How disinterested you are! How truly you care for me! When I am married we will be great friends, more than brother and sister; I shall care almost as I do for him . . . '

I felt horribly sad at that moment, yet something like laughter was stirring in my soul.

'You are very much upset,' I said; 'you are frightened; you think he won't come.'

'Oh dear!' she answered; 'if I were less happy, I believe I should cry at your lack of faith, at your reproaches. However, you have made me think and have given me a lot to think about; but I shall think later, and now I will own that you are right. Yes, I am somehow not myself; I am all suspense, and feel everything as it were too lightly. But hush! that's enough about feelings . . . '

At that moment we heard footsteps, and in the darkness we saw a figure coming towards us. We both started; she almost cried out; I dropped her hand and made a movement as though to walk away. But we were mistaken, it was not he.

'What are you afraid of? Why did you let go of my hand?' she said, giving it to me again. 'Come, what is it? We will meet him together; I want him to see how fond we are of each other.'

'How fond we are of each other!' I cried. ('Oh, Nastenka, Nastenka,' I thought, 'how much you have told me in that saying! Such fondness at *certain* moments makes the heart cold and the soul heavy. Your hand is cold, mine burns like fire. How blind you are, Nastenka! . . . Oh, how unbearable a happy person is sometimes! But I could not be angry with you!')

At last my heart was too full.

'Listen, Nastenka!' I cried. 'Do you know how it has been with me all day.'

'Why, how, how? Tell me quickly! Why have you said nothing all this time?'

'To begin with, Nastenka, when I had carried out all your commissions, given the letter, gone to see your good friends, then . . . then I went home and went to bed.'

'Is that all?' she interrupted, laughing.

'Yes, almost all,' I answered restraining myself, for foolish tears were already starting into my eyes. 'I woke an hour before our appointment, and yet, as it were, I had not been asleep. I don't know what happened to me. I came to tell you all about it, feeling as though time were standing still, feeling as though one sensation, one feeling must remain with me from that time for ever; feeling as though one minute must go on for all eternity, and as though all life had come to a standstill for me . . . When I woke up it seemed as though some musical motive long familiar, heard somewhere in the past, forgotten and voluptuously sweet, had come back to me now. It seemed to me that it had been clamouring at my heart all my life, and only now . . . '

'Oh my goodness, my goodness,' Nastenka interrupted, 'what does all that mean? I don't understand a word.'

'Ah, Nastenka, I wanted somehow to convey to you that strange impression . . . ' I began in a plaintive voice, in which there still lay hid a hope, though a very faint one.

'Leave off. Hush!' she said, and in one instant the sly puss had guessed.

Suddenly she became extraordinarily talkative, gay, mischievous; she took my arm, laughed, wanted me to laugh too, and every confused word I uttered evoked from her prolonged ringing laughter . . . I began to feel angry, she had suddenly begun flirting.

'Do you know,' she began, 'I feel a little vexed that you are not in love with me? There's no understanding human nature! But all the same, Mr Unapproachable, you cannot blame me for being so simple; I tell you everything, everything, whatever foolish thought comes into my head.'

'Listen! That's eleven, I believe,' I said as the slow chime of a bell rang out from a distant tower. She suddenly stopped, left off laughing and began to count.

'Yes, it's eleven,' she said at last in a timid, uncertain voice.

I regretted at once that I had frightened her, making her count the strokes, and I cursed myself for my spiteful impulse; I felt sorry for her, and did not know how to atone for what I had done.

I began comforting her, seeking for reasons for his not coming, advancing various arguments, proofs. No one could have been easier to deceive than she was at that moment; and, indeed, anyone at such a moment listens gladly to any consolation, whatever it may be, and is overjoyed if a shadow of excuse can be found.

'And indeed it's an absurd thing,' I began, warming to my task and admiring the extraordinary clearness of my argument; 'why, he could not have come; you have muddled and confused me, Nastenka, so that I too, have lost count of the time . . . Only think: he can scarcely have received the letter; suppose he is not able to come, suppose he is going to answer the letter, could not come before tomorrow. I will go for it as soon as it's light tomorrow and let you know at once. Consider, there are thousands of possibilities; perhaps he was not at home when the letter came, and may not have read it even now! Anything may happen, you know.'

'Yes, yes!' said Nastenka. 'I did not think of that. Of course anything may happen?' she went on in a tone that offered no opposition, though some other faraway thought could be heard like a vexatious discord in it. 'I tell you what you must do,' she said, 'you go as early as possible tomorrow morning, and if you get anything let me know at once. You know where I live, don't you?'

And she began repeating her address to me.

Then she suddenly became so tender, so solicitous with me. She seemed to listen attentively to what I told her; but when I asked her some question she was silent, was confused, and turned her head away. I looked into her eyes – yes, she was crying.

'How can you? How can you? Oh, what a baby you are! what childishness! . . . Come, come!'

She tried to smile, to calm herself, but her chin was quivering and her bosom was still heaving.

'I was thinking about you,' she said after a minute's silence. 'You are so kind that I should be a stone if I did not feel it. Do you know what has occurred to me now? I was comparing you two. Why isn't he you? Why isn't he like you? He is not as good as you, though I love him more than you.'

I made no answer. She seemed to expect me to say something.

'Of course, it may be that I don't understand him fully yet. You know I was always as it were afraid of him; he was always so grave, as it were so proud. Of course I know it's only that he seems like that. I know there is more tenderness in his heart than in mine . . . I remember how he looked at me when I went in to him – do you remember? – with my bundle; but yet I respect him too much, and doesn't that show that we are not equals?'

'No, Nastenka, no,' I answered, 'it shows that you love him more than anything in the world, and far more than yourself.'

'Yes, I suppose that is so,' answered Nastenka naïvely. 'But do you know what strikes me now? Only I am not talking about him now, but speaking generally; all this came into my mind some time ago. Tell me, how is it that we can't all be like brothers together? Why is it that even the best of men always seem to hide something from other people and to keep something back? Why not say straight out what is in one's heart, when one knows that one is not speaking idly? As it is everyone seems harsher than he really is, as though all were afraid of doing injustice to their feelings by being too quick to express them.'

'Oh, Nastenka, what you say is true; but there are many reasons for that,' I broke in suppressing my own feelings at that moment more than ever.

'No, no!' she answered with deep feeling. 'Here you, for instance, are not like other people! I really don't know how to tell you what I feel; but it seems to me that you, for instance . . . at the present moment . . . it seems to me that you are sacrificing something for me,' she added timidly, with a fleeting glance at me. 'Forgive me for saying so; I am a simple girl, you know. I have seen very little of life, and I really sometimes don't know how to say things,' she added in a voice that quivered with some hidden feeling, while she tried to smile; 'but I only wanted to tell you that I am grateful, that I feel it all too . . . Oh, may God give you happiness for it! What you told me about your dreamer is quite untrue now – that is, I mean, it's not true of you. You are recovering, you are quite a different man from what you described. If you ever fall in love with someone, God give you happiness with her! I won't wish anything for her, for she will be happy with you. I know, I am a woman myself, so you must believe me when I tell you so.'

She ceased speaking, and pressed my hand warmly. I too could not speak without emotion. Some minutes passed.

'Yes, it's clear he won't come tonight,' she said at last raising her head. 'It's late.'

'He will come tomorrow,' I said in the most firm and convincing tone.

'Yes,' she agreed with no sign of her former depression. 'I see for myself now that he could not come till tomorrow. Well, goodbye, till tomorrow. If it rains perhaps I shall not come. But the day after tomorrow, I shall come. I shall come for certain, whatever happens; be sure to be here, I want to see you, I will tell you everything.'

And then when we parted she gave me her hand and said, looking at me candidly: 'We shall always be together, shan't we?'

Oh, Nastenka, Nastenka! If only you knew how lonely I am now!

As soon as it struck nine o'clock I could not stay indoors, but put on my things, and went out in spite of the weather. I was there, sitting on our seat. I went to her street, but I felt ashamed, and turned back without looking at their windows when I was two steps from her door. I went home more depressed than I had ever been before. What a damp, dreary day! If it had been fine I should have walked about all night . . . But tomorrow, tomorrow! Tomorrow she will tell me everything. The letter has not come today, however. But that was to be expected. They are together by now . . .

FOURTH NIGHT

My God, how it has all ended! What it has all ended in! I arrived at nine o'clock. She was already there. I noticed her a good way off; she was standing as she had been that first time, with her elbows on the railing, and she did not hear me coming up to her.

'Nastenka!' I called to her, suppressing my agitation with an effort.

She turned to me quickly.

'Well?' she said. 'Well? Make haste!'

I looked at her in perplexity.

'Well, where is the letter? Have you brought the letter?' she repeated clutching at the railing.

'No, there is no letter,' I said at last. 'Hasn't he been to you yet?' She turned fearfully pale and looked at me for a long time without moving. I had shattered her last hope.

'Well, God be with him,' she said at last in a breaking voice; 'God be with him if he leaves me like that.'

She dropped her eyes, then tried to look at me and could not. For several minutes she was struggling with her emotion. All at once she turned away, leaning her elbows against the railing, and burst into tears.

'Oh don't, don't!' I began; but looking at her I had not the heart to go on, and what was I to say to her?

'Don't try and comfort me,' she said; 'don't talk about him; don't tell me that he will come, that he has not cast me off so cruelly and so inhumanly as he has. What for – what for? Can there have been something in my letter, that unlucky letter?'

At that point sobs stifled her voice; my heart was torn as I looked at her.

'Oh, how inhumanly cruel it is!' she began again. 'And not a line, not a line! He might at least have written that he does not want me, that he rejects me – but not a line for three days! How easy it is for him to wound, to insult a poor, defenceless girl, whose only fault is that she loves him! Oh, what I've suffered during these three days! Oh, dear! When I think that I was the first to go to him, that I humbled myself before him, cried, that I begged of him a little love! . . . and after that! Listen,' she said, turning to me, and her black eyes flashed, 'it isn't so! It can't be so; it isn't natural. Either you are mistaken or I; perhaps he has not received the letter? Perhaps he still knows nothing about it? How could anyone – judge for yourself, tell me, for goodness' sake explain it to me, I can't understand it – how could anyone behave with such barbarous coarseness as he has behaved to me? Not one word! Why, the lowest creature on earth is treated more compassionately. Perhaps he has heard something, perhaps someone has told him something about me,' she cried, turning to me enquiringly: 'What do you think?'

'Listen, Nastenka, I shall go to him tomorrow in your name.'

'Yes?'

'I will question him about everything; I will tell him everything.'

'Yes, yes?'

'You write a letter. Don't say no, Nastenka, don't say no! I will make him respect your action, he shall hear all about it, and if – '

'No, my friend, no,' she interrupted. 'Enough! Not another word, not another line from me – enough! I don't know him; I don't love him any more. I will . . . forget him.'

She could not go on.

'Calm yourself, calm yourself! Sit here, Nastenka,' I said, making her sit down on the seat.

'I am calm. Don't trouble. It's nothing! It's only tears, they will soon dry. Why, do you imagine I shall do away with myself, that I shall throw myself into the river?'

My heart was full: I tried to speak, but I could not.

'Listen,' she said taking my hand. 'Tell me: you wouldn't have behaved like this, would you? You would not have abandoned a girl who had come to you of herself, you would not have thrown into her face a shameless taunt at her weak foolish heart? You would have taken care of her? You would have realised that she was alone, that she did not know how to look after herself, that she could not guard herself from loving you, that it was not her fault, not her fault – that she had done nothing . . . Oh dear, oh dear!'

'Nastenka!' I cried at last, unable to control my emotion. 'Nastenka, you torture me! You wound my heart, you are killing me, Nastenka! I cannot be silent! I must speak at last, give utterance to what is surging in my heart!'

As I said this I got up from the seat. She took my hand and looked at me in surprise.

'What is the matter with you?' she said at last.

'Listen,' I said resolutely. 'Listen to me, Nastenka! What I am going to say to you now is all nonsense, all impossible, all stupid! I know that this can never be, but I cannot be silent. For the sake of what you are suffering now, I beg you beforehand to forgive me!'

'What is it? What is it?' she said drying her tears and looking at me intently, while a strange curiosity gleamed in her astonished eyes. 'What is the matter?'

'It's impossible, but I love you, Nastenka! There it is! Now everything is told,' I said with a wave of my hand. 'Now you will see whether you can go on talking to me as you did just now, whether you can listen to what I am going to say to you . . . '

'Well, what then?' Nastenka interrupted me. 'What of it? I knew you loved me long ago, only I always thought that you simply liked me very much . . . Oh dear, oh dear!'

'At first it was simply liking, Nastenka, but now, now! I am just in the same position as you were when you went to him with your bundle. In a worse position than you, Nastenka, because he cared for no one else as you do.'

'What are you saying to me! I don't understand you in the least. But tell me, what's this for; I don't mean what for, but why are you . . . so suddenly . . . Oh dear, I am talking nonsense! But you . . . '

And Nastenka broke off in confusion. Her cheeks flamed; she dropped her eyes.

'What's to be done, Nastenka, what am I to do? I am to blame. I have abused your . . . But no, no, I am not to blame, Nastenka; I feel that, I know that, because my heart tells me I am right, for I cannot hurt you in any way, I cannot wound you! I was your friend, but I am still your friend, I have betrayed no trust. Here my tears are falling, Nastenka. Let them flow, let them flow – they don't hurt anybody. They will dry, Nastenka.'

'Sit down, sit down,' she said, making me sit down on the seat. 'Oh, my God!'

'No, Nastenka, I won't sit down; I cannot stay here any longer, you cannot see me again; I will tell you everything and go away. I only want to say that you would never have found out that I loved you. I should have kept my secret. I would not have worried you at such a moment with my egoism. No! But I could not resist it now; you spoke of it yourself, it is your fault, your fault and not mine. You cannot drive me away from you . . . '

'No, no, I don't drive you away, no!' said Nastenka, concealing her confusion as best she could, poor child.

'You don't drive me away? No! But I meant to run from you myself. I will go away, but first I will tell you all, for when you were crying here I could not sit unmoved, when you wept, when you were in torture at being – at being – I will speak of it, Nastenka – at being forsaken, at your love being repulsed, I felt that in my heart there was so much love for you, Nastenka, so much love! And it seemed so bitter that I could not help you with my love, that my heart was breaking and I . . . I could not be silent I had to speak, Nastenka, I had to speak!'

'Yes, yes! tell me, talk to me,' said Nastenka with an indescribable gesture. 'Perhaps you think it strange that I talk to you like this, but . . . speak! I will tell you afterwards! I will tell you everything.'

'You are sorry for me, Nastenka, you are simply sorry for me, my dear little friend! What's done can't be mended. What is said cannot be taken back. Isn't that so? Well, now you know. That's the starting-point. Very well. Now it's all right, only listen. When you were sitting crying I thought to myself (oh, let me tell you what I was thinking!), I thought, that (of course it cannot be, Nastenka), I thought that you . . . I thought that you somehow . . . quite apart from me, had ceased to love him. Then – I thought that yesterday and the day before yesterday, Nastenka – then I would – I certainly would – have succeeded in making you love me; you know, you said yourself, Nastenka, that you almost loved me. Well, what next? Well, that's nearly all I wanted to tell you; all that is left to say is how it would be if you loved me, only that, nothing more! Listen, my friend – for anyway you are my friend – I am, of course, a poor, humble man, of no great consequence; but that's not the point (I don't seem to be able to say what I mean, Nastenka, I am so confused), only I would love you, I would love you so, that even if you still loved him, even if you went on loving the man I don't know, you would never feel that my love was a burden to you. You would only feel every minute that at your side was beating a grateful, grateful heart, a warm heart ready for your sake . . . Oh Nastenka, Nastenka! What have you done to me?'

'Don't cry; I don't want you to cry,' said Nastenka getting up quickly from the seat. 'Come along, get up, come with me, don't cry, don't cry,' she said, drying her tears with her handkerchief; 'let us go now; maybe I will tell you something . . . If he has forsaken me now, if he has forgotten me, though I still love him (I do not want to deceive you) . . . but listen, answer me. If I were to love you, for instance, that is, if I only . . . Oh my friend, my friend! To think, to think how I wounded you when I laughed at your love, when I praised you for not falling in love with me. Oh dear! How was it I did not foresee this, how was it I did not foresee this, how could I have been so stupid? But . . . Well, I have made up my mind, I will tell you.'

'Look here, Nastenka, do you know what? I'll go away, that's what I'll do. I am simply tormenting you. Here you are remorseful for having laughed at me, and I won't have you . . . in addition to your sorrow . . . Of course it is my fault, Nastenka, but goodbye!'

'Stay, listen to me: can you wait?'

'What for? How?'

'I love him; but I shall get over it, I must get over it, I cannot fail to get over it; I am getting over it, I feel that . . . Who knows? Perhaps it will all end today, for I hate him, for he has been laughing at me, while you have been weeping here with me, for you have not repulsed me as he has, for you love me while he has never loved me, for in fact, I love you myself . . . Yes, I love you! I love you as you love me; I have told you so before, you heard it yourself – I love you because you are better than he is, because you are nobler than he is, because, because he – '

The poor girl's emotion was so violent that she could not say more; she laid her head upon my shoulder, then upon my bosom, and wept bitterly. I comforted her, I persuaded her, but she could not stop crying; she kept pressing my hand, and saying between her sobs: 'Wait, wait, it will be over in a minute! I want to tell you . . . you mustn't think that these tears – it's nothing, it's weakness, wait till it's over.' . . . At last she left off crying, dried her eyes and we walked on again. I wanted to speak, but she still begged me to wait. We were silent . . . At last she plucked up courage and began to speak.

'It's like this,' she began in a weak and quivering voice, in which, however, there was a note that pierced my heart with a sweet pang; 'don't think that I am so light and inconstant, don't think that I can forget and change so quickly. I have loved him for a whole year, and I swear by God that I have never, never, even in thought, been unfaithful to him . . . He has despised me, he has been laughing at me – God forgive him! But he has insulted me and wounded my heart. I . . . I do not love him, for I can only love what is magnanimous, what understands me, what is generous; for I am like that myself and he is not worthy of me – well, that's enough of him. He has done better than if he had deceived my expectations later, and shown me later what he was . . . Well, it's over! But who knows, my dear friend,' she went on pressing my hand, 'who knows, perhaps my whole love was a mistaken feeling, a delusion – perhaps it began in mischief, in nonsense, because I was kept so strictly by grandmother? Perhaps I ought to love another man, not him, a different man, who would have pity on me and . . . and . . . But don't let us say any more about that,' Nastenka broke off, breathless with emotion, 'I only wanted to tell you . . . I wanted to tell you that if, although I love him (no, did love him), if, in spite of this you still say . . . If you feel that your love is so great that it may at last drive from my heart my old feeling – if you will have pity on me – if you do not want to leave me alone to my fate, without hope, without consolation – if you are ready to love me always as you do now – I swear to you that gratitude . . . that my love will be at last worthy of your love . . . Will you take my hand?'

'Nastenka!' I cried breathless with sobs. 'Nastenka, oh Nastenka!'

'Enough, enough! Well, now it's quite enough,' she said, hardly able to control herself. 'Well, now all has been said, hasn't it! Hasn't it? You are happy – I am happy too. Not another word about it; wait; spare me . . . talk of something else, for God's sake.'

'Yes, Nastenka, yes! Enough about that, now I am happy. I – Yes, Nastenka, yes, let us talk of other things, let us make haste and talk. Yes! I am ready.'

And we did not know what to say: we laughed, we wept, we said thousands of things meaningless and incoherent; at one moment we walked along the pavement, then suddenly turned back and crossed the road; then we stopped and went back again to the embankment; we were like children.

'I am living alone now, Nastenka,' I began, 'but tomorrow! Of course you know, Nastenka, I am poor, I have only got twelve hundred roubles, but that doesn't matter.'

'Of course not, and granny has her pension, so she will be no burden. We must take granny.'

'Of course we must take granny. But there's Matrona.'

'Yes, and we've got Fekla too!'

'Matrona is a good woman, but she has one fault: she has no imagination, Nastenka, absolutely none; but that doesn't matter.'

'That's all right – they can live together; only you must move to us tomorrow.'

'To you? How so? All right, I am ready.'

'Yes, hire a room from us. We have a top floor, it's empty. We had an old lady lodging there, but she has gone away; and I know granny would like to have a young man. I said to her, "Why a young man?" And she said, "Oh, because I am old; only don't you fancy, Nastenka, that I want him as a husband for you." So I guessed it was with that idea.'

'Oh, Nastenka!'

And we both laughed.

'Come, that's enough, that's enough. But where do you live? I've forgotten.'

'Over that way, near X bridge, Barannikov's Buildings.'

'It's that big house?'

'Yes, that big house.'

'Oh, I know, a nice house; only you know you had better give it up and come to us as soon as possible.'

'Tomorrow, Nastenka, tomorrow; I owe a little for my rent there but that doesn't matter. I shall soon get my salary.'

'And do you know I will perhaps give lessons; I will learn something myself and then give lessons.'

'Capital! And I shall soon get a bonus.'

'So by tomorrow you will be my lodger.'

'And we will go to *The Barber of Seville*, for they are soon going to give it again.'

'Yes, we'll go,' said Nastenka, 'but better see something else and not *The Barber of Seville*.'

'Very well, something else. Of course that will be better, I did not think – '

As we talked like this we walked along in a sort of delirium, a sort of intoxication, as though we did not know what was happening to us. At one moment we stopped and talked for a long time at the same place; then we went on again, and goodness knows where we went; and again tears and again laughter. All of a sudden Nastenka would want to go home, and I would not dare to detain her but would want to see her to the house; we set off, and in a quarter of an hour found ourselves at the embankment by our seat. Then she would sigh, and tears would come into her eyes again; I would turn chill with dismay . . . But she would press my hand and force me to walk, to talk, to chatter as before.

'It's time I was home at last; I think it must be very late,' Nastenka finally said. 'We must give over being childish.'

'Yes, Nastenka, only I shan't sleep tonight; I am not going home.'

'I don't think I shall sleep either; only see me home.'

'I should think so!'

'Only this time we really must get to the house.'

'We must, we must.'

'Honour bright? For you know one must go home some time!'

'Honour bright,' I answered laughing.

'Well, come along!'

'Come along! Look at the sky, Nastenka. Look! Tomorrow it will be a lovely day; what a blue sky, what a moon! Look; that yellow cloud is covering it now, look, look! No, it has passed by. Look, look!'

But Nastenka did not look at the cloud; she stood mute as though turned to stone; a minute later she huddled timidly close up to me. Her hand trembled in my hand; I looked at her. She pressed still more closely to me.

At that moment a young man passed by us. He suddenly stopped, looked at us intently, and then again took a few steps on. My heart began throbbing.

'Who is it, Nastenka?' I said in an undertone.

'It's he,' she answered in a whisper, huddling up to me, still more closely, still more tremulously . . . I could hardly stand on my feet.

'Nastenka, Nastenka! It's you!' I heard a voice behind us and at the same moment the young man took several steps towards us.

My God, how she cried out! How she started! How she tore herself out of my arms and rushed to meet him! I stood and looked at them, utterly crushed. But she had hardly given him her hand, had hardly flung herself into his arms, when she turned to me again, was beside me again in a flash, and before I knew where I was she threw both arms round my neck and gave me a warm, tender kiss. Then, without saying a word to me, she rushed back to him again, took his hand, and drew him after her.

I stood a long time looking after them. At last the two vanished from my sight.

MORNING

My night ended with the morning. It was a wet day. The rain was falling and beating disconsolately upon my window pane; it was dark in the room and grey outside. My head ached and I was giddy; fever was stealing over my limbs.

'There's a letter for you, sir; the postman brought it,' Matrona said, stooping over me.

'A letter? From whom?' I cried jumping up from my chair.

'I don't know, sir, better look – maybe it is written there whom it is from.'

I broke the seal. It was from her!

Oh, forgive me, forgive me! I beg you on my knees to forgive me! I deceived you and myself. It was a dream, a mirage . . . My heart aches for you today; forgive me, forgive me!

Don't blame me, for I have not changed to you in the least. I told you that I would love you, I love you now, I more than love you.

Oh, my God! If only I could love you both at once! Oh, if only you were he!'

['Oh, if only he were you,' echoed in my mind. I remembered your words, Nastenka!]

God knows what I would do for you now! I know that you are sad and dreary. I have wounded you, but you know when one loves a wrong is soon forgotten. And you love me.

Thank you, yes, thank you for that love! For it will live in my memory like a sweet dream which lingers long after awakening; for I shall remember for ever that instant when you opened your heart to me like a brother and so generously accepted the gift of my shattered heart, to care for it, nurse it, and heal it . . . If you forgive me, the memory of you will be exalted by a feeling of everlasting gratitude which will never be effaced from my soul . . . I will treasure that memory: I will be true to it, I will not betray it, I will not betray my heart: it is too constant. It returned so quickly yesterday to him to whom it has always belonged.

We shall meet, you will come to us, you will not leave us, you will be for ever a friend, a brother to me. And when you see me you will give me your hand . . . yes? You will give it to me; you have forgiven me, haven't you? You love me *as before*?

Oh, love me, do not forsake me, because I love you so at this moment, because I am worthy of your love, because I will deserve it . . . my dear! Next week I am to be married to him. He has come back in love, he has never forgotten me. You will not be angry at my writing about him. But I want to come and see you with him; you will like him, won't you?

Forgive me, remember and love your

NASTENKA

I read that letter over and over again for a long time; tears gushed to my eyes. At last it fell from my hands and I hid my face.

'Dearie! I say, dearie – ' Matrona began.

'What is it, Matrona?'

'I have taken all the cobwebs off the ceiling; you can have a wedding or give a party.'

I looked at Matrona. She was still a hearty, *youngish* old woman, but I don't know why all at once I suddenly pictured her with lustreless eyes, a wrinkled face, bent, decrepit . . . I don't know why I suddenly pictured my room grown old like Matrona. The walls and the floors looked discoloured, everything seemed dingy; the spiders' webs were thicker than ever. I don't know why, but when I looked out of the window it seemed to me that the house opposite had grown old and dingy too, that the stucco on the columns was peeling off and crumbling, that the cornices were cracked and blackened, and that the walls, of a vivid deep yellow, were patchy.

Either the sunbeams suddenly peeping out from the clouds for a moment were hidden again behind a veil of rain, and everything had grown dingy again before my eyes; or perhaps the whole vista of my future flashed before me so sad and forbidding, and I saw myself just as I was now, fifteen years hence, older, in the same room, just as solitary, with the same Matrona grown no cleverer for those fifteen years.

But to imagine that I should bear you a grudge, Nastenka! That I should cast a dark cloud over your serene, untroubled happiness; that by my bitter reproaches I should cause distress to your heart, should poison it with secret remorse and should force it to throb with anguish at the moment of bliss; that I should crush a single one of those tender blossoms which you have twined in your dark tresses when you go with him to the altar . . . Oh never, never! May your sky be clear, may your sweet smile be bright and untroubled, and may you be blessed for that moment of blissful happiness which you gave to another – lonely and grateful – heart!

My God, a whole moment of happiness! Is that too little for the whole of a man's life?

A Little Hero

AT THAT TIME I was nearly eleven, I had been sent in July to spend the holiday in a village near Moscow with a relation of mine called T., whose house was full of guests, fifty, or perhaps more . . . I don't remember, I didn't count. The house was full of noise and gaiety. It seemed as though it were a continual holiday, which would never end. It seemed as though our host had taken a vow to squander all his vast fortune as rapidly as possible, and he did indeed succeed, not long ago, in justifying this surmise, that is, in making a clean sweep of it all to the last stick.

Fresh visitors used to drive up every minute. Moscow was close by, in sight, so that those who drove away only made room for others, and the everlasting holiday went on its course. Festivities succeeded one another, and there was no end in sight to the entertainments. There were riding parties about the environs; excursions to the forest or the river; picnics, dinners in the open air; suppers on the great terrace of the house, bordered with three rows of gorgeous flowers that flooded with their fragrance the fresh night air, and illuminated the brilliant lights which made our ladies, who were almost every one of them pretty at all times, seem still more charming, with their faces excited by the impressions of the day, with their sparkling eyes, with their interchange of spritely conversation, their peals of ringing laughter; dancing, music, singing; if the sky were overcast *tableaux vivants*, charades, proverbs were arranged, private theatricals were got up. There were good talkers, storytellers, wits.

Certain persons were prominent in the foreground. Of course backbiting and slander ran their course, as without them the world could not get on, and millions of persons would perish of boredom, like flies. But as I was at that time eleven I was absorbed by very different interests, and either failed to observe these people, or if I noticed anything, did not see it all. It was only afterwards that some things came back to my mind. My childish eyes could only see the brilliant side of the picture, and the general animation, splendour and bustle – all that, seen and heard for the first time, made such an impression upon me that for the first few days I was completely bewildered and my little head was in a whirl.

I keep speaking of my age, and of course I was a child, nothing more than a child. Many of these lovely ladies petted me without dreaming of considering my age. But strange to say, a sensation which I did not myself understand already had possession of me; something was already whispering in my heart, of which till then it had had no knowledge, no conception, and for some reason it began all at once to burn and throb, and often my face glowed with a sudden flush. At times I felt as it were abashed, and even resentful of the various privileges of my childish years. At other times a sort of wonder overwhelmed me, and I would go off into some corner where I could sit unseen, as though to take breath and remember something – something which it seemed to me I had remembered perfectly till then, and now had suddenly forgotten, something without which I could not show myself anywhere, and could not exist at all.

At last it seemed to me as though I were hiding something from everyone. But nothing would have induced me to speak of it to anyone, because, small boy that I was, I was ready to weep with shame. Soon in the midst of the vortex around me I was conscious of a certain loneliness. There were other children, but all were either much older or younger than I; besides, I was in no mood for them. Of course nothing would have happened to me if I had not been in an exceptional position. In the eyes of those charming ladies I was still the little unformed creature whom they at once liked to pet, and with whom they could play as though he were a little doll. One of them particularly, a fascinating, fair woman, with very thick luxuriant hair, such as I had never seen before and probably shall never see again, seemed to have taken a vow never to leave me in peace. I was confused, while she was amused by the laughter which she continually provoked from all around us by her wild, giddy pranks with me, and this apparently gave her immense enjoyment. At school among her schoolfellows she was probably nicknamed the Tease. She was wonderfully good-looking, and there was something in her beauty which drew one's eyes from the first moment. And certainly she had nothing in common with the ordinary modest little fair girls, white as down and soft as white mice or pastors' daughters. She was not very tall, and was rather plump, but had soft, delicate, exquisitely cut features. There was something quick as lightning in her face, and indeed she was like fire all over, light, swift, alive. Her big open eyes seemed to flash sparks; they glittered like diamonds, and I would never exchange such blue sparkling eyes for any black ones, were they blacker than any Andalusian orb. And, indeed, my blonde was fully a match for the famous brunette whose praises were sung by a great and well-known poet,[97] who, in a superb poem, vowed by all Castille[98] that he was ready to break his bones to be permitted only to touch the mantle of his divinity with the tip of his finger. Add to that, that *my* charmer was the merriest in the world, the wildest giggler, playful as a child, although she had been married for the last five years. There was a continual laugh upon her lips, fresh as the morning rose that, with the first ray of sunshine, opens its fragrant crimson bud with the cool dewdrops still hanging heavy upon it.

I remember that the day after my arrival private theatricals were being got up. The drawing-room was, as they say, packed to overflowing; there was not a seat empty, and as I was somehow late I had to enjoy the performance standing. But the amusing play attracted me to move forwarder and forwarder, and unconsciously I made my way to the first row, where I stood at last leaning my elbows on the back of an armchair, in which a lady was sitting. It was my blonde divinity, but we had not yet made acquaintance. And I gazed, as it happened, at her marvellous, fascinating shoulders, plump and white as milk, though it did not matter to me in the least whether I stared at a woman's exquisite shoulders or at the cap with flaming ribbons that covered the grey locks of a venerable lady in the front row. Near my blonde divinity sat a spinster lady not in her first youth, one of those who, as I chanced to observe later, always take refuge in the immediate neighbourhood of young and pretty women, selecting such as are not fond of cold-shouldering young men. But that is not the point, only this lady, noting my fixed gaze, bent down to her neighbour and with a simper whispered something in her ear. The blonde lady turned at once, and I remember that her glowing eyes so flashed upon me in the half dark that, not prepared to meet them, I started as though I were scalded. The beauty smiled.

'Do you like what they are acting?' she asked, looking into my face with a shy and mocking expression.

'Yes,' I answered, still gazing at her with a sort of wonder that evidently pleased her.

'But why are you standing? You'll get tired. Can't you find a seat?'

'That's just it, I can't,' I answered, more occupied with my grievance than with the beauty's sparkling eyes, and rejoicing in earnest at having found a kind heart to whom I could confide my troubles. 'I have looked everywhere, but all the chairs are taken,' I added, as though complaining to her that all the chairs were taken.

'Come here,' she said briskly, quick to act on every decision, and, indeed, on every mad idea that flashed on her giddy brain, 'come here, and sit on my knee.'

'On your knee,' I repeated, taken aback. I have mentioned already that I had begun to resent the privileges of childhood and to be ashamed of them in earnest. This lady, as though in derision, had gone ever so much further than the others. Moreover, I had always been a shy and bashful boy, and of late had begun to be particularly shy with women.

'Why yes, on my knee. Why don't you want to sit on my knee?' she persisted, beginning to laugh more and more, so that at last she was simply giggling, goodness knows at what, perhaps at her own capriciousness, or perhaps at my confusion. But that was just what she wanted.

I flushed, and in my confusion looked round trying to find where to escape; but seeing my intention she managed to catch hold of my hand to prevent me from going away, and pulling it towards her, suddenly, quite unexpectedly, to my intense astonishment, squeezed it in her mischievous warm fingers, and began to pinch my fingers till they hurt so much that I had to do my very utmost not to cry out, and in my effort to control myself made the most absurd grimaces. I was, besides, moved to the greatest amazement, perplexity, and even horror, at the discovery that there were ladies so absurd and spiteful as to talk nonsense to boys, and even pinch their fingers, for no earthly reason and before everybody. Probably my unhappy face reflected my bewilderment, for the mischievous creature laughed in my face, as though she were crazy, and meantime she was pinching my fingers more and more vigorously. She was highly delighted in playing such a mischievous prank and completely mystifying and embarrassing a poor boy. My position was desperate. In the first place I was hot with shame, because almost everyone near had turned round to look at us, some in wonder, others with laughter, grasping at once that the beauty was up to some mischief. I dreadfully wanted to scream, too, for she was wringing my fingers with positive fury just because I didn't scream; while I, like a Spartan, made up my mind to endure the agony, afraid by crying out of causing a general fuss, which was more than I could face. In utter despair I began at last struggling with her, trying with all my might to pull away my hand, but my persecutor was much stronger than I was. At last I could bear it no longer, and uttered a shriek – that was all she was waiting for! Instantly she let me go, and turned away as though nothing had happened, as though it was not she who had played the trick but someone else, exactly like some schoolboy who, as soon as the master's back is turned, plays some trick on someone near him, pinches some small weak boy, gives him a flip, a kick or a nudge with his elbows, and instantly turns again, buries himself in his book and begins repeating his lesson, and so makes a fool of the infuriated teacher who flies down like a hawk at the noise.

But luckily for me the general attention was distracted at the moment by the masterly acting of our host, who was playing the chief part in the performance, some comedy of Scribe's.[99] Everyone began to applaud; under cover of the noise I stole away and hurried to the farthest end of the room, from which, concealed behind a column, I looked with horror towards the place where the treacherous beauty was sitting. She was still laughing, holding her handkerchief to her lips. And for a long time she was continually turning round, looking for me in every direction, probably regretting that our silly tussle was so soon over and hatching some other trick to play on me.

That was the beginning of our acquaintance, and from that evening she would never let me alone. She persecuted me without consideration or conscience, she became my tyrant and tormentor. The whole absurdity of her jokes with me lay in the fact that she pretended to be head over ears in love with me, and teased me before everyone. Of course for a wild creature as I was all this was so tiresome and vexatious that it almost reduced me to tears, and I was sometimes put in such a difficult position that I was on the point of fighting with my treacherous admirer. My naïve confusion, my desperate distress, seemed to egg her on to persecute me more; she knew no mercy, while I did not know how to get away from her. The laughter which always accompanied us, and which she knew so well how to excite, roused her to fresh pranks. But at last people began to think that she went a little too far in her jests. And, indeed, as I remember now, she did take outrageous liberties with a child such as I was.

But that was her character; she was a spoilt child in every respect. I heard afterwards that her husband, a very short, very fat and very red-faced man, very rich and apparently very much occupied with business, spoilt her more than anyone. Always busy and flying round, he could not stay two hours in one place. Every day he drove into Moscow, sometimes twice in the day, and always, as he declared himself, on business. It would be hard to find a livelier and more good-natured face than his facetious but always well-bred countenance. He not only loved his wife to the point of weakness, softness: he simply worshipped her like an idol.

He did not restrain her in anything. She had masses of friends, male and female. In the first place, almost everybody liked her; and secondly, the feather-headed creature was not herself over particular in the choice of her friends, though there was a much more serious foundation to her character than might be supposed from what I have just said about her. But of all her friends she liked best of all one young lady, a distant relation, who was also of our party now. There existed between them a tender and subtle affection, one of those attachments which sometimes spring up at the meeting of two dispositions often the very opposite of each other, of which one is deeper, purer and more austere, while the other, with lofty humility and generous self-criticism, lovingly gives way to the other, conscious of the friend's superiority and cherishing the friendship as a happiness. Then begins that tender and noble subtlety in the relations of such characters, love and infinite indulgence on the one side, on the other love and respect – a respect approaching awe, approaching anxiety as to the impression made on the friend so highly prized, and an eager, jealous desire to get closer and closer to that friend's heart in every step in life.

These two friends were of the same age, but there was an immense difference between them in everything – in looks, to begin with. Madame M. was also very handsome, but there was something special in her beauty that strikingly distinguished her from the crowd of pretty women; there was something in her face that at once drew the affection of all to her, or rather, which aroused a generous and lofty feeling of kindliness in everyone who met her. There are such happy faces. At her side everyone grew as it were better, freer, more cordial; and yet her big mournful eyes, full of fire and vigour, had a timid and anxious look, as though every minute dreading something antagonistic and menacing, and this strange timidity at times cast so mournful a shade over her mild, gentle features which recalled the serene faces of Italian madonnas,[100] that looking at her one soon became oneself sad, as though for some trouble of one's own. The pale, thin face, in which, through the irreproachable beauty of the pure, regular lines and the mournful severity of some mute hidden grief, there often flitted the clear looks of early childhood, telling of trustful years and perhaps simple-hearted happiness in the recent past, the gentle but diffident, hesitating smile, all aroused such unaccountable sympathy for her that every heart was unconsciously stirred with a sweet and warm anxiety that powerfully interceded on her behalf even at a distance, and made even strangers feel akin to her. But the lovely creature seemed silent and reserved, though no one could have been more attentive and loving if anyone needed sympathy. There are women who are like sisters of mercy[101] in life. Nothing can be hidden from them, nothing, at least, that is a sore or wound of the heart. Anyone who is suffering may go boldly and hopefully to them without fear of being a burden, for few men know the infinite patience of love, compassion and forgiveness that may be found in some women's hearts. Perfect treasures of sympathy, consolation and hope are laid up in these pure hearts, so often full of suffering of their own – for a heart which loves much grieves much – though their wounds are carefully hidden from the curious eye, for deep sadness is most often mute and concealed. They are not dismayed by the depth of the wound, nor by its foulness and its stench; anyone who comes to them is deserving of help; they are, as it were, born for heroism . . . Mme M. was tall, supple and graceful, but rather thin. All her movements seemed somehow irregular, at times slow, smooth and even dignified, at times childishly hasty; and yet, at the same time, there was a sort of timid humility in her gestures, something tremulous and defenceless, though it neither desired nor asked for protection.

I have mentioned already that the outrageous teasing of the treacherous fair lady abashed me, flabbergasted me and wounded me to the quick. But there was for all that another secret, strange and foolish reason, which I concealed, at which I shuddered as at a skeleton. At the very thought of it, brooding, utterly alone and overwhelmed, in some dark mysterious corner to which the inquisitorial mocking eye of the blue-eyed rogue could not penetrate, I almost gasped with confusion, shame and fear – in short, I was in love; that perhaps is nonsense, that could hardly have been. But why was it, of all the faces surrounding me, only her face caught my attention? Why was it that it was only she whom I cared to follow with my eyes, though I certainly had no inclination in those days to watch ladies and seek their acquaintance? This happened most frequently on the evenings when we were all kept indoors by bad weather, and when, lonely, hiding in some corner of the big drawing-room, I stared about me aimlessly, unable to find anything to do, for except my teasing ladies, few people ever addressed me, and I was insufferably bored on such evenings. Then I stared at the people round me, listened to the conversation, of which I often did not understand one word, and at that time the mild eyes, the gentle smile and lovely face of Mme M. (for she was the object of my passion) for some reason caught my fascinated attention; and the strange, vague, but unutterably sweet impression remained with me. Often for hours together I could not tear myself away from her; I studied every gesture, every movement she made, listened to every vibration of her rich, silvery, but rather muffled voice; but strange to say, as the result of all my observations, I felt, mixed with a sweet and timid impression, a feeling of intense curiosity. It seemed as though I were on the verge of some mystery.

Nothing distressed me so much as being mocked at in the presence of Mme M. This mockery and humorous persecution, as I thought, humiliated me. And when there was a general burst of laughter at my expense, in which Mme M. sometimes could not help joining, in despair, beside myself with misery, I used to tear myself from my tormentor and run away upstairs, where I remained in solitude the rest of the day, not daring to show my face in the drawing-room. I did not yet, however, understand my shame nor my agitation; the whole process went on in me unconsciously. I had hardly said two words to Mme M., and indeed I should not have dared to. But one evening after an unbearable day I turned back from an expedition with the rest of the company. I was horribly tired and made my way home across the garden. On a seat in a secluded avenue I saw Mme M. She was sitting quite alone, as though she had purposely chosen this solitary spot, her head was drooping and she was mechanically twisting her handkerchief. She was so lost in thought that she did not hear me till I reached her.

Noticing me, she got up quickly from her seat, turned round, and I saw her hurriedly wipe her eyes with her handkerchief. She was crying. Drying her eyes, she smiled to me and walked back with me to the house. I don't remember what we talked about; but she frequently sent me off on one pretext or another, to pick a flower or to see who was riding in the next avenue. And when I walked away from her, she at once put her handkerchief to her eyes again and wiped away rebellious tears, which would persist in rising again and again from her heart and dropping from her poor eyes. I realised that I was very much in her way when she sent me off so often, and, indeed, she saw herself that I noticed it all, but yet could not control herself, and that made my heart ache more and more for her. I raged at myself at that moment and was almost in despair; cursed myself for my awkwardness and lack of resource, and at the same time did not know how to leave her tactfully, without betraying that I had noticed her distress, but walked beside her in mournful bewilderment, almost in alarm, utterly at a loss and unable to find a single word to keep up our scanty conversation.

This meeting made such an impression on me that I stealthily watched Mme M. the whole evening with eager curiosity, and never took my eyes off her. But it happened that she twice caught me unawares watching her, and on the second occasion, noticing me, she gave me a smile. It was the only time she smiled that evening. The look of sadness had not left her face, which was now very pale. She spent the whole evening talking to an ill-natured and quarrelsome old lady, whom nobody liked owing to her spying and back-biting habits, but of whom everyone was afraid, and consequently everyone felt obliged to be polite to her . . . At ten o'clock Mme M.'s husband arrived. Till that moment I watched her very attentively, never taking my eyes off her mournful face; now at the unexpected entrance of her husband I saw her start, and her pale face turned suddenly as white as a handkerchief. It was so noticeable that other people observed it. I overheard a fragmentary conversation from which I guessed that Mme M. was not quite happy; they said her husband was as jealous as an Arab, not from love, but from vanity. He was before all things a European, a modern man, who sampled the newest ideas and prided himself upon them. In appearance he was a tall, dark-haired, particularly thickset man, with European whiskers, with a self-satisfied, red face, with teeth white as sugar, and with an irreproachably gentlemanly deportment. He was called a *clever man*. Such is the name given in certain circles to a peculiar species of mankind which grows fat at other people's expense, which does absolutely nothing and has no desire to do anything, and whose heart has turned into a lump of fat from everlasting slothfulness and idleness. You continually hear from such men that there is nothing they can do owing to certain very complicated and hostile circumstances, which 'thwart their genius', and that it is 'sad to see the waste of their talents'. This is a fine phrase of theirs, their *mot d'ordre*, their watchword, a phrase which these well-fed, fat friends of ours bring out at every minute, so that it has long ago bored us as an arrant Tartuffism, an empty form of words. Some, however, of these amusing creatures, who cannot succeed in finding anything to do – though, indeed, they never seek it – try to make everyone believe that they have not a lump of fat for a heart, but on the contrary, something *very deep*, though what precisely the greatest surgeon would hardly venture to decide – from civility, of course. These gentlemen make their way in the world through the fact that all their instincts are bent in the direction of coarse sneering, short-sighted censure and immense conceit. Since they have nothing else to do but note and emphasise the mistakes and weaknesses of others, and as they have precisely as much good feeling as an oyster, it is not difficult for them with such powers of self-preservation to get on with people fairly successfully. They pride themselves extremely upon that. They are, for instance, as good as persuaded that almost the whole world owes them something; that it is theirs, like an oyster which they keep in reserve; that all are fools except themselves; that everyone is like an orange or a sponge, which they will squeeze as soon as they want the juice; that they are the masters everywhere, and that all this acceptable state of affairs is solely due to the fact that they are people of so much intellect and character. In their measureless conceit they do not admit any defects in themselves, they are like that species of practical rogues, innate Tartuffes[102] and Falstaffs,[103] who are such thorough rogues that at last they have come to believe that that is as it should be, that is, that they should spend their lives in knavishness; they have so often assured everyone that they are honest men, that they have come to believe that they are honest men, and that their roguery is honesty. They are never capable of inner judgement before their conscience, of generous self-criticism; for some things they are too fat. Their own priceless personality, their Baal[104] and Moloch,[105] their magnificent ego is always in their foreground everywhere. All nature, the whole world for them is no more than a splendid mirror created for the little god to admire himself continually in it, and to see no one and nothing behind himself; so it is not strange that he sees everything in the world in such a hideous light. He has a phrase in readiness for everything and – the acme of ingenuity on his part – the most fashionable phrase. It is just these people, indeed, who help to make the fashion, proclaiming at every crossroad an idea in which they scent success. A fine nose is just what they have for sniffing a fashionable phrase and making it their own before other people get hold of it, so that it seems to have originated with them. They have a particular store of phrases for proclaiming their profound sympathy for humanity, for defining what is the most correct and rational form of philanthropy, and continually attacking romanticism, in other words, everything fine and true, each atom of which is more precious than all their mollusc tribe. But they are too coarse to recognise the truth in an indirect, roundabout and unfinished form, and they reject everything that is immature, still fermenting and unstable. The well-nourished man has spent all his life in merry-making, with everything provided, has done nothing himself and does not know how hard every sort of work is, and so woe betide you if you jar upon his fat feelings by any sort of roughness; he'll never forgive you for that, he will always remember it and will gladly avenge it. The long and short of it is that my hero is neither more nor less than a gigantic, incredibly swollen bag, full of sentences, fashionable phrases and labels of all sorts and kinds.

Monsieur M., however, had a speciality and was a very remarkable man; he was a wit, good talker and storyteller, and there was always a circle round him in every drawing-room. That evening he was particularly successful in making an impression. He took possession of the conversation; he was in his best form, gay, pleased at something, and he compelled the attention of all; but Mme M. looked all the time as though she were ill; her face was so sad that I fancied every minute that tears would begin quivering on her long eyelashes. All this, as I have said, impressed me extremely and made me wonder. I went away with a feeling of strange curiosity, and dreamed all night of Monsieur M., though till then I had rarely had dreams.

Next day, early in the morning, I was summoned to a rehearsal of some *tableaux vivants* in which I had to take part. The *tableaux vivants*, theatricals, and afterwards a dance were all fixed for the same evening, five days later – the birthday of our host's younger daughter. To this entertainment, which was almost improvised, another hundred guests were invited from Moscow and from surrounding villas, so that there was a great deal of fuss, bustle and commotion. The rehearsal, or rather review of the costumes, was fixed so early in the morning because our manager, a well-known artist, a friend of our host's, who had consented through affection for him to undertake the arrangement of the *tableaux* and the training of us for them, was in haste now to get to Moscow to purchase properties and to make final preparations for the fête, as there was no time to lose. I took part in one *tableau* with Mme M. It was a scene from medieval life and was called 'The Lady of the Castle and Her Page'.

I felt unutterably confused on meeting Mme M. at the rehearsal. I kept feeling that she would at once read in my eyes all the reflections, the doubts, the surmises, that had arisen in my mind since the previous day. I fancied, too, that I was, as it were, to blame in regard to her, for having come upon her tears the day before and hindered her grieving, so that she could hardly help looking at me askance, as an unpleasant witness and unforgiven sharer of her secret. But, thank goodness, it went off without any great trouble; I was simply not noticed. I think she had no thoughts to spare for me or for the rehearsal; she was absent-minded, sad and gloomily thoughtful; it was evident that she was worried by some great anxiety. As soon as my part was over I ran away to change my clothes, and ten minutes later came out on the verandah into the garden. Almost at the same time Mme M. came out by another door, and immediately afterwards coming towards us appeared her self-satisfied husband, who was returning from the garden, after just escorting into it quite a crowd of ladies and there handing them over to a competent *cavaliere servente*.[106] The meeting of the husband and wife was evidently unexpected. Mme M., I don't know why, grew suddenly confused, and a faint trace of vexation was betrayed in her impatient movement. The husband, who had been carelessly whistling an air and with an affectation of profundity stroking his whiskers, now, on meeting his wife, frowned and scrutinised her, as I remember now, with a markedly inquisitorial stare.

'You are going into the garden?' he asked, noticing the parasol and book in her hand.

'No, into the copse,' she said, with a slight flush.

'Alone?'

'With him,' said Mme M., pointing to me. 'I always go for a walk alone in the morning,' she added, speaking in an uncertain, hesitating voice, as people do when they tell their first lie.

'H'm ... and I have just taken the whole party there. They have all met there together in the flower arbour to see N. off. He is going away, you know ... Something has gone wrong in Odessa.[107] Your cousin' (he meant the fair beauty) 'is laughing and crying at the same time; there is no making her out. She says, though, that you are angry with N. about something and so wouldn't go and see him off. Nonsense, of course?'

'She's laughing,' said Mme M., coming down the verandah steps.

'So this is your daily *cavalieré servente*,' added Monsieur M., with a wry smile, turning his lorgnette upon me.

'Page!' I cried, angered by the lorgnette and the jeer; and laughing straight in his face I jumped down the three steps of the verandah at one bound.

'A pleasant walk,' muttered Monsieur M., and went on his way.

Of course, I immediately joined Mme M. as soon as she indicated me to her husband, and looked as though she had invited me to do so an hour before, and as though I had been accompanying her on her walks every morning for the last month. But I could not make out why she was so confused, so embarrassed, and what was in her mind when she brought herself to have recourse to her little lie? Why had she not simply said that she was going alone? I did not know how to look at her, but overwhelmed with wonder I began by degrees very naïvely peeping into her face; but just as an hour before at the rehearsal she did not notice either my looks or my mute question. The same anxiety, only more intense and more distinct, was apparent in her face, in her agitation, in her walk. She was in haste, and walked more and more quickly and kept looking uneasily down every avenue, down every path in the wood that led in the direction of the garden. And I, too, was expecting something. Suddenly there was the sound of horses' hoofs behind us. It was the whole party of ladies and gentlemen on horseback escorting N., the gentleman who was so suddenly deserting us.

Among the ladies was my fair tormentor, of whom Monsieur M. had told us that she was in tears. But characteristically she was laughing like a child, and was galloping briskly on a splendid bay horse. On reaching us, N. took off his hat, but did not stop, nor say one word to Mme M. Soon all the cavalcade disappeared from our sight. I glanced at Mme M. and almost cried out in wonder; she was standing as white as a handkerchief and big tears were gushing from her eyes. By chance our eyes met: Mme M. suddenly flushed and turned away for an instant, and a distinct look of uneasiness and vexation flitted across her face. I was in the way, worse even than last time, that was clearer than day, but how was I to get away?

And, as though guessing my difficulty, Mme M. opened the book which she had in her hand, and colouring and evidently trying not to look at me she said, as though she had only suddenly realised it: 'Ah! It is the second part. I've made a mistake; please bring me the first.'

I could not but understand. My part was over, and I could not have been more directly dismissed.

I ran off with her book and did not come back. The first part lay undisturbed on the table that morning . . . But I was not myself; in my heart there was a sort of haunting terror. I did my utmost not to meet Mme M. But I looked with wild curiosity at the self-satisfied person of Monsieur M., as though there must be something special about him now. I don't understand what was the meaning of my absurd curiosity. I only remember that I was strangely perplexed by all that I had chanced to see that morning. But the day was only just beginning and it was fruitful in events for me.

Dinner was very early that day. An expedition to a neighbouring hamlet to see a village festival that was taking place there had been fixed for the evening, and so it was necessary to be in time to get ready. I had been dreaming for the last three days of this excursion, anticipating all sorts of delights. Almost all the company gathered together on the verandah for coffee. I cautiously followed the others and concealed myself behind the third row of chairs. I was attracted by curiosity, and yet I was very anxious not to be seen by Mme M. But as luck would have it I was not far from my fair tormentor. Something miraculous and incredible was happening to her that day; she looked twice as handsome. I don't know how and why this happens, but such miracles are by no means rare with women. There was with us at this moment a new guest, a tall, pale-faced young man, the official admirer of our fair beauty, who had just arrived from Moscow as though on purpose to replace N., of whom rumour said that he was desperately in love with the same lady. As for the newly arrived guest, he had for a long time past been on the same terms as Benedick with Beatrice, in Shakespeare's

Much Ado about Nothing.[108] In short, the fair beauty was on her very best form that day. Her chatter and her jests were so full of grace, so trustfully naïve, so innocently careless, she was persuaded of the general enthusiasm with such graceful self-confidence that she really was all the time the centre of peculiar adoration. A throng of surprised and admiring listeners was continually round her, and she had never been so fascinating. Every word she uttered was marvellous and seductive, was caught up and handed round in the circle, and not one word, one jest, one sally was lost. I fancy no one had expected from her such taste, such brilliance, such wit. Her best qualities were, as a rule, buried under the most harum-scarum wilfulness, the most schoolboyish pranks, almost verging on buffoonery; they were rarely noticed, and, when they were, were hardly believed in, so that now her extraordinary brilliancy was accompanied by an eager whisper of amazement among all. There was, however, one peculiar and rather delicate circumstance, judging at least by the part in it played by Mme M.'s husband, which contributed to her success. The madcap ventured – and I must add to the satisfaction of almost everyone or, at any rate, to the satisfaction of all the young people – to make a furious attack upon him, owing to many causes, probably of great consequence in her eyes. She carried on with him a regular crossfire of witticisms, of mocking and sarcastic sallies, of that most illusive and treacherous kind that, smoothly wrapped up on the surface, hit the mark without giving the victim anything to lay hold of, and exhaust him in fruitless efforts to repel the attack, reducing him to fury and comic despair.

I don't know for certain, but I fancy the whole proceeding was not improvised but premeditated. This desperate duel had begun earlier, at dinner. I call it desperate because Monsieur M. was not quick to surrender. He had to call upon all his presence of mind, all his sharp wit and rare resourcefulness not to be completely covered with ignominy. The conflict was accompanied by the continual and irrepressible laughter of all who witnessed and took part in it. That day was for him very different from the day before. It was noticeable that Mme M. several times did her utmost to stop her indiscreet friend, who was certainly trying to depict the jealous husband in the most grotesque and absurd guise, in the guise of 'a bluebeard'[109] it must be supposed, judging from all probabilities, from what has remained in my memory and finally from the part which I myself was destined to play in the affair.

I was drawn into it in a most absurd manner, quite unexpectedly. And as ill-luck would have it at that moment I was standing where I could be seen, suspecting no evil and actually forgetting the precautions

I had so long practised. Suddenly I was brought into the foreground as a sworn foe and natural rival of Monsieur M., as desperately in love with his wife, of which my persecutress vowed and swore that she had proofs, saying that only that morning she had seen in the copse ... But before she had time to finish I broke in at the most desperate minute. That minute was so diabolically calculated, was so treacherously prepared to lead up to its finale, its ludicrous dénouement, and was brought out with such killing humour that a perfect outburst of irrepressible mirth saluted this last sally. And though even at the time I guessed that mine was not the most unpleasant part in the performance, yet I was so confused, so irritated and alarmed that, full of misery and despair, gasping with shame and tears, I dashed through two rows of chairs, stepped forward, and addressing my tormentor, cried, in a voice broken with tears and indignation: 'Aren't you ashamed ... aloud ... before all the ladies ... to tell such a wicked ... lie? ... Like a small child ... before all these men ... What will they say? ... A big girl like you ... and married! ... '

But I could not go on, there was a deafening roar of applause. My outburst created a perfect furore. My naïve gesture, my tears, and especially the fact that I seemed to be defending Monsieur M., all this provoked such fiendish laughter that even now I cannot help laughing at the mere recollection of it. I was overcome with confusion, senseless with horror and, burning with shame, hiding my face in my hands rushed away, knocked a tray out of the hands of a footman who was coming in at the door, and flew upstairs to my own room. I pulled out the key, which was on the outside of the door, and locked myself in. I did well, for there was a hue and cry after me. Before a minute had passed my door was besieged by a mob of the prettiest ladies. I heard their ringing laughter, their incessant chatter, their trilling voices; they were all twittering at once, like swallows. All of them, every one of them, begged and besought me to open the door, if only for a moment; swore that no harm should come to me, only that they wanted to smother me with kisses. But ... what could be more horrible than this novel threat? I simply burned with shame the other side of the door, hiding my face in the pillows, and did not open, did not even respond. The ladies kept up their knocking for a long time, but I was deaf and obdurate as only a boy of eleven could be.

But what could I do now? Everything was laid bare, everything had been exposed, everything I had so jealously guarded and concealed! ... Everlasting disgrace and shame had fallen on me! But it is true that I could not myself have said why I was frightened and what I wanted to hide; yet I was frightened of something and had trembled like a leaf at the thought of *that something*'s being discovered. Only till that minute I had not known what it was: whether it was good or bad, splendid or shameful, praiseworthy or reprehensible? Now in my distress, in the misery that had been forced upon me, I learned that it was *absurd* and *shameful*. Instinctively I felt at the same time that this verdict was false, inhuman and coarse; but I was crushed, annihilated; consciousness seemed checked in me and thrown into confusion; I could not stand up against that verdict, nor criticise it properly. I was befogged; I only felt that my heart had been inhumanly and shamelessly wounded, and was brimming over with impotent tears. I was irritated; but I was boiling with indignation and hate such as I had never felt before, for it was the first time in my life that I had known real sorrow, insult and injury – and it was truly that, without any exaggeration. The first untried, unformed feeling had been so coarsely handled in me, a child. The first fragrant, virginal modesty had been so soon exposed and insulted, and the first and perhaps very real and aesthetic impression had been so outraged. Of course there was much my persecutors did not know and did not divine in my sufferings. One circumstance, which I had not succeeded in analysing till then, of which I had been as it were afraid, partly entered into it. I went on lying on my bed in despair and misery, hiding my face in my pillow, and I was alternately feverish and shivery. I was tormented by two questions: first, what had the wretched fair beauty seen, and, in fact, what could she have seen that morning in the copse between Mme M. and me? And secondly, how could I now look Mme M. in the face without dying on the spot of shame and despair?

An extraordinary noise in the yard roused me at last from the state of semi-consciousness into which I had fallen. I got up and went to the window. The whole yard was packed with carriages, saddle-horses and bustling servants. It seemed that they were all setting off; some of the gentlemen had already mounted their horses, others were taking their places in the carriages . . . Then I remembered the expedition to the village fête, and little by little an uneasiness came over me; I began anxiously looking for my pony in the yard; but there was no pony there, so they must have forgotten me. I could not restrain myself, and rushed headlong downstairs, thinking no more of unpleasant meetings or my recent ignominy . . . Terrible news awaited me. There was neither a horse nor seat in any of the carriages to spare for me; everything had been arranged, all the seats were taken, and I was forced to give place to others. Overwhelmed by this fresh blow, I stood on the steps and looked mournfully at the long rows of coaches, carriages and chaises, in which there was not the tiniest corner left for me, and at the smartly dressed ladies, whose horses were restlessly curvetting.

One of the gentlemen was late. They were only waiting for his arrival to set off. His horse was standing at the door, champing the bit, pawing the earth with his hoofs, and at every moment starting and rearing. Two stable-boys were carefully holding him by the bridle and everyone else apprehensively stood at a respectful distance from him.

A most vexatious circumstance had occurred, which prevented my going. In addition to the fact that new visitors had arrived, filling up all the seats, two of the horses had fallen ill, one of them being my pony. But I was not the only person to suffer: it appeared that there was no horse for our new visitor, the pale-faced young man of whom I have spoken already. To get over this difficulty our host had been obliged to have recourse to the extreme step of offering his fiery unbroken stallion, adding, to satisfy his conscience, that it was impossible to ride him, and that they had long intended to sell the beast for its vicious character, if only a purchaser could be found.

But, in spite of his warning, the visitor declared that he was a good horseman, and in any case ready to mount anything rather than not go. Our host said no more, but now I fancied that a sly and ambiguous smile was straying on his lips. He waited for the gentleman who had spoken so well of his own horsemanship, and stood, without mounting his horse, impatiently rubbing his hands and continually glancing towards the door; some similar feeling seemed shared by the two stable-boys, who were holding the stallion, almost breathless with pride at seeing themselves before the whole company in charge of a horse which might any minute kill a man for no reason whatever. Something akin to their master's sly smile gleamed, too, in their eyes, which were round with expectation, and fixed upon the door from which the bold visitor was to appear. The horse himself, too, behaved as though he were in league with our host and the stable-boys. He bore himself proudly and haughtily, as though he felt that he were being watched by several dozen curious eyes and were glorying in his evil reputation exactly as some incorrigible rogue might glory in his criminal exploits. He seemed to be defying the bold man who would venture to curb his independence.

That bold man did at last make his appearance. Conscience-stricken at having kept everyone waiting, hurriedly drawing on his gloves, he came forward without looking at anything, ran down the steps, and only raised his eyes as he stretched out his hand to seize the mane of the waiting horse. But he was at once disconcerted by his frantic rearing and a warning scream from the frightened spectators. The young man stepped back and looked in perplexity at the vicious horse, which was quivering all over, snorting with anger and rolling his bloodshot eyes ferociously, continually rearing on his hind legs and flinging up his fore legs as though he meant to bolt into the air and carry the two stable-boys with him. For a minute the young man stood completely non-plussed; then, flushing slightly with some embarrassment, he raised his eyes and looked at the frightened ladies.

'A very fine horse!' he said, as though to himself, 'and to my thinking it ought to be a great pleasure to ride him; but . . . but do you know, I think I won't go?' he concluded, turning to our host with the broad, good-natured smile which so suited his kind and clever face.

'Yet I consider you are an excellent horseman, I assure you,' answered the owner of the unapproachable horse, delighted, and he warmly and even gratefully pressed the young man's hand, 'just because from the first moment you saw the sort of brute you had to deal with,' he added with dignity. 'Would you believe me, though I have served twenty-three years in the hussars, yet I've had the pleasure of being laid on the ground three times, thanks to that beast, that is, as often as I mounted the useless animal. Tancred, my boy, there's no one here fit for you! Your rider, it seems, must be some Ilya Muromets,[110] and he must be sitting quiet now in the village of Kapatcharovo, waiting for your teeth to fall out. Come, take him away, he has frightened people enough. It was a waste of time to bring him out,' he cried, rubbing his hands complacently.

It must be observed that Tancred[111] was no sort of use to his master and simply ate corn for nothing; moreover, the old hussar had lost his reputation for a knowledge of horseflesh by paying a fabulous sum for the worthless beast, which he had purchased only for his beauty . . . yet he was delighted now that Tancred had kept up his reputation, had disposed of another rider, and so had drawn closer on himself fresh senseless laurels.

'So you are not going?' cried the blonde beauty, who was particularly anxious that her *cavalieré servente* should be in attendance on this occasion. 'Surely you are not frightened?'

'Upon my word I am,' answered the young man.

'Are you in earnest?'

'Why, do you want me to break my neck?'

'Then make haste and get on my horse; don't be afraid, it is very quiet. We won't delay them, they can change the saddles in a minute! I'll try to take yours. Surely Tancred can't always be so unruly.'

No sooner said than done, the madcap leaped out of the saddle and was standing before us as she finished the last sentence.

'You don't know Tancred, if you think he will allow your wretched side-saddle to be put on him! Besides, I would not let you break your neck, it would be a pity!' said our host, at that moment of inward gratification affecting, as his habit was, a studied brusqueness and even coarseness of speech which he thought in keeping with a jolly good fellow and an old soldier, and which he imagined to be particularly attractive to the ladies. This was one of his favourite fancies, his favourite whim, with which we were all familiar.

'Well, cry-baby, wouldn't you like to have a try? You wanted so much to go?' said the valiant horsewoman, noticing me and pointing tauntingly at Tancred, because I had been so imprudent as to catch her eye, and she would not let me go without a biting word, that she might not have dismounted from her horse absolutely for nothing.

'I expect you are not such a — We all know you are a hero and would be ashamed to be afraid; especially when you will be looked at, you fine page,' she added, with a fleeting glance at Mme M., whose carriage was the nearest to the entrance.

A rush of hatred and vengeance had flooded my heart when the fair Amazon had approached us with the intention of mounting Tancred. But I cannot describe what I felt at this unexpected challenge from the madcap. Everything was dark before my eyes when I saw her glance at Mme M. For an instant an idea flashed through my mind . . . but it was only a moment, less than a moment, like a flash of gunpowder; perhaps it was the last straw, and I suddenly now was moved to rage as my spirit rose, so that I longed to put all my enemies to utter confusion, and to revenge myself on all of them and before everyone by showing the sort of person I was. Or whether by some miracle, some prompting from medieval history, of which I had known nothing till then, sent whirling through my giddy brain images of tournaments, paladins, heroes, lovely ladies, the clash of swords, shouts and the applause of the crowd, and amidst those shouts the timid cry of a frightened heart, which moves the proud soul more sweetly than victory and fame – I don't know whether all this romantic nonsense was in my head at the time, or whether, more likely, only the first dawning of the inevitable nonsense that was in store for me in the future, anyway, I felt that my hour had come. My heart leaped and shuddered, and I don't remember how, at one bound, I was down the steps and beside Tancred.

'You think I am afraid?' I cried, boldly and proudly, in such a fever that I could hardly see, breathless with excitement and flushing till the tears scalded my cheeks. 'Well, you shall see!' And clutching at Tancred's mane I put my foot in the stirrup before they had time to make a movement to stop me; but at that instant Tancred reared, jerked his head, and with a mighty bound forward wrenched himself out of the hands of the petrified stable-boys and dashed off like a hurricane, while everyone cried out in horror.

Goodness knows how I got my other leg over the horse while it was in full gallop; I can't imagine, either, how I did not lose hold of the reins. Tancred bore me beyond the trellis gate, turned sharply to the right and flew along beside the fence regardless of the road. Only at that moment I heard behind me a shout from fifty voices, and that shout was echoed in my swooning heart with such a feeling of pride and pleasure that I shall never forget that mad moment of my boyhood. All the blood rushed to my head, bewildering me and overpowering my fears. I was beside myself. There certainly was, as I remember it now, something of the knight-errant about the exploit.

My knightly exploits, however, were all over in an instant or it would have gone badly with the knight. And, indeed, I do not know how I escaped as it was. I did know how to ride, I had been taught. But my pony was more like a sheep than a riding horse. No doubt I should have been thrown off Tancred if he had had time to throw me, but after galloping fifty paces he suddenly took fright at a huge stone which lay across the road and bolted back. He turned sharply, galloping at full speed, so that it is a puzzle to me even now that I was not sent spinning out of the saddle and flying like a ball for twenty feet, that I was not dashed to pieces, and that Tancred did not dislocate his leg by such a sudden turn. He rushed back to the gate, tossing his head furiously, bounding from side to side as though drunk with rage, flinging his legs at random in the air, and at every leap trying to shake me off his back as though a tiger had leaped on him and were thrusting its teeth and claws into his back.

In another instant I should have flown off; I was falling; but several gentlemen flew to my rescue. Two of them intercepted the way into the open country, two others galloped up, closing in upon Tancred so that their horses' sides almost crushed my legs, and both of them caught him by the bridle. A few seconds later we were back at the steps.

They lifted me down from the horse, pale and scarcely breathing. I was shaking like a blade of grass in the wind; it was the same with Tancred, who was standing, his hoofs as it were thrust into the earth and his whole body thrown back, puffing his fiery breath from red and streaming nostrils, twitching and quivering all over, seeming overwhelmed with wounded pride and anger at a child's being so bold with impunity. All around me I heard cries of bewilderment, surprise and alarm.

At that moment my straying eyes caught those of Mme M., who looked pale and agitated, and – I can never forget that moment – in one instant my face was flooded with colour, glowed and burned like fire; I don't know what happened to me, but confused and frightened by my own feelings I timidly dropped my eyes to the ground. But my glance was noticed, it was caught, it was stolen from me. All eyes turned on Mme M., and finding herself unawares the centre of attention, she, too, flushed like a child from some naïve and involuntary feeling and made an unsuccessful effort to cover her confusion by laughing . . . All this, of course, was very absurd-looking from outside, but at that moment an extremely naïve and unexpected circumstance saved me from being laughed at by everyone, and gave a special colour to the whole adventure. The lovely persecutor who was the instigator of the whole escapade, and who till then had been my irreconcilable foe, suddenly rushed up to embrace and kiss me. She had hardly been able to believe her eyes when she saw me dare to accept her challenge, and pick up the gauntlet she had flung at me by glancing at Mme M. She had almost died of terror and self-reproach when I had flown off on Tancred; now, when it was all over, and particularly when she caught the glance at Mme M., my confusion and my sudden flush of colour, when the romantic strain in her frivolous little head had given a new secret, unspoken significance to the moment – she was moved to such enthusiasm over my 'knightliness', that touched, joyful and proud of me, she rushed up and pressed me to her bosom. She lifted the most naïve, stern-looking little face, on which there quivered and gleamed two little crystal tears, and gazing at the crowd that thronged about her said in a grave, earnest voice, such as they had never heard her use before, pointing to me: 'Mais c'est très sérieux, messieurs, ne riez pas!'[112] She did not notice that all were standing, as though fascinated, admiring her bright enthusiasm. Her swift, unexpected action, her earnest little face, the simple-hearted naïveté, the unexpected feeling betrayed by the tears that welled in her invariably laughter-loving eyes, were such a surprise that everyone stood before her as though electrified by her expression, her rapid, fiery words and gestures. It seemed as though no one could take his eyes off her for fear of missing that rare moment in her enthusiastic face. Even our host flushed crimson as a tulip, and people declared that they heard him confess afterwards that 'to his shame' he had been in love for a whole minute with his charming guest. Well, of course, after this I was a knight, a hero.

'De Lorge! Toggenburg!'[113] was heard in the crowd.

There was a sound of applause.

'Hurrah for the rising generation!' added the host.

'But he is coming with us, he certainly must come with us,' said the beauty; 'we will find him a place, we must find him a place. He shall sit beside me, on my knee ... but no, no! That's a mistake! ... ' she corrected herself, laughing, unable to restrain her mirth at our first encounter. But as she laughed she stroked my hand tenderly, doing all she could to soften me, that I might not be offended.

'Of course, of course,' several voices chimed in; 'he must go, he has won his place.'

The matter was settled in a trice. The same old maid who had brought about my acquaintance with the blonde beauty was at once besieged with entreaties from all the younger people to remain at home and let me have her seat. She was forced to consent, to her intense vexation, with a smile and a stealthy hiss of anger. Her protectress, who was her usual refuge, my former foe and new friend, called to her as she galloped off on her spirited horse, laughing like a child, that she envied her and would have been glad to stay at home herself, for it was just going to rain and we should all get soaked.

And she was right in predicting rain. A regular downpour came on within an hour and the expedition was done for. We had to take shelter for some hours in the huts of the village, and had to return home between nine and ten in the evening in the damp mist that followed the rain. I began to be a little feverish. At the minute when I was starting, Mme M. came up to me and expressed surprise that my neck was uncovered and that I had nothing on over my jacket. I answered that I had not had time to get my coat. She took out a pin and pinned up the turned down collar of my shirt, took off her own neck a crimson gauze kerchief, and put it round my neck that I might not get a sore throat. She did this so hurriedly that I had not time even to thank her.

But when we got home I found her in the little drawing-room with the blonde beauty and the pale-faced young man who had gained glory for horsemanship that day by refusing to ride Tancred. I went up to thank her and give back the scarf. But now, after all my adventures, I felt somehow ashamed. I wanted to make haste and get upstairs, there at my leisure to reflect and consider. I was brimming over with impressions. As I gave back the kerchief I blushed up to my ears, as usual.

'I bet he would like to keep the kerchief,' said the young man laughing. 'One can see that he is sorry to part with your scarf.'

'That's it, that's it!' the fair lady put in. 'What a boy! Oh!' she said, shaking her head with obvious vexation, but she stopped in time at a grave glance from Mme M., who did not want to carry the jest too far.

I made haste to get away.

'Well, you are a boy,' said the madcap, overtaking me in the next room and affectionately taking me by both hands, 'why, you should have simply not returned the kerchief if you wanted so much to have it. You should have said you put it down somewhere, and that would have been the end of it. What a simpleton! Couldn't even do that! What a funny boy!'

And she tapped me on the chin with her finger, laughing at my having flushed as red as a poppy.

'I am your friend now, you know; am I not? Our enmity is over, isn't it? Yes or no?'

I laughed and pressed her fingers without a word.

'Oh, why are you so . . . why are you so pale and shivering? Have you caught a chill?'

'Yes, I don't feel well.'

'Ah, poor fellow! That's the result of over-excitement. Do you know what? You had better go to bed without sitting up for supper, and you will be all right in the morning. Come along.'

She took me upstairs, and there was no end to the care she lavished on me. Leaving me to undress she ran downstairs, got me some tea, and brought it up herself when I was in bed. She brought me up a warm quilt as well. I was much impressed and touched by all the care and attention lavished on me; or perhaps I was affected by the whole day, the expedition and feverishness. As I said good-night to her I hugged her warmly, as though she were my dearest and nearest friend, and in my exhausted state all the emotions of the day came back to me in a rush; I almost shed tears as I nestled to her bosom. She noticed my overwrought condition, and I believe my madcap herself was a little touched.

'You are a very good boy,' she said, looking at me with gentle eyes, 'please don't be angry with me. You won't, will you?'

In fact, we became the warmest and truest of friends.

It was rather early when I woke up, but the sun was already flooding the whole room with brilliant light. I jumped out of bed feeling perfectly well and strong, as though I had had no fever the day before; indeed, I felt now unutterably joyful. I recalled the previous day and felt that I would have given any happiness if I could at that minute have embraced my new friend, the fair-haired beauty, again, as I had the night before; but it was very early and everyone was still asleep. Hurriedly dressing I went out into the garden and from there into the copse. I made my way where the leaves were thickest, where the fragrance of the trees was more resinous, and where the sun peeped in most gaily, rejoicing that it could penetrate the dense darkness of the foliage. It was a lovely morning.

Going on farther and farther, before I was aware of it I had reached the further end of the copse and came out on the Rver Moskva.[114] It flowed at the bottom of the hill two hundred paces below. On the opposite bank of the river they were mowing. I watched whole rows of sharp scythes gleam all together in the sunlight at every swing of the mower and then vanish again like little fiery snakes going into hiding; I watched the cut grass flying on one side in dense rich swathes and being laid in long straight lines. I don't know how long I spent in contemplation. At last I was roused from my reverie by hearing a horse snorting and impatiently pawing the ground twenty paces from me, in the track which ran from the high road to the manor house. I don't know whether I heard this horse as soon as the rider rode up and stopped there, or whether the sound had long been in my ears without rousing me from my dreaming. Moved by curiosity I went into the copse, and before I had gone many steps I caught the sound of voices speaking rapidly, though in subdued tones. I went up closer, carefully parting the branches of the bushes that edged the path, and at once sprang back in amazement. I caught a glimpse of a familiar white dress and a soft feminine voice resounded like music in my heart. It was Mme M. She was standing beside a man on horseback who, stooping down from the saddle, was hurriedly talking to her, and to my amazement I recognised him as N., the young man who had gone away the morning before and over whose departure Monsieur M. had been so busy. But people had said at the time that he was going far away to somewhere in the South of Russia, and so I was very much surprised at seeing him with us again so early, and alone with Mme M.

She was moved and agitated as I had never seen her before, and tears were glistening on her cheeks. The young man was holding her hand and stooping down to kiss it. I had come upon them at the moment of parting. They seemed to be in haste. At last he took out of his pocket a sealed envelope, gave it to Mme M., put one arm round her, still not dismounting, and gave her a long, fervent kiss. A minute later he lashed his horse and flew past me like an arrow. Mme M. looked after him for some moments, then pensively and disconsolately turned homewards. But after going a few steps along the track she seemed suddenly to recollect herself, hurriedly parted the bushes and walked on through the copse.

I followed her, surprised and perplexed by all that I had seen. My heart was beating violently, as though from terror. I was, as it were, benumbed and befogged; my ideas were shattered and turned upside down; but I remember I was, for some reason, very sad. I got glimpses from time to time through the green foliage of her white dress before me: I followed her mechanically, never losing sight of her, though I trembled at the thought that she might notice me. At last she came out on the little path that led to the house. After waiting half a minute I, too, emerged from the bushes; but what was my amazement when I saw lying on the red sand of the path a sealed packet, which I recognised, from the first glance, as the one that had been given to Mme M. ten minutes before.

I picked it up. On both sides the paper was blank, there was no address on it. The envelope was not large, but it was fat and heavy, as though there were three or more sheets of notepaper in it.

What was the meaning of this envelope? No doubt it would explain the whole mystery. Perhaps in it there was said all that N. had scarcely hoped to express in their brief, hurried interview. He had not even dismounted . . . Whether he had been in haste or whether he had been afraid of being false to himself at the hour of parting – God only knows . . . I stopped, without coming out on the path, threw the envelope in the most conspicuous place on it, and kept my eyes upon it, supposing that Mme M. would notice the loss and come back and look for it. But after waiting four minutes I could stand it no longer, I picked up my find again, put it in my pocket, and set off to overtake Mme M. I came upon her in the big avenue in the garden. She was walking straight towards the house with a swift and hurried step, though she was lost in thought, and her eyes were on the ground. I did not know what to do. Go up to her, give it her? That would be as good as saying that I knew everything, that I had seen it all. I should betray myself at the first word. And how should I look at her? How would she look at me. I kept expecting that she would discover her loss and return on her tracks. Then I could, unnoticed, have flung the envelope on the path and she would have found it. But no! We were approaching the house; she had already been noticed . . . As ill-luck would have it everyone had got up very early that day, because, after the unsuccessful expedition of the evening before, they had arranged something new, of which I had heard nothing. All were preparing to set off, and were having breakfast in the verandah. I waited for ten minutes, that I might not be seen with Mme M., and making a circuit of the garden approached the house from the other side a long time after her. She was walking up and down the verandah with her arms folded, looking pale and agitated, and was obviously trying her utmost to suppress the agonising, despairing misery which could be plainly discerned in her eyes, her walk, her every movement. Sometimes she went down the verandah steps and walked a few paces among the flower-beds in the direction of the garden; her eyes were impatiently, greedily, even incautiously, seeking something on the sand of the path and on the floor of the verandah. There could be no doubt she had discovered her loss and imagined she had dropped the letter somewhere here, near the house – yes, that must be so, she was convinced of it.

Someone noticed that she was pale and agitated, and others made the same remark. She was besieged with questions about her health and condolences. She had to laugh, to jest, to appear lively. From time to time she looked at her husband, who was standing at the end of the terrace talking to two ladies, and the poor woman was overcome by the same shudder, the same embarrassment, as on the day of his first arrival. Thrusting my hand into my pocket and holding the letter tight in it, I stood at a little distance from them all, praying to fate that Mme M. should notice me. I longed to cheer her up, to relieve her anxiety if only by a glance; to say a word to her on the sly. But when she did chance to look at me I dropped my eyes.

I saw her distress and I was not mistaken. To this day I don't know her secret. I know nothing but what I saw and what I have just described. The intrigue was not such, perhaps, as one might suppose at the first glance. Perhaps that kiss was the kiss of farewell, perhaps it was the last slight reward for the sacrifice made to her peace and honour. N. was going away, he was leaving her, perhaps for ever. Even that letter I was holding in my hand – who can tell what it contained! How can one judge? and who can condemn? And yet there is no doubt that the sudden discovery of her secret would have been terrible – would have been a fatal blow for her. I still remember her face at that minute, it could not have shown more suffering. To feel, to know, to be convinced, to expect, as though it were one's execution, that in a quarter of an hour, in a minute perhaps, all might be discovered, the letter might be found by someone, picked up; there was no address on it, it might be opened, and then . . . What then? What torture could be worse than what was awaiting her? She moved about among those who would be her judges. In another minute their smiling flattering faces would be menacing and merciless. She would read mockery, malice and icy contempt on those faces, and then her life would be plunged in everlasting darkness, with no dawn to follow . . . Yes, I did not understand it then as I understand it now. I could only have vague suspicions and misgivings, and a heartache at the thought of her danger, which I could not fully understand. But whatever lay hidden in her secret, much was expiated, if expiation were needed, by those moments of anguish of which I was witness and which I shall never forget.

But then came a cheerful summons to set off; immediately every one was bustling about gaily; laughter and lively chatter were heard on all sides. Within two minutes the verandah was deserted. Mme M. declined to join the party, acknowledging at last that she was not well. But, thank God, all the others set off, everyone was in haste, and there was no time to worry her with commiseration, enquiries and advice. A few remained at home. Her husband said a few words to her; she answered that she would be all right directly, that he need not be uneasy, that there was no occasion for her to lie down, that she would go into the garden, alone ... with me ... here she glanced at me. Nothing could be more fortunate! I flushed with pleasure, with delight; a minute later we were on the way.

She walked along the same avenues and paths by which she had returned from the copse, instinctively remembering the way she had come, gazing before her with her eyes fixed on the ground, looking about intently without answering me, possibly forgetting that I was walking beside her.

But when we had already reached the place where I had picked up the letter, and the path ended, Mme M. suddenly stopped, and in a voice faint and weak with misery said that she felt worse, and that she would go home. But when she reached the garden fence she stopped again and thought a minute; a smile of despair came on her lips, and utterly worn out and exhausted, resigned, and making up her mind to the worst, she turned without a word and retraced her steps, even forgetting to tell me of her intention.

My heart was torn with sympathy, and I did not know what to do.

We went, or rather I led her, to the place from which an hour before I had heard the tramp of a horse and their conversation. Here, close to a shady elm tree, was a seat hewn out of one huge stone, about which grew ivy, wild jasmine and dog-rose; the whole wood was dotted with little bridges, arbours, grottoes and similar surprises. Mme M. sat down on the bench and glanced unconsciously at the marvellous view that lay open before us. A minute later she opened her book, and fixed her eyes upon it without reading, without turning the pages, almost unconscious of what she was doing. It was about half-past nine. The sun was already high and was floating gloriously in the deep, dark-blue sky, as though melting away in its own light. The mowers were by now far away; they were scarcely visible from our side of the river; endless ridges of mown grass crept after them in unbroken succession, and from time to time the faintly stirring breeze wafted their fragrance to us. The never ceasing concert of those who 'sow not, neither do they reap' and are free as the air they cleave with their sportive wings was all about us. It seemed as though at that moment every flower, every blade of grass was exhaling the aroma of sacrifice, was saying to its Creator, 'Father, I am blessed and happy.'

I glanced at the poor woman, who alone was like one dead amidst all this joyous life; two big tears hung motionless on her lashes, wrung from her heart by bitter grief. It was in my power to relieve and console this poor, fainting heart, only I did not know how to approach the subject, how to take the first step. I was in agonies. A hundred times I was on the point of going up to her, but every time my face glowed like fire.

Suddenly a bright idea dawned upon me. I had found a way of doing it; I revived.

'Would you like me to pick you a nosegay?' I said, in such a joyful voice that Mme M. immediately raised her head and looked at me intently.

'Yes, do,' she said at last in a weak voice, with a faint smile, at once dropping her eyes on the book again.

'Or soon they will be mowing the grass here and there will be no flowers,' I cried, eagerly setting to work.

I had soon picked my nosegay, a poor, simple one I should have been ashamed to take indoors; but how light my heart was as I picked the flowers and tied them up! The dog-rose and the wild jasmine I picked close to the seat. I knew that not far off there was a field of rye, not yet ripe. I ran there for cornflowers; I mixed them with tall ears of rye, picking out the finest and most golden. Close by I came upon a perfect nest of forget-me-nots, and my nosegay was almost complete. Farther away in the meadow there were dark-blue campanulas and wild pinks, and I ran down to the very edge of the river to get yellow water-lilies. At last, making my way back, and going for an instant into the wood to get some bright green fan-shaped leaves of the maple to put round the nosegay, I happened to come across a whole family of pansies, close to which, luckily for me, the fragrant scent of violets betrayed the little flowers hiding in the thick lush grass and still glistening with drops of dew. The nosegay was complete. I bound it round with fine long grass which twisted into a rope, and I carefully laid the letter in the centre, hiding it with the flowers, but in such a way that it could be very easily noticed if the slightest attention were bestowed upon my nosegay.

I carried it to Mme M.

On the way it seemed to me that the letter was lying too much in view: I hid it a little more. As I got nearer I thrust it still further in the flowers; and finally, when I was on the spot, I suddenly poked it so deeply into the centre of the nosegay that it could not be noticed at all from outside. My cheeks were positively flaming. I wanted to hide my face in my hands and run away at once, but she glanced at my flowers as though she had completely forgotten that I had gathered them. Mechanically, almost without looking, she held out her hand and took my present; but at once laid it on the seat as though I had handed it to her for that purpose and dropped her eyes to her book again, seeming lost in thought. I was ready to cry at this mischance. 'If only my nosegay were close to her,' I thought; 'if only she had not forgotten it!' I lay down on the grass not far off, put my right arm under my head, and closed my eyes as though I were overcome by drowsiness. But I waited, keeping my eyes fixed on her.

Ten minutes passed, it seemed to me that she was getting paler and paler . . . fortunately a blessed chance came to my aid.

This was a big, golden bee, brought by a kindly breeze, luckily for me. It first buzzed over my head, and then flew up to Mme M. She waved it off once or twice, but the bee grew more and more persistent. At last Mme M. snatched up my nosegay and waved it before my face. At that instant the letter dropped out from among the flowers and fell straight upon the open book. I started. For some time Mme M., mute with amazement, stared first at the letter and then at the flowers which she was holding in her hands, and she seemed unable to believe her eyes. All at once she flushed, started, and glanced at me. But I caught her movement and I shut my eyes tight, pretending to be asleep. Nothing would have induced me to look her straight in the face at that moment. My heart was throbbing and leaping like a bird in the grasp of some village boy. I don't remember how long I lay with my eyes shut, perhaps two or three minutes. At last I ventured to open them. Mme M. was greedily reading the letter, and from her glowing cheeks, her sparkling, tearful eyes, her bright face, every feature of which was quivering with joyful emotion, I guessed that there was happiness in the letter and all her misery was dispersed like smoke. An agonising, sweet feeling gnawed at my heart, it was hard for me to go on pretending . . . I shall never forget that minute!

Suddenly, a long way off, we heard voices: 'Mme M.! Natalie! Natalie!'

Mme M. did not answer, but she got up quickly from the seat, came up to me and bent over me. I felt that she was looking straight into my face. My eyelashes quivered, but I controlled myself and did not open my eyes. I tried to breathe more evenly and quietly, but my heart smothered me with its violent throbbing. Her burning breath scorched my cheeks; she bent close down to my face as though trying to make sure. At last a kiss and tears fell on my hand, the one which was lying on my breast.

'Natalie! Natalie! where are you,' we heard again, this time quite close.

'Coming,' said Mme M., in her mellow, silvery voice, which was so choked and quivering with tears and so subdued that no one but I could hear that, 'Coming!'

But at that instant my heart at last betrayed me and seemed to send all my blood rushing to my face. At that instant a swift, burning kiss scalded my lips. I uttered a faint cry. I opened my eyes, but at once the same gauze kerchief fell upon them, as though she meant to screen me from the sun. An instant later she was gone. I heard nothing but the sound of rapidly retreating steps. I was alone . . . I pulled off her kerchief and kissed it, beside myself with rapture; for some moments I was almost frantic . . . Hardly able to breathe, leaning on my elbow on the grass, I stared unconsciously before me at the surrounding slopes, streaked with cornfields, at the river that flowed twisting and winding far away, as far as the eye could see, between fresh hills and villages that gleamed like dots all over the sunlit distance – at the dark-blue, hardly visible forests, which seemed as though smoking at the edge of the burning sky, and a sweet stillness inspired by the triumphant peacefulness of the picture gradually brought calm to my troubled heart. I felt more at ease and breathed more freely, but my whole soul was full of a dumb, sweet yearning, as though a veil had been drawn from my eyes as though at a foretaste of something. My frightened heart, faintly quivering with expectation, was groping timidly and joyfully towards some conjecture . . . and all at once my bosom heaved, began aching as though something had pierced it, and tears, sweet tears, gushed from my eyes. I hid my face in my hands, and quivering like a blade of grass, gave myself up to the first consciousness and revelation of my heart, the first vague glimpse of my nature. My childhood was over from that moment.

When two hours later I returned home I did not find Mme M. Through some sudden chance she had gone back to Moscow with her husband. I never saw her again.

Uncle's Dream

From the Annals of Mordasov

1

MARYA ALEXANDROVNA MOSKALEV is the leading lady in Mordasov, and of that there can be no possible question. She behaves as though she were independent of everyone and everyone else were dependent on her. It is true that scarcely anyone likes her and, indeed, very many people sincerely hate her; but on the other hand everyone is afraid of her, and that is just what she wants. Such a desire betokens a high degree of diplomacy. How is it, for instance, that Marya Alexandrovna, who is desperately fond of gossip, and cannot sleep at night if she has not heard something new the day before, how is it that with all that she knows how to deport herself so that it would never occur to anyone looking at her that this majestic lady was the greatest gossip in the world, or at any rate in Mordasov. One would suppose, on the contrary, that gossip would die away in her presence, that backbiters would blush and tremble like schoolboys confronting their teacher, and that the conversation would not deal with any but the loftiest subjects. She knows about some of the Mordasov people facts so scandalous and so important that if she were to tell them on a suitable occasion and to make them public, as she so well knows how to do, there would be a regular earthquake of Lisbon[115] in Mordasov. And at the same time she is very reserved over these secrets and will only tell them in extreme cases, and then only to her most intimate female friends. She confines herself to frightening people, with hints at what she knows, and likes better to keep a man or a lady in continual apprehension than to deal them a final blow. That is intelligence, that is diplomacy! Marya Alexandrovna was always distinguished among us by her irreproachable *comme il faut*, upon which we all model ourselves. As regards *comme il faut* she is without a rival in Mordasov. She can, for instance, kill, tear to pieces, annihilate a rival with a single word, a performance we have witnessed; and at the same time she will have the air of not observing that she has uttered that word. And we all know that this ability is characteristic of the very highest society. In fact, at all such tricks she is a match for Pinetti.[116] Her connections are immense. Many persons who have visited Mordasov have been delighted with her hospitality, and have even kept up a correspondence with her after their departure. Someone even wrote her a poem, and Marya Alexandrovna showed it to us all with pride. One literary visitor dedicated to her his novel, which he read aloud to her in the evenings, and this made an extremely agreeable impression. A learned German, who came from Carlsruhe[117] expressly to study some kind of worm with horns, which is found in our province, and who wrote four quarto volumes on the creature in question, was so enchanted by Marya Alexandrovna's hospitality and politeness that to this day he keeps up with her a correspondence of the most respectful and highly moral tone, from Carlsruhe. Marya Alexandrovna has even been compared in one respect with Napoleon. This comparison was of course made in jest by her enemies, more by way of sarcasm than truth. But while fully admitting the oddity of the comparison I make bold to ask one innocent question: why was Napoleon's head turned at last when he was too greatly exalted? The champions of the old dynasty used to ascribe this to the fact that Napoleon was not only not of royal blood, but was not even a *gentilhomme* of good family, and so was naturally alarmed at last by his own exalted state and was conscious of his real position. In spite of the obvious cleverness of this surmise, which recalls the most brilliant period of the old French court, I venture to add in my turn: how was it that Marya Alexandrovna's head was never under any circumstances turned, how was it that she always remained the leading lady in Mordasov? There were occasions when everybody asked: 'How will Marya Alexandrovna act now in such difficult circumstances?' But the circumstances arrived and passed and – all went well! Everything remained satisfactory, as before; even better than before. Everyone remembers, for instance, how her husband, Afanasy Matveyitch, was deprived of his post owing to his incompetence and feeble-mindedness, which excited the wrath of an inspector from the capital. Everyone thought that Marya Alexandrovna would be depressed, would be humbled, would entreat and petition, would, in short, be crestfallen. Nothing of the sort: Marya Alexandrovna grasped that nothing could be gained by petitioning, and played her cards so well that she lost nothing of her influence in society, and her house is still looked upon as the house of most consequence in Mordasov. Anna Nikolaevna Antipov, the Public Prosecutor's wife, a sworn foe of Marya Alexandrovna's, though externally her friend, was already trumpeting her victory; but when we saw that Marya Alexandrovna could not be easily put to confusion, we realised that she had sent her roots far more deeply down than we had supposed.

By the way, since we have mentioned him we will say a few words about Afanasy Matveyitch, Marya Alexandrovna's husband. In the first place he was a man of very presentable exterior, and indeed of very correct principles, only on critical occasions he somehow lost his head, and looked like a sheep facing a new gate. He was extraordinarily dignified, especially in his white tie at nameday dinners, but his dignified air and presentability only lasted till the minute when he began to speak. Then there was nothing for it, if I may say so, but cotton wool in one's ears. He certainly was not worthy to belong to Marya Alexandrovna; that was the universal opinion, he had only kept his position through the genius of his wife; in my private judgement he ought long ago to have been in the kitchen garden scaring sparrows. There and only there he might have been of real unquestionable service to his fellow-countrymen. And so Marya Alexandrovna acted admirably in sending Afanasy Matveyitch to their country place, two and a half miles from Mordasov, where she had a hundred and twenty serfs – in parenthesis I may say, the whole property, the whole fortune upon which she so worthily maintained the dignity of her household. Everybody knew that she had kept Afanasy Matveyitch about her solely because he was in the government service and in receipt of a salary and . . . of other sums. As soon as he ceased to receive a salary and other sums, she immediately removed him to a distance on account of his incompetence and absolute uselessness. And everyone commended Marya Alexandrovna's clear-sightedness and decision of character. In the country Afanasy Matveyitch is in clover. I went to see him and spent a whole hour with him fairly pleasantly. He tries on his white cravats, cleans his boots with his own hands, not from necessity but simply for love of the art, because he likes his boots to shine; he drinks tea three times a day, is exceedingly fond of going to the bath-house, and – is contented. Do you remember the horrid scandal that was concocted among us a year and a half ago concerning Zinaida Afanasyevna, the only daughter of Marya Alexandrovna and Afanasy Matveyitch? Zinaida Afanasyevna is unquestionably beautiful, and is extremely well educated, yet she is three-and-twenty and is still unmarried. Among the reasons people give for Zina's being unmarried, one of the chief is considered to be the sinister rumour of some strange intimacy a year and a half ago with a wretched district schoolmaster – a rumour which has persisted to this day. Even now there is talk of some love-letter written by Zina and said to have been passed from hand to hand in Mordasov; but I should like to know if anyone has seen that letter. If it has passed from hand to hand what has become of it? Everyone has heard about it, but nobody has seen it. I, at any rate, have never come across anyone who has seen this letter with his own eyes. If you drop a hint about it to Marya Alexandrovna she simply fails to understand you. Now let us assume that there really was something, and Zina did write the love-letter (I fancy, indeed, that it must have been so), how skilful it all was on Marya Alexandrovna's part! How adroitly was this awkward, scandalous affair suppressed and stifled! Not a trace, not a hint! Marya Alexandrovna takes no notice now of this ignoble slander, and at the same time, God knows how she may have worked to save the honour of her only daughter from the slightest slur. And as for Zina's not being married, that's very natural: there are no eligible young men here. The only fitting match for Zina would be a reigning prince. Have you ever seen a beauty like her? It is true that she is proud – too proud. They say that Mozglyakov is paying her his addresses, but it is hardly likely to come to a marriage. What is Mozglyakov? It is true that he is young, not bad looking, a dandy, has a hundred and fifty serfs not mortgaged, and comes from Petersburg. But in the first place, you know he is not quite sound in the upper storey. He is feather-headed, a chatterbox, and has some very new-fangled ideas. And after all what is an estate of a hundred and fifty serfs, especially with new-fangled ideas! That marriage won't come off.

All that the kind reader has read so far was written by me five months ago entirely from excess of feeling. I may as well confess betimes I have rather a partiality for Marya Alexandrovna. I wanted to write something like a eulogy on that magnificent lady, and to put it in the shape of a playful letter to a friend, on the model of the letters which used, at one time, in the old golden days that, thank God, will never return, to be published in the *Northern Bee*[118] and other periodicals. But as I have no friend, and have, moreover, a certain innate literary timidity, my work has remained in my table drawer as my first literary effort and a memento of peaceful recreation in hours of leisure and comfort.

Five months have passed, and all at once a wonderful event has occurred in Mordasov: early one morning Prince K. arrived in the town and stopped at Marya Alexandrovna's house. The consequences of this arrival have been innumerable. The prince spent only three days in Mordasov, but those three days have left behind them momentous memories that will never be effaced. I will say more: Prince K. produced, in a certain sense, a revolution in our town. The story of that revolution is, of course, one of the most significant pages in the annals of Mordasov. That page I have made up my mind at last, after some hesitation, to put into literary shape and lay before the criticism of the honoured public. My story will contain the full and remarkable history of the exaltation, glory and solemn downfall of Marya Alexandrovna and all her family: a worthy and alluring theme for an author. First of all, of course, I must explain what there was wonderful in Prince K.'s arriving in our town and staying at Marya Alexandrovna's – and to do that I must, of course, say a few words about Prince K. himself. And that I will do. Besides, the biography of that personage is absolutely essential for all the further development of our story. And so I will begin.

2

I will begin by saying that Prince K. was not so extraordinarily aged, but yet he was so decrepit, so worn out, that as one looked at him the thought instinctively occurred to one that in another minute he might drop to pieces. Extremely queer stories of the most fantastic kind were repeated in Mordasov about this prince. People even said that the old man was off his head. Everyone thought it very strange that the owner of an estate of four thousand serfs, a man of distinguished family, who might, if he had chosen, have had a great influence in the province, should live in solitude on his magnificent estate, a complete hermit. Many had known Prince K. when he was staying in Mordasov six or seven years before, and they declared that in those days he could not endure solitude and had not the faintest resemblance to a hermit.

All that I could ascertain about him, on good authority, however, was this:

In his young days, which were, however, long ago, the prince had made a brilliant début, he had led a gay life, flirted, had made several tours abroad, sang songs, made puns, and had at no period been distinguished by the brilliance of his intellectual gifts. Of course he had squandered all his fortune, and found himself in his old age without a farthing. Someone advised him to visit his estate, which was beginning to be sold by auction. He set off and arrived in Mordasov, where he stayed six months. He liked provincial life extremely. During those six months he dissipated all he had left, to the last halfpenny, spending his whole time in gambling and getting up various intrigues with the ladies of the province. He was, moreover, extremely good-natured, though of course not without certain princely airs, which were, however, regarded in Mordasov as characteristic of the highest society, and so, instead of annoying people, they positively impressed them favourably. The ladies especially were in perpetual ecstasy over their charming visitor. A number of curious reminiscences of him were preserved. People said among other things that the prince spent more than half the day over his toilet, and was, it appeared, entirely made up of different little bits. No one knew when and where he had managed to become so dilapidated. He wore a wig, moustaches, whiskers, and even a little 'imperial' – all, every hair of it, false, and of a magnificent black colour; he rouged and powdered every day. It was said that he had little springs to smooth away the wrinkles on his face, and these springs were in some peculiar way concealed in his hair. It was asserted, too, that he wore corsets, because he had lost a rib jumping somewhat clumsily out of a window on one of his amorous adventures in Italy. He limped with the left leg; it was maintained that the leg in question was an artificial one, and that the real one had been broken in the course of another similar adventure in Paris, and that he had been provided with a new cork leg of a special pattern. But what will not people say? It certainly was true that his right eye was a glass one, though it was a most skilful imitation. His teeth, too, were false. He spent whole days washing in various patent waters, scenting and pomading himself. It was recalled, however, that even then the prince was perceptibly beginning to grow feeble, and that he had become insufferably garrulous. It seemed as though his career were drawing to its close. Everyone knew that he had not a farthing. And all of a sudden, quite unexpectedly, one of his nearest relations, a very aged lady who had lived for many years in Paris and from whom he could have had no expectations, died, just a month after the funeral of her legal heir. The prince found himself quite unexpectedly the heir to her fortune. A magnificent estate of four thousand serfs, about forty miles from Mordasov, all came to him. He at once prepared to go to Petersburg to settle his affairs. Our ladies got up a magnificent subscription dinner in his honour. It is recalled that the prince was enchantingly gay at this farewell banquet, he made puns, made everyone laugh, told the most extraordinary anecdotes, vowed that he would return as quickly as possible to Duhanovo (his new property), and promised that on his return there would be a continual round of fêtes, picnics, balls, and fireworks. For a whole year after his departure the ladies talked of this promise, and awaited their charming old friend with immense impatience. While awaiting his return they even made up parties to Duhanovo, where there was an old-world manor-house and garden, with acacias lopped into the shape of lions, with artificial mounds, with lakes, upon which boats sailed up and down with wooden images of Turks playing a pipe for figureheads, with arbours, with pavilions, with pleasure grounds and other attractions.

At last the prince returned, but to the general surprise and disappointment he did not even call at Mordasov on his way, but settled at Duhanovo and lived like a hermit. Strange rumours began to circulate, and altogether from that period the prince's history became obscure and fantastic. To begin with, it was asserted that he had not been altogether successful in Petersburg, that some of his relations and future heirs tried to take advantage of the prince's mental feebleness in order to get him put under some sort of supervision, fearing that he would squander everything again. What was more, some people declared that they had tried to put him in a lunatic asylum, but that one of his relations, a gentleman of consequence, had taken his part, explaining frankly to the others that the poor prince, half dead and half a dummy already, would probably soon die altogether, and then the property would come to them without the help of a lunatic asylum. I repeat again: what will not people say? especially in our town, Mordasov. All this, so it was said, scared the prince terribly, so much so that he became a transformed character and turned into a hermit. Some of the Mordasov gentry went from curiosity to call upon him, but were either not received or met with a very strange reception. The prince did not even recognise his old acquaintances. It was asserted that he did not want to recognise them. The Governor, too, paid him a visit.

He returned with the news, that in his opinion the prince really was a little off his head, and ever afterwards he made a wry face at any allusion to his visit to Duhanovo. The ladies were loud in their indignation. At last a fact of prime importance was discovered, namely, that the prince was entirely in the power of one Stepanida Matveyevna, a woman no one knew anything about, who had come with him from Petersburg, was stout and elderly, and went about in cotton dresses with the keys in her hands; that the prince obeyed her in everything like a child and did not dare to take a step without her permission, that she even washed him with her own hands, that she spoilt him, dandled him and comforted him like a child, and that finally she kept away from him all visitors, and especially the relations, who had been gradually beginning to visit Duhanovo to see how things were going. People in Mordasov discussed this incomprehensible relationship a great deal, especially the ladies. It was added that Stepanida Matveyevna had unchecked and independent control of the prince's whole estate; that she dismissed the stewards, the bailiffs and the servants, and collected the revenues; but that she ruled it well, so that the peasants blessed their fate. As regards the prince himself, it was learned that his days were spent almost entirely on his toilet, in trying on wigs and dress coats; that he spent the rest of his time with Stepanida Matveyevna, that he played his game of cards with her, tried his fortune with the cards, only now and then going for a ride on a quiet English mare, on which occasions Stepanida Matveyevna invariably accompanied him in a closed chaise in case of mishap, for the prince rode on horseback chiefly for effect, and could hardly keep in the saddle. He was sometimes seen also on foot, wearing an overcoat and wide-brimmed straw hat; with a lady's pink neckerchief round his neck, with an eyeglass in his eye and a wicker basket for mushrooms, cornflowers and other wild flowers; Stepanida Matveyevna always accompanied him, while behind them walked two tall footmen, and the carriage followed to be ready in case of need. When he was met by a peasant, who stepped aside, took off his hat, bowed low and said: 'Good-day, prince, your excellency, our sunshine,' the prince promptly turned his lorgnette upon him, nodded graciously and said to him affably: '*Bonjour, mon ami, bonjour!*'[119] Many such rumours were current in Mordasov; they could not forget the prince: he was such a near neighbour! What was the general amazement when one fine day there was a report that the prince, the eccentric hermit, had arrived in Mordasov in person and was staying at Marya Alexandrovna's! All was bustle and excitement. Everyone was eager for an explanation, all asked one another what it meant? Some prepared to call on Marya Alexandrovna. The prince's arrival struck everyone as a wonder. The ladies sent one another notes, prepared to call on one another, sent their maids and their husbands to make enquiries. It seemed particularly strange and hard to understand why the prince should stay at Marya Alexandrovna's rather than at anyone else's. Anna Nikolaevna Antipov was particularly annoyed, because the prince was a very distant relation of hers. But to solve all these questions it is absolutely necessary to call on Marya Alexandrovna herself, and we cordially invite the kind reader to do so. It is true that it is only ten o'clock in the morning, but I don't think she will refuse to receive an intimate friend. Us, at any rate, she will certainly admit.

3

Ten o'clock in the morning. We are in Marya Alexandrovna's house in the main street, in the very room which the lady of the house on solemn occasions calls her *salon*. Marya Alexandrovna has also a boudoir. In this *salon* there are well-painted floors, and rather nice wallpapers that were ordered expressly for the walls. In the rather clumsy furniture red is the predominating colour. There is an open fireplace, over the mantelpiece a mirror, before the looking-glass a bronze clock, with a cupid on it in very bad taste. In the space between the windows there are two looking-glasses from which they have already removed the covers. On little tables in front of the looking-glasses there are two more clocks. Against the wall at the farther end is a magnificent piano, which was procured for Zina. Zina is musical. Round the glowing fire armchairs are set, as far as possible in picturesque confusion; among them a little table. At the other end of the room another table covered with a cloth of dazzling whiteness; on it a silver samovar is boiling and a pretty tea-service is set out. The samovar and the tea are presided over by Nastasya Petrovna Zyablov, a lady who lives with Marya Alexandrovna in the capacity of a distant relation. Two words about this lady. She is a widow, she is over thirty, a brunette, with a fresh complexion, and with lively dark-brown eyes. Altogether she is good-looking. She is of a gay disposition and much given to laughter, rather sly, of course, a scandalmonger, and very capable of managing any little affair of her own. She has two children, they are somewhere at school. She would very much like to get married again. She is rather independent in her behaviour. Her husband was an officer in the army. Marya Alexandrovna herself is sitting by the fire, in the very best of spirits, and in a becoming light-green dress. She is highly delighted at the arrival of the prince, who is at this moment upstairs, engaged in his toilet. She is so delighted that she does not even think it necessary to conceal her joy. Before her stands a young man, telling her something with animation. It is evident from his eyes that he is anxious to please his listeners. He is five-and-twenty. His manners would not be bad, but he frequently flies into raptures, and he has, besides, pretensions to wit and humour. He is very well dressed, fair, and rather nice looking. But we have spoken of him already; he is Mr Mozglyakov, of whom great things are expected. Marya Alexandrovna privately thinks that he is rather empty-headed, but gives him a warm welcome. He is a suitor for the hand of her daughter Zina, with whom, in his own words, he is madly in love. He turns every moment to Zina, trying to extract a smile from her lips by his wit and gaiety. But she is perceptibly cold and careless in her manner to him. At this instant, she is standing apart, at the piano, and turning over a calendar with her fingers. She is one of those women who excite general enthusiasm and wonder whenever they appear in society. She is incredibly beautiful; tall, a brunette, with exquisite, almost black eyes, a graceful figure and a superb bust. Her shoulders and arms are antique, her foot is fascinating, she has the step of a queen. She is a little pale today; but her full, crimson, exquisitely chiselled lips, between which gleam even little teeth like threaded pearls, will haunt your dreams for the next three days if once you glance at them. Her expression is grave and severe. Monsieur Mozglyakov seems to fear her intent gaze, at least he winces when he ventures to glance at her. Her movements are disdainfully careless. She is dressed in simple white muslin, which suits her exquisitely, but then everything suits her. On her finger is a ring woven of hair, and from the colour, not her mamma's. Mozglyakov has never dared to ask her whose hair it is. That morning Zina is particularly silent and over-melancholy, as though preoccupied. Marya Alexandrovna, on the other hand, is ready to talk without stopping, though she, too, glances at her daughter from time to time with a peculiar, suspicious look; she does so, however, stealthily, as though she, too, were afraid of her.

'I am so delighted, so delighted, Pavel Alexandrovitch!' she prattles, 'that I am ready to cry aloud my joy out of the window to every passer-by. To say nothing of the charming surprise you have given Zina and me by returning a fortnight earlier than you promised; that goes without saying! I am awfully glad that you have brought the dear prince with you. You know how fond I am of the fascinating old darling! But no, no! You won't understand me. You young people can't understand my enthusiasm, however much I might assure you of it! You don't know what he was to me in the past, six years ago. Do you remember, Zina? I forgot, though, you were staying with your aunt at that time . . . You would not believe it, Pavel Alexandrovitch, I was his mentor, sister, mother! He did what I told him like a child! There was something naïve, tender and ennobling in our relations; something even, as it were, Arcadian . . . I really don't know what to call it! That is why he thinks of my house alone with gratitude, *ce pauvre prince*!¹²⁰ Do you know, Pavel Alexandrovitch, you may perhaps have saved him by bringing him to me! I have thought of him with a pang at my heart these last six years. You wouldn't believe it, he positively haunted my dreams. They say that monstrous woman has bewitched him, ruined him. But at last you have torn him out of her clutches! Yes, we must take advantage of the opportunity and save him altogether! But tell me once more how did you succeed in doing it? Describe your whole meeting as fully as possible. Just now I was in such excitement that I only attended to the central fact, though all the little details, so to speak, make up the real flavour of it! I am awfully fond of trifling details, even on most important occasions what I notice first is the small points . . . and . . . while he is still engaged in his toilet . . . '

'But it is all just what I have told you already, Marya Alexandrovna,' Mozglyakov responds with readiness, perfectly willing to tell his story for the tenth time, it is a pleasure to him. 'I was travelling all night, of course I did not sleep all night, you can imagine what haste I was in,' he adds, turning to Zina; 'in short, I swore, I shouted, I demanded horses. I even made a row at the posting stations over getting horses; if it were printed it would make quite a poem in the latest fashion! But that is off the point! At six o'clock in the morning I reached the last station, Igishevo. I was all of a shiver, but I did not want to warm myself; I called for horses! I frightened the overseer's wife, who had a baby at the breast. I think I must have upset her milk . . . The sunrise was enchanting. The hoar frost, you know, all crimson and silver! I took no notice of anything; in short, I was in desperate haste! I took the horses by storm; I snatched them from a collegiate councillor, and almost challenged him to a duel. I was told that a quarter of an hour before some prince had set off from the station travelling with his own horses; he had spent the night there. I scarcely listened. I got into my sledge, flew off, as though I were let off the chain. There is something like it in Fet, in some elegy of his.[121] Just six miles from the town, at the cross-road leading to the Svyetozersky Monastery, I saw that something surprising had happened. A huge travelling coach was lying on its side, a coachman and two footmen were standing beside it in perplexity, and heart-rending shrieks and wails were coming from the carriage, that lay on its side. I was thinking of driving by: "Let it lie on its side; it is no business of mine." But I was overcome by a feeling of humanity, which, as Heine expresses it,[122] pokes its nose into everything. I stopped. I, my Semyon and the driver – another true Russian heart – hastened to their assistance, and so the six of us together hoisted up the coach at last and set it on its legs, though indeed it had none, for it was on runners. Some peasants on their way to the town with wood helped too. I gave them a trifle. I thought, no doubt this is the same prince! I looked. My goodness! It was he, Prince Gavrila! "What a meeting!" I cried out to him. "Prince! Uncle!" Of course he scarcely recognised me at first sight; however, he almost knew me . . . at a second look. I must confess, however, that he hardly understands who I am now, and I believe he takes me for someone else and not a relation. I saw him seven years ago in Petersburg; but of course I was a boy then. I remembered him; he impressed me – but how should he remember me! I introduced myself;

he was enchanted, embraced me, and at the same time he was trembling all over with fright and crying – he really was crying, I saw that with my own eyes! One thing and another – I persuaded him at last to get into my sledge and to come for at least one day to Mordasov, to rest and recover. He agreed without any ado . . . He told me he was going to the Svyetozersky Monastery to visit the monk Misail, whom he honours and reveres; that Stepanida Matveyevna – and which of us relations has not heard of Stepanida Matveyevna? she drove me off with a broom from Duhanovo last year – that this Stepanida Matveyevna had even received a letter telling her that someone of her folks in Moscow was at the last gasp; her father, or her daughter, I don't remember which exactly, and I am not interested to know, possibly father and daughter both together, with, maybe, the addition of a nephew, a potman in some public-house . . . In short, she was so upset that she made up her mind to part from her prince for ten days, and flew off to adorn the capital with her presence. The prince stayed quiet for one day, for another, tried on his wigs, pomaded and painted himself; he tried to tell his fortune with the cards (maybe with beans too), but could not put up with it without Stepanida Matveyevna. He ordered his horses and set off to the Svyetozersky Monastery. Someone of his household, fearing the absent Stepanida Matveyevna, ventured to protest, but the prince persisted. He set off yesterday, after dinner, stayed the night at Igishevo. He left the station at daybreak, and just at the turning that leads to Father Misail's, went flying with his carriage almost into a ravine. I rescued him, persuaded him to visit our common and deeply respected friend, Marya Alexandrovna; he said that you were the most fascinating lady he had ever known – and here we are, and at this moment the prince is upstairs adjusting his toilet with the assistance of his valet, whom he has not forgotten to bring with him, and whom he never will, under any circumstances, forget to take with him, for he would sooner die than consent to appear before ladies without certain preliminary preparations, or rather, adjustments . . . That's the whole story! *Eine allerliebste Geschichte!*[123]

'But what a humorist he is, Zina!' cries Marya Alexandrovna, after hearing his story. 'How charmingly he tells it. But listen, *Paul,* one question: explain to me exactly what relation you are to the prince! You call him uncle?'

'Upon my word, Marya Alexandrovna, I do not know how or in what way I am related to him; it's seven times removed, I believe, maybe even seventy times seven.[124] It's not a bit my fault; it's all Aunt Aglaya Mihalovna. Aunt Aglaya Mihalovna does nothing but count over the relations on her fingers, though; it was she forced me to go to see him last summer at Duhanovo. She should have gone herself! I simply call him uncle, he answers to that name. That's all our relationship for today, anyway . . . '

'All the same, I repeat that it must have been a prompting from on High that led you to bring him straight to me! I tremble to think what would have happened to him, poor darling, if he had got into anyone else's hands instead of mine. They would have pounced upon him, torn him to pieces, devoured him! They would have fallen upon him as though he were a gold mine – I dare say they would have robbed him! You cannot imagine what low, greedy, artful people there are here, Pavel Alexandrovitch! . . . '

'Upon my soul, to whom should he have been taken if not to you? What are you saying, Marya Alexandrovna?' puts in the widow, Nastasya Petrovna, as she pours out the tea. 'You don't suppose he might have been taken to Anna Nikolaevna's?'

'But why is he so long coming? It's really strange,' says Marya Alexandrovna, getting up from her seat impatiently.

'Uncle, do you mean? Why, I expect he will be another five hours up there dressing! Besides, as he had quite lost his memory, he has perhaps forgotten that he is on a visit to you. You know he is a most extraordinary person, Marya Alexandrovna!'

'Oh, come, come! What nonsense.'

'Not nonsense at all, Marya Alexandrovna! He is half a made-up dummy, not a man! You saw him six years ago, but it is only an hour since I have seen him. He is half a corpse. He is only a reminiscence of a man; they have forgotten to bury him, you know! His eyes are artificial, his legs are made of cork, he is all worked by springs, he even talks by machinery.'

'My goodness, what a giddy fellow you are, to listen to you!' exclaims Marya Alexandrova, assuming a stern air. 'Aren't you ashamed, a young man, and a relation, to talk like that about that venerable old man? To say nothing of his boundless kindliness' – and her voice takes a touching note – 'remember that he is a relic, a scion, so to speak, of our aristocracy. My friend, *mon ami!* I understand that you are led into this frivolity by those modern ideas of which you are always talking. But, my goodness! I share those new ideas myself. I realise that what is at the root of your views is generous and creditable. I realise that there is, indeed, something lofty in those new ideas; but all that does not prevent my seeing the direct, so to speak, practical side of things. I have seen something of the world, I have seen more than you have, and, last of all, I am a mother, and you are still young. He is an old man, and so in our eyes he is absurd! What is more, last time you said that you would certainly emancipate your serfs, and that you must do something for the public weal, and all that comes from poring so much over your Shakespeare[125] or somebody! Believe me, Pavel Alexandrovitch, your Shakespeare has had his day, and if he were to rise again he would not with all his cleverness understand anything about our life. If there is anything chivalrous and sublime in our contemporary society it is to be found only in the highest rank. A prince in a sack is still a prince; a prince in a hovel is as good as a prince in a palace! Here Natalya Dmitryevna's husband has built himself something like a palace – and yet he is Natalya Dmitryevna's husband and no more! And if Natalya Dmitryevna were to stick on fifty crinolines she would still remain the same Natalya Dmitryevna, and would add nothing to herself by it. You, too, represent the highest rank to some extent because you are descended from it. I consider myself not far removed from it, and it's an ill bird that fouls its own nest! But you will find out all this of yourself, *mon cher Paul*,[126] better than I can tell you, and will forget your Shakespeare. I predict it. I am persuaded that you are not in earnest even now, but are talking like that because it is chic. But I have been chattering too long. You stay here, *mon cher Paul*, I will go upstairs and find out about the prince. Perhaps he wants something, and with my stupid servants . . . '

And Marya Alexandrovna goes hurriedly out of the room at the thought of her stupid servants.

'Marya Alexandrovna seems very much pleased that that dressed-up creature, Anna Nikolaevna, has not got hold of the prince. And you know she keeps declaring that she is related to him. She must be bursting with spite now!' remarked Nastasya Petrovna; but observing that she received no answer and glancing at Zina and Pavel Alexandrovitch, she grasped the situation at once and went out of the room as though on some errand. But to reward herself for her discretion she stopped just outside and listened at the door.

Pavel Alexandrovitch turned at once to Zina. He was in great agitation, his voice was quivering.

'Zinaida Afanasyevna, you are not angry with me?' he asked, with a timid and imploring air.

'With you! What for?' said Zina, raising her wonderful eyes and looking at him with a faint flush.

'For coming back so soon, Zinaida Afanasyevna! I could not resist it, I could not wait another fortnight . . . I positively dreamed of you. I flew back to hear my fate . . . But you frown, you are angry! Surely you will not refuse to let me hear something decisive?'

Zinaida certainly did frown.

'I expected you would talk of that,' she answered, dropping her eyes again, in a firm and severe voice, in which there was a note of vexation. 'And as that expectation was very dainful to me, the sooner it is over the better. Again you insist, that is, beg for an answer. Very well, I will repeat it to you again, for my answer is still the same as before; wait! I tell you again – I have not made up my mind yet, and cannot promise to be your wife. That is not exacted by force, Pavel Alexandrovitch. But to comfort you, I will add I do not definitely refuse you. Note, too, in giving you hope now of a favourable decision, I do this entirely out of consideration for your impatience and anxiety. I repeat that I wish to remain perfectly free in my decision, and if I tell you in the end that I do not consent, you must not blame me for having given you hope. And so realise that!'

'And so what does that amount to?' cried Mozglyakov in a plaintive voice. 'Is that hope? Can I extract any hope at all from your words, Zinaida Afanasyevna?'

'Remember all I have told you and extract what you choose. It is for you to decide, but I will add nothing more. I do not refuse you yet, but only tell you, wait. I tell you again I reserve a perfect right to refuse you if I think fit. There is another thing I must tell you, Pavel Alexandrovitch; if you have returned before the time fixed for my answer in order to work upon me in indirect ways, relying on outside support, on the influence of mamma, for instance, you have made a great mistake in your calculations. Then I shall refuse you straight out. Do you hear? And now – that's enough, and please, until the right time, do not utter one word more on this subject.'

All this speech was pronounced dryly, firmly, and without hesitation, as though it had been studied beforehand. Monsieur Paul felt that he had been made a fool of. At that moment Marya Alexandrovna returned. And almost immediately after her Madame Zyablov.

'He will be down directly, I fancy, Zina! Nastasya Petrovna, be quick, make some fresh tea!' Marya Alexandrovna was positively a little excited.

'Anna Nikolaevna has already sent to enquire. Her Anyutka has come flying to the kitchen to ask questions. I bet she's cross now!' Nastasya Petrovna announced, rushing up to the samovar.

'What is that to me!' Marya Alexandrovna said over her shoulder to Madame Zyablov. 'As though I were interested to know what your Anna Nikolaevna is thinking. You may be sure I shan't send anyone to her kitchen. And I wonder, I really wonder why you persist in regarding me as an enemy to poor Anna Nikolaevna, and not you only, but everybody in the town. I appeal to you, Pavel Alexandrovitch! You know us both. Come, what reason have I to be her enemy? Over precedence? But I don't care in the least about precedence. Let her be first, let her. I am ready to be the first to go and congratulate her on being first. And, after all, it's quite unfair. I will take her part – I am bound to take her part! She is maligned. Why do you all attack her? She is young and fond of fine clothes – is that a reason, pray? To my thinking fine clothes are better than something else – like Natalya Dmitryevna, who is fond – of what one really can't talk about. Is it because Anna Nikolaevna is always gadding about and can't stay at home? But my goodness! She has had no education, and of course she finds it tedious to open a book or occupy herself with anything for two minutes together. She flirts and makes eyes out of the window at anyone who passes in the street. But why do people assure her she is so pretty when she has nothing but a white face? She is ridiculous at dances, I admit. But why assure her she dances the polka so splendidly? She wears impossible hats and headdresses; but is it her fault that God has given her no taste, but has made her so easily taken in? Assure her that it looks nice to pin a bit of coloured paper in her hair, and she would stick it in her hair. She is a scandalmonger – but that's the way here: there is no one in the town who does not talk scandal. Sushilov, with his whiskers, is always there, morning, noon, and almost night. But, dear me! No wonder, when her husband plays cards till five in the morning. Besides, there are so many bad examples here! Moreover, it *may be* only scandal. In short, I shall always stand up for her, always. But, good gracious, here is the prince! It is he, it is he! I should know him among a thousand! At last I see you, *mon prince*!' cried Marya Alexandrovna, and she flew to meet the prince as he entered.

4

At the first casual glance you would not have taken the prince for an old man at all, it was only on a closer and more attentive inspection that you discerned that he was a sort of corpse worked by mechanism. All the resources of art were utilised to disguise this mummy as a young man. A marvellous wig, whiskers, moustaches and a little imperial, all of a superb black, covered half his face. His face was whitened and rouged with extraordinary skill, and there was not a trace of wrinkles upon it.

What had become of them? There is no knowing. He was dressed in the height of fashion, as though he had stepped out of a fashion plate. He had on a visiting jacket or something of the sort, upon my word I don't know what exactly, but it was something extremely fashionable and up-to-date, created especially for morning calls. His gloves, his cravat, his waistcoat, his linen, and so on, were all of dazzling freshness and artistic taste. The prince limped a little, but limped so elegantly that it seemed as though it were prescribed by fashion. He had an eyeglass in his eye, the very eye that was itself of glass. The prince was saturated with scent. In talking he drawled certain words in a peculiar way, perhaps from the weakness of old age, perhaps because all his teeth were false, perhaps for the sake of greater dignity. Certain syllables he pronounced with extraordinary sweetness, with a special stress on certain vowels. *Yes* with him was turned into *ye-ess*. In all his manners there was a certain carelessness, acquired in the course of his life as a dandy. But if anything of his old fashionable life was still preserved, it was preserved as it were unconsciously in the form of some vague reminiscence, in the form of some outlived buried past, which, alas! no cosmetics, corsets, perfumers or barbers could bring to life again. And so we shall do well to begin by confessing that if the man had not lost his wits he had long ago lost his memory, and was now constantly muddled, repeating himself, and even babbling at random. One needed a special knack to talk to him. But Marya Alexandrovna could rely upon herself, and at the sight of the prince she flew into unutterable ecstasy.

'But you have not changed, not changed in the least!' she exclaimed, seizing her visitor by both hands and making him sit down in a comfortable armchair. 'Sit down, prince, sit down! It's six years, six whole years since we have met, and not a single letter, not one line all that time! Oh, how badly you have treated me, prince! How angry I have been with you, *mon cher prince*! But – tea, tea! Oh, my goodness, Nastasya Petrovna, tea!'

'Thank you, tha-ank you. I am sor-ry,' the prince lisped (we forgot to say that he lisped a little, but that, too, he did as though it were the fashion). 'I am so-or-ry! And only fancy, last year I qui-ite meant to come here,' he added, looking round the room through his lorgnette. 'But they scared me: you had cho-le-ra here, I was told . . .'

'No, prince, we haven't had cholera here,' said Marya Alexandrovna.

'There was the cattle plague here, uncle!' Mozglyakov put in, anxious to distinguish himself. Mary Alexandrovna looked him up and down with a stern expression.

'To be sure, cattle pla-ague or something of the sort . . . So I stayed at home. But how is your husband, my dear Anna Nikolaevna? Still at his pro-se-cuting duties?'

'N-no, prince,' said Marya Alexandrovna, a little disconcerted; 'my husband is not Prosecutor . . . '

'I'll bet uncle has got mixed up and takes you for Anna Nikolaevna Antipov!' cried the sharp-witted Mozglyakov, but he pulled himself up at once, observing that Marya Alexandrovna seemed to be wincing enough without these explanations.

'Oh, yes, yes, Anna Nikolaevna, and . . . and . . . (I keep forgetting!) Oh, yes, Antipov, An-ti-pov it is,' the prince acquiesced.

'N-no, prince, you are very much mistaken,' said Marya Alexandrovna, with a bitter smile. 'I am not Anna Nikolaevna, and I must say I didn't at all expect that you wouldn't know me. You have surprised me, prince. I am your old friend Marya Alexandrovna Moskalev. Do you remember, prince, Marya Alexandrovna? . . . '

'Marya A-lex-and-rovna, only fancy! And I actually supposed that you were (what's her name) – oh, yes, Anna Vassilyevna . . . *C'est délicieux!* So I have come to the wrong place. And I thought, my dear fellow, that you were taking me to Anna Matveyevna. *C'est charmant!* It often happens like that with me, though . . . I often go to the wrong place! I am satisfied, always satisfied, whatever happens. So you are not Nastasya Vassilyevna? That's interesting . . . '

'Marya Alexandrovna, prince, Marya Alexandrovna! Oh, how badly you have treated me! To forget your best, best friend!'

'Oh, yes, my be-est friend . . . *pardon, pardon!*' the prince lisped, gazing at Zina.

'That is my daughter, Zina. You don't know her, prince; she was away when you were here last, in the year 18—; do you remember?'

'Is that your daughter? *Charmante, charmante!*' muttered the prince, eyeing Zina with avidity through his lorgnette. '*Mais quelle beauté!*[127] he murmured, evidently struck by her.

'Tea, prince,' said Marya Alexandrovna, calling the prince's attention to the page standing before him with the tray in his hands. The prince took the cup and looked attentively at the boy, who had pink and chubby cheeks.

'A-ah, is this your boy?' he said. 'What a pret-ty boy! A-and I am sure he behaves ni-icely . . . '

'But, prince,' Marya Alexandrovna interposed hurriedly, 'I have heard of your terrible adventure! I must confess I was frightened out of my wits . . . Weren't you hurt? Make sure! It is not a thing to neglect.'

'He upset me! He upset me! The coachman upset me!' the prince exclaimed, with extraordinary animation. 'I thought the end of the world was coming or something of the sort, and I must own I was so frightened that – holy saints forgive me! – I didn't know whether I was on my head or my feet! I hadn't expected it, I hadn't expected it! I did not ex-pect it at all. And it's all the fault of my coachman, Fe-o-fil. I rely upon you now entirely, my dear fellow: do what is necessary and investigate the matter thoroughly. I am per-suaded that it was an at-tempt on my life.'

'All right, uncle; all right,' answered Pavel Alexandrovitch. 'I will investigate it thoroughly. Only listen, uncle! Forgive him this once, won't you? What do you say?'

'I won't forgive him on any account. I am persuaded that he was trying to ta-ake my life. He, together with Lavrenty, whom I left at home. Only fancy, he has got hold of some new ideas, you know! There is a sort of scepticism in him . . . in short, he is a communist[128] in the fullest sense of the word! I am positively afraid to meet him.'

'Ah, what you say is so true, prince!' exclaimed Marya Alexandrovna. 'You wouldn't believe what I suffer from these good-for-nothing servants myself! Imagine, I have two new servants, and I must say they are so stupid that I am simply struggling with them from morning till night. You wouldn't believe how stupid they are, prince!'

'Oh, yes; oh, yes. But I must say, I really prefer to have a footman rather stupid,' observed the prince, who like all old men was delighted when people listened to his chatter with obsequious attention; 'it some-how suits a footman, and really is a vir-tue in him if he is simple-hearted and stupid. Only in certain cases, of course. It makes him more im-pos-ing, it gives a solem-nity to his countenance; it gives him a greater air of good breeding, and what I insist on most is a servant's good bre-ed-ing. Here I have my Te-ren-ty. You remember my Te-ren-ty, my dear fellow, don't you? As soon as I looked at him I predicted that he was destined to be a hall-porter! Stupid – phe-nom-enally. He stares like a sheep looking at water. But what imposing dignity! What solemnity! Such a pale-pink double chin! You know, with a white cravat in full get-up, it does produce an effect. I took the greatest fancy to him. Some-times I look at him and feel quite fascinated; he might be writing a dissertation – such a solemn air! In fact he is a regular German philosopher, a Kant,[129] or perhaps more truly, a fat, over-fed turkey-cock. Perfectly *comme il faut*[130] for a manservant.'

Marya Alexandrovna laughed with enthusiasm, and even clapped her hands. Pavel Alexandrovitch seconded her with all his heart; he was extremely entertained by his 'uncle'. Nastasya Petrovna laughed too – even Zina gave a smile.

'But what humour, what gaiety, what wit you have, prince!' exclaimed Marya Alexandrovna. 'What a precious gift for noting the most subtle, the most amusing point! . . . And to vanish from society, to shut yourself up for five whole years! With such a talent! But you might write, prince! You might be another Von Vizin,[131] another Griboyedov, another Gogol! . . . '

'Oh, yes; oh, yes!' said the prince, highly delighted; 'I might, and do you know I used to be remarkably witty in the old days. I actually wrote a vau-de-ville for the stage. There were several ex-qui-site lines in it! It was never acted, though . . . '

'Ah, how charming it would be to read it, and, do you know, Zina, it would be apropos now! They are getting up theatricals here – for a patriotic object, prince – for the benefit of the wounded . . . Your vaudeville would be the thing!'

'Of course! I am ready to write it again, indeed . . . though I have completely forgotten it. But I remember there were two or three puns, such that . . . ' (and the prince kissed his fingertips) 'and altogether when I was abro-ad I made a re-gu-lar fu-rore. I remember Lord Byron.[132] We were on friendly terms. He danced the Cracoviana[133] enchantingly at the Vienna Congress.'[134]

'Lord Byron, uncle! Upon my word, uncle, what do you mean?'

'Oh, yes, Lord Byron. Though perhaps it wasn't Lord Byron, but someone else. Quite so; not Lord Byron, but a Pole, I remember perfectly now. And that Pole was ve-ry ori-gi-nal, he gave himself out for a count, and it afterwards turned out that he was some sort of head cook, but he did dance the Cracoviana most en-chant-ing-ly, and at last he broke his leg. I wrote some verses on that occasion too:

> Our dear little Pole
> To dance was his role.

And what came then, I can't remember.'

> 'When he broke his limb
> No more capers for him.

Oh, that must be how it went, uncle,' exclaimed Mozglyakov, entering more and more into the spirit of the thing.

'I think that is what it was, my dear fellow,' answered the old man, 'or something like it. But perhaps it wasn't it, but anyway, the verses turned out very successfully . . . The fact is I've forgotten some things that have happened. It comes from being so busy.'

'But tell us, prince, what have you been doing all this time in your solitude?' Marya Alexandrovna enquired with interest. 'I have so often thought of you, *mon cher prince*,[135] that I must confess I am burning now with impatience to have a full account of it all.'

'What have I been doing? Well, altogether, you know, I have a great de-al to do. Sometimes – one rests; and sometimes, you know, I go for walks and imagine all sorts of things . . .'

'You must have a very powerful imagination, uncle!'

'Extremely powerful, my dear boy. I sometimes imagine such things that I won-der at myself afterwards. When I was in Kaduev . . . Apropos! I believe you used to be Deputy Governor at Kaduev?'

'I! uncle? Upon my soul, what do you mean?' exclaimed Pavel Alexandrovitch.

'Fancy, my dear fellow, and I have been taking you all the while for the Deputy Governor, and I was wondering to myself how it is that all of a sudden you had got quite a different face . . . He had such a dig-ni-fied face – intelligent, you know. He was an exceptionally intelligent man, and he was always com-pos-ing verses, on all sorts of occasions. He was a bit like the king of diamonds in profile . . .'

'No, prince,' Marya Alexandrovna interposed, 'I vow you will ruin yourself by living like that! To shut yourself up in solitude for five years, to see no one, to hear nothing! But you are a doomed man, prince. Ask anyone among those who are devoted to you, and everyone will tell you that you are a doomed man!'

'Really!' exclaimed the prince.

'I assure you it is so; I am speaking to you as a friend, as a sister. I am speaking to you because you are dear to me, because the memory of the past is sacred to me! What have I to gain by pretending? No, you must reform your life fundamentally, or you will fall sick, you will waste away, you will die . . .'

'Oh, dear me! Am I really going to die so soon?' exclaimed the prince, panic-stricken. 'And do you know, you have guessed right! I am frightfully troubled by haemorrhoids, especially at certain times . . . And when I have attacks of it I generally have the most re-mark-able symptoms (I will tell you all about them) . . . To begin with . . .'

'Uncle, you will tell about that another time,' Pavel Alexandrovitch interposed, 'but now . . . isn't it time for us to start?'

'Oh, yes! Another time if you like. Possibly it is not so very interesting to listen to now I come to think of it . . . At the same time it is a very curious complaint. It has several stages . . . Remind me, my dear boy, I will describe this evening in de-tail one thing that happened . . . '

'But listen, prince, you ought to try a cure abroad,' Marya Alexandrovna intervened again.

'Abroad? Oh, yes; oh, yes! I certainly shall go abroad. I remember when I was abroad in the twenties, it was won-derfully gay. I almost got married to a French *vicomtesse*. I was tremendously in love with her at the time, and wanted to devote my life to her. I did not marry her, though; somebody else did. And such a strange thing happened, I was absent only two hours and the other man won the day, a German baron, he was; he was put into a madhouse for a time afterwards.'

'But, *cher prince*, what I meant was that you must think seriously about your health. There are such doctors abroad . . . and besides, a change of life does so much! You really must abandon your Duhanovo, if only for a time.'

'Ce-er-tain-ly! I have made up my mind to do so long ago, and, do you know, I mean to try hy-drop-athy.'

'Hydropathy?'

'Hydropathy. I have tried hy-drop-athy once already. I was at the waters then. There was a Moscow lady there, I have forgotten her surname, only she was a very poetical lady, about seventy; she had a daughter, too, about fifty, a widow with cataract in her eye. She, too, almost talked in verse. Afterwards she had a very unfortunate mishap: she killed one of her serf girls in a rage and was tried for it. And, do you know, they took it into their heads to make me try the water cure. I must say I had nothing the matter with me; but they kept in-sisting: "Try the cure, try the cure!" Simply from delicacy I began to drink the waters; I thought I really should be better for it; I drank and drank and drank and drank. I drank up a perfect waterfall, and, do you know, hydropathy is really a very good thing and did me a very great deal of good, so that if I had not fallen ill, I assure you I should have been perfectly well . . . '

'That is a very just conclusion, uncle. Tell me, uncle, have you studied logic?'

'Upon my word, what questions you ask,' Marya Alexandrovna observed sternly, much scandalised.

'I did study it, my dear boy, but very long ago. I studied philosophy, too, in Germany. I went through a whole course, but even at the time I couldn't remember it. But . . . I must own . . . you have so frightened me about this illness that I feel quite upset. I'll come back directly though . . . '

'But where are you going, prince?' cried Marya Alexandrovna in amazement.

'I will be back directly, directly . . . I simply want to note down a new idea . . . *Au revoir* . . .'

'What a specimen!' cried Pavel Alexandrovitch, and he went off into a fit of laughter.

Marya Alexandrovna lost patience.

'I don't understand, I don't understand in the least what you are laughing at,' she began with heat. 'To laugh at a venerable old man, at a relation, to take advantage of his angelic kindness and to turn every word he utters into ridicule! I blushed for you, Pavel Alexandrovitch! Tell me, please, what do you find absurd in him? I saw nothing to laugh at in him.'

'When he does not know people, when he sometimes talks nonsense?'

'But that is the effect of the awful life he is leading, of his horrible imprisonment for the last five years under the eye of that fiendish woman. One ought to pity him and not to laugh at him. He did not even know me, you were a witness of that yourself. That was, so to speak, a flagrant example! He absolutely must be saved! I suggested to him to go abroad simply in the hope that he might get rid of that . . . market woman!'

'Do you know what? We ought to find him a wife, Marya Alexandrovna,' cried Pavel Alexandrovitch.

'Again! You are incorrigible, Monsieur Mozglyakov!'

'No, Marya Alexandrovna, no! This time I am speaking seriously! Why shouldn't we marry him? It's an idea. *C'est une idée comme une autre.*[136] What harm could it do him, kindly tell me that? On the contrary, he is in such a position that only such a step could save him! He is still legally able to marry. To begin with, he would be rescued from that trollop (excuse the expression). Secondly and chiefly – imagine that he picks out a girl or, better still, a widow – sweet, kind, sensible, tender and, above all, poor, who will look after him like a daughter and realise that he has been a benefactor to her in giving her the title of his wife. And what could be better for him than a noble and upright creature who would belong to him and would be continually at his side, instead of that . . . female. Of course she ought to be pretty, for even to this day uncle loves a pretty face. Did you notice how he kept looking at Zinaida Afanasyevna?'

'But where will you find such a bride?' asked Nastasya Petrovna, listening attentively.

'Ah, there it is: why, you, for instance, if you were willing! Allow me to ask: aren't you perfectly suitable as a match for the prince? In the first place you are pretty, secondly you are a widow, thirdly you are a lady, fourthly poor (for you really are not very well off), fifthly you are a very sensible woman and consequently will love him, keep him in cotton wool, send that person about her business, take him abroad, will feed him on semolina pudding and sweetmeats, all that up to the time when he leaves this transitory world, which will happen within a year and possibly within two or three months. Then you will be a princess, a wealthy widow, and as a reward for your pluck you can marry a *marquis* or a general! *C'est joli*,[137] isn't it?'

'Why, my gracious! I believe I should fall in love with him, poor dear gentleman, out of mere gratitude if only he made me an offer!' exclaimed Madame Zyablov, and her dark expressive eyes gleamed. 'But that's – all nonsense.'

'Nonsense? If you like, it needn't be nonsense! Ask me nicely and then you may cut off my finger if you are not engaged to him today! Why, there is nothing easier than to persuade or tempt uncle into anything! He always says, "Oh, yes; oh, yes!" You have heard him yourself. We will marry him so that he will hardly notice it. We will deceive him and marry him, perhaps: why, it is for his benefit, mercy upon us! . . . You might dress up in your best to be ready for anything, Nastasya Petrovna.'

Monsieur Mozglyakov's enthusiasm knew no bounds. Sensible though she might be, Madame Zyablov's mouth watered.

'I know I look a perfect slut today without you telling me,' she replied. 'I have grown shockingly careless, I have no ambition. That's how it is I go about such a grub. Why, do I really look like a cook?'

All this time Marya Alexandrovna was sitting with a strange look on her face. I am not mistaken if I say that she heard Pavel Alexandrovitch's strange proposition with a sort of dismay, as though disconcerted by it . . .

At last she recovered herself.

'All this is very nice, no doubt, but it is all nonsense and absurdity, and what is more – quite out of place,' she interrupted Mozglyakov sharply.

'But why, my dear Marya Alexandrovna, why is it nonsense and out of place?'

'For many reasons, and first of all because you are in my house and the prince is my guest, and I allow no one to show a lack of respect for my house. I look upon your words as nothing but a jest, Pavel Alexandrovitch. But, thank goodness, here is the prince!'

'Here I am,' cried the prince, walking into the room. 'It's wonderful, *cher ami*,[138] how many different ideas I've had today. And at other times, perhaps you wouldn't believe it, I seem to have none at all. Nothing all day.'

'That's probably from your tumble today, uncle. It has upset your nerves, and that is how it is . . . '

'I put it down to that myself, my dear fellow, and think that the accident has been really ben-i-fi-cial. So that I have made up my mind to forgive my Feo-fil. Do you know what, I believe he was not trying to take my life after all, what do you think? Besides, he has been punished only lately by having his beard shaved off.'

'His beard shaved off, uncle! Why, he has a beard as big as the German Empire.'

'Oh, yes, as big as the German Empire. You are generally very correct in your con-clu-sions, my dear boy. But it is a false one. And only fancy how it happened; I was sent a price list. The superbest beards for coachmen and gentlemen newly imported from abroad, also whiskers, imperials, moustaches and so on, and all of the best qual-i-ty and at the most moderate prices. I thought I would send for a beard just to see what it was like. So I wrote for a coachman's beard, it really was a beard worth seeing! But it turned out that Feofil had a beard of his own almost twice as big. Of course we were puzzled what to do: to shave his off, or to send back the one they had sent us and let him wear his natural one? I thought and thought about it, and came to the conclusion that it was better for him to have the artificial one.'

'Probably because art is better than nature, uncle!'

'That was just it. And what distress it caused him when his beard was shaved off! As though he had parted with his whole career together with his beard. But isn't it time for us to start, my dear boy?'

'I am ready, uncle.'

'But I hope, prince, that you are only going to the Governor's,' Marya Alexandrovna exclaimed in excitement. 'You are mine now, prince, and belong to my family for the whole day. I am not going to tell you anything about the society here, of course. Perhaps you want to go to Anna Nikolaevna's, and I have not the right to disillusion you; besides, I am fully persuaded that time will tell its own story. But remember that I am your hostess, sister, nurse for the whole of today, and I must own that I tremble for you, prince! You don't know these people, you don't know them.'

'Rely on me, Marya Alexandrovna. Everything shall be as I promised you,' said Mozglyakov.

'Oh, you feather-head! Rely on you! I expect you to dinner, prince. We dine early. And how I regret that on this occasion my husband is in the country. How delighted he would have been to see you. He has such a respect for you, he has such a genuine affection for you.'

'Your husband? So you have a husband, too?' the prince queried.

'Oh, my goodness, how forgetful you are, prince! Why, you have utterly, utterly forgotten all the past! My husband, Afanasy Matveyitch, surely you have not forgotten him? He is in the country now, but you saw him a thousand times in the old days. Do you remember, prince, Afanasy Matveyitch?'

'Afanasy Matveyitch! In the country, only fancy! *Mais c'est délicieux!* So you have a husband too? What a strange thing, though? That's exactly like some vaudeville: "The husband's on the stair, but the wife has gone to . . . " Excuse me, I have forgotten! Only the wife had gone off somewhere also, to Tula or to Yaroslav, anyway it's very funny.'

' "The husband is on the stair, but the wife has gone to Tver," uncle,' Mozglyakov prompted him.

'Oh, yes! Oh, yes! Thank you, my dear boy, Tver it was. *Charmant, charmant.* So that it rhymes also. You always drop into rhyme, my dear boy. I didn't remember whether it was to Yaroslav or to Kostroma,[139] but only that his wife had gone off somewhere too. *Charmant, charmant!* I have a little forgotten what I was beginning to speak about, though . . . Ah, yes, so we are starting, my dear fellow. *Au revoir, Madame. Adieu, ma charmante demoiselle,*[140] added the prince, turning to Zina and kissing his fingertips.

'To dinner, to dinner, prince! Don't forget to make haste back,' Marya Alexandrovna called after him.

5

'You might just glance into the kitchen, Nastasya Petrovna,' she said, after seeing the prince out. 'I have a presentiment that that monster Nikita will be sure to spoil the dinner! I am convinced that he is drunk by now . . . '

Nastasya Petrovna obeyed. As she went out she looked suspiciously at Marya Alexandrovna and observed in her signs of exceptional agitation. Instead of going to look after the monster Nikita, Nastasya Petrovna went into the bigger drawing-room, from there through the corridor to her own room, from there into a little dark apartment, something like a lumber-room, where there were trunks standing, garments of some sort hanging and the dirty linen of the whole family stored in bags. She went on tiptoe to the closed door, held her breath, stooped down, looked through the keyhole and listened. This door was one of the three doors of the very room in which Marya Alexandrovna and Zina had remained, and was always kept shut and locked.

Marya Alexandrovna considered Nastasya Petrovna a sly but exceedingly frivolous woman. No doubt the idea did at times occur to her that Nastasya Petrovna had no scruples and was given to eavesdropping. But at the present moment Marya Alexandrovna was so much engrossed and excited that she quite forgot to take certain precautions. She sat down in an easy chair and looked significantly at Zina. Zina was conscious of that gaze fixed upon her, and a feeling of uneasy depression began to weigh upon her heart.

'Zina!'

Zina slowly turned her pale face towards her, and lifted her dreamy black eyes.

'Zina, I intend to speak to you about an extremely important matter.'

Zina turned completely round to her mother, folded her hands, and stood waiting. There was a look in her face of vexation and sarcasm, which she tried, however, to conceal.

'I want to ask you, Zina, what you thought today of *that* Mozglyakov?'

'You have known what I think of him for ever so long,' answered Zina reluctantly.

'Yes, *mon enfant*; but it seems to me that he is becoming too persistent with his . . . attentions.'

'He says he is in love with me, and his persistency is excusable.'

'Strange; you used not to be so . . . ready to excuse him. On the contrary, you invariably attacked him whenever I spoke of him.'

'It is strange, too, that you always defended him and were so set on my marrying him, and now you attack him.'

'That is almost so. I don't deny it, Zina; I did desire to see you married to Mozglyakov. It was painful for me to see your continual depression, your unhappiness, which I am quite capable of understanding (whatever you may think of me) and which poisons my sleep at night. I felt sure at last that nothing but a complete change of life could save you! And that change must be – marriage. We are not well off and cannot, for instance, go abroad. The asses here are surprised that you are three-and-twenty and not yet married, and concoct a regular legend to explain it. But is it likely I should make a match for you with a local councillor, or with Ivan Ivanitch, our attorney here? Is there a husband here for you? Mozglyakov is empty-headed, of course, but he is the best of the lot. He is of a decent family, he has connections, he has a hundred and fifty serfs; that is better anyway than living by tricks and bribes, and God knows what shifts, that's why I turned my eyes upon him. But I swear I never had a real liking for him. I am persuaded that it was the hand of the Almighty that forewarned me. And if God were to send you even now something better – oh! what a good thing it will be that you have not pledged your word! You have not said anything positive to him today, have you, Zina?'

'Why all this pretence, mamma, when the whole thing could be said in two words?' Zina brought out irritably.

'Pretence, Zina, pretence! And you can use a word like that to your mother? But what am I saying? For a long while past you have put no faith in your mother! For a long while past you have looked on me as your enemy and not your mother.'

'Oh, do leave off, mamma! Surely you and I need not dispute about words! Don't we understand each other? I should have thought it was high time we did.'

'You wound me, my child! You do not believe that I am ready to do absolutely anything, anything, anything to secure your future.'

Zina looked at her mother sarcastically and with annoyance.

'You don't want to marry me to that prince to *secure* my future, do you?' she asked, with a queer smile.

'I have not said a word of that, but since you have mentioned it, I will say that if it were your lot to marry the prince, it would be a great happiness for you and not at all senseless.'

'And I consider that's simply nonsense!' cried Zina passionately. 'Nonsense, nonsense! I also think, mamma, that you have too much romantic inspiration, you are a poetess, in the fullest sense of the word; that's what they call you here. You are continually having projects. Their impossibility and absurdity do not deter you. I had a foreboding while the prince was sitting here that you had this in your mind. When Mozglyakov began playing the fool and declaring that we ought to find a wife for the old man, I read all you were thinking in your face. I am ready to bet that you are thinking of that, and that is what you are leading up to with me. But as your incessant scheming on my behalf is beginning to bore me to death, is beginning to torture me, I beg you not to say one word about it to me; do you hear, mamma? not one word, and I should be glad if you would remember that!' She was breathless with anger.

'You are a child, Zina, a sick, irritable child,' answered Marya Alexandrovna in a tearful voice full of emotion. 'You speak disrespectfully to me

and hurt my feelings. No mother would put up with what I endure
from you every day! But you are nervous, you are ill, you are suffering,
and I am a mother and, above all, a Christian. I must bear it and forgive.
But one word, Zina: if I really were dreaming of that union – why do
you look upon it as nonsense? To my mind Mozglyakov never spoke
more sensibly than just now when he pointed out that it was essential
for the prince to marry – of course, not that slut Nastasya. He was
talking wildly about that.'

'Listen, mamma! Tell me straight out: are you questioning me like
this out of curiosity, or with a motive?'

'I ask you only, why does it seem to you such nonsense?'

'Oh, how annoying! What a life!' exclaimed Zina, stamping with
impatience. 'I'll tell you why, if you still don't know: to say nothing of
all the other absurdities – to take advantage of a wretched old man's
having fallen into dotage, to deceive him, to marry him, a wreck, in
order to get hold of his money and then every day, every hour, to long
for his death, to my mind is not simply nonsense, but so base, so base,
that I can't congratulate you on such ideas, mamma!'

The silence lasted for a minute.

'Zina, do you remember what happened two years ago?' Marya
Alexandrova asked suddenly.

Zina started.

'Mamma,' she said in a severe voice, 'you promised me solemnly
never to speak of that again.'

'And now I solemnly beg you, my child, to allow me only once to
break that promise which I have never broken till now, Zina! The time
has come for a full explanation between us. These two years of silence
have been awful! It can't go on like this! . . . I am ready to beg you on
my knees to let me speak. Listen, Zina, your own mother begs you on
her knees! At the same time I give you my solemn promise – the promise
of an unhappy mother who adores her daughter – that I will never
under any circumstances whatever, even if it were a question of my life,
I will never speak of it again. This shall be the last time, but now – it is
essential!'

Marya Alexandrovna was calculating on her words having their full
effect.

'Speak,' said Zina, turning perceptibly pale.

'Thank you, Zina. Two years ago poor dear Mitya, your little brother,
had a tutor . . .'

'But why do you begin in this solemn way, mamma! Why all this fine
speaking, all these details, which are utterly unnecessary, which are

painful, which are only too well known to both of us?' Zina cut her short with a kind of angry repulsion.

'Because, my child, I, your mother, am compelled to justify myself before you! Because I want to put it all before you from an absolutely different point of view, and not from the mistaken point of view from which you are in the habit of looking at it. In fact, that you might understand better the conclusion I am meaning to draw from all this. Do not imagine, my child, that I want to play with your feelings. No, Zina, you will find in me a true mother, and perhaps shedding tears at my feet, the feet of the *base woman* you have just called me, you will yourself implore the reconciliation you have so long, so haughtily rejected; that is why I wish to speak out the whole truth, Zina, the whole from the very beginning; otherwise I will be silent!'

'Speak,' Zina repeated, cursing her mother's love of fine speeches from the bottom of her heart.

'I will continue, Zina: how this district schoolteacher, hardly more than a boy, made an impression upon you, I could never understand. I put too much confidence in your good sense, in your honourable pride, and above all, in his utter insignificance (for one must tell the whole truth), to suspect there could be anything between you. And all of a sudden you come to me and announce that you intend to marry him! Zina! It was a dagger in my heart! I uttered a shriek and fell into a swoon. But . . . you remember all that? I need not say, I thought it needful to use all my authority, which you call tyranny. Only think, a boy, the son of a sacristan hired for twelve roubles a month, a scribbler of wretched doggerel, published out of kindness in the *Library of Good Reading*,[141] a fellow who could talk of nothing but that cursed Shakespeare – that boy, your husband, the husband of Zinaida Moskalev! Why, it is worthy of Florian and his shepherdesses![142] Forgive me, Zina, but the mere remembrance moves me to frenzy! I refused him, but no authority could keep you in check. Your father could do nothing but blink his eyes, and did not even understand when I tried to explain to him. You maintained your relations with that boy, even had interviews with him, and most awful of all, you even ventured to correspond with him. Rumours were spreading all over the town. Our neighbours began stabbing me with hints: they were already in high glee, they were already blowing their trumpets, and suddenly all my predictions were fulfilled in the most flagrant way. You quarrelled over something; he showed himself utterly unworthy of you . . . the wretched boy (I cannot call him a man), and threatened to show your letters about the town. At that threat, full of indignation, you were wild with anger and gave him a slap in the face. Yes, Zina, that circumstance, too, is known to me! I know all about it, all. That very day the miserable boy showed one of your letters to that scoundrel Zaushin, and within an hour that letter was already in the hands of Natalya Dmitryevna, my deadly enemy. The same evening that madman, overcome with remorse, made an absurd attempt to poison himself. In a word, there was a most appalling scandal! That slut Nastasya ran to me in alarm with the terrible intelligence: the letter had been for a full hour in Natalya Dmitryevna's hands; within two hours the whole town would know of your disgrace! I controlled myself, I did not swoon – but with what blows you struck at my heart, Zina! That shameless hussy, that monster, Nastasya, demanded two hundred roubles, and for that sum swore to get that letter back. I myself ran through the snow in my thin slippers to the Jew Burnstein and pawned my jewel-case – a keepsake from my sainted mother! Within two hours the letter was in my hands: Nastasya had stolen it. She broke open a box and your reputation was saved – there was nothing to prove the story! But in what anxiety you made me pass that awful day! The next day I noticed, for the first time in my life, some grey hairs in my head, Zina! You have formed your own judgement now of that boy's conduct. You will agree now yourself, and perhaps with a bitter smile, that it would have been the acme of folly to entrust your future to his keeping. But from that time you have been fretting, you have been tormenting yourself, my child; you cannot forget him, or rather not him, he was always unworthy of you, but the phantom of your past happiness. That unhappy youth is lying on his deathbed now, I am told he is in consumption, and you – angel of goodness! – you will not marry during his lifetime that you may not lacerate his feelings; for to this day he is tortured by jealousy, though I am persuaded that he never loved you with true exalted love! I know that when he heard of Mozglyakov's attentions, he spied on you, sent to find out, made enquiries. You are sparing him, my child; I have guessed your secret and God knows with what bitter tears I have wetted my pillow!'

'Oh, do drop all that, mamma!' Zina interrupted in unspeakable misery. 'I think you might have left your pillow out,' she added bitingly. 'You can't speak without all this declamation and flourish!'

'You do not believe me, Zina! Do not look upon me with antagonism, my child! My eyes have not been dry for these two years, but I hid my tears from you, and I swear that I, too, have greatly changed during that time! I have long understood your feelings and, I regret to say, that it is only now that I have realised all the depth of your grief. Can you blame me, my dear, for looking on this attachment as a romantic folly inspired by that cursed Shakespeare who will poke his nose where he is not wanted. What mother will blame me for my terror, for the steps I took, for the sternness of my decision? But now, now after seeing your suffering for these two years, I understand and appreciate your feelings. Believe me that I understand you, perhaps far better than you understand yourself. I am persuaded you love not him, that unnatural boy, but your golden dreams, your lost happiness, your exalted ideals. I, too, have loved, and perhaps more ardently than you. I have suffered myself; I, too, have had my exalted ideals. And so who can blame me now; and above all, can you blame me for regarding a match with the prince as the thing best fitted to save you, most essential for you in your present position?'

Zina had been listening with wonder to this long tirade, knowing perfectly well that her mother would not take up this tone without some object. But the unexpected conclusion in her mother's last words utterly amazed her.

'Can you really propose to marry me to that prince?' she cried, looking at her mother in astonishment and almost alarm. 'Then it is not a mere dream, not a project, but your firm intention. So I guessed right? And . . . and . . . and in what way will such a marriage save me and be essential in my position? And . . . and . . . and in what way is all this worked in with what you have been saying just now – with all this story? . . . I really don't understand you, mamma!'

'And I wonder how anyone can fail to understand, *mon ange*!'[143] exclaimed Marya Alexandrovna, growing excited in her turn. 'In the first place the mere fact that you will move into a different society, a different world! You will leave for ever this detestable little town, full of terrible memories for you; where you have no friend, no welcome; where you have been slandered; where all these magpies hate you for your beauty. You may even go abroad this spring to Italy, to Switzerland, to Spain; to Spain, Zina, to Spain, where there is the Alhambra[144] and the Guadalquivir,[145] not this wretched, miserable river here with its unseemly name . . . '

'But excuse me, mamma, you are talking as if I were already married, or at least as though the prince had made me an offer.'

'Don't trouble about that, my angel; I know what I am talking about. But – allow me to proceed. I have already mentioned the *first* point, now for the *second*: I understand, my child, with what repugnance you would give your hand to that Mozglyakov.'

'I know without your telling me that I never shall be his wife!' Zina answered with heat, and her eyes flashed.

'And if you knew how well I understand your repugnance, my dear! It is an awful thing to swear before the altar of God to love one for whom you can feel no love! It is awful to belong to one whom you cannot even respect! And he will have your love; it is for that he will marry you. I can tell that by the look in his eyes when you turn away from him. How awful to keep up the pretence! I have endured that trial for twenty-five years. Your father has wrecked my life. He has, so to speak, sapped my youth, and how often you have seen my tears!'

'Papa is in the country, please let him alone,' answered Zina.

'I know you always take his part. Ah, Zina! My heart ached, when from motives of prudence I desired your marriage with Mozglyakov. But there would be no need to dissemble with the prince. Of course I need not say that you cannot care for him . . . with love, and indeed he is not capable of requiring such love . . . '

'My goodness, what nonsense! But I assure you that you are mistaken from the very beginning upon the most essential point. Let me tell you that I don't want to sacrifice myself for no reason that I know of. Let me tell you that I don't want to be married to anybody, and that I shall remain single. For the last two years you have been nagging at me for not getting married. Well, you will have to make up your mind to accept it. I don't want to, and that is all! And so it shall be.'

'But, Zinotchka darling, for goodness' sake don't fly into a passion before you have heard what I have to say! What a hot-headed child you are, to be sure. Allow me to look at it from my point of view, and you will agree with me at once. The prince will live for a year or two at the utmost, and to my mind it is better to be a young widow than an old maid, to say nothing of your being at his death a princess, free, wealthy and independent! My dear, you may look with contempt on these calculations – calculations on his death! But I am a mother, and what mother would condemn me for my far-sightedness? Finally, if like an angel of goodness you still feel compassion for that boy, such compassion that you are unwilling to be married so long as he lives (as I conjecture is the case), reflect that you will give him fresh courage and relieve his mind by marrying the prince! If he has a spark of common sense, he will understand, of course, that jealousy of the prince would be misplaced, absurd; he will understand that you have married from motives of prudence, from necessity. He will understand, indeed, that is – I merely mean to say, you can marry anyone you like when the prince is dead.'

'To put it plainly, it comes to this: marry the prince, plunder him, reckoning on his death to marry a lover afterwards. You balance your accounts cleverly. You try to tempt me, offering me . . . I understand you, mamma, I quite understand you! You can never resist a display of noble sentiments, even in the nastiest action. You had better have said simply and straightforwardly: "Zina, it is base, but it is profitable, and so consent to do it!" that would be more candid, anyway.'

'But why, my child, persist in looking at it from that point of view – from the point of view of deception, artfulness, self-interest? You regard my calculation as base, deceitful. But by all that is holy, what deceit is there about it, where is the baseness? Look at yourself in the glass; you are so lovely that one might give up a kingdom for your sake! And you, you a beauty, sacrifice your best years to an old man! Like a lovely star you will shed light on his declining hours; you, like the green ivy, will twine about his age; you, and not that nettle, that abominable woman, who has cast a spell on him, and from greed is sapping his existence. Do you think that his money, his princely rank, is more precious than you? Where is the deceit, where is the baseness in that? You don't know what you are saying, Zina!'

'They evidently are more precious, since I have to marry a decrepit wreck. Deceit is always deceit, mamma, whatever the object may be.'

'On the contrary, my dear, on the contrary! You may look at it from a lofty, indeed from a Christian point of view, my child! You said yourself on one occasion, in a moment of frenzy, that you would like to be a sister of mercy. Your heart had suffered, had grown hard. You said (I know this) that it could not love now. If you do not believe in love, turn your feelings to another loftier subject, turn it genuinely, like a child with all faith and reverence – and God will bless you. This old man has suffered too, he is unhappy, he is persecuted; I have known him for some years and have always cherished for him an incomprehensible sympathy, akin to love, as though I had a presentiment. Be his friend, be his daughter, be perhaps even his plaything – if one is to speak plainly. But warm his heart, and you will be doing an act godly and virtuous! He is ridiculous – don't think of that. He is half a man – have compassion on him; you are a Christian! Master yourself; such deeds are done by self-mastery. To our minds it is hard to bandage wounds in a hospital; it is revolting to breathe the infected air of the sickroom. But there are angels of mercy who do that and thank God for their vocation. Here is balm for your wounded heart, occupation, self-sacrifice – and you will heal your own wounds. Where is the egotism in it, where is the baseness? But you don't believe me. You imagine, perhaps, that I am dissimulating when I talk of duty, of self-sacrifice. You can't conceive that I, a frivolous, worldly woman, can have a heart, feelings, principles. Well, refuse to believe, insult your mother, but admit that what she says is reasonable and helpful. Imagine that it is not I who am speaking but someone else; shut your eyes, turn round to the corner, imagine that some unseen voice is speaking to you . . . What troubles you most is that it is all for the sake of money, as though it were some sale or purchase. Well, renounce the money if money is so hateful to you. Keep only what is barely necessary for yourself, and give away the rest to the poor. Help him, for instance, that luckless boy lying now on his deathbed.'

'He will take no help,' Zina said softly, as though to herself.

'He will not take it, but his mother will take it,' Marya Alexandrovna answered triumphantly. 'She will take it without his knowing. You sold your earrings, your aunt's present, and helped her six months ago; I know that. I know the old woman takes in washing to keep her unhappy son.'

'He will soon have no need of help.'

'I know what you are hinting at, too,' Marya Alexandrovna caught her up; and an inspiration, a genuine inspiration, dawned upon her. 'I know what you are alluding to. They say he is in consumption and will not live long. But who says that? The other day I purposely questioned Kalist Stanislavitch; I was anxious about him, because I have a heart, Zina. Kalist Stanislavitch answered me that the illness was, of course, serious, but that he was convinced that, so far, the poor boy was not in consumption, but that it was only a rather severe affection of the chest. Question him yourself. He told me, as a fact, that under different circumstances, especially with a change of climate and surroundings, the patient might recover. He told me that in Spain – and I had heard it before and even read it – that in Spain there is some extraordinary island, I believe it is called Malaga – like some wine, in fact[146] – where not only persons with weak lungs, but even consumptives recover simply from the climate, and that people go there on purpose to be treated, people of rank and consequence, of course; or commercial people too, if only they are rich. But the magical Alhambra, the myrtles, the lemons, the Spaniards on their mules! That alone would make an extraordinary impression on a poetical nature. You think he will not take your help, your money for the journey? Well, deceive him, then, if you are sorry for him! Deception is pardonable when it is to save a man's life. Give him hope, even promise him your love; tell him you will marry him when you are left a widow. Anything in the world can be said in an honourable way. Your mother will not teach you anything dishonourable, Zina; you will do this to save his life, so anything is permissible! You will restore him to life through hope; he will begin to take trouble over his health, to try and cure himself, to obey the doctors. He will try to regain his health for the sake of happiness. If he recovers, even though you do not marry him, anyway he will be well again, and anyway you will have saved him, you will have brought him back to life. And indeed one may even look at him with sympathy; perhaps fate has taught him a lesson and changed him for the better, and if only he is worthy of you – marry him, if you like, when you are left a widow. You will be wealthy and independent. If you restore him to health, you can give him a position in the world – a career. Your marriage will be more excusable then than now, when it is out of the question. What would be in store for you both if you were to venture on such madness now? Universal contempt, beggary, the task of pulling the nasty urchins' ears, for that is part of his duties, the reading of Shakespeare together, staying on for ever in Mordasov; and lastly, his speedy and inevitable death. While if you restore him to health you will be restoring him for a useful, virtuous life; if you forgive him, you will make him adore you. He is fretting over his abominable action, and opening a new life to him, forgiving him, you will give him hope and reconcile him to himself. He may enter the service, may rise to a good grade; and indeed, even if he does not recover, he will die happy, at peace with himself, in your arms – for you will be able to be with him at that moment – trusting in your love, forgiven by you, in the shade of the myrtles and lemons, under the azure exotic sky! Oh, Zina! all that is in your power! There is every advantage for you in it – and all that through marriage with the prince.'

Marya Alexandrovna had finished. Rather a prolonged silence followed. Zina's agitation was inexpressible.

We will not undertake to describe Zina's feelings; we cannot even conjecture them. But it seemed that Marya Alexandrovna had found the way to her heart. Not knowing what was the present state of her daughter's feelings, she had gone over every mood in which she might possibly be, and guessed that she had at last hit on the true path. She coarsely touched upon the sorest spot in Zina's heart. And, from old habit, she could not refrain from the exhibition of noble sentiments, which of course did not hoodwink Zina. 'What does it matter if she does not believe me,' thought Marya Alexandrovna. 'If only I have made her think things over! If only I have clearly hinted at what I could not say outright!' So she argued, and she attained her object. The effect was produced. Zina listened greedily. Her cheeks glowed, her bosom heaved.

'Listen, mamma,' she said resolutely at last, though the sudden pallor of her face betrayed what that resolution cost her. 'Listen, mamma.'

But at that moment a sudden noise in the entrance hall, and a harsh, shrill voice asking for Marya Alexandrovna, made Zina pause. Marya Alexandrovna jumped from her seat.

'Oh, my goodness!' she cried, 'the devil has sent that magpie, the colonel's wife; why, I all but turned her out of the house a fortnight ago!' she added, almost in despair. 'But . . . but it is impossible not to receive her now! Impossible! She most likely has news, or she would not have dared to come. It is important, Zina! I must know . . . We must neglect nothing now! – Oh, how grateful I am for your visit!' she cried, hastening to meet her guest. 'How did you come to think of me, my precious Sofya Petrovna? What an enchanting surprise.'

Zina ran out of the room.

6

The colonel's wife, Sofya Petrovna Karpuhin, had only a moral resembl- ance to a magpie. Physically she was more like a sparrow. She was a little lady, about fifty, with sharp little eyes, with freckles and yellow patches all over her face. On her little dried-up body, perched on strong, thin, sparrow-like little legs, was a dark silk dress which was always rustling, for the colonel's lady could not keep still for two seconds. She was a spiteful and malignant gossip. She was mad on the fact of being a colonel's wife. She very often fought with her husband, the retired colonel, and used to scratch his face. Moreover, she used to drink four glasses of vodka in the morning, and as many in the evening, and had an insane hatred for Anna Nikolaevna Antipov, who had turned her out of her house the week before, as well as for Natalya Dmitryevna Paskudin, who had assisted in the operation.

'I have only looked in for a minute, *mon ange*,' she twittered. 'I really ought not to have sat down. I have only come to tell you what mar- vellous things are going on among us. The whole town has gone off its head about that prince! Our wily ones – *vous comprenez*[147] – are chasing him, hunting him down, snatching him from one another, regaling him with champagne – you wouldn't believe it! You wouldn't believe it! How could you bring yourself to let him go? Do you know that he is at Natalya Dmitryevna's now?'

'At Natalya Dmitryevna's!' cried Marya Alexandrovna, jumping up from her seat. 'Why, he was only going to see the Governor, and afterwards, perhaps, to Anna Nikolaevna's, and was not going to stay long even there!'

'Not for long, I dare say; catch him now if you can! He did not find the Governor at home, then he went to Anna Nikolaevna's, promised to dine with her, and Natalya Dmitryevna, who is always with her nowadays, has carried him off to her house for lunch. There's your prince!'

'And what . . . about Mozglyakov? Why, he promised . . . '

'Yes, your Mozglyakov, indeed! You think a lot of him, don't you? . . . Why, he has gone with him. You see if they don't get up a game of cards there, and he loses all his money as he did last year! Yes, and they'll make the prince take a hand too, and strip him like bark. And the things she is spreading about, that Natalya! She is crying aloud that you are trying to ensnare the prince, you know, with certain objects – *vous comprenez*? She is talking to him about it. Of course he doesn't understand; he sits like a wet cat and says, "Oh, yes! oh, yes!" at every word. And she, she brought out her Sonka – only fancy! fifteen, and she still keeps her in short skirts, only down to the knee, so you can imagine . . . They sent for that little orphan Mashka; she is in short skirts too, only above the knee – I looked through my lorgnette . . . they put some sort of red caps with feathers on their heads – I really don't know what it was meant for! And they made the two little magpies dance the Cossack dance[148] to the piano before the prince! Well, you know his weakness; he was melting with ecstasy. "Contours! contours!" He looked at them through his lorgnette, and they did distinguish themselves, the magpies! They got red in the face, they twirled their legs, and it was such an exhibition that I was shocked, and that was all about it. Tfoo! Call that a dance! I've danced myself, the shawl dance, at the breaking-up party at Madame Jarnis's select boarding school – and it really was a distinguished performance. I was applauded by senators! The daughters of princes and counts were educated there! But this was simply a *cancan*![149] I grew hot with shame, I grew hot, hot! I simply could not sit it out! . . . '

'But . . . surely you have not been at Natalya Dmitryevna's yourself? Why, you . . . '

'Why, yes, she did insult me last week. I say that straight out to everyone. *Mais, ma chère*, I wanted to have a peep at that prince, if it was only through a crack in the door. I did go. For where else could I have seen him? I shouldn't have been to see her, if it hadn't been for that horrid old prince! Only fancy, chocolate was handed round to everyone, but not offered to me, and they did not say a word to me all the time. She did that on purpose, you know. The tub of a woman, I'll pay her out! But goodbye, *mon ange*. I am in a hurry now, a great hurry . . . I must find Akulina Panfilovna, and tell her . . . only you may as well say

goodbye to the prince now, he won't come back to you. You know he
has no memory, so Anna Nikolaevna will certainly carry him off! They
are all afraid that you ... do you understand? on Zina's account.'

'*Quelle horreur!*'[150]

'I assure you the whole town is talking of it! Anna Nikolaevna is set on
keeping him to dinner, and then to stay altogether. She is doing that to
spite you, *mon ange*. I peeped into the servants' quarters; such a bustle
going on there: they are preparing the dinner, such a clatter of knives ...
They have sent for champagne. Make haste, make haste, and catch him
on the road when he is on his way to her. Why, he promised to dine
with you first! He is your visitor, and not hers! To think of her having
the laugh of you, the sly jade, the marplot, the filthy slut! Why, she is
not worth the sole of my shoe, though she is the Prosecutor's wife! I am
a colonel's wife myself! I was brought up at Madame Jarnis's select
establishment ... Tfoo! *Mais adieu, mon ange!*[151] I have my own sledge
waiting, or I would have gone with you ... '

The walking newspaper vanished. Marya Alexandrovna was all of a
tremble with excitement, but her visitor's advice was extremely clear
and practical. There was no reason to delay, and indeed no time to be
lost. But the chief difficulty still remained. Marya Alexandrovna flew to
Zina's room.

Zina, pale and troubled, was walking up and down the room, with her
arms crossed and her head bowed. There were tears in her eyes, but
there was a gleam of determination in the look she cast upon her
mother. She made haste to hide her tears, and a sarcastic smile came on
to her lips.

'Mamma,' she said, before her mother could speak, 'you wasted a
great deal of your eloquence on me just now, far too much. But you did
not blind me – I am not a child. To persuade myself that I am sacrificing
myself like a sister of mercy though I have no vocation for such a life,
to justify the base deeds one commits from simple egoism with the
pretence of honourable motives – all that is casuistry which cannot
deceive me. Do you hear? That could not deceive me, and I want you
to know that!'

'But, *mon ange*,' cried Marya Alexandrovna, crestfallen.

'Do not speak, mamma. Have the patience to hear me to the end.
Though I fully recognise that it is jesuitical casuistry, though I fully
realise the utter baseness of such a proceeding, I fully accept your
proposition – do you hear? – *fully*; and I tell you I am ready to marry the
prince, and even ready to second all your efforts to induce him to marry
me. With what object I do so there is no need for you to know. It is

enough that I have made up my mind. I have made up my mind to everything: I will put on his boots for him; I will be his servant; I will dance to please him, to make up for my baseness to him; I will do anything in the world that he may not regret having married me! But in return for my decision, I insist that you tell me openly by what means you are going to arrange it all. Since you have begun speaking so insistently about it, you could not – I know you – have done so without having some definite plan in your head. Be open for once in your life at least. Openness is the indispensable condition! I cannot decide without knowing exactly how you intend to do it all.'

Marya Alexandrovna was so much taken aback by Zina's unexpected conclusion that for some time she stood facing her, dumb and motionless with amazement, and stared at her open-eyed. She had prepared herself to combat the obstinate romanticism of her daughter, of whose severe rectitude she stood in constant dread, and now she suddenly heard that her daughter agreed with her, and was ready to do anything, even in opposition to her principles! The whole affair was, in consequence, immensely simplified; and there was a gleam of joy in her eyes.

'Zinotchka!' she cried enthusiastically. 'Zinotchka, you are my own flesh and blood!'

She could say no more, but flew to embrace her daughter.

'Oh, my goodness! I did not ask for your endearments, mamma,' cried Zina, with impatient repulsion. 'I don't want your raptures! I ask you for an answer to my question, and nothing more.'

'But, Zina, I love you! I adore you, and you repulse me . . . You know I am doing my best for your happiness . . . '

And unfeigned tears glistened in her eyes. Marya Alexandrovna really did love Zina in *her own way*, and on this occasion, in her success and her excitement, she was brimming over with sentimental emotion; in spite of a certain narrowness in her outlook, Zina understood that her mother loved her and – that love was burdensome to her. She would have been more at ease, indeed, if her mother had hated her . . . .

'Well, don't be angry, mamma; I am so agitated,' she said, to soothe her.

'I am not angry, I am not angry, my angel,' Marya Alexandrovna twittered, reviving instantly. 'Of course I know that you are agitated. Well, my dear, you insist on openness . . . certainly I will be open, entirely open, I assure you! If only you would trust me! And to begin with, I must tell you that I have not yet a definite plan – that is, in full detail, Zinotchka; and indeed I could not have; a clever girl like you will see why. I foresee some obstacles, in fact . . . That magpie just now babbled all sorts of nonsense . . . (oh, my goodness, I must make haste). You see, I am entirely open! But I swear I will attain my object,' she added, with enthusiasm. 'My confidence is not romancing, as you called it just now, my angel; it rests on a basis of reality. It is founded on the absolute feeble-mindedness of the prince, that is the canvas on which I can embroider what I like. The great thing is that they should not prevent me! As though those fools could outwit me!' she cried, bringing her hand down on the table, with a gleam in her eye. 'That is my affair! And what is most necessary is to begin as quickly as we can, so as to settle what is most important today, if only it is possible.'

'Very good, mamma; only listen to one more . . . piece of openness: do you know why I am so interested to know your plan and have no faith in it? Because I cannot rely upon myself. I have said already that I have made up my mind to this base action; but if the details of your plan are really too revolting, too dirty, I warn you that I shan't be able to endure it, and I shall fling it all up. I know that that is only an added baseness: to resolve upon vileness, and to be afraid of the filth in which it is swimming; but there is no help for it. It will inevitably be so! . . . '

'But, Zinotchka, what is there particularly vile in it, *mon ange*?' Marya Alexandrovna was protesting timidly. 'It is nothing but making an advantageous marriage, and everybody does that, you know! You have only to look at it from that point of view, and it all seems perfectly honourable . . . '

'Ah, mamma, for God's sake, don't try to deceive me! You see, I agree to anything, anything! What more do you want? Please don't be alarmed if I call things by their names. That is perhaps my only comfort now.'

And a bitter smile came upon her lips.

'Well, well! that's all right, my angel; we can differ in our opinions and yet mutually respect each other. Only if you are anxious about the details and are afraid they will be nasty, leave all that business to me; I assure you that not a speck of dirt shall fall on you. Should I be willing to compromise you in people's eyes? Only rely on me and everything shall be settled capitally with the utmost decorum, above all, with the utmost decorum! There shall not be the slightest scandal, and if there should be the tiniest, unavoidable, little bit of scandal – well, what of it? Why, we shall be far away then! We shan't stay here, you know! They can talk as much as they like, we can despise them! They will be envious. And they are not worth worrying about! I wonder at you, Zinotchka – but don't be angry with me – how can you, with your pride, be afraid of them?'

'Oh, mamma, I am not in the least afraid of them! You don't understand me a bit,' Zina answered irritably.

'Well, well, my love, don't be angry. All I mean is that they are contriving some nasty plots every day of their lives, and here, just for once in your life . . . But how silly I am! What am I saying? It is not nasty at all! What is there nasty about it? On the contrary, it is perfectly honourable! I will prove that to you conclusively, Zina. I repeat, it all depends on how you look at it . . . '

'Oh, do leave off, mamma, with your arguments,' Zina cried wrathfully, and she stamped impatiently.

'Well, my love, I'll say no more, I'll say no more! I have said something foolish again . . . '

A brief silence followed. Marya Alexandrovna meekly waited for Zina to speak, and looked uneasily into her eyes, as a little dog who has done wrong watches its mistress.

'I don't understand how you are going to set to work,' Zina continued, with repugnance. 'I feel sure that you will only meet with ignominy. I despise their opinion, but for you it will mean disgrace.'

'Oh, if that's all that is worrying you, my angel, please don't worry yourself! I beg you, I entreat you. If only we are agreed, you need not be anxious about me. Oh, if only you knew the storms I have weathered unharmed! The scrapes I have had to get out of! Well, only let me have a try. In any case we must lose no time in getting the prince tête-à-tête. That is the very first thing. And all the rest will depend on it! But I can foresee the rest. They will all be up in arms, but . . . that does not matter. I'll settle their business! I am frightened of Mozglyakov, too . . . '

'Mozglyakov!' Zina pronounced with contempt.

'Why, yes, Mozglyakov; only don't you be frightened, Zinotchka! I declare I'll bring him to such a pass that he will help us of himself! You don't know me, Zinotchka! You don't know what I am equal to in an emergency! Ah, Zinotchka, darling! When I heard about the prince a little while ago, the thought flashed upon my brain even then. My whole mind seemed full of light at once. And who, who could expect that he would come to us? Why, such an opportunity might not occur once in a thousand years! Zinotchka, my angel, there is no dishonour in your marrying an old man and a broken-down cripple, but there would be in your marrying a man you could not endure, though you would *really* be his wife. And you won't be a real wife to the prince, you know. Why, it is not marriage. It is only a domestic contract! Why, of course, it will be a benefit to him, the fool! Why, it is bestowing priceless happiness on an old fool like that! Ah, how beautiful you are today,

Zinotchka! Not beautiful, but a queen of beauty! Why, if I were a man I would win you half a kingdom if you wanted it! They are all asses! How resist kissing this hand!' And Marya Alexandrovna kissed her daughter's hand warmly. 'Why, this is my flesh and blood! We will marry him by force, if need be, the old fool! And how we will arrange life, you and I, Zinotchka! You won't drive away your old mother, when you are in luck will you? Though we do quarrel, my angel, you have never had another friend like me; anyway . . . '

'Mamma! If you have decided, perhaps it is time . . . you were doing something. You are simply wasting time here!' said Zina impatiently.

'It is time, Zina, it is. Oh, I have been letting myself chatter too long!' cried Marya Alexandrovna, catching herself up. 'They are trying to entice the prince away altogether. I'll get into the sledge and set off at once. I'll drive round, call Mozglyakov out, and then . . . Yes, I'll bring him away by force, if need be! Goodbye, Zinotchka, goodbye, darling; don't grieve, have no doubts, don't be sad – above all, don't be sad. Everything will turn out splendidly; everything shall be done with dignity and decorum! It makes all the difference how you look at it . . . Well, goodbye, goodbye.'

Marya Alexandrovna made the sign of the cross over Zina, whisked out of the room, twisted and turned before the looking-glass in her own room for a brief instant, and two minutes later was being whirled along the streets of Mordasov in her sledge, which was always at the door at that hour in readiness for paying calls. Marya Alexandrovna lived *en grand*.[152]

'No, you won't outwit me,' she thought, as she sat in her sledge. 'Zina consents, and that means half my task is done. And break down now! Nonsense! Ah, that Zina! She has agreed, anyway, at last! So some considerations do affect even her darling brain! I drew a tempting prospect for her! I touched her! But it is terrific how beautiful she is today! With her beauty I would have had Europe upside down to suit me. Oh, well, we'll wait and see . . . Shakespeare will fade away when she becomes a princess and gets to know a thing or two. What does she know? Mordasov and her schoolmaster . . . H'm! . . . But what a princess she will be! I love in her that pride, that boldness. She is so unapproachable! She glances at you – it is the look of a queen. Why, how could she, how could she fail to see her advantage? She saw it at last! She'll see the rest . . . I shall be with her, of course! In the end she will agree with me on every point! And she won't be able to get on without me. I shall be a princess myself. I shall be known in Petersburg. Farewell, horrid little town! The prince will die and that boy will die, and then I will marry her to a reigning prince. Only one thing I am afraid of: didn't I confide too much in her? Wasn't I too open? Didn't I let myself be carried away by my feelings? She frightens me; oh, she frightens me!'

And Marya Alexandrovna became engrossed in her meditations; needless to say that they were of an active nature. But as the proverb has it: 'A good will does more than compulsion.'

Left alone, Zina spent a long time walking up and down the room, with her arms crossed. She pondered over many things. Often, and almost unconsciously, she repeated, 'It's time, it's time, it's high time!' What did that fragmentary exclamation mean? More than once tears glistened on her long, silky eyelashes. She did not think of checking them or wiping them away. But there was no need for her mother to be anxious, and to try to penetrate into her daughter's thoughts. Zina had fully made up her mind, and was prepared for all the consequences.

'Wait a bit,' thought Nastasya Petrovna, threading her way out of the lumber-room on the departure of the colonel's wife. 'And I was meaning to put on a pink ribbon for the benefit of that wretched prince, and was fool enough to believe that he would marry me! Ah, Marya Alexandrovna, I am a slut, I am a beggar, I take bribes of two hundred roubles, do I? I dare say I ought to have let you off and taken nothing from a swell like you. I took the money honourably; I took it for the expenses connected with the job . . . I might have had to give a bribe myself. What do you care that I demeaned myself to break the lock with my own hands? I did the dirty work for your benefit, while you sit with your hands in your lap! You have only to embroider on the canvas; wait a bit, I'll show you the canvas! I'll show you both whether I am a slut! You will appreciate Nastasya Petrovna and her kindness.'

7

But Marya Alexandrovna was led by her good genius. The project she was planning was a grand and daring one. To marry her daughter to a wealthy man, to a prince and to a wreck, to marry her without anyone's knowing it, taking advantage of the feeble-mindedness and defence-lessness of her guest, to do this by stealth like a thief, as Marya Alexandrovna's enemies would say, was not only bold but audacious. It was of course a profitable scheme, but in case of failure the schemers would be covered with disgrace. Marya Alexandrovna knew this, but she did not despair. 'You don't know what storms I have weathered unharmed,' she had said to Zina, and she had spoken truly. Otherwise she would not have been much of a heroine.

There is no disputing that all this was something like highway robbery; but Marya Alexandrovna did not take much notice of that. On that score she had one wonderful and unfailing reflection: 'Once married, you can't be unmarried.' A simple thought, but alluring the imagination with such extraordinary advantages that the mere conception of them sent thrills and shudders all over her. Altogether she was in great excitement, and sat in her sledge as though she were on thorns. Like a woman of inspiration with an unmistakable creative gift, she had already formed a plan of action. But this plan was still a rough sketch, altogether *en grand*, and still loomed somewhat dimly before her. A mass of details and unforeseen possibilities of all sorts awaited her. But Marya Alexandrovna had confidence in herself; she was agitated, not by fear of failure – no! she longed only to begin the fray as soon as possible. Impatience, a laudable impatience, fired at the thought of delays and obstacles. But as we are speaking of obstacles we will ask leave to explain our meaning more fully. The chief trouble Marya Alexandrovna foresaw and expected was from her excellent fellow-citizens, and especially from the highly respectable ladies of Mordasov. She knew by experience their implacable hatred for herself. She was perfectly certain, for instance, that at that moment everyone in the town probably knew of her designs, although no one had been told anything about them. She knew from bitter experience on more than one occasion, that no incident, even of the most private nature, happened in her house in the morning without being known by the evening to the humblest market-woman, the humblest individual sitting behind a counter. Of course Marya Alexandrovna, so far, had only a presentiment of trouble. But such presentiments had never deceived her. She was not deceived now. This was what had actually happened, though she knew nothing positive about it. About midday, that is just three hours after the prince's arrival in Mordasov, strange rumours were circulating about the town. No one knew where they had begun, but they spread instantly. All began assuring one another that Marya Alexandrovna had already made a match between the prince and her Zina, her portionless, twenty-three-year-old Zina; that Mozglyakov had been dismissed, and that it was all signed and settled. What was the cause of these rumours? Could it be that everyone knew Marya Alexandrovna so well that they instantly hit on the very centre of her secret thoughts and ideals? Neither the incongruity of such a rumour with the usual order of things, for such affairs can very rarely be settled in an hour, nor the obvious lack of any foundation for the story, for no one could discover whence it had arisen, could shake the conviction of the people of Mordasov. The rumour grew and took root with extraordinary obstinacy. What is most remarkable is that they began to circulate at the very time when Marya Alexandrovna was beginning her conversation with Zina on that very subject. So sharp are the noses of the provincials! The instinct of provincial newsmongers sometimes approaches the miraculous, and of course there is some reason for it. It is founded on the closest and most interested study of one another, pursued through many years. Every provincial lives, as it were, under a glass case. There is no possibility of concealing anything from your excellent fellow-citizens. They know you by heart, they know even what you don't know about yourself. The provincial ought, one would think, by his very nature to be a psychologist and a specialist on human nature. That is why I have been sometimes genuinely amazed at meeting in the provinces not psychologists and specialists on human nature, but a very great number of asses. But that is aside; that is a superfluous reflection.

The news was like a thunderclap. A marriage with the prince appeared to everyone so advantageous, so dazzling, that even the strangeness of the affair did not occur to anyone. We will observe one other circumstance: Zina was almost more hated than Marya Alexandrovna – why? – I cannot tell. Possibly Zina's beauty may have been partly the reason. Perhaps the fact, too, that Marya Alexandrovna was anyway recognised as one of themselves by all the ladies of Mordasov, she was a berry off the same bush. If she had vanished from the town – who knows? – they might have regretted her. She enlivened their society by her goings on. It would have been dull without her. Zina, on the contrary, behaved as if she were living in the clouds and not in Mordasov. She was somehow not on a level with these people, not their equal, and, possibly without being aware of it, behaved with insufferable haughtiness in their company! And now all of a sudden, that Zina, concerning whom there was a scandalous story, that proud, that haughty Zina was becoming a millionaire and a princess, was rising to a rank and distinction. In a couple of years, when she would be a widow, she would marry a duke or maybe a general, who knows, perhaps a governor (and the Governor of Mordasov was, as luck would have it, a widower with a great weakness for the fair sex). Then she would be the lady of the greatest consequence in the province, and of course the mere thought of that was insufferable, and no news could ever have aroused more indignation in Mordasov

then the news of Zina's marrying the prince. Instantly a furious outcry
rose on all sides. People declared that it was wicked, positively vile; that
the prince was out of his mind; that the old man was being deceived,
that they were taking advantage of his feeble-mindedness to deceive
him, to dupe him, to cheat him; that the old man must be saved from
their bloodthirsty claws; that it was robbery and immorality, and finally
that other girls were just as good as Zina; and other girls might just
as well marry the prince. All these objections and opinions, Marya
Alexandrovna, so far, only surmised, but that was enough for her. She
knew for certain that everyone, absolutely everyone, was ready to do
everything possible, and even impossible, to frustrate her designs. Here
they were trying to kidnap the prince so that she would have to get him
back almost by force. Besides, if she did succeed in catching the prince
and luring him back, she could not keep him for ever on the lead.
Besides, who could guarantee that that day, within a couple of hours,
the whole solemn conclave of Mordasov ladies would not be sitting in
her drawing-room, would not call on her on some pretext which would
make it impossible to refuse to see them. If they were refused admittance
at the door, they would climb in at the window – a feat almost
impossible, though it did happen in Mordasov. In short, there was not
an hour, not a second to be lost, and meanwhile nothing had yet been
begun. All at once an idea that was a stroke of genius flashed upon
Marya Alexandrovna's brain, and was instantly matured there. Of that
new idea we shall not neglect to speak in its proper place. Here we will
only say that at that moment, our heroine was dashing along the streets
of Mordasov full of menace and inspiration, resolving even upon actual
violence should it prove necessary in order to get the prince back. She
did not yet know how it would be done and where she would meet him,
but she did know positively that Mordasov would sink into the earth
sooner than one jot of her present plans should fail of accomplishment.

Her first step could not have been more successful. She succeeded in
waylaying the prince in the street and taking him back to dinner. If I am
asked how, in spite of all her enemies' devices, she managed to insist on
getting her own way, so making Anna Nikolaevna look rather a fool – I
am bound to say that I regard such a question as insulting to Marya
Alexandrovna. Could she fail to triumph over any Anna Nikolaevna
Antipov? She simply stopped the prince on his way to her rival's house,
and in spite of everything (including the protests of Mozglyakov, who
was afraid of a scandal) transferred the old gentleman to her sledge. It
was this that distinguished Marya Alexandrovna from her rivals, that on
critical occasions she did not hesitate for fear of a scandal, taking as her

motto, that success justifies everything. The prince, of course, made no great resistance, and, as usual, quickly forgot all about it and was highly delighted. At dinner he babbled away without ceasing, was exceedingly lively, made jokes and puns, began telling anecdotes which he did not finish, or jumped from one story to another without being aware of it. At Natalya Dmitryevna's he had drunk three glasses of champagne; at dinner he drank more, and was completely fuddled. Marya Alexandrovna herself kept filling up his glass. The dinner was a very good one. The monster Nikita had not spoilt it. The lady of the house enlivened the party with the most fascinating graciousness. But the others, as though of design, seemed extraordinarily depressed. Zina maintained a sort of solemn silence. Mozglyakov was evidently put out and ate little. He was absorbed in thought, and as that was very exceptional with him, Marya Alexandrovna felt very uneasy. Nastasya Petrovna sat glum, and actually made signs to Mozglyakov which the latter entirely failed to observe. Had it not been for the enchanting suavity and vivacity of the hostess, the dinner would have been like a funeral.

Yet Marya Alexandrovna was inexpressibly excited. Zina alarmed her dreadfully with her mournful air and tear-stained eyes. And another difficulty was that there was need of haste, of prompt action; and that 'accursed Mozglyakov' sitting on like a blockhead, troubling about nothing, and simply in the way! It was, of course, impossible to begin on such a subject before him. Marya Alexandrovna rose from the table in terrible uneasiness. What was her amazement, her delighted horror, if one may use such an expression, when, as soon as they arose from the table, Mozglyakov came up to her and suddenly, quite unexpectedly, announced – that to his great regret, of course – he was absolutely forced to take leave of them at once.

'Where are you going?' Marya Alexandrovna asked, with a note of extreme regret.

'Well, you see, Marya Alexandrovna,' Mozglyakov began, with some uneasiness and even hesitation, 'a very queer thing has happened to me. I really don't know how to tell you . . . For goodness sake give me advice.'

'Why, what is it?'

'My godfather Boroduev, the merchant, you know, met me today. The old fellow was quite huffy, he scolded me and said I had grown proud. This is the third time I have been in Mordasov without his having a glimpse of me. "Come to tea today," he said. It is four o'clock now, and he drinks tea in the old-fashioned way – when he wakes up. What am I to do? It is a bore of course, Marya Alexandrovna, but think. He saved my poor father from hanging, you know, when he gambled away the government money. It was owing to that that he stood godfather to me. If I am so happy as to marry Zinaida Afanasyevna I have only a hundred and fifty serfs, while he has a million, people say, even more. He is childless. Seventy, think of it! If one pleases him he may leave one a hundred thousand in his will.'

'Oh, my goodness! What are you about! Why are you delaying?' cried Marya Alexandrovna, scarcely concealing her relief. 'Go to him, go to him! You must not let it slip. To be sure, I was noticing at dinner – you seemed so dull! Go, *mon ami*, go. Why, you ought to have paid a call in the morning to show that you appreciate, that you value his kindness. Ah, you young people, you young people!'

'Why, Marya Alexandrovna,' cried Mozglyakov in amazement, 'you yourself attacked me for that acquaintance. Why, you said that he was a peasant with a great beard, connected with innkeepers, low-class people and attorneys.'

'Oh! *mon ami*! We say a great many thoughtless things. I may make mistakes like anyone else – I am not a saint. I don't remember, but I may have easily been in that mood . . . Besides, you were not at that time paying your addresses to Zina . . . Of course it is egoism on my part, but now I am forced to look at it from a different point of view, and what mother could blame me in the circumstances? Go, do not delay for a minute! Spend the evening with him too . . . and, listen! Say something to him about me. Tell him that I have a great regard, a great liking, a respect for him; and do it tactfully, nicely! Oh, my goodness, why it quite went out of my head! I ought to have thought to suggest it to you!'

'You have quite reassured me, Marya Alexandrovna,' Mozglyakov cried, enchanted. 'I swear I will obey you in everything now! Why, I was simply afraid to tell you! . . . Well, goodbye, I am off. Make my apologies to Zinaida Afanasyevna. Though I shall certainly . . . '

'I give you my blessing, *mon ami*. Be sure you speak of me to him! He certainly is a very dear old man. I changed my opinion of him long ago. Though, indeed, I have always liked in him all those old-fashioned truly Russian ways of his . . . *Au revoir, mon ami, au revoir!*'

'Oh, what a blessing that the devil has taken him off! No, it was the hand of God helping us!' she thought, breathless with joy.

Pavel Alexandrovitch went out into the hall, and was putting on his fur coat when Nastasya Petrovna seemed suddenly to spring from nowhere. She was lying in wait for him.

'Where are you going?' she said, holding him by the arm.

'To see Boroduev my godfather, Nastasya Petrovna, who graciously stood sponsor at my christening . . . He's a wealthy old man, he will leave me something, I must make up to him.'

Pavel Alexandrovitch was in the best of spirits.

'To see Boroduev! Very well then, say goodbye to your bride,' Nastasya Petrovna said, abruptly.

'How do you mean goodbye?'

'Why, what I say! You imagine she is yours already! While they are trying to marry her to the prince. I have heard it myself.'

'To the prince? Mercy on us, Nastasya Petrovna!'

'Mercy on us, to be sure! Now wouldn't you like to look on and overhear? Put down your coat and come this way.'

Pavel Alexandrovitch, petrified, put down his fur coat and followed Nastasya Petrovna on tiptoe; she led him to the same little lumber-room in which she had listened that morning.

'But upon my word, Nastasya Petrovna, I really don't understand.'

'Oh, well, you'll understand when you bend down and listen. The farce will begin at once, no doubt.'

'What farce?'

'Sh! don't speak so loud! The farce is that they are simply hoaxing you. This morning when you had gone away with the prince, Marya Alexandrovna was a whole hour persuading Zina to consent to marry this prince; she said that nothing would be easier than to get round him and force him to get married, and she pitched such a fine tale that I felt quite sick. I overheard it all from here. Zina consented. How flattering they both were to you! They look upon you simply as a fool, and Zina said straight out that nothing would induce her to marry you. I am a fool, too! I meant to pin on a pink ribbon! Listen now, listen!'

'But I say, it's the most unholy treachery, if so!' whispered Pavel Alexandrovitch, looking into Nastasya Petrovna's face in the most foolish way.

'Well, you only listen, and that's not all you'll hear.'

'But listen where?'

'Why, stoop down here – to this keyhole . . . '

'But Nastasya Petrovna . . . I . . . I am really not capable of listening at keyholes.'

'Pooh, it's a bit late to think of that. It's a case of putting your honour in your pocket; since you've come you had better listen!'

'But really . . . '

'If you are incapable of it, then be made a fool of! One takes pity on you and you give yourself airs. What is it to me? I am not doing it for my own sake. I shall be gone from here before evening!'

Pavel Alexandrovitch, overcoming his scruples, stooped down to the keyhole. His heart was beating, there was a throbbing in his temples. He scarcely understood what was happening to him.

8

'So you had a very gay time at Natalya Dmitryevna's, prince?' queried Marya Alexandrovna, surveying the field of the approaching conflict with a predatory eye, and desiring to begin the conversation as innocently as possible. Her heart was beating with excitement and anticipation.

After dinner they had taken the prince at once to the *salon*, in which he had been received that morning. All solemn functions and receptions at Marya Alexandrovna's took place in this *salon*. She was proud of the room. The old man seemed rather limp after his six glasses of wine, and could hardly keep on his legs. But he chattered away without ceasing. His garrulousness was only intensified. Marya Alexandrovna realised that this spurt of excitement was only momentary, and that her guest, heavy from his potations, would soon be drowsy. She must seize the moment. Scanning the field of battle, she noticed with satisfaction that the lascivious old man was fixing upon Zina glances of peculiar avidity, and her maternal heart fluttered with joy.

'Ex-ceed-ing-ly gay,' answered the prince, 'and you know Natalya Dmitryevna is an absolutely in-com-parable woman, in-com-parable!'

Though Marya Alexandrovna was so absorbed in her great plans, yet such ringing praise of her rival stabbed her to the heart.

'Upon my word, prince,' she cried, with flashing eyes, 'I really don't know what to think if your Natalya Dmitryevna is an incomparable woman! You say that because you don't known our society, you don't know it at all! Why, it is a mere exhibition of fictitious qualities, of noble sentiments, a farce, an outer husk of gold. Remove that husk and you will find a perfect hell under the flowers; a perfect wasp's nest, where you will be devoured to the last bone!'

'Is it possible!' exclaimed the prince; 'you surprise me!'

'But I vow that it is so! Ah, *mon prince*. Do you know, Zina, I really ought to tell the prince that absurd and undignified incident with Natalya Dmitryevna last week – do you remember? Yes, prince – it is about your vaunted Natalya Dmitreyvna, with whom you are so fascinated. Oh, my dearest prince! I vow I am not a scandalmonger! But I certainly must tell you this, simply to amuse you, to show you in a living instance, in a magnifying glass, so to speak, what people here are like. A fortnight ago Natalya Dmityevna came to see me. Coffee was served, and I went out of the room for something. I remember perfectly well how much sugar there was in my silver sugar-basin: it was quite full. I came back and looked: there were only three lumps lying at the bottom of the basin. No one had been left in the room but Natalya Dmitryevna. What do you say to that! She has a brick house of her own and heaps of money! It's an absurd, comical incident, but you can judge from that of the lofty tone of our society.'

'Is it pos-si-ble!' exclaimed the prince, genuinely surprised. 'What unnatural greediness! Did she eat it all up alone?'

'So you see what an *incomparable* woman she is, prince! How do you like that disgraceful incident? I believe I should have died on the spot if I had brought myself to commit such a revolting action.'

'To be sure; to be sure . . . But, you know, she really is such a *belle femme*.'

'Natalya Dmitryevna! Upon my word, prince, she is a perfect tub! Oh, prince, prince! What are you saying? I did expect better taste from you . . . '

'To be sure, a tub . . . only, you know, she has such a fine figure . . . and that girl who da-anced, she has . . . such a good figure too . . . '

'Sonitchka? But she is quite a child! She is only fourteen!'

'To be sure . . . only, you know, she is so agile and she has . . . such contours . . . too . . . they are developing, such a cha-arm-ing girl! And the other who da-an-ced with her, she is developing too . . . '

'Ah, that is a luckless orphan, prince! She often stays with them.'

'An orph-an! She is a dirty girl, though, she might wash her hands, anyway . . . Though she was at-tra-active, too . . . '

As he said this the prince scrutinised Zina through his lorgnette with a sort of growing avidity. '*Mais quelle charmante personne!*' he muttered in an undertone melting with gratification.

'Zina, play us something, or better still, sing! How she sings, prince! She is equal to a professional, a professional! And if you only knew, prince,' Marya Alexandrovna went on in a low voice, when Zina had moved away to the piano with her soft swimming gait, which sent a thrill through the poor old man. 'If only you knew what a daughter she is! What a loving nature she has, how tender she is with me! What feeling, what heart!'

'To be sure . . . feeling . . . and do you know, I have only known one woman in my life who could be compared with her for beau-uty,' the prince interrupted, with his mouth watering. 'That was Countess Nainsky, she died thirty years ago. A most fas-cin-ating woman she was, an indescribable beauty, afterwards she married her cook . . . '

'Her cook, prince!'

'To be sure, her cook . . . a Frenchman, abroad. She got a count's title for him, abroad. He was a good-looking man, extremely well educated, with little moustaches like this.'

'And . . . and . . . how did they get on together, prince?'

'To be sure, they got on very well together. Though they separated soon afterwards. He robbed her and went off. They quarrelled about some sauce . . . '

'Mamma, what shall I play?' asked Zina.

'You had better sing us something, Zina. How she sings, prince! Are you fond of music?'

'Oh, yes! *Charmant, charmant!* I am very fond of music. I used to know Beethoven when I was abroad.'

'Beethoven! Only fancy, Zina, the prince used to know Beethoven,' Marya Alexandrovna cried rapturously. 'Oh, prince, did you really know Beethoven?'

'To be sure . . . we were quite fri-ends, and he always had his nose in the snuff-box. Such a funny fellow.'

'Beethoven!'

'To be sure, Beethoven, but perhaps it was not Beet-hoven, though, but some other Ger-man. There are such a lot of Germans out there . . . I believe I have mix-ed them up.'

'What am I to sing, mamma?' asked Zina.

'Oh, Zina! Sing that song in which there is so much chivalry, the one in which there is the lady of the castle and her troubadour . . . Oh, prince! How I love all that age of chivalry! Those castles, those castles! That medieval life. Those troubadours, heralds, tournaments . . . I will accompany you, Zina. Come here closer, prince! Ah, those castles, those castles!'

'To be sure . . . those castles. I love castles, too,' muttered the prince rapturously, transfixing Zina with his solitary eye. 'But . . . my goodness!' he exclaimed, 'that so-ong, why, I know that so-ong! I heard that song long ago . . . It brings back such memories . . . Ah, my goodness!'

I will not undertake to describe what happened to the prince while Zina was singing. She sang an old French song, which had once been in fashion. Zina sang it beautifully. Her pure resonant contralto went straight to the heart. Her lovely face, her wonderful eyes, the wonderful delicately moulded fingers with which she turned the music, her thick brilliant black hair, her heaving bosom, her whole figure, proud, lovely, noble, all this bewitched the poor old man completely. He did not take his eyes off her while she was singing, he gasped with emotion. His aged heart, warmed by the champagne, the music and rising memories (what man has not favourite memories?), was throbbing faster and faster, as it had not beat for ages . . . He was ready to fall on his knees before Zina, and was almost weeping when she finished.

'*Oh, ma charmante enfant!*' he cried, kissing her fingers, '*vous me ravissez.*'[153] Only just now, just now I remembered . . . But . . . but . . . *Oh, ma charmante enfant . . .*'

And the prince could not go on.

Marya Alexandrovna felt that her moment had come.

'Why are you wasting your life, prince?' she exclaimed solemnly. 'What feeling, what vital energy, what spiritual riches, and to bury yourself for your whole life in solitude! To run away from people, from your friends! But it is unpardonable! Think better of it, prince! Look at life, so to speak, with a fresh eye! Evoke from your heart your memories of the past – the memories of your golden youth, of those golden days free from care; bring them back to life, restore yourself to life! Begin to live again in society among your fellows! Go abroad, go to Italy, to Spain – to Spain, prince! . . . You want someone to guide you, a heart that would love you, that would honour you and feel with you. But you have friends! Summon them, call them to you and they will flock in crowds to your side! I would be the first to throw up everything and fly at your summons. I remember our friendship, prince; I would abandon my husband and follow you . . . and, indeed, if I were younger, if I were as good and as lovely as my daughter, I would be your travelling companion, your friend, your wife, if that was your wish.'

'And I am sure you were *une charmante personne* in your da-ay,' said the prince, blowing his nose. His eyes were moist with tears.

'We live again in our children, prince,' Marya Alexandrovna answered, with lofty feeling. 'I, too, have my guardian angel! And that is my daughter, the friend of my heart, the partner of my thoughts, prince. She has already refused seven offers, unwilling to part from me.'

'So she would come with you when you ac-com-pan-y me abroad? In that case I will certainly go abroad,' cried the prince, growing more animated. 'I will cer-er-tain-ly go! And if I might flatter myself with the ho-ope . . . But she is a fascinating, fas-cin-na-ting child! *Oh, ma charmante enfant! . . .*' and the prince began kissing her hand again. The poor man would have liked to drop on his knees before her.

'But . . . but, prince, you say: can you flatter yourself with hope?'
Marya Alexandrovna caught him up, conscious of a fresh rush of
eloquence. 'But you are strange, prince. Can you consider yourself
unworthy of a woman's devotion? It is not youth that makes a man
handsome. Remember, that you, so to speak, are a scion of the old
aristocracy. You are the embodiment of the most refined, the most
chivalrous sentiments and . . . manners! Did not Maria love Mazeppa[154]
in his old age? I remember, I have read that Lauzun, that enchanting
marquis at the court of Louis the . . . [155]I have forgotten which, in his
declining years, when he was an old man, won the heart of one of the
leading court beauties! . . . And who has told you that you are old? Who
has instilled that idea into you? Men like you do not grow old! You,
with such wealth of feeling, of gaiety, of wit, of vital energy, of brilliant
manners! Only show yourself at some spa abroad with a young wife, as
beautiful as my Zina – for instance – I am not speaking of her, I only
mention her for example – and you will see what a colossal sensation it
will make! You a scion of the aristocracy, she – a queen of beauty! You
will walk with her on your arm in triumph; she will sing in brilliant
society, you, for your part, will scintillate with wit – and all the visitors
at the spa will flock to look at you! All Europe will be ringing with your
name, for all the newspapers, all the *feuilletons* at the watering-places,
will tell the same story . . . '

'The *feuilletons* . . . Oh, yes; oh, yes. That's in the newspapers . . . '
muttered the prince, not understanding half Marya Alexandrovna's
babble, and growing more and more limp every moment. 'But . . . my
chi-ild, if you are not ti-ired, sing that song you sang just now, once
more.'

'Oh, prince! But she has other songs better still . . . Do you remember
'L'Hirondelle',[156] prince? No doubt you have heard it?'

'Yes, I remember, or, rather, I have forgotten it. No, no; the same
so-ong as be-fore, the same that she sang just now! I don't want
'L'Hirondelle'! I want the same song . . . ' said the prince, entreating
like a child.

Zina sang it over again. The prince could not restrain himself, and
sank on his knees before her.

'*Oh, ma belle châtelaine!*'[157] he cried, in a voice quavering with age
and excitement. '*Oh, ma charmante châtelaine!* Oh, my sweet child! You
have re-min-ded me of so much . . . of what was in the distant past . . .
I thought then that everything would be better than it was afterwards.
In those days I used to sing duets . . . with the vicomtesse . . . that very
song . . . and now . . . I don't know what now . . . '

All this speech the prince uttered breathless and gasping. His tongue was perceptibly faltering. Some words were almost impossible to understand. It could only be seen that he was in an extremely maudlin state; Marya Alexandrovna promptly threw oil on the flames.

'Prince! But perhaps you are falling in love with my Zina!' she cried, feeling that it was a solemn moment.

The prince's answer surpassed her highest expectations.

'I am madly in love with her,' cried the old man suddenly reviving, still on his knees and trembling all over with excitement. 'I am ready to devote my life to her, and if I could only ho-ope . . . But lift me up, I feel ra-ather we-eak . . . I . . . if I could only hope to offer her my heart, then . . . I . . . she would sing me so-ongs eve-ry day, and I could always look at her . . . always look at her . . . Oh, my goodness!'

'Prince, prince! You offer her your hand! You want to rob me of my Zina, my darling, my angel, Zina! But I will not let you go, Zina! You will have to tear her from my arms, from the arms of her mother!' Marya Alexandrovna rushed at her daughter and folded her tightly in her arms, though she was conscious of being somewhat violently repulsed . . . The mamma was rather overdoing it. Zina felt that in every fibre of her being, and looked on at the farce with indescribable disgust. She was silent, however, and that was all Marya Alexandrovna wanted.

'She has refused nine offers, simply to avoid being parted from her mother!' she cried. 'But now, my heart forebodes separation! This morning I noticed how she looked at you . . . You have impressed her with your aristocratic ways, prince, with that refinement! . . . Oh! you are parting us; I have a presentiment of it.'

'I ado-ore her!' muttered the prince, still quivering like an aspen leaf.

'And so you will forsake your mother?' exclaimed Marya Alexandrovna, dashing at her daughter once again.

Zina was in haste to put an end to the painful scene. She held out her lovely hand to the prince, and even forced herself to smile. The prince took the hand with reverence and covered it with kisses.

'Only now, I be-gin to live,' he muttered, gasping with ecstasy.

'Zina,' Marya Alexandrovna pronounced solemnly. 'Look at this man! He is the noblest, the most honourable of all the men I know! He is a medieval knight! But she knows that, prince; she knows it to my sorrow . . . Oh, why did you come! I am giving you my treasure, my angel. Take care of her, prince! That is the earnest prayer of a mother, and what mother will censure me for my sorrow!'

'Mamma, that is enough!' whispered Zina.

'You will protect her from insult, prince. Your sword will flash in the face of any slanderer or backbiter who dare malign my Zina!'

'That is enough, mamma, or I'll . . . '

'Yes, yes, it will flash . . . ' muttered the prince. 'Only now I begin to live . . . I want the wedding to be at once, this minute . . . I . . . I want to send to Du-ha-no-vo at once. I have dia-monds there. I want to lay them at her feet.'

'What fire, what fervour! What nobility of feeling!' exclaimed Marya Alexandrovna. 'And you could waste yourself, waste yourself, withdrawing from the world! I shall say that a thousand times over! I am beside myself when I think of that diabolical . . . '

'How co-ould I help it, I was so fri-ghtened!' muttered the prince, whimpering and growing maudlin. 'They wa-an-ted to put me in a ma-adhouse . . . I was frightened.'

'In a madhouse! Oh, the monsters! Oh, the inhuman creatures! Oh, the base treachery! Prince, I had heard that. But that was insanity on the part of those people! What for, whatever for?'

'I don't know myself, what for!' answered the old man, feeling weak, and sitting down in an easy chair. 'I was at a ba-all, you know, and I to-old some anecdote; and they did not li-ike it. And so there was a fuss.'

'Really only for that, prince?'

'No. I played cards afterwards with Prince Pyotr Demen-ti-tich. I couldn't make my tricks. I had two ki-ings and three queens . . . or, rather, three queens and two ki-ings . . . No; one ki-ing! And afterwards I had the queens . . . '

'And for that! For that! Oh, the fiendish inhumanity! You are weeping, prince! But now that will not happen again! Now I shall be at your side, my prince; I shall not part from Zina, and we shall see if they dare to say a word! . . . And indeed you know, prince, your marriage will impress them. It will put them to shame! They will see that you are still quite competent . . . that is, they will realise that such a beauty would not have married a madman! Now you can hold up your head proudly. You can look them straight in the face . . . '

'Oh, yes; I will look them stra-aight in the face,' muttered the prince, closing his eyes.

'He's nearly asleep, though,' thought Marya Alexandrovna; 'it is merely wasting words.'

'Prince, you are agitated, I see that; you absolutely must be quiet; rest after your emotion,' she said, bending over him maternally.

'Oh, yes; I should like to li-ie down a little,' he said.

'Yes, yes! Calm yourself, prince! This agitation . . . Stay I will accompany you myself . . . I will put you to bed, myself, if need be. Why are you looking at that portrait, prince? It is the portrait of my mother, an angel, not a woman! Oh, why is she not with us now! She was a saintly woman, prince, a saintly woman! I can call her nothing else.'

'A sa-aintly woman? *C'est joli* . . . I had a mother too . . . *princesse* . . . and only fancy, she was an ex-tra-or-din-arily fat woman . . . But that wasn't what I meant to say . . . I am a lit-tle tired. *Adieu, ma charmante enfant!* . . . I . . . de-ligh-ted . . . today . . . tomorrow . . . But no ma-atter! *au revoir, au revoir!*' At this point he tried to wave a kiss, but slipped and almost fell down in the doorway.

'Take care, prince! Lean on my arm,' cried Marya Alexandrovna.

'*Charmant, charmant!*' he muttered as he went out. 'Only now I am be-gin-ning to live!'

Zina was left alone; unutterable bitterness weighed upon her heart. She felt sick with repulsion. She was ready to despise herself. Her cheeks were burning. Clenching her fists and setting her teeth, she stood motionless with bowed head. Tears of shame gushed from her eyes . . . At that moment the door opened and Mozglyakov ran into the room.

9

He had heard all, all!

He did not walk into the room, but actually ran in, pale with emotion and with fury. Zina gazed at him in amazement.

'So that's how it is,' he shouted, panting. 'At last I have found out what you are!'

'What I am!' repeated Zina, staring at him as though he were mad; and all at once her eyes flashed with anger. 'How dare you speak like that, to me?' she cried, going up to him.

'I have heard it all!' Mozglyakov repeated solemnly, though he involuntarily drew back a step.

'You heard? You've been listening,' said Zina, looking at him disdainfully.

'Yes! I've been listening. Yes, I brought myself to do a low thing, but I learned what you are, the most . . . I don't know what words to use to tell you . . . what you have shown yourself to be!' he answered, quailing more and more before Zina's eyes.

'If you have heard, what can you blame me for? What right have you to blame me? What right have you to speak so rudely to me?'

'I? What right have I? And you can ask that? You are going to marry the prince, and I have no right! . . . Why, you gave me your word!'

'When?'

'How can you ask when?'

'Why, only this morning, when you were pestering me, I told you straight out that I could say nothing positive.'

'But you did not drive me away, you did not refuse me altogether. So you were keeping me in reserve! So you were drawing me on!'

A look of suffering as though from an acute, piercing, internal pain came into Zina's irritated face; but she mastered her feeling.

'That I did not drive you away,' she said, clearly and emphatically, though there was a scarcely perceptible quiver in her voice, 'was solely through pity. You implored me yourself to take time, not to say no, but to get to know you better, and "then", you said, "then, when you are convinced that I am an honourable man, perhaps you will not refuse me". Those were your own words when first you pressed your suit. You cannot draw back from them. You had the insolence to say just now that I drew you on. But you saw yourself my aversion when I met you today, a fortnight earlier than you promised. That aversion I did not conceal from you; on the contrary, I displayed it. You noticed it yourself, for you asked me whether I was angry with you for coming back sooner. You know one is not drawing a man on if one cannot and does *not care* to conceal one's aversion. You have had the insolence to say that I was keeping you in reserve. To that I will answer that what I thought about you was, "though he is not endowed with very much intelligence, he may yet be a good man, and so one might marry him". But now I am convinced, to my relief, that you are a fool, and what's more, an ill-natured fool. I have only now to wish you every happiness and *bon voyage*. Goodbye!'

Saying this, Zina turned from him and walked slowly towards the door.

Mozglyakov, guessing that all was lost, boiled with rage.

'Ah, so I am a fool,' he cried, 'so now I am a fool! Very well! Goodbye. But before I go away I'll tell the whole town how you and your mamma have tricked the old prince, after making him drunk! I'll tell everyone! I'll show you what Mozglyakov can do!'

Zina shuddered, and was stopping to answer; but after a moment's thought, she merely shrugged her shoulders contemptuously, and slammed the door after her.

At that moment Marya Alexandrovna appeared in the doorway. She had heard Mozglyakov's exclamation, in an instant guessed what it meant and shuddered with alarm. Mozglyakov had not gone yet, Mozglyakov near the prince, Mozglyakov would spread it all over the town, and secrecy for a short time at least was essential! Marya Alexandrovna had her own calculations. She instantly grasped the situation, and the plan for subduing Mozglyakov was already formed.

'What is the matter, *mon ami*?' she said, going up to him and holding out her hand affectionately.

'What? *mon ami*!' he cried furiously. 'After what you have been plotting, you call me *mon ami*! You don't catch me, honoured madam! And do you suppose you can deceive me again?'

'I am grieved, very much grieved to see you in such a *strange* state of mind, Pavel Alexandrovitch. What an expression to use! You do not even curb your language before a lady.'

'Before a lady! You . . . you may be anything you like, but not a lady!' cried Mozglyakov.

I don't know what he meant to express by this exclamation, but probably something very tremendous.

Marya Alexandrovna looked blandly into his face.

'Sit down,' she said mournfully, motioning him to the chair on which a quarter of an hour before the prince had been reposing.

'But, do listen, Marya Alexandrovna!' cried Mozglyakov in perplexity. 'You look at me as though you were not to blame in any way, but as though I had treated you badly! You can't go on like that, you know! . . . Such a tone! . . . Why, it is beyond all human endurance . . . Do you know that?'

'My friend!' answered Marya Alexandrovna, 'you must still allow me to call you that, for you have no better friend than I; my friend! You are unhappy, you are distressed, you are wounded to the heart – and so it is not to be wondered at that you speak to me in such a tone. But I am resolved to reveal to you everything, to open my whole heart, the more readily as I feel myself somewhat to blame in regard to you. Sit down, let us talk.'

There was a sickly softness in Marya Alexandrovna's voice. There was a look of suffering in her face. Mozglyakov, astounded, sat down in an easy chair beside her.

'You have been listening?' she said, looking reproachfully into his face.

'Yes, I have been listening! If I hadn't listened I should have been a duffer. Anyway, I have found out all that you were plotting against me,' Mozglyakov answered rudely, growing bolder and working himself into a passion.

'And you, you, with your breeding, with your principles, could bring yourself to such an action? Oh, good heavens!'

Mozglyakov positively jumped up from his chair.

'But, Marya Alexandrovna!' he cried, 'it is insufferable to listen to this! Think what you have brought yourself to do with your principles, and then you judge other people!'

'Another question,' she said, without answering him. 'Who put you up to listening, who told you, who is the spy here? That's what I want to know.'

'Excuse me, but I won't tell you that.'

'Very well, I shall find out for myself. I said, *Paul*, that I had treated you badly. But if you go into it all, into all the circumstances, you will see that, even if I am to blame, it is solely through a desire for your good.'

'Mine? My good? That is beyond everything! I warn you, you won't delude me again! I am not such a child as that.'

And he writhed in the armchair with such violence that it creaked.

'Please, my dear boy, keep cool, if you can. Listen to me attentively, and you will agree with everything yourself. To begin with, I intended to tell you about it at once, everything, everything, and you would have heard the whole business from me in the fullest details, without demeaning yourself to listen. That I did not explain it to you before was simply because it was only a project. It might not have come off. You see, I am being perfectly open with you. Secondly, do not blame my daughter. She loves you madly, and it cost me incredible effort to draw her away from you, and to induce her to consent to accept the prince.'

'I have just had the happiness to receive the fullest proof of that *mad* love,' Mozglyakov pronounced ironically.

'Very good. But how were you speaking to her? Was that the way that a lover should speak? Was that the way, indeed, for a well-bred man to speak? You wounded and irritated her!'

'It is not a question of breeding now, Marya Alexandrovna. And this morning, after you had both treated me to such honied looks, I went off with the prince and you blackguarded me behind my back! You called me names – let me tell you that. I know all about it, I know!'

'And no doubt from the same foul source?' said Marya Alexandrovna, with a contemptuous smile. 'Yes, Pavel Alexandrovitch, I did disparage you, I did talk against you, and I must confess I had a hard struggle. But the very fact that I had to abuse you to her, even to slander you, that very fact proves how hard it was for me to extort her consent to abandon you! You short-sighted man! If she did not care for you, would there have been any need for me to blacken your character, to put you in an undignified and ridiculous light, to resort to such extreme measures. But you do not know everything yet! I had to use my maternal authority to eradicate you from her heart, and after incredible efforts I wrung from her only the appearance of agreement. If you were listening just now you must have noticed that she did not support me with the prince by one word, one gesture. Throughout the whole scene she scarcely uttered a single word: she sang like an automaton. Her whole soul was aching with despondency, and it was from pity for her that, at last, I got the prince away. I am sure that she wept as soon as she was alone. When you came in here you must have noticed her tears.'

Mozglyakov did, in fact, remember that when he ran into the room he had noticed that Zina was in tears.

'But you, you, why were you against me, Marya Alexandrovna?' he cried. 'Why did you blacken my character? why did you slander me, as you yourself confess you did?'

'Ah, that is a different matter. If you had asked that question sensibly in the beginning, you would have had an answer to it long ago. Yes, you are right! It has all been my doing, and only mine. Don't mix Zina up in it. What was my object? I answer, in the first place, it was for Zina's sake. The prince is a man of rank and fortune, he has connections, and marrying him, Zina would make a splendid match. Besides, if he dies, perhaps before long, indeed, for we are all more or less mortal, then Zina will be a young widow, a princess, in the highest society, and perhaps very wealthy. Then she can marry anyone she likes; she would be able to make a still wealthier match. But of course she will marry the man she loves, the man she loved before, whose heart she wounded by marrying the prince. Remorse alone would force her to atone for her treatment of the man she loved before.'

'H'm!' mumbled Mozglyakov, looking thoughtfully at his boots.

'And the second thing is, and I will only mention it briefly,' Marya Alexandrovna went on, 'for perhaps you will not understand it. You read your Shakespeare, and draw all your lofty sentiments from him, but in real life, though you are *very good*, you are too young and I am a *mother*, Pavel Alexandrovitch. Listen: I am giving Zina to the prince, partly for his sake, to save him by this marriage. I loved that noble, most kindly, chivalrously honourable old man in the past. We were friends. He is unhappy in the claws of that hellish woman. She will bring him to his grave. God is my witness that I only persuaded Zina to consent to marry the prince by putting before her all the greatness of her heroic self-sacrifice. She was carried away by the nobility of her feelings, by the fascination of an act of sacrifice. There is something chivalrous in her, too. I put before her what a lofty Christian act it was to be the prop, the comfort, the friend, the child, the lovely idol of one who has perhaps but one year yet to live. No hateful woman, no terror, no despondency should be about him in the last days of his life, but brightness, affection, love. These last declining days would seem like Paradise to him! Where is the egoism in that? Tell me pray. It is more like the noble deed of a sister of mercy than egoism!'

'So you are doing this simply for the sake of the old prince, simply as the sacrifice of a sister of mercy?' muttered Mozglyakov in an ironical voice.

'I understand that question, Pavel Alexandrovitch, it is clear enough. You imagine, perhaps, that the interests of the prince are jesuitically intertwined with our own advantage? Well? Possibly those considerations were present in my brain, only they were not jesuitical, but unconscious. I know that you will be amazed at so open a confession, but one thing I do beg of you, Pavel Alexandrovitch: don't mix Zina up in that! She is pure as a dove; she is not calculating; she is capable of nothing but love, my sweet child! If anyone has been calculating, it is I, and I alone! But in the first place, search your own conscience sternly, and tell me: who would not calculate in my position, in a case like this. We consider our interests even in the most magnanimous, even in the most disinterested of our actions, inevitably, involuntarily we consider them. No doubt we all deceive ourselves when we assure ourselves that we are acting solely from noble motives. I don't want to deceive myself; I admit that for all the purity of my motives I was calculating. But ask yourself, am I interested on my own behalf? I want nothing, Pavel Alexandrovitch, I have lived my life. I am calculating for her sake, for the sake of my angel, for my child, and – what mother can blame me for it?'

Tears glistened in Marya Alexandrovna's eyes. Pavel Alexandrovitch listened in astonishment to this candid confession, and blinked incredulously.

'Well, yes, what mother would?' he said at last. 'You pitch a fine tale, Marya Alexandrovna, but . . . but, you know, you gave me your word! You gave me hopes . . . How about me? Only think! You've made me look a pretty fool, haven't you?'

'But surely you don't imagine that I haven't thought of you, *mon cher Paul*; the advantage for you in all this was so immense, that it was that, indeed, that chiefly impelled me to undertake it all.'

'Advantage for me!' cried Mozglyakov, completely dumb-foundered this time. 'How so?'

'My goodness! Can anyone be so simple and short-sighted!' cried Marya Alexandrovna, turning up her eyes to the ceiling. 'Oh, youth! youth! That is what comes of burying oneself in that Shakespeare, of dreaming, and of imagining that one is thinking for oneself when one is following the thoughts and the mind of others! You ask, my *good* Pavel Alexandrovitch, where your advantage is to be found in it. Allow me, for the sake of clearness, to make a digression. Zina loves you – that is beyond doubt! But I have noticed that, in spite of her obvious feeling for you, she has a secret lack of confidence in you, in your good feelings, in your propensities. I have noticed that at times she behaves to you, as it were intentionally, with coldness, the result of uncertainty and lack of confidence. Have you noticed that yourself, Pavel Alexandrovitch?'

'I have noticed it, and today indeed . . . But what do you mean to say, Marya Alexandrovna?'

'There, you see you have noticed it yourself. So I was not mistaken then. She has a strange lack of confidence in the stability of your character. I am a mother – and is it not for me to divine the secrets of my child's heart? Imagine now that instead of rushing into the room with reproaches, and even with abuse, irritating her, wounding and insulting her in her purity, her goodness and her pride, and so unwittingly confirming her suspicions of your evil propensities – imagine that you had accepted it all mildly, with tears of regret, perhaps, even, of despair, but with lofty nobility of feeling . . .'

'H'm! . . .'

'No, do not interrupt me, Pavel Alexandrovitch. I want to paint the whole picture which will strike your imagination. Imagine that you had gone to her and said: "Zinaida! I love you more than life itself, but family reasons divide us. I understand those reasons. They are for your happiness, and I do not venture to rebel against them, Zinaida! I forgive you. Be happy if you can!" And at that point you would fix your gaze upon her, the gaze of a lamb at the sacrifice, if I may so express myself – imagine all that and only think what effect such words would have had on her heart!'

'Yes, Marya Alexandrovna, let us suppose all that; I understand all that . . . But after all, if I had said all that I should have gained nothing by it.'

'No, no, no, my dear! Don't interrupt me. I want to picture the scene in every detail that it may make the right impression on you. Imagine that you meet her again a little later in the highest society; meet her at some ball, in a brilliantly lighted room, to the intoxicating strains of music, in the midst of magnificent women, and in the midst of this gay festival you alone mournful, melancholy, pale, leaning somewhere against a column (but so that you can be seen), watch her in the whirl of the ball. She dances. Around you flow the intoxicating strains of Strauss[158] and the scintillating wit of the highest society – while you stand alone, pale and crushed by your passion. What will Zinaida feel then, do you suppose? With what eyes will she look at you. "And I," she will think, "I doubted of that man who has sacrificed for me all – all, and has rent his heart for my sake." Her old love would, of course, rise up again with irresistible force.'

Marya Alexandrovna stopped to take breath. Mozglyakov wriggled in his easy chair with such violence that it creaked again. Marya Alexandrovna went on: 'For the prince's health Zina will go abroad, to Italy, to Spain – to Spain where there are myrtles, lemons, where the sky is blue, where there is the Guadalquivir; the land of love, where one cannot live without loving: the land of roses, where kisses, so to speak, float in the air. You will follow her there; you will sacrifice your past in the service, your connections, everything. There your love will begin with irresistible force; love, youth! Spain – my God! Your love of course is untainted, holy; though you will languish gazing at one another. You understand me, *mon ami*! Of course there will be base, treacherous people, monsters who will declare that you have not been tempted abroad by family feeling for a suffering old relation. I have purposely called your love untainted, because such people will perhaps give it a very different significance. But I am a mother, Pavel Alexandrovitch, and am I likely to lead you astray! . . . Of course the prince will not be in a condition to look after you both, but – what of that? Could such an abominable calumny be based on that? At last he will die, blessing his fate. Tell me: whom would Zina marry if not you? You are such a distant relation of the prince's that that can be no hindrance to your marriage. You will wed her, young, wealthy, distinguished and, only think! – when the grandest of our noblemen would be proud to marry her. Through her you will gain a footing in the highest circles of society, through her you will gain the highest rank and position. Now you have a hundred and fifty serfs but then you will be rich; the prince will arrange everything in his will. I will see to that. And, lastly and most important, she will have gained complete confidence in you, in your heart, in your feelings, and you will become in her eyes a hero of goodness and self-sacrifice! . . . And after that you ask where your advantage comes in? Why, you must be blind not to reflect, not to consider that advantage, when it stands not two steps from you, staring you in the face, smiling at you and crying out to you: "Here I am, your advantage!" Pavel Alexandrovitch, upon my word!'

'Marya Alexandrovna!' cried Mozglyakov in extraordinary excitement, 'now I understand it all. I have behaved coarsely, basely and caddishly!'

He leapt up from his seat and clutched his hair.

'And unreflectingly,' added Marya Alexandrovna. 'Above all, unreflectingly!'

'I am an ass, Marya Alexandrovna!' he cried, almost in despair. 'Now all is lost, because I loved her so madly.'

'Perhaps all is not lost,' said Madame Moskalev softly, as though pondering something.

'Oh, if that were possible! Help me! Teach me! Save me!'

And Mozglyakov burst into tears.

'My dear!' said Marya Alexandrovna with commiseration, giving him her hand, 'you have acted from excess of ardour, from the fervour of your passion, that is, from love for her! You were in despair, you did not know what you were doing! She ought to understand all that . . . '

'I love her to madness, and am ready to sacrifice anything for her!' cried Mozglyakov.

'I tell you what, I will set you right with her . . . '

'Marya Alexandrovna?'

'Yes, I will undertake to do that! I will bring you together. You must tell her everything – everything as I have told it you, just now.'

'Oh, God! How kind you are, Marya Alexandrovna! But . . . would it be impossible to do it at once?'

'God forbid! Oh, how inexperienced you are, my dear! She is so proud. She will take this as a fresh insult, as insolence! Tomorrow I will arrange it all; but now go away – to see that merchant, for instance . . . come in the evening, perhaps, but I would not advise you to.'

'I will go away, I will! My God! You bring me back to life! But one more question. What if the prince doesn't die so soon?'

'Oh, my God! how naïve you are, *mon cher Paul*. On the contrary, you must pray for his health. We must, with all our hearts, hope for length of days for that dear, kind, chivalrously honourable old man. I shall be the first to pray, night and day, with tears in my eyes, for my daughter's happiness. But, alas! I fear the prince's health is hopeless. Moreover, he will have now to visit Petersburg, to take Zina into society. I fear, oh, I fear that this may be too much for him! But we will pray for the best, *cher Paul*, and the rest is – in God's hands! . . . You are going now? I bless you, *mon ami*! Hope, be patient, be manly above all things, be manly! I never doubted the nobility of your sentiments . . . '

She pressed his hand warmly, and Mozglyakov walked out of the room on tiptoe.

'Well, I have got rid of one fool!' she said triumphantly. 'There are others left . . .'

The door opened and Zina came in. She was paler than usual. Her eyes were flashing.

'Mamma,' she said, 'finish it quickly or I can't endure it! It's all so vile and nasty that I am ready to run out of the house. Don't torture me, don't irritate me! I feel sick – do you hear? – sick of all this filth!'

'Zina! What is the matter with you, my angel? You . . . you have been listening!' cried Marya Alexandrovna, looking intently and uneasily at Zina.

'Yes, I have been listening. Do you want to put me to shame as you did that fool! Listen, I swear that if you go on torturing me like this, and assign to me all sorts of low parts in this low farce, I will throw it all up and make an end of it at one blow. It is enough that I have brought myself to do the vile thing that is most important. But . . . I did not know myself! I shall be stifled in this filth.'

And she went out, slamming the door.

Marya Alexandrovna gazed after her and pondered.

'Haste! haste!' she cried, starting. 'She is the chief trouble, the chief danger, and if all these scoundrels won't let us alone, if they spread it all over the town – as they probably have done by now – all is lost! She will never endure the hubbub and will refuse. At all costs we must take the prince into the country, and promptly too! I will fly off first myself, will haul along my blockhead and bring him here, he must make himself useful at last; meanwhile the old man will have had his sleep out, and we will set off.'

She rang the bell.

'The horses?' she asked the servant who came in.

'They have been ready a long while,' answered the footman.

The horses had been ordered at the moment when Marya Alexandrovna was taking the prince upstairs.

She dressed, but first ran into Zina to tell her in rough outline her decision and to give her some instructions. But Zina could not listen to her. She was lying on her bed, with her face in her pillow, and her white arms bare to the elbows; she was shedding tears and tearing her long, exquisite hair. At moments she shuddered all over as though a cold shiver were running over her limbs. Marya Alexandrovna began talking, but Zina did not even lift her head.

After standing for some time beside her, Marya Alexandrovna went out in confusion, and to vent her feelings, got into the carriage and told her coachman to drive as fast as he could.

'It's a nuisance that Zina overheard it,' she thought as she got into the carriage. 'I brought Mozglyakov round with the same words that I used with her. She is proud, and perhaps was wounded . . . Hm! But the great thing, the great thing is to make haste and settle it all before they have got wind of it! It's a pity! Well, and what if by ill luck the fool is not at home!'

And at the mere thought of that she was overcome with a fury that boded nothing pleasant to Afanasy Matveyitch; she could hardly sit still for impatience. The horses whirled her along full speed.

10

The carriage flew along. We mentioned before that an idea that was a stroke of genius had flashed into Marya Alexandrovna's brain that morning when she was hunting all over the town for the prince. We promised to refer to that idea in its proper place. But the reader knows it already. The idea was to kidnap the prince in her turn, and to carry him off as quickly as possible to their estate in the neighbourhood, where the blissful Afanasy Matveyitch flourished in tranquillity. There is no disguising the fact that Marya Alexandrovna was more and more overcome by an inexplicable uneasiness. This does happen at times to real heroes at the very moment when they are attaining their object. Some instinct suggested to her that it was dangerous to remain at Mordasov. 'But once we are in the country,' she thought, 'the whole town may be upside down for all I care!' Of course, no time was to be lost even in the country. Anything might happen – anything, absolutely anything; though, of course, we put no faith in the rumours, circulated later about my heroine by her enemies, that at this juncture she was actually afraid of the police. In short she saw that she must get the marriage of Zina and the prince solemnised as quickly as possible. She had the means for doing so at hand. The village priest could celebrate the nuptials in their own home. The ceremony might actually be performed the day after tomorrow; at the last resort, even tomorrow. There were cases of weddings within two hours of the betrothal! They could present the haste, the absence of festivities, of betrothal, of bridesmaids, to the prince as essentially *comme il faut*; they could impress upon him that it would be more in keeping with decorum and aristocratic style. In fact, it might all be made to appear as a romantic adventure, and so the most susceptible chord in the prince's heart would be struck. If all else failed, they could always make him drunk or, still better, keep him in a state of perpetual drunkenness. And afterwards, come what may, Zina would anyway be a princess! Even if they did not get off afterwards without a scandal – in Petersburg or Moscow, for instance, where the prince had relations – even that had its consolations. In the first place, all that was in the future; and in the second, Marya Alexandrovna believed that in the best society scarcely anything ever happened without a scandal, especially in the matrimonial line; that this was, in fact, *chic*, though the scandals of the best society were, she imagined, necessarily all of a special stamp – on a grand scale, something after the style of *Monte Cristo*[159] or *Les Mémoires du Diable*.[160] That, in fact, Zina need only show herself in the best society, and her mamma need only be there to support her, and everyone – absolutely everyone – would instantly be conquered, and that not one of all those countesses and princesses would be capable of withstanding the sousing which Marya Alexandrovna alone was capable of giving them, collectively or individually, in true Mordasov style. In consequence of these reflections, Marya Alexandrovna was now flying to her country seat to fetch Afanasy Matveyitch, whose presence, she calculated, was now indispensable. Indeed, to take the prince to the country would mean taking him to see Afanasy Matveyitch, whose acquaintance the prince might not be anxious to make. If Afanasy Matveyitch were to give the invitation it would put quite a different complexion upon it. Moreover, the arrival of an elderly and dignified paterfamilias in a white cravat and a dress-coat, with a hat in his hand, who had come from distant parts at once on hearing about the prince, might produce a very agreeable effect, might even flatter the *amour-propre* of the latter. It would be difficult to refuse an invitation so pressing and so ceremonious, thought Marya Alexandrovna. At last the carriage had driven the two and a half miles, and Sofron, the coachman, pulled up his horses at the front door of a rambling wooden building of one storey, somewhat dilapidated and blacked by age, with a long row of windows, and old lime trees standing round it on all sides. This was the country house and summer residence of Marya Alexandrovna. Lights were already burning in the house.

'Where is the blockhead?' cried Marya Alexandrovna, bursting into the rooms like a hurricane. 'What is that towel here for? Ah! he has been drying himself! Have you been to the baths again? And he is forever swilling his tea! Well, why are you staring at me like that, you perfect fool? Why hasn't his hair been cut? Grishka! Grishka! Grishka! Why haven't you cut your master's hair, as I told you to last week?'

As she went into the room Marya Alexandrovna intended to greet her spouse far more gently, but seeing that he had just come from the bathhouse and was sipping his tea with great enjoyment, she could not refrain from the bitterest indignation. And, indeed, her cares and anxieties were only equalled by the blissful quietism of the useless and incompetent Afanasy Matveyitch; the contrast instantly stung her to the heart. Meanwhile the blockhead, or to speak more respectfully, he who was called the blockhead, sat behind the samovar, and in senseless panic gazed at his better half with open mouth and round eyes, almost petrified by her appearance. The drowsy and clumsy figure of Grishka blinking at this scene was thrust in from the entry.

'He wouldn't let me, that is why I didn't cut it,' he said in a grumbling and husky voice. 'A dozen times I went up to him with the scissors, and said, "The mistress will be coming directly, and then we shall both catch it; and what shall we do then?" "No," he said; "wait a little. I am going to curl it on Sunday, so I must have my hair long."'

'What? So he curls his hair. So you have begun curling your hair while I am away? What new fashion is this? Why, does it suit you – does it suit your wooden head? My goodness, how untidy it is here! What is this smell? I am asking you, you monster, what is this horrid smell here?' shouted his wife, scolding her innocent and completely flabbergasted husband more and more angrily.

'Mo . . . mother!' muttered her panic-stricken spouse, gazing with imploring eyes at his domineering tyrant, and not getting up from his seat. 'Mo . . . mother! . . .'

'How often have I knocked into your ass's head that I am not to be called "mother"? Mother, indeed, to you, a pigmy! How dare you use such a mode of address to a refined lady, whose proper place is in the best society, instead of beside an ass like you!'

'But . . . but you know, Marya Alexandrovna, you are my lawful wedded wife, and so I speak to you . . . as to my wife,' Afanasy Matveyitch protested, and at the same moment put up both hands to his head to protect his hair.

'Oh, you ugly creature! Oh, you aspen post! Was anything ever more stupid than your answer? Lawful wedded wife? Lawful wedded wife, indeed, nowadays! Does anybody in good society make use of that stupid clerical, that revoltingly vulgar expression, "*lawful wedded*"? And how dare you remind me that I am your wife, when I am doing my best, my very utmost, to forget it! Why are you putting your hands over your head? Look what his hair is like! Sopping, absolutely sopping! It won't be dry for another three hours! How can I take him now – how can I let people see him! What's to be done now?'

And Marya Alexandrovna wrung her hands in fury, running backwards and forwards in the room. The trouble, of course, was a small one, and could easily be set right; but the fact was that Marya Alexandrovna could not control her all-conquering and masterful spirit. She felt an irresistible craving to be constantly venting her wrath upon Afanasy Matveyitch, for tyranny is a habit which becomes an irresistible craving. And we all know what a contrast some refined ladies of a certain position are capable of at home behind the scenes; and it is just that contrast I wish to reproduce. Afanasy Matveyitch watched his wife's evolution with a tremor, and positively broke into a perspiration as he looked at her.

'Grishka,' she cried at last, 'dress your master at once: his dress-coat, his trousers, his white tie, his waistcoat. Look sharp! But where is his hairbrush? Where is the brush?'

'Mother! Why, I have just come from the bath; I shall catch cold if I drive to the town . . . '

'You won't catch cold!'

'But my hair is wet . . . '

'Well, we will dry it directly. Grishka, take the hairbrush; brush him till he is dry. Harder, harder, harder! That's it! That's it!'

At this command the zealous and devoted Grishka began brushing his master's hair with all his might, clutching him by the shoulder to get a more convenient grip, and pressing him down to the sofa. Afanasy Matveyitch frowned and almost wept.

'Now come here! Lift him up, Grishka! Where is the pomatum? Bend down, bend down, you good-for-nothing; bend down, you sluggard!'

And Marya Alexandrovna set to work to pomade her husband's head with her own hands, ruthlessly tugging at his thick, grizzled locks, which, to his sorrow, he had not had cut. Afanasy Matveyitch cleared his throat, gasped, but did not scream, and endured the whole operation submissively.

'You have sucked the life-blood out of me, you sloven!' said Marya Alexandrovna. 'Bend down more, bend down!'

'How have I sucked your life-blood, mother?' mumbled her husband, bending his head as far as he could.

'Blockhead! He doesn't understand allegory! Now comb your hair; and you, dress him, and look sharp!'

Our heroine sat down in an easy chair and kept an inquisitorial watch on the whole ceremony of arraying Afanasy Matveyitch. Meanwhile he succeeded in getting his breath and recovering himself a little, and when the tying of his cravat was reached he even ventured to express an opinion of his own on the style and beauty of the knot. Finally, putting on his dress-coat, the worthy man was restored to cheerfulness, and looked at himself in the glass with some respect.

'Where are you taking me, Marya Alexandrovna?' he said, prinking before the looking-glass.

Marya Alexandrovna could not believe her ears. 'Hear him! Oh, you dummy! How dare you ask me where I am taking you!'

'Mother, but, you know, one must know . . . '

'Hold your tongue! Only I tell you if you call me "mother" once more, especially where we are going now, you shall be cut off tea for a month!'

The panic-stricken husband held his tongue.

'Ugh! Not a single decoration has he gained, the sloven!' she went on, looking at Afanasy Matveyitch's black coat contemptuously.

At last her husband was offended.

'It's the government gives decorations, mother; and I am a councillor and not a sloven,' he said, with honourable indignation.

'What, what, what? So you have learnt to argue out here! Ah, you peasant! Ah, you sniveller! It's a pity I haven't time to see to you, or I'd . . . But I shan't forget it later on. Give him his hat, Grishka! Give him his overcoat! While I'm away get these three rooms ready; get the green corner room ready, too. Fetch your brooms instantly! Take the covers off the looking-glasses, off the clocks, too, and within an hour let everything be ready; and put on your swallowtail yourself and give the servants gloves! Do you hear, Grishka, do you hear?'

They got into the carriage. Afanasy Matveyitch was puzzled and wondering. Meanwhile Marya Alexandrovna was deliberating how she could most intelligently knock into her husband's brain certain admonitions indispensable in his present position. But her husband anticipated her.

'Do you know, Marya Alexandrovna, I had a most original dream this morning,' he informed her quite unexpectedly, in the midst of silence on both sides.

'Phoo! you confounded dummy! Goodness knows what I thought you were going to say! Some stupid dream! How dare you interrupt me with your loutish dreams! Original! Do you understand what original means? Listen: I tell you for the last time, if you dare to say one word today about your dream or anything else, I'll . . . I don't know what I'll do to you! Listen attentively. Prince K. has come to stay with me. Do you remember Prince K.?'

'I remember him, mother, I remember him. What has he come for?'

'Be quiet; that is not your business. You must, as master of the house, invite him, with special politeness, to stay with us in the country. That is what I am taking you for. We shall set off and drive back today. But if you dare to utter one single word the whole evening, or tomorrow, or the day after tomorrow, or at any time, I'll set you to herd the geese for a whole year! Don't say anything, not a single word. That's the whole of your duty. Do you understand?'

'But if I am asked a question?'

'Never mind, hold your tongue.'

'But you know it's impossible to hold one's tongue all the while, Marya Alexandrovna.'

'In that case, answer in monosyllables; something, for instance, such as "H'm!" or something of that kind, to show you are a sensible man and think before you speak.'

'H'm!'

'Understand me: I am taking you because you have heard about the prince, and, delighted at his visit, have hastened to pay your respects to him and to ask him to visit you in the country. Do you understand?'

'H'm!'

'None of your h'mming now, you idiot! You answer me.'

'Very good, mother, it shall all be as you say. Only why am I to invite the prince?'

'What, what? Arguing again! What business is it of yours what for? And how dare you ask questions about it?'

'But I keep wondering, mother, how I am to invite him if I hold my tongue, as you tell me.'

'I will speak for you, and you've simply got to bow – do you hear? to bow – and hold your hat in your hand. Do you understand?'

'I understand, moth . . . Marya Alexandrovna.'

'The prince is extremely witty. If he says anything, even though it is not to you, you must respond to everything with a bright and good-humoured smile. Do you understand?'

'H'm!'

'H'mming again! Don't say "H'm!" to me. Answer simply and directly. Do you hear?'

'I hear, Marya Alexandrovna; of course I hear. And I am saying "H'm!" to practise saying it, as you told me. Only I keep wondering about the same thing, mother: how it is to be. If the prince says anything, you tell me to look at him and smile. Well, but if he asks me something?'

'You slow-witted dolt! I have told you already: hold your tongue. I will answer for you; you simply look at him and smile.'

'Why, but he'll think I am dumb,' grumbled Afanasy Matveyitch.

'As though that mattered! Let him think it; you'll conceal the fact that you are a fool, anyway.'

'H'm! . . . But what if other people ask me some question?'

'Nobody will ask you; no one will be there. But in case – which God forbid! – somebody does come in, and if anybody does ask you a question, or say something to you, you must answer at once by a sarcastic smile. Do you know what is meant by a sarcastic smile?'

'It means witty, doesn't it, mother?'

'I'll teach you to be witty, you blockhead! And who would ask a fool like you to be witty? A mocking smile – don't you understand? – mocking and contemptuous.'

'H'm!'

'Oh, I do feel uneasy about this blockhead!' Marya Alexandrovna murmured to herself. 'He certainly has taken a vow to be the death of me! It really would have been better not to have brought him at all.'

Absorbed in such reflections, in regret and anxiety, Marya Alexandrovna was continually popping her head out of the window and urging on the coachman. The horses raced along, but still it seemed too slow for her. Afanasy Matveyitch sat silently in his corner, inwardly repeating his lesson. At last the carriage drove into the town and stopped at Marya Alexandrovna's house. But our heroine had hardly had time to alight at the front door, when all at once she saw driving up to the house a two-seated sledge with a hood – the very sledge in which Anna Nikolaevna Antipov usually drove about. In the sledge were sitting two ladies. One of them was, of course, Anna Nikolaevna herself, the other Natalya Dmitryevna, who had of late been her devoted friend and follower. Marya Alexandrovna's heart sank. But before she had time to cry out, another carriage drove up – a sledge, in which there was evidently another visitor.

There was a sound of joyful exclamations: 'Marya Alexandrovna! And with Afanasy Matveyitch, too! You have just arrived? Where from? How lucky! And we have come to spend the whole evening! What a surprise!'

The visitors sprang out at the front door, and chattered like swallows. Marya Alexandrovna could not believe her eyes or her ears.

'I'll see you further,' she thought to herself. 'It looks like a plot! I must enquire into it. But . . . you won't outwit me, you magpies . . . You wait a bit . . .'

11

As Mozglyakov left Marya Alexandrovna, he was apparently quite comforted. She had completely inflamed his imagination. He did not go to see Boroduev, feeling that he wanted to be alone. A perfect flood of heroic and romantic dreams would not let him rest. He dreamed of a solemn explanation with Zina, then of generous tears of forgiveness on his part, pallor and despair at the gorgeous ball in Petersburg, Spain, the Guadalquivir, love and the dying prince joining their hands on his deathbed. Then his lovely wife devoted to him and for ever lost in admiration of his heroism and lofty feelings; incidentally, on the quiet, the attentions of some countess belonging to the best society into which he would certainly be brought by his marriage with Zina, the widow of Prince K.; a post as vice-governor, money – in fact, everything so eloquently described by Marya Alexandrovna passed once more through his gratified soul, caressing and attracting it, and, above all, flattering his vanity. But – and I really don't know how to explain it – as he began to be wearied by these raptures, the extremely vexatious reflection occurred to him: that all this was, in any case, in the future, while now anyway he had been made a fool of. When this thought came into his mind, he noticed that he had wandered a long way into some solitary and unfamiliar suburb of Mordasov. It had grown dark. In the streets, with their rows of little houses sunk into the earth, there was a savage barking of the dogs which abound in provincial towns in alarming numbers, precisely in those quarters where there is nothing to guard and nothing to steal. Snow was beginning to fall and melting as it fell. From time to time he met a belated workman or a peasant woman in a sheepskin and high boots. All this, for some unknown reason, began to irritate Pavel Alexandrovitch – a very bad sign, for when things are going well everything strikes us in a charming and attractive light. Pavel Alexandrovitch could not help remembering that hitherto he had always been a leading figure in Mordasov. He had been highly gratified when in every house he had heard it hinted that he was an eligible *parti* and had been congratulated on that distinction. He was actually proud of being an eligible young man. And now he would appear before everyone as on the shelf! There would be laughter at his expense. Of course he could not enlighten them, he could not talk to them about Petersburg ballrooms with columns, and about the Guadalquivir! Thinking of all this, full of dejection and regret, he stumbled at last upon a thought which had for a long while been rankling unnoticed in his heart: 'Was it all true? Would it all come to pass as Marya Alexandrovna had described it?' At that point he remembered very opportunely that Marya Alexandrovna was a very designing woman, that however worthy of general respect she might be, she was gossiping and lying from morning till night; that in getting rid of him now, she probably had her own reasons, and that drawing fancy pictures of the future was a thing that anybody could do. He thought of Zina, too, recalled her parting look at him, which expressed anything rather than concealed passion; and therewith appropriately remembered that an hour before she had called him a fool. At that recollection Pavel Alexandrovitch stopped short as though rooted to the spot, and flushed with shame till the tears came into his eyes. As ill-luck would have it, the next minute he had an unpleasant adventure: he stepped back and went flying from the wooden pavement into a heap of snow. While he was floundering in the snow a pack of dogs, which had been pursuing him with their barking for some time, flew at him on all sides. One of them, the smallest and most aggressive, hung on to him, fastening its teeth into his fur coat. Fighting off the dogs, swearing aloud, and even cursing his fate, Pavel Alexandrovitch, with a torn coat and insufferable despondency in his heart, reached the corner of the street and only then realised that he had lost his way. We all know that a man who has lost his way in an unknown part of the town, especially at night, can never walk straight along the streets. Some unknown force seems at every moment to impel him to turn down every side street he comes to on his way. Following this system, Pavel Alexandrovitch was soon hopelessly lost. 'Deuce take all these exalted notions!' he said to himself, spitting with anger. 'And the devil himself take you with your lofty feelings and your Guadalquivirs!' I cannot say that Mozglyakov was attractive at that moment. After wandering about for a couple of hours, he arrived exhausted and harassed at Marya Alexandrovna's front door. He was surprised at seeing a number of carriages. 'Can there be visitors, can it be an evening party?' he thought. 'What's the object of it?' Questioning a servant he met, and learning that Mary Alexandrovna had been to their country house and had brought back with her Afanasy Matveyitch in a white cravat, and that the prince was awake but had not yet come downstairs to join the visitors, Pavel Alexandrovitch went upstairs to his "uncle" without saying a word to anyone. He was at the moment in that state of mind when a man of weak character is capable of committing some horrible, malignant and nasty action from revenge, without considering that he may have to regret it all his life afterwards.

Going upstairs, he saw the prince sitting in an easy chair before his travelling dressing-case, with an absolutely bald head, though he had his "imperial" and whiskers on. The wig was in the hands of his grey-haired old valet and favourite, Ivan Pahomitch. Pahomitch was combing it with an air of deep reflection and respect. As for the prince, he presented a very sorry spectacle, having hardly recovered from his recent potations. He was sitting, as it were, all of a heap, blinking, crumpled and out of sorts, and he looked at Mozglyakov as though he did not recognise him.

'How are you feeling, uncle?' asked Mozglyakov.

'What! . . . That's you,' said his "uncle" at last. 'I've had a little nap, my boy. Oh, my goodness!' he cried, suddenly reviving, 'why, I . . . haven't got my wi-ig on.'

'Don't disturb yourself, uncle. I . . . I will help you, if you like.'

'But now you've learnt my secret! I said we ought to lo-ock the door. Come, my dear, you must give me your wo-ord of honour at once that you won't give away my secret and won't tell anyone that my hair is fa-alse.'

'Upon my word, uncle! Can you think me capable of anything so base!' cried Mozglyakov, anxious to please the old gentleman, with . . . ulterior aims.

'Oh, yes; oh, yes! And as I see you are an honourable man, so be it, I will surprise you . . . and will tell you all my secrets. How do you like my moustaches, my dear?'

'They are superb, uncle! Marvellous! How can you have preserved them so long?'

'Don't deceive yourself, my dear, they are ar-ti-fi-cial,' said the prince, looking with triumph at Pavel Alexandrovitch.

'Is it possible? I can hardly believe it. And the whiskers? Confess, uncle, you must darken them?'

'Darken them? They are not dyed, they are artificial.'

'Artificial? No, uncle, you may say what you like, but I don't believe it. You are laughing at me!'

'*Parole d'honneur,*[161] *mon ami!*' the prince cried triumphantly; 'and only fan-cy, everyone is de-ceived, like you. Even Stepanida Matveyevna cannot believe it, though she sometimes fi-xes them on herself. But, I am sure, my boy, you will keep my secret. Give me your word of honour . . . '

'On my word of honour, uncle, I will keep it. I ask you again, can you think me capable of anything so base?'

'Oh, my dear, what a fall I have had while you were away today. Feofil upset me out of the carriage again.'

'Upset you again! When?'

'We were on our way to the mon-as-tery . . . '

'I know, uncle, this morning.'

'No, no, two hours ago, not more. I set off to the monastery and he upset me. How frigh-tened I was, even now my heart isn't right.'

'But you've been asleep, uncle!' said Mozglyakov, wondering.

'Oh, yes, I've been asleep . . . and afterwards I drove out, though indeed . . . though perhaps I . . . oh, how strange it is!'

'I assure you, uncle, that you have been dreaming it! You have been quietly dozing ever since dinner.'

'Really?' and the prince pondered. 'Oh, yes, perhaps I really did dream it, though I remember everything I dreamed. At first I dreamt of a very dreadful bull with horns; and then I dreamt of some pub-lic pro-se-cu-tor who seemed to have ho-orns, too . . . '

'I suppose that was Nikolay Vassilitch Antipov, uncle?'

'Oh, yes, perhaps it was he; and then I dreamt of Napoleon Bona-parte. Do you know, my dear, they all tell me that I am like Napoleon Bonaparte . . . and in profile I am strikingly like some pope of old days! What do you think, my dear, am I like a pope?'

'I think you are more like Napoleon, uncle.'

'Oh, yes, full face. I think so myself, too, my dear. And I dreamt about him, when he was on the island, and you know he was so talkative, so springhtly, such a jo-olly fel-low that he quite amused me.'

'Are you speaking of Napoleon, uncle?' said Pavel Alexandrovitch, looking at the old man reflectively. A strange idea was beginning to dawn upon his mind, an idea which he could not yet define clearly to himself.

'Oh, yes, of Na-po-leon. We were discussing philosophy to-gether. And do you know, my dear, that I am really sorry the En-glish treated him so harshly. Of course, if he had not been kept on the chain he would have been attacking people again. He was a desperate man, but still I am sorry for him. I wouldn't have treated him so. I would have put him upon an un-in-habited island . . . '

'Why on an uninhabited one?' asked Mozglyakov absent-mindedly.

'Well, perhaps, on an inhabited one; but inhabited only by sensible people. And I would have got up entertainments of all sorts for him: a theatre, concerts, ballets, and all at the government expense. I would have let him go for walks, under supervision, of course, or else he would have slipped away at once. He was very fond of little pies. Well, I would have made him little pies every day. I would have looked after him like a father, so to speak. He would have re-pen-ted in my care . . . '

Mozglyakov listened absent-mindedly to the babble of the old man not yet fully awake, and bit his nails with impatience. He wanted to turn the conversation upon marriage, though he scarcely yet knew why; and unbounded anger was surging in his heart.

All at once the old man cried out in surprise: 'Oh, *mon ami*! Why, I forgot to tell you. Only fancy, I made a pro-po-sal today.'

'A proposal uncle!' cried Mozglyakov, waking up.

'Why, yes, a pro-po-sal. Pahomitch, are you going? Very good. *C'est une charmante personne* . . . But . . . I confess, my dear boy, I acted thoughtlessly. I only se-ee that now. Oh, dear me!'

'But excuse me, uncle, when did you make this proposal?'

'I own, my dear boy, that I really don't quite know when it was. Didn't I dream it, perhaps? Ah, how queer it is, though!'

Mozglyakov shuddered with delight. A new idea flashed upon his mind.

'But who was it you made an offer to, and when did you make it, uncle?' he repeated impatiently.

'The daughter of the house, *mon ami . . . cette belle personne* . . . I have for-got-ten her name, though. Only you see, my dear, I really can't get ma-arried. What am I to do now?'

'Yes, it will certainly be your ruin if you get married. But allow me to ask you one question, uncle. You seem to be convinced that you really have made an offer?'

'Oh, yes . . . I am sure of it.'

'But what if you have dreamed it all, just as you dreamed you had been upset out of your carriage a second time?'

'Oh, my goodness! Perhaps this really was a dream, too! So that I really don't know how to behave with them. How is one to find out for certain, my dear boy, whether I did make a proposal or not? But now fancy what a position I am in?'

'Do you know, uncle, I fancy there is no need to find out.'

'How so?'

'I feel sure that you dreamed it.'

'I think so, too, my dear, especially as I often have dreams of that sort.'

'There you see, uncle. Remember that you had a little wine at lunch, and then again at dinner, and in the end . . . '

'Oh, yes, my dear; it very like-ly was due to that.'

'Besides, uncle, however exhilarated you may have been, you couldn't possibly under any circumstances have made such a nonsensical proposal in reality. As far as I know you, uncle, you are a man of the greatest good sense, and . . . '

'Oh, yes; oh, yes.'

'Only consider one point: if your relations, who have nothing but ill-will for you in any case, were to hear of it, what would happen then?'

'Oh, my goodness!' cried the prince in alarm, 'what would happen then?'

'Upon my word! Why, they would all cry out in chorus that you were out of your mind when you did it, that you had gone mad, that you must be put under restraint, that you had been taken advantage of, and perhaps they would put you somewhere under supervision.'

Mozglyakov knew what would frighten the prince most.

'Oh, my God!' cried the prince, trembling like a leaf. 'Could they possibly shut me up?'

'And then only think, uncle, could you possibly have made such an imprudent offer when you were awake? You understand your own interests. I assure you solemnly that it was all a dream.'

'It cer-tain-ly must have been a dream, it cer-tain-ly must!' the prince repeated in a panic. 'Oh, how sensibly you've thought it out, my de-ear boy! I am sincerely grateful to you for setting me right.'

'I am awfully glad, uncle, that I have met you today. Only fancy, if I had not been here you might really have been muddled, have thought that you were engaged, and have gone down to them as though you were. Think how dangerous!'

'Oh, yes . . . yes, dangerous.'

'Remember that young lady is three-and-twenty; nobody wants to marry her, and all at once you, a man of wealth and rank, appear as a suitor! Why, they would snatch at the idea at once, would assure you you were engaged, and would force you perhaps into marriage. And they would calculate on the possibility of your dying before long.'

'Really?'

'And remember, uncle, a man of your qualities . . . '

'Oh, yes, with my qualities . . . '

'With your intelligence, with your politeness . . . '

'Oh, yes, with my intelligence, yes! . . . '

'And last, but not least, you are a prince. What a splendid match you might make if, for some reason, you really did want to marry! Only think what your relations would say!'

'Oh, my dear, why they would be the death of me! I have endured such treachery, such ill-treatment at their hands . . . Would you believe it, I suspect they wanted to put me into a lu-na-tic asylum. Upon my word, my dear, wasn't that absurd? Why, what could I have done there . . . in a lu-na-tic asylum?'

'Quite so, uncle, and so I won't leave your side when you go downstairs. There are visitors there now.'

'Visitors? Oh, my goodness!'

'Don't be uneasy, uncle, I will keep with you.'

'But how grate-ful I am to you, my dear, you are simply my saviour! But do you know, I think I had better go away.'

'Tomorrow morning, uncle, at seven o'clock tomorrow morning. But today you can take leave of everyone and tell them you are going away.'

'I will certainly go away . . . to Father Misail . . . But my dear boy – what if they do make a match of it?'

'Don't be afraid, uncle, I shall be with you, and whatever they say to you, whatever they hint at, you say straight out that it was all a dream, as it certainly was . . . '

'Oh, yes, it cer-tain-ly must have been a dream. Only do you know, my dear, it was a most en-chan-ting dream! She is wonderfully good-looking, and do you know, such a figure . . . '

'Well, farewell, uncle. I am going downstairs, and you . . . '

'What! Are you going to leave me alone?' cried the prince in alarm.

'No, uncle, we'll both go down but separately; I'll go first, and then you. That will be better.'

'Oh, ve-ry well. And by the way, I must jot down an idea.'

'Quite so, uncle, jot down your idea and then come down, don't delay. Tomorrow morning . . . '

'And tomorrow morning to Father Misail, cer-tain-ly to Father Misail! *Charmant, charmant*! But do you know, my dear, she is won-der-ful-ly good-looking . . . such contours . . . and if I really had to be married . . . '

'God preserve you, uncle.'

'Oh, yes, God preserve me! . . . Well, goodbye, my dear, I'll come directly . . . only I will just jot down . . . Apropos, I have been meaning to ask you for a long time. Have you read the memoirs of Casanova?'[162]

'Yes, I have, uncle, why?'

'Oh, well . . . I have forgotten now what I meant to say . . . '

'You will think of it later, uncle. Goodbye for the present!'

'Goodbye, my dear, goodbye. Though it really was a fascinating dream, a fa-as-cin-a-ting dream! . . . '

12

'We've all come to see you, all of us! and Praskovya Ilyinitchna is coming too, and Luiza Karlovna meant to come too,' twittered Anna Nikolaevna, walking into the *salon* and looking about her greedily.

She was a rather pretty little lady, dressed expensively but in gaudy colours, and very well aware that she was pretty. She fancied that the prince was hidden somewhere in a corner with Zina.

'And Katerina Petrovna is coming, and Felisata Mihalovna meant to be here too,' added Natalya Dmitryevna, the lady of colossal proportions, remarkably like a grenadier, whose appearance had so delighted the prince.

She had on an extraordinary small pink hat perched on the back of her head. For the last three weeks she had been the devoted friend of Anna Nikolaevna, whose good graces she had long been trying to win, and whom, to judge by appearances, she could have swallowed up at one gulp, bones and all.

'I won't speak of the delight, I may call it, of seeing you both here and in the evening too,' Marya Alexandrovna chanted, recovering from her first stupefaction. 'But tell me, please, what miracle has brought you to me tonight, when I quite despaired of such an honour.'

'Oh, my goodness, Marya Alexandrovna, what a forgetful lady you are!' said Natalya Dmitryevna in honied accents, mincing and speaking in a bashful and squeaky voice which was a very curious contrast to her appearance.

'*Mais ma charmante*,' twittered Anna Nikolaevna, 'we must, you know, we really must complete our arrangements for these theatricals. Only today Pyotr Mihalovitch said to Kalist Stanislavitch that he was very much disappointed that it was not coming off well, and that we did nothing but fall out over it. So we met together this evening and thought: let us go to Marya Alexandrovna's and settle it all right away. Natalya Dmitryevna let the others know. They are all coming. So we will talk it all over together and all will go well. We won't let them say that we do nothing but quarrel, will we, *mon ange*?' she added playfully, kissing Marya Alexandrovna. 'Oh, my goodness! Zinaida Afanasyevna! Why, you grow prettier every day!'

Anna Nikolaevna flew to shower kisses on Zina.

'Indeed, she has nothing else to do but grow prettier,' Natalya Dmitryevna added in sugary accents, rubbing her huge hands.

'The devil take them! I did not think about those theatricals! They have been sharp, the magpies!' Marya Alexandrovna murmured, beside herself with fury.

'Especially, my angel, since that darling prince is staying with you. You know there used to be a theatre at Duhanovo in the time of the late owners. We have made enquiries already and know that all the old scenery, the curtain, and even the costumes are put away somewhere. The prince called on me today, and I was so surprised at seeing him that I quite forgot to speak of it. Now we will introduce the subject of the theatre, you must help us, and the prince will order all the old trappings to be sent us. For who is there here you can trust to make anything like scenery? And what is more, we want to interest the prince in our theatricals. He must subscribe, you see it is for charity. Perhaps he will even take a part – he is so sweet and obliging. Then it will be a wonderful success.'

'Of course he will take a part. Why, he can be made to play any part,' Natalya Dmitryevna added with vast significance.

Anna Nikolaevna had not misinformed Marya Alexandrovna: ladies kept arriving every minute. Marya Alexandrovna hardly had time to receive them and utter the exclamations demanded on such occasions by propriety and the rules of *comme il faut*.

I will not undertake to describe all the visitors. I will only mention that each one wore a look of extraordinary wiliness. Anticipation and a sort of wild impatience was expressed on every face. Some of the ladies had come with the express object of witnessing an extraordinary and scandalous scene, and would have been exceedingly wroth if they had had to drive home again without having seen it. On the surface they behaved with the utmost amiability, but Marya Alexandrovna resolutely prepared herself for the attack. There was a shower of questions about the prince; they sounded most natural, yet each seemed to contain an allusion or innuendo. Tea was brought in; everyone sat down. One group took possession of the piano. On being asked to play and sing, Zina answered that she did not feel quite well. The paleness of her face confirmed her words. Sympathetic enquiries were showered upon her, and the ladies even seized the opportunity to ask questions and drop hints. They enquired about Mozglyakov, too, and addressed these enquiries to Zina. Marya Alexandrovna displayed ten times her usual energy at that moment; she saw everything that was going on in every corner of the room, heard what was said by each one of her visitors, though there were nearly a dozen of them, and answered every question immediately, without hesitating for a word. She was trembling for Zina and was surprised that she did not go away, as she had always done before on such occasions. She kept her eye, too, on Afanasy Matveyitch. Everybody always made fun of him in order to pique Marya Alexandrovna through her husband. On this occasion it might be possible to learn something from the simple-minded and open-hearted Afanasy Matveyitch. Marya Alexandrovna looked with anxiety at the way in which her husband was being besieged. Moreover, to every question he answered, 'H'm,' with an expression so unhappy and unnatural that it might well have driven her to fury.

'Marya Alexandrovna, Afanasy Matveyitch won't talk to us at all!' cried one bold, sharp-eyed little lady, who was afraid of nobody and never embarrassed by anything. 'Do tell him to be more polite with ladies.'

'I really don't know what has come over him today,' answered Marya Alexandrovna, interrupting her conversation with Anna Nikolaevna and Natalya Dmitryevna, with a gay smile. 'He certainly is uncommunicative! He has scarcely said a word to me. Why don't you answer Felisata Mihalovna, Athanase? What did you ask him?'

'But . . . but . . . you know, mother, you told me yourself . . . ' Afanasy Matveyitch began muttering in his surprise and confusion. At that moment he was standing by the lighted fire, with his hands thrust into his waistcoat in a picturesque attitude which he had chosen for himself. He was sipping tea. The ladies' questions so embarrassed him that he blushed like a girl. When he began justifying himself, he caught such a terrible glance from his infuriated wife that he almost lost consciousness from terror. Not knowing what to do, anxious to put himself right and regain respect, he took a gulp at his tea; but the tea was too hot. Having taken it so hastily he burnt himself terribly, dropped the cup, spluttered and choked so violently that he had to go out of the room to the surprise of all present. In fact, everything was clear. Marya Alexandrovna realised that her visitors knew all about it and had met together with the worst intentions. The position was dangerous. They might talk to the feeble-minded old man and turn him from his purpose even in her presence. They might even take the prince away from her, set him against her that very evening, and entice him away with them. She might expect anything. But fate had another ordeal in store for her; the door opened, and she beheld Mozglyakov, whom she had believed to be at Boroduev's and did not in the least expect that evening. She started as though something had stabbed her.

Mozglyakov stopped in the doorway and looked round at everyone a little confused. He was not able to control his emotion, which was clearly apparent in his face.

'Oh, my goodness, Pavel Alexandrovitch!' cried several voices.

'Oh, my goodness! Why, it is Pavel Alexandrovitch. How was it you told us he had gone to Boroduev's, Marya Alexandrovna? We were told you were hiding at Boroduev's, Pavel Alexandrovitch!' Natalya Dmitryevna piped.

'Hiding?' repeated Mozglyakov, with a rather wry smile. 'It is a strange expression! Excuse me, Natalya Dmitryevna! I don't conceal myself from anyone, and I don't want to conceal anybody else, either,' he added, looking significantly at Marya Alexandrovna.

Marya Alexandrovna was in a tremor.

'Can the blockhead be mutinous?' she wondered, looking searchingly at Mozglyakov. 'No, that will be worse than anything . . . '

'Is it true, Pavel Alexandrovitch, that they have given you the sack . . . at your office, I mean, of course?' the impudent Felisata Mihalovna asked pertly, sarcastically looking him straight in the face.

'The sack? What sack? I am simply transferring from one branch to another. I have a post in Petersburg,' Mozglyakov answered coldly.

'Oh, I congratulate you, then,' Felisata Mihalovna went on. 'We were positively scared when we heard you were trying to get a post in Mordasov. The posts here can't be relied upon, Pavel Alexandrovitch, there is no keeping them.'

'It is only as a teacher in the district school that you might find a vacancy,' observed Natalya Dmitryevna.

The hint was so obvious and so crude that Anna Nikolaevna, confused, gently nudged her malicious friend with her foot.

'Do you imagine that Pavel Alexandrovitch would be willing to take the place of a wretched teacher?' put in Felisata Mihalovna.

But Pavel Alexandrovitch could not find an answer. He turned round and jostled against Afanasy Matveyitch, who held out his hand to him. Mozglyakov very stupidly did not take his hand, but gave him a low and ironical bow. Exceedingly irritated, he went up to Zina, and looking angrily into her face, muttered: 'This is all thanks to you. Wait a bit, I'll show you this very evening whether I am a fool.'

'Why put it off? One can see that now,' Zina answered aloud, looking her former suitor up and down with an air of aversion.

Mozglyakov turned away hurriedly, frightened by her loud voice.

'Have you been to see Boroduev's,' Marya Alexandrovna ventured to enquire at last.

'No, I have been seeing uncle.'

'Uncle? So you have just been with the prince, then?'

'Oh, my goodness! Then the prince is awake? And we were told that he was still resting,' added Natalya Dmitryevna, with a malignant look at Marya Alexandrovna.

'Don't trouble about the prince, Natalya Dmitryevna,' answered Mozglyakov; 'he is awake, and now, thank God, he has all his senses about him. This morning he was given too much wine; first when he was with you, and afterwards here, till his head, never over-strong, was completely muddled. But now, thank God, we have had a little talk, and he has recovered his common sense. He will be here directly to take leave of you, Marya Alexandrovna, and thank you for all your hospitality. Tomorrow at daybreak we are setting off together to the monastery, and then I shall certainly escort him back to Duhanovo myself, to avoid a second accident like that of today; and then I shall hand him over to Stepanida Matveyevna, who by that time will certainly be back from Moscow and will not let him go on his travels a second time – I can answer for that.'

As he said this, Mozglyakov looked spitefully at Marya Alexandrovna. She was sitting as though petrified with amazement. I admit with grief that my heroine was, perhaps for the first time in her life, cowed.

'So he is going away at daybreak tomorrow! How's that?' said Natalya Dmitryevna, addressing Marya Alexandrovna.

'How is that?' the visitors were heard saying naïvely. 'Why, we heard that . . . why, that's very odd.'

But their hostess did not know what answer to make. Suddenly the general attention was diverted in the most strange and eccentric way. In the adjoining room a strange noise was heard, and abrupt exclamations, and all at once, utterly unexpectedly, Sofya Petrovna Karpuhin dashed into Marya Alexandrovna's *salon*. Sofya Petrovna was unquestionably the most eccentric lady in Mordasov, so eccentric that it had even been decided of late not to receive her in society. It must be observed, too, that regularly every evening at seven o'clock it was her habit to take a nip of something – for the sake of her stomach, as she explained – and after it, she was as a rule in an emancipated state of mind, to put it mildly. She was in that state of mind now at the moment when she so unexpectedly burst in upon Marya Alexandrovna.

'So this is the way, Marya Alexandrovna,' she shouted to be heard all over the room. 'So this is the way you treat me! Don't disturb yourself, I have only come for a minute, I won't sit down. I've come on purpose to find out whether it is true what I am told! So you have balls, banquets, a betrothal party, but Sofya Petrovna must sit at home and knit a stocking! You've asked the whole town, but not me! Though this morning I was your friend and *mon ange* when I came to tell you what they were doing with the prince at Natalya Dmitryevna's. And now here's Natalya Dmitryevna, whom you were abusing like a pickpocket, and who was abusing you, paying you a visit. Don't disturb yourself, Natalya Dmitryevna. I don't want your chocolate *à la sante*, at twopence a stick. I have better to drink at home! Tfoo!'

'One can see you have,' observed Natalya Dmitryevna.

'But upon my word, Sofya Petrovna,' cried Marya Alexandrovna, flushing with vexation, 'what is the matter with you? Do control yourself at least.'

'Don't trouble about me, Marya Alexandrovna, I know all about it, all about it!' cried Sofya Petrovna in her harsh, shrill voice. She was surrounded by the other visitors, who seemed to be enjoying this unexpected scene. 'I have found out all about it. Your Nastasya ran round and told me the whole story. You pounced on this wretched prince, made him drunk, and made him propose to your daughter whom nobody wants to marry now, and you imagine that you've become a fine bird now yourself – a duchess in lace! Tfoo! Don't disturb yourself, I am a colonel's wife myself. I don't care if you don't invite me to your betrothal party. I have mixed with better people than you. I have dined with Countess Zalihvatsky. The head commissary, Kurotchkin, paid me his addresses. As though I wanted your invitation! Tfoo!'

'Come, Sofya Petrovna,' answered Marya Alexandrovna, losing patience, 'I must tell you, this is not the way to burst into a lady's house, especially in *such a condition*, and if you do not relieve me of your presence and your eloquent remarks, I shall promptly take steps to get rid of you.'

'I know you will tell your nasty servants to turn me out! Don't excite yourself, I can find the way for myself. Goodbye; make any marriage you like. And you, Natalya Dmitryevna, don't laugh at me, if you please; I don't care a damn about your chocolate! Though I am not invited here, I don't go dancing jigs to amuse princes. What are you laughing at, Anna Nikolaevna? Sushilov has broken his leg; they've just carried him home! And you, Felisata Mihalovna, if you don't tell your bare-legged Matryoshka to drive your cow home in good time so she's not mooing under my window every day, I will break her legs. Goodbye, Marya Alexandrovna, good luck to you! Tfoo!'

Sofya Petrovna vanished. The visitors laughed. Marya Alexandrovna was thrown into extreme embarrassment.

'I think the lady has had a little too much,' Natalya Dmitryevna brought out in her sugary voice.

'But what insolence!'

'*Quelle abominable femme!*'[163]

'How funny she was, though!'

'Ah, what shocking things she said!'

'But what was it she said about a betrothal party? What betrothal party?' Felisata Mihalovna asked sarcastically.

'But this is awful!' Marya Alexandrovna burst out at last. 'It is these monsters who scatter these absurd rumours by handfuls! It is not so strange, Felisata Mihalovna, that such ladies are to be found in our midst, no; what is more surprising is that these ladies are sought after, are listened to, are encouraged, are believed, are . . . '

'The prince! the prince!' all voices cried suddenly at once.

'Oh, my goodness! *Le cher prince!*'

'Oh, thank goodness. Now we shall find out all the details,' Felisata Mihalovna whispered to her neighbour.

13

The prince came in with a honied smile on his lips. The alarm which Mozglyakov had inspired in his chicken heart entirely disappeared at the sight of the ladies. He melted at once like a sweetmeat. The ladies greeted him with shrill cries of delight. Ladies always made a great deal of our old friend, and were very familiar with him. He was able to afford them incredible entertainment. Felisata Mihalovna had declared that morning (not in earnest, of course) that she was ready to sit on his knee, if that would give him any pleasure, 'because he was a darling, darling old man, sweet beyond all bounds!' Marya Alexandrovna transfixed him with her eyes, trying to read something from his face and to divine from it the way out of her critical position. It was evident that Mozglyakov had said horrible things about her, and that her plans were in jeopardy. But nothing could be read from the prince's face. He was the same as he had been that morning and as he always was.

'Ah, my goodness, here is the prince! We have been waiting and waiting for you,' cried several of the ladies.

'With impatience, prince, with impatience!' piped others.

'That's extremely flat-ter-ing,' lisped the prince, sitting down at the table on which the samovar was boiling. The ladies immediately surrounded him. Anna Nikolaevna and Natalya Dmitryevna were the only ones left by the side of Marya Alexandrovna. Afanasy Matveyitch smiled respectfully. Mozglyakov smiled too, and with a defiant air looked at Zina, who, without taking the slightest notice of him, went and sat down by her father near the fire.

'Oh, prince, is it true what they say, that you are leaving us?' piped Felisata Mihalovna.

'Oh, yes, *mesdames*, I am going away, I want to go abro-oad im-med-iately.'

'Abroad, prince, abroad!' they all cried in chorus. 'What an idea!'

'Abro-oad,' repeated the prince, prinking. 'And do you know, I want to go abroad particularly for the sake of the new ideas.'

'How do you mean for the sake of the new ideas? New ideas about what?' said the ladies, exchanging glances with one another.

'Oh, yes, for the sake of the new ideas,' repeated the prince, with an air of the deepest conviction. 'Everyone now goes abroad for the sake of the new i-deas, and so I, too, want to gain ne-ew i-ideas.'

'Don't you want, perhaps, to enter a masonic lodge,[164] uncle?' put in Mozglyakov, who evidently wished to impress the ladies by his wit and his ease.

'Oh, yes, my dear, you are quite right,' the old man answered un-expectedly. 'In the old days I reall-y did belong to a masonic lodge abroad, and I, too, had a number of noble ideas. I intended, indeed, at that time to do a great deal for the enlighten-ment of the peo-ple, and I quite decided at Frankfurt to set free my man Sidor, whom I had brought with me from Russia. But to my surprise he ran away from me himself. He was an ex-treme-ly odd man. Afterwards I met him in Paris, such a swell, with whiskers; he was walking along the boulevard with a mamselle. He looked at me, gave me a nod, and the mamselle with him was such a brisk, sharp-eyed, alluring creature . . . '

'Come, uncle! Why, you'll be setting all your peasants free next, if you go abroad this time,' cried Mozglyakov, laughing loudly.

'You have gu-essed perfectly right, my dear boy, what I desire to do,' the prince answered without hesitation. 'I do want to set them all fre-ee.'

'But upon my word, prince, they will all run away from you directly, and then where will you get your money?' cried Felisata Mihalovna.

'Of course they would all run away,' Anna Nikolaevna echoed, with a note of alarm.

'Oh, dear me, do you really think they would run away?' cried the prince in astonishment.

'They would run away, they would all run away at once and would leave you alone,' Natalya Dmitryevna confirmed.

'Oh, dear me! Well, then I shall not se-et them free. But of course I did not mean it.'

'So much the better, uncle,' Mozglyakov said approvingly.

Till then, Marya Alexandrovna had been listening and watching in silence. It seemed to her that the prince had entirely forgotten her, and that that was not natural.

'Allow me, prince,' she began in a loud and dignified voice, 'to introduce my husband, Afanasy Matveyitch. He came expressly from our country house as soon as he heard you were staying with us.'

Afanasy Matveyitch smiled and looked dignified. It seemed to him as though he were being praised.

'Ah, I am delighted,' said the prince, 'A-fa-nasy Matveyitch! To be sure, I believe I remember something. A-fa-nasy Mat-ve-yitch. To be sure, that is the gentleman in the country. *Charmant, charmant*, delighted. My dear!' cried the prince, turning to Mozglyakov. 'Why, that's the very man, do you remember, who was in that rhyme this morning. How did it go? "The husband's on the stair, and the wife has gone." . . . Oh, yes, the wife has gone away to some town.'

'Oh, prince, why that's true; "The husband's on the stair, while the wife has gone to Tver," the very vaudeville the actors played here last year,' Felisata Mihalovna put in.

'Oh, yes, precisely: to Tver; I always forget. *Charmant, charmant!* So you are that very man? Extremely glad to make your ac-quaint-ance,' said the prince, holding out his hand to the smiling Afanasy Matveyitch without getting up from his chair. 'Well, I hope you are well?'

'H'm . . . '

'He is quite well, prince, quite well,' Marya Alexandrovna answered hurriedly.

'Oh, yes, one can see he is quite well. And are you always in the country? Well, I am delighted. Why, what red che-eeks he has and how he keeps laughing!'

Afanasy Matveyitch continued smiling, bowing, and even scraping with his foot. But at the prince's last observation he could not restrain himself, and all of a sudden, apropos of nothing, in the most foolish way burst into a loud laugh. Everybody laughed. The ladies squealed with delight. Zina flushed and with flashing eyes looked at Marya Alexandrovna, who in her turn was bursting with anger. It was high time to change the conversation.

'How did you sleep, prince?' she asked in a honied voice, at the same time turning a menacing look upon Afanasy Matveyitch to indicate that he should take himself off as quickly as possible.

'Oh, I had a very good sleep,' answered the prince; 'and do you know, I had a most en-chan-ting dream, an en-chan-ting dream!'

'A dream! I love to hear people tell their dreams,' cried Felisata Mihalovna.

'And I, too, I love it!' added Natalya Dmitryevna.

'An en-chan-ting dream!' repeated the prince, with a mawkish smile; 'but the dream is a dead secret!'

'How so, prince, do you really mean you can't tell it us? It must have been a wonderful dream!' observed Anna Nikolaevna.

'A dead secret,' repeated the prince, gleefully tantalising the ladies' curiosity.

'Oh, then it must be very interesting!' cried the ladies.

'I bet that the prince dreamed that he fell on his knees before some beautiful young lady and made her an offer of marriage!' cried Felisata Mihalovna. 'Come, prince, own up that that's right! Darling prince, confess!'

'Confess, prince, confess,' the others chimed in on all sides.

The prince listened triumphantly and ecstatically to all their outcries. The ladies' supposition flattered his vanity extremely, and he almost licked his lips.

'Though I said that my dream was a dead secret,' he answered at last, 'yet I must admit, madam, that to my great surprise, you have guessed al-most per-fect-ly right.'

'Guessed right!' cried Felisata Mihalovna rapturously. 'Well, prince! Well, now you absolutely must tell us who the beautiful young lady was!'

'You must tell us!'

'Does she live in these parts?'

'Darling prince, do tell us! You must tell us, whatever happens!' they cried on all sides.

'*Mesdames, mesdames!*[165] . . . If you are so very in-sis-tent to know, I can only tell you one thing, that it was the most fas-ci-na-ting and, I may say, the most vir-tu-ous young lady I know,' mumbled the prince, melting like wax.

'Most fascinating and . . . someone living here! Who could it be?' the ladies kept asking, exchanging significant glances and winking at one another.

'Of course, the one who is considered the chief belle here,' said Natalya Dmitryevna, rubbing her huge red hands and looking with her cat-like eyes at Zina. All the others looked at Zina with her.

'Well, prince, if you have such dreams, why don't you get married in reality?' asked Felisata Mihalovna, with a significant look at the others.

'What a splendid match we would make for you!' another lady put in.

'Prince, darling! do get married!' piped a third.

'Get married, get married!' they cried on all sides. 'Why shouldn't you get married?'

'Oh, yes, why not get married,' the prince assented, completely confused by these outcries.

'Uncle!' cried Mozglyakov.

'Oh, yes, my dear, I un-der-stand. I meant to tell you, *mesdames*, that I am not able to get married and that, when I have spent a delightful evening with our fascinating hostess, I shall set off tomorrow to Father Misail at the monastery, and then I am going straight abroad so as to keep up with the progress of European enlightenment.'

Zina turned pale and looked at her mother with inexpressible misery. But Marya Alexandrovna had already made up her mind. Hitherto she had only been waiting, testing things, though she did realise that her project was ruined and that her enemies had circumvented her successfully. At last she grasped the whole position, she made up her mind at one blow to crush the many-headed hydra. She got up from her easy chair majestically and with resolute steps approached the table, scanning with haughty eyes her pigmy foes. There was the light of inspiration in that look. She determined to impress, to disconcert all these venomous scandalmongers, to squash Mozglyakov as though he were a beetle, and by one bold resolute stroke to recapture all her lost influence over the imbecile prince. Exceptional audacity was of course needed; but Marya Alexandrovna had no lack of audacity!

'*Mesdames*,' she began solemnly and with dignity (Marya Alexandrovna was particularly fond of a solemn manner), '*mesdames*, I have been listening for some time to your conversation, to your gay and witty jests, and I think it is time for me to put in my word. You know we have met together this evening – quite by chance (and I am so glad, so glad of it) . . . I should never have brought myself of my own accord to announce to you an important family secret and to publish it abroad sooner than the most ordinary feeling of decorum would dictate. Especially I must beg the forgiveness of my dear guest; but I fancied that he himself, by indirect hints at the very circumstance, gives me to understand that a formal and ceremonious announcement of our family secret will not be disagreeable, that, in fact, he desires this announcement . . . Is it not so, prince, I am not mistaken?'

'Oh, yes, you are not mistaken . . . and I am delighted!' said the prince, without the faintest idea of what she was talking about.

For the sake of greater effect, Marya Alexandrovna stopped to take breath and looked round at the whole company. All the visitors were listening to her words with spiteful and uneasy curiosity. Mozglyakov started. Zina flushed crimson and got up from her chair. Afanasy Matveyitch, in anticipation of something extraordinary, blew his nose to be ready for anything.

'Yes, *mesdames*, I am ready joyfully to confide to you my family secret. After dinner today the prince, captivated by the beauty and . . . virtues of my daughter, did her the honour of offering her his hand. Prince!' she concluded in a voice quivering with tears and emotion, 'dear prince, you must not, you cannot by angry with me for my indiscretion! Nothing but my great joy as a mother could have torn from my heart this precious secret before the fitting time, and . . . what mother could blame me in this case.'

I cannot find words to describe the effect produced by Marya Alexandrovna's unexpected outburst. Everyone seemed as though petrified with amazement. The treacherous visitors, who had thought they would frighten Marya Alexandrovna by their knowledge of her secret, had expected to crush her with the premature disclosure of that secret, who had expected to torment her, at first simply by allusions, were dumbfounded by such audacious candour. Such fearless audacity was a sure sign of power. 'Then was the prince really going to marry Zina of his own free will? Then had they not allured him, made him drunk, deceived him? Then he was not being forced into marriage in an underhand, dishonest way? Then Marya Alexandrovna was not afraid of anybody? Then it would be impossible to prevent the marriage since the prince was not being forced into it?' For a moment there was a sound of whispering which turned at once into shrill cries of delight. Natalya Dmitryevna was the first to embrace Marya Alexandrovna; Anna Nikolaevna followed her example, and after her Felisata Mihalovna. They all jumped up from their seats, they were all thrown into confusion, some of the ladies were pale from spite. They began to congratulate the embarrassed Zina; they even fastened on Afanasy Matveyitch. Marya Alexandrovna held out her arms in a picturesque attitude, and almost by force enfolded her daughter in her embrace. The prince alone looked on at the scene with strange surprise, though he went on smiling as before. The scene pleased him in a way, however. At the sight of the mother embracing the daughter, he took out his handkerchief and wiped his eyes in which there gleamed a tear. Of course, people rushed to congratulate him too.

'We congratulate you, prince! We congratulate you!' the ladies cried on all sides.

'So you are going to get married?'

'So you are really going to get married?'

'Darling prince, so you are going to get married?'

'Oh, yes; oh, yes,' answered the prince, extremely delighted with their raptures and their congratulations. 'And I must say, that nothing gives me more pleasure than your kind sympathy, which I shall ne-ever forget, ne-ever forget. *Charmant! charmant!* You've brought tears into my eyes.'

'Kiss me, prince,' Felisata Mihalovna cried, louder than all the rest.

'And I must say,' the prince went on, interrupted on all sides, 'I am most of all surprised that Marya I-van-ov-na, our honoured hostess, has guessed my dream with such ex-tra-or-di-nary insight. It is as though she had dreamed it instead of me. Ex-tra-or-di-nary insight! Ex-tra-or-di-nary insight!'

'Oh, prince, the dream again?'

'Come, confess, prince, confess!' they all cried, surrounding him.

'Yes, prince, there is no need for concealment, the time has come to reveal our secret!' Marya Alexandrovna said sternly and resolutely. 'I understand your subtle allegory, the enchanting delicacy with which you tried to hint to me your desire to make public your engagement. Yes, *mesdames*, it is true: this afternoon the prince went down on his knees to my daughter, and not in a dream but in reality, and made her a formal offer.'

'Exactly as though it were real and actually with the very same circumstances,' repeated the prince. '*Mademoiselle*,' he said, turning with marked courtesy to Zina, who had not yet recovered from her amazement, '*mademoiselle!* I swear that I would never have made so bold as to pronounce your name if others had not ut-tered it before me. It was a fascinating dream, a fa-sci-na-ting dream, and I am doubly happy that I am now permitted to tell it to you. *Charmant, charmant!* . . .'

'But upon my word how is this? He is still talking about a dream,' whispered Anna Nikolaevna to Marya Alexandrovna, who was somewhat fluttered and had turned a little pale.

Alas! There was an ache and a tremor in Marya Alexandrovna's heart already, apart from those warning words.

'How is this?' whispered the ladies, looking at one another.

'Why, prince,' began Marya Alexandrovna, with a wry and sickly smile. 'I protest, you surprise me! What is this strange idea about a dream? I confess I thought till now that you were jesting, but . . . if it is a joke, it is rather an inappropriate one . . . I should desire, I should wish to put it down to your absent-mindedness, but . . .'

'Perhaps it really is the result of his absent-mindedness,' hissed Natalya Dmitryevna.

'Oh, yes, perhaps it is absent-mindedness,' the prince assented, still not fully grasping what they were trying to get out of him. 'And only fancy, I must tell you an a-nec-dote. In Petersburg I was invited to a fu-ne-ral to some people, *maison bourgeoise, mais honnête*,[166] and I muddled it up and thought it was a nameday party. The nameday party had been the week before. I got ready a bouquet of camelias for the lady whose nameday it was. I go in and what do I see, a respectable, dignified man lying on the table, so that I was quite sur-prised. I simply did not know what to do with myself and the bou-quet.'

'Come, prince, this is not a time for anecdotes!' Marya Alexandrovna interrupted with vexation. 'Of course my daughter has no need to run after suitors, but this afternoon, beside that piano, you made her a proposal. I did not invite you to do so . . . I was, I may say, astounded . . . I was, of course, struck by one idea at the time, and I put it all off till you should wake. But I am a mother . . . she is my daughter . . . You spoke yourself just now of a dream, and I thought that you wished, under the guise of allegory, to tell us of your engagement. I know very well that you will be dissuaded . . . and I suspect who it is . . . but . . . explain yourself, prince, make haste and explain satisfactorily. You cannot jest like this with a respectable family.'

'Oh, no, one cannot jest like this with a respectable family,' the prince assented mechanically, though he was beginning to be a little uneasy.

'But that is no answer, prince, to my question. I beg you to give a definite answer; repeat at once, repeat before everyone that you did make my daughter an offer this afternoon.'

'Oh, yes, I am ready to repeat it, though I have already told the whole story, and Felisata Yakovlevna guessed my dream exactly.'

'It was not a dream, it was not a dream!' cried Marya Alexandrovna in exasperation. 'It was not a dream, it was reality, prince; reality – do you hear? – reality!'

'Reality!' cried the prince, getting up from his chair in his surprise. 'Well, my dear, it is just as you foretold upstairs!' he added, turning to Mozglyakov. 'But I assure you, honoured Marya Stepanovna, that you are in error! I am quite persuaded that I only dreamed it.'

'Lord have mercy upon us!' cried Marya Alexandrovna.

'Don't upset yourself, Marya Alexandrovna,' Natalya Dmitryevna put in. 'Perhaps the prince has forgotten . . . He will remember.'

'I wonder at you, Natalya Dmitryevna,' retorted Marya Alexandrovna indignantly. 'Can such things be forgotten? Can one forget it? Upon my word, prince, are you laughing at us? Or you are, perhaps, playing the part of a profligate beau of the days of the Regency depicted by

Dumas.[167] Some Faire-la-Cour[168] or Lauzun? But apart from that not being in keeping with your years, I assure you that you will not succeed in it. My daughter is not a vicomtesse. Here, this afternoon, on this spot she sang to you, and carried away by her singing you dropped on your knees and made her an offer! Can I be dreaming? Can I be sleeping? Speak, prince: am I awake or sleeping?'

'Oh, yes . . . or rather, perhaps, no . . . ' answered the bewildered prince. 'I mean that I believe I am not dreaming now. You see, I was asleep this afternoon, and so I had a dream that in my sleep . . . '

'Tfoo, my goodness, what does it mean? Not asleep – asleep, dreaming – not dreaming! Why, goodness knows what it means. Are you raving, prince?'

'Oh, yes, goodness knows . . . though I believe I'm utterly at sea now,' said the prince, turning uneasy glances around him.

'But how could you have dreamed it?' Marya Alexandrovna insisted in distress, 'when I tell you your own dream in such detail, though you had not yet told anyone of us about it!'

'But perhaps the prince did tell somebody,' said Natalya Dmitryevna.

'Oh, yes, perhaps I did tell somebody,' the prince repeated, utterly bewildered.

'Here's a farce,' whispered Felisata Mihalovna to her neighbour.

'Good heavens, this is past all endurance!' cried Marya Alexandrovna, wringing her hands in a frenzy. 'She sang to you, she sang a ballad! Did you dream that too?'

'Oh, yes; yes, indeed, I fancy she did sing a ballad,' the prince muttered meditatively.

And his face lightened up at some sudden recollection.

'My dear,' he cried, addressing Mozglyakov, 'I forgot to tell you just now that there really was a ballad, and there were continually castles in that ballad, so that it seemed as if there were a great many castles; and then there was a troubadour! Oh, yes, I remember it all . . . So that I even shed tears . . . And now I am puzzled, it seems as if that really did happen and was not a dream.'

'I must say, uncle,' answered Mozglyakov, speaking as calmly as he could, though his voice quivered from some emotion, 'I must say it seems to me that it is very easy to account for that and make it fit in. I believe you really did listen to singing. Zinaida Afanasyevna sings beautifully. After dinner you were brought in here and Zinaida Afanasyevna sang the ballad to you. I was not there at the time, but you were probably touched by its recalling old days; perhaps remembering that very vicomtesse with whom you used once to sing ballads, and about whom you told us this morning. And then afterwards when you went to bed, in consequence of your pleasant impressions you dreamed that you were in love and had made an offer.'

Marya Alexandrovna was positively petrified by this audacity.

'Ah, my dear, that is just as it really was!' cried the prince, delighted. 'It was just in consequence of those pleasant impressions. I certainly remember the ballad being sung to me, and it was because of that, that in my dream I wanted to get married. And it is true about the vicomtesse too . . . Oh, how clever of you, my dear, to see it all! Well, now I am quite convinced that I dreamed all that! Marya Vassilyevna! I assure you that you are mistaken! It was a dream. Otherwise I should not be playing with your estimable feelings . . . '

'Ah, now I see clearly who has been at work in this!' cried Marya Alexandrovna, beside herself with fury, addressing Mozglyakov. 'It is you, you sir; you dishonourable man, it is all your doing. You have muddled this unhappy imbecile, because you were refused! But you shall pay for this insult, you blackguard! You shall pay for it. You shall pay for it!'

'Marya Alexandrovna!' cried Mozglyakov, turning as red as a crab. 'Your words are so . . . I really don't know what to say of your words . . . No well-bred lady would allow herself . . . I am defending my kinsman, anyway. You must admit that to ensnare him like this . . . '

'Oh, yes, to ensnare like this . . . ' the prince chimed in, trying to hide behind Mozglyakov.

'Afanasy Matveyitch!' shirieked Marya Alexandrovna, in an unnatural voice. 'Don't you hear how we are being outraged and dishonoured? Or have you lost all sense of your duties? Are you not the head of your family, but a repulsive wooden post? Why do you keep blinking? Any other husband would long ago have washed out such an insult to his family in blood! . . . '

'Wife,' Afanasy Matveyitch began with dignity, proud that he was needed at last. 'Wife! Didn't you perhaps dream it all, and afterwards when you woke up, you muddled it all to suit yourself! . . . '

But Afanasy Matveyitch was not destined to give full expression to his witty surmise. To that point the visitors had restrained themselves and had treacherously assumed an air of demure dignity. But at this point a loud burst of laughter that could not be restrained resounded through the room. Marya Alexandrovna, forgetting all propriety, rushed at her husband, probably with the intention of immediately scratching his eyes out. But she was restrained by force. Natalya Dmitryevna took advantage of the occasion to add just one drop more of venom.

'Oh, Marya Alexandrovna, perhaps that is just how it was, and you are upsetting yourself,' she said, in a most honeyed voice.

'What was? How was it?' cried Marya Alexandrovna, not yet fully understanding it.

'Oh, Marya Alexandrovna, you know it sometimes does happen.'

'What happens? Do you want to drive me crazy?'

'Perhaps you really did dream it?'

'Dream it, I? Dream it! And you dare to tell me that to my face?'

'Well, perhaps that is really how it was,' responded Felisata Mihalovna.

'Oh, yes, perhaps that is how it really was,' the prince, too, muttered.

'He too, he too! Lord have mercy on us!' cried Marya Alexandrovna, clasping her hands.

'How you do upset yourself, Marya Alexandrovna! Remember that dreams are sent us from on high. If it is God's will, there is none can oppose Him, and we are all in His hands. It's no use being angry about it.'

'Oh, yes, it's no good being angry about it,' the prince chimed in.

'Do you take me for a lunatic?' Marya Alexandrovna articulated faintly, gasping from wrath. This was beyond human endurance. She hastily sought a chair and sank into a swoon. A hubbub followed.

'It was to do the correct thing that she fainted,' Natalya Dmitryevna whispered to Anna Nikolaevna.

But at that instant, at the moment when the general bewilderment was greatest and the position was at its tensest, a person who had hitherto remained silent suddenly stepped forward – and immediately the whole character of the scene was changed . . . .

14

Zinaida Afanasyevna was, speaking generally, of an extremely romantic disposition. I don't know whether this was, as Marya Alexandrovna maintained, due to too much reading of 'that fool Shakespeare' with 'her wretched little schoolmaster'. But never in the course of her life at Mordasov had Zina permitted herself such an extraordinary romantic or rather heroic action as the one which we are just about to describe.

Pale, with a look of determination in her eyes, but almost shaking with excitement, wonderfully lovely in her indignation, she stepped forward. Scanning the whole company with a slow, challenging look in the midst of the sudden silence, she turned to her mother, who at her first movement had promptly recovered from her swoon and opened her eyes.

'Mamma,' said Zina, 'why keep up deception? Why defile ourselves further by lying? It has all been made so foul that it is not worth taking degrading pains to cover up that foulness!'

'Zina, Zina! What is the matter with you? Think what you are doing!' cried Marya Alexandrovna, leaping up from her chair.

'I told you, I told you beforehand, mamma, that I could not bear all this disgrace,' Zina went on. 'Is it necessary to degrade oneself even more, to defile oneself still further? But do you know, mamma, that I take it all upon myself, for I am more to blame than anyone. I, I by consenting, set this vile . . . intrigue . . . going! You are a mother; you love me, you meant to secure my happiness, in your own way, according to your own ideas. You may be forgiven; but I, I, never.'

'Zina, surely you don't mean to speak? . . . Oh, my God! I foresaw that that dagger would stab me to the heart!'

'Yes, mamma, I shall speak out. I am disgraced, you . . . we are all disgraced! . . .'

'You are exaggerating, Zina! You are not yourself and don't understand what you are saying! And what is the use of telling it? There is no sense in it . . . The disgrace is not ours. I will show at once that the disgrace is not ours.'

'No, mamma,' cried Zina, with an angry quiver in her voice, 'I will not remain silent longer before these people, whose opinion I despise and who have come to jeer at us. I will not endure insult from them; not one of them has the right to throw dirt at me. They are all ready any minute to do thirty times worse than you or I! Dare they, can they be our judges? . . .'

'That's a nice thing! Do you hear what she says? What does it mean? It's insulting us!' was heard on all sides.

'The young lady simply does not know what she is saying,' said Natalya Dmitryevna.

We may observe in parenthesis that Natalya Dmitryevna's remark was a true one. If Zina did not consider those ladies worthy to judge her, what was the object of rushing into such publicity, into such confessions before them? Zinaida Afanasyevna was, in fact, extremely hasty, such was the opinion of the best heads in Mordasov later on. Everything could have been set right, everything could have been smoothed over. It is true that Marya Alexandrovna, too, had damaged their position that evening by her hastiness and presumption. They need only have derided the imbecile old gentleman and have sent him about his business. But as though of design, Zina, contrary to all good sense and Mordasov prudence, addressed herself to the prince.

'Prince,' she said to the old man, who was so impressed by her at that moment that he got up from his chair as a sign of respect. 'Prince, forgive me, forgive us. We deceived you! We drew you on . . . '

'Oh, will you be silent, unhappy girl!' Marya Alexandrovna cried in a frenzy.

'Madam, madam! *Ma charmante enfant* . . . ' muttered the prince, much impressed.

But Zina's proud, impulsive and extremely idealistic character carried her at that instant far away from every propriety demanded by the reality of the position. She even forgot her mother, who was writhing in agony at her confession.

'Yes, we both deceived you, prince; mamma, by determining to make you marry me, and I, by consenting to it. You were given too much wine, I consented to sing and play a part before you. We, as Pavel Alexandrovitch has expressed it, have tricked you when you were weak and helpless, tricked you for the sake of your fortune, for the sake of your rank. All this was horribly base and I repent of it. But I swear to you, prince, that it was from no base impulse that I brought myself to that base act. I meant . . . but what am I saying, it is twice as base to justify oneself for a thing like that! But I assure you, prince, that if I had taken anything from you, I would have paid for it by being your play-thing, your handmaid, your dancing girl, your slave . . . I had vowed it, and would have kept my vow!'

A lump in her throat prevented her from going on. All the visitors seemed petrified and listened with their eyes starting out of their heads. Zina's strange and, to them, utterly unintelligible outbreak completely perplexed them; only the prince was touched to tears, though he did not understand half of what Zina was saying.

'But I will marry you, *ma belle enfant*, if you wi-ish it so much,' he muttered, 'and it will be a gre-at honour to me! Only I assure you that it real-ly was like a dream . . . Why, I dream all sorts of things. Why are you so tro-oubled? I really don't understand it at all, *mon ami*,' he went on, addressing Mozglyakov. 'You explain to me, please . . . '

'And you, Pavel Alexandrovitch,' said Zina, turning too to Mozglyakov, 'you, on whom I once brought myself to look as my future husband, you who have now so cruelly revenged yourself on me, can you really have joined with these people to torture me and cover me with ignominy? And you told me you loved me! But it is not for me to preach to you, I am more to blame than you . . . I have injured you, for I really did lure you on with promises, and my statements were lies and a tissue of falsehoods! I never loved you, and if I had brought myself to marry you it would simply have been to get away from here, from this accursed town, and to escape from all this corruption . . . But, I swear to you, that if I had married you I would have made you a good and faithful wife . . . You have cruelly revenged yourself on me, and if that flatters your pride . . . '

'Zinaida Afanasyevna!' cried Mozglyakov.

'If you still harbour a feeling of hatred for me . . . '

'Zainaida Afanasyevna! ! !'

'If you ever,' said Zina, stifling her tears, 'if you ever did love me! ! !'

'Zinaida Afanasyevna! ! !'

'Zina, Zina, my daughter,' wailed Marya Alexandrovna.

'I am a scoundrel, Zinaida Afanasyevna. I am a scoundrel and nothing else,' declared Mozglyakov, and general excitement followed. Cries of surprise and indignation were raised, but Mozglyakov stood as though rooted to the spot, incapable of thought or speech.

For weak and shallow characters accustomed to habitual subordination who have dared at last to be moved to wrath and to protest, in short, to be resolute and consistent, there is always a line – a limit – to their resolution and consistency, which is soon reached. Their protest is apt at first to be most vigorous. Their energy even approaches frenzy. They fling themselves against obstacles as though with closed eyes, and always take upon themselves burdens beyond their strength. But reaching a certain point, the frenzied man, as though frightened at himself, stops short, dumbfounded with the awful question, 'What is this that I have done?' Then at once he grows limp, whimpers, asks for explanations, drops on his knees, begs forgiveness, implores that all shall be as before, only quickly, as quickly as possible . . . This is almost exactly what happened now with Mozglyakov. After having been beside himself with fury, having invited trouble which now he ascribed entirely to himself alone, having satisfied his vanity and indignation and beginning to hate himself for it, he stopped short, conscience-stricken, before Zina's unexpected outbreak. Her last words crushed him completely. To rush from one extreme to another was the work of a minute.

'I am an ass, Zinaida Afanasyevna!' he cried, in a rush of frantic penitence. 'No! What's an ass? An ass would be nothing. I am incomparably worse than an ass! But I will show you, Zinaida Afanasyevna, I will show you that even an ass may be an honourable man! . . . Uncle! I deceived you. It was I, I deceived you! You were not asleep; you really did make an offer, and I, I, like a scoundrel, out of revenge for having been refused, persuaded you that it had all been a dream.'

'Wonderfully interesting things are coming out,' whispered Natalya Dmitryevna in Anna Nikolaevna's ear.

'My dear,' answered the prince, 'ple-ease calm yourself; you really frighten me with your shouting. I assure you that you are mis-ta-ken . . . I am ready to be married by all means if it is necessary; but, you know, you assured me yourself that it was only a dream . . . '

'Oh, how can I convince you! Tell me how to convince him! Uncle, uncle! You know it's an important matter, most important, affecting family honour. Reflect! Consider!'

'My dear, certainly I will re-flect. Stay, let me recall it all in order. At first I dreamed of my coachman, Fe-o-fi-il . . . '

'Oh! it is not a question of Feofil now, uncle.'

'Oh, well, I suppose it is not a question of him now. Then there was Na-po-le-on, and then we seemed to be drinking tea and a lady came and ate up all the sugar.'

'But, uncle' – Mozglyakov bawled in the confusion of his mind – 'why, it was Marya Alexandrovna herself told us that this morning about Natalya Dmitryevna! Why, I was here and heard it myself! I was hiding and looking at you through the keyhole . . . '

'What, Marya Alexandrovna,' Natalya Dmitryevna broke in; 'so you told the prince too that I stole the sugar out of your sugar-basin! So I come to steal your sugar, do I?'

'Get away with you!' cried Marya Alexandrovna, reduced to despair.

'No, I won't go away, Marya Alexandrovna. Don't dare to speak to me like that! . . . So I stole your sugar, did I? I have been hearing for a long time that you tell such nasty stories about me. Sofya Petrovna gave me an exact account of it . . . So I steal your sugar, do I?'

'But, *mesdames*,' cried the prince, 'it was only a dream, you know. Why, I dream all sorts of things . . . '

'Cursed tub,' Marya Alexandrovna muttered in an undertone.

'So I am a tub, am I!' shrieked Natalya Dmitryevna. 'And who are you? I have known for ever so long that you called me a tub. I have got a husband, anyway, while you've got a fool . . . '

'Oh, yes, I remember there was a tub too,' muttered the prince, unconsciously recalling his conversation with Marya Alexandrovna that morning.

'So you're insulting a lady too? How dare you, prince, insult a lady? If I am a tub, you have no legs . . . '

'Who? I have no legs?'

'Yes, indeed, no legs and no teeth either, so that's what you are.'

'Yes, and only one eye, too,' shouted Marya Alexandrovna.

'You have stays instead of ribs,' said Natalya Dmitryevna.

'Your face is worked by springs.'

'You've no hair! . . . '

'And the idiot has a false moustache,' cried Marya Alexandrovna.

'Do at least leave me my nose, Marya Stepanovna,' cried the prince, overwhelmed by such sudden candour. 'My dear! Was it you gave me away? Did you tell them that my hair was false?'

'Uncle!'

'No, my dear, I really can't stay here any longer. Take me away . . . *quelle société*! What have you brought me to, my goodness?'

'Imbecile, scoundrel!' cried Marya Alexandrovna.

'Oh dear!' said the poor prince. 'I've forgotten for the minute why I came here, but I shall re-mem-ber di-rect-ly. Take me away, dear boy, or they will te-ar me to pieces! Mean-while . . . I must at once no-ote down a new idea . . . '

'Let us go, uncle, it is not too late; I will take you at once to a hotel and I will go with you . . . '

'Oh, yes, to a ho-tel. *Adieu, ma charmante enfant* . . . You alone . . . you alone . . . are good and vir-tu-ous. You are an hon-ou-rable girl. Come along, my dear boy. Oh, dear; oh, dear!'

But I will not describe the conclusion of the unpleasant scene which took place on the prince's departure. The visitors dispersed with shrill scoldings and abuse. Marya Alexandrovna was left at last alone in the midst of the ruins of her former glory. Alas! Power, glory, consequence – all had vanished in that one evening. Marya Alexandrovna realised that she could never rise to her former height. Her despotic rule over local society which had lasted long years was annihilated for ever. What was left her now? To be philosophical? But she was not philosophical. She was in a paroxysm of rage all night. Zina was dishonoured, there would be endless gossip and scandal! Horrors!

As a faithful historian I ought to mention that from this frenzy the chief sufferer was Afanasy Matveyitch, who took refuge at last in the lumber-room, and stayed there freezing till morning; at last the morning came, but it brought nothing good. Misfortunes never come singly.

15

If destiny once begins to pursue someone with misfortune there is no end to its blows. That has been noticed long ago. Was the shame and disgrace of the previous day not enough for Marya Alexandrovna? No! Fate was preparing something more, something better.

Before ten o'clock in the morning a strange and almost incredible rumour was suddenly all over the town, welcomed by all with the most spiteful and venomous glee – as we generally do welcome any extra-ordinary scandal connected with any of our neighbours. 'To be so lost to all shame and conscience!' people cried on all sides; 'to demean herself to such a degree, to disregard all decorum, so utterly to cast off all restraint!' and so on, and so on.

This was what had happened, however. Early in the morning, a little before six o'clock, a poor and pitiful-looking old woman in tears and despair ran up to Marya Alexandrovna's house and besought the maid-servant to wake the young lady immediately, only the young lady, and in secret, so that Marya Alexandrovna should in no way hear of it: Zina, pale and shattered, ran out to the old woman at once. The latter fell at her feet, kissed them, bathed them with her tears, and besought her to come with her to her sick Vasya, who had been so bad, so bad all night that he might perhaps not last through the day. The old woman, sobbing, told Zina that Vasya himself begged her to go for a last farewell before he died, implored her by all the holy angels, by all that had been in the past, and said that if she did not come he would die in despair. Zina at once resolved to go, though yielding to this entreaty would obviously confirm all the old malicious gossip about the intercepted letter, about her scandalous behaviour, and so on. Saying nothing to her mother, she threw on a cloak and at once hastened with the old woman right across the town to one of the poorest quarters of Mordasov, to the most out-of-the-way street, in which there was a little dilapidated house, with little slits for windows, fallen aslant, as it were sunken into the ground and almost buried under huge drifts of snow.

In this little house, in a little, low-pitched, musty room in which the huge stove filled up half the floor space, a young man was lying covered with an old greatcoat, on an unpainted wooden bed with a mattress as thin as a pancake. His face was pale and exhausted, his eyes glittered with a feverish glow, his hands were thin and dry as sticks, his breathing was laboured and husky. It could be seen that he had once been handsome; but disease had disfigured the delicate features of his hand-some face, which was terrible and pitiful to look at, as the face of a consumptive, or rather of a dying man, always is. His old mother, who had been for a whole year, almost to the last hour, hoping for her Vasya's recovery, saw at last that he was not long for this world. She stood over him now crushed with grief, but tearless, clasping her hands and gazing at him as though she could never look at him enough; and though she knew it, she could not grasp that in a few days her Vasya, the apple of her eye, would be covered by the frozen earth out yonder under the snowdrifts in the wretched graveyard. But Vasya was not looking at her at that moment. His whole face, wasted and marked by suffering, was full of bliss. He saw before him, at last, her of whom he had been dreaming, asleep and awake, for the last year and a half in the long, dreary nights of his sickness. He saw that she had forgiven him, coming to him like the angel of the Lord as he lay at death's door. She was pressing his hands, was weeping over him, smiling at him, looking at him again with her wonderful eyes and – and all the past, never to return, rose up in the dying man's soul. Life glowed again in his heart, and seemed at parting from him as though it would make the sufferer feel how hard it was to part.

'Zina,' he said, 'Zinotchka! Don't weep over me, don't mourn, don't grieve, don't remind me that I shall soon die. I shall look at you – yes, as I am looking at you now – I shall feel that our souls are together again, that you have forgiven me; I shall kiss your hands again as in the old days, and die, perhaps, without noticing death! You have grown thin, Zinotchka! My angel, with what kindness you are looking at me now. And do you remember how you used to laugh in the old days? Do you remember? . . . Ah, Zina, I will not ask your forgiveness, I do not want to remember what happened, because, Zina, because though you have forgiven me I shall never forgive myself. There have been long nights, Zina, long, sleepless nights, awful nights, and in those nights on this bed I thought for long hours over many things, and made up my mind long ago that it is better for me to die; yes, by God, it is better! . . . I am not fit for life, Zinotchka!'

Zina was weeping and mutely pressing his hands as though she would check his words.

'Why are you crying, my angel?' the sick man went on; 'because I am dying – only for that? But you know all the past has been dead and buried long ago! You are cleverer than I, you are more pure-hearted, and so you have known a long time that I am a bad man. Can you still love me? And what it has cost me to endure the thought that you know

I am a bad and shallow man. And how much pride there was in that, perhaps honourable pride . . . I don't know. Oh, my dear, all my life has been a dream. I was always dreaming, forever dreaming, but did not live. I was proud, I despised the herd; and in what was I superior to other people? I don't know. Purity of heart, generosity of feeling? But all that was dreaming, Zina, when we read Shakespeare together; but when it came to action I showed my purity and generosity of feeling.'

'Hush!' said Zina, 'hush! . . . All that is not so, it is useless . . . you are killing yourself.'

'Why do you stop me, Zina? I know you have forgiven me, and perhaps you forgave me long ago; but you judged me – and understood the sort of man I am; that is what torments me. I am unworthy of your love, Zina! You were honest and you went to your mother and said that you would marry me and no one else, and you would have kept your word because with you words were not apart from action. While I, I! when it came to action . . . Do you know, Zina, I did not understand then what you would be sacrificing in marrying me! did not even understand that marrying me you might die of starvation. I never even thought of it; I only thought that you would marry me, a great poet (a future one, that is). I would not understand the reasons you brought forward begging me to put off our marriage; I tormented you, bullied you, reproached you, despised you, and it came at last to my threatening you with that letter. I was not even a scoundrel at that moment. I was simply a worm! Oh, how you must have despised me! Yes, it is well that I am dying! It is well that you did not marry me! I should have understood nothing of your sacrifice, I should have tormented you, I should have worried you over our poverty; the years would have passed, and who knows! – Perhaps I should have grown to hate you, as a hindrance in my life. Now it is better. Now at least my bitter tears have purified my heart. Ah, Zinotchka! love me a little as you used to love me once . . . in this last hour at least . . . I know, of course, that I do not deserve your love, but . . . but . . . Oh, my angel!'

Several times in the course of this speech, Zina, sobbing herself, tried to stop him. But he did not listen to her; he was tormented by a longing to express himself, and he went on speaking, though with difficulty, gasping in a hoarse and choking voice.

'If you hadn't met me, if you hadn't loved me, you would have lived!' said Zina. 'Oh, why, why did we meet!'

'No, my darling, do not reproach yourself with my dying,' the sick man went on. 'I am the only person to blame for everything! How much vanity there was in it! Romantic foolishness! Have they told you my foolish history, Zina? You see, two years ago there was a convict here, a criminal and murderer; but when it came to punishment, he turned out to be the most cowardly creature. Knowing that they would not flog a sick man, he got hold of some spirit, put tobacco in it and drank it. He was attacked with such violent sickness, vomiting blood, and it lasted so long, that it affected his lungs. He was moved to the hospital, and within a few months he died of rapid consumption. Well, my angel, I thought of that convict that very day . . . you know, after that note . . . and made up my mind to destroy myself in the same way; but why do you think I chose consumption? Why didn't I strangle myself or drown myself? Was I afraid of immediate death? Perhaps it was that; but I keep fancying, Zinotchka, that even in this I could not lay aside romantic foolishness! Anyway, I had in my mind at the time the thought: how picturesque it would be, here I should lie in bed dying of consumption, while you would be distressed and unhappy at having sent me into consumption; you would come to me confessing yourself guilty, would fall on your knees before me . . . I should forgive you, should die in your arms. It was silly, Zinotchka, silly, wasn't it?'

'Don't speak of it!' said Zina; 'don't say that! You are not like that. Let us rather remember something else, that was good and happy in our past!'

'It is bitter to me, my darling, that is why I talk of it. I haven't seen you for a year and a half. I should like to open my heart to you now. You know ever since then I have been utterly alone, and I think there has not been one moment when I have not thought of you, my precious one. And do you know what, Zinotchka? How I longed to do something, to deserve that you should change your opinion of me! Until lately I did not believe that I should die. You know I was not laid up at first, for a long time I was walking about after my lungs were affected. And what absurd projects I had! I dreamed, for instance, of becoming all at once a great poet and publishing in the *Notes of the Fatherland* a poem unlike anything in the world. I thought of pouring into it all my feelings, all my soul, so that wherever you might be, I should be with you, always reminding you of me with my poem, and the very best of my dreams was that you would think at last and say, "No! he is not such a bad man as I thought!" It was stupid, Zinotchka, wasn't it?'

'No, no, Vasya, no!' said Zina.

She fell on his breast and kissed his hands.

'And how jealous I was of you all this time! I believe I should have died if I had heard of your marriage. I sent, I kept watch on you, I spied . . . She was constantly going' (and he nodded towards his mother). 'You did not love Mozglyakov, did you, Zinotchka? Oh, my angel! Will you remember me when I am dead? I know you will remember; but years will pass, the heart will grow harder, you will grow cold, there will be winter in your soul, and you will forget me, Zinotchka! . . . '

'No, no, never! I shall not marry . . . You are my first . . . and mine for ever . . . '

'Everything dies, Zinotchka, even memories . . . And our noble feelings die. Common sense takes their place. What is the use of repining? Make use of life, Zina. Live long, live happily. Love someone else, if you can love; there is no loving the dead! Only think of me from time to time; do not remember what was bad, forgive the bad; but you know there was good, too, in our love, Zinotchka. Oh, golden days that never can return! . . . Listen, my angel, I always loved the evening hour of sunset. Think of me sometimes at that hour! Oh, no, no! Why die? Oh, how I long to come back to life again! Remember, my dear, remember, remember that time. It was spring then, the sun was shining so brightly, the flowers were in blossom, it was like a holiday all round us; and now look, look!'

And with a wasted hand the poor fellow pointed to the dingy, frozen window. Then he clutched Zina's hands, pressed them to his eyes and sobbed bitterly, bitterly. His sobs almost lacerated his racked breast.

And the whole day he was sobbing in anguish and misery. Zina did her best to comfort him, but she was half dead with misery. She told him that she would never forget him, and that she would never love another man as she loved him. He believed her, smiled, kissed her hands, but memories of the past only kindled fresh suffering in his soul. So passed the whole day. Meanwhile Marya Alexandrovna in alarm sent a dozen times to Zina entreating her to return home and not to ruin herself completely in public opinion. At last, when it was getting dark, almost beside herself with horror, she made up her mind to go to Zina herself. Calling her daughter out into the other room, she besought her almost on her knees 'to turn aside this last worst dagger from her heart'. Zina went out to her feeling ill, her head was burning. She listened and did not understand her mother. Marya Alexandrovna went away at last in despair, for Zina was determined to stay the night in the dying man's house. She did not leave his bedside all night. But the sick-man grew worse and worse. The day came at last, but there was no hope that the sufferer would live through it. The old mother seemed frantic, she walked about as though she could not take it in, giving her son medicines which he would not take. His agony lasted a long time. He could not speak, and only incoherent, husky sounds broke from his throat. Up to the very last moment he gazed at Zina, still sought her with his eyes, and when the light in his eyes was beginning to grow dim, he still, with a straying, uncertain hand, felt for her hand to press it in his. Meanwhile the short winter day was passing. And when the last farewell gleam of sunshine gilded the solitary frozen window of the little room, the soul of the sufferer parted from his exhausted body and floated after that last ray. The old mother, seeing her adored boy lying dead before her, clasped her hands, uttered a shriek, and threw herself upon his breast.

'It is you, you snake in the grass, have been his ruin! You accursed girl, with your ill deeds have parted us and been his undoing.'

But Zina did not hear her. She stood over the dead man as though she had lost all comprehension. At last she bent down, made the sign of the cross over him, kissed him, and walked mechanically out of the room. Her eyes were burning, her head was going round. Her agonising experiences, her two nights without sleep, almost deprived her of reason. She vaguely felt that all her past had been, as it were, torn out of her heart, and that a new life was beginning, gloomy and menacing. But before she had gone ten paces, Mozglyakov seemed to spring out of the earth before her; he seemed to be purposely lying in wait for her at that spot.

'Zinaida Afanasyevna,' he began in a timorous whisper, looking nervously around him, for it was hardly dark yet, 'Zinaida Afanasyevna, of course I am an ass. That is, if you like I am not an ass now, for you see, anyway, I have behaved honourably. But still I am sorry for having been an ass . . . I am afraid I am muddled, Zinaida Afanasyevna, but that is due to all sorts of reasons . . . '

Zina gazed at him almost unconsciously, and went on her way in silence. As it was difficult for two to go abreast on the raised wooden pavement, and as Zina did not move aside, Pavel Alexandrovitch jumped off the pavement and ran by her side below, peeping up continually into her face.

'Zinaida Afanasyevna,' he went on, 'I have reflected, and if you are willing, I am prepared to renew my offer. I am ready to forget everything, Zinaida Afanasvevna, the whole disgrace, and to forgive it, but only on one condition: so long as we are here – let it all be kept secret. You will go away from here as soon as possible; I shall follow you secretly; we will be married in some remote place so that no one shall see it, and then at once we will go to Petersburg, travelling with posting horses, so you should only take a little portmanteau. Eh? Do you agree,

Zinaida Afanasyevna? Tell me quickly! I can't wait about, we might be seen together.'

Zina made no answer, she only looked at Mozglyakov; but the look was such that he understood at once, took off his hat, bowed himself off, and vanished at the first turning into a side street.

'What is the meaning of it?' he thought. 'That evening, the day before yesterday, she was all softness and sentiment, and took all the blame on herself? She changes from day to day, it seems!'

And meanwhile one event was following another in Mordasov. A tragic circumstance had occurred. After being driven to the hotel by Mozglyakov, the old prince was taken ill the same night, and dangerously ill. The people of Mordasov heard the news next morning. Kalist Stanislavitch scarcely left his bedside. In the evening there was a consultation of all the Mordasov doctors. The invitations to request their attendance were written in Latin. But in spite of the Latin the prince had already lost consciousness, was delirious, kept asking Kalist Stanislavitch to sing him a ballad, kept talking about wigs; at times he seemed frightened and cried out. The doctors decided that the hospitality of Mordasov had set up inflammation of the stomach, which had somehow passed (probably on the journey) to the brain. They admitted the possibility also of some moral shock. They summed up in conclusion by saying that the prince had been for a long time past predisposed to death, and so would certainly die. On the last point they were not mistaken, for three days later the poor old man died at the hotel. This was a great shock to the people of Mordasov. No one had expected the affair to take such a serious turn. They flocked in crowds to the hotel where the dead body was lying; they discussed and debated, nodded their heads, and ended by severely censuring 'the luckless prince's murderers', understanding, of course, by that term, Marya Alexandrovna and her daughter. Everyone felt that this affair from its extremely scandalous character might easily gain an unpleasant publicity, would perhaps reach faraway parts, and all sorts of possibilities were talked over and discussed. All this time Mozglyakov was in the greatest fuss and flurry, and at last his head was in a perfect whirl. He was in that state of mind when he saw Zina. His position was certainly difficult. He had brought the prince into the town, he had moved him to the hotel, and now he did not know what to do with the dead man, where to bury him, whom to inform of his death! Should the body be taken to Duhanovo? Besides, he considered himself a nephew. He trembled with apprehension that he might be blamed for the venerable old man's death. 'Very likely there will be talk of it in Petersburg in the

best society!' he thought with a shudder. He could not extract advice of
any sort from his Mordasov acquaintances; they were all overcome
by sudden consternation, they rushed away from the dead body and
left Mozglyakov in gloomy isolation. But all at once the scene was
completely transformed. Early the next morning a new visitor arrived
in the town. Of this visitor all Mordasov instantly began talking, but
they spoke of him mysteriously in a whisper, staring at him out of every
chink and every window when he drove along the High Street on his
way to the governor's. Even Pyotr Mihalovitch seemed overawed, and
did not know what tone to take with his visitor. The visitor was no
other than the renowned Prince Shtchepetilov, a relative of the old
prince's, a man still youngish, about thirty-five, with shoulder-knots
and the epaulets of a colonel. The sight of those shoulder-knots struck
awe into the hearts of all subordinate officials. The police-master,
for instance, completely lost his head – in a moral sense, of course;
physically he put in an appearance, though it was a very stiff and
constrained appearance. It was at last learned that Prince Shtchepetilov
had come from Petersburg, calling on the way at Duhanovo. Finding
no one at Duhanovo, he flew off in pursuit of his uncle to Mordasov,
where he had been thunderstruck by the news of the old man's death
and the rumours concerning the circumstances attending it. Pyotr
Mihalovitch was actually a little nervous as he gave the necessary
explanations; and indeed everyone in Mordasov had a guilty air. Moreover, the visitor had such a stern, such a dissatisfied face, though
one would have thought it impossible to be dissatisfied with the fortune
he was inheriting. He at once took everything into his own hands;
Mozglyakov promptly and with shame effaced himself before the real,
not self-styled, nephew and vanished – no one knew where. It was
decided to move the dead body at once to the monastery, where a
requiem service was arranged. All the directions were given by the old
prince's kinsman briefly, drily and sternly, but with tact and decorum.
Next day, all the town assembled at the monastery to hear the requiem
service. An absurd rumour was current among the ladies that Marya
Alexandrovna would appear at the church in person, and on her knees
before the coffin would pray aloud for forgiveness, and that this all had
to be in accordance with the law. All this, of course, proved to be
nonsense, and Marya Alexandrovna did not come to the church. We
forgot to say that immediately after Zina's return to the house, her
mother decided that very evening to move to their country-house,
considering it impossible to remain longer in the town. There she
listened anxiously from her seclusion to the rumours from the town,

sent to find out about the new arrival, and was all the time in a state of fever. The road from the monastery to Duhavono passed less than three-quarters of a mile from her windows, and so Marya Alexandrovna could command a convenient view of the long procession which stretched from the monastery to Duhavono after the service. The coffin was upon a high hearse; and after it stretched a long string of carriages escorting it to the point where the road turns off to the town. And that gloomy hearse could be seen a long way farther, a black patch against the white snow-covered plain, moving slowly with becoming dignity. But Marya Alexandrovna could not look at it long, she walked away from the window.

A week later she moved to Moscow with her daughter and Afanasy Matveyitch, and a month later the news reached Mordasov that Marya Alexandrovna's country house as well as her town house were for sale. And so this *comme-il-faut* lady was lost to Mordasov for ever! Even this could not pass without ill-natured jibes. It was asserted, for instance, that Afanasy Matveyitch was being sold with their country place . . . One year passed and then a second, and Marya Alexandrovna was almost forgotten. Alas! that is how it always is in life! It was said, however, that she had bought another country place, and had moved to another provincial town, where, of course, she had already taken control of everything; that Zina was still unmarried, that Afanasy Matveyitch . . . However, it is hardly worth while to repeat these rumours, they were all very untrustworthy.

Three years have passed since I wrote the last line of the first part of my Mordasov chronicle, and who would have supposed that I should have occasion to open my manuscript again and to add another piece of news to my story? Well, here it is! I will begin with Pavel Alexandrovitch Mozglyakov. When he disappeared from Mordasov he went straight to Petersburg, where he successfully obtained the post in the service that had long been promised him. He soon forgot all the incidents at Mordasov, threw himself into the vortex of social life on Vassilyevsky Island and had a gay time of it, flirted, kept up with the times, fell in love, made an offer, swallowed another refusal, and before he had digested it, was led by idleness and the frivolity of his character to get for himself a post on an expedition which was being sent to one of the remotest borders of our boundless fatherland, for inspection or for some other object, I don't know for certain what. The party successfully traversed all the forests and deserts, and at last, after long peregrinations, arrived in the chief town of that remote region to call on the governor-general. He was a tall, lean, stern general, an old military man, who had been often wounded in battle, and had two stars and a white cross on his breast. He received the expedition with dignity and decorum, and invited all the officials to a ball which was to be given that very evening on the occasion of the nameday of the governor's wife. Pavel Alexandrovitch was very much pleased. Attiring himself in his Petersburg suit in which he intended to produce an effect, he walked with a free and easy air into the big reception hall, but he was at once somewhat taken aback at the sight of the numbers of thick and plaited epaulets and civilian uniforms with stars on their breasts. He had to pay his respects to the governor's wife, of whom he had heard that she was young and very good-looking. He went up to her, indeed, with aplomb, but was suddenly petrified with amazement. Before him stood Zina in a resplendent ball-dress and diamonds, looking proud and haughty. She completely failed to recognise Pavel Alexandrovitch. Her eyes glided over his face and at once turned to someone else. Astounded, Pavel Alexandrovitch moved to one side, and in the crowd came into collision with a timid young official who seemed to be frightened at finding himself at the governor's ball. Pavel Alexandrovitch immediately began to question him, and learned the most interesting facts. He learned that the governor had married two years ago, when he had visited Moscow, and that he had married a very wealthy young lady of a distinguished family; that the governor's wife 'was awfully good-looking, even one might say a beauty of the first order, but that she behaved extremely proudly, and only danced with generals'; that at the present ball there were in all nine generals, their own and visitors, including the actual civil councillors; 'that the governor's wife had a mamma who lived with her, and that this mamma belonged to the highest society, and was very clever', but that the mamma herself was completely dominated by the daughter, while the general himself simply doted on his spouse. Mozglyakov faltered a question about Afanasy Matveyitch, but they had no conception of his existence in 'the remote region'. Regaining his confidence a little, Mozglyakov walked about the rooms and soon saw Marya Alexandrovna, gorgeously attired, brandishing a costly fan and talking with animation to a personage of the fourth class. Round her clustered several ladies evidently anxious to propitiate her, and Marya Alexandrovna was apparently very gracious to all of them. Mozglyakov ventured to introduce himself. Marya Alexandrovna seemed a little startled, but almost instantly recovered herself. She graciously con-descended to recognise Pavel Alexandrovitch, questioned him about Petersburg acquaintances, asked him why he was not abroad. To

Mordasov she made no allusion whatever, as though such a place had no existence on earth. At last, after mentioning the name of a distinguished Petersburg prince and enquiring after his health, though Mozglyakov had no acquaintance whatever with the prince in question, she turned imperceptibly to a grand personage who was approaching, whose grey locks were fragrant with scent, and a minute later had completely forgotten Pavel Alexandrovitch, though he remained standing before her. With his hat in his hand and a sarcastic smile on his face, Mozglyakov returned to the great hall. Considering for some unknown reasons that he was insulted and even wounded, he resolved not to dance. A morose and absent expression and a biting Mephistophelean smile never left his face the whole evening. He leaned in a picturesque attitude against a column (as luck would have it, there were columns in the hall), and during the whole ball, that is for several hours together, he remained standing at the same place watching Zina. But alas! all his antics, all his striking attitudes, his disillusioned air and all the rest of it were thrown away. Zina completely failed to observe him. At last, enraged and with legs aching from long standing, hungry because as an unhappy lover he could not remain to supper, he returned to his lodgings quite worn out and feeling as though he had been beaten by someone. For a long while he did not go to bed, recalling the past which he had so long forgotten. Next morning new instructions arrived, and with relief Mozglyakov succeeded in being entrusted with the execution of them. He felt positively lighter-hearted as he drove out of the town. Snow was lying like a dazzling shroud over the boundless, deserted plain. In the distance on the very horizon stretched dark forests.

The mettlesome horses dashed along, flinging the powdery snow with their hoofs. The sledge bell tinkled, Pavel Alexandrovitch sank into thought, and then into dreams, and then into a sweet sleep. He woke at the third posting station, feeling fresh and well, with quite different thoughts in his mind.

An Unpleasant Predicament

THIS UNPLEASANT BUSINESS occurred at the epoch when the regeneration of our beloved fatherland[169] and the struggle of her valiant sons towards new hopes and destinies was beginning with irresistible force and with a touchingly näive impetuosity. One winter evening in that period, between eleven and twelveo'clock, three highly respectable gentlemen were sitting in a comfortable and even luxuriously furnished room in a handsome house of two storeys on the Petersburg Side,[170] and were engaged in a staid and edifying conversation on a very interesting subject. These three gentlemen were all of generals' rank. They were sitting round a little table, each in a soft and handsome armchair, and as they talked, they quietly and luxuriously sipped champagne. The bottle stood on the table on a silver stand with ice round it. The fact was that the host, a privy councillor called Stepan Nikiforovitch Nikiforov, an old bachelor of sixty-five, was celebrating his removal into a house he had just bought, and as it happened, also his birthday, which he had never kept before. The festivity, however, was not on a very grand scale; as we have seen already, there were only two guests, both of them former colleagues and former subordinates of Mr Nikiforov; that is, an actual civil councillor called Semyon Ivanovitch Shipulenko, and another actual civil councillor, Ivan Ilyitch Pralinsky. They had arrived to tea at nine o'clock, then had begun upon the wine, and knew that at exactly half-past eleven they would have to set off home. Their host had all his life been fond of regularity. A few words about him.

He had begun his career as a petty clerk with nothing to back him, had quietly plodded on for forty-five years, knew very well what to work towards, had no ambition to draw the stars down from heaven, though he had two stars already, and particularly disliked expressing his own opinion on any subject. He was honest, too, that is, it had not happened to him to do anything particularly dishonest; he was a bachelor because he was an egoist; he had plenty of brains, but he could not bear showing his intelligence; he particularly disliked slovenliness and enthusiasm, regarding it as moral slovenliness; and towards the end of his life had become completely absorbed in a voluptuous, indolent comfort and systematic solitude. Though he sometimes visited people of a rather higher rank than his own, yet from his youth up he could never endure entertaining visitors himself; and of late he had, if he did not play a game of patience, been satisfied with the society of his dining-room clock, and would spend the whole evening dozing in his armchair, listening placidly to its ticking under its glass case on the chimneypiece. In appearance he was closely shaven and extremely proper-looking, he was well-preserved, looking younger than his age; he promised to go on living many years longer, and closely followed the rules of the highest good breeding. His post was a fairly comfortable one: he had to preside somewhere and to sign something. In short, he was regarded as a first-rate man. He had only one passion, or more accurately, one keen desire: that was, to have his own house, and a house built like a gentleman's residence, not a commercial investment. His desire was at last realised: he looked out and bought a house on the Petersburg Side, a good way off, it is true, but it had a garden and was an elegant house. The new owner decided that it was better for being a good way off: he did not like entertaining at home, and for driving to see anyone or to the office he had a handsome carriage of a chocolate hue, a coachman, Mihey, and two little but strong and handsome horses. All this was honourably acquired by the careful frugality of forty years, so that his heart rejoiced over it.

This was how it was that Stepan Nikiforovitch felt such pleasure in his placid heart that he actually invited two friends to see him on his birthday, which he had hitherto carefully concealed from his most intimate acquaintances. He had special designs on one of these visitors. He lived in the upper storey of his new house; and he wanted a tenant for the lower half, which was built and arranged in exactly the same way. Stepan Nikiforovitch was reckoning upon Semyon Ivanovitch Shipulenko, and had twice that evening broached the subject in the course of conversation. But Semyon Ivanovitch made no response. The latter, too, was a man who had doggedly made a way for himself in the course of long years. He had black hair and whiskers, and a face that always had a shade of jaundice. He was a married man of morose disposition who liked to stay at home; he ruled his household with a rod of iron; in his official duties he had the greatest self-confidence. He, too, knew perfectly well what goal he was making for, and better still, what he never would reach. He was in a good position, and he was sitting tight there. Though he looked upon the new reforms with a certain distaste, he was not particularly agitated about them: he was extremely self-confident, and listened with a shade of ironical malice to Ivan Ilyitch Pralinsky expatiating on new themes. All of them had been drinking rather freely, however, so that Stepan Nikiforovitch himself condescended to take part in a slight discussion with Mr Pralinsky concerning the latest reforms. But we must say a few words about his excellency, Mr Pralinsky, especially as he is the chief hero of the present story.

The actual civil councillor Ivan Ilyitch Pralinsky had only been 'his excellency' for four months; in short, he was a young general. He was young in years, too – only forty-three, no more – and he looked and liked to look even younger. He was a tall, handsome man, he was smart in his dress, and he prided himself on its solid, dignified character; with great aplomb he displayed an order of some consequence on his breast. From his earliest childhood he had known how to acquire the airs and graces of aristocratic society, and being a bachelor, dreamed of a wealthy and even aristocratic bride. He dreamed of many other things, though he was far from being stupid. At times he was a great talker, and even liked to assume a parliamentary pose. He came of a good family. He was the son of a general, and brought up in the lap of luxury; in his tender childhood he had been dressed in velvet and fine linen, had been educated at an aristocratic school, and though he acquired very little learning there he was successful in the service, and had worked his way up to being a general. The authorities looked upon him as a capable man, and even expected great things from him in the future. Stepan Nikiforovitch, under whom Ivan Ilyitch had begun his career in the service, and under whom he had remained until he was made a general, had never considered him a good business man and had no expectations of him whatever. What he liked in him was that he belonged to a good family, had property – that is, a big block of buildings, let out in flats, in charge of an overseer – was connected with persons of consequence, and what was more, had a majestic bearing. Stepan Nikiforovitch blamed him inwardly for excess of imagination and instability. Ivan Ilyitch himself felt at times that he had too much *amour propre* and even sensitiveness. Strange to say, he had attacks from time to time of morbid tenderness of conscience and even a kind of faint remorse. With bitterness and a secret soreness of heart he recognised now and again that he did not fly so high as he imagined. At such moments he sank into despondency, especially when he was suffering from haemorrhoids, called his life *une existence manquée*,[171] and ceased – privately, of course – to believe even in his parliamentary capacities, calling himself a talker, a maker of phrases; and though all that, of course, did him great credit, it did not in the least prevent him from raising his head again half an hour later, and growing even more obstinately, even more conceitedly self-confident, and assuring himself that he would yet succeed in making his mark, and that he would be not only a great official, but a statesman whom Russia would long remember. He actually dreamed at times of monuments. From this it will be seen that Ivan Ilyitch aimed high, though he hid his vague hopes and dreams deep in his heart, even with a certain trepidation. In short, he was a good-natured man and a poet at heart. Of late years these morbid moments of disillusionment had begun to be more frequent. He had become peculiarly irritable, ready to take offence, and was apt to take any contradiction as an affront. But reformed Russia gave him great hopes. His promotion to general was the finishing touch. He was roused; he held his head up. He suddenly began talking freely and eloquently. He talked about the new ideas, which he very quickly and unexpectedly made his own and professed with vehemence. He sought opportunities for speaking, drove about the town, and in many places succeeded in gaining the reputation of a desperate Liberal, which flattered him greatly. That evening, after drinking four glasses, he was particularly exuberant. He wanted on every point to confute Stepan Nikiforovitch, whom he had not seen for some time past, and whom he had hitherto always respected and even obeyed. He considered him for some reason reactionary, and fell upon him with exceptional heat. Stepan Nikiforovitch hardly answered him, but only listened slyly, though the subject interested him. Ivan Ilyitch got hot, and in the heat of the discussion sipped his glass more often than he ought to have done. Then Stepan Nikiforovitch took the bottle and at once filled his glass again, which for some reason seemed to offend Ivan Ilyitch, especially as Semyon Ivanovitch Shipulenko, whom he particularly despised and indeed feared on account of his cynicism and ill-nature, preserved a treacherous silence and smiled more frequently than was necessary. 'They seem to take me for a schoolboy,' flashed across Ivan Ilyitch's mind.

'No, it was time, high time,' he went on hotly. 'We have put it off too long, and to my thinking humanity is the first consideration, humanity with our inferiors, remembering that they, too, are men. Humanity will save everything and bring out all that is . . . '

'He-he-he-he!' was heard from the direction of Semyon Ivanovitch.

'But why are you giving us such a talking to?' Stepan Nikiforovitch protested at last, with an affable smile. 'I must own, Ivan Ilyitch, I have not been able to make out, so far, what you are maintaining. You advocate humanity. That is love of your fellow-creatures, isn't it?'

'Yes, if you like. I . . . '

'Allow me! As far as I can see, that's not the only thing. Love of one's fellow-creatures has always been fitting. The reform movement is not confined to that. All sorts of questions have arisen relating to the peasantry, the law courts, economics, government contracts, morals and . . . and . . . and those questions are endless, and all together may give rise to great upheavals, so to say. That is what we have been anxious about, and not simply humanity . . . '

'Yes, the thing is a bit deeper than that,' observed Semyon Ivanovitch.

'I quite understand, and allow me to observe, Semyon Ivanovitch, that I can't agree to being inferior to you in depth of understanding,' Ivan Ilyitch observed sarcastically and with excessive sharpness. 'However, I will make so bold as to assert, Stepan Nikiforovitch, that you have not understood me either . . . '

'No, I haven't."

'And yet I maintain and everywhere advance the idea that humanity and nothing else with one's subordinates, from the official in one's department down to the copying clerk, from the copying clerk down to the house serf, from the servant down to the peasant – humanity, I say, may serve, so to speak, as the cornerstone of the coming reforms and the reformation of things in general. Why? Because. Take a syllogism. I am human, consequently I am loved. I am loved, so confidence is felt in me. There is a feeling of confidence, and so there is trust. There is trust, and so there is love . . . that is, no, I mean to say that if they trust me they will believe in the reforms, they will understand, so to speak, the essential nature of them, will, so to speak, embrace each other in a moral sense, and will settle the whole business in a friendly way, fundamentally. What are you laughing at, Semyon Ivanovitch? Can't you understand?'

Stepan Nikiforovitch raised his eyebrows without speaking; he was surprised.

'I fancy I have drunk a little too much,' said Semyon Ivanovitch sarcastically, 'and so I am a little slow of comprehension. Not quite all my wits about me.'

Ivan Ilyitch winced.

'We should break down,' Stepan Nikiforovitch pronounced suddenly, after a slight pause of hesitation.

'How do you mean we should break down?' asked Ivan Ilyitch, surprised at Stepan Nikiforovitch's abrupt remark.

'Why, we should break under the strain.' Stepan Nikiforovitch evidently did not care to explain further.

'I suppose you are thinking of new wine in old bottles?' Ivan Ilyitch replied, not without irony. 'Well, I can answer for myself, anyway.'

At that moment the clock struck half-past eleven.

'One sits on and on, but one must go at last,' said Semyon Ivanovitch, getting up. But Ivan Ilyitch was before him; he got up from the table and took his sable cap from the chimneypiece. He looked as though he had been insulted.

'So how is it to be, Semyon Ivanovitch? Will you think it over?' said Stepan Nikiforovitch, as he saw the visitors out.

'About the flat, you mean? I'll think it over, I'll think it over.'

'Well, when you have made up your mind, let me know as soon as possible.'

'Still on business?' Mr Pralinsky observed affably, in a slightly ingratiating tone, playing with his hat. It seemed to him as though they were forgetting him.

Stepan Nikiforovitch raised his eyebrows and remained mute, as a sign that he would not detain his visitors. Semyon Ivanovitch made haste to bow himself out.

'Well . . . after that what is one to expect . . . if you don't understand the simple rules of good manners . . . ' Mr Pralinsky reflected to himself, and held out his hand to Stepan Nikiforovitch in a particularly offhand way.

In the hall Ivan Ilyitch wrapped himself up in his light, expensive fur coat; he tried for some reason not to notice Semyon Ivanovitch's shabby raccoon, and they both began descending the stairs.

'The old man seemed offended,' said Ivan Ilyitch to the silent Semyon Ivanovitch.

'No, why?' answered the latter with cool composure.

'Servile flunkey,' Ivan Ilyitch thought to himself.

They went out at the front door. Semyon Ivanovitch's sledge with a grey ugly horse drove up.

'What the devil! What has Trifon done with my carriage?' cried Ivan Ilyitch, not seeing his carriage.

The carriage was nowhere to be seen. Stepan Nikiforovitch's servant knew nothing about it. They appealed to Varlam, Semyon Ivanovitch's coachman, and received the answer that he had been standing there all the time and that the carriage had been there, but now there was no sign of it.

'An unpleasant predicament,' Mr Shipulenko pronounced. 'Shall I take you home?'

'Scoundrelly people!' Mr Pralinsky cried with fury. 'He asked me, the rascal, to let him go to a wedding here on the Petersburg Side; some crony of his was getting married, deuce take her! I sternly forbade him to absent himself, and now I'll bet he has gone off there.'

'He certainly has gone there, sir,' observed Varlam; 'but he promised to be back in a minute, to be here in time, that is.'

'Well, there it is! I had a presentiment that this would happen! I'll give it to him!'

'You'd better give him a good flogging once or twice at the police station, then he will do what you tell him,' said Semyon Ivanovitch, as he wrapped the rug round him.

'Please don't you trouble, Semyon Ivanovitch!'

'Well, won't you let me take you along?'

'*Merci, bon voyage.*'

Semyon Ivanovitch drove off, while Ivan Ilyitch set off on foot along the wooden pavement, conscious of a rather acute irritation.

*   *   *

'Yes, indeed I'll give it to you now, you rogue! I am going on foot on purpose to make you feel it, to frighten you! He will come back and hear that his master has gone off on foot . . . the blackguard!'

Ivan Ilyitch had never abused anyone like this, but he was greatly angered, and besides, there was a buzzing in his head. He was not given to drink, so five or six glasses soon affected him. But the night was enchanting. There was a frost, but it was remarkably still and there was no wind. There was a clear, starry sky. The full moon was bathing the earth in soft silver light. It was so lovely that after walking some fifty paces Ivan Ilyitch almost forgot his troubles. He felt particularly pleased. People quickly change from one mood to another when they are a little drunk. He was even pleased with the ugly little wooden houses of the deserted street.

'It's really a capital thing that I am walking,' he thought; 'it's a lesson to Trifon and a pleasure to me. I really ought to walk oftener. And I shall soon pick up a sledge on the Great Prospect. It's a glorious night. What little houses they all are! I suppose small fry live here, clerks, tradesmen, perhaps . . . That Stepan Nikiforovitch! What reactionaries they all are, those old fogies! Fogies, yes, *c'est le mot*. He is a sensible man, though; he has that *bon sens*,[172] sober, practical understanding of things. But they are old, old. There is a lack of . . . what is it? There is a lack of something . . . "We shall break down." What did he mean by that? He actually pondered when he said it. He didn't understand me a bit. And yet how could he help understanding? It was more difficult not to understand it than to understand it. The chief thing is that I am convinced, convinced in my soul. Humanity . . . the love of one's kind. Restore a man to himself, revive his personal dignity, and then . . .

when the ground is prepared, get to work. I believe that's clear? Yes! Allow me, your excellency; take a syllogism, for instance: we meet, for instance, a clerk, a poor, downtrodden clerk. "Well . . . who are you?" Answer: "A clerk." Very good, a clerk; further: "What sort of clerk are you?" Answer: "I am such and such a clerk," he says. "Are you in the service?" "I am." "Do you want to be happy?" "I do." "What do you need for happiness?" "This and that." "Why?" "Because . . ." and there the man understands me with a couple of words, the man's mine, the man is caught, so to speak, in a net, and I can do what I like with him, that is, for his good. Horrid man that Semyon Ivanovitch! And what a nasty phiz he has! . . . "Flog him in the police station," he said that on purpose. No, you are talking rubbish; you can flog, but I'm not going to; I shall punish Trifon with words, I shall punish him with reproaches, he will feel it. As for flogging, h'm! . . . it is an open question, h'm! . . . What about going to Emerance? Oh, damnation take it, the cursed pavement!' he cried out, suddenly tripping up. 'And this is the capital. Enlightenment! One might break one's leg. H'm! I detest that Semyon Ivanovitch; a most revolting phiz. He was chuckling at me just now when I said they would embrace each other in a moral sense. Well, and they will embrace each other, and what's that to do with you? I am not going to embrace you; I'd rather embrace a peasant . . . If I meet a peasant, I shall talk to him. I was drunk, though, and perhaps did not express myself properly. Possibly I am not expressing myself rightly now . . . H'm! I shall never touch wine again. In the evening you babble, and next morning you are sorry for it. After all, I am walking quite steadily . . . But they are all scoundrels, anyhow!'

So Ivan Ilyitch meditated incoherently and by snatches as he went on striding along the pavement. The fresh air began to affect him, set his mind working. Five minutes later he would have felt soothed and sleepy. But all at once, scarcely two paces from the Great Prospect, he heard music. He looked round. On the other side of the street, in a very tumble-down-looking long wooden house of one storey, there was a great fete, there was the scraping of violins and the droning of a double bass, and the squeaky tooting of a flute playing a very gay quadrille tune. Under the windows stood an audience, mainly of women in wadded pelisses with kerchiefs on their heads; they were straining every effort to see something through a crack in the shutters. Evidently there was a gay party within. The sound of the thud of dancing feet reached the other side of the street. Ivan Ilyitch saw a policeman standing not far off, and went up to him.

'Whose house is that, brother?' he asked, flinging his expensive fur coat open, just far enough to allow the policeman to see the imposing decoration on his breast.

'It belongs to the registration clerk Pseldonimov,'[173] answered the policeman, drawing himself up instantly, discerning the decoration.

'Pseldonimov? Bah! Pseldonimov! What is he up to? Getting married?'

'Yes, your honour, to a daughter of a titular councillor, Mlekopitaev,[174] a titular councillor . . . used to serve in the municipal department. That house goes with the bride.'

'So that now the house is Pseldonimov's and not Mlekopitaev's?'

'Yes, Pseldonimov's, your Honour. It was Mlekopitaev's, but now it is Pseldonimov's.'

'H'm! I am asking you, my man, because I am his chief. I am a general in the same office in which Pseldonimov serves.'

'Just so, your excellency.'

The policeman drew himself up more stiffly than ever, while Ivan Ilyitch seemed to ponder. He stood still and meditated . . .

Yes, Pseldonimov really was in his department and in his own office; he remembered that. He was a little clerk with a salary of ten roubles a month. As Mr Pralinsky had received his department very lately he might not have remembered precisely all his subordinates, but Pseldonimov he remembered just because of his surname. It had caught his eye from the very first, so that at the time he had had the curiosity to look with special attention at the possessor of such a surname. He remembered now a very young man with a long hooked nose, with tufts of flaxen hair, lean and ill-nourished, in an impossible uniform, and with unmentionables so impossible as to be actually unseemly; he remembered how the thought had flashed through his mind at the time: shouldn't he give the poor fellow ten roubles for Christmas, to spend on his wardrobe? But as the poor fellow's face was too austere., and his expression extremely unprepossessing, even exciting repulsion, the good-natured idea somehow faded away of itself, so Pseldonimov did not get his tip. He had been the more surprised when this same Pseldonimov had not more than a week before asked for leave to be married. Ivan Ilyitch remembered that he had somehow not had time to go into the matter, so that the matter of the marriage had been settled offhand, in haste. But yet he did remember exactly that Pseldonimov was receiving a wooden house and four hundred roubles in cash as dowry with his bride. The circumstance had surprised him at the time; he remembered that he had made a slight jest over the juxtaposition of the names Pseldonimov and Mlekopitaev. He remembered all that clearly.

He recalled it, and grew more and more pensive. It is well known that whole trains of thought sometimes pass through our brains instantaneously as though they were sensations without being translated into human speech, still less into literary language. But we will try to translate these sensations of our hero's, and present to the reader at least the kernel of them, so to say, what was most essential and nearest to reality in them. For many of our sensations when translated into ordinary language seem absolutely unreal. That is why they never find expression, though everyone has them. Of course Ivan Ilyitch's sensations and thoughts were a little incoherent. But you know the reason.

'Why,' flashed through his mind, 'here we all talk and talk, but when it comes to action – it all ends in nothing. Here, for instance, take this Pseldonimov: he has just come from his wedding full of hope and excitement, looking forward to his wedding feast . . . This is one of the most blissful days of his life . . . Now he is busy with his guests, is giving a banquet, a modest one, poor, but gay and full of genuine gladness . . . What if he knew that at this very moment I, I, his superior, his chief, am standing by his house listening to the music? Yes, really how would he feel? No, what would he feel if I suddenly walked in? H'm! . . . Of course at first he would be frightened, he would be dumb with embarrassment . . . I should be in his way, and perhaps should upset everything. Yes, that would be so if any other general went in, but not I . . . That's a fact, anyone else, but not I . . .

'Yes, Stepan Nikiforovitch! You did not understand me just now, but here is an example ready for you.

'Yes, we all make an outcry about acting humanely, but we are not capable of heroism, of fine actions.

'What sort of heroism? This sort. Consider: in the existing relations of the various members of society, for me, for me, after midnight to go into the wedding of my subordinate, a registration clerk, at ten roubles the month – why, it would mean embarrassment, a revolution, the last days of Pompeii,[175] a nonsensical folly. No one would understand it. Stepan Nikiforovitch would die before he understood it. Why, he said we should break down. Yes, but that's you old people, inert, paralytic people; but I shan't break down, I will transform the last day of Pompeii to a day of the utmost sweetness for my subordinate, and a wild action to an action normal, patriarchal, lofty and moral. How? Like this. Kindly listen . . .

'Here . . . I go in, suppose; they are amazed, leave off dancing, look wildly at me, draw back. Quite so, but at once I speak out : I go straight up to the frightened Pseldonimov, and with a most cordial, affable smile, in the simplest words, I say: "This is how it is, I have been at his excellency Stepan Nikiforovitch's. I expect you know, close here in the neighbourhood . . . " Well, then, lightly, in a laughing way, I shall tell him of my adventure with Trifon. From Trifon I shall pass on to saying how I walked here on foot . . . "Well, I heard music, I enquired of a policeman, and learned, brother, that it was your wedding. Let me go in, I thought, to my subordinate's; let me see how my clerks enjoy themselves and . . . celebrate their wedding. I suppose you won't turn me out?" Turn me out! What an idea for a subordinate! How the devil could he dream of turning me out! I fancy that he would be half crazy, that he would rush headlong to seat me in an armchair, would be trembling with delight, would hardly know what he was doing for the first minute!

'Why, what can be simpler, more elegant than such an action? Why did I go in? That's another question! That is, so to say, the moral aspect of the question. That's the pith,

'H'm, what was I thinking about, yes!

'Well, of course they will make me sit down with the most important guest, some titular councillor or a relation who's a retired captain with a red nose. Gogol[176] describes these eccentrics so capitally. Well, I shall make acquaintance, of course, with the bride, I shall compliment her, I shall encourage the guests. I shall beg them not to stand on ceremony. To enjoy themselves, to go on dancing. I shall make jokes, I shall laugh; in fact, I shall be affable and charming. I am always affable and charming when I am pleased with myself . . . H'm . . . the point is that I believe I am still a little, well, not drunk exactly, but . . .

'Of course, as a gentleman I shall be quite on an equality with them, and shall not expect any especial marks of . . . But morally, morally, it is a different matter; they will understand and appreciate it . . . My actions will evoke their nobler feelings . . . Well, I shall stay for half an hour . . . even for an hour; I shall leave, of course, before supper; but they will be bustling about, baking and roasting, they will be making low bows, but I will only drink a glass, congratulate them and refuse supper. I shall say – "business". And as soon as I pronounce the word "business", all of them will at once have sternly respectful faces. By that I shall delicately remind them that there is a difference between them and me. The earth and the sky. It is not that I want to impress that on them, but it must be done . . . it's even essential in a moral sense, when all is said and done. I shall smile at once, however, I shall even laugh, and then they will all pluck up courage again . . . I shall jest a little again with the bride; h'm! I may even hint that I shall come again in just nine months to stand godfather, he-he! And she will be sure to be brought to bed by then.

They multiply, you know, like rabbits. And they will all roar with laughter and the bride will blush; I shall kiss her feelingly on the forehead, even give her my blessing . . . and next day my exploit will be known at the office. Next day I shall be stern again, next day I shall be exacting again, even implacable, but they will all know what I am like. They will know my heart, they will know my essential nature: "He is stern as a chief, but as a man he is an angel!" And I shall have conquered them; I shall have captured them by one little act which would never have entered your head; they would be mine; I should be their father, they would be my children . . . Come now, your excellency Stepan Nikiforovitch, go and do likewise . . .

'But do you know, do you understand, that Pseldonimov will tell his children how the general himself feasted and even drank at his wedding! Why you know those children would tell their children, and those would tell their grandchildren as a most sacred story that a grand gentleman, a statesman (and I shall be all that by then), did them the honour, and so on, and so on. Why, I am morally elevating the humiliated, I restore him to himself . . . Why, he gets a salary of ten roubles a month! . . . If I repeat this five or ten times, or something of the sort, I shall gain popularity all over the place . . . My name will be printed on the hearts of all, and the devil only knows what will come of that popularity! . . . '

These, or something like these, were Ivan Ilyitch's reflections (a man says all sorts of things sometimes to himself, gentlemen, especially when he is in rather an eccentric condition). All these meditations passed through his mind in something like half a minute, and of course he might have confined himself to these dreams and, after mentally putting Stepan Nikiforovitch to shame, have gone very peacefully home and to bed. And he would have done well. But the trouble of it was that the moment was an eccentric one.

As ill-luck would have it, at that very instant the self-satisfied faces of Stepan Nikiforovitch and Semyon Ivanovitch suddenly rose before his heated imagination.

'We shall break down!' repeated Stepan Nikiforovitch, smiling disdainfully.

'He-he-he,' Semyon Ivanovitch seconded him with his nastiest smile.

'Well, we'll see whether we do break down!' Ivan Ilyitch said resolutely, with a rush of heat to his face.

He stepped down from the pavement and with firm steps went straight across the street towards the house of his registration clerk Pseldonimov.

*　　*　　*

His star carried him away. He walked confidently in at the open gate and contemptuously thrust aside with his foot the shaggy, husky little sheepdog who flew at his legs with a hoarse bark, more as a matter of form than with any real intention. Along a wooden plank he went to the covered porch which led like a sentry box to the yard, and by three decaying wooden steps he went up to the tiny entry. Here, though a tallow candle or something in the way of a night light was burning somewhere in a corner, it did not prevent Ivan Ilyitch from putting his left foot just as it was, in its golosh, into a galantine[177] which had been stood out there to cool. Ivan Ilyitch bent down, and looking with curiosity, he saw that there were two other dishes of some sort of jelly and also two shapes apparently of blancmange. The squashed galantine embarrassed him, and for one brief instant the thought flashed through his mind, whether he should not slink away at once. But he considered this too low. Reflecting that no one would have seen him, and that they would never think he had done it, he hurriedly wiped his golosh to conceal all traces, fumbled for the felt-covered door, opened it and found himself in a very little anteroom. Half of it was literally piled up with greatcoats, wadded jackets, cloaks, capes, scarves and goloshes. In the other half the musicians had been installed; two violins, a flute and a double bass, a band of four, picked up, of course, in the street. They were sitting at an unpainted wooden table, lighted by a single tallow candle, and with the utmost vigour were sawing out the last figure of the quadrille. From the open door into the drawing-room one could see the dancers in the midst of dust, tobacco smoke and fumes. There was a frenzy of gaiety. There were sounds of laughter, shouts and shrieks from the ladies. The gentlemen stamped like a squadron of horses. Above all the bedlam there rang out words of command from the leader of the dance probably an extremely free and easy and even unbuttoned gentleman: 'Gentlemen advance, ladies' chain, set to partners!'[178] and so on, and so on. Ivan Ilyitch in some excitement cast off his coat and goloshes, and with his cap in his hand went into the room. He was no longer reflecting, however.

For the first minute nobody noticed him; all were absorbed in dancing the quadrille to the end. Ivan Ilyitch stood as though entranced, and could make out nothing definite in the chaos. He caught glimpses of ladies' dresses, of gentlemen with cigarettes between their teeth. He caught a glimpse of a lady's pale-blue scarf which flicked him on the nose. After the wearer, a medical student, with his hair blown in all directions on his head, pranced by in wild delight and jostled violently against him on the way. He caught a glimpse, too, of an officer of some description, who looked half a mile high. Someone in an unnaturally shrill voice shouted, 'O-o-oh, Pseldonimov!' as the speaker flew by stamping. It was sticky under Ivan Ilyitch's feet; evidently the floor had been waxed. In the room, which was a very small one, there were about thirty people.

But a minute later the quadrille was over, and almost at once the very thing Ivan Ilyitch had pictured when he was dreaming on the pavement took place.

A stifled murmur, a strange whisper passed over the whole company, including the dancers, who had not yet had time to take breath and wipe their perspiring faces. All eyes, all faces began quickly turning towards the newly arrived guest. Then they all seemed to draw back a little and beat a retreat. Those who had not noticed him were pulled by their coats or dresses and informed. They looked round and at once beat a retreat with the others. Ivan Ilyitch was still standing at the door without moving a step forward, and between him and the company there stretched an ever widening empty space of floor strewn with countless sweetmeat wrappings, bits of paper and cigarette ends. All at once a young man in a uniform, with a shock of flaxen hair and a hooked nose, stepped timidly out into that empty space. He moved forward, hunched up, and looked at the unexpected visitor exactly with the expression with which a dog looks at its master when the latter has called him up and is going to kick him.

'Good-evening, Pseldonimov, do you know me?' said Ivan Ilyitch, and felt at the same minute that he had said this very awkwardly; he felt, too, that he was perhaps doing something horribly stupid at that moment.

'You-our ex-cel-len-cy!' muttered Pseldonimov.

'To be sure . . . I have called in to see you quite by chance, my friend, as you can probably imagine . . . '

But evidently Pseldonimov could imagine nothing. He stood with staring eyes in the utmost perplexity.

'You won't turn me out, I suppose . . . Pleased or not, you must make a visitor welcome . . . ' Ivan Ilyitch went on, feeling that he was confused to a point of unseemly feebleness; that he was trying to smile and was utterly unable; that the humorous reference to Stepan Niki-forovitch and Trifon was becoming more and more impossible. But as ill luck would have it, Pseldonimov did not recover from his stupefaction, and still gazed at him with a perfectly idiotic air. Ivan Ilyitch winced, he felt that in another minute something incredibly foolish would happen.

'I am not in the way, am I? . . . I'll go away,' he faintly articulated, and there was a tremor at the right corner of his mouth.

But Pseldonimov had recovered himself.

'Good heavens, your excellency . . . the honour . . . ' he muttered, bowing hurriedly. 'Graciously sit down, your excellency . . . ' And recovering himself still further, he motioned him with both hands to a sofa before which a table had been moved away to make room for the dancing.

Ivan Ilyitch felt relieved and sank on the sofa; at once someone flew to move the table up to him. He took a cursory look round and saw that he was the only person sitting down, all the others were standing, even the ladies. A bad sign. But it was not yet time to reassure and encourage them. The company still held back, while before him, bending double, stood Pseldonimov, utterly alone, still completely at a loss and very far from smiling. It was horrid; in short, our hero endured such misery at that moment that his Haroun al-Raschid-like[179] descent upon his subordinates for the sake of principle might well have been reckoned an heroic action. But suddenly a little figure made its appearance beside Pseldonimov, and began bowing. To his inexpressible pleasure and even happiness, Ivan Ilyitch at once recognised him as the head clerk of his office, Akim Petrovitch Zubikov, and though, of course, he was not acquainted with him, he knew him to be a businesslike and exemplary clerk. He got up at once and held out his hand to Akim Petrovitch – his whole hand, not two fingers. The latter took it in both of his with the deepest respect. The general was triumphant, the situation was saved.

And now indeed Pseldonimov was no longer, so to say, the second person, but the third. It was possible to address his remarks to the head clerk in his necessity, taking him for an acquaintance and even an intimate one, and Pseldonimov meanwhile could only be silent and be in a tremor of reverence. So that the proprieties were observed. And some explanation was essential, Ivan Ilyitch felt that; he saw that all the guests were expecting something, that the whole household was gathered together in the doorway, almost creeping, climbing over one another in their anxiety to see and hear him. What was horrid was that the head clerk in his foolishness remained standing.

'Why are you standing?' said Ivan Ilyitch, awkwardly motioning him to a seat on the sofa beside him.

'Oh, don't trouble . . . I'll sit here.' And Akim Petrovitch hurriedly sat down on a chair, almost as it was being put for him by Pseldonimov, who remained obstinately standing.

'Can you imagine what happened,' addressing himself exclusively to Akim Petrovitch, he spoke in a rather quavering, though free and easy voice. He even drawled out his words, with special emphasis on some syllables, pronounced the vowel *ah* like *eh*; in short, felt and was conscious that he was being affected but could not control himself: some external force was at work. He was painfully conscious of many things at that moment.

'Can you imagine, I have only just come from Stepan Nikiforovitch Nikiforov's, you have heard of him perhaps, the privy councillor. You know . . . on that special committee . . . '

Akim Petrovitch bent his whole person forward respectfully: as much as to say, 'Of course, we have heard of him.'

'He is your neighbour now,' Ivan Ilyitch went on, for one instant for the sake of ease and good manners addressing Pseldonimov, but he quickly turned away again, on seeing from the latter's eyes that it made absolutely no difference to him.

'The old fellow, as you know, has been dreaming all his life of buying himself a house . . . Well, and he has bought it. And a very pretty house too. Yes . . . And today was his birthday and he had never celebrated it before; he used even to keep it secret from us, he was too stingy to mark it, he-he. But now he is so delighted over his new house, that he invited Semyon Ivanovitch Shipulenko and me, you know.'

Akim Petrovitch bent forward again. He bent forward zealously. Ivan Ilyitch felt somewhat comforted. It had struck him, indeed, that the head clerk possibly was guessing that he was an indispensable point *d'appui*[180] for his excellency at that moment. That would have been more horrid than anything.

'So we sat together, the three of us; he gave us champagne, we talked about problems . . . even dis-pu-ted . . . He-he!'

Akim Petrovitch raised his eyebrows respectfully.

'Only that is not the point. When I take leave of him at last – he is a punctual old fellow, goes to bed early, you know, in his old age – I go out . . . My Trifon is nowhere to be seen! I am anxious, I make enquiries. "What has Trifon done with the carriage?" It comes out that hoping I should stay on, he had gone off to the wedding of some friend of his, or sister maybe . . . Goodness only knows. Somewhere here on the Petersburg Side. And took the carriage with him while he was about it.'

Again for the sake of good manners the general glanced in the direction of Pseldonimov. The latter promptly gave a wriggle, but not at all the sort of wriggle the general would have liked. 'He has no sympathy, no heart,' flashed through his brain.

'You don't say so!' said Akim Petrovitch, greatly impressed. A faint murmur of surprise ran through all the crowd.

'Can you fancy my position . . . ' (Ivan Ilyitch glanced at them all.) 'There was nothing for it, I set off on foot. I thought I would trudge to the Great Prospect, and there find some cabby . . . he-he!'

'He-he-he!' Akim Petrovitch echoed. Again a murmur, but this time on a more cheerful note, passed through the crowd. At that moment the chimney of a lamp on the wall broke with a crash. Someone rushed zealously to see to it. Pseldonimov started and looked sternly at the lamp, but the general took no notice of it, and all was serene again.

'I walked . . . and the night was so lovely, so still. All at once I heard a band, stamping, dancing. I enquired of a policeman; it is Pseldonimov's wedding. Why, you are giving a ball to all Petersburg Side, my friend. Ha-ha.' He turned to Pseldonimov again.

'He-he-he! To be sure,' Akim Petrovitch responded. There was a stir among the guests again, but what was most foolish was that Pseldonimov, though he bowed, did not even now smile, but seemed as though he were made of wood. 'Is he a fool or what?' thought Ivan Ilyitch. 'He ought to have smiled at that point, the ass, and everything would have run easily.' There was a fury of impatience in his heart.

'I thought I would go in to see my clerk. He won't turn me out I expect . . . pleased or not, one must welcome a guest. You must please excuse me, my dear fellow. If I am in the way, I will go . . . I only came in to have a look . . . '

But little by little a general stir was beginning.

Akim Petrovitch looked at him with a mawkishly sweet expression as though to say, 'How could your excellency be in the way?' all the guests stirred and began to display the first symptoms of being at their ease. Almost all the ladies sat down. A good sign and a reassuring one. The boldest spirits among them fanned themselves with their handkerchiefs. One of them, in a shabby velvet dress, said something with intentional loudness. The officer addressed by her would have liked to answer her as loudly, but seeing that they were the only ones speaking aloud, he subsided. The men, for the most part government clerks, with two or three students among them, looked at one another as though egging each other on to unbend, cleared their throats, and began to move a few steps in different directions. No one, however, was particularly timid, but they were all restive, and almost all of them looked with a hostile expression at the personage who had burst in upon them, to destroy their gaiety. The officer, ashamed of his cowardice, began to edge up to the table.

'But I say, my friend, allow me to ask you your name,' Ivan Ilyitch asked Pseldonimov.

'Porfiry Petrovitch, your excellency,' answered the latter, with staring eyes as though on parade.

'Introduce me, Porfiry Petrovitch, to your bride . . . Take me to her . . . I . . . '

And he showed signs of a desire to get up. But Pseldonimov ran full speed to the drawing-room. The bride, in fact, was standing close by at the door, but as soon as she heard herself mentioned, she hid. A minute later Pseldonimov led her up by the hand. The guests all moved aside to make way for them. Ivan Ilyitch got up solemnly and addressed himself to her with a most affable smile.

'Very, very much pleased to make your acquaintance,' he pronounced with a most aristocratic half-bow, 'especially on such a day . . . '

He gave a meaning smile. There was an agreeable flutter among the ladies.

'*Charmée*,' the lady in the velvet dress pronounced, almost aloud.

The bride was a match for Pseldonimov. She was a thin little lady not more than seventeen, pale, with a very small face and a sharp little nose. Her quick, active little eyes were not at all embarrassed; on the contrary, they looked at him steadily and even with a shade of resentment. Evidently Pseldonimov was marrying her for her beauty. She was dressed in a white muslin dress over a pink slip. Her neck was thin, and she had a figure like a chicken's with the bones all sticking out. She was not equal to making any response to the general's affability.

'But she is very pretty,' he went on, in an undertone, as though addressing Pseldonimov only, though intentionally speaking so that the bride could hear.

But on this occasion, too, Pseldonimov again answered absolutely nothing, and did not even wriggle. Ivan Ilyitch fancied that there was something cold, suppressed in his eyes, as though he had something peculiarly malignant in his mind. And yet he had at all costs to wring some sensibility out of him. Why, that was the object of his coming.

'They are a couple, though!' he thought.

And he turned again to the bride, who had seated herself beside him on the sofa, but in answer to his two or three questions he got nothing but 'yes' or 'no', and hardly that.

'If only she had been overcome with confusion,' he thought to himself, 'then I should have begun to banter her. But as it is, my position is impossible.'

And as ill-luck would have it, Akim Petrovitch, too, was mute; though this was only due to his foolishness, it was still unpardonable.

'My friends! Haven't I perhaps interfered with your enjoyment?' he said, addressing the whole company.

He felt that the very palms of his hands were perspiring.

'No . . . don't trouble, your excellency; we are beginning directly, but now . . . we are getting cool,' answered the officer.

The bride looked at him with pleasure; the officer was not old, and wore the uniform of some branch of the service. Pseldonimov was still standing in the same place, bending forward, and it seemed as though his hooked nose stood out further than ever. He looked and listened like a footman standing with the greatcoat on his arm, waiting for the end of his master's farewell conversation. Ivan Ilyitch made this comparison himself. He was losing his head; he felt that he was in an awkward position, that the ground was giving way under his feet, that he had got in somewhere and could not find his way out, as though he were in the dark.

*　　*　　*

Suddenly the guests all moved aside, and a short, thickset, middle-aged woman made her appearance, dressed plainly though she was in her best, with a big shawl on her shoulders, pinned at her throat, and on her head a cap to which she was evidently unaccustomed. In her hands she carried a small round tray on which stood a full but uncorked bottle of champagne and two glasses, neither more nor less. Evidently the bottle was intended for only two guests.

The middle-aged lady approached the general.

'Don't look down on us, your excellency,' she said, bowing. 'Since you have deigned to do my son the honour of coming to his wedding, we beg you graciously to drink to the health of the young people. Do not disdain us; do us the honour.'

Ivan Ilyitch clutched at her as though she were his salvation. She was by no means an old woman – forty-five or forty-six, not more; but she had such a good-natured, rosy-cheeked, such a round and candid Russian face, she smiled so good-humouredly, bowed so simply, that Ivan Ilyitch was almost comforted and began to hope again.

'So you are the mo-other of your so-on?' he said, getting up from the sofa.

'Yes, my mother, your Excellency,' mumbled Pseldonimov, craning his long neck and thrusting forward his long nose again.

'Ah! I am delighted – de-ligh-ted to make your acquaintance.'

'Do not refuse us, your excellency.'

'With the greatest pleasure.'

The tray was put down. Pseldonimov dashed forward to pour out the wine. Ivan Ilyitch, still standing, took the glass.

'I am particularly, particularly glad on this occasion, that I can . . . ' he began, 'that I can . . . testify before all of you . . . In short, as your chief . . . I wish you, madam' (he turned to the bride), 'and you, friend Porfiry, I wish you the fullest, completest happiness for many long years.'

And he positively drained the glass with feeling, the seventh he had drunk that evening. Pseldonimov looked at him gravely and even sullenly. The general was beginning to feel an agonising hatred of him.

'And that scarecrow' (he looked at the officer) 'keeps obtruding himself. He might at least have shouted, "Hurrah!" and it would have gone off, it would have gone off . . . '

'And you too, Akim Petrovitch, drink a glass to their health,' added the mother, addressing the head clerk. 'You are his superior, he is under you. Look after my boy, I beg you as a mother. And don't forget us in the future, our good, kind friend, Akim Petrovitch.'

'How nice these old Russian women are,' thought Ivan Ilyitch. 'She has livened us all up. I have always loved the democracy . . . '

At that moment another tray was brought to the table; it was brought in by a maid wearing a crackling cotton dress that had never been washed, and a crinoline. She could hardly grasp the tray in both hands, it was so big. On it there were numbers of plates of apples, sweets, fruit meringues and fruit cheeses, walnuts and so on, and so on. The tray had been till then in the drawing-room for the delectation of all the guests, and especially the ladies. But now it was brought to the general alone.

'Do not disdain our humble fare, your excellency. What we have we are pleased to offer,' the old lady repeated, bowing.

'Delighted!' said Ivan Ilyitch, and with real pleasure took a walnut and cracked it between his fingers. He had made up his mind to win popularity at all costs.

Meantime the bride suddenly giggled.

'What is it?' asked Ivan Ilyitch with a smile, encouraged by this sign of life.

'Ivan Kostenkinitch, here, makes me laugh,' she answered, looking down.

The general distinguished, indeed, a flaxen-headed young man, exceedingly good-looking, who was sitting on a chair at the other end of the sofa, whispering something to Madame Pseldonimov. The young man stood up. He was apparently very young and very shy.

'I was telling the lady about a "dream book", your excellency,' he muttered as though apologising.

'About what sort of "dream book"?' asked Ivan Ilyitch condescendingly.

'There is a new "dream book", a literary one. I was telling the lady that to dream of Mr Panaev means spilling coffee on one's shirt front.'[181]

'What innocence!' thought Ivan Ilyitch, with positive annoyance.

Though the young man flushed very red as he said it, he was incredibly delighted that he had said this about Mr Panaev.

'To be sure, I have heard of it . . . ' responded his excellency.

'No, there is something better than that,' said a voice quite close to Ivan Ilyitch. 'There is a new encyclopaedia being published, and they say Mr Kraevsky[182] will write articles . . . and satirical literature.'

This was said by a young man who was by no means embarrassed, but rather free and easy. He was wearing gloves and a white waistcoat, and carried a hat in his hand. He did not dance, and looked condescending, for he was on the staff of a satirical paper called the *Firebrand*,[183] and gave himself airs accordingly. He had come casually to the wedding, invited as an honoured guest of the Pseldonimovs', with whom he was on intimate terms and with whom only a year before he had lived in very poor lodgings, kept by a German woman. He drank vodka, however, and for that purpose had more than once withdrawn to a snug little back room to which all the guests knew their way. The general disliked him extremely.

'And the reason that's funny,' broke in joyfully the flaxen-headed young man, who had talked of the shirt front and at whom the young man on the comic paper looked with hatred in consequence, 'it's funny, your excellency, because it is supposed by the writer that Mr Kraevsky does not know how to spell, and thinks that 'satirical' ought to be written with a "y" instead of an "i". '

But the poor young man scarcely finished his sentence; he could see from his eyes that the general knew all this long ago, for the general himself looked embarrassed, evidently because he knew it. The young man seemed inconceivably ashamed. He succeeded in effacing himself completely, and remained very melancholy all the rest of the evening.

But to make up for that the young man on the staff of the *Firebrand* came up nearer, and seemed to be intending to sit down somewhere close by. Such free and easy manners struck Ivan Ilyitch as rather shocking.

'Tell me, please, Porfiry,' he began, in order to say something, 'why – I have always wanted to ask you about it in person – why you are called Pseldonimov instead of Pseudonimov? Your name surely must be Pseudonimov.'

'I cannot inform you exactly, your excellency,' said Pseldonimov.

'It must have been that when his father went into the service they made a mistake in his papers, so that he has remained now Pseldonimov,' put in Akim Petrovitch. 'That does happen.'

'Un-doubted-ly,' the general said with warmth, 'un-doubted-ly; for only think, Pseudonimov comes from the literary word pseudonym, while Pseldonimov means nothing.'

'Due to foolishness,' added Akim Petrovitch.

'You mean what is due to foolishness?'

'The Russian common people in their foolishness often alter letters, and sometimes pronounce them in their own way. For instance, they say nevalid instead of invalid.'

'Oh, yes, nevalid, he-he-he . . . '

'Mumber, too, they say, your excellency,' boomed out the tall officer, who had long been itching to distinguish himself in some way.

'What do you mean by mumber?'

'Mumber instead of number, your excellency.'

'Oh, yes, mumber . . . instead of number . . . To be sure, to be sure . . . He-he-he!' Ivan Ilyitch had to do a chuckle for the benefit of the officer too.

The officer straightened his tie.

'Another thing they say is nigh by,' the young man on the comic paper put in. But his excellency tried not to hear this. His chuckles were not at everybody's disposal.

'Nigh by, instead of near,' the young man on the comic paper persisted, in evident irritation.

Ivan Ilyitch looked at him sternly.

'Come, why persist?' Pseldonimov whispered to him.

'Why, I was talking. Mayn't one speak?' the latter protested in a whisper; but he said no more and with secret fury walked out of the room.

He made his way straight to the attractive little back room where, for the benefit of the dancing gentlemen, vodka of two sorts, salt fish, caviare arranged in slices and a bottle of very strong sherry of Russian make had been set early in the evening on a little table, covered with a Yaroslav cloth.[184] With anger in his heart he was pouring himself out a glass of vodka, when suddenly the medical student with the dishevelled locks, the foremost dancer and cutter of capers at Pseldonimov's ball, rushed in. He fell on the decanter with greedy haste.

'They are just going to begin!' he said rapidly, helping himself. 'Come and look, I am going to dance a solo on my head; after supper I shall risk the fish dance.[185] It is just the thing for the wedding. So to speak, a friendly hint to Pseldonimov. She's a jolly creature that Kleopatra Semyonovna, you can venture on anything you like with her.'

'He's a reactionary,' said the young man on the comic paper gloomily, as he tossed off his vodka.

'Who is a reactionary?'

'Why, the personage before whom they set those sweetmeats. He's a reactionary, I tell you.'

'What nonsense!' muttered the student, and he rushed out of the room, hearing the opening bars of the quadrille.

Left alone, the young man on the comic paper poured himself out another glass to give himself more assurance and independence; he drank and ate a snack of something, and never had the actual civil councillor Ivan Ilyitch made for himself a bitterer foe more implacably bent on revenge than the young man on the staff of the *Firebrand* whom he had so slighted, especially after the latter had drunk two glasses of vodka. Alas! Ivan Ilyitch suspected nothing of the sort. He did not suspect another circumstance of prime importance either, which had an influence on the mutual relations of the guests and his excellency. The fact was that though he had given a proper and even detailed explanation of his presence at his clerk's wedding, this explanation did not really satisfy anyone, and the visitors were still embarrassed. But suddenly everything was transformed as though by magic, all were reassured and ready to enjoy themselves, to laugh, to shriek, to dance, exactly as though the unexpected visitor were not in the room. The cause of it was a rumour, a whisper, a report which spread in some unknown way that the visitor was not quite . . . it seemed – was, in fact, 'a little top-heavy'. And though this seemed at first a horrible calumny, it began by degrees to appear to be justified; suddenly everything became clear. What was more, they felt all at once extraordinarily free. And it was just at this moment that the quadrille for which the medical student was in such haste, the last before supper, began.

And just as Ivan Ilyitch meant to address the bride again, intending to provoke her with some innuendo, the tall officer suddenly dashed up to her and with a flourish dropped on one knee before her. She immediately jumped up from the sofa, and whisked off with him to take her place in the quadrille. The officer did not even apologise, and she did not even glance at the general as she went away; she seemed, in fact, relieved to escape.

'After all she has a right to be,' thought Ivan Ilyitch, 'and of course they don't know how to behave. Hm! Don't you stand on ceremony, friend Porfiry,' he said, addressing Pseldonimov. 'Perhaps you have . . . arrangements to make . . . or something . . . please don't put yourself out. Why does he keep guard over me?' he thought to himself.

Pseldonimov, with his long neck and his eyes fixed intently upon him, began to be insufferable. In fact, all this was not the thing, not the thing at all, but Ivan Ilyitch was still far from admitting this.

*   *   *

The quadrille began.

'Will you allow me, your excellency?' asked Akim Petrovitch, holding the bottle respectfully in his hands and preparing to pour from it into his excellency's glass.

'I . . . I really don't know, whether . . . '

But Akim Petrovitch, with reverent and radiant face, was already filling the glass. After filling the glass, he proceeded, writhing and wriggling, as it were stealthily, as it were furtively, to pour himself out some, with this difference, that he did not fill his own glass to within a finger length of the top, and this seemed somehow more respectful. He was like a woman in travail as he sat beside his chief. What could he talk about, indeed? Yet to entertain his excellency was an absolute duty since he had the honour of keeping him company. The champagne served as a resource, and his excellency, too, was pleased that he had filled his glass – not for the sake of the champagne, for it was warm and perfectly abominable, but just morally pleased.

'The old chap would like to have a drink himself,' thought Ivan Ilyitch, 'but he doesn't venture till I do. I mustn't prevent him. And indeed it would be absurd for the bottle to stand between as untouched.'

He took a sip, anyway it seemed better than sitting doing nothing.

'I am here,' he said, with pauses and emphasis, 'I am here, you know, so to speak, accidentally, and, of course, it may be . . . that some people would consider . . . it unseemly for me to be at such . . . a gathering.'

Akim Petrovitch said nothing, but listened with timid curiosity.

'But I hope you will understand with what object I have come . . . I haven't really come simply to drink wine . . . he-he!'

Akim Petrovitch tried to chuckle, following the example of his excellency, but again he could not get it out, and again he made absolutely no consolatory answer.

'I am here . . . in order, so to speak, to encourage . . . to show, so to speak, a moral aim,' Ivan Ilyitch continued, feeling vexed at Akim

Petrovitch's stupidity, but he suddenly subsided into silence himself. He saw that poor Akim Petrovitch had dropped his eyes as though he were in fault. The general in some confusion made haste to take another sip from his glass, and Akim Petrovitch clutched at the bottle as though it were his only hope of salvation and filled the glass again.

'You haven't many resources,' thought Ivan Ilyitch, looking sternly at poor Akim Petrovitch. The latter, feeling that stern general-like eye upon him, made up his mind to remain silent for good and not to raise his eyes. So they sat beside each other for a couple of minutes – two sickly minutes for Akim Petrovitch.

A couple of words about Akim Petrovitch. He was a man of the old school, as meek as a hen, reared from infancy to obsequious servility, and at the same time a good-natured and even honourable man. He was a Petersburg Russian; that is, his father and his father's father were born, grew up and served in Petersburg and had never once left Petersburg. That is quite a special type of Russian. They have hardly any idea of Russia, though that does not trouble them at ail. Their whole interest is confined to Petersburg and chiefly the place in which they serve. All their thoughts are concentrated on preference for farthing points,[186] on the shop, and their month's salary. They don't know a single Russian custom, a single Russian song except 'Lutchinushka',[187] and that only because it is played on the barrel organs. However, there are two fundamental and invariable signs by which you can at once distinguish a Petersburg Russian from a real Russian. The first sign is the fact that Petersburg Russians, all without exception, speak of the newspaper as the *Academic News* and never call it the *Petersburg News*.[188] The second and equally trustworthy sign is that Petersburg Russians never make use of the word 'breakfast', but always call it 'Fruhstück', with especial emphasis on the first syllable. By these radical and distinguishing signs you can tell them apart; in short, this is a humble type which has been formed during the last thirty-five years. Akim Petrovitch, however, was by no means a fool. If the general had asked him a question about anything in his own province he would have answered and kept up a conversation; as it was, it was unseemly for a subordinate even to answer such questions as these, though Akim Petrovitch was dying from curiosity to know something more detailed about his excellency's real intentions.

And meanwhile Ivan Ilyitch sank more and more into meditation and a sort of whirl of ideas; in his absorption he sipped his glass every half-minute. Akim Petrovitch at once zealously filled it up. Both were silent. Ivan Ilyitch began looking at the dances, and immediately something attracted his attention. One circumstance even surprised him . . .

The dances were certainly lively. Here people danced in the simplicity of their hearts to amuse themselves and even to romp wildly. Among the dancers few were really skilful, but the unskilled stamped so vigorously that they might have been taken for agile ones. The officer was among the foremost; he particularly liked the figures in which he was left alone, to perform a solo. Then he performed the most marvellous capers. For instance, standing upright as a post, he would suddenly bend over to one side, so that one expected him to fall over; but with the next step he would suddenly bend over in the opposite direction at the same acute angle to the floor. He kept the most serious face and danced in the full conviction that everyone was watching him. Another gentleman, who had had rather more than he could carry before the quadrille, dropped asleep beside his partner so that his partner had to dance alone. The young registration clerk, who had danced with the lady in the blue scarf through all the figures and through all the five quadrilles which they had danced that evening, played the same prank the whole time: that is, he dropped a little behind his partner, seized the end of her scarf, and as they crossed over succeeded in imprinting some twenty kisses on the scarf. His partner sailed along in front of him, as though she noticed nothing. The medical student really did dance on his head, and excited frantic enthusiasm, stamping and shrieks of delight. In short, the absence of constraint was very marked. Ivan Ilyitch, whom the wine was beginning to affect, began by smiling, but by degrees a bitter doubt began to steal into his heart; of course he liked free and easy manners and unconventionality. He desired, he had even inwardly prayed for free and easy manners, when they had all held back, but now that unconventionality had gone beyond all limits. One lady, for instance, the one in the shabby dark-blue velvet dress, bought fourth-hand, in the sixth figure pinned her dress so as to turn it into – something like trousers. This was the Kleopatra Semyonovna with whom one could venture to do anything, as her partner, the medical student, had expressed it. The medical student defied description: he was simply a Fokin.[189] How was it? They had held back and now they were so quickly emancipated! One might think it nothing, but this transformation was somehow strange; it indicated something. It was as though they had forgotten Ivan Ilyitch's existence. Of course he was the first to laugh, and even ventured to applaud. Akim Petrovitch chuckled respectfully in unison, though, indeed, with evident pleasure and no suspicion that his excellency was beginning to nourish in his heart a new gnawing anxiety.

'You dance capitally, young man,' Ivan Ilyitch was obliged to say to the medical student as he walked past him.

The student turned sharply towards him, made a grimace, and bringing his face close into unseemly proximity to the face of his excellency, crowed like a cock at the top of his voice. This was too much. Ivan Ilyitch got up from the table. In spite of that, a roar of inexpressible laughter followed, for the crow was an extraordinarily good imitation, and the whole performance was utterly unexpected. Ivan Ilyitch was still standing in bewilderment, when suddenly Pseldonimov himself made his appearance, and with a bow, began begging him to come to supper. His mother followed him.

'Your excellency,' she said, bowing, 'do us the honour, do not disdain our humble fare.'

'I . . . I really don't know,' Ivan Ilyitch was beginning. 'I did not come with that idea . . . I . . . meant to be going . . . '

He was, in fact, holding his hat in his hands. What is more, he had at that very moment taken an inward vow at all costs to depart at once and on no account whatever to consent to remain, and . . . he remained. A minute later he led the procession to the table. Pseldonimov and his mother walked in front, clearing the way for him. They made him sit down in the seat of honour, and again a bottle of champagne, opened but not begun, was set beside his plate. By way of *hors d'oeuvres* there were salt herrings and vodka. He put out his hand, poured out a large glass of vodka and drank it off. He had never drunk vodka before. He felt as though he were rolling down a hill, were flying, flying, flying, that he must stop himself, catch at something, but there was no possibility of it.

His position was certainly becoming more and more eccentric. What is more, it seemed as though fate were mocking at him. God knows what had happened to him in the course of an hour or so. When he went in he had, so to say, opened his arms to embrace all humanity, all his subordinates; and here not more than an hour had passed and in all his aching heart he felt and knew that he hated Pseldonimov and was cursing him, his wife and his wedding. What was more, he saw from his face, from his eyes alone, that Pseldonimov himself hated him, that he was looking at him with eyes that almost said: 'If only you would take yourself off, curse you! Foisting yourself on us!' All this he had read for some time in his eyes.

Of course as he sat down to table, Ivan Ilyitch would sooner have had his hand cut off than have owned, not only aloud but even to himself, that this was really so. The moment had not fully arrived yet. There was still a moral vacillation. But his heart, his heart . . . it ached! It was clamouring for freedom, for air, for rest. Ivan Ilyitch was really too good-natured.

He knew, of course, that he ought long before to have gone away, not merely to have gone away but to have made his escape. That all this was not the same, but had turned out utterly different from what he had dreamed of on the pavement.

'Why did I come? Did I come here to eat and drink?' he asked himself as he tasted the salt herring. He even had attacks of scepticism. There was at moments a faint stir of irony in regard to his own fine action at the bottom of his heart. He actually wondered at times why he had come in.

But how could he go away? To go away like this without having finished the business properly was impossible. What would people say? They would say that he was frequenting low company. Indeed it really would amount to that if he did not end it properly. What would Stepan Nikiforovitch, Semyon Ivanovitch say (for of course it would be all over the place by tomorrow)? What would be said in the offices, at the Shembels', at the Shubins'? No. he must take his departure in such a way that all should understand why he had come, he must make clear his moral aim . . . And meantime the dramatic moment would not present itself. 'They don't even respect me,' he went on, thinking. 'What are they laughing at? They are as free and easy as though they had no feeling . . . But I have long suspected that all the younger generation are without feeling! I must remain at all costs! They have just been dancing, but now at table they will all be gathered together . . . I will talk about questions, about reforms, about the greatness of Russia . . . I can still win their enthusiasm! Yes! Perhaps nothing is yet lost . . . Perhaps it is always like this in reality. What should I begin upon with them to attract them? What plan can I hit upon? I am lost, simply lost . . . And what is it they want, what is it they require? . . . I see they are laughing together there. Can it be at me, merciful heavens! But what is it I want . . . why is it I am here, why don't I go away, why do I go on persisting?' . . . He thought this, and a sort of shame, a deep unbearable shame, rent his heart more and more intensely.

*   *   *

But everything went on in the same way, one thing after another.

Just two minutes after he had sat down to the table one terrible thought overwhelmed him completely. He suddenly felt that he was horribly drunk, that is, not as he was before, but hopelessly drunk. The cause of this was the glass of vodka which he had drunk after the champagne, and which had immediately produced an effect. He was conscious, he felt in every fibre of his being, that he was growing hopelessly feeble. Of course his assurance was greatly increased, but consciousness had not deserted him, and it kept crying out: 'It is bad, very bad and, in fact, utterly unseemly!' Of course his unstable drunken reflections could not rest long on one subject; there began to be apparent and unmistakably so, even to himself, two opposite sides. On one side there was swaggering assurance, a desire to conquer, a disdain of obstacles and a desperate confidence that he would attain his object. The other side showed itself in the aching of his heart, and a sort of gnawing in his soul. 'What would they say? How would it all end? What would happen tomorrow, tomorrow, tomorrow? . . . '

He had felt vaguely before that he had enemies in the company. 'No doubt that was because I was drunk,' he thought with agonising doubt. What was his horror when he actually, by unmistakable signs, convinced himself now that he really had enemies at the table, and that it was impossible to doubt it.

'And why – why?' he wondered.

At the table there were all the thirty guests, of whom several were quite tipsy. Others were behaving with a careless and sinister in-dependence, shouting and talking at the top of their voices, bawling out the toasts before the time, and pelting the ladies with pellets of bread. One unprepossessing personage in a greasy coat had fallen off his chair as soon as he sat down, and remained so till the end of supper. Another one made desperate efforts to stand on the table, to propose a toast, and only the officer, who seized him by the tails of his coat, moderated his premature ardour. The supper was a pell-mell affair, although they had hired a cook who had been in the service of a general; there was the galantine, there was tongue and potatoes, there were rissoles with green peas, there was, finally, a goose, and last of all blancmange. Among the drinks were beer, vodka and sherry. The only bottle of champagne was standing beside the general, which obliged him to pour it out for himself and also for Akim Petrovitch, who did not venture at supper to officiate on his own initiative. The other guests had to drink the toasts in Caucasian wine or anything else they could get. The table was made up of several tables put together, among them even a card-table. It was covered with many tablecloths, among them one coloured Yaroslav cloth; the gentlemen sat alternately with the ladies. Pseldonimov's mother would not sit down to the table; she bustled about and supervised. But another sinister female figure, who had not shown herself till then, appeared on the scene, wearing a reddish silk dress, with a very high cap on her head and a bandage round her face for toothache. It appeared that this was the bride's mother, who had at last consented to emerge from a back room for supper. She had refused to appear till then owing to her implacable hostility to Pseldonimov's mother, but to that we will refer later. This lady looked spitefully, even sarcastically, at the general, and evidently did not wish to be presented to him. To Ivan Ilyitch this figure appeared suspicious in the extreme. But apart from her, several other persons were suspicious and inspired involuntary apprehension and uneasiness. It even seemed that they were in some sort of plot together against Ivan Ilyitch. At any rate it seemed so to him, and throughout the whole supper he became more and more convinced of it. A gentleman with a beard, some sort of free artist, was particularly sinister; he even looked at Ivan Ilyitch several times, and then turning to his neighbour, whispered something. Another person present was unmistakably drunk, but yet, from certain signs, was to be regarded with suspicion. The medical student, too, gave rise to unpleasant expectations. Even the officer himself was not quite to be depended on. But the young man on the comic paper was blazing with hatred, he lolled in his chair, he looked so haughty and conceited, he snorted so aggressively! And though the rest of the guests took absolutely no notice of the young journalist, who had contributed only four wretched poems to the *Firebrand*, and had consequently become a Liberal and evidently, indeed, disliked him, yet when a pellet of bread aimed in his direction fell near Ivan Ilyitch, he was ready to stake his head that it had been thrown by no other than the young man in question.

All this, of course, had a pitiable effect on him.

Another observation was particularly unpleasant. Ivan Ilyitch became aware that he was beginning to articulate indistinctly and with difficulty, that he was longing to say a great deal, but that his tongue refused to obey him. And then he suddenly seemed to forget himself, and worst of all he would suddenly burst into a loud guffaw of laughter, apropos of nothing. This inclination quickly passed off after a glass of champagne which Ivan Ilyitch had not meant to drink, though he had poured it out; he suddenly drank it quite by accident. After that glass he felt at once almost inclined to cry. He felt that he was sinking into a most peculiar state of sentimentality; he began to be again filled with love, he loved everyone, even Pseldonimov, even the young man on the comic paper. He suddenly longed to embrace all of them, to forget everything and to be reconciled. What is more, to tell them everything openly, all, all; that is, to tell them what a good, nice man he was, with what wonderful talents. What services he would do for his country, how good he was at entertaining the fair sex, and above all, how progressive he was, how humanely ready he was to be indulgent to all, to the very lowest; and finally in conclusion to tell them frankly all the motives that had impelled him to turn up at Pseldonimov's uninvited, to drink two bottles of champagne and to make him happy with his presence.

'The truth, the holy truth and candour before all things! I will capture them by candour. They will believe me, I see it clearly; they actually look at me with hostility, but when I tell them all I shall conquer them completely. They will fill their glasses and drink my health with shouts. The officer will break his glass on his spur. Perhaps they will even should hurrah! Even if they want to toss me after the Hussar fashion I will not oppose them, and indeed it would be very jolly! I will kiss the bride on her forehead; she is charming. Akim Petrovitch is a very nice man, too. Pseldonimov will improve, of course, later on. He will acquire, so to speak, a society polish . . . And although, of course, the younger generation has not that delicacy of feeling, yet . . . yet I will talk to them about the contemporary significance of Russia among the European States. I will refer to the peasant question, too; yes, and . . . and they will all like me and I shall leave with glory! . . . '

These dreams were, of course, extremely agreeable, but what was unpleasant was that in the midst of these roseate anticipations, Ivan Ilyitch suddenly discovered in himself another unexpected propensity, that was to spit. Indeed saliva began running from his mouth apart from any will of his own. He observed the effect on Akim Petrovitch, whose cheek he spluttered upon and who sat not daring to wipe it off from respectfulness. Ivan Ilyitch took his dinner napkin and wiped it himself, but this immediately struck him himself as so incongruous, so opposed to all common sense, that he sank into silence and began wondering. Though Akim Petrovitch emptied his glass, yet he sat as though he were scalded. Ivan Ilyitch reflected now that he had for almost a quarter of an hour been talking to him about some most interesting subject, but that Akim Petrovitch had not only seemed embarrassed as he listened, but positively frightened. Pseldonimov, who was sitting one chair away from him, also craned his neck towards him, and bending his head sideways, listened to him with the most unpleasant air. He actually seemed to be keeping a watch on him. Turning his eyes upon the rest of the company, he saw that many were looking straight at him and laughing. But what was strangest of all was that he was not in the least embarrassed by it; on the contrary, he sipped his glass again and suddenly began speaking so that all could hear: 'I was saying just now,' he began as loudly as possible, 'I was saying just now, ladies and gentlemen, to Akim Petrovitch, that Russia . . . yes, Russia . . . in short, you understand, that I mean to s-s-say . . . Russia is living, it is my profound conviction, through a period of hu-hu-manity . . . '

'Hu-hu-manity . . . ' was heard at the other end of the table.

'Hu-hu . . . '

'Tu-tu!'

Ivan Ilyitch stopped. Pseldonimov got up from his chair and began trying to see who had shouted. Akim Petrovitch stealthily shook his head, as though admonishing the guests. Ivan Ilyitch saw this distinctly, but in his confusion said nothing.

'Humanity!' he continued obstinately; 'and this evening . . . and only this evening I said to Stepan Niki-ki-forovitch . . . yes . . . that . . . that the regeneration, so to speak, of things . . . '

'Your excellency!' came a loud exclamation from the other end of the table.

'What is your pleasure?' answered Ivan Ilyitch, pulled up short and trying to distinguish who had called to him.

'Nothing at all, your excellency. I was carried away, continue! Con-ti-nue!' the voice was heard again.

Ivan Ilyitch felt upset.

'The regeneration, so to speak, of those same things.'

'Your excellency!' the voice shouted again.

'What do you want?'

'How do you do!'

This time Ivan Ilyitch could not restrain himself. He broke off his speech and turned to the assailant who had disturbed the general harmony. He was a very young lad, still at school, who had taken more than a drop too much, and was an object of great suspicion to the general. He had been shouting for a long time past, and had even broken a glass and two plates, maintaining that this was the proper thing to do at a wedding. At the moment when Ivan Ilyitch turned towards him, the officer was beginning to pitch into the noisy youngster.

'What are you about? Why are you yelling? We shall turn you out, that's what we shall do – I don't mean you, your excellency, I don't mean you.

'Continue!' cried the hilarious schoolboy, lolling back in his chair. 'Continue, I am listening, and am very, ve-ry, ve-ry much pleased with you! Praisewor-thy, praisewor-thy!'

'The wretched boy is drunk,' said Pseldonimov in a whisper.

'I see that he is drunk, but . . . '

'I was just telling a very amusing anecdote, your excellency!' began the officer, 'about a lieutenant in our company who was talking just like that to his superior officers; so this young man is imitating him now. To every word of his superior officers he said, "Praiseworthy, praiseworthy!" He was turned out of the army ten years ago on account of it.'

'Wha-at lieutenant was that?'

'In our company, your excellency, he went out of his mind over the word praiseworthy. At first they tried gentle methods, then they put him under arrest . . . His commanding officer admonished him in the most fatherly way, and he answered, "Praiseworthy, praiseworthy!" And strange to say, the officer was a fine-looking man, over six feet. They meant to court-martial him, but then they perceived that he was mad.'

'So . . . a schoolboy. A schoolboy's prank need not be taken seriously. For my part I am ready to overlook it . . . '

'They held a medical enquiry, your excellency.'

'Upon my word, but he was alive, wasn't he? What! Did they dissect him?'

A loud and almost universal roar of laughter resounded among the guests, who had till then behaved with decorum. Ivan Ilyitch was furious.

'Ladies and gentlemen!' he shouted, at first scarcely stammering, 'I am fully capable of apprehending that a man is not dissected alive. I imagined that in his derangement he had ceased to be alive . . . that is, that he had died . . . that is, I mean to say . . . that you don't like me . . . and yet I like you all . . . Yes, I like Por . . . Porfiry . . . I am lowering myself by speaking like this . . . '

At that moment Ivan Ilyitch spluttered so that a great dab of saliva flew on to the tablecloth in a most conspicuous place. Pseldonimov flew to wipe it off with a table-napkin.

This last disaster crushed him completely. 'My friends, this is too much,' he cried in despair.

'The boy is drunk, your excellency,' Pseldonimov assured him again.

'Porfiry, I see that you . . . all . . . yes! I say that I hope . . . yes, I call upon you all to tell me in what way have I lowered myself?' Ivan Ilyitch was almost crying.

'Your excellency, good heavens!'

'Porfiry, I appeal to you . . . Tell me, when I came . . . yes . . . yes, to your wedding, I had an object. I was aiming at moral elevation . . . I wanted it to be felt . . . I appeal to all: am I greatly lowered in your eyes or not?'

A deathlike silence. That was just it, a deathlike silence, and to such a downright question. 'They might at least shout at this minute!' flashed through his excellency's head. But the guests only looked at one another. Akim Petrovitch sat more dead than alive, while Pseldonimov, numb with terror, was repeating to himself the awful question which had occurred to him more than once already. 'What shall I have to pay for all this tomorrow?'

At this point the young man on the comic paper, who was very drunk but who had hitherto sat in morose silence, addressed Ivan Ilyitch directly, and with flashing eyes began answering in the name of the whole company.

'Yes,' he said in a loud voice, 'yes, you have lowered yourself. Yes, you are a reactionary . . . re-ac-tion-ary!'

'Young man, you are forgetting yourself! To whom are you speaking, so to express it?' Ivan Ilyitch cried furiously, jumping up from his seat again.

'To you; and secondly, I am not a young man . . . You've come to give yourself airs and try to win popularity.'

'Pseldonimov, what does this mean?' cried Ivan Ilyitch.

But Pseldonimov was reduced to such horror that he stood still like a post and was utterly at a loss what to do. The guests, too, sat mute in their seats. All but the artist and the schoolboy, who applauded and shouted, 'Bravo, bravo!'

The young man on the comic paper went on shouting with unrestrained violence: 'Yes, you came to show off your humanity! You've hindered the enjoyment of everyone. You've been drinking champagne without thinking that it is beyond the means of a clerk at ten roubles a month. And I suspect that you are one of those high officials who are a little too fond of the young wives of their clerks! What is more, I am convinced that you support State monopolies . . . Yes, yes, yes!'

'Pseldonimov, Pseldonimov,' shouted Ivan Ilyitch, holding out his hands to him. He felt that every word uttered by the comic young man was a fresh dagger at his heart.

'Directly, your excellency; please do not disturb yourself!' Pseldonimov cried energetically, rushing up to the comic young man, seizing him by the collar and dragging him away from the table. Such physical strength could indeed not have been expected from the weakly looking Pseldonimov. But the comic young man was very drunk, while Pseldonimov was perfectly sober. Then he gave him two or three cuffs in the back, and thrust him out of the door.

'You are all scoundrels!' roared the young man of the comic paper. 'I will caricature you all tomorrow in the *Firebrand*.'

They all leapt up from their seats.

'Your excellency, your excellency!' cried Pseldonimov, his mother and several others, crowding round the general; 'your excellency, do not be disturbed!'

'No, no,' cried the general, 'I am annihilated . . . I came . . . I meant to bless you, so to speak. And this is how I am paid, for everything, everything! . . . '

He sank on to a chair as though unconscious, laid both his arms on the table, and bowed his head over them, straight into a plate of blancmange. There is no need to describe the general horror. A minute later he got up, evidently meaning to go out, gave a lurch, stumbled against the leg of a chair, fell full length on the floor and snored . . .

This is what is apt to happen to men who don't drink when they accidentally take a glass too much. They preserve their consciousness to the last point, to the last minute, and then fall to the ground as though struck down. Ivan Ilyitch lay on the floor absolutely unconscious. Pseldonimov clutched at his hair and sat as though petrified in that position. The guests made haste to depart, commenting each in his own way on the incident. It was about three o'clock in the morning.

*   *   *

The worst of it was that Pseldonimov's circumstances were far worse than could have been imagined, in spite of the unattractiveness of his present surroundings. And while Ivan Ilyitch is lying on the floor and Pseldonimov is standing over him tearing his hair in despair, we break off the thread of our story and say a few explanatory words about Porfiry Petrovitch Pseldonimov.

Not more than a month before his wedding he was in a state of hopeless destitution. He came from a province where his father had served in some department and where he had died while awaiting his trial on some charge. When five months before his wedding, Pseldonimov, who had been in hopeless misery in Petersburg for a whole year before, got his berth at ten roubles a month, he revived both physically and mentally, but he was soon crushed by circumstances again. There were only two Pseldonimovs left in the world, himself and his mother, who had left the province after her husband's death. The mother and son barely existed in the freezing cold, and sustained life on the most dubious substances. There were days when Pseldonimov himself went with a jug to the Fontanka for water to drink. When he got his place he succeeded in settling with his mother in a 'corner'. She took in washing, while for four months he scraped together every farthing to get himself boots and an overcoat. And what troubles he had to endure at his office; his superiors approached him with the question: 'How long was it since he had had a bath?' There was a rumour about him that under the collar of his uniform there were nests of bugs. But Pseldonimov was a man of strong character. On the surface he was mild and meek; he had the merest smattering of education, he was practically never heard to talk of anything. I do not know for certain whether he thought, made plans and theories, had dreams. But on the other hand there was being formed within him an instinctive, furtive, unconscious determination to fight his way out of his wretched circumstances. He had the persistence of an ant. Destroy an ants' nest, and they will begin at once re-erecting it; destroy it again, and they will begin again without wearying. He was a constructive house-building animal. One could see from his brow that he would make his way, would build his nest, and perhaps even save for a rainy day. His mother was the only creature in the world who loved him, and she loved him beyond everything. She was a woman of resolute character, hard-working and indefatigable, and at the same time good-natured. So perhaps they might have lived in their corner for five or six years till their circumstances changed, if they had not come across the retired titular councillor Mlekopitaev, who had been a clerk in the treasury and had served at one time in the provinces, but had latterly settled in Petersburg and had established himself there with his family. He knew Pseldonimov, and had at one time been under some obligation to his father. He had a little money, not a large sum, of course, but there it was; how much it was no one knew, not his wife, nor his elder daughter, nor his relations. He had two daughters, and as he was an awful bully, a drunkard, a domestic tyrant and, in addition to that, an invalid, he took it into his head one day to marry one of his daughters to Pseldonimov: 'I knew his father,' he would say, 'he was a good fellow and his son will be a good fellow.' Mlekopitaev did exactly as he liked, his word was law. He was a very queer bully. For the most part he spent his time sitting in an armchair, having lost the use of his legs from some disease which did not, however, prevent him from drinking vodka. For days together he would be drinking and swearing. He was an ill-natured man. He always wanted to have someone whom he could be continually tormenting. And for that purpose he kept several distant relations: his sister, a sickly and peevish woman; two of his wife's sisters, also ill-natured and very free with their tongues, and his old aunt, who had through some accident a broken rib; he kept another dependent also, a Russianised German, for the sake of her talent for entertaining him with stories from *The Arabian Nights*.[190] His sole gratification consisted in jeering at all these unfortunate women and abusing them every minute with all his energies; though the latter, not excepting his wife, who had been born with toothache, dared not utter a word in his presence. He set them at loggerheads with one another, inventing and fostering spiteful back-biting and dissension among them, and then laughed and rejoiced seeing how they were ready to tear one another to pieces. He was very much delighted when his elder daughter, who had lived in great poverty for ten years with her husband, an officer of some sort, and was at last left a widow, came to live with him with three little sickly children. He could not endure her children, but as her arrival had increased the material upon which he could work his daily experiments, the old man was very much pleased. All these ill-natured women and sickly children, together with their tormentor, were crowded together in a wooden house on Petersburg Side, and did not get enough to eat because the old man was stingy and gave out to them money a farthing at a time, though he did not grudge himself vodka; they did not get enough sleep because the old man suffered from sleeplessness and insisted on being amused. In short, they all were in misery and cursed their fate. It was at that time that Mlekopitaev's eye fell upon Pseldonimov. He was struck by his long nose and submissive air. His weakly and unprepossessing younger daughter had just reached the age of seventeen. Though she had at one time attended a German school, she had acquired scarcely anything but the alphabet. Then she grew up rickety and anaemic, in fear of her crippled drunken father's crutch, in a bedlam of domestic back-biting, eavesdropping and scolding. She had never had any friends or any brains. She had for a long time been eager to be married. In company she sat mute, but at home with her mother and the women of the household she was spiteful and cantankerous. She was particularly fond of pinching and smacking her sister's children, telling tales of their pilfering bread and sugar, and this led to endless and implacable strife with her elder sister.

Her old father himself offered her to Pseldonimov. Miserable as the latter's position was, he yet asked for a little time to consider. His mother and he hesitated for a long time. But with the young lady there was to come as dowry a house, and though it was a nasty little wooden house of one storey, yet it was property of a kind. Moreover, they would give with her four hundred roubles, and how long would it take him to save that up himself? 'What am I taking the man into my house for?' shouted the drunken bully. 'In the first place because you are all females, and I am sick of female society. I want Pseldonimov, too, to dance to my piping. For I am his benefactor. And in the second place I am doing it because you are all cross and don't want it, so I'll do it to spite you. What I have said, I have said! And you beat her, Porfiry, when she is your wife; she has been possessed of seven devils ever since she was born. You beat them out of her, and I'll get the stick ready.' Pseldonimov made no answer, but he was already decided. Before the wedding his mother and he were taken into the house, washed, clothed, provided with boots and money for the wedding. The old man took them under his protection possibly just because the whole family was prejudiced against them. He positively liked Pseldonimov's mother, so that he actually restrained himself and did not jeer at her. On the other hand, he made Pseldonimov dance the Cossack dance a week before the wedding. 'Well, that's enough. I only wanted to see whether you remembered your position before me or not,' he said at the end of the dance.

He allowed just enough money for the wedding, with nothing to spare, and invited all his relations and acquaintances. On Pseldonimov's side there was no one but the young man who wrote for the *Firebrand*, and Akim Petrovitch, the guest of honour. Pseldonimov was perfectly aware that his bride cherished an aversion for him, and that she was set upon marrying the officer instead of him. But he put up with everything, he had made a compact with his mother to do so. The old father had been drunk and abusive and foul-tongued the whole of the wedding day and during the party in the evening. The whole family took refuge in the back rooms and were crowded there to suffocation. The front rooms were devoted to the dance and the supper. At last when the old man fell asleep dead drunk at eleven o'clock, the bride's mother, who had been particularly displeased with Pseldonimov's mother that day, made up her mind to lay aside her wrath, become gracious and join the company. Ivan Ilyitch's arrival had turned everything upside down. Madame Mlekopitaev was overcome with embarrassment, and began grumbling that she had not been told that the general had been invited. She was assured that he had come uninvited, but was so stupid as to refuse to believe it. Champagne had to be got. Pseldonimov's mother had only one rouble, while Pseldonimov himself had not one farthing. He had to grovel before his ill-natured mother-in-law, to beg for the money for one bottle and then for another. They pleaded for the sake of his future position in the service, for his career, they tried to persuade her. She did at last give from her own purse, but she forced Pseldonimov to swallow such a cupful of gall and bitterness[191] that more than once he ran into the room where the nuptial couch had been prepared, and madly clutching at his hair and trembling all over with impotent rage, he buried his head in the bed destined for the joys of paradise. No, indeed, Ivan Ilyitch had no notion of the price paid for the two bottles of Jackson he had drunk that evening. What was the horror, the misery and even the despair of Pseldonimov when Ivan Ilyitch's visit ended in this unexpected way. He had a prospect again of no end of misery, and perhaps a night of tears and outcries from his peevish bride, and upbraidings from her unreasonable relations. Even apart from this his head ached already, and there was dizziness and mist before his eyes. And here Ivan Ilyitch needed looking after, at three o'clock at night he had to hunt for a doctor or a carriage to take him home, and a carriage it must be, for it would be impossible to let an ordinary cabby take him home in that condition. And where could he get the money for a carriage? Madame Mlekopitaev, furious that the general had not addressed two words to her, and had not even looked at her at supper, declared that she had not a farthing. Possibly she really had not a farthing. Where could he get it? What was he to do? Yes, indeed, he had good cause to tear his hair.

*　　*　　*

Meanwhile Ivan Ilyitch was moved to a little leather sofa that stood in the dining-room. While they were clearing the tables and putting them away, Pseldonimov was rushing all over the place to borrow money; he even tried to get it from the servants, but it appeared that nobody had any. He ventured to trouble Akim Petrovitch, who had stayed after the other guests. But good-natured as he was, the latter was reduced to such bewilderment and even alarm at the mention of money that he uttered the most unexpected and foolish phrases: 'Another time, with pleasure,' he muttered, 'but now . . . you really must excuse me . . . ' And taking his cap, he ran as fast as he could out of the house. Only the good-natured youth who had talked about the dream book was any use at all; and even that came to nothing. He, too, stayed after the others, showing genuine sympathy with Pseldonimov's misfortunes. At last Pseldonimov, together with his mother and the young man, decided in consultation not to send for a doctor, but rather to fetch a carriage and take the invalid home, and meantime to try certain domestic remedies till the carriage arrived, such as moistening his temples and his head with cold water, putting ice on his head, and so on. Pseldonimov's mother undertook this task. The friendly youth flew off in search of a carriage. As there were not even ordinary cabs to be found on the Petersburg Side at that hour, he went off to some livery stables at a distance to wake up the coachmen. They began bargaining, and declared that five roubles would be little to ask for a carriage at that time of night. They agreed to come, however, for three. When at last, just before five o'clock, the young man arrived at Pseldonimov's with the carriage, they had changed their minds. It appeared that Ivan Ilyitch, who was still unconscious, had become so seriously unwell, was moaning and tossing so terribly, that to move him and take him home in such a condition was impossible and actually unsafe. 'What will it lead to next?' said Pseldonimov, utterly disheartened. What was to be done?

A new problem arose: if the invalid remained in the house, where could they put him? There were only two bedsteads in the house: one large double bed in which old Mlekopitaev and his wife slept, and another double bed of imitation walnut which had just been purchased and was destined for the newly married couple. All the other inhabitants of the house slept on the floor side by side on feather beds, for the most part in bad condition and under-stuffed, anything but presentable in fact, and even of these the supply was insufficient; there was not one to spare. Where could the invalid be put? A feather bed might perhaps have been found – it might in the last resort have been pulled from under someone, but where and on what could a bed have been made up? It seemed that the bed must be made up in the drawing-room, for that room was the farthest from the bosom of the family and had a door into the passage. But on what could the bed be made? Surely not upon chairs. We all know that beds can only be made up on chairs for school-boys when they come home for the weekend, and it would be terribly lacking in respect to make up a bed in that way for a personage like Ivan Ilyitch. What would be said next morning when he found himself lying on chairs? Pseldonimov would not hear of that. The only alternative was to put him on the bridal couch. This bridal couch, that we have mentioned already, was in a little room that opened out of the dining-room; on the bedstead was a double mattress actually newly bought first-hand, clean sheets, four pillows in pink calico covered with frilled muslin cases. The quilt was of pink satin, and it was quilted in patterns. Muslin curtains hung down from a golden ring overhead, in fact it was all just as it should be, and the guests who had all visited the bridal chamber had admired the decoration of it; though the bride could not endure Pseldonlmov, she had several times in the course of the evening run in to have a look at it on the sly. What was her indignation, her wrath, when she learned that they meant to move an invalid, suffering from something not unlike a mild attack of cholera, to her bridal couch! The bride's mother took her part, broke into abuse and vowed she would complain to her husband next day, but Pseldonimov asserted himself and insisted: Ivan Ilyitch was moved into the bridal chamber, and a bed was made up on chairs for the young people. The bride whimpered, would have liked to pinch him, but dared not disobey; her papa had a crutch with which she was very familiar, and she knew that her papa would call her to account next day. To console her they carried the pink satin quilt and the pillows in muslin cases into the drawing-room. At that moment the youth arrived with the carriage, and was horribly alarmed that the carriage was not wanted. He was left to pay for it himself, and he never had as much as a ten-kopeck piece. Pseldonimov explained that he was utterly bankrupt. They tried to parley with the driver. But he began to be noisy and even to batter on the shutters. How it ended I don't know exactly. I believe the youth was carried off to Peski by way of a hostage, to Fourth Rozhdensky Street[192] where he hoped to rouse a student who was spending the night at a friend's, and to try to borrow the money from him. It was going on for six o'clock in the morning when the young people were left alone and shut up in the drawing-room. Pseldonimov's mother spent the whole night by the bedside of the sufferer. She installed herself on a rug on the floor and covered herself with an old coat, but could not sleep because she had to get up every minute: Ivan Ilyitch had a terrible attack of colic. Madame Pseldonimov, a woman of courage and greatness of soul, undressed him with her own hands, took off all his things, looked after him as if he were her own son, and spent the whole night carrying basins, etc., from the bedroom across the passage and bringing them back again empty. And yet the misfortunes of that night were not yet over.

*   *   *

Not more than ten minutes after the young people had been shut up alone in the drawing-room, a piercing shriek was suddenly heard, not a cry of joy, but a shriek of the most sinister kind. The screams were followed by a noise, a crash, as though of the falling of chairs, and instantly there burst into the still dark room a perfect crowd of exclaiming and frightened women, attired in every kind of dishabille.[193] These women were the bride's mother, her elder sister, abandoning for the moment the sick children, and her three aunts; the great-aunt with a broken rib dragged herself in too. Even the cook was there, and the German lady who told stories (whose own feather bed, the best in the house, and her only property, had been forcibly dragged from under her for the young couple), trailed in together with the others. All these respectable and sharp-eyed ladies had, a quarter of an hour before, made their way on tiptoe from the kitchen across the passage, and were listening in the anteroom, devoured by unaccountable curiosity. Meanwhile someone lighted a candle, and a surprising spectacle met the eyes of all. The chairs supporting the broad feather bed only at the sides had parted under the weight, and the feather bed had fallen between them on to the floor. The bride was sobbing with anger, this time she was mortally offended. Pseldonimov, morally shattered, stood like a criminal caught in a crime. He did not even attempt to defend himself. Shrieks and exclamations sounded on all sides. Pseldonimov's mother ran up at the noise, but the bride's mamma on this occasion got the upper hand. She began by showering strange and for the most part quite undeserved reproaches, such as: 'A nice husband you are, after this. What are you good for after such a disgrace?" and so on; and at last carried her daughter away from her husband, undertaking to bear the full responsibility for doing so with her ferocious husband, who would demand an explanation. All the others followed her out exclaiming and shaking their heads. No one remained with Pseldonimov except his mother, who tried to comfort him. But he sent her away at once.

He was beyond consolation. He made his way to the sofa and sat down in the most gloomy confusion of mind just as he was, barefooted and in nothing but his night attire. His thoughts whirled in a tangled crisscross in his mind. At times he mechanically looked about the room where only a little while ago the dancers had been whirling madly, and in which the cigarette smoke still lingered. Cigarette ends and sweetmeat papers still littered the slopped and dirty floor. The wreck of the nuptial couch and the overturned chairs bore witness to the transitoriness of the fondest and surest earthly hopes and dreams. He sat like this almost an hour. The most oppressive thoughts kept coming into his mind, such as the doubt: What was in store for him in the office now? He recognised with painful clearness that he would have, at all costs, to exchange into another department; that he could not possibly remain where he was after all that had happened that evening. He thought, too, of Mlekopitaev, who would probably make him dance the Cossack dance next day to test his meekness. He reflected, too, that though Mlekopitaev had given fifty roubles for the wedding festivities, every farthing of which had been spent, he had not thought of giving him the four hundred roubles yet, no mention had been made of it, in fact. And, indeed, even the house had not been formally made over to him. He thought, too, of his wife who had left him at the most critical moment of his life, of the tall officer who had dropped on one knee before her. He had noticed that already; he thought of the seven devils which according to the testimony of her own father were in possession of his wife, and of the crutch in readiness to drive them out . . . Of course he felt equal to bearing a great deal, but destiny had let loose such surprises upon him that he might well have doubts of his fortitude. So Pseldonimov mused dolefully. Meanwhile the candle end was going out, its fading light, falling straight upon Pseldonimov's profile, threw a colossal shadow of it on the wall, with a drawn-out neck, a hooked nose, and with two tufts of hair sticking out on his forehead and the back of his head. At last, when the air was growing cool with the chill of early morning, he got up, frozen and spiritually numb, crawled to the feather bed that was lying between the chairs, and without rearranging anything, without putting out the candle end, without even laying the pillow under his head, fell into a leaden, deathlike sleep, such as the sleep of men condemned to flogging on the morrow must be.

* * *

On the other hand, what could be compared with the agonising night spent by Ivan Ilyitch Pralinsky on the bridal couch of the unlucky Pseldonimov! For some time, headache, vomiting and other most unpleasant symptoms did not leave him for one second. He was in the torments of hell. The faint glimpses of consciousness that visited his brain, lighted up such an abyss of horrors, such gloomy and revolting pictures, that it would have been better for him not to have returned to consciousness. Everything was still in a turmoil in his mind, however. He recognised Pseldonimov's mother, for instance, heard her gentle admonitions, such as: 'Be patient, my dear; be patient, good sir, it won't be so bad presently.' He recognised her, but could give no logical explanation of her presence beside him. Revolting phantoms haunted him, most frequently of all he was haunted by Semyon Ivanitch; but looking more intently, he saw that it was not Semyon Ivanitch but Pseldonimov's nose. He had visions, too, of the free-and-easy artist, and the officer and the old lady with her face tied up. What interested him most of all was the gilt ring which hung over his head, through which the curtains hung. He could distinguish it distinctly in the dim light of the candle end which lighted up the room, and he kept wondering inwardly: what was the object of that ring, why was it there, what did it mean? He questioned the old lady several times about it, but apparently did not say what he meant; and she evidently did not understand it, however much he struggled to explain. At last, by morning, the symptoms had ceased and he fell into a sleep, a sound sleep without dreams. He slept about an hour, and when he woke he was almost completely conscious, with an insufferable headache and a disgusting taste in his mouth and on his tongue, which seemed turned into a piece of cloth. He sat up in the bed, looked about him, and pondered. The pale light of morning, peeping through the cracks of the shutters in a narrow streak, quivered on the wall. It was about seven o'clock. But when Ivan Ilyitch suddenly grasped the position and recalled all that had happened to him since last evening; when he remembered all his adventures at supper, the failure of his magnanimous action, his speech at table; when he realised all at once with horrifying clearness all that might come of this now, all that people would say and think of him; when he looked round and saw to what a mournful and hideous condition he had reduced the peaceful bridal couch of his clerk – oh, then such deadly shame, such agony overwhelmed him, that he uttered a shriek, hid his face in his hands and fell back on the pillow in despair. A minute later he jumped out of bed, saw his clothes carefully folded and brushed on a chair beside him, seized them, and as best as he could, in desperate haste, began putting them on, looking round and seeming terribly frightened at something. On another chair close by lay his greatcoat and fur cap, and his yellow gloves were in his cap. He meant to steal away secretly. But suddenly the door opened and the elder Madame Pseldonimov walked in with an earthenware jug and basin. A towel was hanging over her shoulder. She set down the jug, and without further conversation told him that he must wash.

'Come, my good sir, wash; you can't go without washing . . .'

And at that instant Ivan Ilyitch recognised that if there was one being in the whole world whom he need not fear, and before whom he need not feel ashamed, it was that old lady. He washed. And long afterwards, at painful moments of his life, he recalled among other pangs of remorse all the circumstances of that waking, and that earthenware basin, and the china jug filled with cold water in which there were still floating icicles, and the oval cake of soap at fifteen kopecks, in pink paper with letters embossed on it, evidently bought for the bridal pair though it fell to Ivan Ilyitch to use it, and the old lady with the linen towel over her left shoulder. The cold water refreshed him, he dried his face, and without even thanking his sister of mercy, he snatched up his hat, flung over his shoulders the coat handed to him by Pseldon-imov, and crossing the passage and the kitchen where the cat was already mewing, and the cook sitting up in her bed staring after him with greedy curiosity, ran out into the yard, into the street, and threw himself into the first sledge he came across. It was a frosty morning. A chilly yellow fog still hid the house and everything. Ivan Ilyitch turned up his collar. He thought that everyone was looking at him, that they were all recognising him, all . . .

*   *   *

For eight days he did not leave the house or show himself at the office. He was ill, wretchedly ill, but more morally than physically. He lived through a perfect hell in those days, and they must have been reckoned to his account in the other world. There were moments when he thought of becoming a monk and entering a monastery. There really were. His imagination, indeed, took special excursions during that period. He pictured subdued subterranean singing, an open coffin, living in a solitary cell, forests and caves; but when he came to himself he recognised almost at once that all this was dreadful nonsense and exaggeration, and was ashamed of this nonsense. Then began attacks of moral agony on the theme of his *existence manquée*. Then shame flamed up again in his soul, took complete possession of him at once, consumed him like fire and reopened his wounds. He shuddered as pictures of all sorts rose before his mind. What would people say about him, what would they think when he walked into his office? what a whisper would dog his steps for a whole year, ten years, his whole life! His story would go down to posterity. He sometimes fell into such dejection that he was ready to go straight off to Semyon Ivanovitch and ask for his forgiveness and friendship. He did not even justify himself, there was no limit to his blame of himself. He could find no extenuating circumstances, and was ashamed of trying to.

He had thoughts, too, of resigning his post at once and devoting himself to human happiness as a simple citizen, in solitude. In any case he would have completely to change his whole circle of acquaintances, and so thoroughly as to eradicate all memory of himself. Then the thought occurred to him that this, too, was nonsense, and that if he adopted greater severity with his subordinates it might all be set right. Then he began to feel hope and courage again. At last, at the expiration of eight days of hesitation and agonies, he felt that he could not endure to be in uncertainty any longer, and *un beau matin*[194] he made up his mind to go to the office.

He had pictured a thousand times over his return to the office as he sat at home in misery. With horror and conviction he told himself that he would certainly hear behind him an ambiguous whisper, would see ambiguous faces, would intercept ominous smiles. What was his surprise when nothing of the sort happened. He was greeted with respect; he was met with bows; everyone was grave; everyone was busy. His heart was filled with joy as he made his way to his own room.

He set to work at once with the utmost gravity, he listened to some reports and explanations, settled doubtful points. He felt as though he had never explained knotty points and given his decisions so intelligently, so judiciously as that morning. He saw that they were satisfied with him, that they respected him, that he was treated with respect. The most thin-skinned sensitiveness could not have discovered anything.

At last Akim Petrovitch made his appearance with some document. The sight of him sent a stab to Ivan Ilyitch's heart, but only for an instant. He went into the business with Akim Petrovitch, talked with dignity, explained things, and showed him what was to be done. The only thing he noticed was that he avoided looking at Akim Petrovitch for any length of time, or rather Akim Petrovitch seemed afraid of catching his eye, but at last Akim Petrovitch had finished and began to collect his papers.

'And there is one other matter,' he began as dryly as he could, 'The clerk Pseldonimov's petition to be transferred to another department. His excellency Semyon Ivanovitch Shipulenko has promised him a post. He begs your gracious assent, your excellency.'

'Oh, so he is being transferred,' said Ivan Ilyitch, and he felt as though a heavy weight had rolled off his heart. He glanced at Akim Petrovitch, and at that instant their eyes met. 'Certainly, I for my part . . . I will assent,' answered Ivan Ilyitch; 'I am ready.'

Akim Petrovitch evidently wanted to slip away as quickly as he could. But in a rush of generous feeling Ivan Ilyitch determined to speak out. Apparently some inspiration had come to him again.

'Tell him,' he began, bending a candid glance full of profound meaning upon Akim Petrovitch, 'tell Pseldonimov that I feel no ill-will, no, I do not! . . . That on the contrary I am ready to forget all that is past, to forget it all . . . '

But all at once Ivan Ilyitch broke off, looking with wonder at the strange behaviour of Akim Petrovitch, who suddenly seemed transformed from a sensible person into a fearful fool. Instead of listening and hearing Ivan Ilyitch to the end, he suddenly flushed crimson in the silliest way, began with positively unseemly haste making strange little bows, and at the same time edged towards the door. His whole appearance betrayed a desire to sink through the floor, or more accurately, to get back to his table as quickly as possible. Ivan Ilyitch, left alone, got up from his chair in confusion; he looked in the looking-glass without noticing his face.

'No, severity, severity and nothing but severity,' he whispered almost unconsciously, and suddenly a vivid flush overspread his face. He felt suddenly more ashamed, more weighed down than he had been in the most insufferable moments of his eight days of tribulation. 'I did break down!' he said to himself, and sank helplessly into his chair.

Notes from Underground

The author of the diary and the diary itself are, of course, imaginary. Nevertheless it is clear that such persons as the writer of these notes not only may, but positively must, exist in our society, when we consider the circumstances in the midst of which our society is formed. I have tried to expose to the view of the public more distinctly than is commonly done, one of the characters of the recent past. He is one of the representatives of a generation still living. In this fragment, entitled 'Underground', this person introduces himself and his views, and, as it were, tries to explain the causes owing to which he has made his appearance and was bound to make his appearance in our midst. In the second fragment there are added the actual notes of this person concerning certain events in his life.   FYODOR DOSTOEVSKY

PART ONE

UNDERGROUND

1

I AM A SICK MAN ... I am a spiteful man. I am an unattractive man. I believe my liver is diseased. However, I know nothing at all about my disease, and do not know for certain what ails me. I don't consult a doctor for it, and never have, though I have a respect for medicine and doctors. Besides, I am extremely superstitious, sufficiently so to respect medicine, anyway (I am well educated enough not to be superstitious, but I am superstitious). No, I refuse to consult a doctor from spite. That you probably will not understand. Well, I understand it, though. Of course, I can't explain who it is precisely that I am mortifying in this case by my spite: I am perfectly well aware that I cannot 'pay out' the doctors by not consulting them; I know better than anyone that by all this I am only injuring myself and no one else. But still, if I don't consult a doctor it is from spite. My liver is bad, well – let it get worse!

I have been going on like that for a long time – twenty years. Now I am forty. I used to be in the government service, but am no longer. I was a spiteful official. I was rude and took pleasure in being so. I did not take bribes, you see, so I was bound to find a recompense in that, at least. (A poor jest, but I will not scratch it out. I wrote it thinking it would sound very witty; but now that I have seen myself that I only wanted to show off in a despicable way, I will not scratch it out on purpose!)

When petitioners used to come for information to the table at which I sat, I used to grind my teeth at them, and felt intense enjoyment when I succeeded in making anybody unhappy. I almost did succeed. For the most part they were all timid people – of course, they were petitioners. But of the uppish ones there was one officer in particular I could not endure. He simply would not be humble, and clanked his sword in a disgusting way. I carried on a feud with him for eighteen months over that sword. At last I got the better of him. He left off clanking it. That happened in my youth, though. But do you know, gentlemen, what was the chief point about my spite? Why, the whole point, the real sting of it lay in the fact that continually, even in the moment of the acutest spleen, I was inwardly conscious with shame that I was not only not a spiteful but not even an embittered man, that I was simply scaring sparrows at random and amusing myself by it. I might foam at the mouth, but bring me a doll to play with, give me a cup of tea with sugar in it, and maybe I should be appeased. I might even be genuinely touched, though probably I should grind my teeth at myself afterwards and lie awake at night with shame for months after. That was my way.

I was lying when I said just now that I was a spiteful official. I was lying from spite. I was simply amusing myself with the petitioners and with the officer, and in reality I never could become spiteful. I was conscious every moment in myself of many, very many elements absolutely opposite to that. I felt them positively swarming in me, these opposite elements. I knew that they had been swarming in me all my life and craving some outlet from me, but I would not let them, would not let them, purposely would not let them come out. They tormented me till I was ashamed: they drove me to convulsions and – sickened me, at last, how they sickened me! Now, are not you fancying, gentlemen, that I am expressing remorse for something now, that I am asking your forgiveness for something? I am sure you are fancying that . . . However, I assure you I do not care if you are . . . It was not only that I could not become spiteful, I did not know how to become anything; neither spiteful nor kind, neither a rascal nor an honest man, neither a hero nor an insect. Now, I am living out my life in my corner, taunting myself with the spiteful and useless consolation that an intelligent man cannot become anything seriously, and it is only the fool who becomes anything. Yes, a man in the nineteenth century must and morally ought to be pre-eminently a characterless creature; a man of character, an active man is pre-eminently a limited creature. That is my conviction of forty years. I am forty years old now, and you know forty years is a whole lifetime; you know it is extreme old age. To live longer than forty years is bad manners, is vulgar, immoral. Who does live beyond forty? Answer that, sincerely and honestly I will tell you who do: fools and worthless fellows. I tell all old men that to their face, all these venerable old men, all these silver-haired and reverend seniors! I tell the whole world that to its face! I have a right to say so, for I shall go on living to sixty myself. To seventy! To eighty! . . . Stay, let me take breath . . .

You imagine no doubt, gentlemen, that I want to amuse you. You are mistaken in that, too. I am by no means such a mirthful person as you imagine, or as you may imagine; however, irritated by all this babble (and I feel that you are irritated) you think fit to ask me who I am – then my answer is, I am a collegiate assessor. I was in the service that I might have something to eat (and solely for that reason), and when last year a distant relation left me six thousand roubles in his will I immediately retired from the service and settled down in my corner. I used to live in this corner before, but now I have settled down in it. My room is a wretched, horrid one in the outskirts of the town. My servant is an old country-woman, ill-natured from stupidity, and, moreover, there is always a nasty smell about her. I am told that the Petersburg climate is bad for me, and that with my small means it is very expensive to live in Petersburg. I know all that better than all these sage and experienced counsellors and monitors . . . But I am remaining in Petersburg; I am not going away from Petersburg! I am not going away because . . . ech! Why, it is absolutely no matter whether I am going away or not going away.

But what can a decent man speak of with most pleasure?

Answer: Of himself.

Well, so I will talk about myself.

I want now to tell you, gentlemen, whether you care to hear it or not, why I could not even become an insect. I tell you solemnly that I have many times tried to become an insect. But I was not equal even to that. I swear, gentlemen, that to be too conscious is an illness – a real thorough-going illness. For man's everyday needs, it would have been quite enough to have the ordinary human consciousness, that is, half or a quarter of the amount which falls to the lot of a cultivated man of our unhappy nineteenth century, especially one who has the fatal ill-luck to inhabit Petersburg, the most theoretical and intentional town on the whole terrestrial globe. (There are intentional and unintentional towns.) It would have been quite enough, for instance, to have the consciousness by which all so-called direct persons and men of action live. I bet you think I am writing all this from affectation, to be witty at the expense of men of action; and what is more, that from ill-bred affectation, I am clanking a sword like my officer. But, gentlemen, whoever can pride himself on his diseases and even swagger over them?

Though, after all, everyone does do that; people do pride themselves on their diseases, and I do, maybe, more than anyone. We will not dispute it; my contention was absurd. But yet I am firmly persuaded that a great deal of consciousness, every sort of consciousness, in fact, is a disease. I stick to that. Let us leave that, too, for a minute. Tell me this: why does it happen that at the very, yes, at the very moments when I am most capable of feeling every refinement of all that is 'sublime and beautiful',[195] as they used to say at one time, it would, as though of design, happen to me not only to feel but to do such ugly things, such that . . . Well, in short, actions that all, perhaps, commit; but which, as though purposely, occurred to me at the very time when I was most conscious that they ought not to be committed. The more conscious I was of goodness and of all that was 'sublime and beautiful', the more deeply I sank into my mire and the more ready I was to sink into it altogether. But the chief point was that all this was, as it were, not accidental in me, but as though it were bound to be so. It was as though it were my most normal condition, and not in the least disease or depravity, so that at last all desire in me to struggle against this depravity passed. It ended by my almost believing (perhaps actually believing) that this was perhaps my normal condition. But at first, in the beginning, what agonies I endured in that struggle! I did not believe it was the same with other people, and all my life I hid this fact about myself as a secret. I was ashamed (even now, perhaps, I am ashamed): I got to the point of feeling a sort of secret abnormal, despicable enjoyment in returning home to my corner on some disgusting Petersburg night, acutely conscious that that day I had committed a loathsome action again, that what was done could never be undone, and secretly, inwardly gnawing, gnawing at myself for it, tearing and consuming myself till at last the bitterness turned into a sort of shameful accursed sweetness, and at last – into positive real enjoyment! Yes, into enjoyment, into enjoyment! I insist upon that. I have spoken of this because I keep wanting to know for a fact whether other people feel such enjoyment? I will explain; the enjoyment was just from the too intense consciousness of one's own degradation; it was from feeling oneself that one had reached the last barrier, that it was horrible, but that it could not be otherwise; that there was no escape for you; that you never could become a different man; that even if time and faith were still left you to change into something different you would most likely not wish to change; or if you did wish to, even then you would do nothing; because perhaps in reality there was nothing for you to change into.

And the worst of it was, and the root of it all, that it was all in accord with the normal fundamental laws of over-acute consciousness, and with the inertia that was the direct result of those laws, and that consequently one was not only unable to change but could do absolutely nothing. Thus it would follow, as the result of acute consciousness, that one is not to blame in being a scoundrel; as though that were any consolation to the scoundrel once he has come to realise that he actually is a scoundrel. But enough . . . Ech, I have talked a lot of nonsense, but what have I explained? How is enjoyment in this to be explained? But I will explain it. I will get to the bottom of it! That is why I have taken up my pen . . . I, for instance, have a great deal of *amour propre*. I am as suspicious and prone to take offence as a humpback or a dwarf. But upon my word I sometimes have had moments when if I had happened to be slapped in the face I should, perhaps, have been positively glad of it. I say, in earnest, that I should probably have been able to discover even in that a peculiar sort of enjoyment – the enjoyment, of course, of despair; but in despair there are the most intense enjoyments, especially when one is very acutely conscious of the hopelessness of one's position. And when one is slapped in the face – why then the consciousness of being rubbed into a pulp would positively overwhelm one. The worst of it is, look at it which way one will, it still turns out that I was always the most to blame in everything. And what is most humiliating of all, to blame for no fault of my own but, so to say, through the laws of nature. In the first place, to blame because I am cleverer than any of the people surrounding me. (I have always considered myself cleverer than any of the people surrounding me, and sometimes, would you believe it, have been positively ashamed of it. At any rate, I have all my life, as it were, turned my eyes away and never could look people straight in the face.) To blame, finally, because even if I had had magnanimity, I should only have had more suffering from the sense of its uselessness. I should certainly have never been able to do anything from being magnanimous – neither to forgive, for my assailant would perhaps have slapped me from the laws of nature, and one cannot forgive the laws of nature; nor to forget, for even if it were owing to the laws of nature, it is insulting all the same. Finally, even if I had wanted to be anything but magnanimous, had desired on the contrary to revenge myself on my assailant, I could not have revenged myself on anyone for anything because I should certainly never have made up my mind to do anything, even if I had been able to. Why should I not have made up my mind? About that in particular I want to say a few words.

3

With people who know how to revenge themselves and to stand up for themselves in general, how is it done? Why, when they are possessed, let us suppose, by the feeling of revenge, then for the time there is nothing else but that feeling left in their whole being. Such a gentleman simply dashes straight for his object like an infuriated bull with its horns down, and nothing but a wall will stop him. (By the way: facing the wall, such gentlemen – that is, the 'direct' persons and men of action – are genuinely nonplussed. For them a wall is not an evasion, as for us people who think and consequently do nothing; it is not an excuse for turning aside, an excuse for which we are always very glad, though we scarcely believe in it ourselves, as a rule. No, they are nonplussed in all sincerity. The wall has for them something tranquillising, morally soothing, final – maybe even something mysterious . . . but of the wall later.)

Well, such a direct person I regard as the real normal man, as his tender mother nature wished to see him when she graciously brought him into being on the earth. I envy such a man till I am green in the face. He is stupid. I am not disputing that, but perhaps the normal man should be stupid, how do you know? Perhaps it is very beautiful, in fact. And I am the more persuaded of that suspicion, if one can call it so, by the fact that if you take, for instance, the antithesis of the normal man, that is, the man of acute consciousness, who has come, of course, not out of the lap of nature but out of a retort (this is almost mysticism, gentlemen, but I suspect this, too), this retort-made man is sometimes so nonplussed in the presence of his antithesis that with all his exaggerated consciousness he genuinely thinks of himself as a mouse and not a man. It may be an acutely conscious mouse, yet it is a mouse, while the other is a man, and therefore, etc., etc. And the worst of it is, he himself, his very own self, looks on himself as a mouse; no one asks him to do so; and that is an important point. Now let us look at this mouse in action. Let us suppose, for instance, that it feels insulted, too (and it almost always does feel insulted), and wants to revenge itself, too. There may even be a greater accumulation of spite in it than in *L'Homme de la Nature et de la Verité*.[196] The base and nasty desire to vent that spite on its assailant rankles perhaps even more nastily in it than in *L'Homme de la Nature et de la Verité*. For through his innate stupidity the latter looks upon his revenge as justice pure and simple; while in consequence of his acute consciousness the mouse does not believe in the justice of it. To come at last to the deed itself, to the very act of revenge. Apart from the one fundamental nastiness, the luckless mouse succeeds in creating around it so many other nastinesses in the form of doubts and questions, adds to the one question so many unsettled questions, that there inevitably works up around it a sort of fatal brew, a stinking mess, made up of its doubts, emotions and of the contempt spat upon it by the direct men of action who stand solemnly about it as judges and arbitrators, laughing at it till their healthy sides ache. Of course the only thing left for it is to dismiss all that with a wave of its paw, and, with a smile of assumed contempt in which it does not even itself believe, creep ignominiously into its mouse-hole. There in its nasty, stinking, underground home our insulted, crushed and ridiculed mouse promptly becomes absorbed in cold, malignant and, above all, everlasting spite. For forty years together it will remember its injury down to the smallest, most ignominious details, and every time will add, of itself, details still more ignominious, spitefully teasing and tormenting itself with its own imagination. It will itself be ashamed of its imaginings, but yet it will recall it all, it will go over and over every detail, it will invent unheard of things against itself, pretending that those things might happen, and will forgive nothing. Maybe it will begin to revenge itself, too, but, as it were, piecemeal, in trivial ways, from behind the stove, incognito, without believing either in its own right to vengeance, or in the success of its revenge, knowing that from all its efforts at revenge it will suffer a hundred times more than he on whom it revenges itself, while he, I dare say, will not even scratch himself. On its deathbed it will recall it all over again, with interest accumulated over all the years and . . .

But it is just in that cold, abominable half despair, half belief, in that conscious burying oneself alive for grief in the underworld for forty years, in that acutely recognised and yet partly doubtful hopelessness of one's position, in that hell of unsatisfied desires turned inward, in that fever of oscillations, of resolutions determined for ever and repented of again a minute later – that the savour of that strange enjoyment of which I have spoken lies. It is so subtle, so difficult of analysis, that persons who are a little limited, or even simply persons of strong nerves, will not understand a single atom of it. 'Possibly,' you will add on your own account with a grin, 'people will not understand it either who have never received a slap in the face,' and in that way you will politely hint to me that I, too, perhaps, have had the experience of a slap in the face in my life, and so I speak as one who knows. I bet that you are thinking that. But set your minds at rest, gentlemen, I have not received a slap in the face, though it is absolutely a matter of indifference to me what you may think about it. Possibly, I even regret, myself, that I have given so few slaps in the face during my life. But enough . . . not another word on that subject of such extreme interest to you.

I will continue calmly concerning persons with strong nerves who do not understand a certain refinement of enjoyment. Though in certain circumstances these gentlemen bellow their loudest like bulls, though this, let us suppose, does them the greatest credit, yet, as I have said already, confronted with the impossible they subside at once. The impossible means the stone wall! What stone wall? Why, of course, the laws of nature, the deductions of natural science, mathematics. As soon as they prove to you, for instance, that you are descended from a monkey, then it is no use scowling, accept it for a fact. When they prove to you that in reality one drop of your own fat must be dearer to you than a hundred thousand of your fellow-creatures, and that this conclusion is the final solution of all so-called virtues and duties and all such prejudices and fancies, then you have just to accept it, there is no help for it, for twice two is a law of mathematics. Just try refuting it.

'Upon my word, they will shout at you, it is no use protesting: it is a case of twice two makes four! Nature does not ask your permission, she has nothing to do with your wishes, and whether you like her laws or dislike them, you are bound to accept her as she is, and consequently all her conclusions. A wall, you see, is a wall . . . and so on, and so on.'

Merciful heavens! but what do I care for the laws of nature and arithmetic, when, for some reason, I dislike those laws and the fact that twice two makes four? Of course I cannot break through the wall by battering my head against it if I really have not the strength to knock it down, but I am not going to be reconciled to it simply because it is a stone wall and I have not the strength.

As though such a stone wall really were a consolation, and really did contain some word of conciliation, simply because it is as true as twice two makes four. Oh, absurdity of absurdities! How much better it is to understand it all, to recognise it all, all the impossibilities and the stone wall; not to be reconciled to one of those impossibilities and stone walls if it disgusts you to be reconciled to it; by the way of the most inevitable, logical combinations to reach the most revolting conclusions on the everlasting theme, that even for the stone wall you are yourself somehow to blame, though again it is as clear as day you are not to blame in the least, and therefore grinding your teeth in silent impotence to sink into luxurious inertia, brooding on the fact that there is no one even for you to feel vindictive against, that you have not, and perhaps never will have, an object for your spite, that it is a sleight of hand, a bit of juggling, a card-sharper's trick, that it is simply a mess, no knowing what and no knowing who, but in spite of all these uncertainties and jugglings, still there is an ache in you, and the more you do not know, the worse the ache.

4

'Ha, ha, ha! You will be finding enjoyment in toothache next,' you cry, with a laugh.

'Well, even in toothache there is enjoyment,' I answer. I had toothache for a whole month and I know there is. In that case, of course, people are not spiteful in silence, but moan; but they are not candid moans, they are malignant moans, and the malignancy is the whole point. The enjoyment of the sufferer finds expression in those moans; if he did not feel enjoyment in them he would not moan. It is a good example, gentlemen, and I will develop it. Those moans express in the first place all the aimlessness of your pain, which is so humiliating to your consciousness; the whole legal system of nature on which you spit disdainfully, of course, but from which you suffer all the same while she does not. They express the consciousness that you have no enemy to punish, but that you have pain; the consciousness that in spite of all possible Vagenheims[197] you are in complete slavery to your teeth; that if someone wishes it, your teeth will leave off aching, and if he does not, they will go on aching another three months; and that finally if you are still contumacious and still protest, all that is left you for your own gratification is to thrash yourself or beat your wall with your fist as hard as you can, and absolutely nothing more. Well, these mortal insults, these jeers on the part of someone unknown, end at last in an enjoyment which sometimes reaches the highest degree of voluptuousness. I ask you, gentlemen, listen sometimes to the moans of an educated man of the nineteenth century suffering from toothache, on the second or third day of the attack, when he is beginning to moan, not as he moaned on the first day, that is, not simply because he has toothache, not just as any coarse peasant, but as a man affected by progress and European civilisation, a man who is 'divorced from the soil and the national elements', as they express it nowadays. His moans become nasty, disgustingly malignant, and go on for whole days and nights. And of course he knows himself that he is doing himself no sort of good with his moans; he knows better than anyone that he is only lacerating and harassing himself and others for nothing; he knows that even the audience before whom he is making his efforts, and his whole family, listen to him with loathing, do not put a ha'porth of faith in him, and inwardly understand that he might moan differently, more simply, without trills and flourishes, and that he is only amusing himself like that from ill-humour, from malignancy. Well, in all these recognitions and disgraces it is that there lies a voluptuous pleasure. As though he would say: 'I am worrying you, I am lacerating your hearts, I am keeping everyone in the house awake. Well, stay awake then, you, too, feel every minute that I have toothache. I am not a hero to you now, as I tried to seem before, but simply a nasty person, an impostor. Well, so be it, then! I am very glad that you see through me. It is nasty for you to hear my despicable moans: well, let it be nasty; here, I will let you have a nastier flourish in a minute . . . ' You do not understand even now, gentlemen? No, it seems our development and our consciousness must go further to understand all the intricacies of this pleasure. You laugh? Delighted. My jests, gentlemen, are of course in bad taste, jerky, involved, lacking self-confidence. But of course that is because I do not respect myself. Can a man of perception respect himself at all?

Come, can a man who attempts to find enjoyment in the very feeling of his own degradation possibly have a spark of respect for himself? I am not saying this now from any mawkish kind of remorse. And, indeed, I could never endure saying, 'Forgive me, papa, I won't do it again,' not because I am incapable of saying that – on the contrary, perhaps just because I have been too capable of it, and in what a way, too. As though of design I used to get into trouble in cases when I was not to blame in any way. That was the nastiest part of it. At the same time I was genuinely touched and penitent, I used to shed tears and, of course, deceived myself, though I was not acting in the least and there was a sick feeling in my heart at the time . . . For that one could not blame even the laws of nature, though the laws of nature have continually all my life offended me more than anything. It is loathsome to remember it all, but it was loathsome even then. Of course, a minute or so later I would realise wrathfully that it was all a lie, a revolting lie, an affected lie, that is, all this penitence, this emotion, these vows of reform. You will ask why did I worry myself with such antics: answer, because it was very dull to sit with one's hands folded, and so one began cutting capers. That is really it. Observe yourselves more carefully, gentlemen, then you will understand that it is so. I invented adventures for myself and made up a life, so as at least to live in some way. How many times it has happened to me – well, for instance, to take offence simply on purpose, for nothing; and one knows oneself, of course, that one is offended at nothing; that one is putting it on, but yet one brings oneself at last to the point of being really offended. All my life I have had an impulse to play such pranks, so that in the end I could not control it in myself. Another time, twice, in fact, I tried hard to be in love. I suffered, too, gentlemen, I assure you. In the depth of my heart there was no faith in my suffering, only a faint stir of mockery, but yet I did suffer, and in the real, orthodox way; I was jealous, beside myself . . . and it was all from *ennui*, gentlemen, all from *ennui*; inertia overcame me. You know the direct, legitimate fruit of consciousness is inertia, that is, conscious sitting-with-the-hands-folded. I have referred to this already. I repeat, I repeat with emphasis: all 'direct' persons and men of action are active just because they are stupid and limited. How explain that? I will tell you: in consequence of their limitation they take immediate and secondary causes for primary ones, and in that way persuade themselves more quickly and easily than other people do that they have found an infallible foundation for their activity, and their minds are at ease and you know that is the chief thing. To begin to act, you know, you must first have your mind completely at ease and no trace of doubt left in it. Why, how am I, for example, to set my mind at rest? Where are the primary causes on which I am to build? Where are my foundations? Where am I to get them from? I exercise myself in reflection, and consequently with me every primary cause at once draws after itself another still more primary, and so on to infinity. That is just the essence of every sort of consciousness and reflection. It must be a case of the laws of nature again. What is the result of it in the end? Why, just the same. Remember I spoke just now of vengeance. (I am sure you did not take it in.) I said that a man revenges himself because he sees justice in it. Therefore he has found a primary cause, that is, justice. And so he is at rest on all sides, and consequently he carries out his revenge calmly and successfully, being persuaded that he is doing a just and honest thing. But I see no justice in it, I find no sort of virtue in it either, and consequently if I attempt to revenge myself, it is only out of spite. Spite, of course, might overcome everything, all my doubts, and so might serve quite successfully in place of a primary cause, precisely because it is not a cause. But what is to be done if I have not even spite (I began with that just now, you know). In consequence again of those accursed laws of consciousness, anger in me is subject to chemical disintegration. You look into it, the object flies off into thin air, your reasons evaporate, the criminal is not to be found, the wrong becomes not a wrong but a phantom, something like the toothache, for which no one is to blame, and consequently there is only the same outlet left again – that is, to beat the wall as hard as you can. So you give it up with a wave of the hand because you have not found a fundamental cause. And try letting yourself be carried away by your feelings, blindly, without reflection, without a primary cause, repelling consciousness at least for a time; hate or love, if only not to sit with your hands folded. The day after tomorrow, at the latest, you will begin despising yourself for having knowingly deceived yourself. Result: a soap-bubble and inertia. Oh, gentlemen, do you know, perhaps I consider myself an intelligent man, only because all my life I have been able neither to begin nor to finish anything. Granted I am a babbler, a harmless vexatious babbler, like all of us. But what is to be done if the direct and sole vocation of every intelligent man is babble, that is, the intentional pouring of water through a sieve?

Oh, if I had done nothing simply from laziness! Heavens, how I should have respected myself, then. I should have respected myself because I should at least have been capable of being lazy; there would at least have been one quality, as it were, positive in me, in which I could have believed myself. Question: What is he? Answer: A sluggard; how very pleasant it would have been to hear that of oneself! It would mean that I was positively defined, it would mean that there was something to say about me. 'Sluggard' – why, it is a calling and vocation, it is a career. Do not jest, it is so. I should then be a member of the best club by right, and should find my occupation in continually respecting myself. I knew a gentleman who prided himself all his life on being a connoisseur of Lafitte.[198] He considered this as his positive virtue, and never doubted himself. He died, not simply with a tranquil, but with a triumphant conscience, and he was quite right, too. Then I should have chosen a career for myself, I should have been a sluggard and a glutton, not a simple one, but, for instance, one with sympathies for everything sublime and beautiful. How do you like that? I have long had visions of it. That 'sublime and beautiful' weighs heavily on my mind at forty. But that is at forty; then – oh, then it would have been different! I should have found for myself a form of activity in keeping with it, to be precise, drinking to the health of everything 'sublime and beautiful'. I should have snatched at every opportunity to drop a tear into my glass and then to drain it to all that is 'sublime and beautiful'. I should then have turned everything into the sublime and the beautiful; in the nastiest, unquestionable trash, I should have sought out the sublime and the beautiful. I should have exuded tears like a wet sponge. An artist, for instance, paints a picture worthy of Gay.[199] At once I drink to the health of the artist who painted the picture worthy of Gay, because I love all that is 'sublime and beautiful'. An author has written *As You Will*:[200] at once I drink to the health of 'anyone you will' because I love all that is 'sublime and beautiful'.

I should claim respect for doing so. I should persecute anyone who would not show me respect. I should live at ease, I should die with dignity, why, it is charming, perfectly charming! And what a good round belly I should have grown, what a treble chin I should have established, what a ruby nose I should have coloured for myself, so that everyone would have said, looking at me: 'Here is an asset! Here is something real and solid!' And, say what you like, it is very agreeable to hear such remarks about oneself in this negative age.

But these are all golden dreams. Oh, tell me, who was it first announced, who was it first proclaimed, that man only does nasty things because he does not know his own interests; and that if he were enlightened, if his eyes were opened to his real normal interests, man would at once cease to do nasty things, would at once become good and noble because, being enlightened and understanding his real advantage, he would see his own advantage in the good and nothing else, and we all know that not one man can, consciously, act against his own interests, consequently, so to say, through necessity, he would begin doing good? Oh, the babe! Oh, the pure, innocent child! Why, in the first place, when in all these thousands of years has there been a time when man has acted only from his own interest? What is to be done with the millions of facts that bear witness that men, *consciously*, that is fully understanding their real interests, have left them in the background and have rushed headlong on another path, to meet peril and danger, compelled to this course by nobody and by nothing, but, as it were, simply disliking the beaten track, and have obstinately, wilfully, struck out another difficult, absurd way, seeking it almost in the darkness. So, I suppose, this obstinacy and perversity were pleasanter to them than any advantage . . . Advantage! What is advantage? And will you take it upon yourself to define with perfect accuracy in what the advantage of man consists? And what if it so happens that a man's advantage, *sometimes*, not only may, but even must, consist in his desiring in certain cases what is harmful to himself and not advantageous. And if so, if there can be such a case, the whole principle falls into dust. What do you think – are there such cases? You laugh; laugh away, gentlemen, but only answer me: have man's advantages been reckoned up with perfect certainty? Are there not some which not only have not been included but cannot possibly be included under any classification? You see, you gentlemen have, to the best of my knowledge, taken your whole register of human advantages from the averages of statistical figures and politico-economical formulas. Your advantages are prosperity, wealth, freedom, peace – and so on, and so on. So that the man who should, for instance, go openly and knowingly in opposition to all that list would to your thinking, and indeed mine, too, of course, be an obscurantist or an absolute madman: would not he? But, you know, this is what is surprising: why does it so happen that all these statisticians, sages and lovers of humanity when they reckon up human advantages invariably leave out one? They don't even take it into their reckoning in the form in which it should be taken, and the whole reckoning depends upon that. It would be no greater matter, they would simply have to take it, this advantage, and add it to the list. But the trouble is that this strange advantage does not fall under any classification and is not in place in any list. I have a friend for instance . . . Ech! gentlemen, but of course he is your friend, too; and indeed there is no one, no one to whom he is not a friend! When he prepares for any undertaking this gentleman immediately explains to you, elegantly and clearly, exactly how he must act in accordance with the laws of reason and truth. What is more, he will talk to you with excitement and passion of the true normal interests of man; with irony he will upbraid the short-sighted fools who do not understand their own interests, nor the true significance of virtue; and, within a quarter of an hour, without any sudden outside provocation, but simply through something inside him which is stronger than all his interests, he will go off on quite a different tack – that is, act in direct opposition to what he has just been saying about himself, in opposition to the laws of reason, in opposition to his own advantage, in fact in opposition to everything . . . I warn you that my friend is a compound personality and therefore it is difficult to blame him as an individual. The fact is, gentlemen, it seems there must really exist something that is dearer to almost every man than his greatest advantages, or (not to be illogical) there is a most advantageous advantage (the very one omitted of which we spoke just now) which is more important and more advantageous than all other advantages, for the sake of which a man if necessary is ready to act in opposition to all laws; that is, in opposition to reason, honour, peace, prosperity – in fact, in opposition to all those excellent and useful things if only he can attain that fundamental, most advantageous advantage which is dearer to him than all. 'Yes, but it's advantage all the same,' you will retort. But excuse me, I'll make the point clear, and it is not a case of playing upon words. What matters is, that this advantage is remarkable from the very fact that it breaks down all our classifications, and continually shatters every system constructed by lovers of mankind for the benefit of mankind. In fact, it upsets everything. But before I mention this advantage to you, I want to compromise myself personally, and therefore I boldly declare that all these fine systems, all these theories for explaining to mankind their real normal interests, in order that inevitably striving to pursue these interests they may at once become good and noble – are, in my opinion, so far, mere logical exercises! Yes, logical exercises. Why, to maintain this theory of the regeneration of mankind by means of the pursuit of his own advantage is to my mind almost the same thing . . . as to affirm, for instance, following Buckle,[201] that through civilisation mankind becomes softer, and consequently less bloodthirsty and less fitted for warfare. Logically it does seem to follow from his arguments. But man has such a predilection for systems and abstract deductions that he is ready to distort the truth intentionally, he is ready to deny the evidence of his senses only to justify his logic. I take this example because it is the most glaring instance of it. Only look about you: blood is being spilt in streams, and in the merriest way, as though it were champagne. Take the whole of the nineteenth century in which Buckle lived. Take Napoleon – the Great and also the present one.[202] Take North America – the eternal union. Take the farce of Schleswig-Holstein[203] . . . And what is it that civilisation softens in us? The only gain of civilisation for mankind is the greater capacity for variety of sensations – and absolutely nothing more. And through the development of this many-sidedness man may come to finding enjoyment in bloodshed. In fact, this has already happened to him. Have you noticed that it is the most civilised gentlemen who have been the subtlest slaughterers, to whom the Attilas[204] and Stenka Razins could not hold a candle, and if they are not so conspicuous as the Attilas and Stenka Razins it is simply because they are so often met with, are so ordinary and have become so familiar to us. In any case civilisation has made mankind if not more bloodthirsty, at least more vilely, more loathsomely bloodthirsty. In the old days he saw justice in bloodshed and with his conscience at peace exterminated those he thought proper. Now we do think bloodshed abominable and yet we engage in this abomination, and with more energy than ever. Which is worse? Decide that for yourselves. They say that Cleopatra (excuse an instance from Roman history) was fond of sticking gold pins into her slave-girls' breasts and derived gratification from their screams and writhings. You will say that that was in the comparatively barbarous times; that these are barbarous times too, because also, comparatively speaking, pins are stuck in even now; that though man has now learned to see more clearly than in barbarous ages, he is still far from having learnt to act as reason and science would dictate. But yet you are fully convinced that he will be sure to learn when he gets rid of certain old bad habits, and when common sense and science have completely re-educated human nature and turned it in a normal direction. You are confident that then man will cease from *intentional* error and will, so to say, be compelled not to want to set his will against his normal interests. That is not all; then, you say, science itself will teach man (though to my mind it's a superfluous luxury) that he never has really had any caprice or will of his own, and that he himself is something of the nature of a piano-key or the stop of an organ, and that there are, besides, things called the laws of nature; so that everything he does is not done by his willing it, but is done of itself, by the laws of nature. Consequently we have only to discover these laws of nature, and man will no longer have to answer for his actions and life will become exceedingly easy for him. All human actions will then, of course, be tabulated according to these laws, mathematically, like tables of logarithms up to 108,000, and entered in an index; or, better still, there would be published certain edifying works of the nature of encyclopaedic lexicons, in which everything will be so clearly calculated and explained that there will be no more incidents or adventures in the world.

Then – this is all what you say – new economic relations will be established, all ready-made and worked out with mathematical exactitude, so that every possible question will vanish in the twinkling of an eye, simply because every possible answer to it will be provided. Then the 'Palace of Crystal'[205] will be built. Then . . . In fact, those will be halcyon days. Of course there is no guaranteeing (this is my comment) that it will not be, for instance, frightfully dull then (for what will one have to do when everything will be calculated and tabulated), but on the other hand everything will be extraordinarily rational. Of course boredom may lead you to anything. It is boredom sets one sticking golden pins into people, but all that would not matter. What is bad (this is my comment again) is that I dare say people will be thankful for the gold pins then. Man is stupid, you know, phenomenally stupid; or rather he is not at all stupid, but he is so ungrateful that you could not find another like him in all creation. I, for instance, would not be in the least surprised if all of a sudden, apropos of nothing, in the midst of general prosperity a gentleman with an ignoble, or rather with a reactionary and ironical, countenance were to arise and, putting his arms akimbo, say to us all: 'I say, gentleman, hadn't we better kick over the whole show and scatter rationalism to the winds, simply to send these logarithms to the devil, and to enable us to live once more at our own sweet foolish will!' That again would not matter, but what is annoying is that he would be sure to find followers – such is the nature of man. And all that for the most foolish reason, which, one would think, was hardly worth mentioning: that is, that man everywhere and at all times, whoever he may be, has preferred to act as he chose and not in the least as his reason and advantage dictated. And one may choose what is contrary to one's own interests, and sometimes one *positively ought* (that is my idea). One's own free unfettered choice, one's own caprice, however wild it may be, one's own fancy worked up at times to frenzy – is that very 'most advantageous advantage' which we have overlooked, which comes under no classification and against which all systems and theories are continually being shattered to atoms. And how do these wiseacres know that man wants a normal, a virtuous choice? What has made them conceive that man must want a rationally advantageous choice? What man wants is simply *independent* choice, whatever that independence may cost and wherever it may lead. And choice, of course, the devil only knows what choice . . .

8

'Ha! ha! ha! But you know there is no such thing as choice in reality, say what you like,' you will interpose with a chuckle. 'Science has succeeded in so far analysing man that we know already that choice and what is called freedom of will is nothing else than – '

Stay, gentlemen, I meant to begin with that myself. I confess, I was rather frightened. I was just going to say that the devil only knows what choice depends on, and that perhaps that was a very good thing, but I remembered the teaching of science . . . and pulled myself up. And here you have begun upon it. Indeed, if there really is someday discovered a formula for all our desires and caprices – that is, an explanation of what they depend upon, by what laws they arise, how they develop, what they are aiming at in one case and in another and so on, that is a real mathematical formula – then, most likely, man will at once cease to feel desire, indeed, he will be certain to. For who would want to choose by rule? Besides, he will at once be transformed from a human being into an organ-stop or something of the sort; for what is a man without desires, without free will and without choice, if not a stop in an organ? What do you think? Let us reckon the chances – can such a thing happen or not?

'H'm!' you decide. 'Our choice is usually mistaken from a false view of our advantage. We sometimes choose absolute nonsense because in our foolishness we see in that nonsense the easiest means for attaining a supposed advantage. But when all that is explained and worked out on paper (which is perfectly possible, for it is contemptible and senseless to suppose that some laws of nature man will never understand), then certainly so-called desires will no longer exist. For if a desire should come into conflict with reason we shall then reason and not desire, because it will be impossible retaining our reason to be *senseless* in our desires, and in that way knowingly act against reason and desire to injure ourselves. And as all choice and reasoning can be really calculated – because there will someday be discovered the laws of our so-called free will – so, joking apart, there may one day be something like a table constructed of them, so that we really shall choose in accordance with it. If, for instance, someday they calculate and prove to me that I made a long nose at someone because I could not help making a long nose at him and that I had to do it in that particular way, what *freedom* is left me, especially if I am a learned man and have taken my degree somewhere? Then I should be able to calculate my whole life for thirty years before-hand. In short, if this could be arranged there would be nothing left for us to do; anyway, we should have to understand that. And, in fact, we ought unwearyingly to repeat to ourselves that at such and such a time and in such and such circumstances nature does not ask our leave; that we have got to take her as she is and not fashion her to suit our fancy, and if we really aspire to formulas and tables of rules, and well, even . . . to the chemical retort, there's no help for it, we must accept the retort too, or else it will be accepted without our consent . . . '

Yes, but here I come to a stop! Gentlemen, you must excuse me for being over-philosophical; it's the result of forty years underground! Allow me to indulge my fancy. You see, gentlemen, reason is an excellent thing, there's no disputing that, but reason is nothing but reason and satisfies only the rational side of man's nature, while will is a manifestation of the whole life, that is, of the whole human life including reason and all the impulses. And although our life, in this manifestation of it, is often worthless, yet it is life and not simply extracting square roots. Here I, for instance, quite naturally want to live, in order to satisfy all my capacities for life, and not simply my capacity for reasoning, that is, not simply one twentieth of my capacity for life. What does reason know? Reason only knows what it has succeeded in learning (some things, perhaps, it will never learn; this is a poor comfort, but why not say so frankly?) and human nature acts as a whole, with everything that is in it, consciously or unconsciously, and, even if it goes wrong, it lives. I suspect, gentlemen, that you are looking at me with compassion; you tell me again that an enlightened and developed man, such, in short, as the future man will be, cannot consciously desire anything disadvantageous to himself, that that can be proved mathematically. I thoroughly agree, it can – by mathematics.

But I repeat for the hundredth time, there is one case, one only, when man may consciously, purposely, desire what is injurious to himself, what is stupid, very stupid – simply in order to have the right to desire for himself even what is very stupid and not to be bound by an obligation to desire only what is sensible. Of course, this very stupid thing, this caprice of ours, may be in reality, gentlemen, more advantageous for us than anything else on earth, especially in certain cases. And in particular it may be more advantageous than any advantage even when it does us obvious harm, and contradicts the soundest conclusions of our reason concerning our advantage – for in any circumstances it preserves for us what is most precious and most important – that is, our personality, our individuality. Some, you see, maintain that this really is the most precious thing for mankind; choice can, of course, if it chooses, be in agreement with reason; and especially if this be not abused but kept within bounds. It is profitable and sometimes even praiseworthy. But very often, and even most often, choice is utterly and stubbornly opposed to reason ... and ... and ... do you know that that, too, is profitable, sometimes even praiseworthy? Gentlemen, let us suppose that man is not stupid. (Indeed one cannot refuse to suppose that, if only from the one consideration, that, if man is stupid, then who is wise?) But if he is not stupid, he is monstrously ungrateful! Phenomenally ungrateful. In fact, I believe that the best definition of man is the ungrateful biped. But that is not all, that is not his worst defect; his worst defect is his perpetual moral obliquity, perpetual – from the days of the Flood to the Schleswig-Holstein period. Moral obliquity and consequently lack of good sense; for it has long been accepted that lack of good sense is due to no other cause than moral obliquity. Put it to the test and cast your eyes upon the history of mankind. What will you see? Is it a grand spectacle? Grand, if you like. Take the Colossus of Rhodes,[206] for instance, that's worth something. With good reason Mr Anaevsky[207] testifies of it that some say that it is the work of man's hands, while others maintain that it has been created by nature herself. Is it many-coloured? Maybe it is many-coloured, too: if one takes the dress uniforms, military and civilian, of all peoples in all ages – that alone is worth something, and if you take the undress uniforms you will never get to the end of it; no historian would be equal to the job. Is it monotonous? Maybe it's monotonous too: it's fighting and fighting; they are fighting now, they fought first and they fought last – you will admit, that it is almost too monotonous. In short, one may say anything about the history of the world – anything that might enter the most disordered imagination. The only thing one can't say is that it's rational. The very word sticks in one's throat. And, indeed, this is the odd thing that is continually happening: there are continually turning up in life moral and rational persons, sages and lovers of humanity who make it their object to live all their lives as morally and rationally as possible, to be, so to speak, a light to their neighbours simply in order to show them that it is possible to live morally and rationally in this world. And yet we all know that those very people sooner or later have been false to themselves, playing some queer trick, often a most unseemly one. Now I ask you: what can be expected of man since he is a being endowed with strange qualities? Shower upon him every earthly blessing, drown him in a sea of happiness, so that nothing but bubbles of bliss can be seen on the surface; give him economic prosperity, such that he should have nothing else to do but sleep, eat cakes and busy himself with the continuation of his species, and even then out of sheer ingratitude, sheer spite, man would play you some nasty trick. He would even risk his cakes and would deliberately desire the most fatal rubbish, the most uneconomical absurdity, simply to introduce into all this positive good sense his fatal fantastic element. It is just his fantastic dreams, his vulgar folly that he will desire to retain, simply in order to prove to himself – as though that were so necessary – that men still are men and not the keys of a piano, which the laws of nature threaten to control so completely that soon one will be able to desire nothing but by the calendar.

And that is not all: even if man really were nothing but a piano-key, even if this were proved to him by natural science and mathematics, even then he would not become reasonable, but would purposely do something perverse out of simple ingratitude, simply to gain his point. And if he does not find means he will contrive destruction and chaos, will contrive sufferings of all sorts, only to gain his point! He will launch a curse upon the world, and as only man can curse (it is his privilege, the primary distinction between him and other animals), maybe by his curse alone he will attain his object – that is, convince himself that he is a man and not a piano-key! If you say that all this, too, can be calculated and tabulated – chaos and darkness and curses, so that the mere possibility of calculating it all beforehand would stop it all, and reason would reassert itself, then man would purposely go mad in order to be rid of reason and gain his point! I believe in it, I answer for it, for the whole work of man really seems to consist in nothing but proving to himself every minute that he is a man and not a piano-key! It may be at the cost of his skin, it may be by cannibalism! And this being so, can one help being tempted to rejoice that it has not yet come off, and that desire still depends on something we don't know?

You will scream at me (that is, if you condescend to do so) that no one is touching my free will, that all they are concerned with is that my will should of itself, of its own free will, coincide with my own normal interests, with the laws of nature and arithmetic.

Good heavens, gentlemen, what sort of free will is left when we come to tabulation and arithmetic, when it will all be a case of twice two makes four? Twice two makes four without my will. As if free will meant that!

9

Gentlemen, I am joking, and I know myself that my jokes are not brilliant, but you know one can take everything as a joke. I am, perhaps, jesting against the grain. Gentlemen, I am tormented by questions; answer them for me. You, for instance, want to cure men of their old habits and reform their will in accordance with science and good sense. But how do you know, not only that it is possible, but also that it is *desirable* to reform man in that way? And what leads you to the conclusion that man's inclinations *need* reforming? In short, how do you know that such a reformation will be a benefit to man? And to go to the root of the matter, why are you so positively convinced that not to act against his real normal interests guaranteed by the conclusions of reason and arithmetic is certainly always advantageous for man and must always be a law for mankind? So far, you know, this is only your supposition. It may be the law of logic, but not the law of humanity. You think, gentlemen, perhaps that I am mad? Allow me to defend myself. I agree that man is pre-eminently a creative animal, predestined to strive consciously for an object and to engage in engineering – that is, incessantly and eternally to make new roads, *wherever they may lead*. But the reason why he wants sometimes to go off at a tangent may just be that he is *predestined* to make the road, and perhaps, too, that however stupid the 'direct' practical man may be, the thought sometimes will occur to him that the road almost always does lead *somewhere*, and that the destination it leads to is less important than the process of making it, and that the chief thing is to save the well-conducted child from despising engineering, and so giving way to the fatal idleness, which, as we all know, is the mother of all the vices. Man likes to make roads and to create, that is a fact beyond dispute. But why has he such a passionate love for destruction and chaos also? Tell me that! But on that point I want to say a couple of words myself. May it not be that he loves chaos and destruction (there can be no disputing that he does sometimes love it) because he is instinctively afraid of attaining his object and completing the edifice he is constructing? Who knows, perhaps he only loves that edifice from a distance, and is by no means in love with it at close quarters; perhaps he only loves building it and does not want to live in it, but will leave it, when completed, for the use of *Les animaux domestiques*[208] – such as the ants, the sheep, and so on. Now the ants have quite a different taste. They have a marvellous edifice of that pattern which endures for ever – the ant-heap.

With the ant-heap the respectable race of ants began and with the ant-heap they will probably end, which does the greatest credit to their perseverance and good sense. But man is a frivolous and incongruous creature, and perhaps, like a chess player, loves the process of the game, not the end of it. And who knows (there is no saying with certainty), perhaps the only goal on earth to which mankind is striving lies in this incessant process of attaining, in other words, in life itself, and not in the thing to be attained, which must always be expressed as a formula, as positive as twice two makes four, and such positiveness is not life, gentlemen, but is the beginning of death. Anyway, man has always been afraid of this mathematical certainty, and I am afraid of it now. Granted that man does nothing but seek that mathematical certainty, he traverses oceans, sacrifices his life in the quest, but to succeed, really to find it, he dreads, I assure you. He feels that when he has found it there will be nothing for him to look for. When workmen have finished their work they do at least receive their pay, they go to the tavern, then they are taken to the police-station – and there is occupation for a week. But where can man go? Anyway, one can observe a certain awkwardness about him when he has attained such objects. He loves the process of attaining, but does not quite like to have attained, and that, of course, is very absurd. In fact, man is a comical creature; there seems to be a kind of jest in it all. But yet mathematical certainty is, after all, something insufferable. Twice two makes four seems to me simply a piece of insolence. Twice two makes four is a pert coxcomb who stands with arms akimbo barring your path and spitting. I admit that twice two makes four is an excellent thing, but if we are to give everything its due, twice two makes five is sometimes a very charming thing too.

And why are you so firmly, so triumphantly, convinced that only the normal and the positive – in other words, only what is conducive to welfare – is for the advantage of man? Is not reason in error as regards advantage? Does not man, perhaps, love something besides well-being? Perhaps he is just as fond of suffering? Perhaps suffering is just as great a benefit to him as well-being? Man is sometimes extraordinarily, passionately, in love with suffering, and that is a fact. There is no need to appeal to universal history to prove that; only ask yourself, if you are a man and have lived at all. As far as my personal opinion is concerned, to care only for well-being seems to me positively ill-bred. Whether it's good or bad, it is sometimes very pleasant, too, to smash things. I hold no brief for suffering nor for well-being either. I am standing for . . . my caprice, and for its being guaranteed to me when necessary. Suffering would be out of place in vaudevilles, for instance; I know that. In the Crystal Palace it is unthinkable; suffering means doubt, negation, and what would be the good of a palace of crystal if there could be any doubt about it? And yet I think man will never renounce real suffering, that is, destruction and chaos. Why, suffering is the sole origin of consciousness. Though I did lay it down at the beginning that consciousness is the greatest misfortune for man, yet I know man prizes it and would not give it up for any satisfaction. Consciousness, for instance, is infinitely superior to twice two makes four. Once you have mathematical certainty there is nothing left to do or to understand. There will be nothing left but to bottle up your five senses and plunge into contemplation. While if you stick to consciousness, even though the same result is attained, you can at least flog yourself at times, and that will, at any rate, liven you up. Reactionary as it is, corporal punishment is better than nothing.

10

You believe in a palace of crystal that can never be destroyed – a palace at which one will not be able to put out one's tongue or make a long nose on the sly. And perhaps that is just why I am afraid of this edifice, that it is of crystal and can never be destroyed and that one cannot put one's tongue out at it even on the sly.

You see, if it were not a palace, but a henhouse, I might creep into it to avoid getting wet, and yet I would not call the henhouse a palace out of gratitude to it for keeping me dry. You laugh and say that in such circumstances a henhouse is as good as a mansion. Yes, I answer, if one had to live simply to keep out of the rain.

But what is to be done if I have taken it into my head that that is not the only object in life, and that if one must live one had better live in a mansion? That is my choice, my desire. You will only eradicate it when you have changed my preference. Well, do change it, allure me with something else, give me another ideal. But meanwhile I will not take a henhouse for a mansion. The palace of crystal may be an idle dream, it may be that it is inconsistent with the laws of nature and that I have invented it only through my own stupidity, through the old-fashioned irrational habits of my generation. But what does it matter to me that it is inconsistent? That makes no difference since it exists in my desires, or rather exists as long as my desires exist. Perhaps you are laughing again? Laugh away; I will put up with any mockery rather than pretend that I am satisfied when I am hungry. I know, anyway, that I will not be put off with a compromise, with a recurring zero, simply because it is consistent with the laws of nature and actually exists. I will not accept as the crown of my desires a block of buildings with tenements for the poor on a lease of a thousand years, and perhaps with a signboard of a dentist hanging out. Destroy my desires, eradicate my ideals, show me something better, and I will follow you. You will say, perhaps, that it is not worth your trouble; but in that case I can give you the same answer. We are discussing things seriously; but if you won't deign to give me your attention, I will drop your acquaintance. I can retreat into my underground hole.

But while I am alive and have desires I would rather my hand were withered off than bring one brick to such a building! Don't remind me that I have just rejected the palace of crystal for the sole reason that one cannot put out one's tongue at it. I did not say because I am so fond of putting my tongue out. Perhaps the thing I resented was that of all your edifices there has not been one at which one could not put out one's tongue. On the contrary, I would let my tongue be cut off out of gratitude if things could be so arranged that I should lose all desire to put it out. It is not my fault that things cannot be so arranged, and that one must be satisfied with model flats. Then why am I made with such desires? Can I have been constructed simply in order to come to the conclusion that all my construction is a cheat? Can this be my whole purpose? I do not believe it.

But do you know what: I am convinced that we underground folk ought to be kept on a curb. Though we may sit forty years underground without speaking, when we do come out into the light of day and break out we talk and talk and talk . . .

11

The long and the short of it is, gentlemen, that it is better to do nothing! Better conscious inertia! And so hurrah for underground! Though I have said that I envy the normal man to the last drop of my bile, yet I should not care to be in his place such as he is now (though I shall not cease envying him). No, no; anyway the underground life is more advantageous. There, at any rate, one can . . . Oh, but even now I am lying! I am lying because I know myself that it is not underground that is better, but something different, quite different, for which I am thirsting, but which I cannot find! Damn underground!

I will tell you another thing that would be better, and that is, if I myself believed in anything of what I have just written. I swear to you, gentlemen, there is not one thing, not one word of what I have written that I really believe. That is, I believe it, perhaps, but at the same time I feel and suspect that I am lying like a cobbler.

'Then why have you written all this?' you will say to me.

'I ought to put you underground for forty years without anything to do and then come to you in your cellar to find out what stage you have reached! How can a man be left with nothing to do for forty years?'

'Isn't that shameful, isn't that humiliating?' you will say, perhaps, wagging your heads contemptuously. 'You thirst for life and try to settle the problems of life by a logical tangle. And how persistent, how insolent are your sallies, and at the same time what a scare you are in! You talk nonsense and are pleased with it; you say impudent things and are in continual alarm and apology for them. You declare that you are afraid of nothing and at the same time try to ingratiate yourself in our good opinion. You declare that you are gnashing your teeth and at the same time you try to be witty so as to amuse us. You know that your witticisms are not witty, but you are evidently well satisfied with their literary value. You may, perhaps, have really suffered, but you have no respect for your own suffering. You may have sincerity, but you have no modesty; out of the pettiest vanity you expose your sincerity to publicity and ignominy. You doubtlessly mean to say something, but hide your last word through fear, because you have not the resolution to utter it, and only have a cowardly impudence. You boast of consciousness, but you are not sure of your ground, for though your mind works, yet your heart is darkened and corrupt, and you cannot have a full, genuine consciousness without a pure heart. And how intrusive you are, how you insist and grimace! Lies, lies, lies!'

Of course I have myself made up all the things you say. That, too, is from underground. I have been for forty years listening to you through a crack in the floor. I have invented them myself, there was nothing else I could invent. It is no wonder that I have learned it by heart and it has taken a literary form . . . But can you really be so credulous as to think that I will print all this and give it to you to read too? And another problem: why do I call you 'gentlemen', why do I address you as though you really were my readers? Such confessions as I intend to make are never printed nor given to other people to read. Anyway, I am not strong-minded enough for that, and I don't see why I should be. But you see a fancy has occurred to me and I want to realise it at all costs. Let me explain.

Every man has reminiscences which he would not tell to everyone, but only to his friends. He has other matters in his mind which he would not reveal even to his friends, but only to himself, and that in secret. But there are other things which a man is afraid to tell even to himself, and every decent man has a number of such things stored away in his mind. The more decent he is, the greater the number of such things in his mind. Anyway, I have only lately determined to remember some of my early adventures. Till now I have always avoided them, even with a certain uneasiness. Now, when I am not only recalling them, but have actually decided to write an account of them, I want to try the experiment whether one can, even with oneself, be perfectly open and not take fright at the whole truth. I will observe, in parenthesis, that Heine says that a true autobiography is almost an impossibility, and that man is bound to lie about himself. He considers that Rousseau certainly told lies about himself in his confessions, and even intentionally lied, out of vanity. I am convinced that Heine is right; I quite understand how sometimes one may, out of sheer vanity, attribute regular crimes to oneself, and indeed I can very well conceive that kind of vanity. But Heine judged of people who made their confessions to the public. I write only for myself, and I wish to declare once and for all that if I write as though I were addressing readers, that is simply because it is easier for me to write in that form. It is a form, an empty form – I shall never have readers. I have made this plain already . . .

I don't wish to be hampered by any restrictions in the compilation of my notes. I shall not attempt any system or method. I will jot things down as I remember them.

But here, perhaps, someone will catch at the word and ask me: if you really don't reckon on readers, why do you make such compacts with yourself – and on paper too – that is, that you won't attempt any system or method, that you will jot things down as you remember them, and so on, and so on? Why are you explaining? Why do you apologise?

Well, there it is, I answer.

There is a whole psychology in all this, though. Perhaps it is simply that I am a coward. And perhaps that I purposely imagine an audience before me in order that I may be more dignified while I write. There are perhaps thousands of reasons. Again, what is my object precisely in writing? If it is not for the benefit of the public why should I not simply recall these incidents in my own mind without putting them on paper?

Quite so; but yet it is more imposing on paper. There is something more impressive in it; I shall be better able to criticise myself and improve my style. Besides, I shall perhaps obtain actual relief from writing. Today, for instance, I am particularly oppressed by one memory of a distant past. It came back vividly to my mind a few days ago, and has remained haunting me like an annoying tune that one cannot get rid of. And yet I must get rid of it somehow. I have hundreds of such reminiscences; but at times some one stands out from the hundred and oppresses me. For some reason I believe that if I write it down I should get rid of it. Why not try?

Besides, I am bored, and I never have anything to do. Writing will be a sort of work. They say work makes man kind-hearted and honest. Well, here is a chance for me, anyway.

Snow is falling today, yellow and dingy. It fell yesterday, too, and a few days ago. I fancy it is the wet snow that has reminded me of that incident which I cannot shake off now. And so let it be a story apropos of the falling snow.

PART TWO

APROPOS OF THE WET SNOW

When from dark error's subjugation
My words of passionate exhortation
Had wrenched thy fainting spirit free;
And writhing prone in thine affliction
Thou didst recall with malediction
The vice that had encompassed thee:
And when thy slumbering conscience, fretting
By recollection's torturing flame,
Thou didst reveal the hideous setting
Of thy life's current ere I came:
When suddenly I saw thee sicken,
And weeping, hide thine anguished face,
Revolted, maddened, horror-stricken,
At memories of foul disgrace, –
etc., etc., etc.

NEKRASSOV

1

At that time I was only twenty-four. My life was even then gloomy, ill-regulated, and as solitary as that of a savage. I made friends with no one and positively avoided talking, and buried myself more and more in my hole. At work in the office I never looked at anyone, and was perfectly well aware that my companions looked upon me, not only as a queer fellow, but even looked upon me – I always fancied this – with a sort of loathing. I sometimes wondered why it was that nobody except me fancied that he was looked upon with aversion? One of the clerks had a most repulsive, pockmarked face, which looked positively villainous. I believe I should not have dared to look at anyone with such an unsightly countenance. Another had such a very dirty old uniform that there was an unpleasant odour in his proximity. Yet not one of these gentlemen showed the slightest self-consciousness – either about their clothes or their countenance or their character in any way. Neither of them ever imagined that they were looked at with repulsion; if they had imagined it they would not have minded – so long as their superiors did not look at them in that way. It is clear to me now that, owing to my unbounded vanity and to the high standard I set for myself, I often looked at myself with furious discontent, which verged on loathing, and so I inwardly attributed the same feeling to everyone. I hated my face, for instance: I thought it disgusting, and even suspected that there was something base in my expression, and so every day when I turned up at the office I tried to behave as independently as possible, and to assume a lofty expression, so that I might not be suspected of being abject. 'My face may be ugly,' I thought, 'but let it be lofty, expressive, and, above all, *extremely* intelligent.' But I was positively and painfully certain that it was impossible for my countenance ever to express those qualities. And what was worst of all, I thought it actually stupid-looking, and I would have been quite satisfied if I could have looked intelligent. In fact, I would even have put up with looking base if, at the same time, my face could have been thought strikingly intelligent.

Of course, I hated my fellow clerks one and all, and I despised them all, yet at the same time I was, as it were, afraid of them. In fact, it happened at times that I thought more highly of them than of myself. It somehow happened quite suddenly that I alternated between despising them and thinking them superior to myself. A cultivated and decent man cannot be vain without setting a fearfully high standard for himself, and without despising and almost hating himself at certain moments. But whether I despised them or thought them superior I dropped my eyes almost every time I met anyone. I even made experiments whether I could face so and so's looking at me, and I was always the first to drop my eyes. This worried me to distraction. I had a sickly dread, too, of being ridiculous, and so had a slavish passion for the conventional in everything external. I loved to fall into the common rut, and had a whole-hearted terror of any kind of eccentricity in myself. But how could I live up to it? I was morbidly sensitive as a man of our age should be. They were all stupid, and as like one another as so many sheep. Perhaps I was the only one in the office who fancied that I was a coward and a slave, and I fancied it just because I was more highly developed. But it was not only that I fancied it, it really was so. I was a coward and a slave. I say this without the slightest embarrassment. Every decent man of our age must be a coward and a slave. That is his normal condition. Of that I am firmly persuaded. He is made and constructed to that very end. And not only at the present time owing to some casual circumstances, but always, at all times, a decent man is bound to be a coward and a slave. It is the law of nature for all decent people all over the earth. If anyone of them happens to be valiant about something, he need not be comforted nor carried away by that; he would show the white feather just the same before something else. That is how it invariably and inevitably ends. Only donkeys and mules are valiant, and they only till they are pushed up to the wall. It is not worth while to pay attention to them for they really are of no consequence.

Another circumstance, too, worried me in those days: that there was no one like me and I was unlike anyone else. 'I am alone and they are *everyone*,' I thought – and pondered.

From that it is evident that I was still a youngster.

The very opposite sometimes happened. It was loathsome sometimes to go to the office; things reached such a point that I often came home ill. But all at once, apropos of nothing, there would come a phase of scepticism and indifference (everything happened in phases to me), and I would laugh myself at my intolerance and fastidiousness, I would reproach myself with being *romantic*. At one time I was unwilling to speak to anyone, while at other times I would not only talk, but go to the length of contemplating making friends with them. All my fastidiousness would suddenly, for no rhyme or reason, vanish. Who knows, perhaps I never had really had it, and it had simply been affected, and got out of books. I have not decided that question even now. Once I quite made friends with them, visited their homes, played preference, drank vodka, talked of promotions . . . But here let me make a digression.

We Russians, speaking generally, have never had those foolish transcendental 'romantics' – German, and still more French – on whom nothing produces any effect; if there were an earthquake, if all France perished at the barricades, they would still be the same, they would not even have the decency to affect a change, but would still go on singing their transcendental songs to the hour of their death, because they are fools. We, in Russia, have no fools; that is well known. That is what distinguishes us from foreign lands. Consequently these transcendental natures are not found among us in their pure form. The idea that they are is due to our 'realistic' journalists and critics of that day, always on the look out for Kostanzhoglos[209] and Uncle Pyotr Ivanitchs[210] and foolishly accepting them as our ideal; they have slandered our romantics, taking them for the same transcendental sort as in Germany or France. On the contrary, the characteristics of our 'romantics' are absolutely and directly opposed to the transcendental European type, and no European standard can be applied to them. (Allow me to make use of this word 'romantic' – an old-fashioned and much respected word which has done good service and is familiar to all.) The characteristics of our romantics are to understand everything, *to see everything and to see it often incomparably more clearly than our most realistic minds see it*; to refuse to accept anyone or anything, but at the same time not to despise anything; to give way, to yield, from policy; never to lose sight of a useful practical object (such as rent-free quarters at the government expense, pensions, decorations), to keep their eye on that object through all the enthusiasms and volumes of lyrical poems, and at the same time to preserve 'the sublime and the beautiful' inviolate within them to the hour of their death, and to preserve themselves also, incidentally, like some precious jewel wrapped in cotton wool if only for the benefit of 'the sublime and the beautiful'. Our 'romantic' is a man of great breadth and the greatest rogue of all our rogues, I assure you . . . I can assure you from experience, indeed. Of course, that is, if he is intelligent. But what am I saying! The romantic is always intelligent, and I only meant to observe that although we have had foolish romantics they don't count, and they were only so because in the flower of their youth they degenerated into Germans, and to preserve their precious jewel more comfortably, settled somewhere out there – by preference in Weimar[211] or the Black Forest.[212]

I, for instance, genuinely despised my official work and did not openly abuse it simply because I was in it myself and got a salary for it. Anyway, take note, I did not openly abuse it. Our romantic would rather go out of his mind – a thing, however, which very rarely happens – than take to open abuse, unless he had some other career in view; and he is never kicked out. At most, they would take him to the lunatic asylum as 'the King of Spain'[213] if he should go very mad. But it is only the thin, fair people who go out of their minds in Russia. Innumerable 'romantics' attain later in life to considerable rank in the service. Their many-sidedness is remarkable! And what a faculty they have for the most contradictory sensations! I was comforted by this thought even in those days, and I am of the same opinion now. That is why there are so many 'broad natures' among us who never lose their ideal even in the depths of degradation; and though they never stir a finger for their ideal, though they are arrant thieves and knaves, yet they tearfully cherish their first ideal and are extraordinarily honest at heart. Yes, it is only among us that the most incorrigible rogue can be absolutely and loftily honest at heart without in the least ceasing to be a rogue. I repeat, our romantics, frequently, become such accomplished rascals (I use the term 'rascals' affectionately), suddenly display such a sense of reality and practical knowledge that their bewildered superiors and the public generally can only ejaculate in amazement.

Their many-sidedness is really amazing, and goodness knows what it may develop into later on, and what the future has in store for us. It is not a poor material! I do not say this from any foolish or boastful patriotism. But I feel sure that you are again imagining that I am joking. Or perhaps it's just the contrary and you are convinced that I really think so. Anyway, gentlemen, I shall welcome both views as an honour and a special favour. And do forgive my digression.

I did not, of course, maintain friendly relations with my comrades and soon was at loggerheads with them, and in my youth and inexperience I even gave up bowing to them, as though I had cut off all relations. That, however, only happened to me once. As a rule, I was always alone.

In the first place I spent most of my time at home, reading. I tried to stifle all that was continually seething within me by means of external impressions. And the only external means I had was reading. Reading, of course, was a great help – exciting me, giving me pleasure and pain. But at times it bored me fearfully. One longed for movement in spite of everything, and I plunged all at once into dark, underground, loathsome vice of the pettiest kind. My wretched passions were acute, smarting, from my continual, sickly irritability. I had hysterical impulses, with tears and convulsions. I had no resource except reading, that is, there was nothing in my surroundings which I could respect and which attracted me. I was overwhelmed with depression, too; I had an hysterical craving for incongruity and for contrast, and so I took to vice. I have not said all this to justify myself . . . But, no! I am lying. I did want to justify myself. I make that little observation for my own benefit, gentlemen. I don't want to lie. I vowed to myself I would not.

And so, furtively, timidly, in solitude, at night, I indulged in filthy vice, with a feeling of shame which never deserted me, even at the most loathsome moments, and which at such moments nearly made me curse. Already even then I had my underground world in my soul. I was fearfully afraid of being seen, of being met, of being recognised. I visited various obscure haunts.

One night as I was passing a tavern I saw through a lighted window some gentlemen fighting with billiard cues, and saw one of them thrown out of the window. At other times I should have felt very much disgusted, but I was in such a mood at the time that I actually envied the gentleman thrown out of the window – and I envied him so much that I even went into the tavern and into the billiard-room. 'Perhaps,' I thought, 'I'll have a fight, too, and they'll throw me out of the window.'

I was not drunk – but what is one to do – depression will drive a man to such a pitch of hysteria? But nothing happened. It seemed that I was not even equal to being thrown out of the window and I went away without having my fight.

An officer put me in my place from the first moment.

I was standing by the billiard-table and in my ignorance blocking up the way, and he wanted to pass; he took me by the shoulders and without a word – without a warning or explanation – moved me from where I was standing to another spot and passed by as though he had not noticed me. I could have forgiven blows, but I could not forgive his having moved me without noticing me.

Devil knows what I would have given for a real regular quarrel – a more decent, a more *literary* one, so to speak. I had been treated like a fly. This officer was over six foot, while I was a spindly little fellow. But the quarrel was in my hands. I had only to protest and I certainly would have been thrown out of the window. But I changed my mind and preferred to beat a resentful retreat.

I went out of the tavern straight home, confused and troubled, and the next night I went out again with the same lewd intentions, still more furtively, abjectly and miserably than before, as it were, with tears in my eyes – but still I did go out again. Don't imagine, though, it was cowardice made me slink away from the officer; I never have been a coward at heart, though I have always been a coward in action. Don't be in a hurry to laugh – I assure you I can explain it all.

Oh, if only that officer had been one of the sort who would consent to fight a duel! But no, he was one of those gentlemen (alas, long extinct!) who preferred fighting with cues or, like Gogol's Lieutenant Pirogov,[214] appealing to the police. They did not fight duels and would have thought a duel with a civilian like me an utterly unseemly procedure in any case – and they looked upon the duel altogether as something impossible, something free-thinking and French. But they were quite ready to bully, especially when they were over six foot.

I did not slink away through cowardice, but through an unbounded vanity. I was afraid not of his six foot, not of getting a sound thrashing and being thrown out of the window; I should have had physical courage enough, I assure you; but I had not the moral courage. What I was afraid of was that everyone present, from the insolent marker down to the lowest little stinking, pimply clerk in a greasy collar, would jeer at me and fail to understand when I began to protest and to address them in literary language. For of the point of honour – not of honour, but of the point of honour (*point d'honneur*) – one cannot speak among us except in literary language. You can't allude to the 'point of honour' in ordinary language. I was fully convinced (the sense of reality, in spite of all my romanticism!) that they would all simply split their sides with laughter, and that the officer would not simply beat me, that is, without insulting me, but would certainly prod me in the back with his knee, kick me round the billiard-table, and only then perhaps have pity and drop me out of the window.

Of course, this trivial incident could not with me end in that. I often met that officer afterwards in the street and noticed him very carefully. I am not quite sure whether he recognised me, I imagine not; I judge from certain signs. But I – I stared at him with spite and hatred and so it went on … for several years! My resentment grew even deeper with years. At first I began making stealthy enquiries about this officer. It was difficult for me to do so, for I knew no one. But one day I heard someone shout his surname in the street as I was following him at a distance, as though I were tied to him – and so I learnt his surname. Another time I followed him to his flat, and for ten kopecks learned from the porter where he lived, on which storey, whether he lived alone or with others, and so on – in fact, everything one could learn from a porter. One morning, though I had never tried my hand with the pen, it suddenly occurred to me to write a satire on this officer in the form of a novel which would unmask his villainy. I wrote the novel with relish. I did unmask his villainy, I even exaggerated it; at first I so altered his surname that it could easily be recognised, but on second thoughts I changed it, and sent the story to the *Otetchestvennye Zapiski*.[215] But at that time such attacks were not the fashion and my story was not printed. That was a great vexation to me.

Sometimes I was positively choked with resentment. At last I determined to challenge my enemy to a duel. I composed a splendid, charming letter to him, imploring him to apologise to me, and hinting rather plainly at a duel in case of refusal. The letter was so composed that if the officer had had the least understanding of the sublime and the beautiful he would certainly have flung himself on my neck and have offered me his friendship. And how fine that would have been! How we should have got on together! 'He could have shielded me with his higher rank, while I could have improved his mind with my culture, and, well … my ideas, and all sorts of things might have happened.' Only fancy, this was two years after his insult to me, and my challenge would have been a ridiculous anachronism, in spite of all the ingenuity of my letter in disguising and explaining away the anachronism. But, thank God (to this day I thank the Almighty with tears in my eyes), I did not send the letter to him. Cold shivers run down my back when I think of what might have happened if I had sent it.

And all at once I revenged myself in the simplest way, by a stroke of genius! A brilliant thought suddenly dawned upon me. Sometimes on holidays I used to stroll along the sunny side of the Nevsky about four o'clock in the afternoon. Though it was hardly a stroll so much as a series of innumerable miseries, humiliations and resentments; but no doubt that was just what I wanted. I used to wriggle along in a most unseemly fashion, like an eel, continually moving aside to make way for generals, for officers of the guards and the hussars, or for ladies. At such minutes there used to be a convulsive twinge at my heart, and I used to feel hot all down my back at the mere thought of the wretchedness of my attire, of the wretchedness and abjectness of my little scurrying figure. This was a regular martyrdom, a continual, intolerable humiliation at the thought, which passed into an incessant and direct sensation, that I was a mere fly in the eyes of all this world, a nasty, disgusting fly – more intelligent, more highly developed, more refined in feeling than any of them, of course – but a fly that was continually making way for everyone, insulted and injured by everyone. Why I inflicted this torture upon myself, why I went to the Nevsky, I don't know. I felt simply drawn there at every possible opportunity.

Already then I began to experience a rush of the enjoyment of which I spoke in the first chapter. After my affair with the officer I felt even more drawn there than before: it was on the Nevsky that I met him most frequently, there I could admire him. He, too, went there chiefly on holidays. He, too, turned out of his path for generals and persons of high rank, and he too, wriggled between them like an eel; but people, like me, or even better dressed than me, he simply walked over; he made straight for them as though there was nothing but empty space before him, and never, under any circumstances, turned aside. I gloated over my resentment watching him and . . . always resentfully made way for him. It exasperated me that even in the street I could not be on an even footing with him.

'Why must you invariably be the first to move aside?' I kept asking myself in hysterical rage, waking up sometimes at three o'clock in the morning. 'Why is it you and not he? There's no regulation about it; there's no written law. Let the making way be equal as it usually is when refined people meet; he moves halfway and you move halfway; you pass with mutual respect.'

But that never happened, and I always moved aside, while he did not even notice my making way for him. And lo and behold a bright idea dawned upon me! 'What,' I thought, 'if I meet him and don't move on one side? What if I don't move aside on purpose, even if I knock up against him? How would that be?' This audacious idea took such a hold on me that it gave me no peace. I was dreaming of it continually, horribly, and I purposely went more frequently to the Nevsky in order to picture more vividly how I should do it when I did do it. I was delighted. This intention seemed to me more and more practical and possible.

'Of course I shall not really push him,' I thought, already more good-natured in my joy. 'I will simply not turn aside, will run up against him, not very violently, but just shouldering each other – just as much as decency permits. I will push against him just as much as he pushes against me.' At last I made up my mind completely. But my preparations took a great deal of time. To begin with, when I carried out my plan I should need to be looking rather more decent, and so I had to think of my get-up. 'In case of emergency, if, for instance, there were any sort of public scandal (and the public there is of the most *recherché*: the Countess walks there; Prince D. walks there; all the literary world is there), I must be well dressed; that inspires respect and of itself puts us on an equal footing in the eyes of the society.'

With this object I asked for some of my salary in advance, and bought at Tchurkin's a pair of black gloves and a decent hat. Black gloves seemed to me both more dignified and *bon ton*[216] than the lemon-coloured ones which I had contemplated at first. 'The colour is too gaudy, it looks as though one were trying to be conspicuous,' and I did not take the lemon-coloured ones. I had got ready long beforehand a good shirt, with white bone studs; my overcoat was the only thing that held me back. The coat in itself was a very good one, it kept me warm; but it was wadded and it had a raccoon collar which was the height of vulgarity. I had to change the collar at any sacrifice, and to have a beaver one like an officer's. For this purpose I began visiting the Gostiny Dvor[217] and after several attempts I pitched upon a piece of cheap German beaver. Though these German beavers soon grow shabby and look wretched, yet at first they look exceedingly well, and I only needed it for the occasion. I asked the price; even so, it was too expensive. After thinking it over thoroughly I decided to sell my raccoon collar. The rest of the money – a considerable sum for me, I decided to borrow from Anton Antonitch Syetotchkin, my immediate superior, an unassuming person, though grave and judicious. He never lent money to anyone, but I had, on entering the service, been specially recommended to him by an important personage who had got me my berth. I was horribly worried. To borrow from Anton Antonitch seemed to me monstrous and shameful. I did not sleep for two or three nights. Indeed, I did not sleep well at that time, I was in a fever; I had a vague sinking at my heart or else a sudden throbbing, throbbing, throbbing! Anton Antonitch was surprised at first, then he frowned, then he reflected, and did after all lend me the money, receiving from me a written authorisation to take from my salary a fortnight later the sum that he had lent me.

In this way everything was at last ready. The handsome beaver replaced the mean-looking raccoon, and I began by degrees to get to work. It would never have done to act offhand, at random; the plan had to be carried out skilfully, by degrees. But I must confess that after many efforts I began to despair: we simply could not run into each other. I made every preparation, I was quite determined – it seemed as though we should run into one another directly – and before I knew what I was doing I had stepped aside for him again and he had passed without noticing me. I even prayed as I approached him that God would grant me determination. One time I had made up my mind thoroughly, but it ended in my stumbling and falling at his feet because at the very last instant when I was six inches from him my courage failed me. He very calmly stepped over me, while I flew on one side like a ball. That night I was ill again, feverish and delirious.

And suddenly it ended most happily. The night before I had made up my mind not to carry out my fatal plan and to abandon it all, and with that object I went to the Nevsky for the last time, just to see how I would abandon it all. Suddenly, three paces from my enemy, I unexpectedly made up my mind – I closed my eyes, and we ran full tilt, shoulder to shoulder, against one another! I did not budge an inch and passed him on a perfectly equal footing! He did not even look round and pretended not to notice it; but he was only pretending, I am convinced of that. I am convinced of that to this day! Of course, I got the worst of it – he was stronger, but that was not the point. The point was that I had attained my object, I had kept up my dignity, I had not yielded a step, and had put myself publicly on an equal social footing with him. I returned home feeling that I was fully avenged for everything. I was delighted. I was triumphant and sang Italian arias. Of course, I will not describe to you what happened to me three days later; if you have read my first chapter you can guess for yourself. The officer was afterwards transferred; I have not seen him now for fourteen years. What is the dear fellow doing now? Whom is he walking over?

But the period of my dissipation would end and I always felt very sick afterwards. It was followed by remorse – I tried to drive it away; I felt too sick. By degrees, however, I grew used to that too. I grew used to everything, or rather I voluntarily resigned myself to enduring it. But I had a means of escape that reconciled everything – that was to find refuge in 'the sublime and the beautiful', in dreams, of course. I was a terrible dreamer, I would dream for three months on end, tucked away in my corner, and you may believe me that at those moments I had no resemblance to the gentleman who, in the perturbation of his chicken heart, put a collar of German beaver on his greatcoat. I suddenly became a hero. I would not have admitted my six-foot lieutenant even if he had called on me. I could not even picture him before me then. What were my dreams and how I could satisfy myself with them – it is hard to say now, but at the time I was satisfied with them. Though, indeed, even now, I am to some extent satisfied with them. Dreams were particularly sweet and vivid after a spell of dissipation; they came with remorse and with tears, with curses and transports. There were moments of such positive intoxication, of such happiness, that there was not the faintest trace of irony within me, on my honour. I had faith, hope, love. I believed blindly at such times that by some miracle, by some external circumstance, all this would suddenly open out, expand; that suddenly a vista of suitable activity – beneficent, good and, above all, *ready made* (what sort of activity I had no idea, but the great thing was that it should be all ready for me) – would rise up before me – and I should come out into the light of day, almost riding a white horse and crowned with laurel. Anything but the foremost place I could not conceive for myself, and for that very reason I quite contentedly occupied the lowest in reality. Either to be a hero or to grovel in the mud – there was nothing between. That was my ruin, for when I was in the mud I comforted myself with the thought that at other times I was a hero, and the hero was a cloak for the mud: for an ordinary man it was shameful to defile himself, but a hero was too lofty to be utterly defiled, and so he might defile himself. It is worth noting that these attacks of the 'sublime and the beautiful' visited me even during the period of dissipation and just at the times when I was touching the bottom. They came in separate spurts, as though reminding me of themselves, but did not banish the dissipation by their appearance. On the contrary, they seemed to add a zest to it by contrast, and were only sufficiently present to serve as an appetising sauce. That sauce was made up of contradictions and sufferings, of agonising inward analysis, and all these pangs and pin-pricks gave a certain piquancy, even a significance to my dissipation – in fact, completely answered the purpose of an appetising sauce. There was a certain depth of meaning in it. And I could hardly have resigned myself to the simple, vulgar, direct debauchery of a clerk and have endured all the filthiness of it. What could have allured me about it then and have drawn me at night into the street? No, I had a lofty way of getting out of it all.

And what loving-kindness, oh Lord, what loving-kindness I felt at times in those dreams of mine! in those 'flights into the sublime and the beautiful'; though it was fantastic love, though it was never applied to anything human in reality, yet there was so much of this love that one did not feel afterwards even the impulse to apply it in reality; that would have been superfluous. Everything, however, passed satisfactorily by a lazy and fascinating transition into the sphere of art, that is, into the beautiful forms of life, lying ready, largely stolen from the poets and novelists and adapted to all sorts of needs and uses. I, for instance, was triumphant over everyone; everyone, of course, was in dust and ashes, and was forced spontaneously to recognise my superiority, and I forgave them all. I was a poet and a grand gentleman, I fell in love; I came in for countless millions and immediately devoted them to humanity, and at the same time I confessed before all the people my shameful deeds, which, of course, were not merely shameful, but had in them much that was 'sublime and beautiful' something in the Manfred style.[218] Everyone would kiss me and weep (what idiots they would be if they did not), while I should go barefoot and hungry preaching new ideas and fighting a victorious Austerlitz[219] against the obscurantists. Then the band would play a march, an amnesty would be declared, the Pope would agree to retire from Rome to Brazil;[220] then there would be a ball for the whole of Italy at the Villa Borghese on the shores of Lake Como,[221] Lake Como being for that purpose transferred to the neighbourhood of Rome; then would come a scene in the bushes, and so on, and so on – as though you did not know all about it? You will say that it is vulgar and contemptible to drag all this into public after all the tears and transports which I have myself confessed. But why is it contemptible? Can you imagine that I am ashamed of it all, and that it was stupider than anything in your life, gentlemen? And I can assure you that some of these fancies were by no means badly composed . . . It did not all happen on the shores of Lake Como. And yet you are right – it really is vulgar and contemptible. And most contemptible of all it is that now I am attempting to justify myself to you. And even more contemptible than that is my making this remark now. But that's enough, or there will be no end to it; each step will be more contemptible than the last . . . I could never stand more than three months of dreaming at a time without feeling an irresistible desire to plunge into society. To plunge into society meant to visit my superior at the office, Anton Antonitch Syetotchkin. He was the only permanent acquaintance I have had in my life, and I wonder at the fact myself now. But I only went to see him when that phase came over me, and when my dreams had reached such a point of bliss that it became essential at once to embrace my fellows and all mankind; and for that purpose I needed at least one human being, actually existing. I had to call on Anton Antonitch, however, on Tuesday – his at-home day; so I had always to time my passionate desire to embrace humanity so that it might fall on a Tuesday.

This Anton Antonitch lived on the fourth storey in a house in Five Corners,[222] in four low-pitched rooms of a particularly frugal and sallow appearance. He had two daughters and there was also an aunt, who used to pour out the tea. Of the daughters one was thirteen and another fourteen, they both had snub noses, and I was awfully shy of them because they were always whispering and giggling together. The master of the house usually sat in his study on a leather couch in front of the table with some grey-headed gentleman, usually a colleague from our office or some other department. I never saw more than two or three visitors there, always the same. They talked about the excise duty, about business in the senate, about salaries, about promotions, about his excellency, and the best means of pleasing him, and so on. I had the patience to sit like a fool beside these people for four hours at a stretch, listening to them without knowing what to say to them or venturing to say a word. I became stupefied, several times I felt myself perspiring, I was overcome by a sort of paralysis; but this was pleasant and good for me. On returning home I deferred for a time my desire to embrace all mankind.

I had however one other acquaintance of a sort, Simonov, who was an old schoolfellow. I had a number of schoolfellows, indeed, in Petersburg, but I did not associate with them and had even given up nodding to them in the street. I believe I had transferred into the department I was in simply to avoid their company and to cut off all connection with my hateful childhood. Curses on that school and all those terrible years of penal servitude! In short, I parted from my schoolfellows as soon as I got out into the world. There were two or three left to whom I nodded in the street. One of them was Simonov, who had in no way been distinguished at school but was of a quiet and equable disposition; I discovered in him a certain independence of character and indeed honesty. I don't even suppose that he was particularly stupid. I had at one time spent some rather soulful moments with him, but these had not lasted long and had somehow been suddenly clouded over. He was evidently uncomfortable at these reminiscences, and was, I fancy, always afraid that I might take up the same tone again. I suspected that he had an aversion for me, but still I went on going to see him, not being quite certain of it.

And so on one occasion, unable to endure my solitude and knowing that as it was Thursday Anton Antonitch's door would be closed, I thought of Simonov. Climbing up to his fourth storey I was thinking that the man disliked me and that it was a mistake to go and see him. But as it always happened that such reflections impelled me, as though purposely, to put myself into a false position, I went in. It was almost a year since I had last seen Simonov.

3

I found two of my old schoolfellows with him. They seemed to be discussing an important matter. All of them took scarcely any notice of my entrance, which was strange, for I had not met them for years. Evidently they looked upon me as something on the level of a common fly. I had not been treated like that even at school, though they all hated me. I knew, of course, that they must despise me now for my lack of success in the service, and for my having let myself sink so low, going about badly dressed and so on – which seemed to them a sign of my incapacity and insignificance. But I had not expected such contempt. Simonov was positively surprised at my turning up. Even in the old days he had always seemed surprised at my coming. All this disconcerted me; I sat down, feeling rather miserable, and began listening to what they were saying.

They were engaged in warm and earnest conversation about a farewell dinner which they wanted to arrange for the next day for a comrade of theirs called Zverkov, an officer in the army, who was going away to a distant province. This Zverkov had been all the time at school with me too. I had begun to hate him particularly in the upper forms. In the lower forms he had simply been a pretty, playful boy whom everybody liked. I had hated him, however, even in the lower forms, just because he was a pretty and playful boy. He was always bad at his lessons and got worse and worse as he went on; however, he left with a good certificate, as he had powerful interests. During his last year at school he came in for an estate of two hundred serfs, and as almost all of us were poor he took up a swaggering tone among us. He was vulgar in the extreme, but at the same time he was a good-natured fellow, even in his swaggering. In spite of superficial, fantastic and sham notions of honour and dignity, all but very few of us positively grovelled before Zverkov, and the more so the more he swaggered. And it was not from any interested motive that they grovelled, but simply because he had been favoured by the gifts of nature. Moreover, it was, as it were, an accepted idea among us that Zverkov was a specialist in regard to tact and the social graces. This last fact particularly infuriated me. I hated the abrupt self-confident tone of his voice, his admiration of his own witticisms, which were often frightfully stupid, though he was bold in his language; I hated his handsome, but stupid face (for which I would, however, have gladly exchanged my intelligent one), and the free-and-easy military manners in fashion in the 'forties. I hated the way in which he used to talk of his future conquests of women (he did not venture to begin his attack upon women until he had the epaulettes of an officer, and was looking forward to them with impatience), and boasted of the duels he would constantly be fighting. I remember how I, invariably so taciturn, suddenly fastened upon Zverkov, when one day talking at a leisure moment with his schoolfellows of his future relations with the fair sex, and growing as sportive as a puppy in the sun, he all at once declared that he would not leave a single village girl on his estate unnoticed, that that was his *droit de seigneur*,²²³ and that if the peasants dared to protest he would have them all flogged and double the tax on them, the bearded rascals. Our servile rabble applauded, but I attacked him, not from compassion for the girls and their fathers, but simply because they were applauding such an insect. I got the better of him on that occasion, but though Zverkov was stupid he was lively and impudent, and so laughed it off, and in such a way that my victory was not really complete; the laugh was on his side. He got the better of me on several occasions afterwards, but without malice, jestingly, casually. I remained angrily and contemptuously silent and would not answer him. When we left school he made advances to me; I did not rebuff them, for I was flattered, but we soon parted and quite naturally. Afterwards I heard of his barrack-room success as a lieutenant, and of the fast life he was leading. Then there came other rumours – of his successes in the service. By then he had taken to cutting me in the street, and I suspected that he was afraid of compromising himself by greeting a personage as insignificant as me. I saw him once in the theatre, in the third tier of boxes. By then he was wearing shoulder-straps. He was twisting and twirling about, ingratiating himself with the daughters of an ancient general. In three years he had gone off considerably, though he was still rather handsome and adroit. One could see that by the time he was thirty he would be corpulent. So it was to this Zverkov that my school-fellows were going to give a dinner on his departure. They had kept up with him for those three years, though privately they did not consider themselves on an equal footing with him, I am convinced of that.

Of Simonov's two visitors, one was Ferfitchkin, a Russianised German – a little fellow with the face of a monkey, a blockhead who was always deriding everyone, a very bitter enemy of mine from our days in the lower forms – a vulgar, impudent, swaggering fellow, who affected a most sensitive feeling of personal honour, though, of course, he was a wretched little coward at heart. He was one of those worshippers of Zverkov who made up to the latter from interested motives, and often borrowed money from him. Simonov's other visitor, Trudolyubov, was a person in no way remarkable – a tall young fellow, in the army, with a cold face, fairly honest, though he worshipped success of every sort, and was only capable of thinking of promotion. He was some sort of distant relation of Zverkov's, and this, foolish as it seems, gave him a certain importance among us. He always thought me of no consequence whatever; his behaviour to me, though not quite courteous, was tolerable.

'Well, with seven roubles each,' said Trudolyubov, 'twenty-one roubles between the three of us, we ought to be able to get a good dinner. Zverkov, of course, won't pay.'

'Of course not, since we are inviting him,' Simonov decided.

'Can you imagine,' Ferfitchkin interrupted hotly and conceitedly, like some insolent flunkey boasting of his master the general's decorations, 'can you imagine that Zverkov will let us pay alone? He will accept from delicacy, but he will order half a dozen bottles of champagne.'

'Do we want half a dozen for the four of us?' observed Trudolyubov, taking notice only of the half-dozen.

'So the three of us, with Zverkov for the fourth, twenty-one roubles, at the Hôtel de Paris at five o'clock tomorrow,' Simonov, who had been asked to make the arrangements, concluded finally.

'How twenty-one roubles?' I asked in some agitation, with a show of being offended; 'if you count me it will not be twenty-one, but twenty-eight roubles.'

It seemed to me that to invite myself so suddenly and unexpectedly would be positively graceful, and that they would all be conquered at once and would look at me with respect.

'Do you want to join, too?' Simonov observed, with no appearance of pleasure, seeming to avoid looking at me. He knew me through and through.

It infuriated me that he knew me so thoroughly.

'Why not? I am an old schoolfellow of his, too, I believe, and I must own I feel hurt that you have left me out,' I said, boiling over again.

'And where were we to find you?' Ferfitchkin put in roughly.

'You never were on good terms with Zverkov,' Trudolyubov added, frowning.

But I had already clutched at the idea and would not give it up.

'It seems to me that no one has a right to form an opinion upon that,' I retorted in a shaking voice, as though something tremendous had happened. 'Perhaps that is just my reason for wishing it now, that I have not always been on good terms with him.'

'Oh, there's no making you out . . . with these refinements,' Trudolyubov jeered.

'We'll put your name down,' Simonov decided, addressing me. 'Tomorrow at five o'clock at the Hôtel de Paris.'

'What about the money?' Ferfitchkin began in an undertone, indicating me to Simonov, but he broke off, for even Simonov was embarrassed.

'That will do,' said Trudolyubov, getting up. 'If he wants to come so much, let him.'

'But it's a private thing, between us friends,' Ferfitchkin said crossly, as he, too, picked up his hat. 'It's not an official gathering.'

'We do not want at all, perhaps . . . '

They went away. Ferfitchkin did not greet me in any way as he went out, Trudolyubov barely nodded. Simonov, with whom I was left *tête-à-tête*, was in a state of vexation and perplexity, and looked at me queerly. He did not sit down and did not ask me to.

'H'm . . . yes . . . tomorrow, then. Will you pay your subscription now? I just ask so as to know,' he muttered in embarrassment.

I flushed crimson; as I did so I remembered that I had owed Simonov fifteen roubles for ages – which I had, indeed, never forgotten, though I had not repaid it.

'You will understand, Simonov, that I could have no idea when I came here . . . I am very much vexed that I have forgotten . . . '

'All right, all right, that doesn't matter. You can pay tomorrow after the dinner. I simply wanted to know . . . Please don't . . . '

He broke off and began pacing the room still more vexed. As he walked he began to stamp with his heels.

'Am I keeping you?' I asked, after two minutes of silence.

'Oh!' he said, starting, 'that is – to be truthful – yes. I have to go and see someone . . . not far from here,' he added in an apologetic voice, somewhat abashed.

'My goodness, why didn't you say so?' I cried, seizing my cap, with an astonishingly free-and-easy air, which was the last thing I should have expected of myself.

'It's close by . . . not two paces away,' Simonov repeated, accompanying me to the front door with a fussy air which did not suit him at all. 'So five o'clock, punctually, tomorrow,' he called down the stairs after me. He was very glad to get rid of me. I was in a fury.

'What possessed me, what possessed me to force myself upon them?' I wondered, grinding my teeth as I strode along the street. 'For a scoundrel, a pig like that Zverkov! Of course I had better not go; of course, I must just snap my fingers at them. I am not bound in any way. I'll send Simonov a note by tomorrow's post . . .'

But what made me furious was that I knew for certain that I should go, that I should make a point of going; and the more tactless, the more unseemly my going would be, the more certainly I would go.

And there was a positive obstacle to my going: I had no money. All I had was nine roubles, I had to give seven of that to my servant, Apollon, for his monthly wages. That was all I paid him – he had to keep himself.

Not to pay him was impossible, considering his character. But I will talk about that fellow, about that plague of mine, another time.

However, I knew I should go and should not pay him his wages.

That night I had the most hideous dreams. No wonder; all the evening I had been oppressed by memories of my miserable days at school, and I could not shake them off. I was sent to the school by distant relations, upon whom I was dependent and of whom I have heard nothing since – they sent me there a forlorn, silent boy, already crushed by their reproaches, already troubled by doubt, and looking with savage distrust at everyone. My schoolfellows met me with spiteful and merciless jibes because I was not like any of them. But I could not endure their taunts; I could not give in to them with the ignoble readiness with which they gave in to one another. I hated them from the first, and shut myself away from everyone in timid, wounded and disproportionate pride. Their coarseness revolted me. They laughed cynically at my face, at my clumsy figure; and yet what stupid faces they had themselves. In our school the boys' faces seemed in a special way to degenerate and grow stupider. How many fine-looking boys came to us! In a few years they became repulsive. Even at sixteen I wondered at them morosely; even then I was struck by the pettiness of their thoughts, the stupidity of their pursuits, their games, their conversations. They had no understanding of such essential things, they took no interest in such striking, impressive subjects, that I could not help considering them inferior to myself. It was not wounded vanity that drove me to it, and for God's sake do not thrust upon me your hackneyed remarks, repeated to nausea, that, 'I was only a dreamer, while they even then had an understanding of life.' They understood nothing, they had no idea of real life, and I swear that that was what made me most indignant with them. On the contrary, the most obvious, striking reality they accepted with fantastic stupidity and even at that time were accustomed to respect success. Everything that was just, but oppressed and looked down upon, they laughed at heartlessly and shamefully. They took rank for intelligence; even at sixteen they were already talking about a snug berth. Of course, a great deal of it was due to their stupidity, to the bad examples with which they had always been surrounded in their childhood and boyhood. They were monstrously depraved. Of course a great deal of that, too, was superficial and an assumption of cynicism; of course there were glimpses of youth and freshness even in their depravity; but even that freshness was not attractive, and showed itself in a certain rakishness. I hated them horribly, though perhaps I was worse than any of them. They repaid me in the same way, and did not conceal their aversion for me. But by then I did not desire their affection: on the contrary, I continually longed for their humiliation.

To escape from their derision I purposely began to make all the progress I could with my studies and forced my way to the very top. This impressed them. Moreover, they all began by degrees to grasp that I had already read books none of them could read, and understood things (not forming part of our school curriculum) of which they had not even heard. They took a savage and sarcastic view of it, but were morally impressed, especially as the teachers began to notice me on those grounds. The mockery ceased, but the hostility remained, and cold and strained relations became permanent between us. In the end I could not put up with it: with years, a craving for society, for friends, developed in me. I attempted to get on friendly terms with some of my schoolfellows; but somehow or other my intimacy with them was always strained and soon ended of itself. Once, indeed, I did have a friend. But I was already a tyrant at heart; I wanted to exercise unbounded sway over him; I tried to instil into him a contempt for his surroundings;

I required of him a disdainful and complete break with those surroundings. I frightened him with my passionate affection; I reduced him to tears, to hysterics. He was a simple and devoted soul; but when he devoted himself to me entirely I began to hate him immediately and repulsed him – as though all I needed him for was to win a victory over him, to subjugate him and nothing else. But I could not subjugate all of them; my friend was not at all like them either, he was, in fact, a rare exception. The first thing I did on leaving school was to give up the special job for which I had been destined so as to break all ties, to curse my past and shake the dust from off my feet . . . And goodness knows why, after all that, I should go trudging off to Simonov's!

Early next morning I roused myself and jumped out of bed with excitement, as though it were all about to happen at once. But I believed that some radical change in my life was coming, and would inevitably come that day. Owing to its rarity, perhaps, any external event, however trivial, always made me feel as though some radical change in my life were at hand. I went to the office, however, as usual, but sneaked away home two hours earlier to get ready. The great thing, I thought, is not to be the first to arrive, or they will think I am overjoyed at coming. But there were thousands of such great points to consider, and they all agitated and overwhelmed me. I polished my boots a second time with my own hands; nothing in the world would have induced Apollon to clean them twice a day, as he considered that it was more than his duties required of him. I stole the brushes to clean them from the passage, being careful he should not detect it, for fear of his contempt. Then I minutely examined my clothes and thought that everything looked old, worn and threadbare. I had let myself get too slovenly. My uniform, perhaps, was tidy, but I could not go out to dinner in my uniform. The worst of it was that on the knee of my trousers was a big yellow stain. I had a foreboding that that stain would deprive me of nine-tenths of my personal dignity. I knew, too, that it was very poor to think so. 'But this is no time for thinking: now I am in for the real thing,' I thought, and my heart sank. I knew, too, perfectly well even then, that I was monstrously exaggerating the facts. But how could I help it? I could not control myself and was already shaking with fever. With despair I pictured to myself how coldly and disdainfully that 'scoundrel' Zverkov would meet me; with what dull-witted, invincible contempt the blockhead Trudolyubov would look at me; with what impudent rudeness the insect Ferfitchkin would snigger at me in order to curry favour with Zverkov; how completely Simonov would take it all in, and how he would despise me for the abjectness of my vanity and lack of spirit –

and, worst of all, how paltry, *unliterary*, commonplace it would all be. Of course, the best thing would be not to go at all. But that was most impossible of all: if I feel impelled to do anything, I seem to be pitch-forked into it. I should have jeered at myself ever afterwards: 'So you funked it, you funked it, you funked the *real thing*!' On the contrary, I passionately longed to show all that 'rabble' that I was by no means such a spiritless creature as I seemed to myself. What is more, even in the acutest paroxysm of this cowardly fever, I dreamed of getting the upper hand, of dominating them, carrying them away, making them like me – if only for my 'elevation of thought and unmistakable wit'. They would abandon Zverkov, he would sit on one side, silent and ashamed, while I should crush him. Then, perhaps, we would be reconciled and drink to our everlasting friendship;[224] but what was most bitter and humiliating for me was that I knew even then, knew fully and for certain, that I needed nothing of all this really, that I did not really want to crush, to subdue, to attract them, and that I did not care a straw really for the result, even if I did achieve it. Oh, how I prayed for the day to pass quickly! In unutterable anguish I went to the window, opened the movable pane and looked out into the troubled darkness of the thickly falling wet snow. At last my wretched little clock hissed out five. I seized my hat and, trying not to look at Apollon, who had been all day expecting his month's wages, but in his foolishness was unwilling to be the first to speak about it, I slipped between him and the door and, jumping into a high-class sledge, on which I spent my last half-rouble, I drove up in grand style to the Hôtel de Paris.

4

I had been certain the day before that I should be the first to arrive. But it was not a question of being the first to arrive. Not only were they not there, but I had difficulty in finding our room. The table was not laid even. What did it mean? After a good many questions I elicited from the waiters that the dinner had been ordered not for five, but for six o'clock. This was confirmed at the buffet too. I felt really ashamed to go on questioning them. It was only twenty-five minutes past five. If they changed the dinner hour they ought at least to have let me know – that is what the post is for, and not to have put me in an absurd position in my own eyes and . . . and even before the waiters. I sat down; the servant began laying the table; I felt even more humiliated when he was present. Towards six o'clock they brought in candles, though there were lamps burning in the room. It had not occurred to the waiter, however, to bring them in at once when I arrived. In the next room two gloomy, angry-looking persons were eating their dinners in silence at two different tables. There was a great deal of noise, even shouting, in a room farther away; one could hear the laughter of a crowd of people, and nasty little shrieks in French: there were ladies at the dinner. It was sickening, in fact. I had rarely passed more unpleasant moments, so much so that when they did arrive all together punctually at six I was overjoyed to see them, as though they were my deliverers, and even forgot that it was incumbent upon me to show resentment.

Zverkov walked in at the head of them; evidently he was the leading spirit. He and all of them were laughing; but, seeing me, Zverkov drew himself up a little, walked up to me deliberately with a slight, rather jaunty bend from the waist. He shook hands with me in a friendly, but not over-friendly, fashion, with a sort of circumspect courtesy like that of a general, as though in giving me his hand he were warding off something. I had imagined, on the contrary, that on coming in he would at once break into his habitual thin, shrill laugh and fall to making his insipid jokes and witticisms. I had been preparing for them ever since the previous day, but I had not expected such condescension, such high-official courtesy. So, then, he felt himself ineffably superior to me in every respect! If he only meant to insult me by that high-official tone, it would not matter, I thought – I could pay him back for it one way or another. But what if, in reality, without the least desire to be offensive, that sheepshead had a notion in earnest that he was superior to me and could only look at me in a patronising way? The very supposition made me gasp.

'I was surprised to hear of your desire to join us,' he began, lisping and drawling, which was something new. 'You and I seem to have seen nothing of one another. You fight shy of us. You shouldn't. We are not such terrible people as you think. Well, anyway, I am glad to renew our acquaintance.'

And he turned carelessly to put down his hat on the window.

'Have you been waiting long?' Trudolyubov enquired.

'I arrived at five o'clock as you told me yesterday,' I answered aloud, with an irritability that threatened an explosion.

'Didn't you let him know that we had changed the hour?' said Trudolyubov to Simonov.

'No, I didn't. I forgot,' the latter replied, with no sign of regret, and without even apologising to me he went off to order the *hors-d'oeuvres*.

'So you've been here a whole hour? Oh, poor fellow!' Zverkov cried ironically, for to his notions this was bound to be extremely funny. That rascal Ferfitchkin followed with his nasty little snigger like a puppy yapping. My position struck him, too, as exquisitely ludicrous and embarrassing.

'It isn't funny at all!' I cried to Ferfitchkin, more and more irritated. 'It wasn't my fault, but other people's. They neglected to let me know. It was . . . it was . . . it was simply absurd.'

'It's not only absurd, but something else as well,' muttered Trudolyubov, naïvely taking my part. 'You are not hard enough upon it. It was simply rudeness – unintentional, of course. And how could Simonov . . . h'm!'

'If a trick like that had been played on me,' observed Ferfitchkin, 'I should . . . '

'But you should have ordered something for yourself,' Zverkov interrupted, 'or simply asked for dinner without waiting for us.'

'You will allow that I might have done that without your permission,' I rapped out. 'If I waited, it was . . . '

'Let us sit down, gentlemen,' cried Simonov, coming in. 'Everything is ready; I can answer for the champagne; it is capitally frozen . . . You see, I did not know your address, where was I to look for you?' he suddenly turned to me, but again he seemed to avoid looking at me. Evidently he had something against me. It must have been what happened yesterday.

All sat down; I did the same. It was a round table. Trudolyubov was on my left, Simonov on my right, Zverkov was sitting opposite, Ferfitchkin next to him, between him and Trudolyubov.

'Tell me, are you . . . in a government office?' Zverkov went on attending to me. Seeing that I was embarrassed he seriously thought that he ought to be friendly to me, and, so to speak, cheer me up.

'Does he want me to throw a bottle at his head?' I thought, in a fury. In my novel surroundings I was unnaturally ready to be irritated.

'In the N— office,' I answered jerkily, with my eyes on my plate.

'And ha-ave you a go-od berth? I say, what ma-a-de you leave your original job?'

'What ma-a-de me was that I wanted to leave my original job,' I drawled more than he, hardly able to control myself. Ferfitchkin went off into a guffaw. Simonov looked at me ironically. Trudolyubov left off eating and began looking at me with curiosity.

Zverkov winced, but he tried not to notice it.

'And the remuneration?'

'What remuneration?'

'I mean, your sa-a-lary?'

'Why are you cross-examining me?' However, I told him at once what my salary was. I turned horribly red.

'It is not very handsome,' Zverkov observed majestically.

'Yes, you can't afford to dine at cafés on that,' Ferfitchkin added insolently.

'To my thinking it's very poor,' Trudolyubov observed gravely.

'And how thin you have grown! How you have changed!' added Zverkov, with a shade of venom in his voice, scanning me and my attire with a sort of insolent compassion.

'Oh, spare his blushes,' cried Ferfitchkin, sniggering.

'My dear sir, allow me to tell you I am not blushing,' I broke out at last; 'do you hear? I am dining here, at this café, at my own expense, not at other people's – note that, Mr Ferfitchkin.'

'Wha-at? Isn't everyone here dining at his own expense? You would seem to be . . . ' Ferfitchkin flew out at me, turning as red as a lobster, and looking me in the face with fury.

'Tha-at,' I answered, feeling I had gone too far, 'and I imagine it would be better to talk of something more intelligent.'

'You intend to show off your intelligence, I suppose?'

'Don't disturb yourself, that would be quite out of place here.'

'Why are you clacking away like that, my good sir, eh? Have you gone out of your wits in your office?'

'Enough, gentlemen, enough!' Zverkov cried, authoritatively.

'How stupid it is!' muttered Simonov.

'It really is stupid. We have met here, a company of friends, for a farewell dinner to a comrade and you carry on an altercation,' said Trudolyubov, rudely addressing himself to me alone. 'You invited yourself to join us, so don't disturb the general harmony.'

'Enough, enough!' cried Zverkov. 'Give over, gentlemen, it's out of place. Better let me tell you how I nearly got married the day before yesterday . . . '

And then followed a burlesque narrative of how this gentleman had almost been married two days before. There was not a word about the marriage, however, but the story was adorned with generals, colonels and kammer-junkers, while Zverkov almost took the lead among them. It was greeted with approving laughter; Ferfitchkin positively squealed.

No one paid any attention to me, and I sat crushed and humiliated.

'Good heavens, these are not the people for me!' I thought. 'And what a fool I have made of myself before them! I let Ferfitchkin go too far, though. The brutes imagine they are doing me an honour in letting me sit down with them. They don't understand that it's an honour to them and not to me! I've grown thinner! My clothes! Oh, damn my trousers! Zverkov noticed the yellow stain on the knee as soon as he came in . . . But what's the use! I must get up at once, this very minute, take my hat and simply go without a word . . . with contempt! And tomorrow I can send a challenge. The scoundrels! As though I cared about the seven roubles. They may think . . . Damn it! I don't care about the seven roubles. I'll go this minute!'

Of course I remained. I drank sherry and Lafitte by the glassful in my discomfiture. Being unaccustomed to it, I was quickly affected. My annoyance increased as the wine went to my head. I longed all at once to insult them all in a most flagrant manner and then go away. To seize the moment and show what I could do, so that they would say, 'He's clever, though he is absurd,' and . . . and . . . in fact, damn them all!

I scanned them all insolently with my drowsy eyes. But they seemed to have forgotten me altogether. They were noisy, vociferous, cheerful. Zverkov was talking all the time. I began listening. Zverkov was talking of some exuberant lady whom he had at last led on to declaring her love (of course, he was lying like a horse), and how he had been helped in this affair by an intimate friend of his, a Prince Kolya, an officer in the hussars, who had three thousand serfs.

'And yet this Kolya, who has three thousand serfs, has not put in an appearance here tonight to see you off,' I cut in suddenly.

For one minute everyone was silent. 'You are drunk already.' Trudolyubov deigned to notice me at last, glancing contemptuously in my direction. Zverkov, without a word, examined me as though I were an insect. I dropped my eyes. Simonov made haste to fill up the glasses with champagne.

Trudolyubov raised his glass, as did everyone else but me.

'Your health and good luck on the journey!' he cried to Zverkov. 'To old times, to our future, hurrah!'

They all tossed off their glasses, and crowded round Zverkov to kiss him. I did not move; my full glass stood untouched before me.

'Why, aren't you going to drink it?' roared Trudolyubov, losing patience and turning menacingly to me.

'I want to make a speech separately, on my own account . . . and then I'll drink it, Mr Trudolyubov.'

'Spiteful brute!' muttered Simonov.

I drew myself up in my chair and feverishly seized my glass, prepared for something extraordinary, though I did not know myself precisely what I was going to say.

'*Silence!*' cried Ferfitchkin. 'Now for a display of wit!'

Zverkov waited very gravely, knowing what was coming.

'Mr Lieutenant Zverkov,' I began, 'let me tell you that I hate phrases, phrase mongers and men in corsets . . . that's the first point, and there is a second one to follow it.'

There was a general stir.

'The second point is: I hate ribaldry and ribald talkers. Especially ribald talkers! The third point: I love justice, truth and honesty.' I went on almost mechanically, for I was beginning to shiver with horror myself and had no idea how I came to be talking like this. 'I love thought, Monsieur Zverkov; I love true comradeship, on an equal footing and not . . . H'm . . . I love . . . But, however, why not? I will drink your health, too, Mr Zverkov. Seduce the Circassian girls,[225] shoot the enemies of the fatherland and . . . and . . . to your health, Monsieur Zverkov!'

Zverkov got up from his seat, bowed to me and said: 'I am very much obliged to you.' He was frightfully offended and turned pale.

'Damn the fellow!' roared Trudolyubov, bringing his fist down on the table.

'Well, he wants a punch in the face for that,' squealed Ferfitchkin.

'We ought to turn him out,' muttered Simonov.

'Not a word, gentlemen, not a movement!' cried Zverkov solemnly, checking the general indignation. 'I thank you all, but I can show him for myself how much value I attach to his words.'

'Mr Ferfitchkin, you will give me satisfaction tomorrow for your words just now!' I said aloud, turning with dignity to Ferfitchkin.

'A duel, you mean? Certainly,' he answered. But probably I was so ridiculous as I challenged him and it was so out of keeping with my appearance that everyone including Ferfitchkin was prostrate with laughter.

'Yes, let him alone, of course! He is quite drunk,' Trudolyubov said with disgust.

'I shall never forgive myself for letting him join us,' Simonov muttered again.

'Now is the time to throw a bottle at their heads,' I thought to myself. I picked up the bottle . . . and filled my glass . . . 'No, I'd better sit on to the end,' I went on thinking; 'you would be pleased, my friends, if I went away. Nothing will induce me to go. I'll go on sitting here and drinking to the end, on purpose, as a sign that I don't think you of the slightest consequence. I will go on sitting and drinking, because this is a public-house and I paid my entrance money. I'll sit here and drink, for I look upon you as so many pawns, as inanimate pawns. I'll sit here and drink . . . and sing if I want to, yes, sing, for I have the right to . . . to sing . . . H'm!'

But I did not sing. I simply tried not to look at any of them. I assumed most unconcerned attitudes and waited with impatience for them to speak *first*. But alas, they did not address me! And oh, how I wished, how I wished at that moment to be reconciled to them! It struck eight, at last nine. They moved from the table to the sofa. Zverkov stretched himself on a lounge and put one foot on a round table. Wine was brought there. He did, as a fact, order three bottles on his own account. I, of course, was not invited to join them. They all sat round him on the sofa. They listened to him, almost with reverence. It was evident that they were fond of him. 'What for? What for?' I wondered. From time to time they were moved to drunken enthusiasm and kissed each other. They talked of the Caucasus, of the nature of true passion, of snug berths in the service, of the income of an hussar called Podharzhevsky, whom none of them knew personally, and rejoiced in the largeness of it, of the extraordinary grace and beauty of a Princess D., whom none of them had ever seen; then it came to Shakespeare's being immortal.

I smiled contemptuously and walked up and down the other side of the room, opposite the sofa, from the table to the stove and back again. I tried my very utmost to show them that I could do without them, and yet I purposely made a noise with my boots, thumping with my heels. But it was all in vain. They paid no attention. I had the patience to walk up and down in front of them from eight o'clock till eleven, in the same place, from the table to the stove and back again. 'I walk up and down to please myself and no one can prevent me.' The waiter who came into the room stopped, from time to time, to look at me. I was somewhat giddy from turning round so often; at moments it seemed to me that I was in delirium. During those three hours I was three times soaked with sweat and dry again. At times, with an intense, acute pang I was stabbed to the heart by the thought that ten years, twenty years, forty years would pass, and that even in forty years I would remember with loathing and humiliation those filthiest, most ludicrous, and most awful moments of my life. No one could have gone out of his way to degrade himself more shamelessly, and I fully realised it, fully, and yet I went on pacing up and down from the table to the stove. 'Oh, if you only knew what thoughts and feelings I am capable of, how cultured I am!' I thought at moments, mentally addressing the sofa on which my enemies were sitting. But my enemies behaved as though I were not in the room. Once – only once – they turned towards me, just when Zverkov was talking about Shakespeare and I suddenly gave a contemptuous laugh. I laughed in such an affected and disgusting way that they all at once broke off their conversation, and silently and gravely for two minutes watched me walking up and down from the table to the stove, *taking no notice of them*. But nothing came of it: they said nothing, and two minutes later they ceased to notice me again. It struck eleven.

'Friends,' cried Zverkov getting up from the sofa, 'let us all be off now, *there*!'

'Of course, of course,' the others assented. I turned sharply to Zverkov. I was so harassed, so exhausted, that I would have cut my throat to put an end to it. I was in a fever; my hair, soaked with perspiration, stuck to my forehead and temples.

'Zverkov, I beg your pardon,' I said abruptly and resolutely. 'Ferfitchkin, yours too, and everyone's, everyone's: I have insulted you all!'

'Aha! A duel is not in your line, old man,' Ferfitchkin hissed venomously.

It sent a sharp pang to my heart.

'No, it's not the duel I am afraid of, Ferfitchkin! I am ready to fight you tomorrow, after we are reconciled. I insist upon it, in fact, and you cannot refuse. I want to show you that I am not afraid of a duel. You shall fire first and I shall fire into the air.'

'He is comforting himself,' said Simonov.

'He's simply raving,' said Trudolyubov.

'But let us pass. Why are you barring our way? What do you want?' Zverkov answered disdainfully. They were all flushed, their eyes were bright: they had been drinking heavily.

'I ask for your friendship, Zverkov; I insulted you, but . . . '

'Insulted? *You* insulted *me*? Understand, sir, that you never, under any circumstances, could possibly insult *me*.'

'And that's enough for you. Out of the way!' concluded Trudolyubov.

'Olympia is mine, friends, that's agreed!' cried Zverkov.

'We won't dispute your right, we won't dispute your right,' the others answered, laughing.

I stood as though spat upon. The party went noisily out of the room. Trudolyubov struck up some stupid song. Simonov remained behind for a moment to tip the waiters. I suddenly went up to him.

'Simonov! give me six roubles!' I said, with desperate resolution.

He looked at me in extreme amazement, with vacant eyes. He, too, was drunk.

'You don't mean you are coming with us?'

'Yes.'

'I've no money,' he snapped out, and with a scornful laugh he went out of the room.

I clutched at his overcoat. It was a nightmare.

'Simonov, I saw you had money. Why do you refuse me? Am I a scoundrel? Beware of refusing me: if you knew, if you knew why I am asking! My whole future, my whole plans depend upon it!'

Simonov pulled out the money and almost flung it at me.

'Take it, if you have no sense of shame!' he pronounced pitilessly, and ran to overtake them.

I was left for a moment alone. Disorder, the remains of dinner, a broken wine glass on the floor, spilt wine, cigarette ends, fumes of drink and delirium in my brain, an agonising misery in my heart and finally the waiter, who had seen and heard all and was looking inquisitively into my face.

'I am going there!' I cried. 'Either they shall all go down on their knees to beg for my friendship, or I will give Zverkov a slap in the face!'

5

'So this is it, this is it at last – contact with real life,' I muttered as I ran headlong downstairs. 'This is very different from the Pope's leaving Rome and going to Brazil, very different from the ball on Lake Como!'

'You are a scoundrel,' a thought flashed through my mind, 'if you laugh at this now.'

'No matter!' I cried, answering myself. 'Now everything is lost!'

There was no trace to be seen of them, but that made no difference – I knew where they had gone.

At the steps was standing a solitary night sledge-driver in a rough peasant coat, powdered over with the still falling, wet, and as it were warm, snow. It was hot and steamy. The little shaggy piebald horse was also covered with snow and coughing, I remember that very well. I made a rush for the roughly made sledge; but as soon as I raised my foot to get into it, the recollection of how Simonov had just given me six roubles seemed to double me up and I tumbled into the sledge like a sack.

'No, I must do a great deal to make up for all that,' I cried. 'But I will make up for it or perish on the spot this very night. Start!'

We set off. There was a perfect whirl in my head.

'They won't go down on their knees to beg for my friendship. That is a mirage, a cheap mirage, revolting, romantic and fantastical – that's

another ball on Lake Como. And so I am bound to slap Zverkov's face!
It is my duty to. And so it is settled; I am flying to give him a slap in the
face. Hurry up!'

The driver tugged at the reins.

'As soon as I go in I'll give it him. Ought I before giving him the slap
to say a few words by way of preface? No. I'll simply go in and give it
him. They will all be sitting in the drawing-room, and he with Olympia
on the sofa. That damned Olympia! She laughed at my looks on one
occasion and refused me. I'll pull Olympia's hair, pull Zverkov's ears!
No, better one ear, and pull him by it round the room. Maybe they will
all begin beating me and will kick me out. That's most likely, indeed.
No matter! Anyway, I shall first slap him; the initiative will be mine;
and by the laws of honour that is everything: he will be branded and
cannot wipe off the slap with any blows, with nothing but a duel. He
will be forced to fight. And let them beat me now. Let them, the
ungrateful wretches! Trudolyubov will beat me hardest, he is so strong;
Ferfitchkin will be sure to catch hold sideways and tug at my hair. But
no matter, no matter! That's what I am going for. The blockheads will
be forced at last to see the tragedy of it all! When they drag me to the
door I shall call out to them that in reality they are not worth my little
finger. Get on, driver, get on!' I cried to the driver. He started and
flicked his whip, I shouted so savagely.

'We shall fight at daybreak, that's a settled thing. I've done with the
office. Ferfitchkin made a joke about it just now. But where can I get
pistols? Nonsense! I'll get my salary in advance and buy them. And
powder, and bullets? That's the second's business. And how can it all
be done by daybreak? and where am I to get a second? I have no
friends. Nonsense!' I cried, lashing myself up more and more. 'It's of
no consequence! The first person I meet in the street is bound to be
my second, just as he would be bound to pull a drowning man out of
water. The most eccentric things may happen. Even if I were to ask the
director himself to be my second tomorrow, he would be bound to
consent, if only from a feeling of chivalry, and to keep the secret!
Anton Antonitch . . . '

The fact is that at that very minute the disgusting absurdity of my
plan and the other side of the question were clearer and more vivid to
my imagination than they could be to anyone on earth. But . . . 'Get on,
driver, get on, you rascal, get on!'

'Ugh, sir!' said the son of toil.

Cold shivers suddenly ran down me. Wouldn't it be better . . . to go
straight home? My God, my God! Why did I invite myself to this

dinner yesterday? But no, it's impossible. And my walking up and down for three hours from the table to the stove? No, they, they and no one else must pay for my walking up and down! They must wipe out this dishonour! Drive on!

And what if they give me into custody? They won't dare! They'll be afraid of the scandal. And what if Zverkov is so contemptuous that he refuses to fight a duel? He is sure to; but in that case I'll show them . . . I will turn up at the posting station when he's setting off tomorrow, I'll catch him by the leg, I'll pull off his coat when he gets into the carriage. I'll get my teeth into his hand, I'll bite him. 'See what lengths you can drive a desperate man to!' He may hit me on the head and they may belabour me from behind. I will shout to the assembled multitude: 'Look at this young puppy who is driving off to captivate the Circassian girls after letting me spit in his face!'

Of course, after that everything will be over! The office will have vanished off the face of the earth. I shall be arrested, I shall be tried, I shall be dismissed from the service, thrown into prison, sent to Siberia. Never mind! In fifteen years when they let me out of prison I will trudge off to him, a beggar in rags. I shall find him in some provincial town. He will be married and happy. He will have a grown-up daughter . . . I shall say to him: 'Look, monster, at my hollow cheeks and my rags! I've lost everything – my career, my happiness, art, science, *the woman I loved*, and all through you. Here are pistols. I have come to discharge my pistol and . . . and I . . . forgive you. Then I shall fire into the air and he will hear nothing more of me . . . '

I was actually on the point of tears, though I knew perfectly well at that moment that all this was out of Pushkin's *Silvio*[226] and Lermontov's *Masquerade*.[227] And all at once I felt horribly ashamed, so ashamed that I stopped the horse, got out of the sledge, and stood still in the snow in the middle of the street. The driver gazed at me, sighing and astonished.

What was I to do? I could not go on there – it was evidently stupid, and I could not leave things as they were, because that would seem as though . . . Heavens, how could I leave things! And after such insults! 'No!' I cried, throwing myself into the sledge again. 'It is ordained! It is fate! Drive on, drive on!' And in my impatience I punched the sledge-driver on the back of the neck.

'What are you up to? What are you hitting me for?' the peasant shouted, but he whipped up his nag so that it began kicking.

The wet snow was falling in big flakes; I unbuttoned myself, regardless of it. I forgot everything else, for I had finally decided on the slap, and felt with horror that it was going to happen *now*, *at once*, and that *no force could stop it*. The deserted street lamps gleamed sullenly in the snowy darkness like torches at a funeral. The snow drifted under my greatcoat, under my coat, under my cravat, and melted there. I did not wrap myself up – all was lost, anyway.

At last we arrived. I jumped out, almost unconscious, ran up the steps and began knocking and kicking at the door. I felt fearfully weak, particularly in my legs and knees. The door was opened quickly as though they knew I was coming. As a fact, Simonov had warned them that perhaps another gentleman would arrive, and this was a place in which one had to give notice and to observe certain precautions. It was one of those 'millinery establishments' which were abolished by the police a good time ago. By day it really was a shop; but at night, if one had an introduction, one might visit it for other purposes.

I walked rapidly through the dark shop into the familiar drawing-room, where there was only one candle burning, and stood still in amazement: there was no one there. 'Where are they?' I asked somebody. But by now, of course, they had separated. Before me was standing a person with a stupid smile, the 'madam' herself, who had seen me before. A minute later a door opened and another person came in.

Taking no notice of anything I strode about the room, and, I believe, I talked to myself. I felt as though I had been saved from death and was conscious of this, joyfully, all over: I should have given that slap, I should certainly, certainly have given it! But now they were not here and . . . everything had vanished and changed! I looked round. I could not realise my condition yet. I looked mechanically at the girl who had come in: and had a glimpse of a fresh, young, rather pale face, with straight, dark eyebrows, and with grave, as it were wondering, eyes that attracted me at once; I should have hated her if she had been smiling. I began looking at her more intently and, as it were, with effort. I had not fully collected my thoughts. There was something simple and good-natured in her face, but something strangely grave. I am sure that this stood in her way here, and no one of those fools had noticed her. She could not, however, have been called a beauty, though she was tall, strong-looking and well built. She was very simply dressed. Something loathsome stirred within me. I went straight up to her.

I chanced to look into the glass. My harassed face struck me as revolting in the extreme, pale, angry, abject, with dishevelled hair. 'No matter, I am glad of it,' I thought; 'I am glad that I shall seem repulsive to her; I like that.'

Somewhere behind a screen a clock began wheezing, as though oppressed by something, as though someone were strangling it. After an unnaturally prolonged wheezing there followed a shrill, nasty, and as it were unexpectedly rapid, chime – as though someone were suddenly jumping forward. It struck two. I woke up, though I had indeed not been asleep but lying half-conscious.

It was almost completely dark in the narrow, cramped, low-pitched room, cumbered up with an enormous wardrobe and piles of cardboard boxes and all sorts of frippery and litter. The candle end that had been burning on the table was going out and gave a faint flicker from time to time. In a few minutes there would be complete darkness.

I was not long in coming to myself; everything came back to my mind at once, without an effort, as though it had been in ambush to pounce upon me again. And, indeed, even while I was unconscious a point seemed continually to remain in my memory unforgotten, and round it my dreams moved drearily. But strange to say, everything that had happened to me on that day seemed to me now, on waking, to be in the far, far away past, as though I had long, long ago lived all that down.

My head was full of fumes. Something seemed to be hovering over me, rousing me, exciting me and making me restless. Misery and spite seemed surging up in me again and seeking an outlet. Suddenly I saw beside me two wide-open eyes scrutinising me curiously and persistently. The look in those eyes was coldly detached, sullen, as it were utterly remote; it weighed upon me.

A grim idea came into my brain and passed all over my body, as a horrible sensation, such as one feels when one goes into a damp and mouldy cellar. There was something unnatural in those two eyes, beginning to look at me only now. I recalled, too, that during those two hours I had not said a single word to this creature, and had, in fact, considered it utterly superfluous; in fact, the silence had for some reason gratified me. Now I suddenly realised vividly the hideous idea – revolting as a spider – of vice, which, without love, grossly and shamelessly begins with that in which true love finds its consummation. For a long time we gazed at each other like that, but she did not drop her eyes before mine and her expression did not change, so that at last I felt uncomfortable.

'What is your name?' I asked abruptly, to put an end to it.

'Liza,' she answered almost in a whisper, but somehow far from graciously, and she turned her eyes away.

I was silent.

'What weather! The snow ... it's disgusting!' I said, almost to myself, putting my arm under my head despondently, and gazing at the ceiling.

She made no answer. This was horrible.

'Have you always lived in Petersburg?' I asked a minute later, almost angrily, turning my head slightly towards her.

'No.'

'Where do you come from?'

'From Riga,' she answered reluctantly.

'Are you a German?'

'No, Russian.'

'Have you been here long?'

'Where?'

'In this house?'

'A fortnight.'

She spoke more and more jerkily. The candle went out; I could no longer distinguish her face.

'Have you a father and mother?'

'Yes ... no ... I have.'

'Where are they?'

'There ... in Riga.'

'What are they?'

'Oh, nothing.'

'Nothing? Why, what class are they?'

'Tradespeople.'

'Have you always lived with them?'

'Yes.'

'How old are you?'

'Twenty.'

'Why did you leave them?'

'Oh, for no reason.'

That answer meant, 'Let me alone; I feel sick, sad.'

We were silent.

God knows why I did not go away. I felt myself more and more sick and dreary. The images of the previous day began of themselves, apart from my will, flitting through my memory in confusion. I suddenly recalled something I had seen that morning when, full of anxious thoughts, I was hurrying to the office.

'I saw them carrying a coffin out yesterday and they nearly dropped it,' I suddenly said aloud, not that I desired to open the conversation, but as it were by accident.

'A coffin?'

'Yes, in the Haymarket; they were bringing it up out of a cellar.'

'From a cellar?'

'Not from a cellar, but a basement. Oh, you know . . . down below . . . from a house of ill-fame. It was filthy all round . . . Eggshells, litter . . . a stench. It was loathsome.'

Silence.

'A nasty day to be buried,' I began, simply to avoid being silent.

'Nasty, in what way?'

'The snow, the wet.' (I yawned.)

'It makes no difference,' she said suddenly, after a brief silence.

'No, it's horrid.' (I yawned again.) 'The gravediggers must have sworn at getting drenched by the snow. And there must have been water in the grave.'

'Why water in the grave?' she asked, with a sort of curiosity, but speaking even more harshly and abruptly than before.

I suddenly began to feel provoked.

'Why, there must have been water at the bottom a foot deep. You can't dig a dry grave in Volkovo Cemetery.'

'Why?'

'Why? Why, the place is waterlogged. It's a regular marsh. So they bury them in water. I've seen it myself . . . many times.' (I had never seen it once, indeed I had never been in Volkovo, and had only heard stories of it.) 'Do you mean to say, you don't mind how you die?'

'But why should I die?' she answered, as though defending herself.

'Why, someday you will die, and you will die just the same as that dead woman. She was . . . a girl like you. She died of consumption.'

'A wench would have died in hospital . . . ' (She knows all about it already: she said 'wench', not 'girl'.)

'She was in debt to her madam,' I retorted, more and more provoked by the discussion; 'and went on earning money for her up to the end, though she was in consumption. Some sledge-drivers standing by were talking about her to some soldiers and telling them so. No doubt they knew her. They were laughing. They were going to meet in a pot-house to drink to her memory.'

A great deal of this was my invention. Silence followed, profound silence. She did not stir.

'And is it better to die in a hospital?'

'Isn't it just the same? Besides, why should I die?' she added irritably.

'If not now, a little later.'

'Why a little later?'

'Why, indeed? Now you are young, pretty, fresh, you fetch a high price. But after another year of this life you will be very different – you will go off.'

'In a year?'

'Anyway, in a year you will be worth less,' I continued malignantly. 'You will go from here to something lower, another house; a year later – to a third, lower and lower, and in seven years you will come to a basement in the Haymarket. That will be if you are lucky. But it would be much worse if you got some disease, consumption, say . . . and caught a chill, or something or other. It's not easy to get over an illness in your way of life. If you catch anything you may not get rid of it. And so you would die.'

'Oh, well, then I shall die,' she answered, quite vindictively, and she made a quick movement.

'But one is sorry.'

'Sorry for whom?'

'Sorry for life.' Silence.

'Have you been engaged to be married? Eh?'

'What's that to you?'

'Oh, I am not cross-examining you. It's nothing to me. Why are you so cross? Of course you may have had your own troubles. What is it to me? It's simply that I felt sorry.'

'Sorry for whom?'

'Sorry for you.'

'No need,' she whispered hardly audibly, and again made a faint movement.

That incensed me at once. What! I was so gentle with her, and she . . . 'Why, do you think that you are on the right path?'

'I don't think anything.'

'That's what's wrong, that you don't think. Realise it while there is still time. There still is time. You are still young, good-looking; you might love, be married, be happy . . . '

'Not all married women are happy,' she snapped out in the rude abrupt tone she had used at first.

'Not all, of course, but anyway it is much better than the life here. Infinitely better. Besides, with love one can live even without happiness. Even in sorrow life is sweet; life is sweet, however one lives. But here what is there but . . . foulness? Phew!'

I turned away with disgust; I was no longer reasoning coldly. I began to feel myself what I was saying and warmed to the subject. I was already longing to expound the cherished ideas I had brooded over in my corner. Something suddenly flared up in me. An object had appeared before me.

'Never mind my being here, I am not an example for you. I am, perhaps, worse than you are. I was drunk when I came here, though,' I hastened, however, to say in self-defence. 'Besides, a man is no example for a woman. It's a different thing. I may degrade and defile myself, but I am not anyone's slave. I come and go, and that's an end of it. I shake it off, and I am a different man. But you are a slave from the start. Yes, a slave! You give up everything, your whole freedom. If you want to break your chains afterwards, you won't be able to; you will be more and more fast in the snares. It is an accursed bondage. I know it. I won't speak of anything else, maybe you won't understand, but tell me: no doubt you are in debt to your madam? There, you see,' I added, though she made no answer, but only listened in silence, entirely absorbed, 'that's a bondage for you! You will never buy your freedom. They will see to that. It's like selling your soul to the devil . . . And besides . . . perhaps, I too, am just as unlucky – how do you know – and wallow in the mud on purpose, out of misery? You know, men take to drink from grief; well, maybe I am here from grief. Come, tell me, what is there good here? Here you and I . . . came together . . . just now and did not say one word to one another all the time, and it was only afterwards you began staring at me like a wild creature, and I at you. Is that loving? Is that how one human being should meet another? It's hideous, that's what it is!'

'Yes!' she assented sharply and hurriedly.

I was positively astounded by the promptitude of this, 'Yes.' So the same thought may have been straying through her mind when she was staring at me just before. So she, too, was capable of certain thoughts? 'Damn it all, this was interesting, this was a point of likeness!' I thought, almost rubbing my hands. And indeed it's easy to turn a young soul like that!

It was the exercise of my power that attracted me most.

She turned her head nearer to me, and it seemed to me in the darkness that she propped herself on her arm. Perhaps she was scrutinising me. How I regretted that I could not see her eyes. I heard her deep breathing.

'Why have you come here?' I asked her, with a note of authority already in my voice.

'Oh, I don't know.'

'But how nice it would be to be living in your father's house! It's warm and free; you have a home of your own.'

'But what if it's worse than this?'

'I must take the right tone,' flashed through my mind. 'I may not get far with sentimentality.' But it was only a momentary thought. I swear she really did interest me. Besides, I was exhausted and moody. And cunning so easily goes hand-in-hand with feeling.

'Who denies it!' I hastened to answer. 'Anything may happen. I am convinced that someone has wronged you, and that you are more sinned against than sinning. Of course, I know nothing of your story, but it's not likely a girl like you has come here of her own inclination . . . '

'A girl like me?' she whispered, hardly audibly; but I heard it.

Damn it all, I was flattering her. That was horrid. But perhaps it was a good thing . . . She was silent.

'See, Liza, I will tell you about myself. If I had had a home from childhood, I shouldn't be what I am now. I often think that. However bad it may be at home, anyway they are your father and mother, and not enemies, strangers. Once a year at least, they'll show their love of you. Anyway, you know you are at home. I grew up without a home; and perhaps that's why I've turned so . . . unfeeling.'

I waited again. 'Perhaps she doesn't understand,' I thought, 'and, indeed, it is absurd – it's moralising.'

'If I were a father and had a daughter, I believe I should love my daughter more than my sons, really,' I began indirectly, as though talking of something else, to distract her attention. I must confess I blushed.

'Why so?' she asked.

Ah! so she was listening!

'I don't know, Liza. I knew a father who was a stern, austere man, but used to go down on his knees to his daughter, used to kiss her hands, her feet, he couldn't make enough of her, really. When she danced at parties he used to stand for five hours at a stretch, gazing at her. He was mad over her: I understand that! She would fall asleep tired at night, and he would wake to kiss her in her sleep and make the sign of the cross over her. He would go about in a dirty old coat, he was stingy to everyone else, but would spend his last penny for her, giving her expensive presents, and it was his greatest delight when she was pleased with what he gave her. Fathers always love their daughters more than the mothers do. Some girls live happily at home! And I believe I should never let my daughters marry.'

'What next?' she said, with a faint smile.

'I should be jealous, I really should. To think that she should kiss anyone else! That she should love a stranger more than her father! It's painful to imagine it. Of course, that's all nonsense, of course every father would be reasonable at last. But I believe before I should let her marry, I should worry myself to death; I should find fault with all her suitors. But I should end by letting her marry whom she herself loved. The one whom the daughter loves always seems the worst to the father, you know. That is always so. So many family troubles come from that.'

'Some are glad to sell their daughters, rather than marrying them honourably.'

Ah, so that was it!

'Such a thing, Liza, happens in those accursed families in which there is neither love nor God,' I retorted warmly, 'and where there is no love, there is no sense either. There are such families, it's true, but I am not speaking of them. You must have seen wickedness in your own family, if you talk like that. Truly, you must have been unlucky. H'm! . . . that sort of thing mostly comes about through poverty.'

'And is it any better with the gentry? Even among the poor, honest people live happily?'

'H'm . . . yes. Perhaps. Another thing, Liza, man is fond of reckoning up his troubles, but does not count his joys. If he counted them up as he ought, he would see that every lot has enough happiness provided for it. And what if all goes well with the family, if the blessing of God is upon it, if the husband is a good one, loves you, cherishes you, never leaves you! There is happiness in such a family! Even sometimes there is happiness in the midst of sorrow; and indeed sorrow is everywhere. If you marry *you will find out for yourself*. But think of the first years of married life with one you love: what happiness, what happiness there sometimes is in it! And indeed it's the ordinary thing. In those early days even quarrels with one's husband end happily. Some women get up quarrels with their husbands just because they love them. Indeed, I knew a woman like that: she seemed to say that because she loved him, she would torment him and make him feel it. You know that you may torment a man on purpose through love. Women are particularly given to that, thinking to themselves, "I will love him so, I will make so much of him afterwards, that it's no sin to torment him a little now." And all in the house rejoice in the sight of you, and you are happy and gay and peaceful and honourable . . . Then there are some women who are jealous. If he went off anywhere – I knew one such woman, she couldn't restrain herself, but would jump up at night and run off on the sly to find out where he was, whether he was with some other woman. That's a pity. And the woman knows herself it's wrong, and her heart fails her and she suffers, but she loves – it's all through love. And how sweet it is to make up after quarrels, to own herself in the wrong or to forgive him! And they both are so happy all at once – as though they had met anew, been married over again; as though their love had begun afresh. And no one, no one should know what passes between husband and wife if they love one another. And whatever quarrels there may be between them they ought not to call in their own mother to judge between them and tell tales of one another. They are their own judges. Love is a holy mystery and ought to be hidden from all other eyes, whatever happens. That makes it holier and better. They respect one another more, and much is built on respect. And if once there has been love, if they have been married for love, why should love pass away? Surely one can keep it! It is rare that one cannot keep it. And if the husband is kind and straightforward, why should not love last? The first phase of married love will pass, it is true, but then there will come a love that is better still. Then there will be the union of souls, they will have everything in common, there will be no secrets between them. And once they have children, the most difficult times will seem to them happy, so long as there is love and courage. Even toil will be a joy; you may deny yourself bread for your children and even that will be a joy, They will love you for it afterwards; so you are laying by for your future. As the children grow up you feel that you are an example, a support for them; that even after you die your children will always keep your thoughts and feelings, because they have received them from you, they will take on your semblance and likeness. So you see this is a great duty. How can it fail to draw the father and mother nearer? People say it's a trial to have children. Who says that? It is heavenly happiness! Are you fond of little children, Liza? I am awfully fond of them. You know – a little rosy baby boy at your bosom, and what husband's heart is not touched, seeing his wife nursing his child! A plump little rosy baby, sprawling and snuggling, chubby little hands and feet, clean tiny little nails, so tiny that it makes one laugh to look at them; eyes that look as if they understand everything. And while it sucks it clutches at your bosom with its little hand, plays. When its father comes up, the child tears itself away from the bosom, flings itself back, looks at its father, laughs, as though it were fearfully funny, and falls to sucking again. Or it will bite its mother's breast when its little teeth are coming, while it looks sideways at her with its little eyes as though to say, "Look, I am biting!" Is not all that happiness when they are the three together, husband, wife and child? One can forgive a great deal for the sake of such moments. Yes, Liza, one must first learn to live oneself before one blames others!'

'It's by pictures, pictures like that one must get at you,' I thought to myself, though I did speak with real feeling, and all at once I flushed crimson. 'What if she were suddenly to burst out laughing, what should I do then?' That idea drove me to fury. Towards the end of my speech I really was excited, and now my vanity was somehow wounded. The silence continued. I almost nudged her.

'Why are you –' she began and stopped. But I understood: there was a quiver of something different in her voice, not abrupt, harsh and unyielding as before, but something soft and shamefaced, so shamefaced that I suddenly felt ashamed and guilty.

'What?' I asked, with tender curiosity.

'Why, you . . . '

'What?'

'Why, you . . . speak somehow like a book,' she said, and again there was a note of irony in her voice.

That remark sent a pang to my heart. It was not what I was expecting.

I did not understand that she was hiding her feelings under irony, that this is usually the last refuge of modest and chaste-souled people when the privacy of their soul is coarsely and intrusively invaded, and that their pride makes them refuse to surrender till the last moment and shrink from giving expression to their feelings before you. I ought to have guessed the truth from the timidity with which she had repeatedly approached her sarcasm, only bringing herself to utter it at last with an effort. But I did not guess, and an evil feeling took possession of me.

'Wait a bit!' I thought.

7

'Oh, hush, Liza! How can you talk about being like a book, when it makes even me, an outsider, feel sick? Though I don't look at it as an outsider, for, indeed, it touches me to the heart . . . Is it possible, is it possible that you do not feel sick at being here yourself? Evidently habit does wonders! God knows what habit can do with anyone. Can you seriously think that you will never grow old, that you will always be good-looking, and that they will keep you here for ever and ever? I say nothing of the loathsomeness of the life here . . . Though let me tell you this about it – about your present life, I mean; here though you are young now, attractive, nice, with soul and feeling, yet you know as soon as I came to myself just now I felt at once sick at being here with you! One can only come here when one is drunk. But if you were anywhere else, living as good people live, I should perhaps be more than attracted by you, should fall in love with you, should be glad of a look from you, let alone a word; I should hang about your door, should go down on my knees to you, should look upon you as my betrothed and think it an honour to be allowed to. I should not dare to have an impure thought about you. But here, you see, I know that I have only to whistle and you have to come with me whether you like it or not. I don't consult your wishes, but you mine. The lowest labourer hires himself as a workman, but he doesn't make a slave of himself altogether; besides, he knows that he will be free again presently. But when are you free? Only think what you are giving up here? What is it you are making a slave of? It is your soul, together with your body; you are selling your soul which you have no right to dispose of! You give your love to be outraged by every drunkard! Love! But that's everything, you know, it's a priceless diamond, it's a maiden's treasure, love – why, a man would be ready to give his soul, to face death to gain that love. But how much is your love worth now? You are sold, all of you, body and soul, and there is no need to strive for love when you can have everything without love. And you know there is no greater insult to a girl than that, do you understand? To be sure, I have heard that they comfort you, poor fools, they let you have lovers of your own here. But you know that's simply a farce, that's simply a sham, it's just laughing at you, and you are taken in by it! Why, do you suppose he really loves you, that lover of yours? I don't believe it. How can he love you when he knows you may be called away from him any minute? He would be a low fellow if he did! Will he have a grain of respect for you? What have you in common with him? He laughs at you and robs you – that is all his love amounts to! You are lucky if he does not beat you. Very likely he does beat you, too. Ask him, if you have got one, whether he will marry you. He will laugh in your face, if he doesn't spit in it or give you a blow – though maybe he is not worth a bad halfpenny himself. And for what have you ruined your life, if you come to think of it? For the coffee they give you to drink and the plentiful meals? But with what object are they feeding you up? An honest girl couldn't swallow the food, for she would know what she was being fed for. You are in debt here, and, of course, you will always be in debt, and you will go on in debt to the end, till the visitors here begin to scorn you. And that will soon happen, don't rely upon your youth – all that flies by express train here, you know. You will be kicked out. And not simply kicked out; long before that she'll begin nagging at you, scolding you, abusing you, as though you had not sacrificed your health for her, had not thrown away your youth and your soul for her benefit, but as though you had ruined her, beggared her, robbed her. And don't expect anyone to take your part: the others, your companions, will attack you, too, to win her favour, for all are in slavery here, and have lost all conscience and pity here long ago. They have become utterly vile, and nothing on earth is viler, more loathsome, and more insulting than their abuse. And you are laying down everything here, unconditionally, youth and health and beauty and hope, and at twenty-two you will look like a woman of five-and-thirty, and you will be lucky if you are not diseased, pray to God for that! No doubt you are thinking now that you have a gay time and no work to do! Yet there is no work harder or more dreadful in the world or ever has been. One would think that the heart alone would be worn out with tears. And you won't dare to say a word, not half a word when they drive you away from here; you will go away as though you were to blame. You will change to another house, then to a third, then somewhere else, till you come down at last to the Haymarket. There you will be beaten at every turn; that is good manners there, the visitors don't know how to be friendly without beating you. You don't believe that it is so hateful there? Go and look for yourself sometime, you can see with your own eyes. Once, one New Year's Day, I saw a woman at a door. They had turned her out as a joke, to give her a taste of the frost because she had been crying so much, and they shut the door behind her. At nine o'clock in the morning she was already quite drunk, dishevelled, half-naked, covered with bruises, her face was powdered, but she had a black-eye, blood was trickling from her nose and her teeth; some cabman had just given her a drubbing. She was sitting on the stone steps, a salt fish of some sort was in her hand; she was crying, wailing something about her luck and beating with the fish on the steps, and cabmen and drunken soldiers were crowding in the doorway taunting her. You don't believe that you will ever be like that? I should be sorry to believe it, too, but how do you know; maybe ten years, eight years ago that very woman with the salt fish came here fresh as a cherub, innocent, pure, knowing no evil, blushing at every word. Perhaps she was like you, proud, ready to take offence, not like the others; perhaps she looked like a queen, and knew what happiness was in store for the man who should love her and whom she should love. Do you see how it ended? And what if at that very minute when she was beating on the filthy steps with that fish, drunken and dishevelled – what if at that very minute she recalled the pure early days in her father's house, when she used to go to school and the neighbour's son watched for her on the way, declaring that he would love her as long as he lived, that he would devote his life to her, and when they vowed to love one another for ever and be married as soon as they were grown up! No, Liza, it would be happy for you if you were to die soon of consumption in some corner, in some cellar like that woman just now. In the hospital, do you say? You will be lucky if they take you, but what if you are still of use to the madam here? Consumption is a queer disease, it is not like fever. The patient goes on hoping till the last minute and says he is all right. He deludes himself And that just suits your madam. Don't doubt it, that's how it is; you have sold your soul, and what is more you owe money, so you daren't say a word. But when you are dying, all will abandon you, all will turn away from you, for then there will be nothing to get from you. What's more, they will reproach you for cumbering the place, for being so long over dying. However you beg you won't get a drink of water without abuse: "Whenever are you going off, you nasty hussy, you won't let us sleep with your moaning, you make the gentlemen sick." That's true, I have heard such things said myself. They will thrust you dying into the filthiest corner in the cellar – in the damp and darkness; what will your thoughts be, lying there alone? When you die, strange hands will lay you out, with grumbling and impatience; no one will bless you, no one will sigh for you, they only want to get rid of you as soon as may be; they will buy a coffin, take you to the grave as they did that poor woman today, and celebrate your memory at the tavern. In the grave, sleet, filth, wet snow – no need to put themselves out for you – "Let her down, Vanuha; it's just like her luck – even here, she is head-foremost, the hussy. Shorten the cord, you rascal." "It's all right as it is." "All right, is it? Why, she's on her side! She was a fellow-creature, after all! But, never mind, throw the earth on her." And they won't care to waste much time quarrelling over you. They will scatter the wet blue clay as quick as they can and go off to the tavern ... and there your memory on earth will end; other women have children to go to their graves, fathers, husbands. While for you neither tear, nor sigh, nor remembrance; no one in the whole world will ever come to you, your name will vanish from the face of the earth – as though you had never existed, never been born at all! Nothing but filth and mud, however you knock at your coffin lid at night, when the dead arise, however you cry: "Let me out, kind people, to live in the light of day! My life was no life at all; my life has been thrown away like a dish-clout; it was drunk away in the tavern at the Haymarket; let me out, kind people, to live in the world again." '

And I worked myself up to such a pitch that I began to have a lump in my throat myself, and ... and all at once I stopped, sat up in dismay and, bending over apprehensively, began to listen with a beating heart. I had reason to be troubled.

I had felt for some time that I was turning her soul upside down and rending her heart, and – and the more I was convinced of it, the more eagerly I desired to gain my object as quickly and as effectually as possible. It was the exercise of my skill that carried me away; yet it was not merely sport ... I knew I was speaking stiffly, artificially, even bookishly, in fact, I could not speak except 'like a book'. But that did not trouble me: I knew, I felt that I should be understood and that this very bookishness might be an assistance. But now, having attained my effect, I was suddenly panic-stricken. Never before had I witnessed such despair! She was lying on her face, thrusting her face into the pillow and clutching it in both hands. Her heart was being torn. Her youthful body was shuddering all over as though in convulsions. Suppressed sobs rent her bosom and suddenly burst out in weeping and wailing, then she pressed closer into the pillow: she did not want anyone here, not a living soul, to know of her anguish and her tears. She bit the pillow, bit her hand till it bled (I saw that afterwards), or, thrusting her fingers into her dishevelled hair, seemed rigid with the effort of restraint, holding her breath and clenching her teeth. I began saying something, begging her to calm herself, but felt that I did not dare; and all at once, in a sort of cold shiver, almost in terror, began fumbling in the dark, trying hurriedly to get dressed to go. It was dark; though I tried my best I could not finish dressing quickly. Suddenly I felt a box of matches and a candlestick with a whole candle in it. As soon as the room was lighted up, Liza sprang up, sat up in bed, and with a contorted face, with a half insane smile, looked at me almost senselessly. I sat down beside her and took her hands; she came to herself, made an impulsive movement towards me, would have caught hold of me, but did not dare, and slowly bowed her head before me.

'Liza, my dear, I was wrong ... forgive me, my dear,' I began, but she squeezed my hand in her fingers so tightly that I felt I was saying the wrong thing and stopped.

'This is my address, Liza, come to me.'

'I will come,' she answered resolutely, her head still bowed.

'But now I am going, goodbye ... till we meet again.'

I got up; she, too, stood up and suddenly flushed all over, gave a shudder, snatched up a shawl that was lying on a chair and muffled herself in it to her chin. As she did this she gave another sickly smile, blushed and looked at me strangely. I felt wretched; I was in haste to get away – to disappear.

'Wait a minute,' she said suddenly, in the passage just at the doorway, stopping me with her hand on my overcoat. She put down the candle in hot haste and ran off; evidently she had thought of something or wanted to show me something. As she ran away she flushed, her eyes shone, and there was a smile on her lips – what was the meaning of it? Against my will I waited: she came back a minute later with an expression that seemed to ask forgiveness for something. In fact, it was not the same face, not the same look as the evening before: sullen, mistrustful and obstinate. Her eyes now were imploring, soft, and at the same time trustful, caressing, timid. The expression with which children look at people they are very fond of, of whom they are asking a favour. Her eyes were a light hazel, they were lovely eyes, full of life, and capable of expressing love as well as sullen hatred.

Making no explanation, as though I, as a sort of higher being, must understand everything without explanations, she held out a piece of paper to me. Her whole face was positively beaming at that instant with naive, almost childish, triumph. I unfolded it. It was a letter to her from a medical student or someone of that sort – a very high-flown and flowery, but extremely respectful, love-letter. I don't recall the words now, but I remember well that through the high-flown phrases there was apparent a genuine feeling, which cannot be feigned. When I had finished reading it I met her glowing, questioning and childishly impatient eyes fixed upon me. She fastened her eyes upon my face and waited impatiently for what I should say. In a few words, hurriedly, but with a sort of joy and pride, she explained to me that she had been to a dance somewhere in a private house, a family of 'very nice people, *who knew nothing*, absolutely nothing, for she had only come here so lately and it had all happened . . . and she hadn't made up her mind to stay and was certainly going away as soon as she had paid her debt . . . ' and at that party there had been the student who had danced with her all the evening. He had talked to her, and it turned out that he had known her in the old days at Riga when he was a child, they had played together, but a very long time ago – and he knew her parents, but *about this* he knew nothing, nothing whatever, and had no suspicion! And the day after the dance (three days ago) he had sent her that letter through the friend with whom she had gone to the party . . . and . . . well, that was all.'

She dropped her shining eyes with a sort of bashfulness as she finished.

The poor girl was keeping that student's letter as a precious treasure, and had run to fetch it, her only treasure, because she did not want me to go away without knowing that she, too, was honestly and genuinely loved; that she, too, was addressed respectfully. No doubt that letter was destined to lie in her box and lead to nothing. But none the less, I am certain that she would keep it all her life as a precious treasure, as her pride and justification, and now at such a minute she had thought of that letter and brought it with naïve pride to raise herself in my eyes that I might see, that I, too, might think well of her. I said nothing, pressed her hand and went out. I so longed to get away . . . I walked all the way home, in spite of the fact that the melting snow was still falling in heavy flakes. I was exhausted, shattered, in bewilderment. But behind the bewilderment the truth was already gleaming. The loathsome truth.

8

It was some time, however, before I consented to recognise that truth. Waking up in the morning after some hours of heavy, leaden sleep, and immediately realising all that had happened on the previous day, I was positively amazed at my last night's *sentimentality* with Liza, at all those 'outcries of horror and pity'. 'To think of having such an attack of womanish hysteria, pah!' I concluded. And what did I thrust my address upon her for? What if she comes? Let her come, though; it doesn't matter . . . But *obviously*, that was not now the chief and the most important matter: I had to make haste and at all costs save my reputation in the eyes of Zverkov and Simonov as quickly as possible; that was the chief business. And I was so taken up that morning that I actually forgot all about Liza.

First of all I had at once to repay what I had borrowed the day before from Simonov. I resolved on a desperate measure: to borrow fifteen roubles straight off from Anton Antonitch. As luck would have it he was in the best of humours that morning, and gave it to me at once, on the first asking. I was so delighted at this that, as I signed the IOU with a swaggering air, I told him casually that the night before 'I had been keeping up with some friends at the Hôtel de Paris; we were giving a farewell party to a comrade, in fact, I might say a friend of my childhood, and you know – a desperate rake, fearfully spoilt – of course, he belongs to a good family, and has considerable means, a brilliant career; he is witty, charming, a regular Lovelace, you understand; we drank an extra "half-dozen" and . . . '

And it went off all right; all this was uttered very easily, unconstrainedly and complacently.

On reaching home I promptly wrote to Simonov.

To this hour I am lost in admiration when I recall the truly gentlemanly, good-humoured, candid tone of my letter. With tact and good-breeding, and, above all, entirely without superfluous words, I blamed myself for all that had happened. I defended myself, 'if I really may be allowed to defend myself,' by alleging that being utterly unaccustomed to wine, I had been intoxicated with the first glass, which I said I had drunk before they arrived, while I was waiting for them at the Hôtel de Paris between five and six o'clock. I begged Simonov's pardon especially; I asked him to convey my explanations to all the others, especially to Zverkov, whom 'I seemed to remember as though in a dream' I had insulted. I added that I would have called upon all of them myself, but my head ached, and besides I had not the face to. I was particularly pleased with a certain lightness, almost carelessness (strictly within the bounds of politeness, however), which was apparent in my style, and better than any possible arguments, gave them at once to understand that I took rather an independent view of 'all that unpleasantness last night'; that I was by no means so utterly crushed as you, my friends, probably imagine; but on the contrary, looked upon it as a gentleman serenely respecting himself should look upon it. 'On a young hero's past no censure is cast!'

'There is actually an aristocratic playfulness about it!' I thought admiringly, as I read over the letter. 'And it's all because I am an intellectual and cultivated man! Another man in my place would not have known how to extricate himself, but here I have got out of it and am as jolly as ever again, and all because I am "a cultivated and educated man of our day". And, indeed, perhaps, everything was due to the wine yesterday. H'm!' . . . No, it was not the wine. I did not drink anything at all between five and six when I was waiting for them. I had lied to Simonov; I had lied shamelessly; and indeed I wasn't ashamed now . . . Hang it all though, the great thing was that I was rid of it.

I put six roubles in the letter, sealed it up, and asked Apollon to take it to Simonov. When he learned that there was money in the letter, Apollon became more respectful and agreed to take it. Towards evening I went out for a walk. My head was still aching and giddy after yesterday. But as evening came on and the twilight grew denser, my impressions and, following them, my thoughts, grew more and more different and confused. Something was not dead within me, in the depths of my heart and conscience it would not die, and it showed itself in acute depression.

For the most part I jostled my way through the most crowded business streets, along Myeshtchansky Street, along Sadovy Street and into Yusupov Garden.[228] I always liked particularly sauntering along these streets in the dusk, just when there were crowds of working people of all sorts going home from their daily work, with faces looking cross with anxiety. What I liked was just that cheap bustle, that bare prose. But on this occasion the jostling of the streets irritated me, I could not make out what was wrong with me, I could not find the clue; something seemed rising up continually in my soul, painfully, and refusing to be appeased. I returned home completely upset, it was just as though some crime were lying on my conscience.

The thought that Liza was coming worried me continually. It seemed queer to me that of all my recollections of yesterday this tormented me, as it were, especially, as it were, quite separately. Everything else I had quite succeeded in forgetting by the evening; I dismissed it all and was still perfectly satisfied with my letter to Simonov. But on this point I was not satisfied at all. It was as though I were worried only by Liza. 'What if she comes,' I thought incessantly, 'well, it doesn't matter, let her come! H'm! it's horrid that she should see, for instance, how I live. Yesterday I seemed such a hero to her, while now, h'm! It's horrid, though, that I have let myself go so, the room looks like a beggar's. And I brought myself to go out to dinner in such a suit! And my American leather sofa with the stuffing sticking out. And my dressing-gown, which will not cover me, such tatters, and she will see all this and she will see Apollon. That beast is certain to insult her. He will fasten upon her in order to be rude to me. And I, of course, shall be panic-stricken as usual, I shall begin bowing and scraping before her and pulling my dressing-gown round me. I shall begin smiling, telling lies. Oh, the beastliness! And it isn't the beastliness of it that matters most! There is something more important, more loathsome, viler! Yes, viler! And to put on that dishonest lying mask again! . . .'

When I reached that thought I fired up all at once.

'Why dishonest? How dishonest? I was speaking sincerely last night. I remember there was real feeling in me, too. What I wanted was to excite an honourable feeling in her . . . Her crying was a good thing, it will have a good effect.'

Yet I could not feel at ease. All that evening, even when I had come back home, even after nine o'clock, when I calculated that Liza could not possibly come, still she haunted me, and what was worse, she came back to my mind always in the same position. One moment out of all that had happened last night stood vividly before my imagination; the moment when I struck a match and saw her pale, distorted face, with its look of torture. And what a pitiful, what an unnatural, what a distorted smile she had at that moment! But I did not know then that fifteen years later I should still in my imagination see Liza, always with the pitiful, distorted, inappropriate smile which was on her face at that minute.

Next day I was ready again to look upon it all as nonsense, as due to over-excited nerves, and, above all, as *exaggerated*. I was always conscious of that weak point of mine, and sometimes very much afraid of it. 'I exaggerate everything, that is where I go wrong,' I repeated to myself every hour. But, however, 'Liza will very likely come all the same,' was the refrain with which all my reflections ended. I was so uneasy that I sometimes flew into a fury: 'She'll come, she is certain to come!' I cried, running about the room; 'if not today, she will come tomorrow; she'll find me out! The damnable romanticism of these pure hearts! Oh, the vileness – oh, the silliness – oh, the stupidity of these "wretched sentimental souls"! Why, how fail to understand? How could one fail to understand? . . .'

But at this point I stopped short, and in great confusion, indeed.

And how few, how few words, I thought, in passing, were needed; how little of the idyllic (and affectedly, bookishly, artificially idyllic, too) had sufficed to turn a whole human life at once according to my will. That's virginity, to be sure! Freshness of soil!

At times a thought occurred to me to go to her, 'to tell her all', and beg her not to come to me. But this thought stirred such wrath in me that I believed I should have crushed that 'damned' Liza if she had chanced to be near me at the time. I should have insulted her, have spat at her, have turned her out, have struck her!

One day passed, however, another and another; she did not come and I began to grow calmer. I felt particularly bold and cheerful after nine o'clock, I even sometimes began dreaming, and rather sweetly: I, for instance, became the salvation of Liza, simply through her coming to me and my talking to her . . . I develop her, educate her. Finally, I notice that she loves me, loves me passionately. I pretend not to understand (I don't know, however, why I pretend, just for effect, perhaps). At last all confusion, transfigured, trembling and sobbing, she flings herself at my feet and says that I am her saviour, and that she loves me better than anything in the world. I am amazed, but . . . 'Liza,' I say, 'can you imagine that I have not noticed your love? I saw it all, I divined it, but I did not dare to approach you first, because I had an influence over you and was afraid that you would force yourself, from gratitude, to respond to my love, would try to rouse in your heart a feeling which was perhaps absent, and I did not wish that ... because it would be tyranny ... it would be indelicate (in short, I launch off at that point into European, inexplicably lofty subtleties *à la* George Sand[229]), but now, now you are mine, you are my creation, you are pure, you are good, you are my noble wife. "Into my house come bold and free, its rightful mistress there to be".'[230]

Then we begin living together, go abroad and so on, and so on. In fact, in the end it seemed vulgar to me myself, and I began putting out my tongue at myself.

Besides, they won't let her out, 'the hussy!' I thought. They don't let them go out very readily, especially in the evening (for some reason I fancied she would come in the evening, and at seven o'clock precisely). Though she did say she was not altogether a slave there yet, and had certain rights; so, h'm! Damn it all, she will come, she is sure to come!

It was a good thing, in fact, that Apollon distracted my attention at that time by his rudeness. He drove me beyond all patience! He was the bane of my life, the curse laid upon me by Providence. We had been squabbling continually for years, and I hated him. My God, how I hated him! I believe I had never hated anyone in my life as I hated him, especially at some moments. He was an elderly, dignified man, who worked part of his time as a tailor. But for some unknown reason he despised me beyond all measure, and looked down upon me insufferably. Though, indeed, he looked down upon everyone. Simply to glance at that flaxen, smoothly brushed head, at the tuft of hair he combed up on his forehead and oiled with sunflower oil, at that dignified mouth, compressed into the shape of the letter V,[231] made one feel one was confronting a man who never doubted of himself. He was a pedant, to the most extreme point, the greatest pedant I had met on earth, and with that had a vanity only befitting Alexander of Macedon.[232] He was in love with every button on his coat, every nail on his fingers – absolutely in love with them, and he looked it! In his behaviour to me he was a perfect tyrant, he spoke very little to me, and if he chanced to glance at me he gave me a firm, majestically self-confident and invariably ironical look that drove me sometimes to fury. He did his work with the air of doing me the greatest favour, though he did scarcely anything for me, and did not, indeed, consider himself bound to do anything. There could be no doubt that he looked upon me as the greatest fool on earth, and that 'he did not get rid of me' was simply because he could get wages from me every month. He consented to do nothing for me for seven roubles a month. Many sins should be forgiven me for what I suffered from him. My hatred reached such a point that sometimes his very step almost threw me into convulsions. What I loathed particularly was his lisp. His tongue must have been a little too long or something of that sort, for he continually lisped, and seemed to be very proud of it, imagining that it greatly added to his dignity. He spoke in a slow, measured tone, with his hands behind his back and his eyes fixed on the ground. He maddened me particularly when he read aloud the Psalms to himself behind his partition. Many a battle I waged over that reading! But he was awfully fond of reading aloud in the evenings, in a slow, even, sing-song voice, as though over the dead. It is interesting that that is how he has ended: he hires himself out to read the Psalms over the dead, and at the same time he kills rats and makes blacking. But at that time I could not get rid of him, it was as though he were chemically combined with my existence. Besides, nothing would have induced him to consent to leave me. I could not live in furnished lodgings: my lodging was my private solitude, my shell, my cave, in which I concealed myself from all mankind, and Apollon seemed to me, for some reason, an integral part of that flat, and for seven years I could not turn him away.

To be two or three days behind with his wages, for instance, was impossible. He would have made such a fuss, I should not have known where to hide my head. But I was so exasperated with everyone during those days, that I made up my mind for some reason and with some object to *punish* Apollon and not to pay him for a fortnight the wages that were owing him. I had for a long time – for the last two years – been intending to do this, simply in order to teach him not to give himself airs with me, and to show him that if I liked I could withhold his wages. I purposed to say nothing to him about it, and was purposely silent indeed, in order to score off his pride and force him to be the first to speak of his wages. Then I would take the seven roubles out of a drawer, show him I have the money put aside on purpose, but that I won't, I won't, I simply won't pay him his wages, I won't just because that is 'what I wish', because 'I am master, and it is for me to decide,' because he has been disrespectful, because he has been rude; but if he were to ask respectfully I might be softened and give it to him, otherwise he might wait another fortnight, another three weeks, a whole month . . . But angry as I was, yet he got the better of me. I could not hold out for four days. He began as he always did begin in such cases, for there had been such cases already, there had been attempts (and it may be observed I knew all this beforehand, I knew his nasty tactics by heart). He would begin by fixing upon me an exceedingly severe stare, keeping it up for several minutes at a time, particularly on meeting me or seeing me out of the house. If I held out and pretended not to notice these stares, he would, still in silence, proceed to further tortures. All at once, apropos of nothing, he would walk softly and smoothly into my room, when I was pacing up and down or reading, stand at the door, one hand behind his back and one foot behind the other, and fix upon me a stare more than severe, utterly contemptuous. If I suddenly asked him what he wanted, he would make me no answer, but continue staring at me persistently for some seconds, then, with a peculiar compression of his lips and a most significant air, deliberately turn round and deliberately go back to his room. Two hours later he would come out again and again present himself before me in the same way. It had happened that in my fury I did not even ask him what he wanted, but simply raised my head sharply and imperiously and began staring back at him. So we stared at one another for two minutes; at last he turned with deliberation and dignity and went back again for two hours.

If I were still not brought to reason by all this, but persisted in my revolt, he would suddenly begin sighing while he looked at me, long, deep sighs as though measuring by them the depths of my moral degradation, and, of course, it ended at last by his triumphing completely: I raged and shouted, but still was forced to do what he wanted.

This time the usual staring manoeuvres had scarcely begun when I lost my temper and flew at him in a fury. I was irritated beyond endurance apart from him.

'Stay,' I cried, in a frenzy, as he was slowly and silently turning, with one hand behind his back, to go to his room. 'Stay! Come back, come back, I tell you!' and I must have bawled so unnaturally, that he turned round and even looked at me with some wonder. However, he persisted in saying nothing, and that infuriated me.

'How dare you come and look at me like that without being sent for? Answer!'

After looking at me calmly for half a minute, he began turning round again.

'Stay!' I roared, running up to him, 'don't stir! There. Answer, now: what did you come in to look at?'

'If you have any order to give me it's my duty to carry it out,' he answered, after another silent pause, with a slow, measured lisp, raising his eyebrows and calmly twisting his head from one side to another, all this with exasperating composure.

'That's not what I am asking you about, you torturer!' I shouted, turning crimson with anger. 'I'll tell you why you came here myself: you see, I don't give you your wages and you are so proud you don't want to bow down and ask for them so you come to punish me with your stupid stares, to worry me and you have no sus-pic-ion how stupid it is – stupid, stupid, stupid, stupid! . . . '

He would have turned round again without a word, but I seized him.

'Listen,' I shouted to him. 'Here's the money, do you see, here it is,' (I took it out of the table drawer); 'here's the seven roubles complete, but you are not going to have it, you . . . are . . . not . . . going . . . to . . . have . . . it . . . until you come respectfully with bowed head to beg my pardon. Do you hear?'

'That cannot be,' he answered, with the most unnatural self-confidence.

'It shall be so,' I said. 'I give you my word of honour, it shall be!'

'And there's nothing for me to beg your pardon for,' he went on, as though he had not noticed my exclamations at all. 'Why, besides, you called me a "torturer", for which I can summons you at the police-station at any time for insulting behaviour.'

'Go, summons me,' I roared, 'go at once, this very minute, this very second! You are a torturer all the same! a torturer!'

But he merely looked at me, then turned, and regardless of my loud calls to him, he walked to his room with an even step and without looking round.

'If it had not been for Liza nothing of this would have happened,' I decided inwardly. Then, after waiting a minute, I went myself behind his screen with a dignified and solemn air, though my heart was beating slowly and violently.

'Apollon,' I said quietly and emphatically, though I was breathless, 'go at once without a minute's delay and fetch the police-officer.'

He had meanwhile settled himself at his table, put on his spectacles and taken up some sewing. But, hearing my order, he burst into a guffaw.

'At once, go this minute! Go on, or else you can't imagine what will happen.'

'You are certainly out of your mind,' he observed, without even raising his head, lisping as deliberately as ever and threading his needle. 'Whoever heard of a man sending for the police against himself? And as for being frightened – you are upsetting yourself about nothing, for nothing will come of it.'

'Go!' I shrieked, clutching him by the shoulder. I felt I should strike him in a minute.

But I did not notice the door from the passage softly and slowly open at that instant and a figure come in, stop short, and begin staring at us in perplexity I glanced, nearly swooned with shame, and rushed back to my room. There, clutching at my hair with both hands, I leaned my head against the wall and stood motionless in that position.

Two minutes later I heard Apollon's deliberate footsteps. 'There is some woman asking for you,' he said, looking at me with peculiar severity. Then he stood aside and let in Liza. He would not go away, but stared at us sarcastically.

'Go away, go away,' I commanded in desperation. At that moment my clock began whirring and wheezing and struck seven.

9

'Into my house come bold and free,
Its rightful mistress there to be.'

I stood before her crushed, crestfallen, revoltingly confused, and I believe I smiled as I did my utmost to wrap myself in the skirts of my ragged wadded dressing-gown – exactly as I had imagined the scene not long before in a fit of depression. After standing over us for a couple of minutes Apollon went away, but that did not make me more at ease. What made it worse was that she, too, was overwhelmed with confusion, more so, in fact, than I should have expected. At the sight of me, of course.

'Sit down,' I said mechanically, moving a chair up to the table, and I sat down on the sofa. She obediently sat down at once and gazed at me open-eyed, evidently expecting something from me at once. This naivety of expectation drove me to fury, but I restrained myself.

She ought to have tried not to notice, as though everything had been as usual, while instead of that, she ... and I dimly felt that I should make her pay dearly for *all this*.

'You have found me in a strange position, Liza,' I began, stammering and knowing that this was the wrong way to begin. 'No, no, don't imagine anything,' I cried, seeing that she had suddenly flushed. 'I am not ashamed of my poverty . . . On the contrary, I look with pride on my poverty. I am poor but honourable . . . One can be poor and honourable,' I muttered. 'However . . . would you like tea? . . . '

'No,' she was beginning.

'Wait a minute.'

I leapt up and ran to Apollon. I had to get out of the room somehow.

'Apollon,' I whispered in feverish haste, flinging down before him the seven roubles which had remained all the time in my clenched fist, 'here are your wages, you see I give them to you; but for that you must come to my rescue: bring me tea and a dozen rusks from the restaurant. If you won't go, you'll make me a miserable man! You don't know what this woman is . . . This is – everything! You may be imagining something . . . But you don't know what that woman is! . . . '

Apollon, who had already sat down to his work and put on his spectacles again, at first glanced askance at the money without speaking or putting down his needle; then, without paying the slightest attention to me or making any answer, he went on busying himself with his needle, which he had not yet threaded. I waited before him for three minutes with my arms crossed *à la Napoléon*.[233] My temples were moist with sweat. I was pale, I felt it. But, thank God, he must have been moved to pity, looking at me. Having threaded his needle he deliberately got up from his seat, deliberately moved back his chair, deliberately took off his spectacles, deliberately counted the money, and finally asking me over his shoulder: 'Shall I get a whole portion?' deliberately walked out of the room. As I was going back to Liza, the thought occurred to me on the way: shouldn't I run away just as I was in my dressing-gown, no matter where, and then let happen what would?

I sat down again. She looked at me uneasily. For some minutes we were silent.

'I will kill him,' I shouted suddenly, striking the table with my fist so that the ink spurted out of the inkstand.

'What are you saying!' she cried, starting.

'I will kill him! kill him!' I shrieked, suddenly striking the table in absolute frenzy, and at the same time fully understanding how stupid it was to be in such a frenzy. 'You don't know, Liza, what that torturer is to me. He is my torturer . . . He has gone now to fetch some rusks; he . . . '

And suddenly I burst into tears. It was an hysterical attack. How ashamed I felt in the midst of my sobs; but still I could not restrain them.

She was frightened.

'What is the matter? What is wrong?' she cried, fussing about me.

'Water, give me water, over there!' I muttered in a faint voice, though I was inwardly conscious that I could have got on very well without water and without muttering in a faint voice. But I was what is called *putting it on*, to save appearances, though the attack was a genuine one.

She gave me water, looking at me in bewilderment. At that moment

Apollon brought in the tea. It suddenly seemed to me that this common-place, prosaic tea was horribly undignified and paltry after all that had happened, and I blushed crimson. Liza looked at Apollon with positive alarm. He went out without a glance at either of us.

'Liza, do you despise me?' I asked, looking at her fixedly, trembling with impatience to know what she was thinking.

She was confused, and did not know what to answer.

'Drink your tea,' I said to her angrily. I was angry with myself, but, of course, it was she who would have to pay for it. A horrible spite against her suddenly surged up in my heart; I believe I could have killed her. To revenge myself on her I swore inwardly not to say a word to her all the time. 'She is the cause of it all,' I thought.

Our silence lasted for five minutes. The tea stood on the table; we did not touch it. I had got to the point of purposely refraining from beginning in order to embarrass her further; it was awkward for her to begin alone. Several times she glanced at me with mournful perplexity. I was obstinately silent. I was, of course, myself the chief sufferer, because I was fully conscious of the disgusting meanness of my spiteful stupidity, and yet at the same time I could not restrain myself.

'I want to ... get away ... from there altogether,' she began, to break the silence in some way, but, poor girl, that was just what she ought not to have spoken about at such a stupid moment to a man so stupid as I was. My heart positively ached with pity for her tactless and unnecessary straightforwardness. But something hideous at once stifled all compassion in me; it even provoked me to greater venom. I did not care what happened. Another five minutes passed.

'Perhaps I am in your way,' she began timidly, hardly audibly, and was getting up.

But as soon as I saw this first impulse of wounded dignity I positively trembled with spite, and at once burst out.

'Why have you come to me, tell me that, please?' I began, gasping for breath and regardless of logical connection in my words. I longed to have it all out at once, at one burst; I did not even trouble how to begin. 'Why have you come? Answer, answer,' I cried, hardly knowing what I was doing. 'I'll tell you, my good girl, why you have come. You've come because I talked sentimental stuff to you then. So now you are soft as butter and longing for fine sentiments again. So you may as well know that I was laughing at you then. And I am laughing at you now. Why are you shuddering? Yes, I was laughing at you! I had been insulted just before, at dinner, by the fellows who came that evening before me. I came to you, meaning to thrash one of them, an officer; but I didn't succeed, I didn't find him; I had to avenge the insult on someone to get my own back again; you turned up, I vented my spleen on you and laughed at you. I had been humiliated, so I wanted to humiliate; I had been treated like a rag, so I wanted to show my power . . . That's what it was, and you imagined I had come there on purpose to save you. Yes? You imagined that? You imagined that?'

I knew that she would perhaps be muddled and not take it all in exactly, but I knew, too, that she would grasp the gist of it, very well indeed. And so, indeed, she did. She turned white as a handkerchief, tried to say something, and her lips worked painfully; but she sank on a chair as though she had been felled by an axe. And all the time afterwards she listened to me with her lips parted and her eyes wide open, shuddering with awful terror. The cynicism, the cynicism of my words overwhelmed her . . . 'Save you!' I went on, jumping up from my chair and running up and down the room before her. 'Save you from what? But perhaps I am worse than you myself. Why didn't you throw it in my teeth when I was giving you that sermon: "But what did you come here yourself for? was it to read us a sermon?" Power, power was what I wanted then, sport was what I wanted; I wanted to wring out your tears, your humiliation, your hysteria – that was what I wanted then! Of course, I couldn't keep it up then, because I am a wretched creature. I was frightened, and, the devil knows why, gave you my address in my folly. Afterwards, before I got home, I was cursing and swearing at you because of that address, I hated you already because of the lies I had told you. Because I only like playing with words, only dreaming, but, do you know, what I really want is that you should all go to hell. That is what I want. I want peace; yes, I'd sell the whole world for a farthing, straight off, so long as I was left in peace. Is the world to go to pot, or am I to go without my tea? I say that the world may go to pot for me so long as I always get my tea. Did you know that, or not? Well, anyway, I know that I am a blackguard, a scoundrel, an egoist, a sluggard. Here I have been shuddering for the last three days at the thought of your coming. And do you know what has worried me particularly for these three days? That I posed as such a hero to you, and now you would see me in a wretched torn dressing-gown, beggarly, loathsome. I told you just now that I was not ashamed of my poverty; so you may as well know that I am ashamed of it; I am more ashamed of it than of anything, more afraid of it than of being found out if I were a thief, because I am as vain as though I had been skinned and the very air blowing on me hurt. Surely by now you must realise that I shall never forgive you for having found me in this wretched dressing-gown, just as I was flying at Apollon like a spiteful cur. The saviour, the former hero, was flying like a mangy, unkempt sheepdog at his lackey, and the lackey was jeering at him! And I shall never forgive you for the tears I could not help shedding before you just now, like some silly woman put to shame! And for what I am confessing to you now, I shall never forgive you either! Yes – you must answer for it all because you turned up like this, because I am a blackguard, because I am the nastiest, stupidest, absurdest and most envious of all the worms on earth, who are not a bit better than I am, but, the devil knows why, are never put to confusion; while I shall always be insulted by every louse, that is my doom! And what is it to me that you don't understand a word of this! And what do I care, what do I care about you, and whether you go to ruin there or not? Do you understand? How I shall hate you now after saying this, for having been here and listening. Why, it's not once in a lifetime a man speaks out like this, and then it is in hysterics! . . . What more do you want? Why do you still stand confronting me, after all this? Why are you worrying me? Why don't you go?'

But at this point a strange thing happened. I was so accustomed to think and imagine everything from books, and to picture everything in the world to myself just as I had made it up in my dreams beforehand, that I could not all at once take in this strange circumstance. What happened was this: Liza, insulted and crushed by me, understood a great deal more than I imagined. She understood from all this what a woman understands first of all, if she feels genuine love, that is, that I was myself unhappy.

The frightened and wounded expression on her face was followed first by a look of sorrowful perplexity. When I began calling myself a scoundrel and a blackguard and my tears flowed (the tirade was accompanied throughout by tears), her whole face worked convulsively. She was on the point of getting up and stopping me; when I finished she took no notice of my shouting: 'Why are you here, why don't you go away?' but realised only that it must have been very bitter to me to say all this. Besides, she was so crushed, poor girl; she considered herself infinitely beneath me; how could she feel anger or resentment? She suddenly leapt up from her chair with an irresistible impulse and held out her hands, yearning towards me, though still timid and not daring to stir . . . At this point there was a revulsion in my heart too. Then she suddenly rushed to me, threw her arms round me and burst into tears. I, too, could not restrain myself, and sobbed as I never had before.

'They won't let me . . . I can't be good!' I managed to articulate; then I went to the sofa, fell on it face downwards, and sobbed on it for a quarter of an hour in genuine hysterics. She came close to me, put her arms round me and stayed motionless in that position. But the trouble was that the hysterics could not go on for ever, and (I am writing the loathsome truth) lying face downwards on the sofa with my face thrust into my nasty leather pillow, I began by degrees to be aware of a faraway, involuntary but irresistible feeling that it would be awkward now for me to raise my head and look Liza straight in the face. Why was I ashamed? I don't know, but I was ashamed. The thought, too, came into my overwrought brain that our parts now were completely changed, that she was now the heroine, while I was just a crushed and humiliated creature as she had been before me that night – four days before . . . And all this came into my mind during the minutes I was lying on my face on the sofa.

My God! surely I was not envious of her then.

I don't know, to this day I cannot decide, and at the time, of course, I was still less able to understand what I was feeling than now. I cannot get on without domineering and tyrannising over someone, but . . . there is no explaining anything by reasoning and so it is useless to reason.

I conquered myself, however, and raised my head; I had to do so sooner or later . . . and I am convinced to this day that it was just because I was ashamed to look at her that another feeling was suddenly kindled and flamed up in my heart . . . a feeling of mastery and possession. My eyes gleamed with passion, and I gripped her hands tightly. How I hated her and how I was drawn to her at that minute! The one feeling intensified the other. It was almost like an act of vengeance. At first there was a look of amazement, even of terror on her face, but only for one instant. She warmly and rapturously embraced me.

10

A quarter of an hour later I was rushing up and down the room in frenzied impatience, from minute to minute I went up to the screen and peeped through the crack at Liza. She was sitting on the ground with her head leaning against the bed, and must have been crying. But she did not go away, and that irritated me. This time she understood it all. I had insulted her finally, but . . . there's no need to describe it. She realised that my outburst of passion had been simply revenge, a fresh humiliation, and that to my earlier, almost causeless hatred was added now a *personal hatred*, born of envy . . . Though I do not maintain positively that she understood all this distinctly; but she certainly did fully understand that I was a despicable man, and, what was worse, incapable of loving her. I know I shall be told that this is incredible – but it is incredible to be as spiteful and stupid as I was; it may be added that it was strange I should not love her, or at any rate, appreciate her love. Why is it strange? In the first place, by then I was incapable of love, for I repeat, with me loving meant tyrannising and showing my moral superiority. I have never in my life been able to imagine any other sort of love, and have nowadays come to the point of sometimes thinking that love really consists in the right – freely given by the beloved object – to tyrannise over her.

Even in my underground dreams I did not imagine love except as a struggle. I began it always with hatred and ended it with moral subjugation, and afterwards I never knew what to do with the subjugated object. And what is there to wonder at in that, since I had succeeded in so corrupting myself, since I was so out of touch with 'real life' as to have actually thought of reproaching her and putting her to shame for having come to me to hear 'fine sentiments'; and did not even guess that she had come not to hear fine sentiments, but to love me, because to a woman all reformation, all salvation from any sort of ruin and all moral renewal is included in love and can only show itself in that form.

I did not hate her so much, however, when I was running about the room and peeping through the crack in the screen. I was only insufferably oppressed by her being here. I wanted her to disappear. I wanted 'peace', to be left alone in my underground world. Real life oppressed me with its novelty so much that I could hardly breathe.

But several minutes passed and she still remained, without stirring, as though she were unconscious. I had the shamelessness to tap softly at the screen as though to remind her . . . She started, sprang up, and flew to seek her kerchief, her hat, her coat, as though making her escape from me . . . Two minutes later she came from behind the screen and looked with heavy eyes at me. I gave a spiteful grin, which was forced, however, to *keep up appearances*, and I turned away from her eyes.

'Goodbye,' she said, going towards the door.

I ran up to her, seized her hand, opened it, thrust something into it and closed it again. Then I turned at once and dashed away in haste to the other corner of the room to avoid seeing, anyway . . . I did mean a moment since to tell a lie – to write that I did this accidentally, not knowing what I was doing through foolishness, through losing my head. But I don't want to lie, and so I will say straight out that I opened her hand and put the money into it . . . from spite. It came into my head to do this while I was running up and down the room and she was sitting behind the screen. But this I can say for certain: though I did that cruel thing purposely, it was not an impulse from the heart but came from my evil brain. This cruelty was so affected, so purposely made up, so completely a product of the brain, of books, that I could not even keep it up a minute – first I dashed away to avoid seeing her, and then in shame and despair rushed after Liza. I opened the door in the passage and began listening.

'Liza! Liza!' I cried on the stairs, but in a low voice, not boldly. There was no answer, but I fancied I heard her footsteps, lower down on the stairs.

'Liza!' I cried, more loudly.

No answer. But at that minute I heard the stiff outer glass door open heavily with a creak and slam violently; the sound echoed up the stairs.

She had gone. I went back to my room in hesitation. I felt horribly oppressed.

I stood still at the table, beside the chair on which she had sat and looked aimlessly before her. A minute passed, suddenly I started; straight before me on the table I saw . . . In short, I saw a crumpled blue five-rouble note, the one I had thrust into her hand a minute before. It was the same note; it could be no other, there was no other in the flat. So she had managed to fling it from her hand onto the table at the moment when I had dashed into the farther corner.

Well! I might have expected that she would do that. Might I have expected it? No, I was such an egoist, I was so lacking in respect for my fellow-creatures that I could not even imagine she would do so. I could not endure it. A minute later I flew like a madman to dress, flinging on what I could at random, and ran headlong after her. She could not have got two hundred paces away when I ran out into the street.

It was a still night and the snow was coming down in masses and falling almost perpendicularly, covering the pavement and the empty street as though with a pillow. There was no one in the street, no sound was to be heard. The street lamps gave a disconsolate and useless glimmer. I ran two hundred paces to the crossroads and stopped short.

Where had she gone? And why was I running after her?

Why? To fall down before her, to sob with remorse, to kiss her feet, to entreat her forgiveness! I longed for that, my whole breast was being rent to pieces, and never, never shall I recall that minute with indifference. But – what for? I thought. Should I not begin to hate her, perhaps, even tomorrow, just because I had kissed her feet today? Should I give her happiness? Had I not recognised that day, for the hundredth time, what I was worth? Should I not torture her?

I stood in the snow, gazing into the troubled darkness and pondered this.

'And will it not be better?' I mused fantastically, afterwards at home, stifling the living pang of my heart with fantastic dreams. 'Will it not be better that she should keep the resentment of the insult for ever? Resentment – why, it is purification; it is a most stinging and painful consciousness! Tomorrow I should have defiled her soul and have exhausted her heart, while now the feeling of insult will never die in her heart, and however loathsome the filth awaiting her – the feeling of insult will elevate and purify her . . . by hatred . . . h'm! . . . perhaps, too, by forgiveness . . . Will all that make things easier for her though? . . . '

And, indeed, I will ask on my own account here, an idle question: which is better – cheap happiness or exalted sufferings? Well, which is better?

So I dreamed as I sat at home that evening, almost dead with the pain in my soul. Never had I endured such suffering and remorse, yet could there have been the faintest doubt when I ran out from my lodging that I should turn back halfway? I never met Liza again and I have heard nothing of her. I will add, too, that I remained for a long time afterwards pleased with the phrase about the benefit from resentment and hatred, in spite of the fact that I almost fell ill from misery . . .

Even now, so many years later, all this is somehow a very evil memory. I have many evil memories now, but . . . hadn't I better end my 'Notes' here? I believe I made a mistake in beginning to write them; anyway I have felt ashamed all the time I've been writing this story, so it's hardly literature so much as a corrective punishment. Why, to tell long stories showing how I have spoiled my life through morally rotting in my corner, through lack of fitting environment, through divorce from real life, consumed with spite in my underground world, would certainly not be interesting; a novel needs a hero, and all the traits for an anti-hero are *expressly* gathered together here, and, what matters most, it all produces an unpleasant impression, for we are all divorced from life, we are all cripples, every one of us, more or less. We are so divorced from it that we feel at once a sort of loathing for real life, and so cannot bear to be reminded of it. Why, we have come almost to looking upon real life as an effort, almost as hard work, and we are all privately agreed that it is better in books. And why do we fuss and fume sometimes? Why are we perverse and ask for something else? We don't know what ourselves. It would be the worse for us if our petulant prayers were answered. Come, try, give any one of us, for instance, a little more independence, untie our hands, widen the spheres of our activity, relax the control and we . . . yes, I assure you . . . we should be begging to be under control again at once. I know that you will very likely be angry with me for that, and will begin shouting and stamping. Speak for yourself, you will say, and for your miseries in your underground hole, and don't dare to say all of us – excuse me, gentlemen, I am not justifying myself with that 'all of us'. As for what concerns me in particular I have only in my life carried to an extreme what you have not dared to carry halfway, and what's more, you have taken your cowardice for good sense, and have found comfort in deceiving yourselves. So that perhaps, after all, there is more life in me than in you. Look into it more carefully! Why, we don't even know what living means now, what it is, and what it is called? Leave us alone without books and we shall be lost and in confusion at once. We shall not know what to join on to, what to cling to, what to love and what to hate, what to respect and what to despise. We are oppressed at being men – men with a real individual body and blood, we are ashamed of it, we think it a disgrace and try to contrive to be some sort of impossible generalised man. We are stillborn, and for generations past have not been begotten by living fathers, and that suits us better and better. We are developing a taste for it. Soon we shall contrive to be born somehow from an idea. But enough; I don't want to write more from 'Underground'.

The notes of this paradoxalist do not end here, however. He could not refrain from going on with them, but it seems to us that we may stop here. FYODOR DOSTOEVSKY

The Crocodile

An Extraordinary Incident

A true story of how a gentleman of a certain age and of respectable appearance was swallowed alive by the crocodile in the Arcade, and of the consequences that followed.

Ohè Lambert! Où est Lambert? As-tu vu Lambert?[234]

1

ON THE THIRTEENTH OF JANUARY of this present year, 1865, at half-past twelve in the day, Elena Ivanovna, the wife of my cultured friend Ivan Matveitch, who is a colleague in the same department, and may be said to be a distant relation of mine, too, expressed the desire to see the crocodile now on view at a fixed charge in the Arcade. As Ivan Matveitch had already in his pocket his ticket for a tour abroad (not so much for the sake of his health as for the improvement of his mind), and was consequently free from his official duties and had nothing whatever to do that morning, he offered no objection to his wife's irresistible fancy, but was positively aflame with curiosity himself.

'A capital idea!' he said, with the utmost satisfaction. 'We'll have a look at the crocodile! On the eve of visiting Europe it is as well to acquaint ourselves on the spot with its indigenous inhabitants.' And with these words, taking his wife's arm, he set off with her at once for the Arcade. I joined them, as I usually do, being an intimate friend of the family. I have never seen Ivan Matveitch in a more agreeable frame of mind than he was on that memorable morning – how true it is that we know not beforehand the fate that awaits us! On entering the Arcade he was at once full of admiration for the splendours of the building and, when we reached the shop in which the monster lately arrived in Petersburg was being exhibited, he volunteered to pay the quarter-rouble for me to the crocodile owner – a thing which had never happened before. Walking into a little room, we observed that besides the crocodile there were in it parrots of the species known as cockatoo, and also a group of monkeys in a special case in a recess. Near the entrance, along the left wall stood a big tin tank that looked like a bath covered with a thin iron grating and filled with water to the depth of two inches. In this shallow pool was kept a huge crocodile, which lay like a log absolutely motionless and apparently deprived of all its faculties by our damp climate, so inhospitable to foreign visitors. This monster at first aroused no special interest in any one of us.

'So this is the crocodile!' said Elena Ivanovna, with a pathetic cadence of regret. 'Why, I thought it was . . . something different.'

Most probably she thought it was made of diamonds. The owner of the crocodile, a German, came out and looked at us with an air of extraordinary pride.

'He has a right to be proud,' Ivan Matveitch whispered to me, 'he knows he is the only man in Russia exhibiting a crocodile.'

This quite nonsensical observation I ascribe also to the extremely good-humoured mood which had overtaken Ivan Matveitch, who was on other occasions of a rather envious disposition.

'I fancy your crocodile is not alive,' said Elena Ivanovna, piqued by the irresponsive stolidity of the proprietor, and addressing him with a charming smile in order to soften his churlishness – a manoeuvre so typically feminine.

'Oh, no, madam,' the latter replied in broken Russian; and instantly moving the grating half off the tank, he poked the monster's head with a stick.

Then the treacherous monster, to show that it was alive, faintly stirred its paws and tail, raised its snout and emitted something like a prolonged snuffle.

'Come, don't be cross, Karlchen,' said the German caressingly, gratified in his vanity.

'How horrid that crocodile is! I am really frightened,' Elena Ivanovna twittered, still more coquettishly. 'I know I shall dream of him now.'

'But he won't bite you if you do dream of him,' the German retorted gallantly, and was the first to laugh at his own jest, but none of us responded.

'Come, Semyon Semyonitch,' said Elena Ivanovna, addressing me exclusively, 'let us go and look at the monkeys. I am awfully fond of monkeys; they are such darlings . . . and the crocodile is horrid.'

'Oh, don't be afraid, my dear!' Ivan Matveitch called after us, gallantly displaying his manly courage to his wife. 'This drowsy denizen of the realms of the Pharaohs will do us no harm.' And he remained by the tank. What is more, he took his glove and began tickling the crocodile's nose with it, wishing, as he said afterwards, to induce him to snort. The proprietor showed his politeness to a lady by following Elena Ivanovna to the case of monkeys.

So everything was going well, and nothing could have been foreseen. Elena Ivanovna was quite skittish in her raptures over the monkeys, and seemed completely taken up with them. With shrieks of delight she was continually turning to me, as though determined not to notice the proprietor, and kept gushing with laughter at the resemblance she detected between these monkeys and her intimate friends and acquaintances. I, too, was amused, for the resemblance was unmistakable. The German did not know whether to laugh or not, and so at last was reduced to frowning. And it was at that moment that a terrible, I may say unnatural, scream set the room vibrating. Not knowing what to think, for the first moment I stood still, numb with horror, but, noticing that Elena Ivanovna was screaming too, I quickly turned round and what did I behold! I saw – oh, heavens! – I saw the luckless Ivan Matveitch in the terrible jaws of the crocodile, held by them round the waist, lifted horizontally in the air and desperately kicking. Then – one moment, and no trace remained of him. But I must describe it in detail, for I stood all the while motionless, and had time to watch the whole process taking place before me with an attention and interest such as I never remember to have felt before. 'What,' I thought at that critical moment, 'what if all that had happened to me instead of to Ivan Matveitch – how unpleasant it would have been for me!'

But to return to my story. The crocodile began by turning the unhappy Ivan Matveitch in his terrible jaws so that he could swallow his legs first; then bringing up Ivan Matveitch, who kept trying to jump out and clutching at the sides of the tank, sucked him down again as far as his waist. Then bringing him up again, gulped him down, and so again and again. In this way Ivan Matveitch was visibly disappearing before our eyes. At last, with a final gulp, the crocodile swallowed my cultured friend entirely, this time leaving no trace of him. From the outside of the crocodile we could see the protuberances of Ivan Matveitch's figure as he passed down the inside of the monster. I was on the point of screaming again when destiny played another treacherous trick upon us. The crocodile made a tremendous effort, probably oppressed by the magnitude of the object he had swallowed, once more opened his terrible jaws, and with a final hiccup he suddenly let the head of Ivan Matveitch pop out for a second, with an expression of despair on his face. In that brief instant the spectacles dropped off his nose to the bottom of the tank. It seemed as though that despairing countenance had only popped out to cast one last look on the objects around it, to take its last farewell of all earthly pleasures. But it had not time to carry out its intention; the crocodile made another effort, gave a gulp and instantly it vanished again – this time for ever. This appearance and disappearance of a still living human head was so horrible, but at the same time – either from its rapidity and unexpectedness or from the dropping of the spectacles – there was something so comic about it, that I suddenly quite unexpectedly exploded with laughter. But pulling myself together and realising that to laugh at such a moment was not the thing for an old family friend, I turned at once to Elena Ivanovna and said with a sympathetic air: 'Now it's all over with our friend Ivan Matveitch!'

I cannot even attempt to describe how violent was the agitation of Elena Ivanovna during the whole process. After the first scream she seemed rooted to the spot, and stared at the catastrophe with apparent indifference, though her eyes looked as though they were starting out of her head; then she suddenly went off into a heart-rending wail, but I seized her hands.

At this instant the proprietor, too, who had at first been also petrified by horror, suddenly elapsed his hands and cried, gazing upwards: 'Oh, my crocodile! *Oh, mein allerliebster Karlchen! Mutter, Mutter, Mutter!*'[235]

A door at the rear of the room opened at this cry, and the *Mutter*, a rosy-cheeked, elderly but dishevelled woman in a cap made her appearance, and rushed with a shriek to her German.

A perfect bedlam followed. Elena Ivanovna kept shrieking out the same phrase, as though in a frenzy, 'Flay him! flay him!' apparently entreating them – probably in a moment of oblivion – to flay somebody for something. The proprietor and *Mutter* took no notice whatever of either of us; they were both bellowing like calves over the crocodile.

'He did for himself! He will burst himself at once, for he did swallow a *ganz* official!'[236] cried the proprietor.

'*Unser Karlchen, unser allerliebster Karlchen wird sterben*,' howled his wife.

'We are bereaved and without bread!' chimed in the proprietor.

'Flay him! flay him! flay him!' clamoured Elena Ivanovna, clutching at the German's coat.

'He did tease the crocodile. For what did your man tease the crocodile?' cried the German, pulling away from her. 'You will, if *Karlchen wird* burst, therefore pay, *das war mein Sohn, das war mein einziger Sohn*.'[237]

I must own I was intensely indignant at the sight of such egoism in the German and the cold-heartedness of his dishevelled *Mutter*; at the same time Elena Ivanovna's reiterated shriek of, 'Flay him! flay him!' troubled me even more and absorbed at last my whole attention, positively alarming me. I may as well say straight off that I entirely misunderstood this strange exclamation: it seemed to me that Elena Ivanovna had for the moment taken leave of her senses, but nevertheless wishing to avenge the loss of her beloved Ivan Matveitch, was demanding by way of compensation that the crocodile should be severely thrashed, while she was meaning something quite different. Looking round at the door, not without embarrassment, I began to entreat Elena Ivanovna to calm herself, and above all not to use the shocking word flay. For such a reactionary desire here, in the midst of the Arcade and of the most cultured society, not two paces from the hall where at this very minute Mr Lavrov was perhaps delivering a public lecture,[238] was not only impossible but unthinkable, and might at any moment bring upon us the hisses of culture and the caricatures of Mr Stepanov.[239] To my horror I was immediately proved to be correct in my alarmed suspicions: the curtain that divided the crocodile room from the little entry where the quarter-roubles were taken suddenly parted, and in the opening there appeared a figure with moustaches and beard, carrying a cap, with the upper part of its body bent a long way forward, though the feet were scrupulously held beyond the threshold of the crocodile room in order to avoid the necessity of paying the entrance money.

'Such a reactionary desire, madam,' said the stranger, trying to avoid falling over in our direction and to remain standing outside the room, 'does no credit to your development, and is conditioned by lack of phosphorus in your brain. You will be promptly held up to shame in the *Chronicle of Progress* and in our satirical prints . . .'

But he could not complete his remarks; the proprietor coming to himself, and seeing with horror that a man was talking in the crocodile room without having paid entrance money, rushed furiously at the progressive stranger and turned him out with a punch from each fist. For a moment both vanished from our sight behind a curtain, and only then I grasped that the whole uproar was about nothing. Elena Ivanovna turned out quite innocent; she had, as I have mentioned already, no idea whatever of subjecting the crocodile to a degrading corporal punishment, and had simply expressed the desire that he should be opened and her husband released from his interior.

'What! You wish that my crocodile be perished!' the proprietor yelled, running in again. 'No! let your husband be perished first, before my crocodile! . . . *Mein Vater* showed crocodile, *mein Grossvater* showed crocodile, *mein Sohn* will show crocodile, and I will show crocodile! All will show crocodile! I am known to *ganz Europa*, and you are not known to *ganz Europa*, and you must pay me a *strafe!'*[240]

'*Ja, ja,*' put in the vindictive German woman, 'we shall not let you go, Pay up, since Karlchen is burst!'

'And, indeed, it's useless to flay the creature,' I added calmly, anxious to get Elena Ivanovna away home as quickly as possible, 'as our dear Ivan Matveitch is by now probably soaring somewhere in the empyrean.'

'My dear' – we suddenly heard, to our intense amazement, the voice of Ivan Matveitch – 'my dear, my advice is to apply direct to the superintendent's office, as without the assistance of the police the German will never be made to see reason.'

These words, uttered with firmness and aplomb, and expressing an exceptional presence of mind, for the first minute so astounded us that we could not believe our ears. But, of course, we ran at once to the crocodile's tank, and with equal reverence and incredulity listened to the unhappy captive. His voice was muffled, thin and even squeaky, as though it came from a considerable distance. It reminded one of a jocose person who, covering his mouth with a pillow, shouts from an adjoining room, trying to mimic the sound of two peasants calling to one another in a deserted plain or across a wide ravine – a performance to which I once had the pleasure of listening in a friend's house at Christmas.

'Ivan Matveitch, my dear, and so you are alive!' faltered Elena Ivanovna.

'Alive and well,' answered Ivan Matveitch, 'and, thanks to the Almighty, swallowed without any damage whatever. I am only uneasy as to the view my superiors may take of the incident; for after getting a permit to go abroad I've got into a crocodile, which seems anything but clever.'

'But, my dear, don't trouble your head about being clever; first of all we must somehow excavate you from where you are,' Elena Ivanovna interrupted.

'Excavate!' cried the proprietor. 'I will not let my crocodile be excavated. Now the *publicum* will come many more, and I will *funfzig* kopecks ask and Karlchen will cease to burst.'

'*Gott sei Dank!*'[241] put in his wife.

'They are right,' Ivan Matveitch observed tranquilly; 'the principles of economics before everything.'

'My dear! I will fly at once to the authorities and lodge a complaint, for I feel that we cannot settle this mess by ourselves.'

'I think so too.' observed Ivan Matveitch; 'but in our age of industrial crisis it is not easy to rip open the belly of a crocodile without economic compensation, and meanwhile the inevitable question presents itself: What will the German take for his crocodile? And with it another: How will it be paid? For, as you know, I have no means . . . '

'Perhaps out of your salary . . . ' I observed timidly, but the proprietor interrupted me at once.

'I will not the crocodile sell; I will for three thousand the crocodile sell! I will for four thousand the crocodile sell! Now the *publicum* will come very many. I will for five thousand the crocodile sell!'

In fact he gave himself insufferable airs. Covetousness and a revolting greed gleamed joyfully in his eyes.

'I am going!' I cried indignantly.

'And I! I too! I shall go to Andrey Osipitch himself. I will soften him with my tears,' whined Elena Ivanovna.

'Don't do that, my dear,' Ivan Matveitch hastened to interpose. He had long been jealous of Andrey Osipitch on his wife's account, and he knew she would enjoy going to weep before a gentleman of refinement, for tears suited her. 'And I don't advise you to do so either, my friend,' he added, addressing me. 'It's no good plunging headlong in that slap-dash way; there's no knowing what it may lead to. You had much better go today to Timofey Semyonitch, as though to pay an ordinary visit; he is an old-fashioned and by no means brilliant man, but he is trustworthy, and what matters most of all, he is straightforward. Give him my greetings and describe the circumstances of the case. And since I owe him seven roubles over our last game of cards, take the opportunity to pay him the money; that will soften the stern old man. In any case his advice may serve as a guide for us. And meanwhile take Elena Ivanovna home . . . Calm yourself, my dear,' he continued, addressing her. 'I am weary of these outcries and feminine squabblings, and should like a nap. It's soft and warm in here, though I have hardly had time to look round in this unexpected haven.'

'Look round! Why, is it light in there?' cried Elena Ivanovna in a tone of relief.

'I am surrounded by impenetrable night,' answered the poor captive, 'but I can feel and, so to speak, have a look round with my hands . . . Goodbye; set your mind at rest and don't deny yourself recreation and diversion. Till tomorrow! And you, Semyon Semyonitch, come to me in the evening, and as you are absent-minded and may forget it, tie a knot in your handkerchief.'

I confess I was glad to get away, for I was overtired and somewhat bored. Hastening to offer my arm to the disconsolate Elena Ivanovna, whose charms were only enhanced by her agitation, I hurriedly led her out of the crocodile room.

'The charge will be another quarter-rouble in the evening,' the proprietor called after us.

'Oh, dear, how greedy they are!' said Elena Ivanovna, looking at herself in every mirror on the walls of the Arcade, and evidently aware that she was looking prettier than usual.

'The principles of economics,' I answered with some emotion, proud that passers-by should see the lady on my arm.

'The principles of economics,' she drawled in a touching little voice. 'I did not in the least understand what Ivan Matveitch said about those horrid economics just now.'

'I will explain to you,' I answered, and began at once telling her of the beneficial effects of the introduction of foreign capital into our country, upon which I had read an article in the *Petersburg News* and the *Voice*[242] that morning.

'How strange it is,' she interrupted, after listening for some time. 'But do leave off, you horrid man. What nonsense you are talking . . . Tell me, do I look purple?'

'You look perfect, and not purple!' I observed, seizing the opportunity to pay her a compliment.

'Naughty man!' she said complacently. 'Poor Ivan Matveitch,' she added a minute later, putting her little head on one side coquettishly. 'I am really sorry for him. Oh, dear!' she cried suddenly, 'how is he going to have his dinner . . . and . . . and . . . what will he do . . . if he wants anything?'

'An unforeseen question,' I answered, perplexed in my turn. To tell the truth, it had not entered my head, so much more practical are women than we men in the solution of the problems of daily life!

'Poor dear! how could he have got into such a mess . . . nothing to amuse him, and in the dark. How vexing it is that I have no photograph of him. And so now I am a sort of widow,' she added, with a seductive smile, evidently interested in her new position. 'Hm! . . . I am sorry for him, though.'

It was, in short, the expression of the very natural and intelligible grief of a young and interesting wife for the loss of her husband. I took her home at last, soothed her, and after dining with her and drinking a cup of aromatic coffee, set off at six o'clock to Timofey Semyonitch, calculating that at that hour all married people of settled habits would be sitting or lying down at home.

Having written this first chapter in a style appropriate to the incident recorded, I intend to proceed in a language more natural though less elevated, and I beg to forewarn the reader of the fact.

2

The venerable Timofey Semyonitch met me rather nervously, as though somewhat embarrassed. He led me to his tiny study and shut the door carefully, 'that the children may not hinder us,' he added with evident uneasiness. There he made me sit down on a chair by the writing-table, sat down himself in an easy chair, wrapped round him the skirts of his old wadded dressing-gown, and assumed an official and even severe air, in readiness for anything, though he was not my chief nor Ivan Matveitch's, and had hitherto been reckoned as a colleague and even a friend.

'First of all,' he said, 'take note that I am not a person in authority, but just such a subordinate official as you and Ivan Matveitch . . . I have nothing to do with it, and do not intend to mix myself up in the affair.'

I was surprised to find that he apparently knew all about it already. In spite of that I told him the whole story over in detail. I spoke with positive excitement, for I was at that moment fulfilling the obligations of a true friend. He listened without special surprise, but with evident signs of suspicion.

'Only fancy,' he said, 'I always believed that this would be sure to happen to him.'

'Why, Timofey Semyonitch? It is a very unusual incident in itself . . . '

'I admit it. But Ivan Matveitch's whole career in the service was leading up to this end. He was flighty – conceited indeed. It was always progress and ideas of all sorts, and this is what progress brings people to!'

'But this is a most unusual incident and cannot possibly serve as a general rule for all progressives.'

'Yes, indeed it can. You see, it's the effect of over-education, I assure you. For over-education leads people to poke their noses into all sorts of places, especially where they are not invited. Though perhaps you know best,' he added, as though offended. 'I am an old man and not of much education. I began as a soldier's son, and this year has been the jubilee of my service.'

'Oh, no, Timofey Semyonitch, not at all. On the contrary, Ivan

Matveitch is eager for your advice; he is eager for your guidance. He implores it, so to say, with tears.'

'So to say, with tears! Hm! Those are crocodile's tears and one cannot quite believe in them. Tell me, what possessed him to want to go abroad? And how could he afford to go? Why, he has no private means!'

'He had saved the money from his last bonus,' I answered plaintively. 'He only wanted to go for three months – to Switzerland . . . to the land of William Tell.'[243]

'William Tell? Hm!'

'He wanted to meet the spring at Naples, to see the museums, the customs, the animals . . . '

'Hm! The animals! I think it was simply from pride. What animals? Animals, indeed! Haven't we animals enough? We have museums, menageries, camels. There are bears quite close to Petersburg! And here he's got inside a crocodile himself . . . '

'Oh, come, Timofey Semyonitch! The man is in trouble, the man appeals to you as to a friend, as to an older relation, craves for advice – and you reproach him. Have pity at least on the unfortunate Elena Ivanovna!'

'You are speaking of his wife? A charming little lady,' said Timofey Semyonitch, visibly softening and taking a pinch of snuff with relish. 'Particularly prepossessing. And so plump, and always putting her pretty little head on one side . . . Very agreeable. Andrey Osipitch was speaking of her only the other day.'

'Speaking of her?'

'Yes, and in very flattering terms. Such a bust, he said, such eyes, such hair . . . A sugar-plum, he said, not a lady – and then he laughed. He is still a young man, of course,' Timofey Semyonitch blew his nose with a loud noise. 'And yet, young though he is, what a career he is making for himself.'

'That's quite a different thing, Timofey Semyonitch.'

'Of course, of course.'

'Well, what do you say then, Timofey Semyonitch?'

'Why, what can I do?'

'Give advice, guidance, as a man of experience, a relative! What are we to do? What steps are we to take? Go to the authorities and . . . '

'To the authorities? Certainly not.' Timofey Semyonitch replied hurriedly. 'If you ask my advice, you had better, above all, hush the matter up and act, so to speak, as a private person. It is a suspicious incident, quite unheard of. Unheard of, above all; there is no precedent for it, and it is far from creditable . . . And so discretion above all . . . Let him lie there a bit. We must wait and see . . . '

'But how can we wait and see, Timofey Semyonitch? What if he is stifled there?'

'Why should he be? I think you told me that he made himself fairly comfortable there?'

I told him the whole story over again. Timofey Semyonitch pondered.

'Hm!' he said, twisting his snuff-box in his hands. 'To my mind it's really a good thing he should lie there a bit, instead of going abroad. Let him reflect at his leisure. Of course he mustn't be stifled, and so he must take measures to preserve his health, avoiding a cough, for instance, and so on . . . And as for the German, it's my personal opinion he is within his rights, and even more so than the other side, because it was the other party who got into *his* crocodile without asking permission, and not *he* who got into Ivan Matveitch's crocodile without asking permission, though, so far as I recollect, the latter has no crocodile. And a crocodile is private property, and so it is impossible to slit him open without compensation.'

'For the saving of human life, Timofey Semyonitch?'

'Oh, well, that's a matter for the police. You must go to them.'

'But Ivan Matveitch may be needed in the department. He may be asked for.'

'Ivan Matveitch needed? Ha-ha! Besides, he is on leave, so that we may ignore him – let him inspect the countries of Europe! It will be a different matter if he doesn't turn up when his leave is over. Then we shall ask for him and make enquiries.'

'Three months! Timofey Semyonitch, for pity's sake!'

'It's his own fault. Nobody thrust him there. At this rate we should have to get a nurse to look after him at government expense, and that is not allowed for in the regulations. But the chief point is that the crocodile is private property, so that the principles of economics apply in this question. And the principles of economics are paramount. Only the other evening, at Luke Andreitch's, Ignaty Prokofyitch was saying so. Do you know Ignaty Prokofyitch? A capitalist, in a big way of business, and he speaks so fluently. We need industrial development, he said; "There is very little development among us. We must create it. We must create capital, so we must create a middle-class, the so-called bourgeoisie. And as we haven't capital we must attract it from abroad. We must, in the first place, give facilities to foreign companies to buy up lands in Russia as is done now abroad. The communal holding of land is poison, is ruin." And, you know, he spoke with such heat; well, that's all right for him – a wealthy man, and not in the service. With the communal system, he said, there will be no improvement in industrial development or agriculture. Foreign companies, he said, must as far as possible buy up the whole of our land in big lots, and then split it up, split it up, split it up, into the smallest parts possible – and do you know he pronounced the words split it up with such determination – and then sell it as private property. Or rather, not sell it, but simply let it. "When," he said, "all the land is in the hands of foreign companies they can fix any rent they like. And so the peasant will work three times as much for his daily bread and he can be turned out at pleasure. So that he will feel it, will be submissive and industrious, and will work three times as much for the same wages. But as it is, with the commune, what does he care? He knows he won't die of hunger, so he is lazy and drunken. And meanwhile money will be attracted into Russia, capital will be created and the bourgeoisie will spring up. The English political and literary paper, *The Times*, in an article the other day on our finances stated that the reason our financial position was so unsatisfactory was that we had no middle-class, no big fortunes, no accommodating proletariat." Ignaty Prokofyitch speaks well. He is an orator. He wants to lay a report on the subject before the authorities, and then to get it published in the *News*. That's something very different from verses like Ivan Matveitch's . . . '

'But how about Ivan Matveitch?' I put in, after letting the old man babble on.

Timofey Semyonitch was sometimes fond of talking and showing that he was not behind the times but knew all about things.

'How about Ivan Matveitch? Why, I am coming to that. Here we are, anxious to bring foreign capital into the country – and only consider: as soon as the capital of a foreigner, who has been attracted to Petersburg, has been doubled through Ivan Matveitch, instead of protecting the foreign capitalist, we are proposing to rip open the belly of his original capital – the crocodile. Is it consistent? To my mind, Ivan Matveitch, as the true son of his fatherland, ought to rejoice and to be proud that through him the value of a foreign crocodile has been doubled and possibly even trebled. That's just what is wanted to attract capital. If one man succeeds, mind you, another will come with a crocodile, and a third will bring two or three of them at once, and capital will grow up about them – there you have a bourgeoisie. It must be encouraged.'

'Upon my word, Timofey Semyonitch!' I cried, 'you are demanding almost supernatural self-sacrifice from poor Ivan Matveitch.'

'I demand nothing, and I beg you, before everything – as I have said already – to remember that I am not a person in authority and so cannot

demand anything of anyone. I am speaking as a son of the fatherland –
that is, not as *the* son of the fatherland, but as *a* son of the fatherland.
Again, what possessed him to get into the crocodile? A respectable man,
a man of good grade in the service, lawfully married – and then to
behave like that! Is it consistent?'

'But it was an accident.'

'Who knows? And where is the money to compensate the owner to
come from?'

'Perhaps out of his salary, Timofey Semyonitch?'

'Would that be enough?'

'No, it wouldn't, Timofey Semyonitch,' I answered sadly. 'The
proprietor was at first alarmed that the crocodile would burst, but as
soon as he was sure that it was all right, he began to bluster and was
delighted to think that he could double the charge for entry.'

'Treble and quadruple perhaps! The public will simply stampede the
place now, and crocodile owners are smart people. Besides, it's not Lent
yet, and people are keen on diversions, and so I say again, the great
thing is that Ivan Matveitch should preserve his incognito, don't let him
be in a hurry. Let everybody know, perhaps, that he is in the crocodile,
but don't let them be officially informed of it. Ivan Matveitch is in
particularly favourable circumstances for that, for he is reckoned to be
abroad. It will be said he is in the crocodile, and we will refuse to believe
it. That is how it can be managed. The great thing is that he should
wait; and why should he be in a hurry?'

'Well, but if . . . '

'Don't worry, he has a good constitution.'

'Well, and afterwards, when he has waited?'

'Well, I won't conceal from you that the case is exceptional in the
highest degree. One doesn't know what to think of it, and the worst of
it is there is no precedent. If we had a precedent we might have something to go by. But as it is, what is one to say? It will certainly take time
to settle it.'

A happy thought flashed upon my mind.

'Cannot we arrange,' I said, 'that, if he is destined to remain in the
entrails of the monster and it is the will of Providence that he should
remain alive, he should send in a petition to be reckoned as still
serving?'

'Hm! . . . Possibly as on leave and without salary . . . '

'But couldn't it be with salary?'

'On what grounds?'

'As sent on a special commission.'

'What commission and where?'

'Why, into the entrails, the entrails of the crocodile . . . So to speak, for exploration, for investigation of the facts on the spot. It would, of course, be a novelty, but that is progressive and would at the same time show zeal for enlightenment.'

Timofey Semyonitch thought a little.

'To send a special official,' he said at last, 'to the inside of a crocodile to conduct a special enquiry is, in my personal opinion, an absurdity. It is not in the regulations. And what sort of special enquiry could there be there?'

'The scientific study of nature on the spot, in the living subject. The natural sciences are all the fashion nowadays, botany . . . He could live there and report his observations . . . For instance, concerning digestion or simply habits. For the sake of accumulating facts.'

'You mean as statistics. Well, I am no great authority on that subject, indeed I am no philosopher at all. You say "facts" – we are overwhelmed with facts as it is, and don't know what to do with them. Besides, statistics are a danger.'

'In what way?'

'They are a danger. Moreover, you will admit he will report facts, so to speak, lying like a log. And, can one do one's official duties lying like a log? That would be another novelty and a dangerous one; and again, there is no precedent for it. If we had any sort of precedent for it, then, to my thinking, he might have been given the job.'

'But no live crocodiles have been brought over hitherto, Timofey Semyonitch.'

'Hm . . . yes,' he reflected again. 'Your objection is a just one, if you like, and might indeed serve as a ground for carrying the matter further; but consider again that if with the arrival of living crocodiles government clerks begin to disappear, and then on the ground that they are warm and comfortable there, expect to receive the official sanction for their position, and then take their ease there . . . you must admit it would be a bad example. We should have everyone trying to go the same way to get a salary for nothing.'

'Do your best for him, Timofey Semyonitch. By the way, Ivan Matveitch asked me to give you the seven roubles he lost to you at cards.'

'Ah, he lost that the other day at Nikifor Nikiforitch's. I remember. And how gay and amusing he was – and now!'

The old man was genuinely touched.

'Intercede for him, Timofey Semyonitch!'

'I will do my best. I will speak in my own name, as a private person, as though I were asking for information. And meanwhile, you find out indirectly, unofficially, how much would the proprietor consent to take for his crocodile?'

Timofey Semyonitch was visibly more friendly.

'Certainly,' I answered. 'And I will come back to you at once to report.'

'And his wife . . . is she alone now? Is she depressed?'

'You should call on her, Timofey Semyonitch.'

'I will. I thought of doing so before; it's a good opportunity . . . And what on earth possessed him to go and look at the crocodile. Though, indeed, I should like to see it myself.'

'Go and see the poor fellow, Timofey Semyonitch.'

'I will. Of course, I don't want to raise his hopes by doing so. I shall go as a private person . . . Well, goodbye, I am going to Nikifor Nikiforitch's again; shall you be there?'

'No, I am going to see the poor prisoner.'

'Yes, now he is a prisoner! . . . Ah, that's what comes of thoughtlessness!'

I said goodbye to the old man. Ideas of all kinds were straying through my mind. A good-natured and most honest man, Timofey Semyonitch, yet, as I left him, I felt pleased at the thought that he had celebrated his fiftieth year of service, and that Timofey Semyonitchs are now a rarity among us. I flew at once, of course, to the Arcade to tell poor Ivan Matveitch all the news. And, indeed, I was moved by curiosity to know how he was getting on in the crocodile and how it was possible to live in a crocodile. And, indeed, was it possible to live in a crocodile at all? At times it really seemed to me as though it were all an outlandish, monstrous dream, especially as an outlandish monster was the chief figure in it.

3

And yet it was not a dream, but actual, indubitable fact. Should I be telling the story if it were not?

But to continue. It was late, about nine o'clock, before I reached the Arcade, and I had to go into the crocodile room by the back entrance, for the German had closed the shop earlier than usual that evening. Now in the seclusion of domesticity he was walking about in a greasy old frock-coat, but he seemed three times as pleased as he had been in the morning. It was evident that he had no apprehensions now, and that the public had been coming 'many more'. The *Mutter* came out later, evidently to keep an eye on me. The German and the *Mutter* frequently whispered together. Although the shop was closed he charged me a quarter-rouble. What unnecessary exactitude!

'You will every time pay; the public will one rouble, and you one quarter pay; for you are the good friend of your good friend; and I a friend respect . . .'

'Are you alive, are you alive, my cultured friend?' I cried, as I approached the crocodile, expecting my words to reach Ivan Matveitch from a distance and to flatter his vanity.

'Alive and well,' he answered, as though from a long way off or from under the bed, though I was standing close beside him. 'Alive and well; but of that later . . . How are things going?'

As though purposely not hearing the question, I was just beginning with sympathetic haste to question him about how he was, what it was like in the crocodile, and what, in fact, there was inside a crocodile. Both friendship and common civility demanded this. But with capricious annoyance he interrupted me.

'How are things going?' he shouted, in a shrill and on this occasion particularly revolting voice, addressing me peremptorily as usual.

I described to him my whole conversation with Timofey Semyonitch down to the smallest detail. As I told my story I tried to show my resentment in my voice.

'The old man is right,' Ivan Matveitch pronounced as abruptly as usual in his conversation with me. 'I like practical people, and can't endure sentimental milksops. I am ready to admit, however, that your idea about a special commission is not altogether absurd. I certainly have a great deal to report, both from a scientific and from an ethical point of view. But now all this has taken a new and unexpected aspect, and it is not worth while to trouble about mere salary. Listen attentively. Are you sitting down?'

'No, I am standing up.'

'Sit down on the floor if there is nothing else, and listen attentively.

Resentfully I took a chair and put it down on the floor with a bang, in my anger.

'Listen,' he began dictatorially. 'The public came today in masses. There was no room left in the evening, and the police came in to keep order. At eight o'clock, that is, earlier than usual, the proprietor thought it necessary to close the shop and end the exhibition to count the money he had taken and prepare for tomorrow more conveniently. So I know there will be a regular fair tomorrow. So we may assume that all the most cultivated people in the capital, the ladies of the best society, the foreign ambassadors, the leading lawyers and so on, will all be present. What's more, people will be flowing here from the remotest provinces of our vast and interesting empire. The upshot of it is that I am the cynosure of all eyes, and though hidden to sight, I am eminent. I shall teach the idle crowd. Taught by experience, I shall be an example of greatness and resignation to fate! I shall be, so to say, a pulpit from which to instruct mankind. The mere biological details I can furnish about the monster I am inhabiting are of priceless value. And so, far from repining at what has happened, I confidently hope for the most brilliant of careers.'

'You won't find it wearisome?' I asked sarcastically.

What irritated me more than anything was the extreme pomposity of his language. Nevertheless, it all rather disconcerted me. 'What on earth, what can this frivolous blockhead find to be so cocky about?' I muttered to myself. 'He ought to be crying instead of being cocky.'

'No!' he answered my observation sharply, 'for I am full of great ideas, only now can I at leisure ponder over the amelioration of the lot of humanity. Truth and light will come forth now from the crocodile. I shall certainly develop a new economic theory of my own and I shall be proud of it – which I have hitherto been prevented from doing by my official duties and by trivial distractions. I shall refute everything and be a new Fourier.[244] By the way, did you give Timofey Semyonitch the seven roubles?'

'Yes, out of my own pocket,' I answered, trying to emphasise that fact in my voice.

'We will settle it,' he answered superciliously. 'I confidently expect my salary to be raised, for who should get a rise if not I? I am of the utmost service now. But to business. My wife?'

'You are, I suppose, enquiring after Elena Ivanovna?'

'My wife?' he shouted, this time in a positive squeal.

There was no help for it! Meekly, though gnashing my teeth, I told him how I had left Elena Ivanovna. He did not even hear me out.

'I have special plans in regard to her,' he began impatiently. 'If I am celebrated *here*, I wish her to be celebrated *there*. Savants, poets, philosophers, foreign mineralogists, statesmen, after conversing in the morning with me, will visit her *salon* in the evening. From next week onwards she must have an At Home every evening. With my salary doubled, we shall have the means for entertaining, but the entertainment must not go beyond tea and hired footmen – that's settled.

Both here and there they will talk of me. I have long thirsted for an opportunity for being talked about, but could not attain it, fettered by my humble position and low grade in the service. And now all this has been attained by a simple gulp on the part of the crocodile. Every word of mine will be listened to, every utterance will be thought over, repeated, printed. And I'll teach them what I am worth! They shall understand at last what abilities they have allowed to vanish in the entrails of a monster. This man might have been Foreign Minister or might have ruled a kingdom, some will say. And that man did all but rule a kingdom, others will say. In what way am I inferior to a Garnier-Pagesishky[245] or whatever they are called? My wife must be a worthy second – I have brains, she has beauty and charm. She is beautiful, and that is why she is his wife, some will say. She is beautiful *because* she is his wife, others will amend. To be ready for anything let Elena Ivanovna buy tomorrow the *Encyclopaedia*,[246] edited by Andrey Kraevsky, that she may be able to converse on any topic. Above all, let her be sure to read the political leader in the *Petersburg News*, comparing it every day with the *Voice*. I imagine that the proprietor will consent to take me sometimes with the crocodile to my wife's brilliant *salon*. I will be in a tank in the middle of the magnificent drawing-room, and I will scintillate with witticisms which I will prepare in the morning. To the statesman I will impart my projects; to the poet I will speak in rhyme; with the ladies I can be amusing and charming without impropriety, since I shall be no danger to their husbands' peace of mind. To all the rest I shall serve as a pattern of resignation to fate and the will of Providence. I shall make my wife a brilliant literary lady; I shall bring her forward and explain her to the public; as my wife she must be full of the most striking virtues; and if they are right in calling Andrey Alexandrovitch our Russian Alfred de Musset, they will be still more right in calling her our Russian Yevgenia Tour.'[247]

I must confess that, although this wild nonsense was rather in Ivan Matveitch's habitual style, it did occur to me that he was in a fever and delirious. It was the same, everyday Ivan Matveitch, but magnified twenty times.

'My friend,' I asked him, 'are you hoping for a long life? Tell me, in fact, are you well? How do you eat, how do you sleep, how do you breathe? I am your friend, and you must admit that the incident is most unnatural, and consequently my curiosity is most natural.'

'Idle curiosity and nothing else,' he pronounced sententiously, 'but you shall be satisfied. You ask how I am managing in the entrails of the monster? To begin with, the crocodile, to my amusement, turns out to be perfectly empty. His inside consists of a sort of huge empty sack made of gutta-percha, like the elastic goods sold in the Gorohovy Street, in the Morskaya and, if I am not mistaken, in the Voznesensky Prospect.[248] Otherwise, if you think of it, how could I find room?'

'Is it possible?' I cried, in a surprise that may well be understood. 'Can the crocodile be perfectly empty?'

'Perfectly,' Ivan Matveitch maintained sternly and impressively. 'And in all probability, it is so constructed by the laws of nature. The crocodile possesses nothing but jaws furnished with sharp teeth, and besides the jaws, a tail of considerable length – that is all, properly speaking. The middle part between these two extremities is an empty space enclosed by something of the nature of gutta-percha, probably really gutta-percha.'

'But the ribs, the stomach, the intestines, the liver, the heart?' I interrupted quite angrily.

'There is nothing, absolutely nothing of all that, and probably there never has been. All that is the idle fancy of frivolous travellers. As one inflates an air-cushion, I am now with my person inflating the crocodile. He is incredibly elastic. Indeed, you might, as the friend of the family, get in with me if you were generous and self-sacrificing enough – and even with you here there would be room to spare. I even think that in the last resort I might send for Elena Ivanovna. However, this void, hollow formation of the crocodile is quite in keeping with the teachings of natural science. If, for instance, one had to construct a new crocodile, the question would naturally present itself: What is the fundamental characteristic of the crocodile? The answer is clear: to swallow human beings. How is one, in constructing the crocodile, to secure that he should swallow people? The answer is clearer still: construct him hollow. It was settled by physics long ago that nature abhors a vacuum. Hence the inside of the crocodile must be hollow so that it may abhor the vacuum, and consequently swallow and so fill itself with anything it can come across. And that is the sole rational cause why every crocodile swallows men. It is not the same in the constitution of man: the emptier a man's head is, for instance, the less he feels the thirst to fill it, and that is the one exception to the general rule. It is all as clear as day to me now. I have deduced it by my own observation and experience, being, so to say, in the very bowels of nature, in its retort, listening to the throbbing of its pulse. Even etymology supports me, for the very word crocodile means voracity. Crocodile – *crocodillo* – is evidently an Italian word, dating perhaps from the Egyptian Pharaohs, and evidently derived from the French verb *croquer*, which means to eat, to devour, in general to absorb nourishment. All these remarks I intend to deliver as my first lecture in Elena Ivanovna's *salon* when they take me there in the tank.'

'My friend, oughtn't you at least to take some purgative?' I cried involuntarily. 'He is in a fever, a fever, he is feverish!' I repeated to myself in alarm.

'Nonsense!' he answered contemptuously. 'Besides, in my present position it would be most inconvenient. I knew, though, you would be sure to talk of taking medicine.'

'But, my friend, how . . . how do you take food now? Have you dined today?'

'No, but I am not hungry, and most likely I shall never take food again. And that, too, is quite natural; filling the whole interior of the crocodile I make him feel always full. Now he need not be fed for some years. On the other hand, nourished by me, he will naturally impart to me all the vital juices of his body; it is the same as with some accomplished coquettes who embed themselves and their whole persons for the night in raw steak, and then, after their morning bath, are fresh, supple, buxom and fascinating. In that way nourishing the crocodile, I myself obtain nourishment from him, consequently we mutually nourish one another. But as it is difficult even for a crocodile to digest a man like me, he must, no doubt, be conscious of a certain weight in his stomach – an organ which he does not, however, possess – and that is why, to avoid causing the creature suffering, I do not often turn over, and although I could turn over I do not do so from humanitarian motives. This is the one drawback of my present position, and in an allegorical sense Timofey Semyonitch was right in saying I was lying like a log. But I will prove that even lying like a log – nay, that only lying like a log – one can revolutionise the lot of mankind. All the great ideas and movements of our newspapers and magazines have evidently been the work of men who were lying like logs; that is why they call them divorced from the realities of life – but what does it matter, their saying that! I am constructing now a complete system of my own, and you wouldn't believe how easy it is! You have only to creep into a secluded corner or into a crocodile, to shut your eyes, and you immediately devise a perfect millennium for mankind. When you went away this afternoon I set to work at once and have already invented three systems; now I am preparing the fourth. It is true that at first one must refute everything that has gone before, but from the crocodile it is so easy to refute it; besides, it all becomes clearer, seen from the inside of the crocodile . . . There are some drawbacks, though small ones, in my position, however; it is somewhat damp here and covered with a sort of slime; moreover, there is rather a smell of india-rubber exactly like the smell of my old goloshes. That is all, there are no other drawbacks.'

'Ivan Matveitch,' I interrupted, 'all this is a miracle in which I can scarcely believe. And can you, can you intend never to dine again?'

'What trivial nonsense you are troubling about, you thoughtless, frivolous creature! I talk to you about great ideas, and you . . . Understand that I am sufficiently nourished by the great ideas which light up the darkness in which I am enveloped. The good-natured proprietor has, however, after consulting the kindly *Mutter*, decided with her that they will every morning insert into the monster's jaws a bent metal tube, something like a whistle pipe, by means of which I can absorb coffee or broth with bread soaked in it. The pipe has already been bespoken in the neighbourhood, but I think this is superfluous luxury. I hope to live at least a thousand years, if it is true that crocodiles live so long, which, by the way – good thing I thought of it – you had better look up in some natural history tomorrow and tell me, for I may have been mistaken and have mixed it up with some excavated monster. There is only one reflection rather troubles me: as I am dressed in cloth and have boots on, the crocodile can obviously not digest me. Besides, I am alive, and so am opposing the process of digestion with my whole will power; for you can understand that I do not wish to be turned into what all nourishment turns into, for that would be too humiliating for me. But there is one thing I am afraid of: in a thousand years the cloth of my coat, unfortunately of Russian make, may decay, and then, left without clothing, I might perhaps, in spite of my indignation, begin to be digested; and though by day nothing would induce me to allow it, at night, in my sleep, when a man's will deserts him, I may be overtaken by the humiliating destiny of a potato, a pancake or veal. Such an idea reduces me to fury. This alone is an argument for the revision of the tariff and the encouragement of the importation of English cloth, which is stronger and so will withstand nature longer when one is swallowed by a crocodile. At the first opportunity I will impart this idea to some statesman and at the same time to the political writers on our Petersburg dailies. Let them publish it abroad. I trust this will not be the only idea they will borrow from me. I foresee that every morning a regular crowd of them, provided with quarter-roubles from the editorial office, will be flocking round me to seize my ideas on the telegrams of the previous day. In brief, the future presents itself to me in the rosiest light.'

'Fever, fever!' I whispered to myself.

'My friend, what of freedom?' I asked, wishing to learn his views thoroughly. 'You are, so to speak, in prison, while every man has a right to the enjoyment of freedom.'

'You are a fool,' he answered. 'Savages love independence, wise men love order; and if there is no order . . . '[249]

'Ivan Matveitch, spare me, please!'

'Hold your tongue and listen!' he squealed, vexed at my interrupting him. 'Never has my spirit soared as now. In my narrow refuge there is only one thing that I dread – the literary criticisms of the monthlies and the lies of our satirical papers. I am afraid that thoughtless visitors, stupid and envious people and nihilists in general, may turn me into ridicule. But I will take measures. I am impatiently awaiting the response of the public tomorrow, and especially the opinion of the newspapers. You must tell me about the papers tomorrow.'

'Very good; tomorrow I will bring a perfect pile of papers with me.'

'Tomorrow it is too soon to expect reports in the newspapers, for it will take four days for it to be advertised. But from today come to me every evening by the back way through the yard. I am intending to employ you as my secretary. You shall read the newspapers and magazines to me, and I will dictate to you my ideas and give you commissions. Be particularly careful not to forget the foreign telegrams. Let all the European telegrams be here every day. But enough; most likely you are sleepy by now. Go home, and do not think of what I said just now about criticisms: I am not afraid of it, for the critics themselves are in a critical position. One has only to be wise and virtuous and one will certainly get on to a pedestal. If not Socrates,[250] then Diogenes,[251] or perhaps both of them together – that is my future role among mankind.'

So frivolously and boastfully did Ivan Matveitch hasten to express himself before me, like feverish weak-willed women who, as we are told by the proverb, cannot keep a secret. All that he told me about the crocodile struck me as most suspicious. How was it possible that the crocodile was absolutely hollow? I don't mind betting that he was bragging from vanity and partly to humiliate me. It is true that he was an invalid and one must make allowances for invalids; but I must frankly confess, I never could endure Ivan Matveitch. I have been trying all my life, from a child up, to escape from his tutelage and have not been able to! A thousand times over I have been tempted to break with him altogether, and every time I have been drawn to him again, as though I were still hoping to prove something to him or to revenge myself on him. A strange thing, this friendship! I can positively assert that nine-tenths of my friendship for him was made up of malice. On this occasion, however, we parted with genuine feeling.

'Your friend a very clever man!' the German said to me in an under-tone as he moved to see me out; he had been listening all the time attentively to our conversation.

'Apropos,' I said, 'while I think of it: how much would you ask for your crocodile in case anyone wanted to buy it?'

Ivan Matveitch, who heard the question, was waiting with curiosity for the answer; it was evident that he did not want the German to ask too little; anyway, he cleared his throat in a peculiar way on hearing my question.

At first the German would not listen – was positively angry.

'No one will dare my own crocodile to buy!' he cried furiously, and turned as red as a boiled lobster. 'Me not want to sell the crocodile! I would not for the crocodile a million thalers take. I took a hundred and thirty thalers from the public today, and I shall tomorrow ten thousand take, and then a hundred thousand every day I shall take. I will not him sell.'

Ivan Matveitch positively chuckled with satisfaction. Controlling myself – for I felt it was a duty to my friend – I hinted coolly and reasonably to the crazy German that his calculations were not quite correct, that if he makes a hundred thousand every day, all Petersburg will have visited him in four days, and then there will be no one left to bring him roubles, that life and death are in God's hands, that the crocodile may burst or Ivan Matveitch may fall ill and die, and so on and so on.

The German grew pensive.

'I will him drops from the chemist's get,' he said, after pondering, 'and will save your friend that he die not.'

'Drops are all very well,' I answered, 'but consider, too, that the thing may get into the law courts. Ivan Matveitch's wife may demand the restitution of her lawful spouse. You are intending to get rich, but do you intend to give Elena Ivanovna a pension?'

'No, me not intend,' said the German in stern decision.

'No, we not intend,' said the *Mutter*, with positive malignancy.

'And so would it not be better for you to accept something now, at once, a secure and solid though moderate sum, than to leave things to chance? I ought to tell you that I am enquiring simply from curiosity.'

The German drew the *Mutter* aside to consult with her in a corner where there stood a case with the largest and ugliest monkey of his collection.

'Well, you will see!' said Ivan Matveitch.

As for me, I was at that moment burning with the desire, first, to give the German a thrashing, next, to give the *Mutter* an even sounder one, and, thirdly, to give Ivan Matveitch the soundest thrashing of all for his boundless vanity. But all this paled beside the answer of the rapacious German.

After consultation with the *Mutter* he demanded for his crocodile fifty thousand roubles in bonds of the last Russian loan with lottery voucher attached, a brick house in Gorohovy Street with a chemist's shop attached, and in addition the rank of Russian colonel.

'You see!' Ivan Matveitch cried triumphantly. 'I told you so! Apart from this last senseless desire for the rank of a colonel, he is perfectly right, for he fully understands the present value of the monster he is exhibiting. The economic principle before everything!'

'Upon my word!' I cried furiously to the German. 'But what should you be made a colonel for? What exploit have you performed? What service have you done? In what way have you gained military glory? You are really crazy!'

'Crazy!' cried the German, offended. 'No, I a person very sensible am, but you very stupid! I have a colonel deserved for that I have a crocodile shown and in him a live *hofrath* sitting! And a Russian can a crocodile not show and a live *hofrath* in him sitting! Me extremely clever man and much wish colonel to be!'

'Well, goodbye, then, Ivan Matveitch!' I cried, shaking with fury, and I went out of the crocodile room almost at a run.

I felt that in another minute I could not have answered for myself. The unnatural expectations of these two blockheads were insupportable. The cold air refreshed me and somewhat moderated my indignation. At last, after spitting vigorously fifteen times on each side, I took a cab, got home, undressed and flung myself into bed. What vexed me more than anything was my having become his secretary. Now I was to die of boredom there every evening, doing the duty of a true friend! I was ready to beat myself for it, and I did, in fact, after putting out the candle and pulling up the bedclothes, punch myself several times on the head and various parts of my body. That somewhat relieved me, and at last I fell asleep fairly soundly, in fact, for I was very tired. All night long I could dream of nothing but monkeys, but towards morning I dreamt of Elena Ivanovna.

The monkeys I dreamed about, I suppose, because they were shut up in the case at the German's; but Elena Ivanovna was a different story.

I may as well say at once, I loved the lady, but I make haste – post-haste – to make a qualification. I loved her as a father, neither more nor less. I judge that because I often felt an irresistible desire to kiss her little head or her rosy cheek. And though I never carried out this inclination, I would not have refused even to kiss her lips. And not merely her lips, but her teeth, which always gleamed so charmingly like two rows of pretty, well-matched pearls when she laughed. She laughed extraordinarily often. Ivan Matveitch in demonstrative moments used to call her his 'darling absurdity' – a name extremely happy and appropriate. She was a perfect sugarplum, and that was all one could say of her. Therefore I am utterly at a loss to understand what possessed Ivan Matveitch to imagine his wife as a Russian Yevgenia Tour? Anyway, my dream, with the exception of the monkeys, left a most pleasant impression upon me, and going over all the incidents of the previous day as I drank my morning cup of tea, I resolved to go and see Elena Ivanovna at once on my way to the office – which, indeed, I was bound to do as the friend of the family.

In a tiny little room out of the bedroom – the so-called little drawing-room, though their big drawing-room was little too – Elena Ivanovna was sitting, in some half-transparent morning wrapper, on a smart little sofa before a little tea-table, drinking coffee out of a little cup in which she was dipping a minute biscuit. She was ravishingly pretty, but struck me as being at the same time rather pensive.

'Ah, that's you, naughty man!' she said, greeting me with an absent-minded smile. 'Sit down, feather-head, have some coffee. Well, what were you doing yesterday? Were you at the masquerade?'

'Why, were you? I don't go, you know. Besides, yesterday I was visiting our captive . . . ' I sighed and assumed a pious expression as I took the coffee.

'Whom? . . . What captive? . . . Oh, yes! Poor fellow! Well, how is he – bored? Do you know . . . I wanted to ask you . . . I suppose I can ask for a divorce now?'

'A divorce!' I cried in indignation and almost spilled the coffee. 'It's that swarthy fellow,' I thought to myself bitterly.

There was a certain swarthy gentleman with little moustaches who was something in the architectural line, and who came far too often to see them, and was extremely skilful in amusing Elena Ivanovna. I must confess I hated him and there was no doubt that he had succeeded in seeing Elena Ivanovna yesterday, either at the masquerade or even here, and putting all sorts of nonsense into her head.

'Why,' Elena Ivanovna rattled off hurriedly, as though it were a lesson she had learnt, 'if he is going to stay on in the crocodile, perhaps not come back all his life, while I sit waiting for him here! A husband ought to live at home, and not in a crocodile . . . '

'But this was an unforeseen occurrence,' I was beginning, in very comprehensible agitation.

'Oh, no, don't talk to me, I won't listen, I won't listen,' she cried, suddenly getting quite cross. 'You are always against me, you wretch! There's no doing anything with you, you will never give me any advice! Other people tell me that I can get a divorce because Ivan Matveitch will not get his salary now.'

'Elena Ivanovna! is it you I hear!' I exclaimed pathetically. 'What villain could have put such an idea into your head? And divorce on such a trivial ground as a salary is quite impossible. And poor Ivan Matveitch, poor Ivan Matveitch is, so to speak, burning with love for you even in the bowels of the monster. What's more, he is melting away with love like a lump of sugar. Yesterday while you were enjoying yourself at the masquerade, he was saying that he might in the last resort send for you as his lawful spouse to join him in the entrails of the monster, especially as it appears the crocodile is exceedingly roomy, not only able to accommodate two but even three persons . . . '

And then I told her all that interesting part of my conversation the night before with Ivan Matveitch.

'What, what!' she cried, in surprise. 'You want me to get into the monster too, to be with Ivan Matveitch? What an idea! And how am I to get in there, in my hat and crinoline? Heavens, what foolishness! And what should I look like while I was getting into it, and very likely there would be someone there to see me! It's absurd! And what should I have to eat there? And . . . and . . . and what should I do there when . . . Oh, my goodness, what will they think of next? . . . And what should I have to amuse me there? . . . You say there's a smell of gutta-percha? And what should I do if we quarrelled – should we have to go on staying there side by side? Foo, how horrid!'

'I agree, I agree with all those arguments, my sweet Elena Ivanovna,' I interrupted, striving to express myself with that natural enthusiasm which always overtakes a man when he feels the truth is on his side. 'But one thing you have not appreciated in all this – you have not realised that he cannot live without you if he is inviting you there; that is a proof of love, passionate, faithful, ardent love . . . You have thought too little of his love, dear Elena Ivanovna!'

'I won't, I won't, I won't hear anything about it!' waving me off with her pretty little hand with glistening pink nails that had just been washed and polished. 'Horrid man! You will reduce me to tears! Get into it yourself, if you like the prospect. You are his friend, get in and keep him company, and spend your life discussing some tedious science . . . '

'You are wrong to laugh at this suggestion' – I checked the frivolous woman with dignity – 'Ivan Matveitch has invited me as it is. You, of course, are summoned there by duty; for me, it would be an act of generosity. But when Ivan Matveitch described to me last night the elasticity of the crocodile, he hinted very plainly that there would be room not only for you two, but for me also as a friend of the family, especially if I wished to join you, and therefore . . . '

'How so, the three of us?' cried Elena Ivanovna, looking at me in surprise. 'Why, how should we . . . are we going to be all three there together? Ha-ha-ha! How silly you both are! Ha-ha-ha! I shall certainly pinch you all the time, you wretch! Ha-ha-ha! Ha-ha-ha!'

And falling back on the sofa, she laughed till she cried. All this – the tears and the laughter were so fascinating that I could not resist rushing eagerly to kiss her hand, which she did not oppose, though she did pinch my ears lightly as a sign of reconciliation.

Then we both grew very cheerful, and I described to her in detail all Ivan Matveitch's plans. The thought of her evening receptions and her *salon* pleased her very much.

'Only I should need a great many new dresses,' she observed, 'and so Ivan Matveitch must send me as much of his salary as possible and as soon as possible. Only . . . only I don't know about that,' she added thoughtfully. 'How can he be brought here in the tank? That's very absurd. I don't want my husband to be carried about in a tank. I should feel quite ashamed for my visitors to see it . . . I don't want that, no, I don't.'

'By the way, while I think of it, was Timofey Semyonitch here yesterday?'

'Oh, yes, he was; he came to comfort me, and do you know, we played cards all the time. He played for sweetmeats, and if I lost he was to kiss my hands. What a wretch he is! And only fancy, he almost came to the masquerade with me, really!'

'He was carried away by his feelings!' I observed. 'And who would not be with you, you charmer?'

'Oh, get along with your compliments! Stay, I'll give you a pinch as a parting present. I've learnt to pinch awfully well lately. Well, what do you say to that? By the way, you say Ivan Matveitch spoke several times of me yesterday?'

'N-no, not exactly . . . I must say he is thinking more now of the fate of humanity, and wants . . . '

'Oh, let him! You needn't go on! I am sure it's fearfully boring. I'll go and see him sometime. I shall certainly go tomorrow. Only not today; I've got a headache, and besides, there will be such a lot of people there today . . . They'll say, "That's his wife," and I shall feel ashamed . . . Goodbye. You will be . . . there this evening, won't you?'

'To see him, yes. He asked me to go and take him the papers.'

'That's capital. Go and read to him. But don't come and see me today. I am not well, and perhaps I may go and see someone. Goodbye, you naughty man.'

'It's that swarthy fellow is going to see her this evening,' I thought.

At the office, of course, I gave no sign of being consumed by these cares and anxieties. But soon I noticed some of the most progressive papers seemed to be passing particularly rapidly from hand to hand among my colleagues, and were being read with an extremely serious expression of face. The first one that reached me was the *Newssheet*, a paper of no particular party but humanitarian in general,[252] for which it was regarded with contempt among us, though it was read. Not without surprise I read in it the following paragraph:

Yesterday strange rumours were circulating among the spacious ways and sumptuous buildings of our vast metropolis. A certain well-known *bon vivant* of the highest society, probably weary of the cuisine at Borel's[253] and at the X Club, went into the Arcade, into the place where an immense crocodile recently brought to the metropolis is being exhibited, and insisted on its being prepared for his dinner. After bargaining with the proprietor he at once set to work to devour him (that is, not the proprietor, a very meek and punctilious German, but his crocodile), cutting juicy morsels with his penknife from the living animal, and swallowing them with extraordinary rapidity. By degrees the whole crocodile disappeared into the vast recesses of his stomach, so that he was even on the point of attacking an ichneumon, a constant companion of the crocodile, probably imagining that the latter would be as savoury. We are by no means opposed to that new article of diet with which foreign gourmands have long been familiar. We have, indeed, predicted that it would come. English lords and travellers make up regular parties for catching crocodiles in Egypt, and consume the back of the monster cooked like beef-steak, with mustard, onions and potatoes. The French who followed in the train of Lesseps[254] prefer the paws baked in hot ashes, which they do, however, in opposition to the English, who laugh at them. Probably both ways would be appreciated among us. For our part, we are delighted at a new branch of industry, of which our great and varied fatherland stands pre-eminently in need. Probably before a year is out crocodiles will be brought in hundreds to replace this first one, lost in the stomach of a Petersburg gourmand. And why should not the crocodile be acclimatised among us in Russia? If the water of the Neva is too cold for these interesting strangers, there are ponds in the capital and rivers and lakes outside it. Why not breed crocodiles at Pargolovo,[255] for instance, or at Pavlovsk,[256] in the Presensky Ponds[257] and in Samoteka[258] in Moscow? While providing agreeable, wholesome nourishment for our fastidious gourmands, they might at the same time entertain the ladies who walk about these ponds and instruct the children in natural history. The crocodile skin might be used for making jewel-cases, boxes, cigar-cases, pocketbooks, and possibly more than one thousand fortunes saved up in the greasy notes that are peculiarly beloved of merchants might be laid by in crocodile skin. We hope to return more than once to this interesting topic.'

Though I had foreseen something of the sort, yet the reckless inaccuracy of the paragraph overwhelmed me. Finding no one with whom to share my impression, I turned to Prohor Savvitch who was sitting opposite to me, and noticed that the latter had been watching me for some time, while in his hand he held the *Voice* as though he were on the point of passing it to me. Without a word he took the *Newssheet* from me, and as he handed me the *Voice* he drew a line with his nail against an article to which he probably wished to call my attention. This Prohor Savvitch was a very queer man: a taciturn old bachelor, he was not on intimate terms with any of us, scarcely spoke to anyone in the office, always had an opinion of his own about everything, but could not bear to impart it to anyone. He lived alone. Hardly anyone among us had ever been in his lodging.

This was what I read in the *Voice*.

Everyone knows that we are progressive and humanitarian and want to be on a level with Europe in this respect. But in spite of all our exertions and the efforts of our paper we are still far from maturity, as may be judged from the shocking incident which took place yesterday in the Arcade and which we predicted long ago. A foreigner arrives in the capital bringing with him a crocodile which he begins exhibiting in the Arcade. We immediately hasten to welcome a new branch of useful industry such as our powerful and varied fatherland stands in great need of. Suddenly yesterday at four o'clock in the afternoon a gentleman of exceptional stoutness enters the foreigner's shop in an intoxicated condition, pays his entrance money, and immediately without any warning leaps into the jaws of the crocodile, who was forced, of course, to swallow him, if only from an instinct of self-preservation, to avoid being crushed. Tumbling into the inside of the crocodile, the stranger at once dropped asleep. Neither the shouts of the foreign proprietor, nor the lamentations of his terrified family, nor threats to send for the police made the slightest impression. Within the crocodile was heard nothing but laughter and a promise to flay him (*sic*), though the poor mammal, compelled to swallow such a mass, was vainly shedding tears. An uninvited guest is worse than a Tartar.[259] But in spite of the proverb the insolent visitor would not leave. We do not know how to explain such barbarous incidents which prove our lack of culture and disgrace us in the eyes of foreigners. The recklessness of the Russian temperament has found a fresh outlet. It may be asked what was the object of the uninvited visitor? A warm and comfortable abode? But there are many excellent houses in the capital with very cheap and comfortable lodgings, with the Neva water laid on, and a staircase lighted by gas, frequently with a hall-porter maintained by the proprietor. We would call our readers' attention to the barbarous treatment of domestic animals: it is difficult, of course, for the crocodile to digest such a mass all at once, and now he lies swollen out to the size of a mountain, awaiting death in insufferable agonies. In Europe persons guilty of inhumanity towards domestic animals have long been punished by law. But in spite of our European enlightenment, in spite of our European pavements, in spite of the European architecture of our houses, we are still far from shaking off our time-honoured traditions.

Though the houses are new, the conventions are old.[260]

And, indeed, the houses are not new, at least the staircases in them are not. We have more than once in our paper alluded to the fact that in the Petersburg Side in the house of the merchant Lukyanov the steps of the wooden staircase have decayed, fallen away, and have long been a danger for Afimya Skapidarov, a soldier's wife who works in the house, and is often obliged to go up the stairs with water or armfuls of wood. At last our predictions have come true: yesterday evening at half-past eight Afimya Skapidarov fell down with a basin of soup and broke her leg. We do not know whether Lukyanov will mend his staircase now, Russians are often wise after the event, but the victim of Russian carelessness has by now been taken to the hospital. In the same way we shall never cease to maintain that the house-porters who clear away the mud from the wooden pavement in the Viborgsky Side ought not to spatter the legs of passers-by, but should throw the mud up into heaps as is done in Europe,' and so on, and so on.

'What's this?' I asked in some perplexity, looking at Prohor Savvitch. 'What's the meaning of it?'

'How do you mean?'

'Why, upon my word! Instead of pitying Ivan Matveitch, they pity the crocodile!'

'What of it? They have pity even for a beast, a mammal. We must be up to Europe, mustn't we? They have a very warm feeling for crocodiles there too. He-he-he!'

Saying this, queer old Prohor Savvitch dived into his papers and would not utter another word.

I stuffed the *Voice* and the *Newssheet* into my pocket and collected as many old copies of the newspapers as I could find for Ivan Matveitch's diversion in the evening, and though the evening was far off, yet on this occasion I slipped away from the office early to go to the Arcade and look, if only from a distance, at what was going on there, and to listen to the various remarks and currents of opinion. I foresaw that there would be a regular crush there, and turned up the collar of my coat to meet it. I somehow felt rather shy – so unaccustomed are we to publicity. But I feel that I have no right to report my own prosaic feelings when faced with this remarkable and original incident.

Bobok

From Somebody's Diary

SEMYON ARDALYONOVITCH said to me all of a sudden the day before yesterday: 'Why, will you ever be sober, Ivan Ivanovitch? Tell me that, pray.'

A strange requirement. I did not resent it, I am a timid man; but here they have actually made me out mad. An artist painted my portrait as it happened: 'After all, you are a literary man,' he said. I submitted, he exhibited it. I read: 'Go and look at that morbid face suggesting insanity.'

It may be so, but think of putting it so bluntly into print. In print everything ought to be decorous; there ought to be ideals, while instead of that . . .

Say it indirectly, at least; that's what you have style for. But no, he doesn't care to do it indirectly. Nowadays humour and a fine style have disappeared, and abuse is accepted as wit. I do not resent it: but God knows I am not enough of a literary man to go out of my mind. I have written a novel, it has not been published. I have written articles – they have been refused. Those articles I took about from one editor to another; everywhere they refused them: you have no salt they told me. 'What sort of salt do you want?' I asked with a jeer. 'Attic salt?'

They did not even understand, For the most part I translate from the French for the booksellers. I write advertisements for shopkeepers too: 'Unique opportunity! Fine tea, from our own plantations . . . ' I made a nice little sum over a panegyric on his deceased excellency Pyotr Matveyitch. I compiled 'The Art of Pleasing the Ladies', a commission from a bookseller. I have brought out some six little works of this kind in the course of my life. I am thinking of making a collection of the *bons mots* of Voltaire,[261] but am afraid it may seem a little flat to our people. Voltaire's no good now; nowadays we want a cudgel, not Voltaire. We knock each other's last teeth out nowadays. Well, so that's the whole extent of my literary activity. Though indeed I do send round letters to the editors gratis and fully signed. I give them all sorts of counsels and admonitions, criticise and point out the true path. The letter I sent last week to an editor's office was the fortieth I had sent in the last two years. I have wasted four roubles over stamps alone for them. My temper is at the bottom of it all.

I believe that the artist who painted me did so not for the sake of literature, but for the sake of two symmetrical warts on my forehead, a natural phenomenon, he would say. They have no ideas, so now they are out for phenomena. And didn't he succeed in getting my warts in his portrait – to the life? That is what they call realism.

And as to madness, a great many people were put down as mad among us last year. And in such language! 'With such original talent . . . and yet, after all, it appears . . . however, one ought to have foreseen it long ago.' That is rather artful; so that from the point of view of pure art one may really commend it. Well, but after all, these so-called madmen have turned out cleverer than ever. So it seems the critics can call them mad, but they cannot produce anyone better.

The wisest of all, in my opinion, is he who can, if only once a month, call himself a fool – a faculty unheard of nowadays. In the old days, once a year at any rate a fool would recognise that he was a fool, but nowadays not a bit of it. And they have so muddled things up that there is no telling a fool from a wise man. They have done that on purpose.

I remember a witty Spaniard saying when, two hundred and fifty years ago, the French built their first madhouses: 'They have shut up all their fools in a house apart, to make sure that they are wise men themselves.' Just so: you don't show your own wisdom by shutting someone else in a madhouse. 'K. has gone out of his mind, means that we are sane now.' No, it doesn't mean that yet.

Hang it though, why am I maundering on? I go on grumbling and grumbling. Even my maidservant is sick of me. Yesterday a friend came to see me. 'Your style is changing,' he said; 'it is choppy: you chop and chop – and then a parenthesis, then a parenthesis in the parenthesis, then you stick in something else in brackets, then you begin chopping and chopping again.'

The friend is right. Something strange is happening to me. My character is changing and my head aches. I am beginning to see and hear strange things, not voices exactly, but as though someone beside me were muttering, 'Bobok, bobok, bobok!' [a *bobok* is a small bean]

What's the meaning of this bobok? I must divert my mind.

I went out in search of diversion, I hit upon a funeral. A distant relation – a collegiate counsellor, however. A widow and five daughters, all marriageable young ladies. What must it come to even to keep them in slippers. Their father managed it, but now there is only a little pension. They will have to eat humble pie. They have always received me ungraciously. And indeed I should not have gone to the funeral now had it not been for a peculiar circumstance. I followed the procession to the cemetery with the rest; they were stuck-up and held aloof from me. My uniform was certainly rather shabby. It's five-and-twenty years, I believe, since I was at the cemetery; what a wretched place!

To begin with, the smell! There were fifteen hearses, with palls varying in expensiveness; there were actually two catafalques. One was a general's and one some lady's. There were many mourners, a great deal of feigned mourning and a great deal of open gaiety. The clergy have nothing to complain of; it brings them a good income. But the smell, the smell. I should not like to be one of the clergy here.

I kept glancing at the faces of the dead cautiously, distrusting my impressionability. Some had a mild expression, some looked unpleasant. As a rule the smiles were disagreeable, and in some cases very much so. I don't like them; they haunt one's dreams.

During the service I went out of the church into the air: it was a grey day, but dry. It was cold too, but then it was October. I walked about among the tombs. They are of different grades. The third grade cost thirty roubles; it's decent and not so very dear. The first two grades are tombs in the church and under the porch; they cost a pretty penny. On this occasion they were burying in tombs of the third grade six persons, among them the general and the lady.

I looked into the graves – and it was horrible: water and such water! Absolutely green, and . . . but there, why talk of it! The gravedigger was baling it out every minute. I went out while the service was going on and strolled outside the gates. Close by was an almshouse, and a little farther off there was a restaurant. It was not a bad little restaurant: there was lunch and everything. There were lots of the mourners here. I noticed a great deal of gaiety and genuine heartiness. I had something to eat and drink.

Then I took part in the bearing of the coffin from the church to the grave. Why is it that corpses in their coffins are so heavy? They say it is due to some sort of inertia, that the body is no longer directed by its owner . . . or some nonsense of that sort, in opposition to the laws of mechanics and common sense. I don't like to hear people who have nothing but a general education venture to solve the problems that require special knowledge; and with us that's done continually. Civilians love to pass opinions about subjects that are the province of the soldier and even of the field-marshal; while men who have been educated as engineers prefer discussing philosophy and political economy.

I did not go to the requiem service. I have some pride, and if I am only received owing to some special necessity, why force myself on their dinners, even if it be a funeral dinner. The only thing I don't understand is why I stayed at the cemetery; I sat on a tombstone and sank into appropriate reflections.

I began with the Moscow Exhibition and ended with reflecting upon astonishment in the abstract. My deductions about astonishment were these: 'To be surprised at everything is stupid of course, and to be astonished at nothing is a great deal more becoming and for some reason accepted as good form. But that is not really true. To my mind to be astonished at nothing is much more stupid than to be astonished at everything. And, moreover, to be astonished at nothing is almost the same as feeling respect for nothing. And indeed a stupid man is incapable of feeling respect.'

'But what I desire most of all is to feel respect. I thirst to feel respect,' one of my acquaintances said to me the other day. He thirsts to feel respect! Goodness, I thought, what would happen to you if you dared to print that nowadays? At that point I sank into forgetfulness. I don't like reading the epitaphs of tombstones: they are everlastingly the same. An unfinished sandwich was lying on the tombstone near me; stupid and inappropriate. I threw it on the ground, as it was not bread but only a sandwich. Though I believe it is not a sin to throw bread on the earth, but only on the floor. I must look it up in Suvorin's calendar.[262]

I suppose I sat there a long time – too long a time, in fact; I must have lain down on a long stone which was of the shape of a marble coffin. And how it happened I don't know, but I began to hear things of all sorts being said. At first I did not pay attention to it, but treated it with contempt. But the conversation went on. I heard muffled sounds as though the speakers' mouths were covered with a pillow, and at the same time they were distinct and very near. I came to myself, sat up and began listening attentively.

'Your excellency, it's utterly impossible. You led hearts, I return your lead, and here you play the seven of diamonds. You ought to have given me a hint about diamonds.'

'What, play by hard and fast rules? Where is the charm of that?'

'You must, your excellency. One can't do anything without something to go upon. We must play with dummy, let one hand not be turned up.'

'Well, you won't find a dummy here.'

What conceited words! And it was queer and unexpected. One was such a ponderous, dignified voice, the other softly suave; I should not have believed it if I had not heard it myself. I had not been to the requiem dinner, I believe. And yet how could they be playing preference here and what general was this? That the sounds came from under the tombstones of that there could be no doubt. I bent down and read on the tomb: 'Here lies the body of Major-General Pervoyedov ... a cavalier of such and such orders.' Hm! 'Passed away in August of this year ... fifty-seven ... Rest, beloved ashes, till the joyful dawn!'

Hm, dash it, it really is a general! There was no monument on the grave from which the obsequious voice came, there was only a tombstone. He must have been a fresh arrival. From his voice he was a lower court councillor.

'Oh-ho-ho-ho!' I heard in a new voice a dozen yards from the general's resting-place, coming from quite a fresh grave. The voice belonged to a man and a plebeian, mawkish with its affectation of religious fervour. 'Oh-ho-ho-ho!'

'Oh, here he is hiccuping again!' cried the haughty and disdainful voice of an irritated lady, apparently of the highest society. 'It is an affliction to be by this shopkeeper!'

'I didn't hiccup; why, I've had nothing to eat. It's simply my nature. Really, madam, you don't seem able to get rid of your caprices here.'

'Then why did you come and lie down here?'

'They put me here, my wife and little children put me here, I did not lie down here of myself. The mystery of death! And I would not have lain down beside you not for any money; I lie here as befitting my fortune, judging by the price. For we can always do that – pay for a tomb of the third grade.'

'You made money, I suppose? You fleeced people?'

'Fleece you, indeed! We haven't seen the colour of your money since January. There's a little bill against you at the shop.'

'Well, that's really stupid; to try and recover debts here is too stupid, to my thinking! Go to the surface. Ask my niece – she is my heiress.'

'There's no asking anyone now, and no going anywhere. We have both reached our limit and, before the judgement seat of God, are equal in our sins.'

'In our sins,' the lady mimicked him contemptuously. 'Don't dare to speak to me.'

'Oh-ho-ho-ho!'

'You see, the shopkeeper obeys the lady, your excellency.'

'Why shouldn't he?'

'Why, your excellency, because, as we all know, things are different here.'

'Different? How?'

'We are dead, so to speak, your excellency.'

'Oh, yes! But still . . . '

Well, this is an entertainment, it is a fine show, I must say! If it has come to this down here, what can one expect on the surface? But what a queer business! I went on listening, however, though with extreme indignation.

'Yes, I should like a taste of life! Yes, you know . . . I should like a taste of life.' I heard a new voice suddenly somewhere in the space between the general and the irritable lady.

'Do you hear, your excellency, our friend is at the same game again. For three days at a time he says nothing, and then he bursts out with, "I should like a taste of life, yes, a taste of life!" And with such appetite, he-he!'

'And such frivolity.'

'It gets hold of him, your excellency, and do you know, he is growing sleepy, quite sleepy – he has been here since April; and then all of a sudden, "I should like a taste of life!" '

'It is rather dull, though,' observed his excellency.

'It is, your excellency. Shall we tease Avdotya Ignatyevna again, he-he?'

'No, spare me, please. I can't endure that quarrelsome virago.'

'And I can't endure either of you,' cried the virago disdainfully. 'You are both of you bores and can't tell me anything ideal. I know one little story about you, your excellency – don't turn up your nose, please – how a manservant swept you out from under a married couple's bed one morning.'

'Nasty woman,' the general muttered through his teeth.

'Avdotya lgnatyevna, ma'am,' the shopkeeper wailed suddenly again, 'my dear lady, don't be angry, but tell me, am I going through the ordeal by torment now, or is it something else?'

'Ah, he is at it again, as I expected! For there's a smell from him which means he is turning round!'

'I am not turning round, ma'am, and there's no particular smell from me, for I've kept my body whole as it should be, while you're regularly high. For the smell is really horrible even for a place like this. I don't speak of it, merely from politeness.'

'Ah, you horrid, insulting wretch. He positively stinks and talks about me.'

'Oh-ho-ho-ho! If only the time for my requiem would come quickly: I should hear their tearful voices over my head, my wife's lament and my children's soft weeping! . . . '

'Well, that's a thing to fret for! They'll stuff themselves with funeral rice and go home . . . Oh, I wish somebody would wake up!'

'Avdotya Ignatyevna,' said the insinuating government clerk, 'wait a bit, the new arrivals will speak.'

'And are there any young people among them?'

'Yes, there are, Avdotya Ignatyevna. There are some not more than lads.'

'Oh, how welcome that would be!'

'Haven't they begun yet?' enquired his excellency.

'Even those who came the day before yesterday haven't awakened yet, your eexcellency. As you know, they sometimes don't speak for a week. It's a good job that today and yesterday and the day before they brought a whole lot. As it is, they are all last year's for seventy feet round.'

'Yes, it will be interesting.'

'Yes, your excellency, they buried Tarasevitch, the privy councillor, today. I knew it from the voices. I know his nephew, he helped to lower the coffin just now.'

'Hm, where is he, then?'

'Five steps from you, your excellency, on the left . . . Almost at your feet. You should make his acquaintance, your excellency.'

'Hm, no – it's not for me to make advances.'

'Oh, he will begin of himself, your excellency. He will be flattered. Leave it to me, your excellency, and I . . . '

'Oh, oh! . . . What is happening to me?' croaked the frightened voice of a new arrival.

'A new arrival, your excellency, a new arrival, thank God! And how quick he's been! Sometimes they don't say a word for a week.'

'Oh, I believe it's a young man!' Avdotya Ignatyevna cried shrilly.

'I . . . I . . . it was a complication, and so sudden!' faltered the young man again. 'Only the evening before, Schultz said to me, "There's a complication," and I died suddenly before morning. Oh! oh!'

'Well, there's no help for it, young man,' the general observed graciously, evidently pleased at a new arrival. 'You must be comforted. You are kindly welcome to our Vale of Jehoshaphat,[263] so to call it. We are kind-hearted people, you will come to know us and appreciate us. Major-General Vassili Vassilitch Pervoyedov, at your service.'

'Oh, no, no! Certainly not! I was at Schultz's; I had a complication, you know, at first it was my chest and a cough, and then I caught a cold:

my lungs and influenza . . . and all of a sudden, quite unexpectedly . . . the worst of all was its being so unexpected.'

'You say it began with the chest,' the government clerk put in suavely, as though he wished to reassure the new arrival.

'Yes, my chest and catarrh and then no catarrh, but still the chest, and I couldn't breathe . . . and you know . . . '

'l know, I know. But if it was the chest you ought to have gone to Ecke and not to Schultz.'

'You know, I kept meaning to go to Botkin's, and all at once . . . '

'Botkin is quite prohibitive,' observed the general.

'Oh, no, he is not forbidding at all; I've heard he is so attentive and foretells everything beforehand.'

'His excellency was referring to his fees,' the government clerk corrected him.

'Oh, not at all, he only asks three roubles, and he makes such an examination, and gives you a prescription . . .and I was very anxious to see him, for I have been told . . . Well, gentlemen, had I better go to Ecke or to Botkin?'[264]

'What? To whom?' The general's corpse shook with agreeable laughter. The government clerk echoed it in falsetto.

'Dear boy, dear, delightful boy, how I love you!' Avdotya Ignatyevna squealed ecstatically. 'I wish they had put someone like you next to me.'

No, that was too much! And these were the dead of our times! Still, I ought to listen to more and not be in too great a hurry to draw conclusions. That snivelling new arrival – I remember him just now in his coffin – had the expression of a frightened chicken, the most revolting expression in the world! However, let us wait and see.

* * *

But what happened next was such a bedlam that I could not keep it all in my memory. For a great many woke up at once; an official – a civil councillor – woke up, and began discussing at once the project of a new sub-committee in a government department and of the probable transfer of various functionaries in connection with the sub-committee – which very greatly interested the general. I must confess I learnt a great deal that was new myself, so much so that I marvelled at the channels by which one may sometimes in the metropolis learn government news. Then an engineer half woke up, but for a long time muttered absolute nonsense, so that our friends left off worrying him and let him lie till he was ready. At last the distinguished lady who had been buried in the morning under the catafalque showed symptoms of the reanimation of the tomb. Lebeziatnikov (for the obsequious lower-court councillor whom I detested and who lay beside General Pervoyedov was called, it appears, Lebeziatnikov) became much excited, and surprised that they were all waking up so soon this time. I must own I was surprised too; though some of those who woke had been buried for three days, as, for instance, a very young girl of sixteen who kept giggling . . . giggling in a horrible and predatory way.

'Your excellency, privy councillor Tarasevitch is waking!' Lebeziatnikov announced with extreme fussiness.

'Eh? What?' the privy councillor, waking up suddenly, mumbled, with a lisp of disgust. There was a note of ill-humoured peremptoriness in the sound of his voice.

I listened with curiosity – for during the last few days I had heard something about Tarasevitch – shocking and upsetting in the extreme.

'It's I, your excellency, so far only I.'

'What is your petition? What do you want?'

'Merely to enquire after your excellency's health; in these unaccustomed surroundings everyone feels at first, as it were, oppressed . . . General Pervoyedov wishes to have the honour of making your excellency's acquaintance, and hopes . . . '

'I've never heard of him.'

'Surely, your excellency! General Pervoyedov, Vassili Vassilitch . . . '

'Are you General Pervoyedov?'

'No, your excellency, I am only the lower-court councillor Lebeziatnikov, at your service, but General Pervoyedov . . . '

'Nonsense! And I beg you to leave me alone.'

'Let him be.' General Pervoyedov at last himself checked with dignity the disgusting officiousness of his sycophant in the grave.

'He is not fully awake, your excellency, you must consider that; it's the novelty of it all. When he is fully awake he will take it differently.'

'Let him be,' repeated the general.

*   *   *

'Vassili Vassilitch! Hey, your Excellency!' a perfectly new voice shouted loudly and aggressively from close beside Avdotya lgnatyevna. It was a voice of gentlemanly insolence, with the languid pronunciation now fashionable and an arrogant drawl. 'I've been watching you all for the last two hours. Do you remember me, Vassili Vassilitch? My name is Klinevitch, we met at the Volokonskys' where you, too, were received as a guest, I am sure I don't know why.'

'What, Count Pyotr Petrovitch? . . . Can it be really you . . . and at such an early age? How sorry I am to hear it.'

'Oh, I am sorry myself, though I really don't mind, and I want to amuse myself as far as I can everywhere. And I am not a count but a baron, only a baron. We are only a set of scurvy barons, risen from being flunkeys, but why I don't know and I don't care. I am only a scoundrel of the pseudo-aristocratic society, and I am regarded as "a charming *polisson*"²⁶⁵. My father is a wretched little general, and my mother was at one time received *en haut lieu*. With the help of the Jew Zifel I forged fifty thousand-rouble notes last year and then I informed against him, while Julie Charpentier de Lusignan carried off the money to Bordeaux. And only fancy, I was engaged to be married – to a girl still at school, three months under sixteen, with a dowry of ninety thousand. Avdotya lgnatyevna, do you remember how you seduced me fifteen years ago when I was a boy of fourteen in the Corps des Pages?'

'Ah, that's you, you rascal! Well, you are a godsend, anyway, for here . . .'

'You were mistaken in suspecting your neighbour, the business gentleman, of unpleasant fragrance . . . I said nothing, but I laughed. The stench came from me: they had to bury me in a nailed-up coffin.'

'Ugh, you horrid creature! Still, I am glad you are here; you can't imagine the lack of life and wit here.'

'Quite so, quite so, and I intend to start here something original. Your excellency – I don't mean you, Pervoyedov – your excellency the other one, Tarasevitch, the privy councillor! Answer! I am Klinevitch, who took you to Mademoiselle Furie in Lent, do you hear?'

'I do, Klinevitch, and I am delighted, and trust me . . .'

'I wouldn't trust you with a halfpenny, and I don't care. I simply want to kiss you, dear old man, but luckily I can't. Do you know, gentlemen, what this *grand-père*'s²⁶⁶ little game was? He died three or four days ago, and would you believe it, he left a deficit of four hundred thousand government roubles from the fund for widows and orphans. He was the sole person in control of it for some reason, so that his accounts were not audited for the last eight years. I can fancy what long faces they all have now, and what they call him. It's a delectable thought, isn't it? I have been wondering for the last year how a wretched old man of seventy, gouty and rheumatic, succeeded in preserving the physical energy for his debaucheries – and now the riddle is solved! Those widows and orphans – the very thought of them must have egged him on! I knew about it long ago, I was the only one who did know; it was Julie told me, and as soon as I discovered it, I attacked him in a friendly way at once in Easter week: "Give me twenty-five thousand, if you don't they'll look into your accounts tomorrow." And just fancy, he had only thirteen thousand left then, so it seems it was very apropos his dying now. *Grand-père, grand-père;* do you hear?'

'*Cher* Klinevitch, I quite agree with you, and there was no need for you . . . to go into such details. Life is so full of suffering and torment and so little to make up for it . . . that I wanted at last to be at rest, and so far as I can see I hope to get all I can from here too.'

'I bet that he has already sniffed Katiche Berestoy!'

'Who? What Katiche?' There was a rapacious quiver in the old man's voice.

'A-ah, what Katiche? Why, here on the left, five paces from me and ten from you. She has been here for five days, and if only you knew, *grand-père*, what a little wretch she is! Of good family and breeding and a monster, a regular monster! I did not introduce her to anyone there, I was the only one who knew her . . . Katiche, answer!'

'He-he-he!' the girl responded with a jangling laugh, in which there was a note of something as sharp as the prick of a needle. 'He-he-he!'

'And a little blonde?' the *grand-père* faltered, drawling out the syllables.

'He-he-he!'

'I . . . have long . . . I have long,' the old man faltered breathlessly, 'cherished the dream of a little fair thing of fifteen and just in such surroundings.'

'Ach, the monster!' cried Avdotya Ignatyevna.

'Enough!' Klinevitch decided. 'I see there is excellent material. We shall soon arrange things better. The great thing is to spend the rest of our time cheerfully; but what time? Hey, you, government clerk, Lebeziatnikov or whatever it is, I hear that's your name!'

'Semyon Yevseitch Lebeziatnikov, lower-court councillor, at your service, very, very, very much delighted to meet you.'

'I don't care whether you are delighted or not, but you seem to know everything here. Tell me first of all how it is we can talk? I've been wondering ever since yesterday. We are dead and yet we are talking and seem to be moving – and yet we are not talking and not moving. What jugglery is this?'

'If you want an explanation, baron, Platon Nikolaevitch could give you one better than I.'

'What Platon Nikolaevitch is that? To the point. Don't beat about the bush.'

'Platon Nikolaevitch is our home-grown philosopher, scientist and

Master of Arts. He has brought out several philosophical works, but for the last three months he has been getting quite drowsy, and there is no stirring him up now. Once a week he mutters something utterly irrelevant.'

'To the point, to the point!'

'He explains all this by the simplest fact, namely, that when we were living on the surface we mistakenly thought that there death was death. The body revives, as it were, here, the remains of life are concentrated, but only in consciousness. I don't know how to express it, but life goes on, as it were, by inertia. In his opinion everything is concentrated somewhere in consciousness and goes on for two or three months . . . sometimes even for half a year . . . There is one here, for instance, who is almost completely decomposed, but once every six weeks he suddenly utters one word, quite senseless of course, about some bobok. "Bobok, bobok," but you see that an imperceptible speck of life is still warm within him.'

'It's rather stupid. Well, and how is it I have no sense of smell and yet I feel there's a stench?'

'That . . . he-he . . . Well, on that point our philosopher is a bit foggy. It's apropos of smell, he said, that the stench one perceives here is, so to speak, moral – he-he! It's the stench of the soul, he says; that in these two or three months it may have time to recover itself . . . and this is, so to speak, the last mercy . . . Only, I think, baron, that these are mystic ravings very excusable in his position . . .

'Enough; all the rest of it, I am sure, is nonsense. The great thing is that we have two or three months more of life and then – bobok! I propose to spend these two months as agreeably as possible, and so to arrange everything on a new basis. Gentlemen! I propose to cast aside all shame.'

'Ah, let us cast aside all shame, let us!' many voices could be heard saying; and strange to say, several new voices were audible, which must have belonged to others newly awakened. The engineer, now fully awake, boomed out his agreement with peculiar delight. The girl Katiche giggled gleefully.

'Oh, how I long to cast off all shame!' Avdotya lgnatyevna exclaimed rapturously.

'I say, if Avdotya lgnatyevna wants to cast off all shame . . . '

'No, no, no, Klinevitch, I was ashamed up there all the time, but here I should like to cast off shame, I should like it awfully.'

'I understand, Klinevitch,' boomed the engineer, 'that you want to rearrange life here on new and rational principles.'

'Oh, I don't care a hang about that! For that we'll wait for Kudeyarov who was brought here yesterday. When he wakes he'll tell you all about it. He is such a personality, such a titanic personality! Tomorrow they'll bring along another natural scientist, I believe, an officer for certain, and three or four days later a journalist, and, I believe, his editor with him. But deuce take them all, there will be a little group of us anyway, and things will arrange themselves. Though meanwhile I don't want us to be telling lies. That's all I care about, for that is one thing that matters. One cannot exist on the surface without lying, for life and lying are synonymous, but here we will amuse ourselves by not lying. Hang it all, the grave has some value after all! We'll all tell our stories aloud, and we won't be ashamed of anything. First of all I'll tell you about myself. I am one of the predatory kind, you know. All that was bound and held in check by rotten cords up there on the surface. Away with cords and let us spend these two months in shameless truthfulness! Let us strip and be naked!'

'Let us be naked, let us be naked!' cried all the voices.

'I long to be naked, I long to be,' Avdotya Ignatyevna shrilled.

'Ah . . . ah, I see we shall have fun here; I don't want Ecke after all.'

'No, I tell you. Give me a taste of life!'

'He-he-he!' giggled Katiche.

'The great thing is that no one can interfere with us, and though I see Pervoyedov is in a temper, he can't reach me with his hand. *Grand-père*, do you agree?'

'I fully agree, fully, and with the utmost satisfaction, but on condition that Katiche is the first to give us her biography.'

'I protest! I protest with all my heart!' General Pervoyedov brought out firmly.

'Your excellency!' the scoundrel Lebeziatnikov persuaded him in a murmur of fussy excitement, 'your excellency, it will be to our advantage to agree. Here, you see, there's this girl's . . . and all their little affairs.'

'There's the girl, it's true, but . . . '

'It's to our advantage, your excellency, upon my word it is! If only as an experiment, let us try it. . . '

'Even in the grave they won't let us rest in peace.'

'In the first place, general, you were playing preference in the grave, and in the second we don't care a hang about you,' drawled Klinevitch.

'Sir, I beg you not to forget yourself.'

'What? Why, you can't get at me, and I can tease you from here as though you were Julie's lapdog. And another thing, gentlemen, how is he a general here? He was a general there, but here he's mere refuse.'

'No, not mere refuse . . . Even here . . . '

'Here you will rot in the grave and six brass buttons will be all that will be left of you.'

'Bravo, Klinevitch, ha-ha-ha!' roared voices.

'I have served my sovereign . . . I have the sword . . . '

'Your sword is only fit to prick mice, and you never drew it even for that.'

'That makes no difference; I formed a part of the whole.'

'There are all sorts of parts in a whole.'

'Bravo, Klinevitch, bravo! Ha-ha-ha!'

'I don't understand what the sword stands for,' boomed the engineer.

'We shall run away from the Prussians like mice, they'll crush us to powder!' cried a voice in the distance that was unfamiliar to me but that was positively spluttering with glee.

'The sword, sir, is an honour,' the general cried, but only I heard him. There arose a prolonged and furious roar, clamour and hubbub, and only the hysterically impatient squeals of Avdotya Ignatyevna were audible.

'But do let us make haste! Ah, when are we going to begin to cast off all shame!'

'Oh-ho-ho! . . . The soul does in truth pass through torments!' exclaimed the voice of the plebeian, 'and . . . '

And here I suddenly sneezed. It happened suddenly and un-intentionally, but the effect was striking: all became as silent as one expects it to be in a churchyard, it all vanished like a dream. A real silence of the tomb set in. I don't believe they were ashamed on account of my presence: they had made up their minds to cast off all shame! I waited five minutes – not a word, not a sound. It cannot be supposed that they were afraid of my informing the police; for what could the police do to them? I must conclude that they had some secret unknown to the living, which they carefully concealed from every mortal.

'Well, my dears,' I thought, 'I shall visit you again.' And with those words, I left the cemetery.

No, that I cannot admit; no, I really cannot! The bobok case does not trouble me (so that is what the bobok signified!).

Depravity in such a place, depravity of the last aspirations, depravity of sodden and rotten corpses – and not even sparing the last moments of consciousness! Those moments have been granted, vouchsafed to them, and . . . and, worst of all, in such a place! No, that I cannot admit.

I shall go to other tombs, I shall listen everywhere. Certainly one ought to listen everywhere and not merely at one spot in order to form an idea. Perhaps one may come across something reassuring.

But I shall certainly go back to those. They promised their biographies and anecdotes of all sorts. Tfoo! But I shall go, I shall certainly go; it is a question of conscience!

I shall take it to the *Citizen*; the editor there has had his portrait exhibited too.[267] Maybe he will print it.

The Heavenly Christmas Tree

I AM A NOVELIST, and I suppose I have made up this story. I write 'I suppose', though I know for a fact that I have made it up, but yet I keep fancying that it must have happened somewhere at sometime, that it must have happened on Christmas Eve in some great town in a time of terrible frost. I have a vision of a boy, a little boy, six years old or even younger. This boy woke up that morning in a cold damp cellar. He was dressed in a sort of little dressing-gown and was shivering with cold. There was a cloud of white steam from his breath, and sitting on a box in the corner, he blew the steam out of his mouth and amused himself in his dullness watching it float away. But he was terribly hungry. Several times that morning he went up to the plank bed where his sick mother was lying on a mattress as thin as a pancake, with some sort of bundle under her head for a pillow. How had she come here? She must have come with her boy from some other town and suddenly fallen ill. The landlady who let the 'corners' had been taken two days before to the police station, the lodgers were out and about as the holiday was so near, and the only one left had been lying for the last twenty-four hours dead drunk, not having waited for Christmas. In another corner of the room a wretched old woman of eighty, who had once been a children's nurse but was now left to die friendless, was moaning and groaning with rheumatism, scolding and grumbling at the boy so that he was afraid to go near her corner. He had got a drink of water in the outer room, but could not find a crust anywhere and had been on the point of waking his mother a dozen times. He felt frightened at last in the darkness: it had long been dusk, but no light was kindled. Touching his mother's face, he was surprised that she did not move at all, and that she was as cold as the wall. 'It is very cold here,' he thought. He stood a little, unconsciously letting his hands rest on the dead woman's shoulders, then he breathed on his fingers to warm them, and then quietly fumbling for his cap on the bed, he went out of the cellar. He would have gone earlier, but was afraid of the big dog which had been howling all day at the neighbour's door at the top of the stairs. But the dog was not there now, and he went out into the street.

Mercy on us, what a town! He had never seen anything like it before. In the town from which he had come, it was always such black darkness at night. There was one lamp for the whole street, the little, low-pitched, wooden houses were closed up with shutters, there was no one to be seen in the street after dusk, all the people shut themselves up in their houses, and there was nothing but the howling of packs of dogs, hundreds and thousands of them barking and howling all night. But there it was so warm and he was given food, while here – oh, dear, if he only had something to eat! And what a noise and rattle here, what light and what people, horses and carriages, and what a frost! The frozen steam hung in clouds over the horses, over their warmly breathing mouths; their hoofs clanged against the stones through the powdery snow, and everyone pushed so, and – oh, dear, how he longed for some morsel to eat, and how wretched he suddenly felt. A policeman walked by and turned away to avoid seeing the boy.

Here was another street – oh, what a wide one, here he would be run over for certain; how everyone was shouting, racing and driving along, and the light, the light! And what was this? A huge glass window, and through the window a tree reaching up to the ceiling; it was a fir tree, and on it were ever so many lights, gold papers and apples and little dolls and horses; and there were children, clean and dressed in their best, running about the room, laughing and playing and eating and drinking something. And then a little girl began dancing with one of the boys, what a pretty little girl! And he could hear the music through the window. The boy looked and wondered and laughed, though his toes were aching with the cold and his fingers were red and stiff so that it hurt him to move them. And all at once the boy remembered how his toes and fingers hurt him, and began crying, and ran on; and again through another window-pane he saw another Christmas tree, and on a table cakes of all sorts – almond cakes, red cakes and yellow cakes, and three grand young ladies were sitting there, and they gave the cakes to anyone who went up to them, and the door kept opening, lots of gentlemen and ladies went in from the street. The boy crept up, suddenly opened the door and went in. Oh, how they shouted at him and waved him back! One lady went up to him hurriedly and slipped a kopeck into his hand, and with her own hands opened the door into the street for him! How frightened he was. And the kopeck rolled away and clinked upon the steps; he could not bend his red fingers to hold it tight. The boy ran away and went on, where he did not know. He was ready to cry again but he was afraid, and ran on and on and blew his fingers. And he was miserable because he felt suddenly so lonely and terrified, and all at once, mercy on us! What was this again? People were standing in a crowd admiring. Behind a glass window there were three little dolls, dressed in red and green clothes, and looking exactly, exactly as though they were alive. One was a little old man sitting and playing a big violin, the two others were standing close by and playing little violins and nodding in time, and looking at one another, and their lips moved, they were speaking, actually speaking, only one couldn't hear through the glass. And at first the boy thought they were alive, and when he grasped that they were dolls he laughed. He had never seen such dolls before, and had no idea there were such dolls! And he wanted to cry, but he felt amused, amused by the dolls. All at once he fancied that someone caught at his smock behind: a wicked big boy was standing beside him and suddenly hit him on the head, snatched off his cap and tripped him up. The boy fell down on the ground; at once there was a shout, he was numb with fright, he jumped up and ran away. He ran, and not knowing where he was going, ran in at the gate of someone's courtyard and sat down behind a stack of wood: 'They won't find me here besides it's dark!'

He sat huddled up and was breathless from fright, and all at once, quite suddenly, he felt so happy: his hands and feet suddenly left off aching and grew so warm, as warm as though he were on a stove; then he shivered all over, then he gave a start, why, he must have been asleep. How nice to have a sleep here! 'I'll sit here a little and go and look at the dolls again,' said the boy, and smiled thinking of them. 'Just as though they were alive! . . . ' And suddenly he heard his mother singing over him. 'Mammy, I am asleep; how nice it is to sleep here!'

'Come to my Christmas tree, little one,' a soft voice suddenly whispered over his head.

He thought that this was still his mother, but no, it was not she. Who it was calling him, he could not see, but someone bent over and embraced him in the darkness; and he stretched out his hands to him, and . . . and all at once – oh, what a bright light! Oh, what a Christmas tree! And yet it was not a fir tree – he had never seen a tree like that! Where was he now? Everything was bright and shining, and all round him were dolls; but no, they were not dolls, they were little boys and girls, only so bright and shining. They all came flying round him, they all kissed him, took him and carried him along with them, and he was flying himself, and he saw that his mother was looking at him and laughing joyfully. 'Mammy, Mammy; oh, how nice it is here, Mammy!' And again he kissed the children and wanted to tell them at once of those dolls in the shop window.

'Who are you, boys? Who are you, girls?' he asked, laughing and admiring them.

'This is Christ's Christmas tree,' they answered. 'Christ always has a Christmas tree on this day, for the little children who have no tree of their own . . .' And he found out that all these little boys and girls were children just like himself: that some had been frozen in the baskets in which they had as babies been laid on the doorsteps of well-to-do Petersburg people; others had been boarded out with Finnish women by the Foundling and had been suffocated; others had died at their starved mother's breasts (in the Samara famine[268]); others had died in the third-class railway carriages from the foul air; and yet they were all here, they were all like angels about Christ, and He was in the midst of them and held out His hands to them and blessed them and their sinful mothers . . . And the mothers of these children stood on one side weeping; each one knew her boy or girl, and the children flew up to them and kissed them and wiped away their tears with their little hands, and begged them not to weep because they were so happy.

And down below in the morning the porter found the little dead body of the frozen child on the wood stack; they sought out his mother too . . . She had died before him. They met before the Lord God in heaven.

Why have I made up such a story, so out of keeping with an ordinary diary, and a writer's above all? And I promised two stories dealing with real events! But that is just it, I keep fancying that all this may have happened really – that is, what took place in the cellar and on the wood stack; but as for Christ's Christmas tree, I cannot tell you whether that could have happened or not.

A Gentle Spirit

From the Author

I ask my readers' forgiveness that this time instead of the *Diary* in its usual form I am giving them only a story. But I really have been working on this story for almost a month. In any case I beg my readers' indulgence.

Now for the story itself. I have called it "fantastic" even though I consider it to be realistic in the highest degree. But there really is something fantastic about it, namely in the actual form of the story, that I think needs to be explained at the outset.

The thing is that this is neither a story nor notes. Imagine a husband, whose wife is lying on a table, a suicide, who a few hours earlier has thrown herself out of a window. He is confused and can't manage to collect his thoughts. He paces about his rooms and tries to make sense of what has happened, to collect his thoughts successfully. What's worse is that he is an inveterate hypochondriac, one of those who talks to himself. Here he is talking to himself, recounting what happened, trying to comprehend it. Despite the seeming coherence of his musings, he contradicts himself several times, both in logic and his feelings. He justifies himself and accuses her and indulges himself in irrelevant clarifications: there is a crudity of mind and heart here, as well as profound feeling. Little by little he really does clarify for himself what has happened and collects his thoughts successfully. The series of memories he evokes irresistibly leads him in the end to the truth; the truth irresistibly ennobles his mind and heart. At the end even the tone of the story changes in comparison with the erratic beginning. The truth reveals itself to this unhappy man very clearly and definitively, at least as far as he is concerned.

That is the subject. Of course the business of telling the story takes several hours, with interruptions and pauses, and the form is inconsistent: sometimes he talks to himself, sometimes he speaks to an invisible listener, some sort of judge. But that is always the way in real life. If a stenographer could listen in on him and record everything verbatim, it would seem more uneven, less polished than I have presented it, but as far as I can tell the psychological coherence would perhaps be the same. But this assumption of a stenographer's recording everything (which I would polish after) is the element I call fantastic in the story. Yet something similar has been attempted in art a number of times: Victor Hugo, for example, in his masterpiece *The Last Day of a Condemned Man*, used almost the same device. Although he didn't create a stenographer he allowed himself an even greater lack of verisimilitude by presuming that someone condemned to death would be able (and have time) to make notes not only on his last day, but even in his last hour and literally his last minute. But if he hadn't permitted himself this fantasy, the work itself would not exist, the most realistic and truthful work Hugo ever wrote.[269]

PART ONE

CHAPTER 1

Who I was and Who She was

H, WHILE she is still here, it is still all right; I go up and look at her every minute; but tomorrow they will take her away – and how shall I be left alone? Now she is on the table in the drawing-room, they put two card tables together; the coffin will be here tomorrow – white, pure white '*gros de Naples*'[270] – but that's not it . . .

I keep walking about, trying to explain it to myself. I have been trying for the last six hours to get it clear, but still I can't think of it all as a whole.

The fact is I walk to and fro, and to and fro.

This is how it was. I will simply tell it in order. (Order!)

Gentlemen, I am far from being a literary man and you will see that; but no matter, I'll tell it as I understand it myself. The horror of it for me is that I understand it all!

It was, if you care to know, that is to take it from the beginning, that she used to come to me simply to pawn things, to pay for advertising in the *Voice* to the effect that a governess was quite willing to travel, to give lessons at home, and so on, and so on. That was at the very beginning, and I, of course, made no difference between her and the others: 'She comes,' I thought, 'like anyone else,' and so on.

But afterwards I began to see a difference. She was such a slender, fair little thing, rather tall, always a little awkward with me, as though embarrassed (I fancy she was the same with all strangers, and in her eyes, of course, I was exactly like anybody else – that is, not as a pawn-broker but as a man).

As soon as she received the money she would turn round at once and go away. And always in silence. Other women argue so, entreat, haggle for me to give them more; this one did not ask for more . . .

I believe I am muddling it up.

Yes; I was struck first of all by the things she brought: poor little silver gilt earrings, a trashy little locket, things not worth sixpence. She knew herself that they were worth next to nothing, but I could see from her face that they were treasures to her, and I found out afterwards as a fact that they were all that was left her belonging to her father and mother.

Only once I allowed myself to scoff at her things. You see I never allow myself to behave like that. I keep up a gentlemanly tone with my clients: few words, politeness and severity. 'Severity, severity!'

But once she ventured to bring her last rag, that is, literally, the remains of an old hare-skin jacket, and I could not resist saying something by way of a joke. My goodness! how she flared up! Her eyes were large, blue and dreamy but – how they blazed. But she did not drop one word; picking up her 'rags', she walked out.

It was then for the first time I noticed her *particularly*, and thought something of the kind about her – that it, something of a particular kind. Yes, I remember another impression – that is, if you will have it, perhaps the chief impression, that summed up everything. It was that she was terribly young, so young that she looked just fourteen. And yet she was within three months of sixteen. I didn't mean that, though, that wasn't what summed it all up. Next day she came again. I found out later that she had been to Dobranravov's and to Mozer's with that jacket, but they take nothing but gold and would have nothing to say to it. I once took some stones from her (rubbishy little ones) and, thinking it over afterwards, I wondered: I, too, only lend on gold and silver, yet from her I accepted stones. That was my second thought about her then; that I remember. That time, that is when she came from Mozer's, she brought an amber cigar-holder. It was a connoisseur's article, not bad, but again, of no value to us, because we only deal in gold. As it was the day after her 'mutiny', I received her sternly. Sternness with me takes the form of dryness. As I gave her two roubles, however, I could not resist saying, with a certain irritation, 'I only do it for you, of course; Mozer wouldn't take such a thing.'

The words 'for *you*' I emphasised particularly, and with a particular implication.

I was spiteful. She flushed up again when she heard that 'for you', but she did not say a word, she did not refuse the money, she took it – that is poverty! But how hotly she flushed! I saw I had stung her. And when she had gone out, I suddenly asked myself whether my triumph over her was worth two roubles. He! He!! He!!! I remember I put that question to myself twice over. 'Was is worth it? Was it worth it?'

And, laughing, I inwardly answered it in the affirmative. And I felt very much elated. But that was not an evil feeling; I said it with design, with a motive; I wanted to test her, because certain ideas with regard to her had suddenly come into my mind. That was the third thing I thought particularly about her . . . Well, it was from that time it all began. Of course, I tried at once to find out all her circumstances indirectly, and awaited her coming with a special impatience. I had a presentiment that she would come soon. When she came, I entered into affable conversation with her, speaking with unusual politeness. I have not been badly brought up and have manners. H'm. It was then I guessed that she was soft-hearted and gentle.

The gentle and soft-hearted do not resist long, and though they are by no means very ready to reveal themselves, they do not know how to escape from a conversation; they are niggardly in their answers, but they do answer, and the more readily the longer you go on. Only, on your side you must not flag, if you want them to talk. I need hardly say that she did not explain anything to me then. About the *Voice* and all that I found out afterwards. She was at that time spending her last farthing on advertising, haughtily at first, of course. 'A governess, prepared to travel, will send terms on application'; but, later on: 'willing to do anything, to teach, to be a companion, to be a house-keeper, to wait on an invalid, plain sewing', and so on, and so on, the usual thing! Of course, all this was added to the advertisement a bit at a time and finally, when she was reduced to despair, it came to: 'without salary in return for board'. No, she could not find a situation. I made up my mind then to test her for the last time. I suddenly took up the *Voice* of the day and showed her an advertisement. 'A young person, without friends and relations, seeks a situation as a governess to young children, preferably in the family of a middle-aged widower. Might be a comfort in the home.'

'Look here how this lady has advertised this morning, and by the evening she will certainly have found a situation. That's the way to advertise.'

Again she flushed crimson and her eyes blazed, she turned round and went straight out. I was very much pleased, though by that time I felt sure of everything and had no apprehensions; nobody will take her cigar-holders, I thought. Besides, she has got rid of them all. And so it was, two days later, she came in again, such a pale little creature, all agitation – I saw that something had happened to her at home, and something really had. I will explain directly what had happened, but now I only want to recall how I did something chic, and rose in her opinion. I suddenly decided to do it. The fact is she was pawning the ikon (she had brought herself to pawn it!) . . Ah! listen! listen! This is the beginning now, I've been in a muddle. You see I want to recall all this, every detail, every little point. I want to bring them all together and look at them as a whole and – I cannot . . . It's these little things, these little things . . . It was an ikon of the Madonna. A Madonna with the Babe, an old-fashioned, homely one, and the setting was silver gilt, worth – well, six roubles perhaps. I could see the ikon was precious to her; she was pawning it whole, not taking it out of the setting. I said to her: 'You had better take it out of the setting, and take the ikon home; for it's not the thing to pawn.'

'Why, are you forbidden to take them?'

'No, it's not that we are forbidden, but you might, perhaps, your-self . . . '

'Well, take it out.'

'I tell you what. I will not take it out, but I'll set it here in the shrine with the other ikons,' I said, on reflection. 'Under the little lamp' (I always had the lamp burning as soon as the shop was opened), 'and you simply take ten roubles.'

'Don't give me ten roubles. I only want five; I shall certainly redeem it.'

'You don't want ten? The ikon's worth it,' I added noticing that her eyes flashed again.

She was silent. I brought out five roubles.

'I don't despise anyone; I've been in such straits myself; and worse too, and that you see me here in this business . . . is owing to what I've been through in the past . . . '

'You're revenging yourself on the world? Yes?' she interrupted sud-denly with rather sarcastic mockery, which, however, was to a great extent innocent (that is, it was general, because certainly at that time she did not distinguish me from others, so that she said it almost without malice).

'Aha,' thought I; 'so that's what you're like. You've got character; you belong to the new movement.'[271]

'You see!' I remarked at once, half-jestingly, half-mysteriously, 'I am part of that part of the Whole that seeks to do ill, but does good . . . '

Quickly and with great curiosity, in which , however, there was something very childlike, she looked at me.

'Stay . . . what's that idea? Where does it come from? I've heard it somewhere . . . '

'Don't rack your brains. In those words Mephistopheles introduces himself to Faust.[272] Have you read *Faust*?'

'Not . . . not attentively.'

'That is, you have not read it at all. You must read it. But I see an ironical look in your face again. Please don't imagine that I've so little taste as to try to use Mephistopheles to commend myself to you and grace the role of pawnbroker. A pawnbroker will still be a pawnbroker. We know.'

'You're so strange . . . I didn't mean to say anything of that sort.'

She meant to say: 'I didn't expect to find you were an educated man;' but she didn't say it; I knew, though, that she thought that. I had pleased her very much.

'You see,' I observed, 'one may do good in any calling – I'm not speaking of myself, of course. Let us grant that I'm doing nothing but harm, yet . . . '

'Of course, one can do good in every position,' she said, glancing at me with a rapid, profound look. 'Yes, in any position,' she added suddenly.

Oh, I remember, I remember all those moments! And I want to add, too, that when such young creatures, such sweet young creatures want to say something so clever and profound, they show at once so truthfully and naïvely in their faces, 'Here I am saying something clever and profound now' – and that is not from vanity, as it is with anyone like me, but one sees that she appreciates it awfully herself, and believes in it, and thinks a lot of it, and imagines that you think a lot of all that, just as she does. Oh, truthfulness! it's by that they conquer us. How exquisite it was in her!

I remember it, I have forgotten nothing! As soon as she had gone, I made up my mind. That same day I made my last investigations and found out every detail of her position at the moment; every detail of her past I had learned already from Lukerya, at that time a servant in the family, whom I had bribed a few days before. This position was so awful that I can't understand how she could laugh as she had done that day and feel interest in the words of Mephistopheles, when she was in such horrible straits. But – that's youth! That is just what I thought about her at the time with pride and joy; for, you know, there's a greatness of soul in it – to be able to say, 'Though I am on the edge of the abyss, yet Goethe's grand words are radiant with light.' Youth always has some greatness of soul, if its only a spark and that distorted. Though it's of her I am speaking, of her alone. And, above all, I looked upon her then as mine and did not doubt of my power. You know, that's a voluptuous idea when you feel no doubt of it.

But what is the matter with me? If I go on like this, when shall I put it all together and look at it as a whole. I must make haste, make haste – that is not what matters, oh, my God!

CHAPTER 2

The Offer of Marriage

The 'details' I learned about her I will tell in one word: her father and mother were dead, they had died three years before, and she had been left with two disreputable aunts: though it is saying too little to call them disreputable. One aunt was a widow with a large family (six children, one smaller than another), the other a horrid old maid. Both were horrid. Her father was in the service, but only as a copying clerk, and was only a gentleman by courtesy; in fact, everything was in my favour. I came as though from a higher world; I was anyway a retired lieutenant of a brilliant regiment, a gentleman by birth, independent and all the rest of it, and as for my pawnbroker's shop, her aunts could only have looked on that with respect. She had been living in slavery at her aunts' for those three years: yet she had managed to pass an examination somewhere – she managed to pass it, she wrung the time for it, weighed down as a she was by the pitiless burden of daily drudgery, and that proved something in the way of striving for what was higher and better on her part! Why, what made me want to marry her? Never mind me, though; of that later on . . . As though that mattered! She taught her aunt's children; she made their clothes; and towards the end not only washed the clothes, but with her weak chest even scrubbed the floors. To put it plainly, they used to beat her, and taunt her with eating their bread. It ended by their scheming to sell her. Tfoo! I omit the filthy details. She told me all about it afterwards.

All this had been watched for a whole year by a neighbour, a fat shopkeeper, and not a humble one but the owner of two grocer's shops. He had ill-treated two wives and now he was looking for a third, and so he cast his eye on her. 'She's a quiet one,' he thought; 'she's grown up in poverty, and I am marrying for the sake of my motherless children.'

He really had children. He began trying to make the match and negotiating with the aunts. He was fifty years old, besides. She was aghast with horror. It was then she began coming so often to me to advertise in the *Voice*. At last she began begging the aunts to give her just a little time to think it over. They granted her that little time, but would not let her have more; they were always at her: 'We don't know where to turn to find food for ourselves, without having an extra mouth to feed.'

I had found all this out already, and the same day, after what had happened in the morning, I made up my mind. That evening the shopkeeper came, bringing with him a pound of sweets from the shop; she was sitting with him, and I called Lukerya out of the kitchen and told her to go and whisper to her that I was at the gate and wanted to say something to her without delay. I felt pleased with myself. And altogether I felt awfully pleased all that day.

On the spot, at the gate, in the presence of Lukerya, before she had recovered from her amazement at my sending for her, I informed her that I should look upon it as an honour and happiness . . . telling her, in the next place, not to be surprised at the manner of my declaration and at my speaking at the gate, saying that I was a straightforward man and had learned the position of affairs. And I was not lying when I said I was straightforward. Well, hang it all. I did not only speak with propriety – that is, showing I was a man of decent breeding, but I spoke with originality and that was the chief thing. After all, is there any harm in admitting it? I want to judge myself and am judging myself. I must speak pro and contra, and I do. I remembered afterwards with enjoyment, though it was stupid, that I frankly declared, without the least embarrassment, that, in the first place, I was not particularly talented, not particularly intelligent, not particularly good-natured, rather a cheap egoist (I remember that expression, I thought of it on the way and was pleased with it) and that very probably there was a great deal that was disagreeable in me in other respects. All this was said with a special sort of pride – we all know how that sort of thing is said. Of course, I had good taste enough not to proceed to enlarge on my virtues after honourably enumerating my defects, not to say 'to make up for that I have this and that and the other'. I saw that she was still horribly frightened I purposely exaggerated. I told her straight out that she would have enough to eat, but that fine clothes, theatres, balls – she would have none of, at any rate not till later on, when I had attained my object. This severe tone was a positive delight to me. I added as cursorily as possible, that in adopting such a calling – that is, in keeping a pawnbroker's shop, I had one object, hinting there was a special circumstance . . . but I really had a right to say so: I really had such an aim and there really was such a circumstance. Wait a minute, gentlemen; I have always been the first to hate this pawnbroking business, but in reality, though it is absurd to talk about oneself in such mysterious phrases, yet, you know, I was 'revenging myself on society', I really was, I was, I was! So that her gibe that morning at the idea of my revenging myself was unjust. That is, do you see, if I had said to her straight out in words: 'Yes, I am revenging myself on society,' she would have laughed as she did that morning, and it would, in fact, have been absurd. But by indirect hints, by dropping mysterious phrases, it appeared that it was possible to work upon her imagination. Besides, I had no fears then: I knew that the fat shopkeeper was anyway more repulsive to her than I was, and that I, standing at the gate, had appeared as a deliverer. I understood that, of course. Oh, what is base a man understands particularly well! But was it base? How can a man judge? Didn't I love her even then?

Wait a bit: of course, I didn't breathe a word to her of doing her a benefit; the opposite, oh, quite the opposite; I made out that it was I that would be under an obligation to her, not she to me. Indeed, I said as much – I couldn't resist saying it – and it sounded stupid, perhaps, for I noticed a shade flit across her face. But altogether I won the day completely. Wait a bit, if I am to recall all that vileness, then I will tell of that worst beastliness. As I stood there what was stirring in my mind was, 'You are tall, a good figure, educated and – speaking without conceit – good-looking.' That is what was at work in my mind. I need hardly say that, on the spot, out there at the gate she said, 'Yes.' But . . . but I ought to add: that out there by the gate she thought a long time before she said yes. She pondered for so long that I said to her, 'Well?' – and could not even refrain from asking it with a certain swagger.

'Wait a little. I'm thinking.'

And her little face was so serious, so serious that even then I might have read it! And I was mortified: 'Can she be choosing between me and the grocer!' I thought. Oh, I did not understand then! I did not understand anything, anything, then! I did not understand till today! I remember Lukerya ran after me as I was going away, stopped me on the road and said, breathlessly: 'God will reward you, sir, for taking our dear young lady; only don't speak of that to her – she's proud.'

Proud, is she! 'I like proud people,' I thought. Proud people are particularly nice when . . . well, when one has no doubt of one's power over them, eh? Oh, base, tactless man! Oh, how pleased I was! You know, when she was standing there at the gate, hesitating whether to say yes to me, and I was wondering at it, you know, she may have had some such thought as this: 'If it is to be misery either way, isn't it best to choose the very worst' – that is, let the fat grocer beat her to death when he was drunk! Eh! what do you think, could there have been a thought like that?

And, indeed, I don't understand it now, I don't understand it at all, even now. I have only just said that she may have had that thought: of two evils choose the worst – that is the grocer. But which was the worst for her then – the grocer or I? The grocer or the pawnbroker who quoted Goethe? That's another question! What a question! And even that you don't understand: the answer is lying on the table and you call it a question! Never mind me, though. It's not a question of me at all . . . and, by the way, what is there left for me now – whether it's a question of me or whether it is not? That's what I am utterly unable to answer. I had better go to bed. My head aches . . .

CHAPTER 3

The Noblest of Men, Though I Don't Believe it Myself

I could not sleep. And how should I? There is a pulse throbbing in my head. One longs to master it all, all that degradation. Oh, the degradation! Oh, what degradation I dragged her out of then! Of course, she must have realised that, she must have appreciated my action! I was pleased, too, by various thoughts – for instance, the reflection that I was forty-one and she was only sixteen. That fascinated me, that feeling of inequality was very sweet, was very sweet.

I wanted, for instance, to have a wedding *à l'anglaise*,[273] that is only the two of us, with just the two necessary witnesses, one of them Lukerya, and from the wedding straight to the train to Moscow (I happened to have business there, by the way), and then a fortnight at the hotel. She opposed it, she would not have it, and I had to visit her aunts and treat them with respect as though they were relations from whom I was taking her. I gave way, and all befitting respect was paid the aunts. I even made the creatures a present of a hundred roubles each and promised them more – not telling her anything about it, of course, that I might not make her feel humiliated by the lowness of her surroundings. The aunts were as soft as silk at once. There was a wrangle about the trousseau, too; she had nothing, almost literally, but she did not want to have anything. I succeeded in proving to her, though, that she must have something, and I made up the trousseau, for who would have given her anything? But there, enough of me. I did, however, succeed in communicating some of my ideas to her then, so that she knew them anyway. I was in too great a hurry, perhaps. The best of it was that, from the very beginning, she rushed to meet me with love, greeted me with rapture, when I went to see her in the evening, told me in her chatter (the enchanting chatter of innocence) all about her childhood and girlhood, her old home, her father and mother. But I poured cold water upon all that at once. That was my idea. I met her enthusiasm with silence, friendly silence, of course . . . but, all the same, she could quickly see that we were different and that I was – an enigma. And being an enigma was what I made a point of most of all! Why, it was just for the sake of being an enigma, perhaps, that I have been guilty of all this stupidity. The first thing was sternness – it was with an air of sternness that I took her into my house. In fact, as I went about then feeling satisfied, I framed a complete system. Oh, it came of itself without any effort. And it could not have been otherwise. I was bound to create that system owing to one inevitable fact – why should I libel myself indeed! The system was a genuine one. Yes, listen; if you must judge a man, better judge him knowing all about it . . . listen.

How am I to begin this, for it is very difficult. When you begin to justify yourself – then it is difficult. You see, for instance, young people despise money – I made money of importance at once; I laid special stress on money. And laid such stress on it that she became more and more silent. She opened her eyes wide, listened, gazed and said nothing. You see, the young are heroic, that is the good among them are heroic and impulsive, but they have little tolerance; if the least thing is not quite right they are full of contempt. And I wanted breadth, I wanted to instil breadth into her very heart, to make it part of her inmost feeling, did I not? I'll take a trivial example: how should I explain my pawn-broker's shop to a character like that? Of course, I did not speak of it directly, or it would have appeared that I was apologising; I, so to speak, worked it through with pride, I almost spoke without words, and I am masterly at speaking without words. All my life I have spoken without words, and I have passed through whole tragedies on my own account without words. Why, I, too, have been unhappy! I was abandoned by everyone, abandoned and forgotten, and no one, no one knew it! And all at once this sixteen-year-old girl picked up details about me from vulgar people and thought she knew all about me, and, meanwhile, what was precious remained hidden in this heart! I went on being silent, with her especially I was silent, with her especially, right up to yesterday – why was I silent? Because I was proud. I wanted her to find out for herself, without my help, and not from the tales of low people; I wanted her to divine of herself what manner of man I was and to understand me! Taking her into my house I wanted all her respect, I wanted her to be standing before me in homage for the sake of my sufferings – and I deserved it. Oh, I have always been proud, I always wanted all or nothing! You see it was just because I am not one who will accept half a happiness, but always wanted all, that I was forced to act like that then: it was as much as to say, 'See into me for yourself and appreciate me!' For you must see that if I had begun explaining myself to her and prompting her, ingratiating myself and asking for her respect – it would have been as good as asking for charity . . . But . . . but why am I talking of that!

Stupid, stupid, stupid, stupid! I explained to her then, in two words, directly, ruthlessly (and I emphasise the fact that it was ruthlessly), that the heroism of youth was charming, but – not worth a farthing. Why not? Because it costs them so little, because it is not gained through life; it is, so to say, merely 'first impressions of existence',[274] but just let us see you at work! Cheap heroism is always easy, and even to sacrifice life is easy too; because it is only a case of hot blood and an overflow of energy,[275] and there is such a longing for what is beautiful! No, take the deed of heroism that is laborious, obscure, without noise or flourish, slandered, in which there is a great deal of sacrifice and not one grain of glory – in which you, a splendid man, are made to look like a scoundrel before everyone, though you might be the most honest man in the world – you try that sort of heroism and you'll soon give it up! While I – I have been bearing the burden of that all my life. At first she argued – ough, how she argued – but afterwards she began to be silent, completely silent, in fact, only opened her eyes wide as she listened, such big, big eyes, so attentive. And . . . and what is more, I suddenly saw a smile, mistrustful, silent, an evil smile. Well, it was with that smile on her face I brought her into my house. It is true that she had nowhere to go.

CHAPTER 4

Plans and Plans

Which of us began it first?

Neither. It began of itself from the very first. I have said that with sternness I brought her into the house. From the first step, however, I softened it. Before she was married it was explained to her that she would have to take pledges and pay out money, and she said nothing at the time (note that). What is more, she set to work with positive zeal. Well, of course, my lodging, my furniture all remained as before. My lodging consisted of two rooms, a large room from which the shop was partitioned off, and a second one, also large, our living room and bedroom. My furniture is scanty: even her aunts had better things. My shrine of ikons with the lamp was in the outer room where the shop is; in the inner room my bookcase with a few books in and a trunk of which I keep the key; of course, there is a bed, tables and chairs. Before she was married I told her that one rouble a day, and not more, was to be spent on our board – that is, on food for me, her and Lukerya, whom I had enticed to come to us. 'I must have thirty thousand in three years,' said I, 'and we can't save the money if we spend more.' She fell in with this, but I raised the sum by thirty kopecks a day. It was the same with the theatre. I told her before marriage that she would not go to the theatre, and yet I decided once a month to go to the theatre, and in a decent way, to the stalls. We went together. We went three times and saw *The Hunt after Happiness*,[276] and *Singing Birds*,[277] I believe. (Oh, what does it matter!) We went in silence and in silence we returned. Why, why, from the very beginning, did we take to being silent? From the very first, you know, we had no quarrels, but always the same silence. She was always, I remember, watching me stealthily in those days; as soon as I noticed it I became more silent that before. It is true that it was I insisted on the silence, not she. On her part there were one or two outbursts, she rushed to embrace me; but as these outbursts were hysterical, painful, and I wanted secure happiness, with respect from her, I received them coldly. And indeed, I was right; each time the outburst was followed next day by a quarrel.

Though, again, there were no quarrels, but there was silence and – and on her side a more and more defiant air. 'Rebellion and independence,' that's what it was, only she didn't know how to show it.

Yes, that gentle creature was becoming more and more defiant. Would you believe it, I was becoming revolting to her? I learned that. And there could be no doubt that she was moved to frenzy at times. Think, for instance, of her beginning to sniff at our poverty, after her coming from such sordidness and destitution – from scrubbing the floors! You see, there was no poverty; there was frugality, but there was abundance of what was necessary, of linen, for instance, and the greatest cleanliness. I always used to dream that cleanliness in a husband attracts a wife. It was not our poverty she was scornful of, but my supposed miserliness in the housekeeping: 'He has his objects,' she seemed to say; 'he is showing his strength of will.' She suddenly refused to go to the theatre. And more and more often wore an ironical look . . . And I was more silent, more and more silent.

I could not begin justifying myself, could I? What was at the bottom of all this was the pawnbroking business. Allow me, I knew that a woman, above all at sixteen, must be in complete subordination to a man. Women have no originality. That – that is an axiom; even now, even now, for me it is an axiom! What does it prove that she is lying there in the outer room? Truth is truth, and even Mill[278] is no use against it! And a woman who loves, oh, a woman who loves idealises even the vices, even the villainies of the man she loves. He would not himself ever succeed in finding such justification for his villanies as she will find for him. That is generous but not original. It is the lack of originality alone that has been the ruin of women, and, I repeat, what is the use of your pointing to that table? Why, what is there original in her being on that table? Oh – Oh – Oh!

Listen. I was convinced of her love at that time. Why, she used to throw herself on my neck in those days. She loved me; that is, more accurately, she wanted to love. Yes, that's just what it was, she wanted to love; she was trying to love. And the point was that in this case there were no villanies for which she had to find justification. You will say, I'm a pawnbroker; and everyone says the same. But what if I am a pawnbroker? It follows that there must be reasons since the most generous of men had become a pawnbroker. You see, gentlemen, there are ideas . . . that is, if one expresses some ideas, utters them in words, the effect is very stupid. The effect is to make one ashamed. For what reason? For no reason. Because we are all wretched creatures and cannot hear the truth, or I do not know why. I said just now, 'the most generous of men' – that is absurd, and yet that is how it was. It's the truth, that is, the absolute, absolute truth! Yes, I *had the right* to want to make myself secure and open that pawnbroker's shop: 'You have rejected me, you –

people, I mean – you have cast me out with contemptuous silence. My passionate yearning towards you you have met with insult all my life. Now I have the right to put up a wall against you, to save up that thirty thousand roubles and end my life somewhere in the Crimea,[279] on the south coast, among the mountains and vineyards, on my own estate bought with that thirty thousand, and above everything, far away from you all, living without malice against you, with an ideal in my soul, with a beloved woman at my heart, and a family, if God sends one, and – helping the inhabitants all around.'

Of course, it is quite right that I say this to myself now, but what could have been more stupid than describing all that aloud to her? That was the cause of my proud silence, that's why we sat in silence. For what could she have understood? Sixteen years old, the earliest youth – yes, what could she have understood of my justification, of my sufferings? Undeviating straightness, ignorance of life, the cheap convictions of youth, the hen-like blindness of those 'noble hearts', and what stood for most was – the pawnbroker's shop and – enough! (And was I a villain in the pawnbroker's shop? Did not she see how I acted? Did I extort too much?)

Oh, how awful is truth on earth! That exquisite creature, that gentle spirit, that heaven – she was a tyrant, she was the insufferable tyrant and torture of my soul! I should be unfair to myself if I didn't say so! You imagine I didn't love her? Who can say that I did not love her! Do you see, it was a case of irony, the malignant irony of fate and nature! We were under a curse, the life of men in general is under a curse! (mine in particular). Of course, I understand now that I made some mistake! Something went wrong. Everything was clear, my plan was clear as daylight: 'Austere and proud, asking for no moral comfort, but suffering in silence.' And that was how it was. I was not lying, I was not lying! 'She will see for herself, later on, that it was heroic, only that she had not known how to see it, and when, someday, she divines it she will prize me ten times more and will abase herself in the dust and fold her hands in homage' – that was my plan. But I forgot something or lost sight of it. There was something I failed to manage. But, enough, enough! And whose forgiveness am I to ask now? What is done is done. Be bolder, man, and have some pride! It is not your fault! . . .

Well, I will tell the truth, I am not afraid to face the truth; it was *her fault, her fault*!

CHAPTER 5

A Gentle Spirit in Revolt

Quarrels began from her suddenly beginning to pay out loans on her own account, to price things above their worth, and even, on two occasions, she deigned to enter into a dispute about it with me. I did not agree. But then the captain's widow turned up.

This old widow brought a medallion – a present from her dead husband, a souvenir, of course. I lent her thirty roubles on it. She fell to complaining, begged me to keep the thing for her – of course we do keep things. Well, in short, she came again to exchange it for a bracelet that was not worth eight roubles; I, of course, refused. She must have guessed something from my wife's eyes, anyway she came again when I was not there and my wife changed it for the medallion.

Discovering it the same day, I spoke mildly but firmly and reasonably. She was sitting on the bed, looking at the ground and tapping with her right foot on the carpet (her characteristic movement); there was an ugly smile on her lips. Then, without raising my voice in the least, I explained calmly that the money was *mine*, that I had a right to look at life with *my own* eyes and – and that when I had offered to take her into my house, I had hidden nothing from her.

She suddenly leapt up, suddenly began shaking all over and – what do you think – she suddenly stamped her foot at me; it was a wild animal, it was a frenzy, it was the frenzy of a wild animal. I was petrified with astonishment; I had never expected such an outburst. But I did not lose my head. I made no movement even, and again, in the same calm voice, I announced plainly that from that time forth I should deprive her of the part she took in my work. She laughed in my face, and walked out of the house.

The fact is, she had not the right to walk out of the house. Nowhere without me, such was the agreement before she was married. In the evening she returned; I did not utter a word.

The next day, too, she went out in the morning, and the day after again. I shut the shop and went off to her aunts. I had cut off all relations with them from the time of the wedding – I would not have them to see me, and I would not go to see them. But it turned out that she had not been with them. They listened to me with curiosity and laughed in my face: 'It serves you right,' they said. But I expected their laughter. At that point, then, I bought over the younger aunt, the unmarried one, for a hundred roubles, giving her twenty-five in advance. Two days later she came to me: 'There's an officer called Efimovitch mixed up in this,' she said; 'a lieutenant who was a comrade of yours in the regiment.'

I was greatly amazed. That Efimovitch had done me more harm than anyone in the regiment, and about a month ago, being a shameless fellow, he once or twice came into the shop with a pretence of pawning something and, I remember, began laughing with my wife. I went up at the time and told him not to dare to come to me, recalling our relations; but there was no thought of anything in my head, I simply thought that he was insolent. Now the aunt suddenly informed me that she had already appointed to see him and that the whole business had been arranged by a former friend of the aunt's, the widow of a colonel, called Yulia Samsonovna. 'It's to her,' she said, 'your wife goes now.'

I will cut the story short. The business cost me three hundred roubles, but in a couple of days it had been arranged that I should stand in an adjoining room, behind closed doors, and listen to the first rendezvous between my wife and Efimovitch, *tête-à-tête*. Meanwhile, the evening before, a scene, brief but very memorable for me, took place between us.

She returned towards evening, sat down on the bed, looked at me sarcastically, and tapped on the carpet with her foot. Looking at her, the idea suddenly came into my mind that for the whole of the last month, or rather, the last fortnight, her character had not been her own; one might even say that it had been the opposite of her own; she had suddenly shown herself a mutinous, aggressive creature; I cannot say shameless, but regardless of decorum and eager for trouble. She went out of her way to stir up trouble. Her gentleness hindered her, though. When a girl like that rebels, however outrageously she may behave, one can always see that she is forcing herself to do it, that she is driving herself to do it, and that it is impossible for her to master and overcome her own modesty and shamefacedness. That is why such people go to such lengths at times that one can hardly believe one's eyes. One who is accustomed to depravity, on the contrary, always softens things, acts more disgustingly, but with a show of decorum and seemliness by which she claims to be superior to you.

'Is it true that you were turned out of the regiment because you were afraid to fight a duel?' she asked suddenly, apropos of nothing – and her eyes flashed.

'It is true that by the sentence of the officers I was asked to give up my commission, though, as a fact, I had sent in my papers before that.'

'You were turned out as a coward?'

'Yes, they sentenced me as a coward. But I refused to fight a duel, not from cowardice, but because I would not submit to their tyrannical decision and send a challenge when I did not consider myself insulted. You know,' I could not refrain from adding, 'that to resist such tyranny and to accept the consequences meant showing far more manliness than fighting any kind of duel.'

I could not resist it. I dropped the phrase, as it were, in self-defence, and that was all she wanted, this fresh humiliation for me.

She laughed maliciously.

'And is it true that for three years afterwards you wandered about the streets of Petersburg like a tramp, begging for coppers and spending your nights in billiard-rooms?'

'I even spent the night in Vyazemsky's House in the Haymarket.[280] Yes, it is true; there was much disgrace and degradation in my life after I left the regiment, but not moral degradation because even at the time I hated what I did more than anyone. It was only the degradation of my will and my mind, and it was only caused by the desperateness of my position. But that is over . . . '

'Oh, now you are a personage – a financier!'

A hint at the pawnbroker's shop. But by then I had succeeded in recovering my mastery of myself. I saw that she was thirsting for explanations that would be humiliating to me and – I did not give them. A customer rang the bell very opportunely, and I went out into the shop. An hour later, when she was dressed to go out, she stood still, facing me, and said: 'You didn't tell me anything about that, though, before our marriage?'

I made no answer and she went away.

And so next day I was standing in that room, the other side of the door, listening to hear how my fate was being decided, and in my pocket I had a revolver. She was dressed better than usual and sitting at the table, and Efimovitch was showing off before her. And after all, it turned out exactly (I say it to my credit) as I had foreseen and had assumed it would, though I was not conscious of having foreseen and assumed it. I do not know whether I express myself intelligibly.

This is what happened.

I listened for a whole hour. For a whole hour I was present at a duel between a noble, lofty woman and a worldly, corrupt, dense man with a crawling soul. And how, I wondered in amazement, how could that naïve, gentle, silent girl have come to know all that? The wittiest author of a society comedy could not have created such a scene of mockery, of naïve laughter, and of the holy contempt of virtue for vice. And how brilliant her sayings, her little phrases were: what wit there was in her rapid answers, what truths in her condemnation. And, at the same time, what almost girlish simplicity. She laughed in his face at his declarations of love, at his gestures, at his proposals. Coming coarsely to the point at once, and not expecting to meet with opposition, he was utterly nonplussed. At first I might have imagined that it was simply coquetry on her part – 'the coquetry of a witty, though depraved creature to enhance her own value'. But no, the truth shone out like the sun, and to doubt was impossible. It was only an exaggerated and impulsive hatred for me that had led her, in her inexperience, to arrange this interview, but, when it came off – her eyes were opened at once. She was simply in desperate haste to mortify me, come what might, but though she had brought herself to do something so low she could not endure unseemliness. And could she, so pure and sinless, with an ideal in her heart, have been seduced by Efimovitch or any worthless snob? On the contrary, she was only moved to laughter by him. All her goodness rose up from her soul and her indignation roused her to sarcasm. I repeat, the buffoon was completely nonplussed at last and sat frowning, scarcely answering, so much so that I began to be afraid that he might insult her, from a mean desire for revenge. And I repeat again: to my credit, I listened to that scene almost without surprise. I met, as it were, nothing but what I knew well. I had gone, as it were, on purpose to meet it, believing not a word of it, not a word said against her, though I did take the revolver in my pocket – that is the truth. And could I have imagined her different? For what did I love her, for what did I prize her, for what had I married her? Oh, of course, I was quite convinced of her hate for me, but at the same time I was quite convinced of her sinlessness. I suddenly cut short the scene by opening the door. Efimovitch leapt up. I took her by the hand and suggested she should go home with me. Efimovitch recovered himself and suddenly burst into loud peals of laughter.

'Oh, to sacred conjugal rights I offer no opposition; take her away, take her away! And you know,' he shouted after me, 'though no decent man could fight you, yet from respect to your lady I am at your service . . . If you are ready to risk yourself.'

'Do you hear?' I said, stopping her for a second in the doorway.

After which not a word was said all the way home. I led her by the arm and she did not resist. On the contrary, she was greatly impressed, and this lasted after she got home. On reaching home she sat down in a chair and fixed her eyes upon me. She was extremely pale; though her lips were compressed ironically yet she looked at me with solemn and austere defiance and seemed convinced in earnest, for the minute, that I should kill her with the revolver. But I took the revolver from my pocket without a word and laid it on the table! She looked at me and at the revolver. (Note that the revolver was already an object familiar to her. I had kept one loaded ever since I opened the shop. I made up my mind when I set up the shop that I would not keep a huge dog or a strong manservant, as Mozer does, for instance. My cook opens the doors to my visitors. But in our trade it is impossible to be without means of self-defence in case of emergency, and I kept a loaded revolver. In early days, when first she was living in my house, she took great interest in that revolver, and asked questions about it, and I even explained its construction and working; I even persuaded her once to fire at a target. Note all that). Taking no notice of her frightened eyes, I lay down on the bed, half-undressed. I felt very much exhausted; it was by then about eleven o'clock. She went on sitting in the same place, not stirring, for another hour. Then she put out the candle and she, too, without undressing, lay down on the sofa near the wall. For the first time she did not sleep with me – note that too . . .

CHAPTER 6

A Terrible Reminiscence

Now for a terrible reminiscence . . .

I woke up, I believe, before eight o'clock, and it was very nearly broad daylight. I woke up completely to full consciousness and opened my eyes. She was standing at the table holding the revolver in her hand. She did not see that I had woken up and was looking at her. And suddenly I saw that she had begun moving towards me with the revolver in her hand. I quickly closed my eyes and pretended to be still asleep.

She came up to the bed and stood over me. I heard everything; though a dead silence had fallen, I heard that silence. All at once there was a convulsive movement and, irresistibly, against my will, I suddenly opened my eyes. She was looking straight at me, straight into my eyes, and the revolver was at my temple. Our eyes met. But we looked at each other for no more than a moment. With an effort I shut my eyes again, and at the same instant I resolved that I would not stir and would not open my eyes, whatever might be awaiting me.

It does sometimes happen that people who are sound asleep suddenly open their eyes, even raise their heads for a second and look about the room, then, a moment later, they lay their heads again on the pillow unconscious, and fall back to sleep without understanding anything. When meeting her eyes and feeling the revolver on my forehead, I closed my eyes and remained motionless, as though in a deep sleep – she certainly might have supposed that I really was asleep, and that I had seen nothing, especially as it was utterly improbable that, after seeing what I had seen, I should shut my eyes again at *such* a moment.

Yes, it was improbable. But she might guess the truth all the same – that thought flashed upon my mind at once, all at the same instant. Oh, what a whirl of thoughts and sensations rushed into my mind in less than a minute. Hurrah for the electric speed of thought! In that case (so I felt), if she guessed the truth and knew that I was awake, I should crush her by my readiness to accept death, and her hand might tremble. Her determination might be shaken by a new, overwhelming impression. They say that people standing on a height have an impulse to throw themselves down. I imagine that many suicides and murders have been committed simply because the revolver has been in the hand. It is like a precipice, with an incline of an angle of forty-five degrees, down which you cannot help sliding, and something impels you irresistibly to pull the trigger. But the knowledge that I had seen, that I knew it all, and was waiting for death at her hands without a word – might hold her back on the incline.

The stillness was prolonged, and all at once I felt on my temple, on my hair, the cold contact of iron. You will ask: did I confidently expect to escape? I will answer you as God is my judge: I had no hope of it, except one chance in a hundred. Why did I accept death? But I will ask, what use was life to me after that revolver had been raised against me by the being I adored? Besides, I knew with the whole strength of my being that there was a struggle going on between us, a fearful duel for life and death, the duel fought by the coward of yesterday, rejected by his comrades for cowardice. I knew that and she knew it, if only she guessed the truth that I was not asleep.

Perhaps that was not so, perhaps I did not think that then, but yet it must have been so, even without conscious thought, because I've done nothing but think of it every hour of my life since.

But you will ask me again: why did you not save her from such wickedness? Oh! I've asked myself that question a thousand times since – every time that, with a shiver down my back, I recall that second. But at that moment my soul was plunged in dark despair! I was lost, I myself was lost – how could I save anyone? And how do you know whether I wanted to save anyone then? How can one tell what I could be feeling then?

My mind was in a ferment, though; the seconds passed; she still stood over me – and suddenly I shuddered with hope! I quickly opened my eyes. She was no longer in the room: I got out of bed: I had conquered – and she was conquered for ever!

I went to the samovar. We always had the samovar brought into the outer room and she always poured out the tea. I sat down at the table without a word and took a glass of tea from her. Five minutes later I looked at her. She was fearfully pale, even paler than the day before, and she looked at me. And suddenly . . . and suddenly, seeing that I was looking at her, she gave a pale smile with her pale lips, with a timid question in her eyes. 'So she still doubts and is asking herself: does he know or doesn't he know; did he see or didn't he?' I turned my eyes away indifferently. After tea I close the shop, went to the market and bought an iron bedstead and a screen. Returning home, I directed that the bed should be put in the front room and shut off with a screen. It was a bed for her, but I did not say a word to her. She understood without words, through that bedstead, that I 'had seen and knew all', and that all doubt was over. At night I left the revolver on the table, as I always did. At night she got into her new bed without a word: our marriage bond was broken, 'she was conquered but not forgiven'. At night she began to be delirious, and in the morning she had brain-fever. She was in bed for six weeks.

PART TWO

CHAPTER 1

The Dream of Pride

Lukerya has just announced that she can't go on living here and that she is going away as soon as her lady is buried. I knelt down and prayed for five minutes. I wanted to pray for an hour, but I keep thinking and thinking, and always sick thoughts, and my head aches – what is the use of praying? – it's only a sin! It is strange, too, that I am not sleepy: in great, too great sorrow, after the first outbursts one is always sleepy. Men condemned to death, they say, sleep very soundly on the last night. And so it must be, it is the law of nature, otherwise their strength would not hold out . . . I lay down on the sofa but I did not sleep . . .

. . . For the six weeks of her illness we were looking after her day and night – Lukerya and I together with a trained nurse whom I had engaged from the hospital. I spared no expense – in fact, I was eager to spend my money on her. I called in Dr Shreder and paid him ten roubles a visit. When she began to get better I did not show myself so much. But why am I describing it? When she got up again, she sat quietly and silently in my room at a special table, which I had bought for her, too, about that time . . . Yes, that's the truth, we were absolutely silent; that is, we began talking afterwards, but only of the daily routine. I purposely avoided expressing myself, but I noticed that she, too, was glad not to have to say a word more than was necessary. It seemed to me that this was perfectly normal on her part: 'She is too much shattered, too completely conquered,' I thought, 'and I must let her forget and grow used to it.' In this way we were silent, but every minute I was preparing myself for the future. I thought that she was too, and it was fearfully interesting to me to guess what she was thinking about to herself then.

I will say more: oh! of course, no one knows what I went through, moaning over her in her illness. But I stifled my moans in my own heart, even from Lukerya. I could not imagine, could not even conceive of her dying without knowing the whole truth. When she was out of danger and began to regain her health, I very quickly and completely, I remember, recovered my tranquillity. What is more, I made up my mind to *defer out future* as long as possible, and meanwhile to leave things just as they were. Yes, something strange and peculiar happened to me then, I cannot call it anything else: I had triumphed, and the mere consciousness of that was enough for me. So the whole winter passed. Oh! I was satisfied as I had never been before, and it lasted the whole winter.

You see, there had been a terrible external circumstance in my life which, up till then – that is, up to the catastrophe with my wife – had weighed upon me every day and every hour. I mean the loss of my reputation and my leaving the regiment. In two words, I was treated with tyrannical injustice. It is true my comrades did not love me because of my difficult character, and perhaps because of my absurd character, though it often happens that what is exalted, precious and of value to one, for some reason amuses the herd of one's companions. Oh, I was never liked, not even at school! I was always and everywhere disliked. Even Lukerya cannot like me. What happened in the regiment, though it was the result of their dislike of me, was in a sense accidental. I mention this because nothing is more mortifying and insufferable than to be ruined by an accident, which might have happened or not have happened, from an unfortunate accumulation of circumstances which might have passed over like a cloud. For an intelligent being it is humiliating. This is what happened.

In an interval, at a theatre, I went out to the refreshment bar. A hussar called A— came in and began, before all the officers present and the public, loudly talking to two other hussars, telling them that Captain Bezumtsev, of our regiment, was making a disgraceful scene in the passage and was, 'he believed, drunk'. The conversation did not go further and, indeed, it was a mistake, for Captain Bezumtsev was not drunk and the 'disgraceful scene' was not really disgraceful. The hussars began talking of something else, and the matter ended there, but the next day the story reached our regiment, and then they began saying at once that I was the only officer of our regiment in the refreshment bar at the time, and that when A— the hussar, had spoken insolently of Captain Bezumtsev, I had not gone up to A— and stopped him by remonstrating. But on what grounds could I have done so? If he had a grudge against Bezumtsev, it was their personal affair and why should I interfere? Meanwhile, the officers began to declare that it was not a personal affair, but that it concerned the regiment, and as I was the only officer of the regiment present I had thereby shown all the officers and other people in the refreshment bar that there could be officers in our regiment who were not over-sensitive on the score of their own honour and the honour of their regiment. I could not agree with this view.

They let me know that I could set everything right if I were willing, even now, late as it was, to demand a formal explanation from A—. I was not willing to do this, and as I was irritated I refused with pride. And thereupon I forthwith resigned my commission – that is the whole story. I left the regiment, proud but crushed in spirit. I was depressed in will and mind. Just then it was that my sister's husband in Moscow squandered all our little property and my portion of it, which was tiny enough, but the loss of it left me homeless, without a farthing. I might have taken a job in a private business, but I did not. After wearing a distinguished uniform I could not take work in a railway office. And so – if it must be shame, let it be shame; if it must be disgrace, let it be disgrace; if it must be degradation, let it be degradation – (the worse it is, the better) that was my choice. Then followed three years of gloomy memories, and even Vyazemsky's House. A year and a half ago my godmother, a wealthy old lady, died in Moscow, and to my surprise left me three thousand in her will. I thought a little and immediately decided on my course of action. I determined on setting up as a pawnbroker, without apologising to anyone: money, then a home, as far as possible from memories of the past, that was my plan. Nevertheless, the gloomy past and my ruined reputation fretted me every day, every hour. But then I married. Whether it was by chance or not I don't know. But when I brought her into my home I thought I was bringing a friend, and I needed a friend so much. But I saw clearly that the friend must be trained, schooled, even conquered. Could I have explained myself straight off to a girl of sixteen with her prejudices? How, for instance, could I, without the chance help of the horrible incident with the revolver, have made her believe I was not a coward, and that I had been unjustly accused of cowardice in the regiment? But that terrible incident came just in the nick of time. Standing the test of the revolver, I scored off all my gloomy past. And though no one knew about it, she knew, and for me that was everything, because she was everything for me, all the hope of the future that I cherished in my dreams! She was the one person I had prepared for myself, and I needed no one else – and here she knew everything; she knew, at any rate, that she had been in haste to join my enemies against me unjustly. That thought enchanted me. In her eyes I could not be a scoundrel, now, but at most a strange person, and that thought after all that had happened was by no means displeasing to me; strangeness is not a vice – on the contrary, it sometimes attracts the feminine heart. In fact, I purposely deferred the climax: what had happened was, meanwhile, enough for my peace of mind and provided a great number of pictures and materials for my dreams. That is what is wrong, that I am a dreamer: I had enough material for my dreams, and about her I thought she could wait.

So the whole winter passed in a sort of expectation. I liked looking at her on the sly, when she was sitting at her little table. She was busy at her needlework, and sometimes in the evening she read books taken from my bookcase. The choice of books in the bookcase must have had an influence in my favour too. She hardly ever went out. Just before dusk, after dinner, I used to take her out every day for a walk. We took a constitutional, but we were not absolutely silent, as we used to be. I tried, in fact, to make a show of our not being silent, but talking harmoniously, but as I have said already, we both avoided letting ourselves go. I did it purposely, I thought it was essential to 'give her time'. Of course, it was strange that almost till the end of the winter it did not once strike me that, though I love to watch her stealthily, I had never once, all the winter, caught her glancing at me! I thought it was timidity in her. Besides, she had an air of such timid gentleness, such weakness after her illness. Yes, better to wait and – 'she will come to you all at once of herself . . . '

That thought fascinated me beyond all words. I will add one thing; sometimes, as it were purposely, I worked myself up and brought my mind and spirit to the point of believing she had injured me. And so it went on for some time. But my anger could never be very real or violent. And I felt myself as though it were only acting. And though I had broken off out marriage by buying that bedstead and screen, I could never, never look upon her as a criminal. And not that I took a frivolous view of her crime, but because I had the sense to forgive her completely, from the very first day, even before I bought the bedstead. In fact, it is strange on my part, for I am strict in moral questions. On the contrary, in my eyes, she was so conquered, so humiliated, so crushed, that sometimes I felt agonies of pity for her, though sometimes the thought of her humiliation was actually pleasing to me. The thought of our inequality pleased me . . .

I intentionally performed several acts of kindness that winter. I excused two debts, I gave one poor woman money without any pledge. And I said nothing to my wife about it, and I didn't do it in order that she should know; but the woman came to thank me, almost on her knees. And in that way it became public property; it seemed to me that she heard about the woman with pleasure.

But spring was coming, it was mid-April, we took out the double windows and the sun began lighting up our silent room with its bright beams. But there was, as it were, a veil before my eyes and a blindness over my mind. A fatal, terrible veil! How did it happen that the scales suddenly fell from my eyes, and I suddenly saw and understood? Was it a chance, or had the hour come, or did a ray of sunshine kindle a thought, a conjecture, in my dull mind? No, it was not a thought, not a conjecture. But a chord suddenly vibrated, a feeling that had long been dead was stirred and came to life, flooding all my darkened soul and devilish pride with light. It was as though I had suddenly leaped up from my place. And, indeed, it happened suddenly and abruptly. It happened towards evening, at five o'clock, after dinner . . .

CHAPTER 2

The Veil Suddenly Falls

Two words first. A month ago I noticed a strange melancholy in her, not simply silence, but melancholy. That, too, I noticed suddenly. She was sitting at her work, her head bent over her sewing, and she did not see that I was looking at her. And it suddenly struck me that she had grown so delicate-looking, so thin, that her face was pale, her lips were white. All this, together with her melancholy, struck me all at once. I had already heard a little dry cough, especially at night. I got up at once and went off to ask Shreder to come, saying nothing to her.

Shreder came next day. She was very much surprised and looked first at Shreder and then at me.

'But I am well,' she said, with an uncertain smile.

Shreder did not examine her very carefully (these doctors are some-times superciliously careless), he only said to me in the other room that it was just the result of her illness, and that it wouldn't be amiss to go for a trip to the sea in the spring, or, if that were impossible, to take a cottage out of town for the summer. In fact, he said nothing except that there was weakness, or something of that sort. When Shreder had gone, she said again, looking at me very earnestly: 'I am quite well, quite well.'

But as she said this she suddenly flushed, apparently from shame. Apparently it was shame. Oh! now I understand: she was ashamed that I was still *her husband*, that I was looking after her still as though I were a real husband. But at the time I did not understand and put down her blush to humility (the veil!).

And so, a month later, in April, at five o'clock on a bright sunny day, I was sitting in the shop making up my accounts. Suddenly I heard her, sitting in our room, at work at her table, begin softly, softly . . . singing. This novelty made an overwhelming impression upon me, and to this day I don't understand it. Till then I had hardly ever heard her sing, unless, perhaps, in those first days, when we were still able to be playful and practise shooting at a target. Then her voice was rather strong, resonant; though not quite true it was very sweet and healthy. Now her little song was so faint – it was not that it was melancholy (it was some sort of ballad), but in her voice there was something jangled, broken, as though her voice were not equal to it, as though the song itself were sick. She sang in an undertone, and suddenly, as her voice rose, it broke – such a poor little voice, it broke so pitifully; she cleared her throat and again began softly, softly singing . . .

My emotions will be ridiculed, but no one will understand why I was so moved! No, I was still not sorry for her, it was still something quite different. At the beginning, for the first minute, at any rate, I was filled with sudden perplexity and terrible amazement – a terrible and strange, painful and almost vindictive amazement: 'She is singing, and before me; *has she forgotten about me?*'

Completely overwhelmed, I remained where I was, then I suddenly got up, took my hat and went out, as it were, without thinking. At least I don't know why or where I was going. Lukerya began giving me my overcoat.

'She is singing?' I said to Lukerya involuntarily. She did not understand, and looked at me still without understanding; and, indeed, I was really unintelligible.

'Is it the first time she is singing?'

'No, she sometimes does sing when you are out,' answered Lukerya.

I remember everything. I went downstairs, went out into the street and walked along at random. I walked to the corner and began looking into the distance. People were passing by, the pushed against me. I did not feel it. I called a cab and told the man, I don't know why, to drive to Politseysky Bridge.[281] Then suddenly changed my mind and gave him twenty kopecks.

'That's for my having troubled you,' I said, with a meaningless laugh, but a sort of ecstasy was suddenly shining within me.

I returned home, quickening my steps. The poor little jangled, broken note was ringing in my heart again. My breath failed me. The veil was falling, was falling from my eyes! Since she sang before me, she had forgotten me – that is what was clear and terrible. My heart felt it. But rapture was glowing in my soul and it overcame my terror.

Oh! the irony of fate! Why, there had been nothing else, and could have been nothing else but that rapture in my soul all the winter, but where had I been myself all the winter? Had I been there together with my soul? I ran up the stairs in great haste, I don't know whether I went in timidly. I only remember that the whole floor seemed to be rocking and I felt as though I were floating on a river. I went into the room. She was sitting in the same place as before, with her head bent over her sewing, but she wasn't singing now. She looked cursorily and without interest at me; it was hardly a look but just a habitual and indifferent movement upon somebody's coming into the room.

I went straight up and sat down beside her in a chair abruptly, as though I were mad. She looked at me quickly, seeming frightened; I took her hand and I don't remember what I said to her – that is, tried to say, for I could not even speak properly. My voice broke and would not obey me and I did not know what to say. I could only gasp for breath.

'Let us talk . . . you know . . . tell me something!' I muttered something stupid. Oh! how could I help being stupid? She started again and drew back in great alarm, looking at my face, but suddenly there was an expression of *stern surprise* in her eyes. Yes, surprise and *stern*. She looked at me with wide-open eyes. That sternness, that stern surprise shattered me at once: 'So you still expect love? Love?' that surprise seemed to be asking, though she said nothing. But I read it all, I read it all. Everything within me seemed quivering, and I simply fell down at her feet. Yes, I grovelled at her feet. She jumped up quickly, but I held her forcibly by both hands.

And I fully understood my despair – I understood it! But, would you believe it? ecstasy was surging up in my head so violently that I thought I should die. I kissed her feet in delirium and rapture. Yes, in immense, infinite rapture, and that, in spite of understanding all the hopelessness of my despair. I wept, said something, but could not speak. Her alarm and amazement were followed by some uneasy misgiving, some grave question, and she looked at me strangely, wildly even; she wanted to understand something quickly and she smiled. She was horribly ashamed at my kissing her feet and she drew them back. But I kissed the place on the floor where her foot had rested. She saw it and suddenly began laughing with shame (you know how it is when people laugh with shame). She became hysterical, I saw that her hands trembled – I did not think about that but went on muttering that I loved her, that I would not get up. 'Let me kiss your dress . . . and worship you like this all my life.' . . . I don't know, I don't remember – but suddenly she broke into sobs and trembled all over. A terrible fit of hysterics followed. I had frightened her.

I carried her to the bed. When the attack had passed off, sitting on the edge of the bed, with a terribly exhausted look, she took my two hands and begged me to calm myself: 'Come, come, don't distress yourself, be calm!' and she began crying again. All that evening I did not leave her side. I kept telling her I should take her to Boulogne[282] to bathe in the sea now, at once, in a fortnight, that she had such a broken voice, I had heard it that afternoon, that I would shut up the shop, that I would sell it to Dobronravov, that everything should begin afresh and, above all, Boulogne, Boulogne! She listened and was still afraid. She grew more and more afraid. But that was not what mattered most for me: what mattered most to me was the more and more irresistible longing to fall at her feet again, and again to kiss and kiss the spot where her foot had rested, and to worship her; and – 'I ask nothing, nothing more of you,' I kept repeating, 'do not answer me, take no notice of me, only let me watch you from my corner, treat me as your dog, your thing . . . ' She was crying.

'*I thought you would let me go on like that*,' suddenly broke from her unconsciously, so unconsciously that, perhaps, she did not notice what she had said, and yet – oh, that was the most significant, momentous phrase she uttered that evening, the easiest for me to understand, and it stabbed my heart as though with a knife! It explained everything to me, everything, but while she was beside me, before my eyes, I could not help hoping and was fearfully happy. Oh, I exhausted her fearfully that evening. I understood that, but I kept thinking that I should alter everything directly. At last, towards night, she was utterly exhausted. I persuaded her to go to sleep and she fell sound asleep at once. I expected her to be delirious and she was a little delirious, but very slightly. I kept getting up every minute in the night and going softly in my slippers to look at her. I wrung my hands over her, looking at that frail creature in that wretched little iron bedstead which I had bought for three roubles. I knelt down, but did not dare to kiss her feet in her sleep (without her consent). I began praying but leapt up again. Lukerya kept watch over me and came in and out from the kitchen. I went in to her, and told her to go to bed, and that tomorrow 'things would be quite different'.

And I believed in this, blindly, madly.

Oh, I was brimming over with rapture, rapture! I was eager for the next day. Above all, I did not believe that anything could go wrong, in spite of the symptoms. Reason had not altogether come back to me, though the veil had fallen from my eyes, and for a long, long time it did not come back – not till today, not till this very day! Yes, and how could it have come back then? why, she was still alive then; why, she was here before my eyes, and I was before her eyes: 'Tomorrow she will wake up and I will tell her all this, and she will see it all.' That was how I reasoned then, simply and clearly, because I was in an ecstasy! My great idea was the trip to Boulogne. I kept thinking for some reason that Boulogne would be everything, that there was something final and decisive about Boulogne. 'To Boulogne, to Boulogne!' . . . I waited frantically for the morning.

CHAPTER 3

I Understand Too Well

But you know that was only a few days ago, five days, only five days ago, last Tuesday! Yes, yes, if there had only been a little longer, if she had only waited a little – and I would have dissipated the darkness! – It was not as though she had not recovered her calmness. The very next day she listened to me with a smile, in spite of her confusion . . . All this time, all these five days, she was either confused or ashamed. She was afraid, too, very much afraid. I don't dispute it, I am not so mad as to deny it. It was terror, but how could she help being frightened? We had so long been strangers to one another, had grown so alienated from one another, and suddenly all this . . . But I did not look at her terror. I was dazzled by the new life beginning! . . . It is true, it is undoubtedly true that I made a mistake. There were even, perhaps, many mistakes. When I woke up next day, the first thing in the morning (that was on Wednesday), I made a mistake: I suddenly made her my friend. I was in too great a hurry, but a confession was necessary, inevitable – more than a confession! I did not even hide what I had hidden from myself all my life. I told her straight out that the whole winter I had been doing nothing but brood over the certainty of her love. I made clear to her that my money-lending had been simply the degradation of my will and my mind, my personal idea of self-castigation and self-exaltation. I explained to her that I really had been cowardly that time in the refreshment bar, that it was owing to my temperament, to my self-consciousness. I was impressed by the surroundings, by the theatre: I was doubtful how I should succeed and whether it would be stupid. I was not afraid of a duel, but of its being stupid . . . and afterwards I would not own it and tormented everyone and had tormented her for it, and had married her so as to torment her for it. In fact, for the most part I talked as though in delirium. She herself took my hands and made me leave off. 'You are exaggerating . . . you are distressing yourself,' and again there were tears, again almost hysterics! She kept begging me not to say all this, not to recall it.

I took no notice of her entreaties, or hardly noticed them: 'Spring, Boulogne! There there would be sunshine, there our new sunshine,' I kept saying that! I shut up the shop and transferred it to Dobronravov. I suddenly suggested to her giving all our money to the poor except the three thousand left me by my godmother, which we would spend on going to Boulogne, and then we would come back and begin a new life of real work. So we decided, for she said nothing . . . She only smiled. And I believe she smiled chiefly from delicacy, for fear of disappointing me. I saw, of course, that I was burdensome to her, don't imagine I was so stupid or egoistic as not to see it. I saw it all, all, to the smallest detail, I saw better than anyone; all the hopelessness of my position stood revealed.

I told her everything about myself and about her. And about Lukerya. I told her that I had wept . . . Oh, of course, I changed the conversation. I tried, too, not to say a word more about certain things. And, indeed, she did revive once or twice – I remember it, I remember it! Why do you say I looked at her and saw nothing? And if only *this* had not happened, everything would have come to life again. Why, only the day before yesterday, when we were talking of reading and what she had been reading all winter, she told me something herself, and laughed as she told me, recalling the scene of Gil Blas and the Archbishop of Granada.[283] And with that sweet, childish laughter, just as in the old days when we were engaged (one instant! one instant!); how glad I was! I was awfully struck, though, by the story of the Archbishop; so she had found peace of mind and happiness enough to laugh at that literary masterpiece while she was sitting there in the winter. So then she had begun to be fully at rest, had begun to believe confidently 'that I should leave her *like that*. I thought you would leave me like that,' those were the words she uttered then on Tuesday! Oh! the thought of a child of ten! And you know she believed it, she believed that really everything would remain *like that*: she at her table and I at mine, and we both should go on like that till we were sixty. And all at once – I come forward, her husband, and the husband wants love! Oh, the delusion! Oh, my blindness!

It was a mistake, too, that I looked at her with rapture; I ought to have controlled myself, as it was my rapture frightened her. But, indeed, I did control myself, I did not kiss her feet again. I never made a sign of . . . well, that I was her husband – oh, there was no thought of that in my mind, I only worshipped her! But, you know, I couldn't be quite silent, I could not refrain from speaking altogether! I suddenly said to her frankly that I enjoyed her conversation and that I thought her incomparably more cultured and developed than I. She flushed crimson and said in confusion that I exaggerated. Then, like a fool, I could not resist telling her how delighted I had been when I had stood behind the door listening to her duel, the duel of innocence with that low cad, and how I had enjoyed her cleverness, the brilliance of her wit, and, at the same time, her childlike simplicity. She seemed to shudder all over, was murmuring again that I exaggerated, but suddenly her whole face darkened, she hid it in her hands and broke into sobs . . . Then I could not restrain myself: again I fell at her feet, again I began kissing her feet, and again it ended in a fit of hysterics, just as on Tuesday. That was yesterday evening – and – in the morning . . .

In the morning! Madman! why, that morning was today, just now, only just now!

Listen and try to understand: why, when we met by the samovar (it was after yesterday's hysterics), I was actually struck by her calmness, that is the actual fact! And all night I had been trembling with terror over what happened yesterday. But suddenly she came up to me and, clasping her hands (this morning, this morning!), began telling me that she was a criminal, that she knew it, that her crime had been torturing her all the winter, was torturing her now . . . That she appreciated my generosity . . . 'I will be your faithful wife, I will respect you . . . '

Then I leapt up and embraced her like a madman. I kissed her, kissed her face, kissed her lips like a husband for the first time after a long separation. And why did I go out this morning, only two hours . . . our passports for abroad . . . Oh, God! if only I had come back five minutes, only five minutes earlier! . . . That crowd at our gates, those eyes all fixed upon me. Oh, God!

Lukerya says (oh! I will not let Lukerya go now for anything. She knows all about it, she has been here all the winter, she will tell me everything!), she says that when I had gone out of the house and only about twenty minutes before I came back – she suddenly went into our room to her mistress to ask her something, I don't remember what, and saw that her ikon (that same ikon of the Mother of God) had been taken down and was standing before her on the table, and her mistress seemed to have only just been praying before it. 'What are you doing, mistress?' 'Nothing, Lukerya, run along.' Then, 'Wait a minute, Lukerya.' 'She came up and kissed me. "Are you happy, mistress?" I said. "Yes, Lukerya," "Master ought to have come to beg your pardon long ago, mistress . . . Thank God that you are reconciled." "Very good, Lukerya," she said. "Go away, Lukerya," and she smiled, but so strangely. So strangely that Lukerya went back ten minutes later to have a look at her.

'She was standing by the wall, close to the window, she had laid her arm against the wall, and her head was pressed on her arm, she was standing like that thinking. And she was standing so deep in thought that she did not hear me come and look at her from the other room. She seemed to be smiling – standing, thinking and smiling. I looked at her, turned softly and went out wondering to myself, and suddenly I heard the window opened. I went in at once to say: "It's fresh, mistress; mind you don't catch cold," and suddenly I saw she had got on the window ledge and was standing there, her full height, in the open window, with her back to me, holding the ikon in her hand. My heart sank on the spot. I cried, "Mistress, mistress." She heard, made a movement to turn back to me, but, instead of turning back, took a step forward, pressed the ikon to her bosom, and flung herself out of the window.'

I only remember that when I went in at the gate she was still warm. The worst of it was they were all looking at me. At first they shouted and then suddenly they were silent, and then all of them moved away from me . . . and she was lying there with the ikon. I remember, as it were, in a darkness, that I went up to her in silence and looked at her a long while. But all came round me and said something to me. Lukerya was there too, but I did not see her. She says she said something to me. I only remember that workman. He kept shouting to me that, 'Only a handful of blood came from her mouth, a handful, a handful!' and he pointed to the blood on a stone. I believe I touched the blood with my finger, I smeared my finger, I looked at my finger (that I remember), and he kept repeating: 'a handful, a handful!'

'What do you mean by a handful?' I yelled with all my might, I am told, and I lifted up my hands and rushed at him.

Oh, wild! wild! Delusion! Monstrous! Impossible!

CHAPTER 4

I was Only Five Minutes Too Late

Is it not so? Is it likely? Can one really say it was possible? What for, why did this woman die?

Oh, believe me, I understand, but why she died is still a question. She was frightened of my love, asked herself seriously whether to accept it or not, could not bear the question and preferred to die. I know, I know, no need to rack my brains: she had made too many promises, she was afraid she could not keep them – it is clear. There are circumstances about it quite awful.

For why did she die? That is still a question, after all. The question hammers, hammers at my brain. I would have left her *like that* if she had wanted to remain *like that*. She did not believe it, that's what it was! No – no. I am talking nonsense, it was not that at all. It was simply because with me she had to be honest – if she loved me, she would have had to love me altogether, and not as she would have loved the grocer. And as she was too chaste, too pure, to consent to such love as the grocer wanted she did not want to deceive me. Did not want to deceive me with half love, counterfeiting love, or a quarter love. They are honest, too honest, that is what it is! I wanted to instil breadth of heart in her, in those days, do you remember? A strange idea.

It is awfully interesting to know: did she respect me or not? I don't know whether she despised me or not. I don't believe she did despise me. It is awfully strange: why did it never once enter my head all the winter that she despised me? I was absolutely convinced of the contrary up to that moment when she looked at me with *stern surprise*. Stern it was. I understood on the spot that she despised me. I understood once for all, for ever! Ah, let her, let her despise me all her life even, only let her be living! Only yesterday she was walking about, talking. I simply can't understand how she threw herself out of the window! And how could I have imagined it five minutes before? I have called Lukerya. I won't let Lukerya go now for anything!

Oh, we might still have understood each other! We had simply become terribly estranged from one another during the winter, but couldn't we have grown used to each other again? Why, why, couldn't we have come together again and begun a new life again? I am generous, she was too – that was a point in common! Only a few more words, another two days – no more, and she would have understood everything.

What is most mortifying of all is that it is chance – simply a barbarous, lagging chance. That is what is mortifying! Five minutes, only five minutes too late! Had I come five minutes earlier, the moment would have passed away like a cloud, and it would never have entered her head again. And it would have ended by her understanding it all. But now again empty rooms, and me alone. Here the pendulum is ticking; it does not care, it has no pity . . . There is no one – that's the misery of it!

I keep walking about, I keep walking about. I know, I know, you need not tell me; it amuses you, you think it absurd that I complain of chance and those five minutes. But it is evident. Consider one thing: she did not even leave a note to say, 'Blame no one for my death,' as people always do. Might she not have thought that Lukerya might get into trouble. 'She was alone with her,' might have been said, 'and pushed her out.' In any case she would have been taken up by the police if it had not happened that four people, from the windows, from the lodge and from the yard, had seen her stand with the ikon in her hands and jump out of herself. But that, too, was a chance, that the people were standing there and saw her. No, it was all a moment, only an irresponsible moment. A sudden impulse, a fantasy! What if she did pray before the ikon? It does not follow that she was facing death. The whole impulse lasted, perhaps, only some ten minutes; it was all decided, perhaps, while she stood against the wall with her head on her arm, smiling. The idea darted into her brain, she turned giddy and – and could not resist it.

Say what you will, it was clearly a misunderstanding. It would have been possible to live with me. And what if it were anaemia? Was it simply from poorness of blood, from the flagging of vital energy? She had grown tired during the winter, that was what it was . . .

I was too late!!!

How thin she is in her coffin, how sharp her nose has grown! Her eyelashes lie straight as arrows. And, you know, when she fell, nothing was crushed, nothing was broken! Nothing but that 'handful of blood'. A dessertspoonful, that is. From internal injury. A strange thought: if only it were possible not to bury her? For if they take her away, then . . . oh, no, it is almost incredible that they should take her away! I am not mad and I am not raving – on the contrary, my mind was never so lucid – but what shall I do when again there is no one, only the two rooms, and me alone with the pledges? Madness, madness, madness! I worried her to death, that is what it is!

What are your laws to me now? What do I care for your customs, your morals, your life, your state, your faith! Let your judge judge me, let me be brought before your court, let me be tried by jury, and I shall say that I admit nothing. The judge will shout, 'Be silent, officer.' And I will shout to him, 'What power have you now that I will obey? Why did blind, inert force destroy that which was dearest of all? What are your laws to me now? They are nothing to me.' Oh, I don't care!

She was blind, blind! She is dead, she does not hear! You do not know with what paradise I would have surrounded you. There was paradise in my soul, I would have made it blossom around you! Well, you wouldn't have loved me – so be it, what of it? Things should still have been *like that*, everything should have remained *like that*. You should only have talked to me as a friend – we could have rejoiced and laughed with joy looking at one another. And so we should have lived. And if you had loved another – well, so be it, so be it! You should have walked with him laughing, and I should have watched you from the other side of the street . . . Oh, anything, anything, if only she would open her eyes just once! For one instant, only one! If she would look at me as she did this morning, when she stood before me and made a vow to be a faithful wife! Oh, in one look she would have understood it all!

Oh, blind force! Oh, nature! Men are alone on earth – that is what is dreadful! 'Is there a living man in the country?' cried the Russian hero. I cry the same, though I am not a hero, and no one answers my cry. They say the sun gives life to the universe. The sun is rising and – look at it, is it not dead? Everything is dead and everywhere there are dead. Men are alone – around them is silence – that is the earth! 'Men, love one another' – who said that?[284] Whose commandment is that? The pendulum ticks callously, heartlessly. Two o'clock at night. Her little shoes are standing by the little bed, as though waiting for her . . . No, seriously, when they take her away tomorrow, what will become of me?

The Peasant Marey

I T WAS THE SECOND DAY in Easter week. The air was warm, the sky was blue, the sun was high, warm, bright, but my soul was very gloomy. I sauntered behind the prison barracks. I stared at the palings of the stout prison fence, counting the movers; but I had no inclination to count them, though it was my habit to do so. This was the second day of the 'holidays' in the prison; the convicts were not taken out to work; there were numbers of men drunk, loud abuse and quarrelling were springing up continually in every corner. There were hideous, disgusting songs and card-parties installed beside the platform-beds. Several of the convicts who had been sentenced by their comrades for special violence, to be beaten till they were half dead, were lying on the platform-beds covered with sheepskins till they should recover and come to themselves again; knives had already been drawn several times. For these two days of holiday all this had been torturing me till it made me ill. And indeed I could never endure without repulsion the noise and disorder of drunken people, and especially in this place. On these days even the prison officials did not look into the prison, made no searches, did not look for vodka, understanding that they must allow even these outcasts to enjoy themselves once a year, and that things would be even worse if they did not. At last a sudden fury flamed up in my heart. A political prisoner called M. met me; he looked at me gloomily, his eyes flashed and his lips quivered. '*Je haïs ces brigands!*'[285] he hissed to me through his teeth, and walked on. I returned to the prison ward, though only a quarter of an hour before I had rushed out of it, as though I were crazy, when six stalwart fellows had all together flung themselves upon the drunken Tatar Gazin to suppress him and had begun beating him; they beat him stupidly, a camel might have been killed by such blows, but they knew that this Herçules[286] was not easy to kill, and so they beat him without uneasiness. Now, on returning, I noticed on the bed in the farthest corner of the room Gazin lying unconscious, almost without sign of life. He lay covered with a sheepskin, and everyone walked round him, without speaking; though they confidently hoped that he would come to himself next morning, yet if luck was against him, maybe from a beating like that, the man would die. I made my way to my own place opposite the window with the iron grating, and lay on my back with my hands behind my head and my eyes shut. I liked to lie like that; a sleeping man is not molested, and meanwhile one can dream and think. But I could not dream, my heart was beating uneasily, and M.'s words, '*Je haïs ces brigands!*' were echoing in my ears. But why describe my impressions; I sometimes dream even now of those times at night, and I have no dreams more agonising. Perhaps it will be noticed that even to this day I have scarcely once spoken in print of my life in prison. *The House of the Dead*[287] I wrote fifteen years ago in the character of an imaginary person, a criminal who had killed his wife. I may add by the way that since then, very many persons have supposed, and even now maintain, that I was sent to penal servitude for the murder of my wife.

Gradually I sank into forgetfulness and by degrees was lost in memories. During the whole course of my four years in prison I was continually recalling all my past, and seemed to live over again the whole of my life in recollection. These memories rose up of themselves, it was not often that of my own will I summoned them. It would begin from some point, some little thing, at times unnoticed, and then by degrees there would rise up a complete picture, some vivid and complete impression. I used to analyse these impressions, give new features to what had happened long ago, and best of all, I used to correct it, correct it continually, that was my great amusement. On this occasion, I suddenly for some reason remembered an unnoticed moment in my early childhood when I was only nine years old – a moment which I should have thought I had utterly forgotten; but at that time I was particularly fond of memories of my early childhood. I remembered the month of August in our country house: a dry bright day but rather cold and windy; summer was waning and soon we should have to go to Moscow to be bored all the winter over French lessons, and I was so sorry to leave the country. I walked past the threshing-floor and, going down the ravine, I went up to the dense thicket of bushes that covered the farther side of the ravine as far as the copse. And I plunged right into the midst of the bushes, and heard a peasant ploughing alone on the clearing about thirty paces away. I knew that he was ploughing up the steep hill and the horse was moving with effort, and from time to time the peasant's call, 'Come up!' floated upwards to me. I knew almost all our peasants, but I did not know which it was ploughing now, and I did not care who it was, I was absorbed in my own affairs. I was busy, too; I was breaking off switches from the nut trees to whip the frogs with. Nut sticks make such fine whips, but they do not last; while birch twigs are just the opposite. I was interested, too, in beetles and other insects; I used to collect them, some were very ornamental. I was very fond, too, of the little nimble red and yellow lizards with black spots on them, but I was afraid of snakes. Snakes, however, were much more rare than lizards. There were not many mushrooms there. To get mushrooms one had to go to the birch wood, and I was about to set off there. And there was nothing in the world that I loved so much as the wood with its mushrooms and wild berries, with its beetles and its birds, its hedgehogs and squirrels, with its damp smell of dead leaves which I loved so much, and even as I write I smell the fragrance of our birch wood: these impressions will remain for my whole life. Suddenly in the midst of the profound stillness I heard a clear and distinct shout, 'Wolf!' I shrieked and, beside myself with terror, calling out at the top of my voice, ran out into the clearing and straight to the peasant who was ploughing.

It was our peasant Marey. I don't know if there is such a name, but everyone called him Marey – a thickset, rather well-grown peasant of fifty, with a good many grey hairs in his dark brown, spreading beard. I knew him, but had scarcely ever happened to speak to him till then. He stopped his horse on hearing my cry, and when, breathless, I caught with one hand at his plough and with the other at his sleeve, he saw how frightened I was.

'There is a wolf!' I cried, panting.

He flung up his head, and could not help looking round for an instant, almost believing me.

'Where is the wolf?'

'A shout . . . someone shouted: "Wolf" . . . ' I faltered out.

'Nonsense, nonsense! A wolf? Why, it was your fancy! How could there be a wolf?' he muttered, reassuring me. But I was trembling all over, and still kept tight hold of his smock frock, and I must have been quite pale. He looked at me with an uneasy smile, evidently anxious and troubled over me.

'Why, you have had a fright, aïe, aïe!' He shook his head. 'There, dear . . . Come, little one, aïe!"

He stretched out his hand, and all at once stroked my cheek.

'Come, come, there; Christ be with you! Cross yourself!'

But I did not cross myself. The corners of my mouth were twitching, and I think that struck him particularly. He put out his thick, black-nailed, earth-stained finger and softly touched my twitching lips.

'Aïe, there, there,' he said to me with a slow, almost motherly smile. 'Dear, dear, what is the matter? There; come, come!'

I grasped at last that there was no wolf, and that the shout that I had heard was my fancy. Yet that shout had been so clear and distinct, but such shouts (not only about wolves) I had imagined once or twice before, and I was aware of that. (These hallucinations passed away later as I grew older.)

'Well, I will go then,' I said, looking at him timidly and enquiringly.

'Well, do, and I'll keep watch on you as you go. I won't let the wolf get at you,' he added, still smiling at me with the same motherly expression. 'Well, Christ be with you! Come, run along then,' and he made the sign of the cross over me and then over himself. I walked away, looking back almost at every tenth step. Marey stood still with his mare as I walked away, and looked after me and nodded to me every time I looked round. I must own I felt a little ashamed at having let him see me so frightened, but I was still very much afraid of the wolf as I walked away, until I reached the first barn halfway up the slope of the ravine; there my fright vanished completely, and all at once our yard-dog Voltchok flew to meet me. With Voltchok I felt quite safe, and I turned round to Marey for the last time; I could not see his face distinctly, but I felt that he was still nodding and smiling affectionately to me. I waved to him; he waved back to me and started his little mare. 'Come up!' I heard his call in the distance again, and the little mare pulled at the plough again.

All this I recalled all at once, I don't know why, but with extra-ordinary minuteness of detail. I suddenly roused myself and sat up on the platform-bed, and, I remember, found myself still smiling quietly at my memories. I brooded over them for another minute.

When I got home that day I told no one of my 'adventure' with Marey. And indeed it was hardly an adventure. And in fact I soon forgot Marey. When I met him now and then afterwards, I never even spoke to him about the wolf or anything else; and all at once now, twenty years afterwards in Siberia, I remembered this meeting with such distinctness to the smallest detail. So it must have lain hidden in my soul, though I knew nothing of it, and rose suddenly to my memory when it was wanted; I remembered the soft motherly smile of the poor serf, the way he signed me with the cross and shook his head. 'There, there, you have had a fright, little one!' And I remembered particularly the thick earth-stained finger with which he softly and with timid tenderness touched my quivering lips. Of course anyone would have reassured a child, but something quite different seemed to have happened in that solitary meeting; and if I had been his own son, he could not have looked at me with eyes shining with greater love. And what made him like that? He was our serf and I was his little master, after all. No one would know that he had been kind to me and reward him for it. Was he, perhaps, very fond of little children? Some people are. It was a solitary meeting in the deserted fields, and only God, perhaps, may have seen from above with what deep and humane civilised feeling, and with what delicate, almost feminine tenderness, the heart of a coarse, brutally ignorant Russian serf, who had as yet no expectation, no idea even of his freedom, may be filled. Was not this, perhaps, what Konstantin Aksakov[288] meant when he spoke of the high degree of culture of our peasantry?

And when I got down off the bed and looked around me, I remember I suddenly felt that I could look at these unhappy creatures with quite different eyes, and that suddenly by some miracle all hatred and anger had vanished utterly from my heart. I walked about, looking into the faces that I met. That shaven peasant, branded on his face as a criminal, bawling his hoarse, drunken song, may be that very Marey; I cannot look into his heart.

I met M. again that evening. Poor fellow! he could have no memories of Russian peasants, and no other view of these people but: '*Je haïs ces brigands!*' Yes, the Polish prisoners had more to bear than I.

The Dream of a Ridiculous Man

1

I AM a ridiculous person. Now they call me a madman. That would be a promotion if it were not that I remain as ridiculous in their eyes as before. But now I do not resent it, they are all dear to me now, even when they laugh at me – and, indeed, it is just then that they are particularly dear to me. I could join in their laughter – not exactly at myself, but through affection for them, if I did not feel so sad as I look at them. Sad because they do not know the truth and I do know it. Oh, how hard it is to be the only one who knows the truth! But they won't understand that. No, they won't understand it.

In the old days I used to be miserable at seeming ridiculous. Not seeming, but being. I have always been ridiculous, and I have known it, perhaps, from the hour I was born. Perhaps from the time I was seven years old I knew I was ridiculous. Afterwards I went to school, studied at the university, and, do you know, the more I learned, the more thoroughly I understood that I was ridiculous. So that it seemed in the end as though all the sciences I studied at the university existed only to prove and make evident to me as I went more deeply into them that I was ridiculous. It was the same with life as it was with science. With every year the same consciousness of the ridiculous figure I cut in every relation grew and strengthened. Everyone always laughed at me. But not one of them knew or guessed that if there were one man on earth who knew better than anybody else that I was absurd, it was myself, and what I resented most of all was that they did not know that. But that was my own fault; I was so proud that nothing would have ever induced me to tell it to anyone. This pride grew in me with the years; and if it had happened that I allowed myself to confess to anyone that I was ridiculous, I believe that I should have blown out my brains the same evening. Oh, how I suffered in my early youth from the fear that I might give way and confess it to my schoolfellows. But since I grew to manhood, I have for some unknown reason become calmer, though I realised my awful characteristic more fully every year. I say 'unknown', for to this day I cannot tell why it was. Perhaps it was owing to the terrible misery that was growing in my soul through something which was of more consequence than anything else about me: that something was the conviction that had come upon me that nothing in the world mattered. I had long had an inkling of it, but the full realisation came last year almost suddenly. I suddenly felt that it was all the same to me whether the world existed or whether there had never been anything at all: I began to feel with all my being that there was nothing existing. At first I fancied that many things had existed in the past, but afterwards I guessed that there never had been anything in the past either, but that it had only seemed so for some reason. Little by little I guessed that there would be nothing in the future either. Then I left off being angry with people and almost ceased to notice them. Indeed this showed itself even in the pettiest trifles: I used, for instance, to knock against people in the street. And not so much from being lost in thought: what had I to think about? I had almost given up thinking by that time; nothing mattered to me. If at least I had solved my problems! Oh, I had not settled one of them, and how many there were! But I gave up caring about anything, and all the problems disappeared.

And it was after that that I found out the truth. I learnt the truth last November – on the third of November, to be precise – and I remember every instant since. It was a gloomy evening, one of the gloomiest possible evenings. I was going home at about eleven o'clock, and I remember that I thought that the evening could not be gloomier. Even physically. Rain had been falling all day, and it had been a cold, gloomy, almost menacing rain, with, I remember, an unmistakable spite against mankind. Suddenly between ten and eleven it had stopped, and was followed by a horrible dampness, colder and damper than the rain, and a sort of steam was rising from everything, from every stone in the street, and from every by-lane if one looked down it as far as one could. A thought suddenly occurred to me that if all the street lamps had been put out it would have been less cheerless, that the gas made one's heart sadder because it lighted it all up. I had had scarcely any dinner that day, and had been spending the evening with an engineer, and two other friends had been there also. I sat silent – I fancy I bored them. They talked of something rousing and suddenly they got excited over it. But they did not really care, I could see that, and only made a show of being excited. I suddenly said as much to them. 'My friends,' I said, 'you really do not care one way or the other.' They were not offended, but they laughed at me. That was because I spoke without any note of reproach, simply because it did not matter to me. They saw it did not, and it amused them.

As I was thinking about the gas lamps in the street I looked up at the sky. The sky was horribly dark, but one could distinctly see tattered clouds, and between them fathomless black patches. Suddenly I noticed in one of these patches a star, and began watching it intently. That was because that star had given me an idea: I decided to kill myself that night. I had firmly determined to do so two months before, and poor as I was, I bought a splendid revolver that very day, and loaded it. But two months had passed and it was still lying in my drawer; I was so utterly indifferent that I wanted to seize a moment when I would not be so indifferent – why, I don't know. And so for two months every night that I came home I thought I would shoot myself. I kept waiting for the right moment. And so now this star gave me a thought. I made up my mind that it should certainly be that night. And why the star gave me the thought I don't know.

And just as I was looking at the sky, this little girl took me by the elbow. The street was empty, and there was scarcely anyone to be seen. A cabman was sleeping in the distance in his cab. It was a child of eight with a kerchief on her head, wearing nothing but a wretched little dress all soaked with rain, but I noticed her wet broken shoes and I recall them now. They caught my eye particularly. She suddenly pulled me by the elbow and called me. She was not weeping, but was spasmodically crying out some words which she could not utter properly because she was shivering and shuddering all over. She was in terror about something, and kept crying, 'Mammy, mammy!' I turned facing her, I did not say a word and went on; but she ran, pulling at me, and there was that note in her voice which in frightened children means despair. I know that sound. Though she did not articulate the words, I understood that her mother was dying, or that something of the sort was happening to them, and that she had run out to call someone, to find something to help her mother. I did not go with her; on the contrary, I had an impulse to drive her away. I told her first to go to a policeman. But clasping her hands, she ran beside me sobbing and gasping, and would not leave me. Then I stamped my foot and shouted at her. She called out, 'Sir! sir! . . . ' but suddenly abandoned me and rushed headlong across the road. Some other passer-by appeared there, and she evidently flew from me to him.

I mounted up to my fifth storey. I have a room in a flat where there are other lodgers. My room is small and poor, with a garret window in the shape of a semicircle. I have a sofa covered with American leather, a table with books on it, two chairs and a comfortable armchair, as old as old can be, but of the good old-fashioned shape. I sat down, lighted the candle, and began thinking. In the room next to mine, through the partition wall, a perfect bedlam was going on. It had been going on for the last three days. A retired captain lived there, and he had half a dozen visitors, gentlemen of doubtful reputation, drinking vodka and playing stoss[289] with old cards. The night before there had been a fight, and I know that two of them had been for a long time engaged in dragging each other about by the hair. The landlady wanted to complain, but she was in abject terror of the captain. There was only one other lodger in the flat, a thin little regimental lady, on a visit to Petersburg with three little children, who had been taken ill since they came into the lodgings. Both she and her children were in mortal fear of the captain, and lay trembling and crossing themselves all night, and the youngest child had a sort of fit from fright. That captain, I know for a fact, sometimes stops people in the Nevsky Prospect and begs. They won't take him into the service, but strange to say (that's why I am telling this), all this month that the captain has been here his behaviour has caused me no annoyance. I have, of course, tried to avoid his acquaintance from the very beginning, and he, too, was bored with me from the first; but I never care how much they shout the other side of the partition nor how many of them there are in there: I sit up all night and forget them so completely that I do not even hear them. I stay awake till daybreak, and have been going on like that for the last year. I sit up all night in my armchair at the table, doing nothing. I only read by day. I sit – don't even think; ideas of a sort wander through my mind and I let them come and go as they will. A whole candle is burnt every night. I sat down quietly at the table, took out the revolver and put it down before me. When I had put it down I asked myself, I remember, 'Is that so?' and answered with complete conviction, 'It is.' That is, I shall shoot myself. I knew that I should shoot myself that night for certain, but how much longer I should go on sitting at the table I did not know. And no doubt I should have shot myself if it had not been for that little girl.

2

You see, though nothing mattered to me, I could feel pain, for instance. If anyone had stuck me it would have hurt me. It was the same morally: if anything very pathetic happened, I should have felt pity just as I used to do in the old days when there were things in life that did matter to me. If I had felt pity that evening, I should have certainly helped a child. Why, then, had I not helped the little girl? Because of an idea that occurred to me at the time: when she was calling and pulling at me, a question suddenly arose before me and I could not settle it. The question was an idle one, but I was vexed. I was vexed at the reflection that if I were going to make an end of myself that night, nothing in life ought to have mattered to me. Why was it that all at once I did not feel that nothing mattered and was sorry for the little girl? I remember that I was very sorry for her, so much so that I felt a strange pang, quite incongruous in my position. Really I do not know better how to convey my fleeting sensation at the moment, but the sensation persisted at home when I was sitting at the table, and I was very much irritated as I had not been for a long time past. One reflection followed another. I saw clearly that so long as I was still a human being and not nothingness, I was alive and so could suffer, be angry and feel shame at my actions. So be it. But if I am going to kill myself, in two hours, say, what is the little girl to me and what have I to do with shame or with anything else in the world? I shall turn into nothing, absolutely nothing. And can it really be true that the consciousness that I shall *completely* cease to exist immediately and so everything else will cease to exist does not in the least affect my feeling of pity for the child nor the feeling of shame after a contemptible action? I stamped and shouted at the unhappy child as though to say – not only do I feel no pity, but even if I behave inhumanly and contemptibly, I am free to, for in another two hours everything will be extinguished. Do you believe that that was why I shouted that? I am almost convinced of it now. It seemed clear to me that life and the world somehow depended upon me now. I may almost say that the world now seemed created for me alone: if I shot myself the world would cease to be at least for me. I say nothing of its being likely that nothing will exist for anyone when I am gone, and that as soon as my consciousness is extinguished the whole world will vanish too and become void like a phantom, as a mere appurtenance of my consciousness, for possibly all this world and all these people are only me myself. I remember that as I sat and reflected, I turned all these new questions that swarmed one after another quite the other way, and thought of something quite new. For instance, a strange reflection suddenly occurred to me, that if I had lived before on the moon or on Mars and there had committed the most disgraceful and dishonourable action and had there been put to such shame and ignominy as one can only conceive and realise in dreams, in nightmares, and if, finding myself afterwards on earth, I were able to retain the memory of what I had done on the other planet and at the same time knew that I should never, under any circumstances, return there, then looking from the earth to the moon – should I care or not? Should I feel shame for that action or not? These were idle and superfluous questions for the revolver was already lying before me, and I knew in every fibre of my being that it would happen for certain, but they excited me and I raged. I could not die now without having first settled something. In short, the child had saved me, for I put off my pistol shot for the sake of these questions. Meanwhile the clamour had begun to subside in the captain's room: they had finished their game, were settling down to sleep, and meanwhile were grumbling and languidly winding up their quarrels. At that point, I suddenly fell asleep in my chair at the table – a thing which had never happened to me before. I dropped asleep quite unawares.

Dreams, as we all know, are very queer things: some parts are presented with appalling vividness, with details worked up with the elaborate finish of jewellery, while others one gallops through, as it were, without noticing them at all, as, for instance, through space and time. Dreams seem to be spurred on not by reason but by desire, not by the head but by the heart, and yet what complicated tricks my reason has played sometimes in dreams, what utterly incomprehensible things happen to it! My brother died five years ago, for instance. I sometimes dream of him; he takes part in my affairs, we are very much interested, and yet all through my dream I quite know and remember that my brother is dead and buried. How is it that I am not surprised that, though he is dead, he is here beside me and working with me? Why is it that my reason fully accepts it? But enough. I will begin about my dream. Yes, I dreamed a dream, my dream of the third of November. They tease me now, telling me it was only a dream. But does it matter whether it was a dream or reality, if the dream made known to me the truth? If once one has recognised the truth and seen it, one knows that it is the truth and that there is no other and there cannot be, whether one is asleep or awake. Let it be a dream, so be it, but that real life of which you make so much I had meant to extinguish by suicide, and my dream, my dream – oh, it revealed to me a different life, renewed, grand and full of power!

Listen.

3

I have mentioned that I dropped asleep unawares and even seemed to be still reflecting on the same subjects. I suddenly dreamt that I picked up the revolver and aimed it straight at my heart – my heart, and not my head; and I had determined beforehand to fire at my head, at my right temple. After aiming at my chest I waited a second or two, and suddenly my candle, my table, and the wall in front of me began moving and heaving. I made haste to pull the trigger.

In dreams you sometimes fall from a height, or are stabbed, or beaten, but you never feel pain unless, perhaps, you really bruise yourself against the bedstead, then you feel pain and almost always wake up from it. It was the same in my dream. I did not feel any pain, but it seemed as though with my shot everything within me was shaken and everything was suddenly dimmed, and it grew horribly black around me. I seemed to be blinded, and benumbed, and I was lying on something hard, stretched on my back; I saw nothing, and could not make the slightest movement. People were walking and shouting around me, the captain bawled, the landlady shrieked – and suddenly another break and I was being carried in a closed coffin. And I felt how the coffin was shaking and reflected upon it, and for the first time the idea struck me that I was dead, utterly dead, I knew it and had no doubt of it, I could neither see nor move and yet I was feeling and reflecting. But I was soon reconciled to the position, and as one usually does in a dream, accepted the facts without disputing them.

And now I was buried in the earth. They all went away, I was left alone, utterly alone. I did not move. Whenever before I had imagined being buried the one sensation I associated with the grave was that of damp and cold. So now I felt that I was very cold, especially the tips of my toes, but I felt nothing else.

I lay still; strange to say I expected nothing, accepting without dispute that a dead man had nothing to expect. But it was damp. I don't know how long a time passed – whether an hour, or several days, or many days. But all at once a drop of water fell on my closed left eye, making its way through the coffin lid; it was followed a minute later by a second, then a minute later by a third – and so on, regularly every minute. There was a sudden glow of profound indignation in my heart, and I suddenly felt in it a pang of physical pain. 'That's my wound,' I thought; 'that's the bullet . . . ' And drop after drop every minute kept falling on my closed eyelid. And all at once, not with my voice, but with my entire being, I called upon the power that was responsible for all that was happening to me:

'Whoever you may be, if you exist, and if anything more rational than what is happening here is possible, suffer it to be here now. But if you are revenging yourself upon me for my senseless suicide by the hideousness and absurdity of this subsequent existence, then let me tell you that no torture could ever equal the contempt which I shall go on dumbly feeling, though my martyrdom may last a million years!'

I made this appeal and held my peace. There was a full minute of unbroken silence and again another drop fell, but I knew with infinite unshakable certainty that everything would change immediately. And behold my grave suddenly was rent asunder, that is, I don't know whether it was opened or dug up, but I was caught up by some dark and unknown being and we found ourselves in space. I suddenly regained my sight. It was the dead of night, and never, never had there been such darkness. We were flying through space far away from the earth. I did not question the being who was taking me; I was proud and waited. I assured myself that I was not afraid, and was thrilled with ecstasy at the thought that I was not afraid. I do not know how long we were flying, I cannot imagine; it happened as it always does in dreams when you skip over space and time, and the laws of thought and existence, and only pause upon the points for which the heart yearns. I remember that I suddenly saw in the darkness a star. 'Is that Sirius?'[290] I asked impulsively, though I had not meant to ask questions.

'No, that is the star you saw between the clouds when you were coming home,' the being who was carrying me replied.

I knew that it had something like a human face. Strange to say, I did not like that being, in fact I felt an intense aversion for it. I had expected complete non-existence, and that was why I had put a bullet through my heart. And here I was in the hands of a creature not human, of course, but yet living, existing. 'And so there is life beyond the grave,' I thought with the strange frivolity one has in dreams. But in its inmost depth my heart remained unchanged. 'And if I have got to exist again,' I thought, 'and live once more under the control of some irresistible power, I won't be vanquished and humiliated.'

'You know that I am afraid of you and you despise me for that,' I said suddenly to my companion, unable to refrain from the humiliating question which implied a confession, and feeling my humiliation stab my heart as with a pin. He did not answer my question, but all at once I felt that he was not even despising me, but was laughing at me and had no compassion for me, and that our journey had an unknown and mysterious object that concerned me only. Fear was growing in my heart. Something was mutely and painfully communicated to me from my silent companion, and permeated my whole being. We were flying through dark, unknown space. I had for some time lost sight of the constellations familiar to my eyes. I knew that there were stars in the heavenly spaces the light of which took thousands or millions of years to reach the earth. Perhaps we were already flying through those spaces. I expected something with a terrible anguish that tortured my heart.

And suddenly I was thrilled by a familiar feeling that stirred me to the depths: I suddenly caught sight of our sun! I knew that it could not be our sun, that gave life to our earth, and that we were an infinite distance from our sun, but for some reason I knew in my whole being that it was a sun exactly like ours, a duplicate of it. A sweet, thrilling feeling resounded with ecstasy in my heart: the kindred power of the same light which had given me light stirred an echo in my heart and awakened it, and I had a sensation of life, the old life of the past for the first time since I had been in the grave.

'But if that is the sun, if that is exactly the same as our sun,' I cried, 'where is the earth?'

And my companion pointed to a star twinkling in the distance with an emerald light. We were flying straight towards it.

'And are such repetitions possible in the universe? Can that be the law of nature? . . . And if that is an earth there, can it be just the same earth as ours . . . just the same, as poor, as unhappy, but precious and beloved for ever, arousing in the most ungrateful of her children the same poignant love for her that we feel for our earth?' I cried out, shaken by irresistible, ecstatic love for the old familiar earth which I had left. The image of the poor child whom I had repulsed flashed through my mind.

'You shall see it all,' answered my companion, and there was a note of sorrow in his voice.

But we were rapidly approaching the planet. It was growing before my eyes; I could already distinguish the ocean, the outline of Europe; and suddenly a feeling of a great and holy jealousy glowed in my heart.

'How can it be repeated and what for? I love and can love only that earth which I have left, stained with my blood, when, in my ingratitude, I quenched my life with a bullet in my heart. But I have never, never ceased to love that earth, and perhaps on the very night I parted from it I loved it more than ever. Is there suffering upon this new earth? On our earth we can only love with suffering and through suffering. We cannot love otherwise, and we know of no other sort of love. I want suffering in order to love. I long, I thirst, this very instant, to kiss with tears the earth that I have left, and I don't want, I won't accept life on any other!'

But my companion had already left me. I suddenly, quite without noticing how, found myself on this other earth, in the bright light of a sunny day, fair as paradise. I believe I was standing on one of the islands that make up on our globe the Greek archipelago, or on the coast of the mainland facing that archipelago. Oh, everything was exactly as it is with us, only everything seemed to have a festive radiance, the splendour of some great, holy triumph attained at last. The caressing sea, green as emerald, splashed softly upon the shore and kissed it with manifest, almost conscious love. The tall, lovely trees stood in all the glory of their blossom, and their innumerable leaves greeted me, I am certain, with their soft, caressing rustle and seemed to articulate words of love. The grass glowed with bright and fragrant flowers. Birds were flying in flocks in the air, and perched fearlessly on my shoulders and arms and joyfully struck me with their darling, fluttering wings. And at last I saw and knew the people of this happy land. That came to me of themselves, they surrounded me, kissed me. The children of the sun, the children of their sun – oh, how beautiful they were! Never had I seen on our own earth such beauty in mankind. Only perhaps in our children, in their earliest years, one might find some remote faint reflection of this beauty. The eyes of these happy people shone with a clear brightness. Their faces were radiant with the light of reason and full of a serenity that comes of perfect understanding, but those faces were gay; in their words and voices there was a note of childlike joy. Oh, from the first moment, from the first glance at them, I understood it all! It was the earth untarnished by the Fall; on it lived people who had not sinned. They lived just in such a paradise as that in which, according to all the legends of mankind, our first parents lived before they sinned; the only difference was that all this earth was the same paradise. These people, laughing joyfully, thronged round me and caressed me; they took me home with them, and each of them tried to reassure me. Oh, they asked me no questions, but they seemed, I fancied, to know everything without asking, and they wanted to make haste to smooth away the signs of suffering from my face.

4

And do you know what? Well, granted that it was only a dream, yet the sensation of the love of those innocent and beautiful people has remained with me for ever, and I feel as though their love is still flowing out to me from over there. I have seen them myself, have known them and been convinced; I loved them, I suffered for them afterwards. Oh, I understood at once even at the time that in many things I could not understand them at all; as an up-to-date Russian progressive and contemptible Petersburger, it struck me as inexplicable that, knowing so much, they had, for instance, no science like ours. But I soon realised that their knowledge was gained and fostered by intuitions different from those of us on earth, and that their aspirations, too, were quite different. They desired nothing and were at peace; they did not aspire to knowledge of life as we aspire to understand it, because their lives were full. But their knowledge was higher and deeper than ours; for our science seeks to explain what life is, aspires to understand it in order to teach others how to live, while they without science knew how to live; and that I understood, but I could not understand their knowledge. They showed me their trees, and I could not understand the intense love with which they looked at them; it was as though they were talking with creatures like themselves. And perhaps I shall not be mistaken if I say that they conversed with them. Yes, they had found their language, and I am convinced that the trees understood them. They looked at all nature like that – at the animals who lived in peace with them and did not attack them, but loved them, conquered by their love. They pointed to the stars and told me something about them which I could not understand, but I am convinced that they were somehow in touch with the stars, not only in thought, but by some living channel. Oh, these people did not persist in trying to make me understand them, they loved me without that, but I knew that they would never understand me, and so I hardly spoke to them about our earth. I only kissed in their presence the earth on which they lived and mutely worshipped them themselves. And they saw that and let me worship them without being abashed at my adoration, for they themselves loved much. They were not unhappy on my account when at times I kissed their feet with tears, joyfully conscious of the love with which they would respond to mine. At times I asked myself with wonder how it was they were able never to offend a creature like me, and never once to arouse a feeling of jealousy or envy in me? Often I wondered how it could be that, boastful and untruthful as I was, I never talked to them of what I knew – of which, of course, they had no notion – that I was never tempted to do so by a desire to astonish or even to benefit them.

They were as gay and sportive as children. They wandered about their lovely woods and copses, they sang their lovely songs; their fare was light – the fruits of their trees, the honey from their woods and the milk of the animals who loved them. The work they did for food and raiment was brief and not laborious. They loved and begot children, but I never noticed in them the impulse of that cruel sensuality which overcomes almost every man on this earth, all and each, and is the source of almost every sin of mankind on earth. They rejoiced at the arrival of children as new beings to share their happiness. There was no quarrelling, no jealousy among them, and they did not even know what the words meant. Their children were the children of all, for they all made up one family. There was scarcely any illness among them, though there was death; but their old people died peacefully, as though falling asleep, giving blessings and smiles to those who surrounded them to take their last farewell with bright and lovely smiles. I never saw grief or tears on those occasions, but only love, which reached the point of ecstasy, but a calm ecstasy, made perfect and contemplative. One might think that they were still in contact with the departed after death, and that their earthly union was not cut short by death. They scarcely understood me when I questioned them about immortality, but evidently they were so convinced of it without reasoning that it was not for them a question at all. They had no temples, but they had a real living and uninterrupted sense of oneness with the whole of the universe; they had no creed, but they had a certain knowledge that when their earthly joy had reached the limits of earthly nature, then there would come for them, for the living and for the dead, a still greater fullness of contact with the whole of the universe. They looked forward to that moment with joy, but without haste, not pining for it, but seeming to have a foretaste of it in their hearts of which they talked to one another.

In the evening before going to sleep they liked singing in musical and harmonious chorus. In those songs they expressed all the sensations that the parting day had given them, sang its glories and took leave of it. They sang the praises of nature, of the sea, of the woods. They liked making songs about one another, and praised each other like children; they were the simplest songs, but they sprang from their hearts and went to one's heart. And not only in their songs but in all their lives they seemed to do nothing but admire one another. It was like being in love with each other, but an all-embracing, universal feeling.

Some of their songs, solemn and rapturous, I scarcely understood at all. Though I understood the words I could never fathom their full significance. It remained, as it were, beyond the grasp of my mind, yet my heart unconsciously absorbed it more and more. I often told them that I had had a presentiment of it long before, that this joy and glory had come to me on our earth in the form of a yearning melancholy that at times approached insufferable sorrow; that I had had a foreknowledge of them all and of their glory in the dreams of my heart and the visions of my mind; that often on our earth I could not look at the setting sun without tears . . . that in my hatred for the men of our earth there was always a yearning anguish: why could I not hate them without loving them? why could I not help forgiving them? and in my love for them there was a yearning grief: why could I not love them without hating them? They listened to me, and I saw they could not conceive what I was saying, but I did not regret that I had spoken to them of it: I knew that they understood the intensity of my yearning anguish over those whom I had left. But when they looked at me with their sweet eyes full of love, when I felt that in their presence my heart, too, became as innocent and just as theirs, the feeling of the fullness of life took my breath away, and I worshipped them in silence.

Oh, everyone laughs in my face now, and assures me that one cannot dream of such details as I am telling now, that I only dreamed or felt one sensation that arose in my heart in delirium and made up the details myself when I woke up. And when I told them that perhaps it really was so, my God, how they shouted with laughter in my face, and what mirth I caused! Oh, yes, of course I was overcome by the mere sensation of my dream, and that was all that was preserved in my cruelly wounded heart; but the actual forms and images of my dream, that is, the very ones I really saw at the very time of my dream, were filled with such harmony, were so lovely and enchanting and were so actual, that on awakening I was, of course, incapable of clothing them in our poor language, so that they were bound to become blurred in my mind; and so perhaps I really was forced afterwards to make up the details, and so of course to distort them in my passionate desire to convey some at least of them as quickly as I could. But on the other hand, how can I help believing that it was all true? It was perhaps a thousand times brighter, happier and more joyful than I describe it. Granted that I dreamed it, yet it must have been real. You know, I will tell you a secret: perhaps it was not a dream at all! For then something happened so awful, something so horribly true, that it could not have been imagined in a dream. My heart may have originated the dream, but would my heart alone have been capable of originating the awful event which happened to me afterwards? How could I alone have invented it or imagined it in my dream? Could my petty heart and fickle, trivial mind have risen to such a revelation of truth? Oh, judge for yourselves: hitherto I have concealed it, but now I will tell the truth. The fact is that I . . . corrupted them all!

Yes, yes, it ended in my corrupting them all! How it could come to pass I do not know, but I remember it clearly. The dream embraced thousands of years and left in me only a sense of the whole. I only know that I was the cause of their sin and downfall. Like a vile trichina,[291] like a germ of the plague infecting whole kingdoms, so I contaminated all this earth, so happy and sinless before my coming. They learnt to lie, grew fond of lying, and discovered the charm of falsehood. Oh, at first perhaps it began innocently, with a jest, coquetry, with amorous play, perhaps indeed with a germ, but that germ of falsity made its way into their hearts and pleased them. Then sensuality was soon begotten, sensuality begot jealousy, jealousy – cruelty ... Oh, I don't know, I don't remember; but soon, very soon the first blood was shed. They marvelled and were horrified, and began to be split up and become divided. They formed into unions, but it was against one another. Reproaches, upbraidings followed. They came to know shame, and shame brought them to virtue. The conception of honour sprang up, and every union began waving its flags. They began torturing animals, and the animals withdrew from them into the forests and became hostile to them. They began to struggle for separation, for isolation, for individuality, for mine and thine. They began to talk in different languages. They became acquainted with sorrow and loved sorrow; they thirsted for suffering, and said that truth could only be attained through suffering. Then science appeared. As they became wicked they began talking of brotherhood and humanitarianism, and understood those ideas. As they became criminal, they invented justice and drew up whole legal codes in order to observe it, and, to ensure their being kept, set up a guillotine. They hardly remembered what they had lost, in fact refused to believe that they had ever been happy and innocent. They even laughed at the possibility of this happiness in the past, and called it a dream. They could not even imagine it in definite form and shape, but, strange and wonderful to relate, though they lost all faith in their past happiness and called it a legend, they so longed to be happy and innocent once more that they succumbed to this desire like children, made an idol of it, set up temples and worshipped their own idea, their own desire; though at the same time they fully believed that it was unattainable and could not be realised, yet they bowed down to it and adored it with tears! Nevertheless, if it could have happened that they had returned to the innocent and happy condition which they had lost, and if someone had shown it to them again and had asked them whether they wanted to go back to it, they would certainly have refused.

They answered me: 'We may be deceitful, wicked and unjust, we know it and weep over it, we grieve over it; we torment and punish ourselves more perhaps than that merciful Judge Who will judge us and whose Name we know not. But we have science, and by the means of it we shall find the truth and we shall arrive at it consciously. Knowledge is higher than feeling, the consciousness of life is higher than life. Science will give us wisdom, wisdom will reveal the laws, and the knowledge of the laws of happiness is higher than happiness.'

That is what they said, and after saying such things everyone began to love himself better than anyone else, and indeed they could not do otherwise. All became so jealous of the rights of their own personality that they did their very utmost to curtail and destroy them in others, and made that the chief thing in their lives. Slavery followed, even voluntary slavery; the weak eagerly submitted to the strong, on condition that the latter aided them to subdue the still weaker. Then there were saints who came to these people, weeping, and talked to them of their pride, of their loss of harmony and due proportion, of their loss of shame. They were laughed at or pelted with stones. Holy blood was shed on the threshold of the temples. Then there arose men who began to think how to bring all people together again, so that everybody, while still loving himself best of all, might not interfere with others, and all might live together in something like a harmonious society. Regular wars sprang up over this idea. All the combatants at the same time firmly believed that science, wisdom and the instinct of self-preservation would force men at last to unite into a harmonious and rational society; and so, meanwhile, to hasten matters, "the wise" endeavoured to exterminate as rapidly as possible all who were "not wise" and did not understand their idea, that the latter might not hinder its triumph. But the instinct of self-preservation grew rapidly weaker; there arose men, haughty and sensual, who demanded all or nothing. In order to obtain everything they resorted to crime, and if they did not succeed – to suicide. There arose religions with a cult of non-existence and self-destruction for the sake of the everlasting peace of annihilation. At last these people grew weary of their meaningless toil, and signs of suffering came into their faces, and then they proclaimed that suffering was a beauty, for in suffering alone was there meaning. They glorified suffering in their songs. I moved about among them, wringing my hands and weeping over them, but I loved them perhaps more than in the days when there was no suffering in their faces and when they were innocent and so lovely. I loved the earth they had polluted even more than when it had been a paradise, if only because sorrow had come to it. Alas! I always loved sorrow and tribulation, but only for myself, for myself; but I wept over them, pitying them. I stretched out my hands to them in despair, blaming, cursing and despising myself. I told them that all this was my doing, mine alone; that it was I had brought them corruption, contamination and falsity. I besought them to crucify me, I taught them how to make a cross. I could not kill myself, I had not the strength, but I wanted to suffer at their hands. I yearned for suffering, I longed that my blood should be drained to the last drop in these agonies. But they only laughed at me, and began at last to look upon me as crazy. They justified me, they declared that they had only got what they wanted themselves, and that all that now was could not have been otherwise. At last they declared to me that I was becoming dangerous and that they would lock me up in a madhouse if I did not hold my tongue. Then such grief took possession of my soul that my heart was wrung, and I felt as though I were dying; and then . . . then I awoke.

It was morning, that is, it was not yet daylight, but about six o'clock. I woke up in the same armchair; my candle had burnt out; everyone was asleep in the captain's room, and there was a stillness all round, rare in our flat. First of all I leapt up in great amazement: nothing like this had ever happened to me before, not even in the most trivial detail; I had never, for instance, fallen asleep like this in my armchair. While I was standing and coming to myself I suddenly caught sight of my revolver lying loaded, ready – but instantly I thrust it away! Oh, now, life, life! I lifted up my hands and called upon eternal truth, not with words, but with tears; ecstasy, immeasurable ecstasy flooded my soul. Yes, life and spreading the good tidings! Oh, I at that moment resolved to spread the tidings, and resolved it, of course, for my whole life. I go to spread the tidings, I want to spread the tidings – of what? Of the truth, for I have seen it, have seen it with my own eyes, have seen it in all its glory.

And since then I have been preaching! Moreover I love all those who laugh at me more than any of the rest. Why that is so I do not know and cannot explain, but so be it. I am told that I am vague and confused, and if I am vague and confused now, what shall I be later on? It is true indeed: I am vague and confused, and perhaps as time goes on I shall be more so. And of course I shall make many blunders before I find out how to preach, that is, find out what words to say, what things to do, for it is a very difficult task. I see all that as clear as daylight, but, listen, who does not make mistakes? An yet, you know, all are making for the same goal, all are striving in the same direction anyway, from the sage to the lowest robber, only by different roads. It is an old truth, but this is what is new: I cannot go far wrong. For I have seen the truth; I have seen and I know that people can be beautiful and happy without losing the power of living on earth. I will not and cannot believe that evil is the normal condition of mankind. And it is just this faith of mine that they laugh at. But how can I help believing it? I have seen the truth – it is not as though I had invented it with my mind, I have seen it, seen it, and *the living image* of it has filled my soul for ever. I have seen it in such full perfection that I cannot believe that it is impossible for people to have it. And so how can I go wrong? I shall make some slips no doubt, and shall perhaps talk in second-hand language, but not for long: the living image of what I saw will always be with me and will always correct and guide me. Oh, I am full of courage and freshness, and I will go on and on if it were for a thousand years! Do you know, at first I meant to conceal the fact that I corrupted them, but that was a mistake – that was my first mistake! Truth whispered to me that I was *lying*, and preserved me and corrected me. But how establish paradise – I don't know, because I do not know how to put it into words. After my dream I lost command of words. All the chief words, anyway, the most necessary ones. But never mind, I shall go and I shall keep talking, I won't leave off, for anyway I have seen it with my own eyes, though I cannot describe what I saw. But the scoffers do not understand that. It was a dream, they say, delirium, hallucination. Oh! As though that meant so much! And they are so proud! A dream! What is a dream? And is not our life a dream? I will say more. Suppose that this paradise will never come to pass (that I understand), yet I shall go on preaching it. And yet how simple it is: in one day, *in one hour* everything could be arranged at once! The chief thing is to love others like yourself, that's the chief thing, and that's everything; nothing else is wanted – you will find out at once how to arrange it all. And yet it's an old truth which has been told and retold a billion times – but it has not formed part of our lives! The consciousness of life is higher than life, the knowledge of the laws of happiness is higher than happiness – that is what one must contend against. And I shall. If only everyone wants it, it can be arranged at once.

And I tracked down that little girl . . . and I shall go on and on!

Abbreviated Table of Civil, Court and Military Ranks

CIVIL RANKS	COURT RANKS	MILITARY RANKS
1 Chancellor of the Empire		
	—	Field Marshal
2 Actual Privy Councillor	Chief Chamberlain	
		General
3 Privy Councillor	Marshall	Lieutenant-General
4 Actual Councillor of State		
	Chamberlain	Major-General
5 Councillor of State	Master of Ceremonies	
		Brigadier
6 Collegiate Councillor	Gentleman of the Bedchamber	
	(ranks 5-8)	Colonel
7 Court Councillor		Lieutenant-Colonel
8 Collegiate Assessor		Major
9 Titular Councillor		Captain
10 Collegiate Secretary		Staff-Captain
11 Naval Secretary		Lieutenant
12 County Secretary		Second-Lieutenant
13 Provincial Secretary		Ensign
14 Collegiate Registrar		

Notes

Mr Prohartchin

1 (p. 1) *Volkovo* a cemetery founded in 1756 on the outskirts of St Petersburg because of the limited spaces in crypts and churchyards

2 (p. 4) *Peski* 'Sands', district in the heart of St Petersburg between Nevsky Prospect and Ligovsky Avenue

3 (p. 4) *faro* popular nineteenth-century card game. It was first played during the reign of Louis XIV.

4 (p. 4) *preference* Preference originated in Austria and was played with a 32-card deck. It became Russia's national card game in the 1840s.

5 (p. 4) *bixe* combination of mini-billiards and pinball

6 (p. 4) *hussars* cavalry regiment created in the eighteenth century in Russia

7 (p. 5) *Tver* powerful medieval centre north of Moscow, rebuilt in the eighteenth century by Catherine the Great

8 (p. 8) *Tolkutchy Market* in the centre of St Petersburg, situated inside Apraksin Dvor, a large market and retail block between Sadovy Street and the Fontanka River. A new department store was built there in 1863.

9 (p. 8) *Crooked Lane* In the 1840s, Crooked Lane linked the Fontanka with Zagorodny Prospect.

10 (p. 10) *flips on the nose* a game played with a 36-card deck, in which the object is to take 7 tricks (also called '7 leaves')

11 (p. 10) *three cards* a cross between whist and three-card monte

12 (p. 10) *Kolomna* area of St Petersburg, first developed by Peter the Great in the 1740s. A number of artists moved there in the first half of the nineteenth century.

13 (p. 12) *Fontanka Embankment* a seven-kilometre stretch of river on which some of St Petersburg's most impressive palaces and

monuments are built. The Fontanka is a canal and a branch of the Neva River that flows through St Petersburg.

14 (p. 18) *if your nose were cut off you would eat it up with a bit of bread and not notice it* In 'The Nose', a story by Nikolay Gogol (1809–1852), dramatist, novelist, and short-story writer, a barber discovers his client's nose in a loaf of bread.

15 (p. 19) *doubting Thomas* One of Christ's Apostles, Thomas refused to believe that Jesus was resurrected until he had seen him and probed the actual wounds himself (John 20:24–9).

16 (p. 20) *Napoleon* leader of France during a time of profound political and social change and one of the greatest military strategists who ever lived (1769–1821)

17 (p. 25) *German Kreutzers* copper and silver coins

The Landlady

18 (p. 31) *flâneur* stroller, loafer

19 (p. 35) *a poor German called Schpies* Here Dostoevsky gives this incidental character the name of a German writer, Christian Spiess (1755–1799), known for his romances.

20 (p. 47) *Stenka Razin* Cossack leader (1630–1671) who conducted a successful and bloody campaign in southern Russia against the nobility and the Tsar

21 (p. 48) *Mother Volga* The longest river in Europe, the Volga plays a central role in Russian literature and folklore.

22 (p. 55) *Pushkin himself mentions a similar case in his works* perhaps a reference to mysterious motifs, as in 'The Queen of Spades', a story in which the the number three figures prominently. Pushkin himself often speculated about the date on which he would die.

23 (p. 90) *the magician's pupil who . . . bade the broom bring him water* The reference is to 'The Sorcerer's Apprentice' (Der Zauberlehrling) a ballad by Johann Wolfgang von Goethe (1749–1832), written in 1797. His extraordinary abilities as a novelist, literary theorist, critic, statesman and scientist made Goethe the quintessential Renaissance man.

A Novel in Nine Letters

24 (p. 95) *patchouli*   herb of the mint family, used in perfume and incense

25 (p. 95) *mignonette*   garden annual with fragrant white flowers

26 (p. 95) *Woe from Wit*   Alexander Griboyedov's (1795–1829) comic play, first circulated in 1825. It rapidly became a Russian classic.

27 (p. 95) *Alexandrinsky Theatre*   St Petersburg theatre built in 1832 near the Anichkov Palace on Nevsky Prospect

28 (p. 100) *Simbirsk*   city and administrative centre on the Volga River, 893 kilometers (555 miles) east of Moscow

29 (p. 104) *Don Quixote de la Mancha*   Spanish novel by Miguel de Cervantes (1547–1616), now generally regarded as the first great foundational work of European literature

Another Man's Wife, or the Husband Under the Bed

30 (p. 110) *Paul de Kock*   prolific French novelist (1793–1871) famous for his depiction of middle-class Parisian life

31 (p. 111) *Voznesensky Bridge*   eighteenth-century bridge over Griboyedov Canal in St Petersburg

32 (p. 114) *To Pokrov*   Pokrovskaya Church on Pokrov Square (present-day Turgenev Square)

33 (p. 119) *c'est vous*   it's you

34 (p. 119) *Izmailovsky Bridge*   bridge across the Fontanka at the end of Voskresenskogo Prospect

35 (p. 121) *Why the prima donna . . . mews a lullaby to you like a little white kitten*   The reference is to the Italian singer Erminia Frezzolini (1818–1884), famous for her bel canto roles in operas by Bellini and Donizetti. She sang in St Petersburg during 1827–8. Dostoevsky described her as a doll with a beautiful voice.

36 (p. 121) *Hamlet, Prince of Denmark upon the evil example set by age to youth*   The reference is to Act 2, Scene 2, in an exchange with Polonius.

37 (p. 122) *those newspapers which are filled with advice, warnings . . . recommendations of the celebrated Mr Princhipi, sworn foe of all beetles in the world* The reference is to the *St Petersburg News* and *St Petersburg Police Gazette*. In 1848 one Mikhail Principe advertised in the *Gazette* a powder that would kill cockroaches and other insects.

38 (p. 123) *prédestiné* predestined

39 (p. 124) *Grand Theatre* From 1818 to 1886 the Bolshoi Kamenny (Stone) Theatre was Russia's main theatre for ballet and opera.

40 (p. 124) *sans faute* without fail

41 (p. 126) *Don Juan* imaginary libertine, the subject of works by Mozart, Byron, Pushkin, etc.

42 (p. 126) *Lovelace* imaginary libertine in *Clarissa*, an epistolary novel by Samuel Richardson (1689–1761)

43 (p. 134) *Nuremburg doll* Nuremberg was well known for the toys manufactured there.

44 (p. 136) *ici, ici* come here, come here

45 (p. 140) *Rinaldo-Rinaldini* a 1797 novel by German writer Christian Vulpius, subtitled *The Robber Captain*. It was one of the most popular penny dreadfuls of the era.

A Faint Heart

46 (p. 153) *façon Manon Lescaut* the heroine of Abbé Prevost's (1697–1763) tragic novel, in which a woman with a passionate nature and luxurious tastes flouts convention and dies as a result

47 (p. 155) *c'est plus coquet* it's more stylish

48 (p. 182) *there was a frost of twenty degrees* equivalent to –25°Celsius. At the time Russia used the Réaumur scale, named after French scientist René Antoine Ferchault de Réaumur, in which the freezing and boiling points of water are 0° and 80° degrees respectively.

Polzunkov

49 (p. 186) *restricted*   the Russian word here is *zamknutaya*, closed

50 (p. 186) *Even the smoke of our native land is sweet to us*   words spoken by Chatsky, the hero of Griboyedov's *Woe from Wit*. Chatsky is quoting Gavrila Derzhavin's (1743–1816) poem 'The Harp', published in 1798.

51 (p. 187) *Homeric laughter*   Homer is the Greek poet who wrote the *Iliad* and the *Odyssey*. He is famous for his larger-than-life epic characters, hence the reference to this laughter.

52 (p. 188) *St Mary of Egypt's day*   This saint (344–c.421) was born in Egypt where she grew up to become a dissolute woman and lived for years as a prostitute. Barred from entering the church in Jerusalem while on what she called an anti-pilgrimage, she begged for forgiveness and embraced an ascetic life. Her feast day is 1 April, an important date in this story.

53 (p. 188) *penates*   household gods and protectors of the Roman state

54 (p. 188) *junker*   young nobleman

55 (p. 189) *prodigal son*   a figure from one of Christ's parables (Luke 15:11–32) about loss and redemption. He leaves his home, falls into profligacy and loses all his money. His father forgives him when he returns and throws a huge party to celebrate. Christ's point is that we need to be generous towards those who disappoint or offend us.

56 (p. 190) *the song about the hussar who leaned upon the sword*   reference to a popular ballad by Mikhail Viyelgorskogo (1788–1856), a Polish composer. He was the son of the Polish Ambassador to Russia and himself had a distinguished career in Russia's foreign service.

57 (p. 191) *They strike you on the cheek and in your joy you offer them your whole back*   an echo of Christ's telling the disciples to 'turn the other cheek' (Matthew 5:39)

An Honest Thief

58 (p. 198) *dvornik*   porter or janitor in a Russian household

A Christmas Tree and a Wedding

59 (p. 213) *con amore*   with great relish

60 (p. 214) *nankin*   yellowish cloth made from cotton

61 (p. 217) *batiste handkerchief*   a fine cloth made from cotton or linen

White Nights

A Sentimental Story from the Diary of a Dreamer

62 (p. 221) *White Nights*   period between late May and early July, associated particularly with St Petersburg, when the sun hardly sets

63 (p. 221) The epigraph is a quotation from Turgenev's (1818–1883) poem 'The Flower', first published in 1843. He soon abandoned poetry and went on to become one of Russia's most important novelists, the author of *Fathers and Sons*, *On the Eve*, *Rudin*, etc.

64 (p. 221) *Nevsky*   Nevsky Prospect is St Petersburg's main street, planned by Peter the Great. It runs east from the Admiralty Building on the Bolshaya Neva, crosses the Fontanka and turns south-east, ending at the Alexander Nevsky Monastery on the Neva.

65 (p. 221) *the Gardens*   Founded in 1704 at the confluence of the Fontanka Canal and the Neva, the Summer Garden is St Petersburg's most famous park, ornamented by rare flowers, beautiful statues and exquisite fountains.

66 (p. 221) *Embankment*   The Admiralty Embankment, one of the most fashionable streets in the city, bifurcates St Petersburg, running from Decembrists' Square (where it becomes the English Embankment) to the Palace Bridge (where it becomes the Palace Embankment).

67 (p. 222) *the Celestial Empire*   one of China's many names. The term 'son of heaven' was used to describe the Chinese Emperor.

68 (p. 223) *Kamenny*   an island in the Neva delta, home to the aristocracy since the time of Peter the Great

69 (p. 223) *Aptekarsky*   a small island in the Neva delta, linked to adjoining islands by ten bridges. It was transformed by Peter the Great into a garden of medicinal plants (hence its name, which means pharmacy).

70 (p. 223) *Peterhof Road*   the road to the most famous palaces built around the city, the imperial palace of Peter the Great

71 (p. 223) *Pargolovo*   northern suburb of St Petersburg, originally an estate belonging to the Shuvalov family

72 (p. 223) *Krestovsky Island*   First owned by the Belosselsky family, this island became a recreational area for the general population in the nineteenth century.

73 (p. 223) *Black River*   river near which Pushkin was ostensibly killed in a duel with a French aristocrat, Georges d'Anthès

74 (p. 223) *the Islands*   In the nineteenth century there were approximately 100 islands comprising St Petersburg, joined by some 340 bridges, canals and rivers.

75 (p. 224) *canal embankment*   street beside the Yekaterininsky Canal

76 (p. 233) *King Solomon*   The illegitimate son of King David, he used his acumen and ruthlessness to become one of the most successful and powerful biblical kings. His counterpart in Arab lore is Allah Suleiman, who seals up a genie in a pitcher until, one thousand eight hundred years later, the seal is broken. The story of the opening of the seven seals is told in Revelation 6–8.

77 (p. 234) *'the Goddess of Fancy' if you have read Zhukovsky*   The reference is to 'My Goddess' (1809), a poem by Vasily Zhukovsky (1783–1852). The poem is a free translation of 'Meine Göttin' by Goethe.

78 (p. 235) *seventh crystal heaven*   In Aristotle's cosmology, the earth is at the centre, surrounded by eight crystal spheres: the moon, the sun, five known planets and the stars were embedded in the spheres themselves.

79 (p. 236) *Hoffmann*   Ernst Theodor Amadeus Hoffmann (1776–1822), German Romantic writer well known in Russia for his fantastic tales

80 (p. 236) *St Bartholomew's Night*   23 August 1572, on the eve of the Feast of St Bartholomew, thousands of Protestants were massacred in France.

81 (p. 236) *Diana Vernon*   shrewd and attractive young woman in Sir Walter Scott's (1771–1832) novel *Rob Roy* (1817)

82 (p. 236) *the taking of Kazan ... Ivan Vassilyevitch*   Ivan the Terrible (1530–1584), whose reign established Russia's power over the Khanates of Kazan, Astrakhan and Siberia

83 (p. 236) *Clara Mowbray*   the heroine of *St Ronan's Well*, a Scott novel published in 1824

84 (p. 236) *Effie Deans*   the protagonist in Scott's *Heart of Midlothian* (1818)

85 (p. 236) *Huss* Jan Hus (1369–1415), a Czech priest whose teachings anticipate the Protestant revolution, was excommunicated for heresy and burned at the stake.

86 (p. 236) *Robert the Devil*   an opera by Meyerbeer (1791–1864), first performed in 1831, which went on to become a huge success and helped make the German composer known throughout Europe

87 (p. 236) *Minna and Brenda*   the names of the Troil girls who are in love with two rival seafaring men in Scott's *The Pirate* (1822)

88 (p. 236) *Battle of Berezina*   battle in late November 1812 between Napoleon's retreating French army and the Russian armies pursuing him. The phrase became synonymous with 'disaster' for the French.

89 (p. 236) *of a poem at Countess V.D.'s*   Princess Yekaterina Romanovna Vorontsova-Dashkova (1743–1810) edited a journal, wrote plays, collaborated with Catherine the Great, befriended Diderot, Voltaire and Benjamin Franklin, was appointed head of two of Russia's most distinguished Academies, and worked tirelessly to promote Russian culture.

90 (p. 236) *Danton*   Georges Danton (1759–1794), a major figure in the French Revolution, who was guillotined by his fellow Jacobins in the vicious in-fighting of the First Republic's bloody final days

91 (p. 236) *Cleopatra e i suoi amanti*   Cleopatra VII Philopater (69–30BC) had children by Julius Ceasar and Mark Antony. Pushkin proposed this as a subject in his *Egyptian Nights* (1835).

92 (p. 236) *'The Little House in Kolomna'*   poem by Pushkin published in 1830 that deals frankly and amusingly with female sexuality

93 (p. 237) *so long and so fondly*   allusion to the Russian poet Mikhail Lermontov's (1814–1841) translation of Heinrich Heine's (1797–1856) 'Sie liebten sich beide' (They loved one another).

94 (p. 243) *Ivanhoe*   the eponymous hero of a Scott romance published in 1820. The novel was an enormously popular work set in the Middle Ages.

95 (p. 244) *The Barber of Seville*   opera buffa by Gioachino Rossini (1792–1868), first performed in 1816. A brilliant comic masterpiece

composed in less than three weeks, it enjoyed a huge success in Russia.

96 (p. 248) *the letter . . . but . . .* In Rossini's opera, the heroine Rosina writes a letter to a young duke whom she admires, and produces it with a flourish as soon as the possibility of writing it is mentioned, much to the surprise of Figaro, the go-between in this affair.

A Little Hero

97 (p. 267) *The famous brunette whose praises were sung by a great and well-known poet* The poet in question is Alfred de Musset (1810–1857). He published 'L'Andalouse' in 1829, which became widely known as a song. Andalusia is an area in southern Spain, comprised of eight provinces, whose capital is Seville.

98 (p. 267) *Castille* a vaguely defined region in the centre of the Iberian peninsular that became part of the Kingdom of Spain

99 (p. 269) *Scribe* Augustin Eugène Scribe (1791–1861), famous for his well-made plays and libretti, usually organised around a carefully contrived plot

100 (p. 270) *madonnas* representations of Mary, mother of Christ

101 (p. 270) *sisters of mercy* philanthropic organisation to help the poor and the sick, founded in St Petersburg in the 1840s

102 (p. 274) *Tartuffe* character in Molière's (1622–1673) play of that name, first performed in 1664. Tartuffe is the archetypal hypocrite.

103 (p. 274) *Falstaff* Shakespeare's greatest comic character, who claims (rightly) that he is not only witty but the source of wit in others. A vain, cowardly, dissolute follower of the future King Henry V, Falstaff is devastatingly rejected by Henry once he ascends the throne.

104 (p. 274) *Baal* a word which, meaning master or lord in Semitic, could be used for a range of local and other deities

105 (p. 274) *Moloch* Moloch ('king' in Semitic) was a god worshipped in different parts of the Middle East and North Africa and often associated with blood sacrifices.

106 (p. 275) *cavaliere servente* courtly lover of a married woman

107 (p. 276) *Odessa* Ukrainian port on the Black Sea, founded by Catherine the Great in 1794

108 (p. 277–8) *Benedick with Beatrice, in Shakespeare's 'Much Ado about Nothing'*   quarrelsome and witty friends who ultimately discover their love for each other

109 (p. 278) *a bluebeard*   'Bluebeard' is a French folktale by Charles Perrault (1628–1703) about a murderous jealous husband.

110 (p. 282) *Ilya Muromets*   famous knight errant in medieval epic poems and tales

111 (p. 282) *Tancred*   the name of the hero of Torquato Tasso's (1544–1595) epic poem *Jerusalem Delivered*, published in 1581

112   (p. 285) *Mais c'est très sérieux, messieurs, ne riez pas!*   But this is serious, gentleman, don't make fun of him!

113 (p. 285) *De Lorge! Toggenburg!*   tragic heroes in ballads by Johann Christoph Friedrich von Schiller (1759–1805)

114 (p. 288) *the River Moskva*   river that rises west of Moscow and ultimately empties into the Caspian Sea

Uncle's Dream

115 (p. 295) *earthquake of Lisbon*   On 1 November 1755, All Saints Day, an earthquake struck the Portuguese capital, killing many thousands and almost totally destroying the city. The catastrophe was much discussed by thinkers and theologians at the time. Enlightenment philosophers – for example, Voltaire in *Candide* – were interested in how such an event squared with the notion of a providential order or beneficent God.

116 (p. 296) *Pinetti*   Giovanni Pinetti (1750–c.1803) was the most famous magician of his day and performed extensively in Russia.

117 (p. 296) *Carlsruhe*   city in south-west Germany. In 1848 it elected a republican government and declared its independence.

118 (p. 298) *Northern Bee*   newspaper founded in 1825 that rapidly became conservative and pro-government. Its editors frequently mocked and criticised writers supposed to have liberal tendencies

119 (p. 302) *Bonjour, mon ami, bonjour!*   Hello, my friend, hello.

120 (p. 304) *ce pauvre prince!*   this poor prince!

121 (p. 305) *something like it in Fet, in some elegy of his*   Mozglyakov is flaunting a suspect erudition here: there is nothing like this scene

at an inn in the poetry of Afanasy Fet (1820–1892), the extraordinarily gifted nineteenth-century Russian poet.

122 (p. 305) *overcome by a feeling of humanity, which, as Heine expresses it* Heinrich Heine (1797–1856) is a German poet, journalist, essayist and literary critic. This is another of Mozglyakov's invented references.

123 (p. 306) *Eine allerliebste Geschichte*   a most delightful story

124 (p. 306) *seventy times seven*   the figure Christ gave those who asked him how many times one should forgive one's brother (Matthew 18:22)

125 (p. 308) *Shakespeare*   William Shakespeare (1564–1616) was a Renaissance playwright who is now universally regarded as the greatest writer who ever lived.

126 (p. 308) *mon cher Paul*   my dear Paul

127 (p. 312) *C'est délicieux! . . . C'est charmante! . . . Mais quelle beauté!* That is wonderful! . . . that is charming! . . . but what beauty!

128 (p. 313) *communist*   believer in a society based on common ownership of property

129 (p. 313) *a regular German philosopher Kant*   Immanuel Kant (1724–1804) was a German thinker whose thought continues to be influential for those interested in metaphysics, epistemology and ethics.

130 (p. 313) *comme il faut*   appropriate

131 (p. 314) *Von Vizin*   Denis Fonvizin (1745–1792), well-known eighteenth-century Russian dramatist

132 (p. 314) *Lord Byron*   George Gordon, 6th Baron Byron (1788–1824), English poet and dramatist who became one of the leading figures of the Romantic movement. He gave his name to the concept of the Byronic hero, brooding, isolated, hypnotically attractive and fated to die unhappy.

133 (p. 314) *Cracoviana*   a lively Polish folk and ballroom dance, usually in 2/4 time. Associated with Cracow, it dates back to the sixteenth century.

134 (p. 314) *Vienna Congress*   In 1814–15, at the end of the Napoleonic Wars, the major European nations met in Vienna to decide the borders, the governments and the future of Europe.

135 (p. 315) *mon cher prince*   my dear prince

136 (p. 317) *C'est une idée comme une autre.*   It's as good an idea as any.

137 (p. 318) *C'est joli.*   It's clever.

138 (p. 319) *cher ami*   dear friend

139 (p. 320) *Tver . . . Yarsolav . . . Kostroma*   three cities north of Moscow on the Volga River

140 (p. 320) *Adieu, ma charmante demoiselle*   Goodbye, my charming young lady

141 (p. 324) *Library of Good Reading*   a monthly publication, subtitled *A Journal of Literature, the Sciences, the Arts, News, and Fashions*, that became popular in the 1830s

142 (p. 324) *Florian and his shepherdesses*   Jean-Pierre Florian (1755–1794), French writer famous for his pastoral novels

143 (p. 326) *mon ange*   my angel

144 (p. 326) *Alhambra*   palace in Granada used by Muslim emirs and Christian rulers for hundreds of years before it fell into disrepair. It became a major tourist attraction in the nineteenth century.

145 (p. 326) *Guadalquivir*   river that goes through Cordoba and Seville before emptying into the Atlantic

146 (p. 329) *there is some extraordinary island, I believe it is called Malaga – like some wine, in fact*   Malaga is a city on the south coast of Spain, not an island, but it has been a tourist attraction for centuries and is known for its sweet wine. Marya Alexandrova is probably confusing it with Majorca.

147 (p. 331) *vous comprenez*   you understand

148 (p. 332) *the Cossack dance*   also known as the national dance of Ukraine or the Hopak. It dates back to the sixteenth century.

149 (p. 332) *cancan*   provocative dance performed in music halls by a chorus line of high-kicking female dancers

150 (p. 333) *Quelle horreur!*   How awful!

151 (p. 333) *Mais adieu, mon ange!*   But goodbye, my angel!

152 (p. 337) *en grand*   a life of luxury

153 (p. 348) *Oh, ma charmante enfant! . . . Vous me ravissez!* Oh, my charming child! . . . You delight me!

154 (p. 349) *Did not Maria love Mazeppa*   characters from Pushkin's *Poltava*. Maria is the daughter of a wealthy Cossack who elopes with Mazeppa, a Ukrainian hetman at the time of Peter the Great.

155   (p. 349) *that Lauzun, that enchanting marquis at the court of Louis the . . .*   Antoine Nompar de Caumont (1633–1723), Count and Duke of Lauzun, favourite at the court of Louis XIV. He prided himself on his many love affairs.

156   (p. 349) *L'Hirondelle*   French song, 'The Swallow' in English, by Johann Burgmüller (1806–1874), a German composer who moved to Paris when he was still a young man

157   (p. 349) *O, ma belle châtelaine!* Oh, my beautiful lady (mistress of a castle)!

158   (p. 359) *Strauss*   Johann Strauss (1825–1899), prolific Austrian composer of light music, dance music and operettas

159   (p. 363) *Monte Cristo   The Count of Monte Cristo*, a historical novel by Alexandre Dumas (1802–1870), an adventure story of a wrongly imprisoned man and his revenge. Dumas's work was translated into Russian, and he lived in Russia for a couple of years.

160   (p. 363) *Les mémoires du diable*   novel by Frédéric Soulié (1800–1847) about mysterious goings on in the castle a young baron has inherited from his father

161   (p. 371) *Parole d'honneur*   word of honour

162   (p. 372) *Casanova*   Giacomo Casanova (1725–1798) was an Italian adventurer and the author of *The Story of My Life*, an account of his extraordinary powers of seduction.

163   (p. 381) *Quelle abominable femme!*   What an abominable woman!

164   (p. 383) *masonic lodge*   A fraternal organisation that traces its origins back to medieval stonemasonry. Its members are committed to perform works that aid the community, yet a considerable amount of secrecy surrounds these activities.

165   (p. 385) *Mesdames*   Ladies

166   (p. 389) *maison bourgeoise, mais honnête*   middle-class home but decent

167   (p. 390) *days of the regency depicted by Dumas*   In his Regency romances, Dumas recounted stories of aristocratic adventures during the Regency, 1717–23, when France was governed by Philippe d'Orléans until the furure Louis XV assumed the throne at the age of twelve.

168   (p. 390) *Some Faire-la-cour*   Some wooer

169 (p. 409) *regeneration of our beloved fatherland*   The serfs were freed in 1861, a year before this story was published. Alexander II (1818–1881), who became Tsar in 1855, was also responsible for a range of educational and political reforms, the abolition of capital punishment and the decentralisation of state power.

170 (p. 409) *Petersburg Side*   area of the city between Vasilyevsky Island and the Vyborg side

171 (p. 411) *amour-propre . . . une existence manqué*   self-esteem . . . a wasted life

172 (p. 415) *c'est le mot . . . bon sens*   that's the word for it . . . common sense

173 (p. 417) *Pseldonimov*   This name is almost *psevdonim* (pseudonym) in Russian, a point made later in the tale (see p. 428).

174 (p. 417) *Mlekopitaev*   'mammal' in Russian

175 (p. 418) *the last days of Pompeii*   painting by Karl Bryullov (1799–1852), which he worked on for three years, 1830 to 1833. The finished work is a massive depiction of the chaos that ensues as Vesuvius erupts and the people of Pompeii try in vain to save themselves from destruction.

176 (p. 419) *Gogol*   Gogol is arguably Russia's most original writer, hence the reference to original characters.

177 (p. 421) *galantine*   deboned meat dish, usually chicken, cooked by poaching or roasting, served cold

178 (p. 421) *Gentlemen advance, ladies' chain, set to partners!*   instructions for the quadrille, a square dance performed by four couples, popular at the end of the eighteenth and beginning of the nineteenth centuries

179 (p. 423) *Haroun al-Raschid*   A resourceful Arab leader and respected intellectual, Haroun al-Raschid (763–809), the Caliph of the Fifth Abbasid, is the subject of a group of tales in *The Thousand and One Nights*.

180 (p. 424) *point d'appui*   foundation

181 (p. 429) *to dream of Mr Panaev means spilling coffee on one's shirt front*   Ivan Panaev (1812–1862), writer, critic, journalist, editor and, like Dostoevsky, an early follower of the radical critic

Vissarion Belinsky. Panaev was the editor of *The Contemporary* in the 1850s. In an article on dreams in contemporary Russian literature, the poet Nikolay Shcherbina (1821–1869) wrote that dreaming of Panaev meant spilling one's coffee or buying half a dozen Dutch shirts.

182 (p. 429) *Kraevsky* Andrey Alexandrovich Kraevsky (1810–1889), best known as the editor of the distinguished literary and political journal *Notes from the Fatherland*

183 (p. 429) *the Firebrand* weekly satirical journal published in St Petersburg in the early 1860s

184 (p. 430) *Yaroslav cloth* Yaroslav is a city 175 miles north-east of Moscow, known for its linen mills from the seventeenth century

185 (p. 431) *the fish dance* folk dance in which a man imitates a fish out of water

186 (p. 433) *preference for farthing points* game resembling bridge played with a 32-card deck for small amounts of money (a farthing is a quarter of a penny)

187 (p. 433) *Lutchinushka* Little Birch Splinter, the title of a popular Russian song

188 (p. 433) *Academic News* or *Petersburg News* The Academy of Sciences published the daily paper, the *Petersburg News*, hence its twofold name.

189 (p. 434) *Fokin* dancer known for his risqué performances of the can-can

190 (p. 444) *Arabian Nights* collection of stories and tales compiled during an age in which Islamic culture flourished, *c.*800–1250

191 (p. 446) *cupful of gall and bitterness* This was what Christ was given to drink before being crucified. See Matthew 27:34: 'They gave him vinegar to drink mingled with gall: and when he had tasted thereof, he would not drink.'

192 (p. 449) *to Peski by way of a hostage to Fourth Rozhdensky Street* across St Petersburg to an area near the central train station

193 (p. 449) *deshabille* state of undress

194 (p. 453) *un beau matin* one fine day

Notes from Underground

195 (p. 458) *'sublime and beautiful'* The reference is to Kant's *Observations on the Feeling of the Beautiful and the Sublime* (1764). Kant claims that tranquil, picturesque nature is beautiful and that stormy, majestic nature is sublime. The Underground Man repeatedly uses the 'sublime and beautiful' phrase ironically.

196 (p. 461) *l'homme de la nature et de la vérité* the man of nature and of truth. Here Dostoevsky is mocking Jean-Jacques Rousseau (1712–1778). A similar phrase occurs in his *Confessions* and on his tombstone. Rousseau argued that the natural man was corrupted by civilisation.

197 (p. 463) *Vagenheims* There were eight dentists with this name in St Petersburg in the 1860s.

198 (p. 476) *connoisseur of Lafitte* one of the world's best known and most expensive wines, now called Lafite Rothschild. The vineyard is in the village of Pauillac near Bordeaux.

199 (p. 467) *a picture worthy of Gay* Nikolay Ge (1831–1894) was a popular Russian painter of historical and religious subjects. The reference is to his 'Last Supper', exhibited at the Academy of Art in St Petersburg in 1863, the year before 'Notes' was published.

200 (p. 467) *an author has written 'As you will'* Satiric novelist Mikhail Saltykov-Shchedrin (1826–1889) wrote an article with this title for the *Contemporary*.

201 (p. 470) *following Buckle* Henry Buckle (1821–1862), English historian who argued that the development of civilisation diminishes the possibility of war between nations. His insistence that human behaviour is guided by fixed laws made him an obvious target for Dostoevsky.

202 (p. 470) *Take Napoleon – the Great and also the present one* Napoleon Bonaparte (see Note 16) and his nephew, Napoleon III, sometimes called 'Le Petit Napoleon'. The latter's adventuristic foreign policy involved France in wars with Russia, Italy, Mexico and finally Prussia, all of which conflicts ended badly for the French.

203 (p. 470) *the farce of Schleswig-Holstein* states fought over by Germany and Denmark for more than eight hundred years. Germany and Austria claimed the two duchies in 1864.

204 (p. 470) *Attila* Attila (*c.*406–453) was the leader of the Huns, a nomadic people who invaded and wrought havoc in the Balkans, Persia, Gaul and Italy.

205 (p. 471) *Palace of Crystal* In 1851, the Crystal Palace was built in Hyde Park for the Great Exhibition. It was then rebuilt in South London, surrounded by a park. In Nikolay Chernyshevsky's *What is to be Done?*, there is a chapter called 'The Fourth Dream of Vera Pavlovna', in which she sees a crystal palace built in the middle of green fields. It is a symbol for the perfect world that socialists can build together.

206 (p. 474) *Colossus of Rhodes* statue of the Greek sun god, Helios, erected in Rhodes to celebrate the victory of Rhodes over Cyprus. Almost a hundred feet high, it was one of the Seven Wonders of the Ancient World.

207 (p. 474) *Mr Anaevsky* A. E. Anaevsky (1788–1866) was a Russian writer who, in an article on the Colossus of Rhodes, quoted authorities who suggested that it was not a man-made creation but a natural one.

208 (p. 477) *les animaux domestiques* domestic animals

209 (p. 485) *Kostanzhoglo* character in Gogol's *Dead Souls* who favours new agricultural methods and advocates adapting to change

210 (p. 485) *Uncle Pyotr Ivanitch* character in 'A Ordinary Story' (1847) by novelist Ivan Goncharov (1812–1891). He epitomises hard-headed practicality.

211 (p. 486) *Weimar* One of Europe's most important cultural centres in the eighteenth and nineteenth centuries, Weimar attracted writers such as Goethe, Schiller, Herder and Wieland, as well as artists, architects and musicians.

212 (p. 486) *Black Forest* area in south-west Germany that features splendid mountain scenery, picturesque villages and dark, brooding forests

213 (p. 486) *to the lunatic asylum as 'the King of Spain'* In Gogol's *Diary of a Madman*, Poprishchin is locked up because he thinks he is the King of Spain.

214 (p. 488) *Lieutenant Pirogov* In Gogol's 'Nevsky Prospect', the lieutenant is thrashed by a German for flirting with his wife. Pirogov intends to go to the authorities to lodge a complaint but on the way he buys a pastry and decides to forget the incident.

215 (p. 489) *Otetchestvennye Zapiski* *Notes of the Fatherland*, a journal that provided liberal writers with an outlet for their vision of how Russia should be ruled and what reforms should be attempted

216 (p. 491) *bon ton* high society

217 (p. 491) *Gostiny Dvor* shopping arcade on Nevsky Prospect

218 (p. 494) *Manfred style* eponymous hero of a poem by Byron. His relation with a woman named Astarte is forbidden for mysterious reasons involving suspicions of incest.

219 (p. 494) *Austerlitz* In December 1805 near Austerlitz (Slavkov u Brna in the modern-day Czech Republic) the French armies under Napoleon won a crushing victory against Russian and Austrian forces. Napoleon cleverly deceived the Allies into taking the offensive, and then routed them with a series of brilliant flank attacks.

220 (p. 494) *the Pope would agree to retire from Rome to Brazil* Napoleon and Pope Pius VII were in constant conflict over the Catholic Church's insistence on maintaining temporal power in a rapidly changing Europe. Napoleon effectively kept the Pope under house arrest from 1809 to 1814.

221 (p. 494) *a ball for the whole of Italy at the Villa Borghese on the shores of the Lake of Como* Lake Como is in the north near the Italian Alps. The Villa Borghese is a summer palace in Rome, built in 1613 on the Pincian Hill, to house the magnificent art collection of Cardinal Scipione Borghese.

222 (p. 495) *Five Corners* the intersection in St Petersburg where Zagorodny Prospect meets Rubinstein, Lomonosov and Razyezzhaya Streets

223 (p. 497) *droit de seigneur* landlord's right. In feudal times, the landlord could assert his right to spend the first night with the bride of a serf.

224 (p. 503) *drink to our everlasting friendship* In the original, the Underground Man is planning to toast shifting from the formal *vy* to the more intimate *ty*

225 (p. 508) *the Circassian girls*   Russia completed its conquest of the Caucasus in 1864, a conflict that displaced a large number of Circassians, a North Caucasian ethnic group.

226 (p. 513) *Silvio*   principal character in Pushkin's story 'The Shot'. Having refused to kill his opponent in a duel because he seems indifferent to the prospect of losing his life, Silvio seeks him out years later when he is engaged to be married.

227 (p. 513) *Lermontov's Masquerade*   a melodramatic play by Lermontov that tells an Othello-type story – insanely jealous husband, innocent wife, hasty inferences – that ends tragically

228 (p. 531) *Myeshtchansky Street, along Sadovy Street and in Yusupov Garden*   Myeshtchansky Street runs from the Griboyedov Canal to Voznesensky Avenue. Nearby Sadovy Street is lined by many historical buildings and monuments, including the Yusupov Palace. This garden was initially part of the estate of Nicolas Yusupov, famous for his palace built by the renowned architect Giacomo Quarenghi in 1790. The mansion was bought by the crown in 1810 and the garden was opened to the public in 1863. Separated from the palace by a fence, the garden featured fountains, a place to rent boats on the pond and bridges linking the small islands together.

229 (p. 533) *George Sand*   The pseudonym of Amantine-Lucile-Aurore Dupin (1804–1876), a prolific French writer of pastoral novels, literary criticism and essays on politics and society. One of Dostoevsky's characters in *The Devils* devotes himself to translating her work.

230 (p. 533) *Into my house come bold and free/ Its rightful mistress there to be*   the last lines of the poem by Nekrasov that introduces Chapter 9 of Part Two

231 (p. 533) *the shape of the letter V*   the last letter of the thousand-year-old forty-three-letter Russian alphabet, used from the eleventh to the thirteenth centuries

232 (p. 533) *Alexander of Macedon*   Alexander the Great (356–323BC) was one of the greatest military figures that the world has ever known. He defeated Persia in a series of pitched battles and eventually ruled over an empire that stretched from modern-day Italy to Kashmir.

233 (p. 538) *à la Napoléon*   in the Napoleonic style

The Crocodile

234 (p. 547) *Ohé Lambert! Où est Lambert? As-tu vu Lambert?* Hey Lambert! Where is Lambert? Have you seen Lambert? This was a popular catchphrase in Paris in the middle of the nineteenth century, the exact origins of which are unknown.

235 (p. 550) *Oh mein allerliebster Karlchen! Mutter, Mutter, Mutter! . . .* Oh my beloved Karlchen! Mama, mama, mama!

236 (p. 550) *swallow a ganz official* swallow an official whole

237 (p. 550) *if Karlchen wird burst . . . das war mein Sohn, das war mein einziger Sohn* if Karlchen does burst . . . that was my son, that was my only son

238 (p. 551) *Mr Lavrov was perhaps delivering a public lecture* Pyotr Lavrov (1823–1900), scientist and philosopher, one of the leaders of the populist revolutionary movement. His November 1860 lectures on the contemporary significance of philosophy elicited a great deal of interest.

239 (p. 551) *the caricatures of M. Stepanov* Nikolay Stepanov (1807–1877) artist, cartoonist and editor of the *Firebrand* and other journals.

240 (p. 552) *Mein Vater . . . mein Grossvater . . . ganz Europa . . . strafe* my father . . . my grandfather . . . all over Europe . . . a fine

241 (p. 552) *fünfzig . . . Gott sei dank!* fifty . . . thank God!

242 (p. 554) *the Voice* In the original, Dostoevsky gave this journal a satiric title, the *Hair* (*Volos*), instead of the *Voice* (*Golos*). The *Voice* was a widely read St Petersburg journal in the 1870s.

243 (p. 556) *William Tell* Swiss folk hero credited with killing an Austrian official in 1307 and starting the movement that resulted in Swiss independence

244 (p. 563) *Fourier* Charles Fourier (1772–1837), influential French political thinker, best known for his plans for utopian communities. He envisioned humanity living in six million *phalensteries*, or communes, each containing exactly 1620 people. Many utopian communities were founded on the principles he outlined, and all sorts of radical thinkers were influenced by his work.

245 (p. 564) *Garnier-Pagesishky* Louis Garnier-Pagès (1803–1878), French political figure, strong supporter of reform during the short-lived Second Republic and the Second Empire

246 (p. 564) *Encyclopaedia* a reference to the *Encyclopaedic Dictionary*, edited by Andrey Kraevsky, the first volume of which came out in 1861. Dostoevsky (and many others) questioned Kraevsky's competence and he was quickly replaced by Lavrov. For the record, it should be noted that Kraevsky was an extremely gifted editor who worked on all the important journals of the day. His moderate stances on many political issues made him a target for writers on the left and right.

247 (p. 564) *Yevgenia Tour* pseudonym of Elizaveta Salias de Turnemir (1815–1892), Russian writer, editor, publisher, translator and literary critic

248 (p. 565) *Voznesensky Prospect* a street in St Petersburg that links Admiralteysky Prospect and Izmailovsky Prospect

249 (p. 568) *Savages love independence, wise men love order; and if there is no order* a slightly altered quotation from Nikolay Karamzin's (1766–1826) short novel *Marfa Posadnitsa* (Martha the Mayoress), published in 1802

250 (p. 568) *Socrates* Socrates (469–399BC) was a Greek teacher and a founder of Western Philosophy. He is best known for what he says in his student Plato's *Dialogues*.

251 (p. 568) *Diogenes* Diogenes (412–323BC) was a Greek philosopher who embaced Cynicism. The Cynics argued against wealth, power and fame, opting instead for a set of ascetic ideals.

252 (p. 574) *Newssheet, a paper of no particular party but humanitarian in general.* The reference is to the *Petersburg Tabloid: A Newspaper of City Life and Literature*, founded in 1864 and published as a daily.

253 (p. 574) *weary of the cuisine at Borel's* a famous restaurant in Pushkin's day, named after its French owner Borelle

254 (p. 575) *the train of Lesseps* Ferdinand de Lesseps (1805–1894), French diplomat who, in the face of widespread scepticism and formidable obstacles, supervised the successful building of the Suez Canal, joining the Mediterranean and the Red Sea

255 (p. 575) *Pargolovo* The Shuvalov Park on this estate north of St Petersburg featured a network of old ponds.

256 (p. 575) *Pavlovsk* A summer retreat for the imperial family, Pavlovsk is a palace situated twenty miles south of St Petersburg. It was built in 1780 by Paul I, son and heir of Catherine the Great, following a design of the Scottish architect Charles Cameron.

257 (p. 575) *Presensky Ponds*   three ponds joined by canals and a waterfall, built in the eighteenth century on the Studenets estate west of Moscow

258 (p. 575) *Samoteka*   area east of Moscow

259 (p. 576) *Tartar*   name of a twelfth-century tribe, subjugated by the Mongol Empire under Genghis Khan

260 (p. 576) *Though the houses are new, the conventions are old*   The character Chatsky says this in Griboyedov's *Woe from Wit* (see Notes 26 and 50).

Bobok

261 (p. 579) *Voltaire*   pseudonym of François Marie Arouet (1694–1778), the most famous philosopher and writer of the French Enlightenment. Devastatingly satirical, extraordinarily witty, astonishingly prolific, Voltaire's attacks on corruption and his championing of social justice made him very popular in Tsarist Russia.

262 (p. 582) *Suvorin's calendar*   Aleksey Suvorin (1834–1912), Russian journalist and publisher, was responsible for publishing more than a thousand books on a vast range of subjects. His *Russian Calendar* became a handbook for many readers.

263 (p. 585) *Vale of Jehoshaphat*   In the Old Testament Book of Joel, God says that he will sit in the Vale of Jehoshaphat 'to judge all the nations on every side'.

264 (p. 586) *had I better go to Ecke or to Botkin?*   V. E. Ecke (1818–1875) and S. P. Botkin (1832–1889) were both well-known doctors in St Petersburg. Botkin was one of the founders of Russian medical science.

265 (p. 588) *polisson . . . en haut lieu*   urchin, ragamuffin . . . in high places

266 (p. 588) *grand-père*   grandfather

267 (p. 593) *I shall take it to the Citizen; the editor there has had his portrait exhibited too*   This is a good example of Dostoevsky's wry humour: he took over as editor of the *Citizen* (*Grazhdanin*) in 1873, and duly published 'Bobok' in it.

The Heavenly Christmas Tree

268 (p. 598) *Samara famine*   In 1873–4, after three years of bad crops, thousands of people living in the Samara region in the south-east of Russia died from lack of food.

A Gentle Spirit: A Fantastic Story

269 (p. 600) *Victor Hugo . . . 'The Last Day of a Condemned Man'* French poet, dramatist and novelist Victor Hugo (1802–1885) spoke out against injustice during his long and distinguished career. The short story about the man condemned to death was published in 1829.

270 (p. 600) *gros de Naples*   a well-woven plain weave silk fabric

271 (p. 603) *new movement*   reform movements in the 1860s and 70s, encouraged by Tsar Alexander II, included agitation for social change, the liberalisation of politics, abolition of censorship, woman's rights, and so on

272 (p. 604) *I'm part of the whole that seeks to do ill . . . Mephistopheles introduces himself to Faust*   the allusion is to Goethe's *Faust* (1808), in which Mephistopheles answers Faust's question about who he is by saying: 'Part of that power, not understood,/ Which always wills the Bad, and always works the Good.'

273 (p. 608) *à l'anglaise*   in the English manner

274 (p. 610) *first impressions of existence*   phrase from 'The Demon', a Pushkin poem in which the upbeat, optimistic view of man and his relations with nature is undermined by a scoffing internal spirit that pours poison into the poet's soul

275 (p. 610) *hot blood and an overflow of energy*   an allusion to an 1839 poem, 'Do not Trust Yourself' by Lermontov. In it, the young idealistic poet is warned against the imagination and its power to elicit destructive yearnings.

276 (p. 601) *The Hunt after Happiness*   play by Pyotr Yurkevich (d. 1884), Russian playwright and translator

277 (p. 602) *Singing Birds*   Russian title of *La Périchole*, an *opera buffa* by Jacques Offenbach (1819–1880)

278 (p. 612) *Mill*   John Stuart Mill (1806–1873) was a British

philosopher and economist who made important contributions to social policy and political theory. He was an early and fervent proponent of rights for women.

279 (p. 613) *the Crimea*   a peninsula surrounded by the Black Sea and the Sea of Azov. In Dostoevsky's time it was part of Russia.

280 (p. 616) *Vyazemsky's House in the Haymarket*   warehouse near Sennaya Ploshchad, a square near the centre of St Petersburg, home to gangs of petty criminals, prostitutes, the poor and the dispossessed

281 (p. 626) *Politseysky Bridge*   Police Bridge. It was called Green Bridge after it was first painted green in 1730, then Police Bridge because St Petersburg's chief police official lived nearby. It is situated where Nevsky Prospect crosses the Moika Canal, and is called Green Bridge once more.

282 (p. 628) *Boulogne*   port city on the northern coast of France

283 (p. 630) *Gil Blas and the Archbishop of Granada*   an episode in the picaresque novel *Gil Blas*, written by Alain René Lesage (1668–1747), in which the Archbishop dismisses his young assistant for daring to offer the slightest of criticisms of the prelate's sermon

284 (p. 635) *'Men, love one another' – who said that?*   The passage is from John 15:17: 'These things I command you, that ye love one another.'

The Peasant Marey

285 (p. 637) *Je hais ces brigands!*   I detest these robbers!

286 (p. 637) *Hercules*   mythical hero (Heracles in Greek), son of Zeus, known for his strength and resourcefulness, as demonstrated by his performance of the famous Twelve Labours imposed upon him by King Eurystheus

287 (p. 638) *The House of the Dead*   novel by Dostoevsky published in 1861 representing lives of convicts in a Siberian prison camp, loosely based on his own experiences

288 (p. 641) *Konstantin Aksakov*   Russian critic and writer (1817–1860), son of the novelist Sergey Aksakov, Konstantin Aksakov was one of the first Slavophiles, a group of thinkers convinced that Russian culture must turn its back on the West and find its own direction.

The Dream of a Ridiculous Man

289 (p. 646) *playing stoss*   German version of faro, a complicated betting game with a stormy history, including widespread cheating by both the bank and the players

290 (p. 650) *Sirius*   the brightest star in the sky, although it is more than fifty trillion miles from earth. It is sometimes called the Dog Star, because it is in the constellation Canis Major.

291 (p. 656) *trichina*   nematode worm that is a parasite of flesh-eating animals